Lecture Notes in Computer Science 2021

Edited by G. Goos, J. Hartmanis and J. van Leeuwen

T0181056

Springer
Berlin
Heidelberg
New York
Barcelona
Hong Kong
London
Milan
Paris
Singapore
Tokyo

José Nuno Oliveira   Pamela Zave (Eds.)

FME 2001:
Formal Methods
for Increasing
Software Productivity

International Symposium of Formal Methods Europe
Berlin, Germany, March 12-16, 2001
Proceedings

 Springer

Series Editors

Gerhard Goos, Karlsruhe University, Germany
Juris Hartmanis, Cornell University, NY, USA
Jan van Leeuwen, Utrecht University, The Netherlands

Volume Editors

José Nuno Oliveira
University of Minho, Computer Science Department
Campus de Gualtar, 4700-320 Braga, Portugal
E-mail: jno@di.uminho.pt

Pamela Zave
AT&T Laboratories – Research
180 Park Avenue, Florham Park, New Jersey 07932, USA
E-mail: pamela@research.att.com

Cataloging-in-Publication Data applied for

Die Deutsche Bibliothek - CIP-Einheitsaufnahme

Formal methods for increasing software productivity : proceedings /
FME 2001, International Symposium of Formal Methods Europe, Berlin,
Germany, March 12 - 16, 2001. José Nuno Oliveira ; Pamela Zave (ed.).
- Berlin ; Heidelberg ; New York ; Barcelona ; Hong Kong ; London ;
Milan ; Paris ; Singapore ; Tokyo : Springer, 2001
   (Lecture notes in computer science ; Vol. 2021)
   ISBN 3-540-41791-5

CR Subject Classification (1998): F.3, D.1-3, J.1, K.6, F.4.1

ISSN 0302-9743
ISBN 3-540-41791-5 Springer-Verlag Berlin Heidelberg New York

Springer-Verlag Berlin Heidelberg New York
a member of BertelsmannSpringer Science+Business Media GmbH

http://www.springer.de
© Springer-Verlag Berlin Heidelberg 2001

Typesetting: Camera-ready by author, data conversion by PTP-Berlin, Stefan Sossna
Printed on acid-free paper   SPIN: 10782329   06/3142   5 4 3 2 1 0

Preface

FME 2001 is the tenth in a series of meetings organized every eighteen months by Formal Methods Europe (FME), an independent association whose aim is to stimulate the use of, and research on, formal methods for software development. It follows four VDM Europe Symposia, four other Formal Methods Europe Symposia, and the 1999 World Congress on *Formal Methods in the Development of Computing Systems*. These meetings have been notably successful in bringing together a community of users, researchers, and developers of precise mathematical methods for software development.

FME 2001 took place in Berlin, Germany and was organized by the Computer Science Department of the Humboldt-Universität zu Berlin. The theme of the symposium was *Formal Methods for Increasing Software Productivity*. This theme recognizes that formal methods have the potential to do more for industrial software development than enhance software quality – they can also increase productivity at many different points in the software life-cycle.

The importance of the theme is borne out by the many contributed papers showing how formal methods can make software development more efficient. There is an emphasis on tools that find errors automatically, or with relatively little human effort. There is also an emphasis on the use of formal methods to assist with critical, labor-intensive tasks such as program design and test-case generation.

The many application areas addressed in the various parts of the symposium (tutorials, workshops, contributed papers, and invited papers) include smart cards, avionic and satellite computers, financial contracts, E-commerce, middleware, security, telecommunications, and the FireWire standard. Many contributions involve multi-disciplinary teams of researchers coming from both industry and academia. We are pleased to see this evidence of the spreading influence of formal methods.

In addition to the 32 papers selected for presentation by the program committee (out of 72 submissions involving authors from 25 countries), this volume contains the abstracts of three invited talks: *Lightweight Formal Methods*, by Daniel Jackson (Laboratory for Computer Science, MIT); *A Programming Model for Wide-Area Computing*, by Jayadev Misra (University of Texas at Austin); and *Composing Contracts: An Adventure in Financial Engineering* by Simon Peyton Jones (Microsoft Research Ltd).

January 2001   José Nuno Oliveira
                                                               Pamela Zave

Acknowledgements

We are very grateful to the members of the program committee and their referees for their care and diligence in reviewing the submitted papers. We are also grateful to the local organizers and the sponsoring institutions.

Program Committee

Eerke Boiten (UK)
Rick Butler (USA)
Lars-Henrik Eriksson (Sweden)
John Fitzgerald (UK)
Peter Gorm Larsen (Denmark)
Yves Ledru (France)
Dominique Méry (France)
Jayadev Misra (USA)
Richard Moore (Macau)
Friederike Nickl (Germany)

Tobias Nipkow (Germany)
José N. Oliveira (co-chair, Portugal)
Paritosh Pandya (India)
Nico Plat (The Netherlands)
Amir Pnueli (Israel)
Augusto Sampaio (Brazil)
Steve Schneider (UK)
Jim Woodcock (UK)
Pamela Zave (co-chair, USA)

Organizing Committee

Birgit Heene
Stefan Jähnichen (co-chair)
Axel Martens

Wolfgang Reisig (co-chair)
Thomas Urban
Tobias Vesper

Sponsoring Institutions

The generous support of the following companies and institutions is gratefully acknowledged:

Humboldt-Universität zu Berlin
GMD FIRST
Formal Methods Europe
Universidade do Minho
DaimlerChrysler AG
WIDIS GmbH Berlin
WISTA Management GmbH

External Referees

All submitted papers were reviewed by members of the program committee and a number of external referees, who produced extensive review reports and without whose work the quality of the symposium would have suffered. To the best of our knowledge the list below is accurate. We apologize for any omissions or inaccuracies.

Tutorials and Workshops

The following tutorials were scheduled for the two days preceding the research symposium:

SDL 2001 — J. Fischer, Andreas Prinz, and Eckhardt Holz (Humboldt-Universität zu Berlin and DResearch Digital Media Systems GmbH)

Modeling for Formal Methods — Mícheál Mac an Airchinnigh, Andrew Butterfield, and Arthur Hughes (University of Dublin)

From UML to Z, Support for Requirements Engineering with RoZ — Yves Ledru and Sophie Dupuy (LSR/IMAG)

Beyond Model Checking: Formal Specification and Verification of Practical Mission-Critical Systems — Ramesh Bharadwaj (Naval Research Laboratory, USA)

We are grateful to all those who kindly submitted tutorial proposals. In addition, two international workshops were co-located with the symposium tutorials:

First International Workshop on Automated Verification of Infinite-State Systems (AVISS'01) — organized by Ramesh Bharadwaj (Naval Research Laboratory, USA) and Steve Sims (Reactive-Systems, Inc.)

Formal Approaches to the IEEE 1394 (FireWire) Identify Protocol — organized by Carron Shankland, Savi Maharaj (University of Stirling), and Judi Romijn (University of Nijmegen).

We thank the organizers of these events for their interest in sharing the atmosphere of the symposium.

Table of Contents

Lightweight Formal Methods 1
  Daniel Jackson

Reformulation: A Way to Combine Dynamic Properties and *B* Refinement   2
  F. Bellegarde, C. Darlot, J. Julliand, O. Kouchnarenko

Mechanized Analysis of Behavioral Conformance in the Eiffel
Base Libraries 20
  Steffen Helke, Thomas Santen

Proofs of Correctness of Cache-Coherence Protocols 43
  Joseph Stoy, Xiaowei Shen, Arvind

Model-Checking Over Multi-valued Logics............................. 72
  Marsha Chechik, Steve Easterbrook, Victor Petrovykh

How to Make FDR Spin: LTL Model Checking of CSP by Refinement 99
  Michael Leuschel, Thierry Massart, Andrew Currie

Avoiding State Explosion for Distributed Systems with Timestamps 119
  Fabrice Derepas, Paul Gastin, David Plainfossé

Secrecy-Preserving Refinement 135
  Jan Jürjens

Information Flow Control and Applications – Bridging a Gap – 153
  Heiko Mantel

A Rigorous Approach to Modeling and Analyzing
E-Commerce Architectures 173
  Vasu S. Alagar, Zheng Xi

A Formal Model for Reasoning about Adaptive QoS-Enabled Middleware . 197
  Nalini Venkatasubramanian, Carolyn Talcott, Gul Agha

A Programming Model for Wide-Area Computing...................... 222
  Jayadev Misra

A Formal Model of Object-Oriented Design and GoF Design Patterns 223
  Andres Flores, Richard Moore, Luis Reynoso

Validation of UML Models Thanks to Z and Lustre 242
  Sophie Dupuy-Chessa, Lydie du Bousquet

Components, Contracts, and Connectors for the Unified
Modelling Language UML 259
    Claus Pahl

An Integrated Approach to Specification and Validation of
Real-Time Systems 278
    Adnan Sherif, Augusto Sampaio, Sérgio Cavalcante

Real-Time Logic Revisited 300
    Stephen E. Paynter

Improvements in BDD-Based Reachability Analysis of Timed Automata . . 318
    Dirk Beyer

Serialising Parallel Processes in a Hardware/Software
Partitioning Context 344
    Leila Silva, Augusto Sampaio, Geraint Jones

Verifying Implementation Relations 364
    Jonathan Burton, Maciej Koutny, Giuseppe Pappalardo

An Adequate Logic for Full LOTOS 384
    Muffy Calder, Savi Maharaj, Carron Shankland

Towards a Topos Theoretic Foundation for the Irish School of Constructive
Mathematics ($M_C^{\clubsuit}$) 396
    Mícheál Mac an Airchinnigh

Faithful Translations among Models and Specifications 419
    Shmuel Katz

Composing Contracts: An Adventure in Financial Engineering 435
    Simon Peyton Jones

From Complex Specifications to a Working Prototype. A Protocol
Engineering Case Study 436
    Manuel J. Fernández Iglesias, Francisco J. González-Castaño,
    José M. Pousada Carballo, Martín Llamas Nistal,
    Alberto Romero Feijoo

Coverage Directed Generation of System-Level Test Cases for the
Validation of a DSP System 449
    Laurent Arditi, Hédi Boufaïed, Arnaud Cavanié, Vincent Stehlé

Using Formal Verification Techniques to Reduce Simulation and
Test Effort 465
    O. Laurent, P. Michel, V. Wiels

Transacted Memory for Smart Cards 478
    Pieter H. Hartel, Michael J. Butler, Eduard de Jong, Mark Longley

Houdini, an Annotation Assistant for ESC/Java 500
    Cormac Flanagan, K. Rustan M. Leino

A Heuristic for Symmetry Reductions with Scalarsets 518
    Dragan Bošnački, Dennis Dams, Leszek Holenderski

View Updatability Based on the Models of a Formal Specification 534
    Michael Johnson, Robert Rosebrugh

Grammar Adaptation 550
    Ralf Lämmel

Test-Case Calculation through Abstraction 571
    Bernhard K. Aichernig

A Modular Approach to the Specification and Validation of an Electrical
Flight Control System 590
    M. Doche, I. Vernier-Mounier, F. Kordon

A Combined Testing and Verification Approach for Software Reliability ... 611
    Natasha Sharygina, Doron Peled

Author Index **629**

Table of Contents XIII

Lightweight Formal Methods

Daniel Jackson

Laboratory for Computer Science
Massachusetts Institute of Technology
Cambridge, Massachusetts, USA
dnj@lcs.mit.edu

Abstract. Formal methods have offered great benefits, but often at a heavy price. For everyday software development, in which the pressures of the market don't allow full-scale formal methods to be applied, a more lightweight approach is called for. I'll outline an approach that is designed to provide immediate benefit at relatively low cost. Its elements are a small and succinct modelling language, and a fully automatic analysis scheme that can perform simulations and find errors. I'll describe some recent case studies using this approach, involving naming schemes, architectural styles, and protocols for networks with changing topologies. I'll make some controversial claims about this approach and its relationship to UML and traditional formal specification approaches, and I'll barbeque some sacred cows, such as the belief that executability compromises abstraction.

J.N. Oliveira and P. Zave (Eds.): FME 2001, LNCS 2021, p. 1, 2001.
© Springer-Verlag Berlin Heidelberg 2001

Reformulation: A Way to Combine Dynamic Properties and B Refinement

F. Bellegarde, C. Darlot, J. Julliand, and O. Kouchnarenko

Laboratoire d'Informatique de l'Université de Franche-Comté
16, route de Gray, 25030 Besançon Cedex
Ph:(33) 3 81 66 64 52, Fax:(33) 3 81 66 64 50
{bellegar,darlot,julliand,kouchna}@lifc.univ-fcomte.fr,
Web : http://lifc.univ-fcomte.fr

Abstract. We are interested in verifying dynamic properties of reactive systems. The reactive systems are specified by B event systems in a refinement development. The refinement allows us to combine proof and model-checking verification techniques in a novel way. Most of the *PLTL* dynamic properties are preserved by refinement, but in our approach, the user can also express how a property evolves during the refinement. The preservation of the abstract property, expressed by a *PLTL* formula F_1, is used as an assumption for proving a *PLTL* formula F_2 which expresses an enriched property in the refined system. Formula F_1 is verified by model-checking on the abstract system. So, to verify the enriched formula F_2, it is enough to prove some propositions depending on the respective patterns followed by F_1 and F_2. In this paper, we show how to obtain these *sufficient* propositions from the refinement relation and the semantics of the *PLTL* formulae. The main advantage is that the user does not need to express a variant or a loop invariant to obtain automatic proofs of dynamic properties, at least for finite state event systems. Another advantage is that the model-checking is done on an abstraction with few states.

Keywords: Verification of *PLTL* properties, Combination of proof and model-checking, Refinement development.

1 Introduction

Most properties of reactive systems [8,2,7] are dynamic. In our approach for the design and verification, reactive systems are expressed by B finite state event systems and their dynamic properties are formulated in the Propositional Linear Temporal Logic [8] (*PLTL*). Recall that the B method is essentially a refinement design.

Our methodological approach as well as our verification techniques for addressing the introduction of dynamic constraints in B (see Fig. 1) is quite different from the propositions of J.–R. Abrial and L. Mussat in [2]. The B event systems can be associated with finite or infinite transition systems. In B, the verification of invariants, *dynamic invariants* and of liveness modalities *leads to*

J.N. Oliveira and P. Zave (Eds.): FME 2001, LNCS 2021, pp. 2–19, 2001.

and *until* uses a proof technique which requires explicit *variants* and *loop invariants* from the users. *Variants* and *loop invariants* are needed for the verification of the liveness modalities. Moreover, a global *variant* is necessary for proving that the refinement introduces no live-lock. Our proposals deal only with the specification and the verification of finite state systems but the specification and the verification of any *PLTL* property (safety, liveness, fairness) is possible.

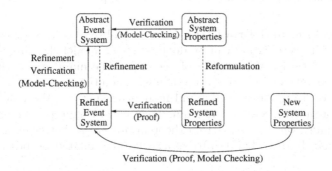

Fig. 1. Specification and verification approach

They differ from [2] in the four essential following points.

1. The dynamic properties are expressed in *PLTL*.
2. As for the events, the dynamic properties that are introduced at the abstract level can be enriched through the refinement. Then, they are formulated anew at the refined level. We say that the formula is *reformulated*.
3. The abstract dynamic properties are model-checked and their *reformulations* are verified by proof.

The motivation behind these propositions is threefold. First and above all, we want to set the user free from looking for a *variant* and a *loop invariant* when expressing dynamic properties. Second, we want to be able to use model-checking and proof for the verification in a way which utilizes them at their best. Third, the user can express its modalities freely using the expressive power of the *PLTL* logic.

B + PLTL versus B + Modalities (see Point 1 above). In [2], J.–R. Abrial and L. Mussat use three patterns of dynamic properties: the *dynamic invariant* and the two modalities *leads to* and *until*. If p and q are propositional predicates, the *dynamic invariants* have the same expressive power as the set of *PLTL* formulae $\Box(p \Rightarrow \bigcirc q)$. The modalities have the same expressive power as a fragment of the *PLTL* using the two kinds of properties $\Box(p \Rightarrow \Diamond q)$, and $\Box(p \Rightarrow (p \mathcal{U} q))$. Moreover, besides the instances for p and q, the user has to specify a *variant*, often a *loop invariant*, and a list of the events which may be taken during the loop.

We use the *PLTL* future operators *Always, Next, Eventually,* and *Until* (denoted respectively by $\Box$, $\bigcirc$, $\Diamond$, and $\mathcal{U}$) with the following meaning. For a path σ,

- $\Box p$ means that the property p holds in each state of σ;
- $\bigcirc p$ means that the property p holds in the next state;
- $\Diamond p$ means that there exists a state in the future which satisfies p;
- $p\mathcal{U}q$ means that p holds until q eventually happens.

Model-Checking and Proof (see Points 3 above). We choose the *PLTL* logic because its verification can be done by *PLTL* model-checking [5] which is entirely automatic for the totality of the logic. The main drawback is that it cannot handle very or infinite state systems. A solution for large finite systems may consist of using jointly proof and model-checking. So, the model-checking explosion is avoided as well as the requirement consisting in providing clues such as *variants* and *loop invariants* to a theorem prover. To better explain how we propose to join both techniques to verify the reformulated properties consider Fig. 1.

First, the user specifies the abstract event system with its invariant and its dynamic properties expressed in *PLTL*. The invariant is proof-checked as in *B*. The dynamic properties are model-checked on the event system operational model, i.e., on the set of paths of a finite state transition system with a small number of states.

Second, the user specifies its refinements introducing new variables. The relation between the set of states S_2 of the refined system and the set of states S_1 of the abstract system is expressed by a *gluing invariant*. New events are introduced, old events are formulated once more, new *PLTL* formulae are introduced, and old *PLTL* formulae are formulated anew.

We do not want to use the *PLTL* model-checking again for the verification of the reformulated properties. So, we propose to use proof techniques, but without requiring a *loop invariant* and of a *variant*. In the paper, we present two kinds of propositions which are associated systematically according to the shapes (called *refinement patterns*) of the abstract *PLTL* formula and the refined formula. The first kind—a weak form, includes propositional sub-formulae and the invariants of the event systems. When they are valid, we know that the refined formula holds. The failure does not mean that the refined formula does not hold. So, the second kind—a strong form, includes either the abstract or the refined events. Again, the success means that the refined formula holds but, from a failure, we cannot conclude. Therefore, these propositions are *sufficient conditions* and not *proof obligations*.

In the paper, we show that if these propositions (weak or strong) are valid, then the reformulated properties hold without the help of neither an user-given *variant* nor a *loop invariant*.

Reformulation versus Preservation (see Point 2 above). In [2], the modalities *leads to* and *until* which hold on the abstract paths are preserved on the refined paths. However, *dynamic invariants*, which could be expressed by an instance of the *PLTL* pattern $\Box(p \Rightarrow \bigcirc q)$, are not preserved on the refined paths since new events may not verify the *dynamic invariant*. Moreover, because the new events are interwoven among the old ones, the refined system does not satisfy the pattern $\Box(p \Rightarrow \bigcirc q)$ but it satisfies an instance of the *PLTL* pattern $\Box(p \Rightarrow \Diamond q)$—a weaker formula. More generally, the preservation technique does not allow the user to indicate how the new events are interwoven among the old events. However, the reformulation can do it. For example, the reformulation of the *PLTL* pattern $\Box(p_1 \Rightarrow \bigcirc q_1)$ by the *PLTL* pattern $\Box(p_2 \Rightarrow \bigcirc q_2)$, allows us to specify that it is forbidden to introduce some of the new events before the old events which are enabled when p_1 holds. The reformulation of the pattern $\Box(p_1 \Rightarrow \bigcirc q_1)$ by the pattern $\Box(p_2 \Rightarrow (r_2 \mathcal{U} q_2))$ allows introducing only the new events which maintain r_2. So, the purpose of the reformulation of a property is that the formula of the refined property specifies explicitly how the new events can be interwoven among the old events. Therefore, the reformulated formula may be richer than the preserved formula. The effect of a reformulated formula compares with the effect of a gluing invariant in the following manner. A *gluing invariant* specifies a relation between the refined and the abstract states whereas a reformulated formula, together with the *gluing invariant*, specifies a relation between the refined and the abstract paths of the operational model. It is redundant with the expression of the events but we think that it is important that the design allows such redundancies in a specification so that the verification can exploit them.

Paper Organization. The paper is organized as follows. Section 2 illustrates our approach on an example. After a short presentation of our refinement relation, we explain how to verify the *reformulated* dynamic properties through refinement in Section 3. Finally, we situate our concerns and give some ideas about future works in Section 4.

2 Example

In this section, we introduce a robot as an example. We will examine the operational specification, and then, we will express some dynamic properties to be verified on this system.

2.1 Operational Description

Figure 2 shows the physical system. The robot must move some parts from the *arrival device* (called AD) to one of the *exit devices* (called resp. LED and RED for the left and right exit devices) using the *carrier device* (called CD).

Here, we show the abstract specification as well as two further levels of refinement called *first refinement* and *second refinement*. We express the specifications using a B event system syntax extended with *PLTL*. Notice that the variables are annotated with a number corresponding to the level of refinement (here: 0, 1 and 2).

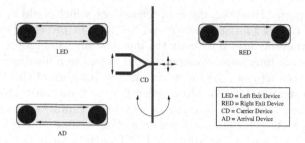

Fig. 2. Physical system

Abstract Specification. The very abstract specification only formalizes the transportation of the parts ignoring the arrival and exit devices and the carrier device movements which will be considered in further refinements. In other words, we only observe the carrier device state. Figure 3 gives the operational semantics of the abstract level specification described as the event system below (for the B syntax, please see [1]). There are two events:

- *Load*: The carrier device takes a part, then it is busy (value b);
- *Unload*: The carrier device drops a part, then it is free (value f).

EVENT SYSTEM ROBOT$_0$
SETS: DEVICE_STATE=$\{f,b\}$
VARIABLES: CD$_0$
INVARIANT: CD$_0 \in$ DEVICE_STATE
INITIALIZATION: CD$_0$:=f
EVENTS:
Load $\hat{=}$**SELECT** CD$_0$=f **THEN** CD$_0$:=b **END**;
Unload $\hat{=}$**SELECT** CD$_0$=b **THEN** CD$_0$:=f **END**
END

Fig. 3. Transition system for the abstract level

First Refinement. We consider now the left and right exit devices. The variables of the abstract and the refined specifications are linked together by a *gluing invariant*. We observe two new events (*LEvac* and *REvac*) which set the exit devices free. These events can happen whenever the exit devices are busy. In the refined specification, the old events keep the same labels. Notice that the guards of the old events (e.g. *Unload*) are strengthened. Also, notice that when both exit devices are free, the carrier device unloads a part nondeterministically either toward the left exit device or toward the right exit device.

The transition system in Fig. 4 shows the first refinement operational semantics. We can notice that if we group the states according to the gluing invariant, we obtain two *modules* (one where in each state the carrier device is empty and one where it is busy) corresponding to the two states of the abstract level.

EVENT SYSTEM $ROBOT_1$ **REFINES** $ROBOT_0$
VARIABLES: LED_1, RED_1, CD_1
INVARIANT:
$LED_1 \in$ DEVICE_STATE $\wedge$ $RED_1 \in$ DEVICE_STATE $\wedge$ $CD_1 = CD_0$
INITIALIZATION: $LED_1 := f \parallel RED_1 := f \parallel CD_1 := f$
EVENTS:
/* Old events */
Load $\hat{=}$**SELECT** $CD_1 = f$ **THEN** $CD_1 := b$ **END**;
Unload $\hat{=}$**SELECT** $(LED_1 = f \vee RED_1 = f) \wedge CD_1 = b$
$\qquad$ **THEN IF** $LED_1 = b$ **THEN** $RED_1 := b$
$\qquad\qquad$ **ELSE IF** $RED_1 = b$ **THEN** $LED_1 := b$
$\qquad\qquad\qquad$ **ELSE CHOICE** $LED_1 := b$
$\qquad\qquad\qquad\qquad$ **OR** $RED_1 := b$ **END**
$\qquad\qquad$ **END**
$\qquad$ **END**
$\qquad\qquad \parallel CD_1 := f$
$\qquad$ **END**;

/* New events */
LEvac $\hat{=}$**SELECT** $LED_1 = b$ **THEN** $LED_1 := f$ **END**;
REvac $\hat{=}$**SELECT** $RED_1 = b$ **THEN** $RED_1 := f$ **END**
END$ROBOT_1$

Second Refinement. Now, we observe two new events (*LRotate* and *RRotate*) which change the carrier device side which is registered in the variable *CDS*. The side value is either left—denoted l, or right—denoted r. We remove the nondeterminism by giving priority to the left exit device whenever possible—this for minimizing the carrier device movements, i.e., we do not unload on the right exit device if the left one is free.

EVENT SYSTEM $ROBOT_2$ **REFINES** $ROBOT_1$
SETS: SIDE$=\{l,r\}$
VARIABLES: LED_2, RED_2, CD_2, CDS_2

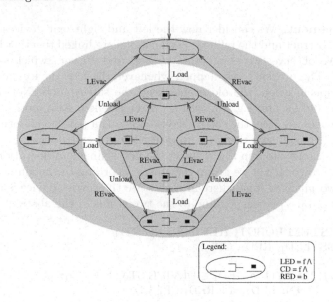

Fig. 4. First refinement transition system

INVARIANT:
$LED_2=LED_1 \wedge RED_2=RED_1 \wedge CD_2=CD_1 \wedge CDS_2 \in SIDE \wedge$
$(CDS_2=r \Rightarrow (CD_2=f \vee RED_2=f))$
INITIALIZATION: $LED_2:=f \parallel RED_2:=f \parallel CD_2:=f \parallel CDS_2:=l$
EVENTS:
/* Old events */
Load $\hat{=}$**SELECT** $CD_2=f \wedge CDS_2=l$ **THEN** $CD_2:=b$ **END**;
Unload $\hat{=}$**SELECT** $CD_2=b \wedge ((LED_2=f \wedge CDS_2=l) \vee$
$(RED_2=f \wedge CDS_2=r \wedge LED_2=b))$
         THEN IF $LED_2=f \wedge CDS_2=l$ **THEN** $LED_2:=b$
            ELSE $RED_2:=b$
            END
            $\parallel CD_2:=f$
      END;
LEvac $\hat{=}$**SELECT** $LED_2=b$ **THEN** $LED_2:=f$ **END**;
REvac $\hat{=}$**SELECT** $RED_2=b$ **THEN** $RED_2:=f$ **END**;

/* New events */
LRotate $\hat{=}$**SELECT** $CDS_2=r \wedge (CD_2=f \vee LED_2=f)$
      THEN $CDS_2:=l$
      END;
RRotate $\hat{=}$**SELECT** $CDS_2=l \wedge CD_2=b \wedge LED_2=b \wedge RED_2=f$
      THEN $CDS_2:=r$
      END
END

Figure 5 shows the second refinement transition system. We can notice that if we group the states according to the gluing invariant, we obtain eight modules.

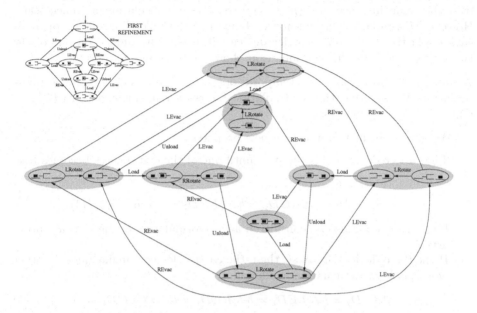

Fig. 5. Second refinement transition system

2.2 Dynamic Properties

We want to express some dynamic properties to be verified on the systems previously described.

Dynamic Properties of the Abstraction. The carrier device should immediately unload. This is expressed by Formula 1 which can be read as follows: "At any time, if the carrier is busy, it is free in the next state".

$$\Box(CD_0 = b \Rightarrow \bigcirc(CD_0 = f)) \tag{1}$$

Dynamic Properties for the First Refinement. The previous property is reformulated either into Formula 2 or into Formula 3.

$$\Box(CD_1 = b \Rightarrow \Diamond(CD_1 = f)) \tag{2}$$

$$\Box(CD_1 = b \Rightarrow \Diamond(CD_1 = f \wedge (LED_1 = b \vee RED_1 = b))) \tag{3}$$

Formula 2 considers that any event which does not modify the carrier state may happen before unloading. If the refinement holds, Formula 2 holds without any further verification since any instance of a formula $\square(p \Rightarrow \bigcirc q)$ refines into the same instance of $\square(p \Rightarrow \Diamond q)$. So, the reformulation is unnecessary. However, Formula 3 expresses more about how the unloading may happen. It says explicitly that a busy carrier device will eventually unload on one of the two exit devices. So, the reformulation allows us to be more accurate.

Remark 1. In both cases, the temporal operator $\bigcirc$ becomes a $\Diamond$ in the reformulation. We say that the reformulation follows a refinement pattern $(\square(p \Rightarrow \bigcirc q), \square(p \Rightarrow \Diamond q))$, for short $\bigcirc\Diamond$.

We also have the two following new properties:

- The carrier device holds the part until one of the exit devices becomes free.

$$\square(CD_1 = b \\ \Rightarrow ((CD_1 = b)\mathcal{U}(CD_1 = b \wedge (LED_1 = f \vee RED_1 = f)))) \tag{4}$$

Formula 4 could also be considered as a reformulation of the abstract property 1.
- If the three devices are busy, then, the carrier device remains busy. In other words, only the evacuation is allowed.

$$\square((CD_1 = b \wedge LED_1 = b \wedge RED_1 = b) \Rightarrow \bigcirc(CD_1 = b)) \tag{5}$$

Dynamic Properties for the Second Refinement. The above properties can be reformulated as follows by taking the carrier device side into consideration.

- Formula 3 is reformulated into Formula 6, following a $\Diamond\Diamond$ pattern:

$$\square(CD_2 = b \Rightarrow \Diamond(CD_2 = f \wedge ((LED_2 = b \wedge CDS_2 = l) \vee \\ (RED_2 = b \wedge CDS_2 = r)))) \tag{6}$$

The enrichment of Formula 3 in Formula 6 consists in expressing that "the carrier device is turned to the side of the previous unloading".
- Formula 4 is reformulated into Formula 7, following a $\mathcal{U}\mathcal{U}$ pattern:

$$\square((CD_2 = b \wedge LED_2 = b \wedge CDS_2 = l) \Rightarrow ((CDS_2 = l \wedge CD_2 = b) \\ \mathcal{U}(CDS_2 = l \wedge CD_2 = b \wedge (LED_2 = f \vee RED_2 = f)))) \tag{7}$$

It can be read as: "If the carrier device is busy and directed toward its left, it stays directed toward the left until it can turn to the right.
- Formula 5 is reformulated into Formula 8. It follows a $\bigcirc\bigcirc$ pattern by expressing that the *new* events *LRotate* and *RRotate* must preserve the $\bigcirc$.

$$\square((CD_2 = b \wedge LED_2 = b \wedge RED_2 = b) \\ \Rightarrow \bigcirc(CD_2 = b)) \tag{8}$$

It can be read as: "The carrier device must stay busy when rotating".

The next section describes how to deduce invariants providing sufficient verification conditions from the $PLTL$ property syntax at both the refined and the abstract levels together with the path refinement relation.

3   Reformulated Dynamic Property Verification

In this section, we explain how to verify the reformulated dynamic properties through refinement. We suppose that the system TS_2 of state space S_2 refines the abstract system TS_1 of state space S_1 and we exploit this refinement to show that if a property P_1 holds on the abstract system then a reformulated property P_2 holds on a refined system.

We hope to avoid the $PLTL$ property model-checking explosion which is likely to happen during the refinement by providing sufficient conditions to verify the reformulated $PLTL$ property P_2 using that η holds between TS_2 and TS_1 and P_1 holds on TS_1 as assumptions.

These conditions are first-order predicate formulae where the predicate domains are limited to finite sets so that these conditions are easily decidable by any theorem prover. Moreover, the conditions depend on the formulation of the $PLTL$ property at both levels.

We determine two kinds of conditions. The first kind does not take into account the events. These conditions are often too weak to prove the $PLTL$ formulae. So, we consider how the new events are interwoven among the old events to exhibit stronger conditions. Therefore, as in the B proof obligations for refinement, these last conditions are formulated using guards and generalized substitutions of the events.

3.1   About Refinement

We use transition systems as operational semantics of the B event systems because of the $PLTL$ semantics. At the abstract level, a $PLTL$ property P is verified for the event system by model-checking on a transition system which is its operational model. This supposes that the set of states of this transition system is finite.

In this section, we give an intuitive presentation of a refinement relation between the set of states S_2 of the refined transition system TS_2 and the set of states S_1 of the abstract transition system TS_1 which determines a relation between the paths of the transition systems modeling the corresponding event systems. This relation has been studied thoroughly in [4].

As in B, the important assumption is that the new events do not take control forever. However, in our approach, this is verified by a model state enumeration. The refinement verification is linear in the number of states of the refined system. This way we prevent the state explosion coming from the $PLTL$ model-checking itself.

As for the refinement in B, the conjunction of the abstract system invariant I_1 and the gluing invariant I_2 determines a relation μ between the refined and abstract states. The refinement relation η restricts μ taking into account that the new events do not take the control forever, and that non-determinism may decrease. The relation η between states implies a relation between the refined paths and some abstract paths of the transition systems. Figure 6 gives an example of two related paths. As usual, the *PLTL* model-checking is based on the labeling of each state by a set of the propositions holding on it. By the refinement definition from [4], it is very important to ensure that any event which is taken on the abstract path is also eventually taken on the refined path preceded by some new events.

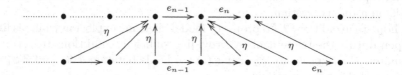

Fig. 6. Path refinement example

3.2   Refinement and Dynamic Properties

The dynamic properties that can be expressed in B event systems are

- either a dynamic invariant which indicates how the variables of the system are authorized to evolve; this corresponds roughly to a *PLTL* formula involving the next operator as $\Box(p \Rightarrow \bigcirc q)$;
- or the B modalities which have *PLTL* equivalences as the patterns $\Box(p \Rightarrow \Diamond q)$ and $\Box(p \Rightarrow (p\mathcal{U}q))$.

Generally, a *PLTL* formula following the pattern $\Box(p_1 \Rightarrow \bigcirc q_1)$ is formulated again at a refined level either as the pattern $\Box(p_2 \Rightarrow \bigcirc q_2)$ or $\Box(p_2 \Rightarrow \Diamond q_2)$ or $\Box(p_2 \Rightarrow (r_2\mathcal{U}q_2))$. It can be a more complicated expression. We call a *refinement pattern* a pair of a *PLTL* pattern and its reformulated pattern. Notice that in a given pattern, the variables are propositional variables.

Our approach allows the user to have more flexibility to express properties through refinement than in B (where the modalities are only *preserved* and cannot be expressed again).

On the one hand, the preservation of dynamic invariant through the B refinement seems to correspond to the refinement pattern $(\Box(p_1 \Rightarrow \bigcirc q_1), \Box(p_2 \Rightarrow \Diamond q_2))$ (for short, $\bigcirc\Diamond$).

On the other hand, the B refinement preserves the modalities patterns. Again the reformulation offers more possibilities. First, the pattern $\mathcal{U}$ is $\Box(p_1 \Rightarrow (r_1\mathcal{U}q_1))$ whereas the B modality *until* corresponds to a pattern $\Box(p_1 \Rightarrow (p_1\mathcal{U}q_1))$. Second, a pattern $\mathcal{U}$ may evolve into a pattern $\Diamond$. Third, the reformulation allows enriching gradually a property through refinement. In contrast, when a property P does not need to be enriched, it is preserved by refinement so that, in such a case, it is useless to reformulate P during further refinements.

Notice that it is inconceivable that a pattern $\Diamond$ evolves into a pattern $\bigcirc$. The direction of the implication between the patterns of the pair is naturally mirrored by the direction of the refinement. We have discussed the pattern evolution through refinement in [6].

The sufficient proof conditions are deduced from the $PLTL$ refinement pattern semantics. So, we are not limited to a small set of refinement patterns. Our experience shows that in most applications the same few refinement patterns are often used. However, a small number of more complicated refinement patterns may be novel to a particular application but it is generally easy to build a corresponding sufficient condition set as it is shown in the next section.

3.3   Weak Sufficient Conditions

Consider the refinement pattern $\mathcal{U}\mathcal{U}$. Suppose a formula of pattern $\Box(p_1 \Rightarrow (r_1\mathcal{U}q_1))$ holds on the paths of the abstract transition system TS_1. We want to have sufficient conditions for the pattern $\Box(p_2 \Rightarrow (r_2\mathcal{U}q_2))$ holding on the paths of a refined transition system TS_2.

From the semantics of $\mathcal{U}$ and from the path refinement relation as shown in Fig. 6, we deduce the following set of sufficient conditions.

- A *beginning condition*. Assume p_2 is satisfied on a state s_2, and s_1 be the abstract state such that s_2 together with s_1 satisfy $I_2 \wedge I_1$. Then, p_1 must be satisfied by s_1. From that we deduce a first condition $p_2 \wedge I_2 \wedge I_1 \Rightarrow p_1$.
- A *maintenance condition*. The proposition r_1 holds on each state s of any path of the abstract system beginning in s_1 before the satisfaction of q_1. So, r_2 must also hold on each state s' of any path of a refined system beginning in s_2 before the satisfaction of q_2. By refinement, s and s' satisfy $I_2 \wedge I_1$. From that we deduce a second condition $r_1 \wedge I_2 \wedge I_1 \Rightarrow r_2$.
- An *ending condition*. On any path after s_1 there exists a state t satisfying q_1. So, if q_2 holds on a state t' such that t and t' satisfy $I_2 \wedge I_1$, we are done. We deduce the third condition $q_1 \wedge I_2 \wedge I_1 \Rightarrow q_2$.

We see that we have two kinds of implications, one from an abstract system property to a refined system property (either for an ending condition or a maintenance condition), and the other from a refined system property to an abstract system property (for a beginning condition) (see Fig. 7).

We now give theorems providing a building block for a beginning condition.

Theorem 1. *Given an abstract transition system TS_1 of state space S_1, and a transition system TS_2 of state space S_2 refining TS_1, let I_1 be the invariant of TS_1, and let I_2 be the gluing invariant. Each state $s_1(\in S_1)$ glued with a state $s_2(\in S_2)$ on which a proposition p_2 holds satisfies a proposition p_1 if the condition $p_2 \wedge I_2 \wedge I_1 \Rightarrow p_1$ holds on $s_2 \wedge s_1$.*

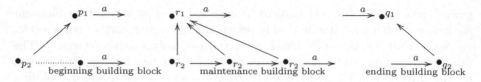

Fig. 7. Building blocks

Proof. Immediate by the following. Let $s_2 \in S_2$ be a state satisfying p_2. Let $s_1 \in S_1$ be a state glued with s_2. Then, s_2 and s_1 satisfy $p_2 \wedge I_1 \wedge I_2$. Since $p_2 \wedge I_2 \wedge I_1 \Rightarrow p_1$, the property p_1 which contains only variables of TS_1, holds on s_1.

Theorem 2. *The condition stated by Theorem 1 is a building block for a beginning condition of any refinement pattern $(\Box(p_1 \Rightarrow Q_1), \Box(p_2 \Rightarrow Q_2))$ where Q_1 and Q_2 are PLTL formulae.*

Proof. Immediate by the following. If a refined path begins in a state satisfying p_2 then it is necessarily glued with all the states in S_1 satisfying p_1.

We propose another building block either for a maintenance condition or for an ending condition.

Theorem 3. *Given an abstract transition system TS_1 and a transition system TS_2 refining TS_1, let I_1 be the invariant of TS_1, and let I_2 be the gluing invariant. Each state $s_2(\in S_2)$ glued with a state $s_1(\in S_1)$ on which a proposition q_1 holds satisfies a proposition q_2 if the condition $q_1 \wedge I_2 \wedge I_1 \Rightarrow q_2$ holds on $s_2 \wedge s_1$.*

Proof. The proof is the same as for Theorem 1.

Theorem 4. *The condition stated by Theorem 3 is a building block for an ending condition of any refinement pattern $(\Box Q_1, \Box Q_2)$ where q_1 is an eventuality which occurs in the PLTL formula Q_1 and q_2 is an eventuality which occurs in the PLTL formula Q_2.*

Proof. Immediate by the following. If an abstract state s_1 satisfying q_1 occurs in a path of S_1 then all the states in S_2 glued with s_1 are compelled to satisfy q_2.

As a consequence of Theorem 3, a maintenance condition can be deduced according to the following argument. Let s_1 be a state in S_1 for which r_1 holds. In a path of TS_2, all the states which begin a transition refining *skip* (these transitions are labeled by new events) that are glued with s_1 verify r_2. Notice how important are the *non τ-divergence* and the *lack of new deadlock* clauses of the refinement relation for reaching the ending condition. However, it may be too weak when new events appear since, in this case, the condition forces q_2 to

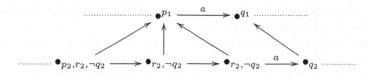

Fig. 8. Pattern $\bigcirc\mathcal{U}$

be true after each of these new events up until the occurrence of the next old event.

We now have a way to construct the set of weak sufficient conditions associated to one of the following often used refinement patterns $\bigcirc\bigcirc$, $\bigcirc\mathcal{U}$, $\bigcirc\Diamond$, $\mathcal{U}\mathcal{U}$, $\mathcal{U}\Diamond$, $\Diamond\Diamond$. For instance, the set of weak sufficient conditions for the refinement pattern $(\Box(p_1 \Rightarrow \bigcirc q_1), \Box(p_2 \Rightarrow (r_2\mathcal{U}q_2)))$ is (see Fig. 8)

$$p_2 \wedge I_2 \wedge I_1 \Rightarrow p_1, \text{ a beginning condition}$$
$$p_1 \wedge I_2 \wedge I_1 \Rightarrow r_2, \text{ a maintenance condition}$$
$$q_1 \wedge I_2 \wedge I_1 \Rightarrow q_2, \text{ an ending condition}$$

Consider the following dynamic property for the event system from Section 2. If the carrier device is busy, and so are both exit devices then, in the next state, the carrier device remains busy while one of the exit devices becomes free.

$$\Box((CD_1 = b \wedge LED_1 = b \wedge RED_1 = b) \Rightarrow \bigcirc((CD_1 = b) \\ \wedge (LED_1 = f \vee RED_1 = f))) \tag{9}$$

Notice that this implies Property 5 from Section 2.2. The above property is reformulated into

$$\Box((CD_2 = b \wedge LED_2 = b \wedge RED_2 = b) \Rightarrow ((CD_2 = b) \\ \mathcal{U}(CD_2 = b \wedge (LED_2 = f \vee RED_2 = f)))) \tag{10}$$

because of the new events. The above set of weak sufficient conditions is enough to ensure the satisfaction of the reformulated property.

Moreover, the building blocks can also be used to deduce weak sufficient conditions for more complex refinement patterns. Consider, for example, a refinement pattern $(\Box(p_1 \Rightarrow \bigcirc(r_1\mathcal{U}q_1)), \Box(p_2 \Rightarrow \Diamond(r_2 \Rightarrow r_2\mathcal{U}q_2)))$. Its set of weak sufficient conditions is the following:

$$p_2 \wedge I_2 \wedge I_1 \Rightarrow p_1, \text{ a beginning condition}$$
$$r_1 \wedge I_2 \wedge I_1 \Rightarrow r_2, \text{ a maintenance condition}$$
$$q_1 \wedge I_2 \wedge I_1 \Rightarrow q_2, \text{ an ending condition}$$

Unfortunately, some of these building blocks are often too weak for the proof because they do not express the semantics of the refinement patterns precisely enough. The next section presents strong sufficient conditions which are used in our verification process when the weak sufficient conditions fail in proving an instance of a refinement pattern.

Obviously, the cause of the failure may not come from the conditions but either from the incorrectness of the refined formula (error of expression or error in the pattern evolution), or even from the incorrectness or the insufficiency of the gluing invariant. The problem with the invariant happens only if the modular refinement relation does not hold. So, the refinement verification eliminates this cause of failure.

3.4   Strong Sufficient Conditions

In the failure case, we have to try a strong sufficient condition based on the new events (refining *skip*) interwoven among the old events. For example, with the refinement pattern $\bigcirc \Diamond$ followed by Formula 1 and its reformulation into Formula 3, the proof of the set of weak conditions fails for the ending condition $q_1 \wedge I_2 \wedge I_1 \Rightarrow q_2$. Then, the weak ending condition has to be replaced by the following strong ending sufficient condition:

$$\forall\, a \in OldEvents, p_1 \wedge G_{1a} \wedge G_{2a} \wedge I_1 \wedge I_2 \Rightarrow [S_{2a}]q_2$$

where S_{2a} is a generalized substitution of an old event a in a refined system, G_{2a} is its guard, and G_{1a} is the guard of the event a in the abstract system. In other words, each old event a enabled by a refined state s_2 which satisfies r_2 and is glued with an abstract state s_1 satisfying p_1, changes s_2 into a state satisfying q_2.

The above condition also can be used as an ending condition for the refinement pattern $\bigcirc \mathcal{U}$. It is used in proving Formula 4 as a reformulation of Formula 1. However, for the pattern $\bigcirc \mathcal{U}$, the left-hand side of the implication often needs to be strengthened with the conjunction of r_2 to better fit the semantics of $\mathcal{U}$.

Strong sufficient conditions are also required by the persistence of the *PLTL* operator $\bigcirc$ in a refinement pattern.

The persistence of the *PLTL* operator $\bigcirc$ in a pattern evolution. We can imagine three plausible refinement patterns coming from the abstract pattern $p_1 \Rightarrow \bigcirc q_1$.

- The more likely the pattern $\bigcirc$ evolves into eventuality patterns either $\Diamond$ (e.g Formula 1 reformulated into Formula 3) or $\mathcal{U}$ (e.g. Formula 1 reformulated into Formula 4) because of transitions refining *skip*.
- However, in a few cases, it may happen that the property is not concerned with the new events. For instance, Formula 5 of the second refinement is satisfied by both of the new events *LRotate* and *RRotate*. With this point of view, it is reformulated into Formula 8.

For a $\bigcirc$ persistence, the weakest set of sufficient conditions we can build is composed of the weak beginning condition, the weak ending condition, and a condition saying that no new event can precede an old event concerned with $\bigcirc$. This condition is

$$\forall\, a \in NewEvents, (p_1 \wedge I_1 \wedge I_2) \Rightarrow \neg G_a$$

where G_a is the guard of an event a. Therefore, any state s_2 satisfying p_2 must not satisfy a guard of a new event which is sufficient to ensure the persistence of $\neg p_2$.

More about strong sufficient conditions. Let us examine strong sufficient conditions for the pattern refinement $\mathcal{U}\mathcal{U}$ followed by Formula 4 and its reformulation into Formula 7 as expressed in Section 2.2. The following strong ending condition

$$\forall\, a \in OldEvents, r_1 \wedge \neg q_1 \wedge r_2 \wedge \neg q_2 \wedge G_{1a} \wedge G_{2a} \wedge I_1 \wedge I_2 \Rightarrow [S_{2a}]q_2$$

is easily built for this refinement pattern (see Fig. 9). However, this condition is likely to fail because of the old events which may be taken before the $\mathcal{U}$ ends. So, the refinement pattern $\mathcal{U}\mathcal{U}$ requires the following stronger sufficient ending

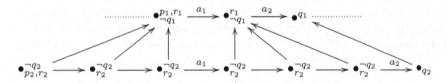

Fig. 9. Pattern $\mathcal{U}\mathcal{U}$

condition which eliminates from the condition the events which might be taken before the $\mathcal{U}$ ends, i.e., the events which do not change the abstract state to an abstract state which satisfies q_1. For that, it is enough to strengthen the implication with the conjunction of $[S_{1a}]q_1$.

$$\forall\ a \in OldEvents,$$
$$r_1 \wedge \neg q_1 \wedge r_2 \wedge \neg q_2 \wedge G_{1a} \wedge G_{2a} \wedge I_1 \wedge I_2 \wedge [S_{1a}]q_1 \Rightarrow [S_{2a}]q_2$$

This stronger sufficient ending condition proves the reformulated Formula 7 of Section 2.2. The refinement pattern $\Diamond\Diamond$ follows the same ending stronger sufficient condition, condition which allows proving that, assuming the satisfaction of Formula 3, its reformulation by Formula 6 holds.

Notice that the strong sufficient conditions are universally quantified on either the set of the new events or the set of the old events of a refined system.

As for the deduction of the weak sufficient conditions, we can exhibit building blocks but they take into account the guards and the generalized substitutions of the involved events. Again, for a given refinement pattern, we get a constructive way to find the set of strong sufficient conditions by using building blocks according to their respective semantics.

3.5 Dynamic Properties Reformulation Versus Variants and Loop Invariants

In this section, we have shown that the verification of *PLTL* reformulation of the dynamic properties can be fully automatic for finite state systems using no variant and no loop invariant.

Given a *PLTL* formula P_1 and its reformulation P_2, we get a systematic construction for finding a set of propositions (building blocks) which suffices to ensure that the refined property holds on the refined system. So, failure does not mean that the property is false. There are two main causes of failure:

- either the gluing invariant is too weak,
- or the property is false, but may be only outside the reachable state set.

Notice that it is the same as in *B* where an invariant which does not hold on the whole state space could be true on the reachable state space.

The sufficient conditions can be viewed as another way to use the preservation of P_1 by refinement as an assumption to verify P_2. Formulating again a property through refinement is useful for three reasons. First, in order to establish the gluing invariant, the user can have a path refinement style of reasoning and not only a variable connection one. Second, it allows us to deal with the model-checking explosion problem since we avoid to model-check the reformulated property by proving either weak or strong sufficient conditions. Third, it opens up an original solution to combine proof and model-checking techniques. This solution is based on refinement.

4 Conclusion and Perspectives

We have proposed a distinctive approach for the verification of finite state reactive systems. The specifications are expressed as *B* finite state event systems, i.e., the variables range over finite domains. A significant number of reactive system, particularly communication and synchronization protocols, are in essence finite state systems. Moreover, the refinement design of event systems requires a decreasing variant for verifying that the new events—the events introduced in the specification during the refinement, do not take control forever. Our goal is to liberate the design from such features. For that purpose, the verification consists in confronting the labeled transition system which models the finite state specification with its dynamic properties expressed by *PLTL* formulae. This can be done automatically by model-checking without additional features. Moreover, the refinement has to relate an abstract transition system and its refinement by the *modular refinement relation* η which is easily verified algorithmically in the particular case of finite state systems. The combination of proof techniques and model-checking relies on a distinction between *reformulated* and *new properties*, the first being verified by a proof technique and the second, by model-checking.

Reformulating a property through refinement is useful for three reasons. First, in order to establish the gluing invariant, the user can have a path refinement style of reasoning and not only a variable relationship one. Second, it allows us to deal with the model-checking explosion problem since we avoid model-checking the reformulated property by proving either weak or strong sufficient conditions. Third, it opens up a peculiar approach for combining proof and model-checking techniques. This approach is based on refinement.

We are currently improving and completing our toolkit (described in [3]) so that we can validate the verification process on larger examples. This is also needed for validating the methodology on industrial size applications. This is essential for our claim about *reformulated/new properties*. Furthermore, we are extending some of the above ideas from finite state systems to a class of parameterized systems which are infinite state systems. The idea is that the abstract system can be finite state whereas the refinements may be infinite state systems.

References

1. J.-R. Abrial. *The B Book*. Cambridge University Press - ISBN 0521-496195, 1996.
2. J.-R. Abrial and L. Mussat. Introducing dynamic constraints in B. In *Second Conference on the B method, France*, volume 1393 of *Lecture Notes in Computer Science*, pages 83–128. Springer Verlag, April 1998.
3. F. Bellegarde, C. Darlot, J. Julliand, and O. Kouchnarenko. Reformulate dynamic properties during B refinement and forget variants and loop invariants. In *Proc. Int. Conf. ZB'2000, York, Angleterre*. Springer-Verlag, August 2000. LNCS to appear.
4. F. Bellegarde, J. Julliand, and O. Kouchnarenko. Ready-simulation is not ready to express a modular refinement relation. In *Proc. Int. Conf. on Fundamental Aspects of Software Engineering, FASE'2000*, volume 1783 of *Lecture Notes in Computer Science*, pages 266–283. Springer-Verlag, April 2000.
5. G. Holzmann. *Design and validation of protocols*. Prentice Hall software series, 1991.
6. J. Julliand, F. Bellegarde, and B. Parreaux. De l'expression des besoins à l'expression formelle des propriétés dynamiques. *Technique et Science Informatiques*, 18(7), 1999.
7. L. Lamport. A temporal logic of actions. *ACM Transactions On Programming Languages And Systems, TOPLAS*, 16(3):872–923, May 1994.
8. Z. Manna and A. Pnueli. *The Temporal Logic of Reactive and Concurrent Systems: Specification*. Springer-Verlag - ISBN 0-387-97664-7, 1992.

Mechanized Analysis of Behavioral Conformance in the Eiffel Base Libraries

Steffen Helke and Thomas Santen

Technische Universität Berlin
Institut für Kommunikations- und Softwaretechnik
FR 5-6, Franklinstrasse 28/29, D-10587 Berlin
email: helke@cs.tu-berlin.de, santen@acm.org

Abstract. We report on an analysis of the inheritance relationships in the Eiffel Base Libraries, a library of container data structures. If inheritance is behaviorally conforming, then polymorphism can be used safely, and the inheritance hierarchy can be considered part of the interface of the library to its clients. We describe a theory of object-oriented specification in higher-order logic that we used to specify part of the Eiffel Base Libraries. With the theorem prover Isabelle/HOL, we mechanically prove conformance relationships between those specifications. This work allows us to draw conclusions about the design of the Eiffel Base Libraries, and about the feasibility of using an interactive theorem prover to apply a strictly formal theory to the specification of a commercial product.

1 Introduction

One of the promises of object-oriented software development is to facilitate the reuse of software components by incremental modification through inheritance, and by decoupling abstract interfaces from concrete implementations through polymorphism. Clients commonly use the components of a library as they are provided. Therefore, the components must have a precisely defined interface. An important piece of information that the interface must make available to the clients are the inheritance relations in the library that the clients may consider part of the interface. Only the inheritance relations of the interface that yield a behaviorally conforming subclass allow clients to use polymorphism *safely*. Therefore, it is worthwhile to study behavioral conformance in a library of components designed for reuse, in particular for inheritance relations that the library designers consider part of the library's interface. Unless clients are sure that abstract classes provide a *behaviorally conforming* interface to more concrete classes of the library, they will pick only a few concrete classes of the library and base their code on the interfaces of those classes. Thus, their code will be more sensitive than necessary to a change of the implementation of a data structure they use. On the other hand, if the clients may trust in the conformance of the inheritance relations in a library, they can design their software to rely on the interfaces to objects provided by abstract classes only. The resulting code will be more abstract and robust to changes of the implementation of objects.

Not all libraries of object-oriented components, however, consider inheritance relations part of their interface to clients. The *Library of Efficient Data Structures and*

J.N. Oliveira and P. Zave (Eds.): FME 2001, LNCS 2021, pp. 20–42, 2001.
© Springer-Verlag Berlin Heidelberg 2001

Algorithms (LEDA) [11], for example, uses inheritance for implementation purposes only. The inheritance "hierarchy" presented to clients basically is flat. Cook [2] investigated behavioral conformance (based on America's [1] notion of behavioral subtyping) between the Smalltalk-80 collection classes. The conformance hierarchy that he derived from the specifications of those classes exhibits multiple relations between the classes. Contrasting the conformance hierarchy with the inheritance hierarchy, he notes that the two are mostly unrelated and in some cases even contradict each other.

In contrast to LEDA and the Smalltalk-80 library, a design goal of the Eiffel Base Libraries [10] was to accomplish a "Linnean reconstruction of the fundamental software structures. ... to devise a coherent overall structure, in which every important variant will have a precise place deduced from the application of a small number of classification criteria" [10]. Therefore, the rich inheritance hierarchy in the Eiffel Base Libraries must be considered part of the interface of the libraries. It is designed to provide various abstractions (or views) of the objects that implement concrete data structures.

Using a theory of object-oriented specification that we have developed with the theorem prover Isabelle/HOL, we have investigated the conformance relations part in the Eiffel Base Libraries. The aim of this work was to provide mechanized tool support for reasoning about software components and to test the feasibility of such an approach on a practically used software product.

In Section 2, we give a brief overview of the part of the Eiffel Base Libraries that we worked on. Section 3 discusses why specifying classes is useful and introduces our specification notation. The representation of specifications in Isabelle/HOL is the topic of Section 4. Section 5 introduces behavioral conformance and the way we have defined it in higher-order logic. We analyze the way classes are built by inheritance in the Eiffel Base Libraries in Section 6. Section 7 shows how those constructions can be mimicked at the specification level. Section 8 summarizes the work on the specifications with Isabelle. We conclude in Section 9 with observations about the Eiffel Base Libraries as a software product and with an analysis of our work with Isabelle/HOL.

2   The Eiffel Base Libraries

The several hundred classes of the Eiffel Base Libraries are grouped into five main libraries: the *kernel*, *data structure*, *iteration*, *Lex*, and *Parse* libraries. We concentrate on the data structure library. It is the largest part of the Eiffel Base Libraries and covers fundamental data structures and algorithms, such as lists, arrays, queues, stacks, trees, and hash tables. Because we investigate the data structure library only, we use the name "Eiffel Base Libraries" as a synonym for the data structure library in the following.

The data structures covered by the Eiffel Base Libraries are container structures: their objects are collections of items that may be changed and accessed according to the specific properties of the data structure. Figure 1 shows the part of the Eiffel Base Libraries on which we focus our investigation. The root of the class hierarchy of the data structure library is the class *CONTAINER* shown in Figure 2. Because the type *G* of the items is irrelevant for a container, the classes of the *CONTAINER* hierarchy are generic in *G*. The interface of the class *CONTAINER* contains three basic features that any container structure must provide: the test *has*(v) determines if the container object

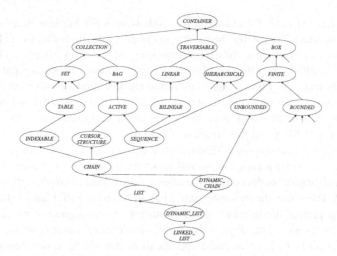

Fig. 1. The *CONTAINER* hierarchy.

contains an item *v*; the attribute *empty* is true if the container does not contain any item; the attribute *linear_representation* provides access to the container as a sequence (of type *LINEAR*[*G*]).

The keywords **require** and **ensure** are part of the assertion language of Eiffel that makes it possible to state preconditions (**require**) and postconditions (**ensure**) of features, and class invariants, and check their validity during execution of an Eiffel program. We will discuss the assertion language in more detail when we consider specifications of Eiffel classes in Section 3.

A major design principle of the Eiffel Base Libraries is to organize the inheritance hierarchy according to a taxonomy of container structures. The three direct descendants of *CONTAINER* represent three criteria – groups of related properties – that serve to describe containers.

- The *access* criterion describes how the clients of a container can access its items. For example, only the top item of a stack is accessible to its clients, whereas the clients of an array can access each of the items of the array by an index. The class *COLLECTION* is the root of the access hierarchy.
- The *traversal* criterion describes how the clients of a container can navigate through the container, accessing each of its items in turn. For example, a particular kind of list may allow traversals only from the front to the back of the list, whereas another kind of list may also allow to traverse it from the back to the front. The class *TRAVERSABLE* is the root of the traversal hierarchy.
- The *storage* criterion describes the cardinality of a container and the ways to change the cardinality. For example, some containers are finite, others are potentially infinite. A finite container may have a fixed size, or its size may be unbounded. The class *BOX* is the root of the storage hierarchy.

```
class CONTAINER [G]
    feature has (v : G) : BOOLEAN is
        deferred
        ensure not_found_in_empty : Result implies not empty
    end;
    feature empty : BOOLEAN is
        deferred
    end;
    feature linear_representation : LINEAR [G] is
        deferred
    end;
    feature object_comparison : BOOLEAN
        ⋮
end
```

```
class COLLECTION [G]
    inherit CONTAINER [G]
    feature extendible : BOOLEAN is          feature prune (v : G) is
        deferred                                 require prunable : prunable
    end;                                         deferred
    feature prunable : BOOLEAN is            end;
        deferred                             feature prune_all (v : G) is
    end;                                         require prunable : prunable
    feature put, extend (v : G) is              do
        require extendible : extendible          ...
        deferred                                 ensure no_more_occurrences : not has(v)
        ensure item_inserted : has(v)        end;
    end;                                     feature wipe_out is
    feature fill (other : CONTAINER [G]) is  require prunable
        do                                       deferred
        ...                                      ensure wiped_out : empty
    end;                                     end;
                                         end
```

```
class BAG [G]
    inherit COLLECTION [G]
        redefine extend
        end
    feature occurrences (v : G) : INTEGER is
        deferred
        ensure not_negative_occurrences : Result >= 0
    end;
    feature extend (v : G) is
        deferred
        ensure then one_more_occurrence : occurrences(v) = old(occurrences(v)) + 1
end
```

Fig. 2. Container classes.

```
class ACTIVE [G]
  inherit BAG [G]
  feature item :  G is            feature replace (v :  G) is
    require readable :  readable      require writable :  writable
    deferred                          deferred
  end;                              ensure item_replaced :  item = v
  feature readable :  BOOLEAN is  end;
    deferred                      feature remove is
  end;                              require prunable :  prunable;
  feature writable :  BOOLEAN is               writable :  writable
    deferred                          deferred
  end;                            end;
  invariant
    writable_constraint :  writable implies readable;
    empty_constraint :  empty implies (not readable) and (not writable)
end
```

Fig. 3. "Active" containers.

Each class in the *CONTAINER* hierarchy provides a view to containers with a particular combination of properties. The (deferred) classes near the root of the hierarchy provide very abstract views of containers. For example the class *BAG* shown in Figure 2 adds only one feature to the ones it inherits from *COLLECTION*: the feature *occurrence*(v) returns the number of occurrences of the item v in the container. Thus, the class *BAG* implicitly represents the property that a bag may store an item more than once. The leaves of the container hierarchy, such as *LINKED_LIST* at the bottom of Figure 1, are effective classes implementing a specific kind of container structure.

The siblings that directly inherit from the same class in some cases represent alternative properties of the class of containers their parent class represents. For example, the classes *SET* and *BAG* represent such a "choice point". The feature *occurrence*(v) provided by *BAG* is useless for sets, because a set may contain an item v at most once. The class *SET* declares an attribute *count*, instead, that holds the number of (different) elements in a set. It also strengthens the postcondition of the feature *prune*(v), which it inherits from *COLLECTION* (c.f. Figure 2). The feature *prune*(v) removes an occurrence of v from the container. For a set, which may contain v at most once, *prune*(v) removes *all* occurrences of v, i.e. it ensures *not has*(v). For a bag, in contrast, *prune_all*(v) establishes that postcondition, but *prune*(v) does not necessarily do so.

Other branches in the inheritance hierarchy represent independent properties, which may be combined further down in the hierarchy by multiple inheritance. For example, the descendant *TABLE* of *BAG* describes containers whose items are accessible through keys. Figure 3 shows the class *ACTIVE*, which is another descendant of *BAG*. The class *ACTIVE* describes containers that have a (possibly undefined) "current item" (called *item*) on which access and modification features work. Being accessible through keys and having a current item are not contradictory properties of a container. The class *CHAIN*, which is a common abstraction of (non-circular) lists and circular containers, combines those properties by multiple inheritance. Thus, the interfaces of *TABLE* and *ACTIVE* both provide valid "views" of a chain.

Fig. 4. Specification of *COLLECTION*.

3 Specification of Library Classes

Eiffel is one of the few programming languages that support *assertions*. Assertions are Boolean expressions that are evaluated at run-time (if the program is compiled with the appropriate compiler option). An assertion that evaluates to *false* raises an exception. Assertions thus provide a valuable tool for debugging programs.

The assertion language is similar to an algebraic specification language that allows one to specify relations between the functions (i.e. the features) of a given signature (i.e. a class). Nevertheless, assertions are too weak to state all relevant properties of a class. In particular for abstract – deferred – classes, it often is impossible to state assertions that describe the intended functionality of a feature. For example, there are no assertions about the attribute *empty* of *CONTAINER* (c.f. Figure 2), because the features available in *CONTAINER* are not expressive enough to state a postcondition on *empty* that captures the intended meaning of that attribute. [1] Similarly, there are no constraints on the attribute *linear_representation* of *CONTAINER*, because it is impossible to state that the items in *linear_representation* are exactly the items in the container object.

---

[1] The characterization of *empty* by $\forall v : G \bullet \neg\ has(v)$ cannot be coded by assertions, because it is impossible to quantify over all elements of G in an assertion

We use a notation similar[2] to Object-Z [17] to specify the intended behavior of classes in a "model-based" way. Refering to a (hidden) mathematical model of containers, we can easily express the effect of features on a container. Figure 4 shows the specification of the class *COLLECTION*, whose Eiffel code is sketched in Figure 2. The semantics of our notation is given by representing it in higher-order logic – a topic that we address in Section 4.

A collection is a mutable container structure storing a number of items of a set G. It can be tested whether a collection is empty and whether it contains a given item. A collection can be extended by a single item (*extend*) or the items of another collection (*fill*). Conversely, duplicate items can be removed from a collection, but once an item with a particular value has been added to the collection, at least one item with an equal value must remain in the collection. The attribute *lin_rep* gives access to a representation of the collection as a sequence.

The constituents of the class specification are gathered in a *class schema* called *Collection[G]*. The parameter indicates that the class is generic in a set G of items. The first component of the class schema is the state schema *STATE*. It describes the valid states of the objects of the class, including attributes of the objects that are observable by other objects. The first component c of the state is the mathematical model of a collection, a bag.

Bags are defined relationally by partial functions from the set of items G to the positive natural numbers, bag $G == G$ $_1$. Bags are formed using double brackets, $v_1, \ldots, v_n$ for items $v_1, \ldots, v_n$, the membership test for bags is v c, $b \uplus d$ is the union of two bags, and $b \sharp v$ is the number of v's in b. The function *items* maps sequences to bags. The domain anti-restriction D R restricts the domain of relation R to items not in D.

In contrast to c, which is not accessible from outside of the class, the state components below the keyword visible are externally visible attributes. Visible state components are a notational abbreviation for methods returning values that depend only on the internal state of an object, so-called *observer methods*. The predicate below the horizontal line of the state schema is the *state invariant*. It describes the relationship between the state components of valid objects.

The schema *INIT* describes the valid initial states of objects: the container c is initially empty, and, because the state invariant is implicitly required by *INIT*, *empty = true* and *lin_rep = ⟨⟩*.

The schemas *has*, *extend*, *fill*, *prune*, and *prune_all* specify the methods of the class. Like in Object-Z, input and output variables are decorated with question marks and exclamation marks, respectively. Undecorated variables refer to the state of the object before executing the method (*pre-state*), primed variables to the state after executing the method (*post-state*). The method schemas of a class *implicitly* refer to the state schema, and the notation $\Delta(x, y, z)$ is used to indicate that the method may change only the state components x, y, and z.

The observation that the assertions of a class are insufficient to specify the intended behavior of its objects properly is also valid for the classes further down in the container

---

[2] The history constraints we use are not part of Object-Z, and we do not support all language features of Object-Z

```
┌─ ACTIVE[G] ─────────────────────────────────────────────────
│ BAG[G]
│ ┌─ STATE ─────────────────────────────────────────────────
│ │ visible
│ │ item : G
│ │ readable : Bool
│ │ writable : Bool
│ ├──────────────────────────────────────────
│ │ readable = true ⇒ item    c
│ │ empty = true ⇒ (readable = false ∧ writable = false)
│ │ writable = true ⇒ readable = true
│ └─────────────────────────────────────────────────────────
│
│ ┌─ replace ───────────────────────────────────────────────
│ │ Δ(c, item, readable, writable, linear_representation)
│ │ v? : G
│ ├──────────────────────────────────────────
│ │ writable = true
│ │ item = v? ⇒ c' = c
│ │ item ≠ v? ⇒ count(c') = count(c) ⊕ {item ↦ (c(item) − 1)}
│ │                                  ⊕{v? ↦ (c ♯ v? + 1)}
│ │ item' = v?
│ └─────────────────────────────────────────────────────────
│
│ ┌─ remove ────────────────────────────────────────────────
│ │ Δ(item, c, readable, writable, extendible, prunable, linear_representation, empty)
│ ├──────────────────────────────────────────
│ │ prunable = true
│ │ writable = true
│ │ count(c') = count(c) ⊕ {item ↦ (c(item) − 1)}
│ └─────────────────────────────────────────────────────────
└──────────────────────────────────────────────────────────────
```

Fig. 5. Specification of *ACTIVE*.

hierarchy, which have a richer structure. The assertions of the class *ACTIVE* (c.f. Figure 3), for example, do not at all clarify the purpose of the new features it declares. The postcondition of *replace(v)*, which shall replace the parameter v for the current item of the container, ensures that the attribute *item* equals v, but it cannot state the effect of *replace(v)* on the container. The method could just set the attribute that holds the value of the current item to v, and leave the container data untouched.

The specification of *ACTIVE* in Figure 5, in contrast, clarifies the effect of *replace(v)* on the internal data of the container, which, for this class, is a bag c : bag G. It relates the value of *item* to the elements of c and requires c to change accordingly. The function *count(c)* maps a bag c to a total function of the same type that maps all items not in the domain of c to 0.

The preceding examples do not question the use of assertions as a documentation of Eiffel code and as a tool for effective debugging, but they show that specifications in a more powerful language than the assertion language of Eiffel can extend the information provided by assertions to include information about the intended functionality of features. That information is not only useful as a documentation for users of the Eiffel Base Libraries, but it also is indispensable for a machine assisted analysis of the library.

4 Representation of Class Specifications in Isabelle/HOL

Since our aim is to come up with tool support for reasoning about class specifications, we must map the Object-Z-like specifications of classes to a logical formalism for which a proof tool exists. To this end, we use Isabelle/HOL, the implementation of higher-order logic (HOL) in the generic theorem prover Isabelle [12]. Our representation of class specifications builds on the representation $\mathcal{HOL\text{-}Z}$ [8] of plain Z in Isabelle/HOL, which we extend by definitions of object-oriented concepts. We have derived an extensive theory about those concepts using Isabelle, and we have implemented a number of tailor-made proof procedures that provide efficient proof support to work with concrete specifications such as the ones describing the Eiffel Base Libraries.

In the following, we can only very briefly introduce the general approach of representing class specifications in HOL and reasoning about them using Isabelle. For a more detailed description of the theory and its implementation, we refer to [8,13]. $\mathcal{HOL\text{-}Z}$ and the complete theory of object-oriented specification in HOL are described in [16].

4.1 The Type of Classes

In $\mathcal{HOL\text{-}Z}$, the schemas of Z are represented by predicates in HOL, i.e. a schema definition of Z is mapped to a function definition in HOL. The defined function maps the tuple of the signature components of the schema to the Boolean values (in HOL, the truth values are just ordinary values). This leads to a so-called shallow embedding of Z in HOL, where the expressions of Z are considered as a concrete syntax for certain expression of HOL. The strong similarity of the semantics of Z and HOL justifies that view [14].

To represent object-oriented specifications, we extend $\mathcal{HOL\text{-}Z}$ by defining a type of classes in HOL. For technical reasons, we distinguish between the constant and the mutable part of the state of an object in that definition: Given that α is the type of method identifiers, the types κ and σ are the types of the immutable and mutable parts of the object state, and the methods of the class have the input type ι and the output type ω, then the type $(\alpha, \kappa, \sigma, \iota, \omega) Class$ consists of all class specifications whose components have the respective types.

$$
\begin{aligned}
(\alpha, \kappa, \sigma, \iota, \omega) \, Class \overset{\mathrm{typ}}{=} \{ &(C, S, I, Mths, H) \mid \\
&(C :: \kappa \, Const) \\
&(S :: (\kappa, \sigma) \, State) \\
&(I :: (\kappa, \sigma) \, Init) \\
&(Mths :: (\alpha, \kappa, \sigma, \iota, \omega) \, Methods) \\
&(H :: (\kappa, \sigma) \, History). \\
&Cls' \, C \, S \, I \, Mths \, H \}
\end{aligned}
\tag{1}
$$

According to that type definition, a class specification is represented by a quintuple $(C, S, I, Mths, H)$. The components C and S are schemas describing invariants over the constant and mutable part of the objects' state. The predicate I represents the initialization schema. The method suite $Mths$ is a (finite) function mapping method identifiers to representations of operation schemas specifying the methods of the class. The predicate

$$Collection\ G \overset{\text{def}}{=} (basicclass\ (CollConst\ G)\ (CollState\ G)\ (CollInit\ G)\ (CollHist\ G))$$
$$\boxdot\ ("empty",\ empty\ G)$$
$$\boxdot\ ("extendible",\ extendible\ G)$$
$$\boxdot\ ("prunable",\ prunable\ G)$$
$$\boxdot\ ("lin\_rep",\ lin\_rep\ G)$$
$$\boxplus\ ("has",\ has\ G)$$
$$\boxplus\ ("extend",\ extend\ G)$$
$$\boxplus\ ("prune",\ prune\ G)$$
$$\boxplus\ ("prune\_all",\ prune\_all\ G)$$
$$\boxplus\ ("fill",\ fill\ G)$$

Fig. 6. Representation of *COLLECTION* in Isabelle/HOL.

H, the *history constraint*, is a relation between before and after states of the objects of the class.

Finally, the predicate $(Cls'\ C\ S\ I\ Mths\ H)$ describes the *internal consistency* of the class. It is defined by four conditions, which ensure that the constituents of a class refer to each other in a way that conforms to our intuition of a class specification:

1. The constant of an object's state can be chosen independently of the mutable part of its state.
2. The initialization establishes a state that satisfies the state invariant.
3. The history constraint relates only states satisfying the state invariant.
4. Each operation schema specifying a method of the class relates only states satisfying the invariant, and it respects the history constraint.

Internal consistency establishes a semantic relation between the components of a class that is in part indicated by the Object-Z-like notation we use to denote class specifications (c.f. Figure 4). For example, it is understood that the methods of a class implicitly refer to the properties of its state schema and constant declarations. The logical representation, however, must make these conditions explicit, because much of the theory about classes derived in Isabelle/HOL relies on them.

4.2 Class Constructors

The type definition (1) abstractly introduces the concept of a class in HOL. Thus, we can define HOL functions that construct class specifications. Those functions take as parameters the representations of Z schemas provided by $\mathcal{HOL\text{-}Z}$ of the component specifications of a class. For example, Figure 6 shows the representation of the specification of *COLLECTION* given in Figure 4.

The function *basicclass* constructs a class specification without methods, the functions $\boxdot$ and $\boxplus$ add the specification of an observer or of an ordinary method to a class specification. Thus, the definition of *Collection G* in Figure 6 first builds a class without methods from the schemas describing the invariant and the initialization of the class. For example, $(CollInit\ G)$ is the HOL predicate representing *INIT* of Figure 4. Then, the definition successively adds the specifications of observers and the other methods of *COLLECTION*, where *extend G*, for example, is the representation of the schema *extend* of Figure 4. The string *"extend"* is the identifier of *extend G* in *Collection G*. We can use it to select the method specification from the class specification, e.g. to model method invocations. The set *ids* (*Collection G*) is the set of method identifiers of *Collection G*.

To be able to work with a class specification in HOL, we must show that its components are internally consistent, i.e. that they satisfy the predicate Cls'. A tactic implemented in Isabelle accomplishes that proof fully automatically for specifications adhering to the usual style of specifying in Z.

5   Behavioral Conformance

Polymorphic assignments in object-oriented languages allow us to express the substitution of (an object of) a data type for another in a program at the level of the programming language. Thus, polymorphism is a means of the object-language to express the meta-language substitution of programs for programs in the context of a client program. We may therefore apply the concept of data type refinement to answer the question whether a variable can safely be bound to an object of a proper subtype of the variable's static type. America [1] coined the term *behavioral subtyping*[3] for this property. Using Hoare-triples to specify the behavior of methods of an object type, he requires that the specification of a subtype *data refines* the specification of a supertype (using a function from subtype to supertype as the simulation relation). He uses the well-known forward simulation rule of data refinement with a retrieve function as it is commonly used for Z (see, e.g., [18]).

5.1   Extra Methods

Rephrased in object-oriented terminology, America's definition of behavioral subtyping requires that no program can distinguish whether a particular variable is bound to an object of its static type or to an object of a proper subtype of that type – provided that the program uses the interface of the supertype only. This restriction on the observing programs is inadequate for most (imperative) object-oriented programming languages, because it is common practice to access the same object via different interfaces.

If we allow sharing of object references in observing programs, we must take the effect of the *extra methods* of a subtype into account in the definition of behavioral subtyping. The *extra methods* of a subtype with respect to a supertype are the methods of the subtype that do not directly correspond to methods of the supertype. Liskov and Wing [9] proposed two modifications of America's definition of subtyping to account for extra methods. We use the relation between the classes *CONTAINER*[G] and *COLLECTION*[G] shown in Figure 2 to illustrate Liskov and Wing's propositions. The purpose of *COLLECTION*[G] (and many other classes of the Eiffel Base Libraries) is

---

[3] The term "behavioral subtyping" is misleading, because the logical relationship that America [1] defines may hold between classes that are not related by inheritance. We call that relationship *behavioral conformance* throughout this paper. Only in the remainder of the present section, where we refer to the terminology of others, will we stay with the term "behavioral subtyping".

to extend *CONTAINER*[G] by several new methods, leaving the inherited methods untouched. Even this small example shows that considering extra methods is indispensable for reasoning about object-oriented component libraries.

Extension Rule. One approach to address subtyping in the presence of extra methods is to interpret a class specification as a complete description of the possible behaviors of all objects of the class – including objects of subclasses. Liskov and Wing [9] call that the *extension rule* of subtyping. In this interpretation, the methods of a class induce the behavior of its objects. All changes of an object's state are caused by the methods defined by its class, and we can identify the objects of a class with the inductively defined set of traces whose starting points are initial objects and which are extended by method applications. Then, extra methods can but mimic the behavior that is already possible without using extra methods.

Consider the relationship between the classes *CONTAINER* and *COLLECTION* shown in Figure 2. The class *CONTAINER* defines the observers *has*, *empty*, and *linear_representation*, but it does not provide a method to change an object's state. The class *COLLECTION* inherits from *CONTAINER* and introduces new methods to add items to a container and remove items from it. According to the extension rule, *COLLECTION* is *not* a behavioral subtype of *CONTAINER*, because the mutators *extend*, *prune*, etc. cannot be explained by the methods inherited from *CONTAINER* (because the latter are observers only).

Constraint Rule. The designers of the Eiffel Base Libraries clearly intended the class *CONTAINER*, which is the root of the inheritance hierarchy of the libraries, to provide the most abstract interface to any object of a container type. A descendant such as *COLLECTION* should be accepted as a behavioral subtype of *CONTAINER*, but the principal assumption underlying the extension rule – that the methods of a class induce all possible behavior of its objects – is obviously not satisfied for that inheritance hierarchy. We must assume that the designers of the library have a more liberal view on subtyping: the description of *CONTAINER* does not forbid that objects change, therefore a subclass may introduce mutators.

The *constraint rule* of subtyping [9] reflects this liberal view: any behavior of an object is admissible unless the specification of its class explicitly disallows it. Liskov and Wing augment class specifications by *history constraints* to restrict the admissible behavior of objects. History constraints are relations of object states describing admissible state changes of objects independently of the changes that the methods make possible. The constraint rule requires that the history constraint of a subclass is sufficient for the one of the superclass. The rule poses the same restrictions on methods as America's definition of subtyping, allowing for weakening of preconditions. Weakening the precondition of a method does not lead to subtyping relations contradicting the intuition that the history constraint describes the possible behaviors of an object, because Liskov and Wing require all methods of a class to satisfy the history constraint. We captured that requirement in the definition of internal consistency.

In the example of Figure 2, we assume an unconstrained history (the full relation on valid states of objects) for *CONTAINER*. With that specification of *CONTAINER*, the constraint rule establishes that *COLLECTION* is a behavioral subtype of *CONTAINER*.

5.2   Behavioral Conformance in Isabelle/HOL

We have defined the analog of Liskov and Wing's constraint rule for our specifications in Isabelle/HOL. That definition is quite lengthy and its exact technical phrasing is not important for this paper. In the following, we therefore paraphrase the definition in a condensed form using Z schema calculus. For more details, we refer the reader to [16].

The predicate *conforms* defines behavioral conformance in HOL. It is declared as follows:

$$conforms :: [\,(\alpha, (\iota, \iota', \omega, \omega')\, IOconv) finmap, (\alpha, \alpha') finmap, (\kappa, \kappa', \sigma, \sigma')\, retrv,$$
$$(\alpha, \kappa, \sigma, \iota, \omega)\, Class, (\alpha', \kappa', \sigma', \iota', \omega')\, Class\,] \rightarrow bool$$

For two class specifications $A = (AConst, AState, AInit, AMeth, AHist)$ and $C = (CConst, CState, CInit, CMeths, CHist)$, the proposition *conforms* $\Theta\, \phi R A C$ is true if C behaviorally conforms to A with the retrieve relation R, the signature morphism ϕ, and the conversion Θ of input/output types between the methods of A and the methods of C.

The relation R relates the states of A to the states of C. Unlike America (and data reification in VDM [6]) we do not require R to be a function, because it turns out that some conformance relationships in the Eiffel Base Libraries require that more liberal view of data refinement, which is also the usual one for Z [4,18].

The signature morphism ϕ maps the names of the methods in *AMeths* to the names of the methods in *CMeths*. For each method of A it thus identifies the method of C that simulates it.

We need the type conversion Θ for technical reasons: HOL is strongly typed. Therefore, we need to inject the different input and output types of the operation schemas specifying the methods of a class into a common type that we can use as *the* type of inputs and outputs, respectively, of the method suite of the class. As a consequence of that representation of classes, the input/output types of different classes, in general, are different. To relate single methods of two classes, we need to map a subset of the input/output type of one class to an isomorphic subset of the input/output type of the other class. The conversion Θ is a family of isomorphisms [15] (indexed by the method identifiers of A) that accomplishes that task.

Paraphrased without the technical overhead we just discussed, *conforms* $\Theta\, \phi R A\, C$ requires the following conditions to hold:

1. The signature morphism ϕ maps all methods of A to some of C:

    $$\mathrm{dom}\, \phi = ids\, A \wedge \mathrm{ran}\, \phi \subseteq ids\, C$$

2. All concrete initial states represent abstract initial states:

    $$\forall CConst;\ CState \bullet CInit \Rightarrow \exists AConst;\ AState \bullet AInit \wedge R$$

3. The preconditions of the abstract methods imply the preconditions of the concrete methods:

$$\forall n : \text{dom } \phi; \; AConst; \; AState; \; CConst; \; CState; \; inp_n? : X_n \bullet$$
$$\text{pre} \, AMeths(n) \wedge R \Rightarrow \text{pre} \, CMeths(\phi(n))$$

4. The concrete methods simulate the abstract methods:

$$\forall n : \text{dom } \phi; \; AConst; \; AState; \; CConst; \; CState; \; CState'; \; inp_n? : X_n; \; out_n! : Y_n \bullet$$
$$\text{pre} \, AMeths(n) \wedge R \wedge CMeths(\phi(n)) \Rightarrow \exists AState' \bullet R' \wedge AMeths(n)$$

5. The concrete history is sufficient for the abstract history:

$$\forall CConst; \; CState \bullet CHist \Rightarrow \exists AConst; \; AState \bullet AHist \wedge R \wedge R'$$

Those conditions are just the conditions of forward simulation rephrased to classes and augmented with the constraint rule that handles extra methods.

5.3   Transitivity of Conformance

Our definition of behavioral conformance in HOL is strictly formal. Therefore, we can derive properties of conformance mechanically within higher order logic using Isabelle/HOL. One important property that we have derived in that way is the transitivity of conformance: Given three classes A, B, and C, and conformance relationships between A and B, and B and C, we know that C also conforms to A:

$$\frac{conforms \, \Theta_{ab} \, \phi_{ab} \, R_{ab} \, A \, B \quad conforms \, \Theta_{bc} \, \phi_{bc} \, R_{bc} \, B \, C \quad \Theta_{ac} = \dots}{conforms \, \Theta_{ac} \, (\phi_{ab} \quad {}_m\phi_{bc}) \, (R_{ab} \quad {}_{\updownarrow} R_{bc}) \, A \, C} \tag{2}$$

6   Inheritance in the Eiffel Base Libraries

In the following, we identify patterns of inheritance in the Eiffel Base Libraries. Each of the patterns corresponds to an operation that constructs a class schema from another one. Those specification building operations do not necessarily produce a behaviorally conforming subclass of their parameter class. Therefore, it would be inadequate to call one of them "the inheritance operation" of our specification language.

There are five ways the classes in the hierarchy[4] of Figure 1 are constructed by inheritance, none of which, in general, yield behaviorally conforming subclasses:

1. *add new methods*: extend the parent by new "extra" methods;
2. *redefine methods*: change the specification or implementation of methods inherited from the parent class;

---

[4] This hierarchy includes just the inheritance relations that we consider part of the interface of the Eiffel Base Libraries; the figure does not show inheritance that is used for implementation purposes only.

3. *add new attributes*: extend the parent by new attributes, thus extending the state of the object;
4. *hide a feature*: export the feature to *NONE*, thus excluding it from the interface of the new class;
5. *combine classes by multiple inheritance*: combine several classes into one, selecting a definition from one class for each feature whose name appears in several of the inherited classes.

Most inheritance relations of the container hierarchy are combinations of those inheritance patterns. For example, the class *BAG* (c.f. Figure 2) extends *COLLECTION* by the new attribute *occurrences*, and it redefines the method *extend*.

We use the following specification building operations to construct specifications according the inheritance patterns: The constructor $\boxplus$ of class schemas (c.f. Section 4.2) extends a class schema by a new method. We can also use it to model redefinition, because if $n \in ids\ Cls$, then $Cls \boxplus (n, OP)$ overrides the definition of n in Cls.

Introducing new attributes involves two modifications of the specification: first, it modifies the state schema to include the new attribute and describe its invariant relations to the other state components; second, it adds a new observer method to the class schema. Modifying the state schema to include a new attribute is a special case of changing the internal model of a class schema such that, under certain conditions, the resulting class schema behaviorally conforms to the original one. We define an operation on class schemas to change the internal model of a class schema and characterize the conditions under which it yields a behaviorally conforming subclass in the following Section 7.

7   Subclass Calculation

Just as it is much more productive to build subclasses from classes by inheritance in Eiffel, it is necessary to construct specifications of subclasses from the specifications of their superclasses. It would be infeasable to specify each class in the Eiffel Base Libraries from scratch, because the resulting specifications would become very large and incomprehensible.

In the preceeding section, we showed that most of the constructions in the Eiffel Base Libraries can be mimicked on the specification level with the class constructors of Section 4. In this section, we define another class constructor, the *subclass calculator*, that allows us to change the mathematical model of a container when constructing the specification from a subclass from the specification of a class. Under certain conditions, the resulting specification behaviorally conforms to the original one.

7.1   The Subclass Calculator

The subclass calculator works dually to a posit-and-prove approach to behavioral conformance. Instead of defining two classes schemas and exhibiting a retrieve relation to establish behavioral conformance, the subclass calculator maps a class schema and a retrieve relation to a new class schema. The calculator uses the conditions of behavioral conformance to specify the components of the resulting concrete class in terms of the given abstract class and the retrieve relation. Roughly, the calculator conjoins the components of the abstract class with the retrieve relation, and existentially quantifies over the abstract constants and states in the resulting formula. The construction for methods relies on the the "data refinement calculator" that Josephs [7] defines to construct a concrete operation schema as a data refinement of an abstract one in Z.

In HOL, the function *SimBy* maps a given class and a retrieve relation to a new class.

$$SimBy :: [\, (\alpha, \kappa, \sigma, \iota, \omega) \; Class, \, (\kappa, \kappa', \sigma, \sigma') \; retrv \,] \rightarrow (\alpha, \kappa', \sigma', \iota, \omega) \; Class$$

The components of *SimBy Cls R* are defined as follows:

- The constant and state schemas of the calculated subclass are defined in terms of the conjunction of the constant and state schemas of *Cls* and the retrieve relation *R*, and hiding the abstract entities.
- For each method *M* of *Cls*, there is a method *M'* of the calculated subclass. The precondition of *M'* contains all pairs of constants and states for which abstract constants and states exist that satisfy the precondition of *M*. For those states, the concrete operation relates the pre- and post-states for which abstract ones exist that satisfy *M*.

$$M' \stackrel{\text{def}}{=} (\exists \, c\, s. \; \text{pre} \; M \, c \, s \, inp \wedge R \, c \, cc \, s \, cs) \wedge$$
$$(\forall \, c\, s. \; \text{pre} \; M \, c \, s \, inp \wedge R \, c \, cc \, s \, cs \Rightarrow$$
$$(\exists \, s'. \; R \, c \, cc \, s' \, cs' \wedge M \, c \, s \, s' \, inp \, out)))$$

- The history schema of the calculated subclass is defined similarly to the constant and state schemas. The retrieve relation *R* establishes correspondences between the abstract and the concrete pre- and post-states.

Josephs [7] already notes that the data refinement calculator for Z does not always yield a refinement. For general retrieve relations *R*, it is still necessary to check the applicability condition relating the preconditions of abstract and concrete operations. (c.f. Section 5.2). If, however, the retrieve relation *R* is a function from the concrete onto the abstract states, then the calculated subclass *SimBy Cls R* behaviorally conforms to *Cls*. That condition on *R* corresponds to the adequacy condition of data reification in VDM [6], which admits functional abstractions only. The predicate *is_surj_fun* defines that condition formally.

$$\frac{is\_surj\_fun \, R \, (cma \; Cls) \, (sma \; Cls) \quad CVs = IdentList \stackrel{io}{\cong} Cls \quad M = id_m \, (ids \; Cls)}{conforms \; CVs \, M \, R \, Cls \, (SimBy \; Cls \, R)} \quad (3)$$

Theorem (3) is of great practical importance. It establishes once and for all the – relatively simple – conditions under which subclass calculation implies behavioral conformance. As the next section will show, subclass calculation is suitable to define the specifications of most classes of the Eiffel Base Libraries. Theorem (3) helps a lot to simplify proofs of behavioral conformance between those specifications – compared to proofs against the definition of behavioral conformance. In particular, the theorem does not require the proof to consider the method suites of the two classes, which otherwise is the major work in a proof of behavioral conformance.

7.2 An Alternative Representation of *Collection*

Using the subclass calculator, we can build a specification of *Collection* from the specification of *Container*. The internal model of *Container* is a set of the items in the
container. The internal model we use in *Collection*, however, is a bag (c.f. Figure 4).
Given a relation R_{Coll}^{Cont} that equates the internal model of *Container* to the domain of c in
Collection, we can construct the specification of *Collection* by calculating a subclass of
Container according to R_{Coll}^{Cont} and augmenting the resulting class with the extra methods
of *Collection*:

$$Collection\ G \stackrel{\text{def}}{=} (SimBy\ (Container\ G)\ R_{Coll}^{Cont})$$
$$\boxplus\ ("prunable", Prunable\ G)$$
$$\boxplus\ \ldots \boxplus\ ("prune\_all", Prune\_all\ G)$$

We used that way of constructing specifications to economically specify the classes
of the Eiffel Base Libraries shown in Figure 1.

8   Conformance Analysis of the Eiffel Base Libraries

We followed a five step procedure to specify classes and analyze behavioral conformance
with Isabelle/HOL (see [5] for the technical details):

1. Specify a class in Object-Z-like notation; represent the specification as a class
   schema in HOL. For the representation, decide whether to construct the class schema
   independently of other class schemas, or to use the subclass calculator to construct
   the class schema from another one. In the latter case, determine an appropriate
   retrieve relation.
2. Prove the internal consistency of the new class schema, and derive unconditional
   equations to select the components of the class schema.
3. Derive the preconditions of the methods of the new class schema.
4. Determine retrieve relations between the new class schema and the specifications of
   the immediate ancestors of the class in the inheritance hierarchy, if such relations
   exist. Analyze whether or not the retrieve relations are surjective functions.
5. Prove behavioral conformance of the new class with its immediate ancestors.

Step 2 is strictly necessary to be able to prove non-trivial propositions about the
specific class schema. Deriving the preconditions in Step 3, however, mainly served to
validate the specifications, because the retrieve relations we considered all were surjective functions such that we could apply Theorem (3) to prove behavioral conformance
in Step 5. If a class schema is constructed by subclass calculation in Step 1, then Step 4
only needs to analyze the function property of the relation used in Step 1.

Figure 7 shows the subgraph of the *CONTAINER* hierarchy that we considered. We
represented the classes in HOL that are shaded gray in the figure. The class schemas
of the *COLLECTION* and *TRAVERSABLE* hierarchies are defined in terms of their immediate ancestors in those hierarchies. The class schema *BAG* is a simple extension of

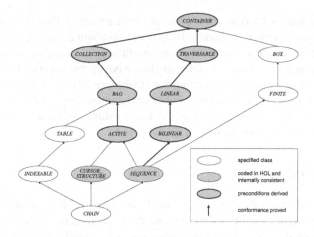

Fig. 7. The specified and analyzed subgraph of the *CONTAINER* hierarchy.

COLLECTION by new methods (using ⊞). All other constructions in the two hierarchies are subclass calculations that are extended by new methods and observers for new attributes. The transitions from *CONTAINER* to *COLLECTION* and to *TRAVERSABLE* involve changes of the mathematical model of the container: in *CONTAINER*, it is a set, whereas it is a bag in *COLLECTION* and a sequence in *TRAVERSABLE*. The constructions of the other classes only extend the state with new attributes. The retrieve relations for those constructions are therefore projections from the extended concrete state to the abstract state.

To derive the internal consistency (Step 2) of the class schemas shaded gray in the figure, we used a tailor-made tactic (c.f. Section 4.2). Deriving the preconditions (Step 3) of the methods of all classes except *CURSOR_STRUCTURE* and *SEQUENCE*, served to validate the specifications. To derive the preconditions, we used a tactic to apply the one-point-rule in a sophisticated way, which included handling subclass calculations. All retrieve relations used in the subclass calculations, and also the one used to analyze the inheritance of *ACTIVE* by *SEQUENCE*, are surjective functions (Step 4). This allowed us to rely on Theorem (3) when proving behavioral conformance relations (Step 5).

To achieve a high degree of automation, we implemented two tactics to prove conformance for the typical construction used in the library. Given an abstract class schema *ACls* that construction consists of two steps: first, we defined an intermediate class schema

$$BCls = SimBy\ ACls\ R$$

by subclass calculation; second, we extended the class schema *BCls* by a number of methods (possibly overriding method definitions of *ACls*):

$$CCls = BCls \boxplus (n_1, Op_1) \ldots \boxplus (n_k, Op_k)$$

Our tactics consider conformance proofs for subclass calculation and extension by methods, respectively. They automatically synthesize appropriate I/O conversions and handle all proof obligations related to class schema constructions. Using the theorems about subclass calculation of Section 7 and similar theorems about extension of a class schema by a method, they reduce a conformance proposition to verification conditions on (the $\mathcal{HOL\text{-}Z}$ representations of) the Z schemas that make up the specification of the class. They present only those verification conditions to the user of Isabelle to prove them interactively. Thus, the two tactics establish behavioral conformance of $BCls$ to $ACls$, and of $CCls$ to $BCls$. An application of Theorem (2), the transitivity of behavioral conformance, completes the proof of conformance of $CCls$ to $ACls$.

9   Conclusions

We conclude with an evaluation of our work on the Eiffel Base Libraries. First, we discuss our experience with the libraries and their specification.. Then we draw some conclusions about the suitability of our framework for applying it to the libraries.

The Eiffel Base Libraries. Setting up the specifications of classes of the library and analyzing their relationships required a detailed examination of their informal description, their specification by assertions, and their implementation code, too. Often, Meyer's [10] informal description of the purpose of classes and their features helped to clarify their functionality, but occasionally it was necessary to inspect the code not only of the class in question but also of its descendants, in particular the effective ones at the leaves of the inheritance hierarchy, to determine the precise function of a feature in a class. This was especially necessary to distinguish between similar features, such as *extend*, *put*, and *replace*, or *prune* and *remove*.

Class specifications concisely describe the possible behavior of objects. The resulting specifications capture not only the information that is directly present in the class description (by assertions and code), which is quite sparse for the deferred classes near the root of the class hierarchy. Capturing information about the descendants of a class, too, the specifications describe the possible "evolution" of features (by late binding) when moving down in the inheritance hierarchy toward effective classes. Thus, the specifications disambiguate the functionality of features and describe – in a single specification – not just a single class but the cluster of classes that inherit from that class. A class specification concisely captures the possible behavior of the objects of a class. Behaviorally conforming subclasses assumed, the specification of a method completely describes the possible effects of an invocation of the method at the presence of late binding and polymorphism. It is not necessary to inspect the different implementations of the method in the descendants of the class.

Inheritance induces behavioral conformance. All inheritance relations in the part of the libraries that we analyzed induce behavioral conformance. Therefore, it is safe to use objects of those classes polymorphically, accessing them through an abstract interface, as it is provided by the deferred classes in the library. This justifies to consider the entire inheritance graph shown in Figure 7, not just the interfaces of the classes, as part of the interface of the Eiffel Base Libraries to their clients.

Table 1. Analysis of Class Specifications.

Class	Number of methods		Proof time (in min.)	
	new	total	Internal consistency	Precondition analysis
CONTAINER	3	3	2	1
COLLECTION	8	11	17	10
BAG	2	12	2	4
ACTIVE	5	17	13	41
CURSOR_STRUCTURE	11	28	125	—
TRAVERSABLE	3	6	3	5
LINEAR	8	14	20	50
BILINEAR	2	16	10	25
SEQUENCE	14	30	130	—

Performance measured on a SUN-Enterprise 3000
with 4 UltraSparc-I processors (167 MHz) and 4 GB main memory.

Retrieve relations are simple. The retrieve relations that relate immediate descendants to their ancestors are relatively simple. Overriding the specifications of inherited methods is rarely necessary. These observations indicate that the individual classes encapsulate few well-defined "properties" or "design decisions" rather than merging many in one class.

Partial conformance can describe the effect of hiding methods. The inheritance relations that are part of the interface of the libraries to clients are designed to ensure behavioral conformance. Hiding features avoids duplicating classes in some places. In a strict sense, hiding destroys conformance, because the signature morphism from the abstract to the concrete class is necessarily partial. But, as Frick et. al. [3] observe, considering all methods of a class often is unnecessary to ensure safe polymorphic uses: the conditions of behavioral conformance need only hold for the methods that a context actually uses. It is, of course, easy to define a weaker notion of conformance in our framework that does not require the signature morphism to be total.

The Framework. Table 1 gives an impression of the size and complexity of the application of our tactics to the classes of Figure 7. It provides data on the sizes of the classes and on the performance of the tactics establishing internal consistency and deriving preconditions. The first two columns show the number of methods that are newly defined in a class and the total number of methods including the ones "inherited" from its parent class (by a subclass calculation). It is common for a class to extend its parent class with approximately ten new methods.

New methods determine the effort of internal consistency and precondition analysis. The third column shows performance figures for proving the class schemas internally

Table 2. Performance for proving behavioral conformance.

Conformance	Proof time in min.
COLLECTION – CONTAINER	2
BAG – COLLECTION	4
ACTIVE – BAG	3
TRAVERSABLE – CONTAINER	4
LINEAR – TRAVERSABLE	4
BILINEAR – LINEAR	4
SEQUENCE – BILINEAR	4
SEQUENCE – ACTIVE (incomplete)	(20)

consistent. The figures increase proportional to the number of *new* methods, because the proofs were carried out starting with *CONTAINER* and moving down in the inheritance hierarchy. Thus, the consistency lemmas for the ancestors of a class were available for proving the internal consistency of the class.

Similarly, the figures for the performance of the precondition analyses indicate that preconditions have been derived for new methods only. Those preconditions served to validate the specifications. The subsequent conformance proofs did not need to consider preconditions, because all retrieve relations were surjective functions, and therefore, the proofs could employ Theorem (3).

Abstract theorems are essential for feasibility. Table 2 shows performance figures for the proofs of behavioral conformance. The conformance proofs required between two and four minutes of computation time. The possibility to apply general theorems, such as Theorem (3) by appropriate tactics helps to keep the effort for conformance proofs low. Isabelle needs two seconds to resolve a proof goal with the transitivity Theorem (2). The theorem about conformance of subclass calculations alone allows for a speed-up of a factor of five in the first conformance proof: Isabelle needs ten minutes to prove that a specification of *COLLECTION* that is *not* based on the one of *CONTAINER* behaviorally conforms to *CONTAINER*.

Non-functional retrieve relations are necessary. There are inheritance relations in the library that require non-functional retrieve relations. An example is the relation between *COLLECTION* and its immediate descendant *SET* (c.f. Figure 1). The model of a container in the specification of *COLLECTION* is a bag, because the specification of *prune* must allow the method to remove some but not all occurrences of the item v. In the specification of *SET*, however, the model of the container is a set (as it is in the specification of *CONTAINER*). To prove behavioral conformance of *SET* to *COLLECTION*, we need a non-functional retrieve relation that relates a set s to all bags b for which dom $b = s$. That observation also illustrates a difference between specifications of classes and specifications of "classical" abstract data types: in an object-oriented context, deferred classes such as *COLLECTION* do not provide a "complete" interface to their objects as an abstract data type does but they provide a restricted "view" of an object of an effected class that has a much larger interface.

Multiple inheritance is hard. In contrast to the other proofs of conformance, the definitions of *SEQUENCE* and *ACTIVE* are independent. We approached the proof of that conformance relation by simplifying the method schemas of the two classes to obtain "explicit" predicates. The figure at the bottom row of Table 2 shows the computation time to derive some simplified forms of the method schemas of *SEQUENCE*. Like for the precondition analyses in Table 1, the need to eliminate the numerous existential quantifications in the definition of the subclass calculator is responsible for the high cost of those simplifications.

The performance figures of Table 2 indicate that the theory of subclass calculations that we sketched in Section 7 is suitable to handle the patterns of single inheritance that we identified in Section 6. To investigate behavioral conformance for multiple inheritance properly, however, we need a more elaborate theory. A "step-wise" approach that, in the example, would establish relations between *SEQUENCE* and the ancestors of *ACTIVE*, moving down in the inheritance hierarchy, seems promising to prove the behavioral conformance induced by multiple inheritance. General theorems about "pushouts" of conformance relations would support such an approach. Our framework is expressive enough to state and prove such theorems.

We consider our work on the Eiffel Base Libraries as a substantial application of our framework to a mature, practically used software product. The specifications of the part of the Eiffel Base Libraries we worked on total about three thousand lines of Isabelle theory files. The proofs about those specifications consist of another three thousand lines of proof scripts written in ML. Although there is potential for optimization, our work shows the practicality of using a mature theorem prover such as Isabelle to develop an abstract theory of object oriented specification and apply it to reason about the specifications of software components.

References

1. P. America. Designing an object-oriented programming language with behavioral subtyping. In J. W. de Bakker, W. P. de Roever, and G. Rozenberg, editors, *Foundations of Object-Oriented Languages*, LNCS 489. Springer-Verlag, 1991.
2. W. R. Cook. Interfaces and specifications for the Smalltalk-80 collection classes. In *Proc. OOPSLA'92*, volume 27(10) of *ACM SIGPLAN Notices*, pages 1–15, 1992.
3. A. Frick, R. Neumann, and W. Zimmermann. Eine Methode zur Konstruktion robuster Klassenhierarchien. In *Softwaretechnik 96*, pages 16–23, 1996.
4. Jifeng He, C. A. R. Hoare, and J. W. Sanders. Data refinement refined. In B. Robinet and R. Wilhelm, editors, *European Symposium on Programming (ESOP'86)*, LNCS 213, pages 187–196. Springer-Verlag, 1986.
5. S. Helke. Maschinengestützte Analyse der Untertypbeziehungen zwischen Klassen der Eiffel Datenstrukturbibliothek. Master's thesis, Dept. of Computer Science, Technical University of Berlin, 1998.
6. C. B. Jones. *Systematic Software Development using VDM*. Prentice Hall, 2nd edition, 1990.

7. M. B. Josephs. The data refinement calculator for Z specifications. *Information Processing Letters*, 27:29–33, 1988.
8. Kolyang, T. Santen, and B. Wolff. A structure preserving encoding of Z in Isabelle/HOL. In J. von Wright, J. Grundy, and J. Harrison, editors, *Theorem Proving in Higher-Order Logics*, LNCS 1125, pages 283–298. Springer-Verlag, 1996.
9. B. Liskov and J. Wing. A behavioral notion of subtyping. *ACM Transactions on Programming Languages and Systems*, 16(6):1811–1841, 1994.
10. B. Meyer. *Reusable Software*. Prentice Hall, 1994.
11. S. Näher. LEDA manual version 3.0. Technical Report MPI-I-93-109, Max-Planck-Institut für Informatik, Saarbrücken, February 1993.
12. L. C. Paulson. *Isabelle – A Generic Theorem Prover*. LNCS 828. Springer-Verlag, 1994.
13. T. Santen. A theory of structured model-based specifications in Isabelle/HOL. In E. L. Gunter and A. Felty, editors, *Proc. International Conference on Theorem Proving in Higher Order Logics*, LNCS 1275, pages 243–258. Springer-Verlag, 1997.
14. T. Santen. On the semantic relation of Z and HOL. In J. Bowen and A. Fett, editors, *ZUM'98: The Z Formal Specification Notation*, LNCS 1493, pages 96–115. Springer-Verlag, 1998.
15. T. Santen. Isomorphisms – a link between the shallow and the deep. In Y. Bertot, G. Dowek, A. Hirschowitz, C. Paulin, and L. Théry, editors, *Theorem Proving in Higher Order Logics*, LNCS 1690, pages 37–54. Springer-Verlag, 1999.
16. T. Santen. *A Mechanized Logical Model of Z and Object-Oriented Specification*. Shaker-Verlag, 2000. Dissertation, Fachbereich Informatik, Technische Universität Berlin, (1999).
17. G. Smith. *The Object-Z Specification Language*. Kluwer Academic Publishers, 1999.
18. J. M. Spivey. *The Z Notation – A Reference Manual*. Prentice Hall, 2nd edition, 1992.

Proofs of Correctness of Cache-Coherence Protocols

Joseph Stoy[1], Xiaowei Shen[2], and Arvind[2]

[1] Oxford University Computing Laboratory
Oxford OX1 3QD, England
Joe.Stoy@comlab.ox.ac.uk
[2] Laboratory for Computer Science
Massachusetts Institute of Technology
Cambridge MA 02139, USA
xwshen, arvind@lcs.mit.edu

Abstract. We describe two proofs of correctness for Cachet, an adaptive cache-coherence protocol. Each proof demonstrates soundness (conformance to an abstract cache memory model CRF) and liveness. One proof is manual, based on a term-rewriting system definition; the other is machine-assisted, based on a TLA formulation and using PVS. A two-stage presentation of the protocol simplifies the treatment of soundness, in the design and in the proofs, by separating all liveness concerns. The TLA formulation demands precision about what aspects of the system's behavior are observable, bringing complication to some parts which were trivial in the manual proof. Handing a completed design over for independent verification is unlikely to be successful: the prover requires detailed insight into the design, and the designer must keep correctness concerns at the forefront of the design process.

1 Introduction: Memory Models and Protocols

Shared memory multiprocessor systems provide a global memory image so that processors running parallel programs can exchange information and synchronize with one another by accessing shared variables. In large-scale systems the physical memory is usually distributed across different sites to achieve better performance. Distributed Shared Memory (DSM) systems implement the shared memory abstraction with a large number of processors connected by a network, combining the scalability of network-based architectures with the convenience of shared memory programming. The technique known as caching allows shared variables to be replicated in multiple sites simultaneously to reduce memory access latency. DSM systems rely on cache-coherence protocols to ensure that each processor can observe the semantic effect of memory access operations performed by another processor.

A shared memory system implements a *memory model*, which defines the semantics of memory access instructions. An ideal memory model should allow efficient and scalable implementations while still having simple semantics

J.N. Oliveira and P. Zave (Eds.): FME 2001, LNCS 2021, pp. 43–71, 2001.

for architects and compiler writers to reason about. Commit-Reconcile-Fences (CRF) [SAR99b] is a mechanism-oriented memory model intended for architects and compiler writers rather than for high-level parallel programming. It is intended to give architects great flexibility for efficient implementations, while giving compiler writers adequate control. It can be used to give precise descriptions of the memory behavior of many existing architectures; moreover, it can be efficiently implemented on these platforms. Conversely, if implemented in its own right, CRF provides a platform for their efficient implementations: thus upward and downward compatibility is obtained.

Caching and instruction reordering are ubiquitous features of modern computer systems and are necessary to achieve high performance. The design of cache-coherence protocols plays a crucial role in the construction of shared memory systems because of its profound impact on the overall performance and implementation complexity. Such protocols can be extremely complicated, especially in the presence of various optimizations. It often takes much more time to verify their correctness than to design them, and the problem of their verification has gained considerable attention in recent years [ABM93,Arc87,Bro90,PD95, PD96a] [PD96b,PD96c,PNAD95,SD95,HQR99,Del00]. Formal methods provide the only way to avoid subtle errors in sophisticated protocols.

This paper addresses the task of implementing CRF in its own right. As part of this task, we propose a cache-coherence protocol, Cachet [SAR99a,She00], which is adaptive in the sense that it can be tuned on the fly to behave efficiently under varying patterns of memory usage. This is a complex protocol; it is an amalgam of several micro-protocols, each intended for a different usage pattern. We show that the design of each micro-protocol, and Cachet itself, is simplified by taking it in two stages: "imperative" rules, which are sufficient to guarantee the protocol's soundness, are specified (and may be proved correct) before adding the "directive" rules, which are needed to ensure its liveness.

Even with this simplifying approach, however, the result is so complex that a formal correctness proof is desirable; and constructing such a proof with confidence calls for machine assistance. In this paper we compare two proof efforts for components of the Cachet protocol: one is manual, rooted in the term-rewriting methodology in which CRF and Cachet are described; the other is machine-assisted, using an implementation of Lamport's TLA [Lam94] in SRI's PVS [COR+95]. The manual proof may be found in [She00]; the PVS version of TLA and the full machine-assisted proofs are available on the web [Sto].

1.1   The CRF Memory Model

The essence of memory models is the correspondence between each load instruction and the store instruction that supplies the data retrieved by the load. The memory model of uniprocessor systems is intuitive: a load operation returns the most recent value written to the address, and a store operation binds the value for subsequent load operations. In parallel systems, notions such as "the most recent value" can become ambiguous since multiple processors access me-

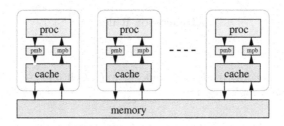

SYS	≡	Sys(MEM, SITEs)	*System*
SITEs	≡	{SITE}	*Set of Sites*
SITE	≡	Site(CACHE, PMB, MPB, PROC)	*Site*
CACHE	≡	{Cell(a,v,CSTATE)}	*Semantic Cache*
CSTATE	≡	Clean ⫿ Dirty	*Cache State*
PMB	≡	[⟨t,INST⟩]	*Processor-to-Memory Buffer*
MPB	≡	{⟨t,REPLY⟩}	*Memory-to-Processor Buffer*
INST	≡	Load(a) ⫿ Store(a,v)	*Transaction Instruction*
		⫿ Commit(a) ⫿ Reconcile(a)	
REPLY	≡	v ⫿ Ack	*Reply*
MEM	≡	A →V	*Main Memory*

Fig. 1. System Configuration of CRF (omitting fences)

mory concurrently. Surveys of some well-known memory models can be found elsewhere [AG96,KPS93].

One motivation underlying CRF is to eliminate the *modèle de l'année* aspect of many existing relaxed memory models while still permitting efficient implementations. It exposes both data replication and instruction reordering at the instruction set architecture level. The CRF model has a semantic notion of caches (referred to as "saches" when there is any danger of confusion with physical caches). Loads and stores are always performed directly on local caches. New instructions are provided to move data between cache and main memory whenever necessary: the Commit instruction ensures that a modified value in the cache is written back, while the Reconcile instruction ensures that a value which might be stale is purged from the cache. CRF also provides fine-grain fence instructions to control the re-ordering of memory-related instructions: they are irrelevant to protocol correctness, and are not treated further in this paper.

The CRF model permits aggressive cache-coherence protocols because no operation explicitly or implicitly involves more than one semantic cache. A novel feature of CRF is that many memory models can be expressed as restricted versions of CRF: programs written under those memory models can be translated into efficient CRF programs. Translations of programs written under memory

---

Processor Rules

CRF-Loadl Rule
 Site($cache$, $\langle t,$Load$(a)\rangle$:pmb, mpb, $proc$) if Cell($a,v,$-$) \in cache$
$\rightarrow$ Site($cache$, pmb, $mpb|\langle t,v\rangle$, $proc$)

CRF-Storel Rule
 Site(Cell($a,$-,-$) \mid cache$, $\langle t,$Store$(a,v)\rangle$:pmb, mpb, $proc$)
$\rightarrow$ Site(Cell($a,v,$Dirty$) \mid cache$, pmb, $mpb|\langle t,$Ack$\rangle$, $proc$)

CRF-Commit Rule
 Site($cache$, $\langle t,$Commit$(a)\rangle$:pmb, mpb, $proc$) if Cell($a,$-,Dirty$) \notin cache$
$\rightarrow$ Site($cache$, pmb, $mpb|\langle t,$Ack$\rangle$, $proc$)

CRF-Reconcile Rule
 Site($cache$, $\langle t,$Reconcile$(a)\rangle$:pmb, mpb, $proc$) if Cell($a,$-,Clean$) \notin cache$
$\rightarrow$ Site($cache$, pmb, $mpb|\langle t,$Ack$\rangle$, $proc$)

Background Rules

CRF-Cache Rule
 Sys(mem, Site($cache$, pmb, mpb, $proc$) $\mid sites$) if $a \notin cache$
$\rightarrow$ Sys(mem, Site(Cell($a,mem[a],$Clean$) \mid cache$, pmb, mpb, $proc$) $\mid sites$)

CRF-Writeback Rule
 Sys(mem, Site(Cell($a,v,$Dirty$) \mid cache$, pmb, mpb, $proc$) $\mid sites$)
$\rightarrow$ Sys($mem[a:=v]$, Site(Cell($a,v,$Clean$) \mid cache$, pmb, mpb, $proc$) $\mid sites$)

CRF-Purge Rule
 Site(Cell($a,$-,Clean$) \mid cache$, pmb, mpb, $proc$)
$\rightarrow$ Site($cache$, pmb, mpb, $proc$)

Fig. 2. The CRF Rules (omitting fences)

models such as sequential consistency and release consistency into CRF programs are straightforward.

Figure 1 shows the system configuration of the CRF model. We use {SITE} to indicate a set of sites, and [< t, INST >] to indicate a list of items of the form < t, INST > (each instruction is associated with a unique tag). Notation A $\rightarrow$ V denotes a function from addresses to values. Note that cache cells have two states, Clean and Dirty. The Clean state indicates that the value has not been modified since it was last cached or last written back; the Dirty state indicates that the value has been changed and has not been written back to the memory

Processor Rules				
Rule Name	**Instruction**	**Cstate**	**Action**	**Next Cstate**
CRF-Loadl	Load(a)	Cell(a,v,Clean)	retire	Cell(a,v,Clean)
		Cell(a,v,Dirty)	retire	Cell(a,v,Dirty)
CRF-Storel	Store(a,v)	Cell(a,-,Clean)	retire	Cell(a,v,Dirty)
		Cell(a,-,Dirty)	retire	Cell(a,v,Dirty)
CRF-Commit	Commit(a)	Cell(a,v,Clean)	retire	Cell(a,v,Clean)
		$a \notin cache$	retire	$a \notin cache$
CRF-Reconcile	Reconcile(a)	Cell(a,v,Dirty)	retire	Cell(a,v,Dirty)
		$a \notin cache$	retire	$a \notin cache$

Background Rules				
Rule Name	**Cstate**	**Mstate**	**Next Cstate**	**Next Mstate**
CRF-Cache	$a \notin cache$	Cell(a,v)	Cell(a,v,Clean)	Cell(a,v)
CRF-Writeback	Cell(a,v,Dirty)	Cell(a,-)	Cell(a,v,Clean)	Cell(a,v)
CRF-Purge	Cell(a,-,Clean)	Cell(a,v)	$a \notin cache$	Cell(a,v)

Fig. 3. Summary of the CRF Rules

since then. Notice that different caches may have cells with the same address but different values.

Figure 2 gives the term-rewriting rules for the CRF model (omitting all mention of fences). As usual for term-rewriting systems, a rule may be applied whenever there is a context matching its left-hand side; if more than one rule is applicable, the choice is non-deterministic. For example, a Commit instruction at the head of the processor-to-memory buffer *pmb* does not in itself imply that the CRF-Commit rule can be applied: the rule is not applicable if the relevant cache cell state is Dirty. In that case, however, the background CRF-Writeback rule is applicable; and when that rule has been applied, the CRF-Commit rule can then be used.

In the CRF specification, we use constructors '|' and ':' to add an element to a set and to prepend an element to a list. For example, the processor-to-memory buffer *pmb* can be thought of as an FIFO queue; this aspect is captured by the use of ':'. The notation *mem*[a] refers to the content of memory location a, and *mem*[a:=v] represents the memory with location a updated with value v.

Figure 3 shows the rules in summarized form. The tabular description are easily translated into formal TRS rules (cases that are not specified represent illegal or unreachable states). The complete definition of CRF can be found elsewhere [SAR99b,She00].

1.2   The Cachet Protocol

The Cachet protocol is a directory-based adaptive cache-coherence protocol to implement the CRF memory model in distributed shared memory systems. It is a seamless integration of several so-called micro-protocols (Base, Writer-Push and Migratory), though each micro-protocol is functionally complete in itself. It provides both intra-protocol and inter-protocol adaptivity which can be exploited by appropriate heuristic mechanisms to achieve optimal performance under changing program behavior. Different micro-protocols can be used by different cache engines, and a cache can dynamically switch from one micro-protocol to another.

The CRF model allows a cache-coherence protocol to use any cache or memory in the memory hierarchy as the rendezvous for processors that access shared memory locations, provided that it maintains the same observable behavior. The micro-protocols differ in the actions they perform when committing dirty cells and reconciling clean ones.

Base: The most straightforward implementation simply uses the memory as the rendezvous. When a Commit instruction is executed for an address that is cached in the Dirty state, the data must be written back to the memory before the instruction can complete. A Reconcile instruction for an address cached in the Clean state requires that the data be purged from the cache before the instruction can complete. An attractive characteristic of Base is its simplicity: no extra state needs to be maintained at the memory side.

Writer-Push (WP): If load operations are far more frequent than store operations, it is desirable to allow a Reconcile instruction to complete even when the address is cached in the Clean state; then a subsequent load access to the address causes no cache miss. This implies, however, that when a Commit instruction is performed on a dirty cell, it cannot complete until any clean copies of the address are purged from all other caches. It can therefore be a lengthy process to commit an address that is cached in the Dirty state.

Migratory: When an address is used exclusively by one processor for a considerable time, it makes sense to give the cache exclusive ownership, so that all instructions on the address become local operations. This is reminiscent of the exclusive state in conventional invalidate-based protocols. The protocol ensures that an address can be stored in at most one cache at any time. A Commit instruction can then complete even when the address is cached in the Dirty state, and a Reconcile instruction can complete even when the address cached in the Clean state. The exclusive ownership can migrate among different caches whenever necessary.

Different micro-protocols are optimized for different access patterns. The Base protocol is ideal when the location is randomly accessed by several processors and only necessary commit and reconcile operations are invoked. The WP protocol is appropriate when some processors are likely to read an address many times before any processor writes the address. The Migratory protocol fits well when one processor is likely to read or write an address many times before any other processor uses the address.

1.3   The Imperative-&-Directive Design Methodology

To simplify the process of designing protocols such as these, we have proposed a two-stage design methodology called Imperative-&-Directive, to separate soundness and liveness concerns. Soundness ensures that the system exhibits only legal behaviors permitted by the specification; liveness ensures that the system eventually performs actions which make progress. The first stage of the design involves only *imperative rules*: these specify actions which can affect the soundness of the system. The messages handled by these rules are known as *imperative messages*. The second stage of the design adds *directive messages*: these can be used to invoke imperative rules, but they are also manipulated by other rules known as *directive rules*. Imperative and directive rules are properly integrated to ensure both soundness and liveness. Directive rules do not change the soundness of a state; moreover, improper conditions for invoking imperative rules can cause deadlock or livelock but cannot affect soundness. It therefore suffices to verify the soundness of the system with respect to the imperative rules, rather than the integrated rules of the integrated protocol.

As an example, the WP protocol includes an imperative rule which allows a cache to purge a clean value, notifying the memory via an imperative Purged message. The imperative rule does not specify when this must be invoked to ensure the liveness of the system. When the memory requires that the cache perform a purge operation (to allow a writeback elsewhere to complete), it sends a directive PurgeReq message to the cache. The integrated protocol ensures both soundness and liveness by requiring that the cache respond appropriately once such a request is received.

We also make an entirely separate classification of the rules of the integrated protocol, dividing them into two disjoint sets: *mandatory rules* and *voluntary rules*. The distinction is that for liveness of the system it is essential that mandatory rules, if they become applicable, are sooner or later actually executed. Voluntary rules, on the other hand, have no such requirement and are provided purely for adaptivity and performance reasons: an enabled voluntary rule may be ignored forever without harm to the protocol's correctness (but possibly with considerable harm to the performance).

Mandatory rules, therefore, require some kind of fairness to ensure the liveness of the system. This can be expressed in terms of weak or strong fairness. *Weak fairness* means that if a mandatory rule remains applicable, it will eventually be applied. *Strong fairness* means that if a mandatory rule continually becomes applicable, it will eventually be applied. When we say a rule is weakly or strongly fair, we mean the application of the rule at each possible site is weakly or strongly fair.

Liveness is not handled by the TRS formalism itself, so needs some extra notation. Temporal logic provides the appropriate repertoire. For example, the "leads to" operator "$\rightsquigarrow$" is defined by $F \rightsquigarrow G \equiv \Box(F \Rightarrow \Diamond G)$, which asserts that whenever F is true, G will be true at some later time. Then our overall liveness criterion (that every processor request is eventually satisfied) may be written as

$$\langle t, - \rangle \in pmb \quad \rightsquigarrow \quad \langle t, - \rangle \in mpb.$$

A mandatory action is usually triggered by events such as an instruction from the processor or a message from the network. A voluntary action, in contrast,

Protocol	Imperative Rules	Integrated Rules
Base	15	27
WP	19	45
Migratory	16	36
Cachet	75	146

Fig. 4. The Number of Imperative and Integrated Rules

is enabled as long as the cache or memory cell is in some appropriate state. For example, the voluntary purge rule allows a cache to drop a clean copy at any time (for example because of more pressing demands on the cache's limited capacity), while the mandatory purge rule requires the same operation once a PurgeReq request is received.

Conventional cache-coherence protocols consist only of mandatory actions. In our view, an adaptive coherence protocol consists of three components: mandatory rules, voluntary rules and heuristic policies. Voluntary rules provide enormous adaptivity, which can be exploited by various heuristic policies. An entirely separate mechanism can use heuristic messages and heuristic states to help determine when one of the voluntary rules should be invoked at a given time. Different heuristic policies can result in different performance, but they cannot affect the soundness and liveness of the system, which are always guaranteed.

The Imperative-&-Directive methodology can dramatically simplify the design and verification of cache-coherence protocols. Protocols designed with this methodology are often easy to understand and modify. Figure 4 illustrates the number of imperative and integrated rules for Cachet and its micro-protocols. Although Cachet consists of 146 rewriting rules, only 75 basic imperative rules need be considered in the soundness proofs, including the proofs of many soundness-related invariants used in the liveness proof. To simplify protocol design and verification still further, protocol rules can be classified in yet another dimension, into *basic* and *composite* rules [She00]. The verification of both soundness and liveness may then be conducted with respect only to the basic rules. The Cachet protocol, for example, contains 60 basic imperative rules and 113 basic integrated rules.

1.4   The Writer-Push Protocol

Our main example is the WP protocol, which is designed to ensure that if an address is cached in the Clean state, the cache cell contains the same value as the memory cell. This is achieved by requiring that all clean copies of an address be purged before the memory cell can be modified. As the name "Writer-Push" suggests, the writer is responsible for informing potential readers to have their stale copies, if any, purged in time. A commit operation on a dirty cell can therefore be a lengthy process, since it cannot complete before clean copies of the address are purged from all other caches.

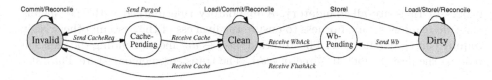

Fig. 5. Cache State Transitions of WP

There are three stable cache states for each address, Invalid, Clean and Dirty. Each memory cell maintains a memory state, which can be $C[dir]$ or $T[dir,sm]$, where C and T stand for cached and transient, respectively. In the transient state, the directory *dir* contains identifiers of the cache sites in which the address is cached (the purpose of the suspended message buffer *sm* will be explained below).

There are five imperative messages, with the following informal meanings:

- Cache: the memory supplies a data copy to the cache.
- WbAck: the memory acknowledges a writeback operation and allows the cache to retain a clean copy.
- FlushAck: the memory acknowledges a writeback operation and requires the cache to purge the address.
- Purged: the cache informs the memory of a purge operation.
- Wb: the cache writes a dirty copy back to the memory.

The full WP protocol has in addition two transient cache states, WbPending and CachePending. The WbPending state means a writeback operation is being performed on the address, and the CachePending state means a cache copy is being requested for the address. There are two directive messages:

- PurgeReq: the memory requests the cache to purge its copy.
- CacheReq: the cache requests a data copy from the memory.

Figure 5 shows the cache state transitions of WP. A cache can purge a clean cell and inform the memory via a Purged message. It can also write the data of a dirty cell to the memory via a Wb message and set the cache state to WbPending, indicating that a writeback operation is being performed on the address. There are two possible acknowledgements for a writeback operation. If a writeback acknowledgement (WbAck) is received, the cache state becomes Clean; if a flush acknowledgement (FlushAck) is received, the cache state becomes Invalid (that is, the address is purged from the cache). When a cache receives a Cache message, it simply caches the data in the Clean state. A cache responds to a purge request on a clean cell by purging the clean data and sending a Purged message to the memory. If the cache copy is dirty, the dirty copy is forced to be written back via a Wb message.

Figure 6 summarizes the rules of the WP protocol. The cache engine and memory engine rules are categorized into mandatory and voluntary rules; the processor rules are all mandatory. A mandatory rule marked with 'SF' means the rule requires strong fairness to ensure the liveness of the system; otherwise it requires only weak fairness. The notation '$msg \to dir$' means sending the message msg to the destinations in directory dir. The transient memory state $T[dir,sm]$

Mandatory Processor Rules					
Instruction	**Cstate**	**Action**	**Next Cstate**		
Load(a)	Cell(a,v,Clean)	*retire*	Cell(a,v,Clean)	P1	SF
	Cell(a,v,Dirty)	*retire*	Cell(a,v,Dirty)	P2	SF
	$a \notin cache$	$\langle$CacheReq,$a\rangle \to$ H	Cell(a,-,CachePending)	P5	
Store(a,v)	Cell(a,-,Clean)	*retire*	Cell(a,v,Clean)	P4	SF
	Cell(a,-,Dirty)	*retire*	Cell(a,v,Dirty)	P5	SF
	$a \notin cache$	$\langle$CacheReq,$a\rangle \to$ H	Cell(a,-,CachePending)	P6	
Commit(a)	Cell(a,v,Clean)	*retire*	Cell(a,v,Clean)	P7	SF
	Cell(a,v,Dirty)	$\langle$Wb,$a,v\rangle \to$ H	Cell(a,v,WbPending)	P8	
	$a \notin cache$	*retire*	$a \notin cache$	P9	SF
Reconcile(a)	Cell(a,v,Clean)	*retire*	Cell(a,v,Clean)	P10	SF
	Cell(a,v,Dirty)	*retire*	Cell(a,v,Dirty)	P11	SF
	$a \notin cache$	*retire*	$a \notin cache$	P12	SF

Voluntary C-engine Rules				
	Cstate	**Action**	**Next Cstate**	
	Cell(a,-,Clean)	$\langle$Purged,$a\rangle \to$ H	$a \notin cache$	VC1
	Cell(a,v,Dirty)	$\langle$Wb,$a,v\rangle \to$ H	Cell(a,v,WbPending)	VC2
	$a \notin cache$	$\langle$CacheReq,$a\rangle \to$ H	Cell(a,-,CachePending)	VC3

Mandatory C-engine Rules				
Msg from H	**Cstate**	**Action**	**Next Cstate**	
$\langle$Cache,$a,v\rangle$	$a \notin cache$		Cell(a,v,Clean)	MC1
	Cell(a,-,CachePending)		Cell(a,v,Clean)	MC2
$\langle$WbAck,$a\rangle$	Cell(a,v,WbPending)		Cell(a,v,Clean)	MC3
$\langle$FlushAck,$a\rangle$	Cell(a,-,WbPending)		$a \notin cache$	MC4
$\langle$PurgeReq,$a\rangle$	Cell(a,-,Clean)	$\langle$Purged,$a\rangle \to$ H	$a \notin cache$	MC5
	Cell(a,v,Dirty)	$\langle$Wb,$a,v\rangle \to$ H	Cell(a,v,WbPending)	MC6
	Cell(a,v,WbPending)		Cell(a,v,WbPending)	MC7
	Cell(a,-,CachePending)		Cell(a,-,CachePending)	MC8
	$a \notin cache$		$a \notin cache$	MC9

Voluntary M-engine Rules				
	Mstate	**Action**	**Next Mstate**	
	Cell(a,v,C[dir]) ($id \notin dir$)	$\langle$Cache,$a,v\rangle \to id$	Cell(a,v,C[$id\,|\,dir$])	VM1
	Cell(a,v,C[dir]) ($dir \neq \epsilon$)	$\langle$PurgeReq,$a\rangle \to dir$	Cell(a,v,T[dir,ϵ])	VM2

Mandatory M-engine Rules				
Msg from id	**Mstate**	**Action**	**Next Mstate**	
$\langle$CacheReq,$a\rangle$	Cell(a,v,C[dir]) ($id \notin dir$)	$\langle$Cache,$a,v\rangle \to id$	Cell(a,v,C[$id\,|\,dir$])	MM1 SF
	Cell(a,v,C[dir]) ($id \in dir$)		Cell(a,v,C[dir])	MM2
	Cell(a,v,T[dir,sm]) ($id \notin dir$)	*stall message*	Cell(a,v,T[dir,sm])	MM3
	Cell(a,v,T[dir,sm]) ($id \in dir$)		Cell(a,v,T[dir,sm])	MM4
$\langle$Wb,$a,v\rangle$	Cell(a,v_1,C[$id\,|\,dir$])	$\langle$PurgeReq,$a\rangle \to dir$	Cell(a,v_1,T[$dir,(id,v)$])	MM5
	Cell(a,v_1,T[$id\,|\,dir,sm$])		Cell(a,v_1,T[$dir,(id,v)\,|\,sm$])	MM6
$\langle$Purged,$a\rangle$	Cell(a,v,C[$id\,|\,dir$])		Cell(a,v,C[dir])	MM7
	Cell(a,v,T[$id\,|\,dir,sm$])		Cell(a,v,T[dir,sm])	MM8
	Cell(a,-,T[$\epsilon,(id,v)\,|\,sm$])	$\langle$FlushAck,$a\rangle \to id$	Cell(a,v,T[ϵ,sm])	MM9
	Cell(a,-,T[$\epsilon,(id,v)$])	$\langle$WbAck,$a\rangle \to id$	Cell(a,v,C[id])	MM10
	Cell(a,v,T[ϵ,ϵ])		Cell(a,v,C[ϵ])	MM11

Fig. 6. The WP Protocol

is used for bookkeeping during a writeback operation: dir represents the cache sites which have not yet acknowledged the broadcast PurgeReq requests, and sm contains the suspended writeback message that the memory has received but has not yet acknowledged (only the source and the data need to be recorded).

2   The Manual Proof of Correctness

One way to show that an implementation is correct with respect to a specification is to show that one can simulate the other. In particular, every sequence of terms generated by the rewriting rules of the implementation ought to be compatible (with respect to some observation function) with some sequence that could be generated by the specification system. (Sometimes it is also possible to show the reverse simulation, but this is not necessary for the correctness of an implementation.)

Accordingly we prove the soundness of WP by showing that CRF can simulate WP. The first stage involves only the imperative messages (not the directives). Queues can be thought of as multi-sets, not ordered FIFO sequences, and messages may be selected from the queues non-deterministically; the soundness property will therefore not be compromised in the presence of specific reordering restrictions introduced later, such as FIFO message passing for each particular address. The second stage adds directives to the repertoire of messages, and operations to handle them. Accordingly, we first show soundness of the imperative subset, by proving that any imperative rule of WP can be simulated in CRF with respect to some particular abstraction function. The soundness of the complete protocol follows from the fact that all the other rules may be derived from the imperative subset.

We first define an abstraction function from WP to CRF. For WP terms in which all message queues are empty, it is straightforward to find the corresponding CRF terms: there is a one-to-one correspondence between these "drained" terms of WP and the terms of CRF. For WP terms that contain non-empty message queues, we apply a set of "draining" rules to extract all the messages from the queues. These rules are derived from a subset of the rules of the protocol, some of them in reverse: we use backward draining for Wb messages and forward draining for all other messages (forwarding draining of Wb messages would lead to non-deterministic drained terms when there are multiple writeback messages regarding the same address). Consequently, all the Cache, WbAck, FlushAck and Wb messages will be drained towards cache sites, while all the Purged messages will be drained towards the memory. The system of draining rules is strongly normalizing and terminating; so it is easy to use it to define an abstraction function.

The liveness proof deals with the integrated protocol, and typically assumes that the queues satisfy FIFO ordering. We prove that whenever a processor initiates an instruction, there will be a later state in which that instruction has been retired. The proof involves showing that the appropriate messages are placed in the queues, that each messages makes progress towards the head of the queue, and that it is dealt with when it arrives at its destination. Each of these requires a fairness constraint on the relevant rules, to guarantee that they are eventually executed; arrival at the head of a queue also requires an induction. Matters are further complicated by the possibility of stalled messages, and transitory states of the main memory.

Many details of this proof are omitted; some arise similarly in the machine-assisted version and are treated below in Section 4. A complete description of the manual proof can be found elsewhere [She00].

3 Setting Up for the Machine-Assisted Verification

3.1 Choice of a Logical System

For systems as complicated as the CRF protocols, correctness proofs become too large to handle reliably by hand. It is therefore necessary to resort to mechanical assistance, and so to choose an appropriate tool. A mechanical tool requires more formality in the expression of a specification; and it is often convenient to adopt some existing formal system as a vehicle. The liveness parts of the CRF specifications find natural expression in terms of temporal logic, and it was therefore in this area that we looked for a formal system.

It takes a good deal of investment of effort to become proficient in the use of any substantial piece of mathematics; so it is worth choosing carefully among the possibilities before one starts. In the choice of a suitable system, we have adopted one engineered to concentrate on the areas in which most of our detailed work will be found. The "actions" of Lamport's Temporal Logic of Actions [Lam94] correspond closely with the transitions of our term-rewriting systems; and its temporal logic provisions seem to cope with the liveness and fairness constraints we need to handle, without burdening us with unnecessary complication.

3.2 Choice of a Tool

In the selection of a mechanical tool, too, a careful choice needs to be made. Lamport correctly points out that when verifying a design one spends most of the time in mundane checking of small print, based on simple arithmetic rather than abstruse logic. So we look for a tool which embodies efficient decision procedures in these areas; indeed, for this it is worth sacrificing the ability to define and to work with non-conventional logics (as will be seen, this trade-off arises in the present work). PVS [COR+95] fits that particular bill. Moreover, PVS now contains a fairly rudimentary model-checker which may be of use in certain parts of our investigations in the future.

We have accordingly implemented [Sto] TLA in PVS. This may be thought of as analogous to implementing the algorithms of Linear Algebra in C, except that instead of developing the subroutines, with the aid of the compiler, we are proving the theorems, with the aid of the proof engine.

3.3 The Move to PVS

In the PVS version of our specification, since we are not concerned with instruction re-ordering, we found it convenient to simplify the processor interface: for this version it is just a $\langle Op, a, v \rangle$ triple, where Op is one of the CRF operations or

In the tabular form:

Rule Name	Instruction	Cstate	Action	Next Cstate
CRF-Loadl	Load(a)	Cell(a,v,Clean)	retire	Cell(a,v,Clean)
		Cell(a,v,Dirty)	retire	Cell(a,v,Dirty)

In TRS:

CRF-Loadl Rule
    Site($cache$, $\langle t,\text{Load}(a)\rangle$:$pmb$, mpb, $proc$)   *if*   Cell(a,v,-) $\in cache$
$\rightarrow$ Site($cache$, pmb, $mpb|\langle t,v\rangle$, $proc$)

CRF-Loadl′ Rule
    Site($cache$, $interface$(Load,a,-))   *if*   Cell(a,v,-) $\in cache$
$\rightarrow$ Site($cache$, $interface$(Ready,a,v)
)

In PVS:

```
CRF_Load(i) : action = LAMBDA s0, s1:

( s0'proc(i)'op = load AND
  full?(s0'cache(i)(a)) AND

  s1 = s0 WITH
  ['proc(i)'op  := ready,
   'proc(i)'val := val(s0'cache(i)(a))] )
  WHERE a = s0'proc(i)'adr
```

Fig. 7. The Load Rule in PVS

Ready). To illustrate how the TRS version is transliterated into PVS, Figure 7 shows various definitions for the Load rule. First we repeat the tabular summary from Figure 3; then we give the TRS rule in full, followed by the version with the simplified interface; finally we give a PVS version (note that the backquote denotes field selection from a record).

It will be seen that there is a fairly obvious correspondence between TRS rules and their equivalents as TLA "actions" in PVS. Indeed, we are planning to automate the translation, so that the same source file can be used both as the basis for our verification proofs and as the starting point for hardware synthesis. Similarly, there is a close correspondence between a TLA behavior and the sequence of states arising in a TRS reduction.

Assertions about states also appear similar in the two systems. For example, the assertion which allows the Reconcile instruction to be a no-op in WP is shown in both forms in Figure 8. These would naturally form part of an "invariant assertion" to be proved true for all states in a behavior (which in TLA would find expression as a temporal formula under the "always" operator $\square$). Since the truth of the assertion in Figure 8 depends on the correct messages being sent at appropriate times, the complete assertion to be proved is much more

---

Assertion about TRS:

$\text{Cell}(a,v,\text{Clean}) \in \text{Cache}_i(s) \Rightarrow \text{Cell}(a,v,-) \in \text{Mem}(s)$

In PVS:

```
clean_w?(s'cache(i)(a)) => s'cache(i)(a)'val = s'mem(a)
```

Fig. 8. Assertions on States

For each site and address,
  The cache state is WbPending **iff**
    (1) there's a Wb in the home queue **or**
    (2) there's a WbAck or FlushAck in the site queue **or**
    (3) the memory state is transient, and a Wb is stalled there
  and never more than one of (1),(2),(3) is true
  and there's never more than one Wb in the home queue
  and there's never more than one Purged in the home queue
  and there's never more than one WbAck or FlushAck in the site queue
  and if the cache is Clean its value is the same as the memory's
  and the site is in the memory directories **iff**
    (a) there's a Cache command in the site queue **or**
    (b) the cache is valid **or**
    (c) the cache is WbPending and there's not a FlushAck in the site
        queue **or**
    (d) there's a Purged in the home queue
  and never more than one of (a),(b),(c),(d) is true
  and any Wb command in the home queue has the same value as the cache
  and any Cache command in the site queue has the same value as the memory
  and any stalled Wb has the same value as the cache
  and if there's a WbAck in the site queue, the cache value is the same as
      the memory's
  and none of the stalled messages in the home queue is
      an imperative message.
(Note that here "a site is in the memory directories" means it's in the directory either of the
C state or the T state, **or** there's a stalled Wb message about it in the sm set of the T state.)

Fig. 9. The Invariant for WP

complicated: the invariant used for the PVS proof is shown, somewhat informally, in Figure 9. In each system the main part of the proof of invariance is a large case analysis, showing that the truth of the assertion is preserved by each of the rules.

The liveness assertions, too, are fairly similar: they are shown in Figure 10. In the PVS notation, the type conversion between predicates on states and on behaviors is supplied automatically by the system.

3.4   Structure of a TLA Specification in PVS

PVS is a strongly typed system, so we must begin by setting out the structure of the state (corresponding to the structure of a complete TRS term). The state contains components for the entire universe with which we shall be concerned: the abstract specification and all its implementations. Of course, not all components will be relevant to each specification; a specification's footprint sets out what is

About the TRS version:

$\text{Proc}_{id}(\sigma) = \langle \text{Op}, -, - \rangle \quad \rightsquigarrow \quad \text{Proc}_{id}(\sigma) = \langle \text{Ready}, -, - \rangle$

In PVS:

```
LET op_is_ready(i) : state_pred =
   LAMBDA s: s'proc(i)'op = ready
IN
LAMBDA b : FORALL i : ( []<>(op_is_ready(i)) )(b)
```

Fig. 10. The Liveness Assertions for WP

relevant and what is not. In the case of CRF, the fields are **proc** (an array of processors, one per site), **mem** (the main memory), and **cache** (an array of caches). The only relevant parts of a processor are its interface with the memory system; and in our simplified version this means that each element in the **proc** array is a triple, **<op, adr, val>**, where **op** is one of the CRF operations (omitting fences) or Ready.

A TLA specification does not usually attempt to regulate the entire state. For one thing, it needs to leave some freedom to the implementer. For example, CRF includes atomic transitions which write back data from cache to memory; this is implemented using queues, and the operation is no longer atomic. TLA allows us to be precise about which parts of the state are constrained by the specification, and which parts are of no concern. (In our example only the processor interfaces will be constrained by the specification; the implementation may use any convenient mechanism to achieve a satisfactory behavior of those interfaces.)

We accordingly say that each specification has a "footprint", which consists just of those parts of the state which it is constraining. If the footprint components in some sequence of states (some behavior) satisfy a specification, changes in other components are irrelevant.

A TLA specification is normally constructed from three principal components. Each component is formally an assertion about behaviors, but each of them has a different thrust. The first specifies the initial state (the first element in the behavior sequence. Each processor interface is ready, and each cache is empty for every address. The obvious definition is:

```
Init_crf : state_pred = LAMBDA s:
  (FORALL i : s'proc(i)'op = ready) AND
  (FORALL i,a : empty?(s'cache(i)(a)))
```

In fact we prefer to define the predicate as a function on the footprint rather than on the whole state. Doing this systematically makes it much simpler to prove that the whole specification has the required footprint, which is necessary later. The type checker automatically inserts the necessary (predefined) type conversions. So the definition becomes

```
Init_crf : state_pred = LAMBDA fp:
 (FORALL i : fp'proc(i)'op = ready) AND
 (FORALL i,a : empty?(fp'cache(i)(a)))
```

The second component specifies the permissible transitions. As we have seen, this part is closely related to the TRS rules: each rules has a corresponding PVS definition. The definitions for the Load rule were given in Figure 7; in the PVS version the first group of terms gives the precondition for the transition, and the second specifies the change. Here again we actually give the assertion in terms of the footprint, using fp0 as the starting footprint and fp1 the resulting one instead of s0 and s1. The rules are grouped together, using appropriate predefined operators, into a composite action, say CRF_N, which specifies that any one of the component transitions may occur.

Since TLA specifications relate only to a particular footprint, and we do not wish in any way to constrain transitions elsewhere in the state, TLA introduces the notion of stuttering. A stutter occurs when two successive states are identical, or (from the point of view of a particular specification) when the footprint in the two states is unchanged. Only stutter-independent specification formulae are allowed by TLA: that is to say, a behavior acceptable to the formula must remain so if stuttering transitions are added or removed. (In TLA itself this is ensured by syntactic restrictions on the grammar of the formula notation; in our PVS version we have to check it semantically when necessary.) Lamport uses the notation $\square[CRF\_N]_{c\_fp}$, which we write as alSQUARE(CRF_N, c_fp), to assert that each state in a behavior is related to the next either by a transition allowed by CRF_N, or by a transition which stutters on the footprint c_fp. This is the second component of our specification.

The third component specifies the "liveness" requirement. Since the component that specifies the transition rules allows the possibility of continuous stuttering, we must specify the requirement that something actually happens. In general, the third component is intended to specify some global requirements of the behavior, without contradicting anything specified in the previous two components. In this case we wish to assert that any operation initiated by any processor interface eventually completes; the form of this assertion was described above, and we use it to define the formula CRF_fair. Notice that we do not impose any requirement that any operation should ever commence: that is up to the processor, and so is no part of the memory specification.

The three components are combined into the formula Crf:

```
Crf : temporal_formula =
 Init_crf AND  alSQUARE(CRF_N, c_fp) AND CRF_fair
```

This formula has a footprint which includes the processor interface, the main memory and the caches. Finally, therefore, we must indicate that we are attempting to specify only the behavior of the processor interface (proc). We use a notation very like an existential quantifier:

```
CRF : temporal_formula = EXISTSV(mem_cache, Crf).
```

Here, `mem_cache` is a variable consisting of the `mem` and the `cache` components of the state. The `EXISTSV` operator, applied to a behavior, asserts that there is a sequence of values for this variable with which the given behavior, or a behavior stutter-equivalent to the given behavior, can be updated, so as to give a behavior acceptable to `Crf`. Thus CRF is also stutter-independent, and constrains only the behavior of the processor interface: its footprint is merely the `proc` component of the state. The formal definition of `EXISTSV` is discussed by Lamport [Lam94]; the PVS definition is given at [Sto].

CRF is our final specification. Notice that the liveness component refers only to the externally visible interface—we find this convenient, as it allows the component to appear unchanged in the specification of the implementation. We later replace this component in an implementation by assertions about the fairness of some of the operations, and prove that they are sufficient to guarantee the original requirement.

3.5   Structure of a TLA-Based Proof

An assertion of correctness is of the form

```
ASSERT(
 EXISTSV(mem_cache_queues, Cbase)
         => EXISTSV(mem_cache, Crf) )
```

The main part of a proof of this assertion is the construction of an "abstraction function". This is a function from the state as manipulated by the implementation (by `Cbase` in our example) to the kind of state acceptable to the abstract specification (`Crf`). More precisely, since it is not allowed to change the externally visible parts of the footprint, it is a substitution for the `mem` and `cache` components. Then we prove that, under this substitution, a state acceptable to `Cbase` is acceptable to `Crf`, i.e. that

```
ASSERT( Cbase => subst(Cbase_bar, mem_cache)(Crf) )
```

where `Cbase_bar` is the state-function giving the value to be substituted for the `mem_cache` variable.

In all but fairly trivial cases (such as our "derived rules" example below), we shall need some extra properties of the state to prove the correctness of this assertion. For example, we may need to prove that values waiting in queue entries remain faithful copies of values in memory, or that queues contain no duplicate entries. So another important part of the proof is the construction and verification of the appropriate "invariant" properties. It may be noted that some investigations of the correctness of protocols amount merely to the demonstration of the invariant; in our approach, invariants are aids to proving the validity of the corresponding implementation.

Once we have proved the substitution assertion above, we may infer (just as with ordinary existential quantification)

```
ASSERT( Cbase => EXISTSV(mem_cache, Crf) )
```

and finally, provided that EXISTSV(mem_cache, Crf) is independent of the variable mem_cache_queues, and that various of the formulae are stutter-independent, we infer

```
ASSERT( EXISTSV(mem_cache_queues, Cbase)
                    => EXISTSV(mem_cache, Crf) )
```

as required. The independence criterion is satisfied, partly because Crf does not involve the queues at all, and partly because for any formula F,

```
    EXISTSV(mem_cache, F)
```

is independent of mem_cache. This final part of the proof is usually fairly formulaic: all the real work is in the previous sections.

In our application, the liveness component of the specification remains unchanged in the implementation, unaffected by the substitution; if this had not been the case, there are TLA rules for dealing with this much more complicated situation. See below for the treatment of liveness in this application.

3.6   Example: Derived Rules

As a simple example of this approach, we consider the validity of some "derived rules" in CRF. For example, CRF requires that an address be cached before a store operation overwrites the value; but clearly this is in some sense equivalent to a single operation which establishes a "dirty" value in a cache which did not previously contain that address. So there are two specifications, one (CRF2) containing the extra store-on-empty rule and the other (CRF) not: in what sense are they equivalent? If we consider the raw behavior, of the mem, cache and proc footprint, they are *not* equivalent: Crf2 can do in a single transition what necessarily takes two in Crf. If we consider the behavior of the "quantified" version, however, in which the changes in mem and cache are invisible, the difference becomes merely an extra stutter (in this case, *before* the transition that affects proc); and we have agreed that behaviors which differ only in stuttering are to be considered equivalent.

To prove this equivalence we must show that each version implies the other. It is easy to show that every behavior acceptable to CRF is also acceptable to CRF2, since CRF2's rules are a superset of CRF's. The argument for the other direction proceeds in two stages. First, we define yet another system, Crf2s, based on Crf2 and involving a new state variable (let us call it stut) to manage the stutter. stut normally has a null value. In this new system we arrange that each occurrence of the store-on-empty rule must be preceded by a transition which merely sets stut to a non-null value; and store-on-empty itself is altered so that it also resets stut to null. Some of the details are shown in Figure 11. We then prove, using a TLA theorem provided for this purpose, that

```
    Crf2 = EXISTSV(stut, Crf2s)
```

```
svquiescent : action =
  (LAMBDA s0,s1: null?(s0'stut) AND null?(s1'stut))

setsv(i, sts) : action =
  (LAMBDA s0,s1:
    null?(s0'stut) AND s1 = s0 WITH [stut := inuse(sts, i)])

resetsv(i, sts) : action =
  (LAMBDA s0,s1: s0'stut = inuse(sts, i) AND null?(s1'stut))

CRF_Ns : action = CRF_N AND svquiescent

dummyCRF_soe : action =
  LAMBDA ss: EXISTS i :
      enabled(CRF_Store_on_empty(i)) AND setsv(i, store_on_empty_flag)

CRF_soe : action =
  LAMBDA ss: EXISTS i :
      Crf_Store_on_empty(i) AND resetsv(i, store_on_empty_flag)

CRF_N2s : action = CRF_Ns OR dummyCRF_soe OR CRF_soe
```

Fig. 11. Part of the "Derived Rule" Specification

```
Crf_bar(s) : sfnval =
  CASES s'stut OF
   nil : mcs(s'mem, s'cache, s'stut),
   inuse(sts, i) :
    IF    sts = store_on_empty_flag THEN
      mcs(s'mem,
          s'cache WITH [(i)(a) := cell(clean, s'mem(a))],
          s'stut)
          WHERE a = s'proc(i)'adr
    ELSE mcs(s'mem, s'cache, s'stut)
    ENDIF
  ENDCASES
```

Fig. 12. The Abstraction Function

Next we define an abstraction function from the Crf2s state to the Crf state; it maps any state in which stut is non-null to the intermediate state in the two-transition equivalent of store_on_empty, and otherwise makes no change (see Figure 12). Using this function we can prove

    ASSERT(EXISTSV(mem_cache_stut, Crf2s)
                    => EXISTSV(mem_cache_stut, Crf))

Then, on the left-hand side, we can argue that

    EXISTSV(mem_cache_stut, Crf2s) =
        EXISTSV(mem_cache, EXISTSV(stut, Crf2s))

and hence (using a previous result)

    EXISTSV(mem_cache_stut, Crf2s) =
        EXISTSV(mem_cache, Crf2)

Similarly for the right-hand side,

```
EXISTSV(mem_cache_stut, Crf) =
    EXISTSV(mem_cache, EXISTSV(stut, Crf))
```

and hence

```
EXISTSV(mem_cache_stut, Crf) = EXISTSV(mem_cache, Crf)
```

since Crf is independent of stut. This gives us the equality of CRF2 and CRF, as required.

4   The Machine-Assisted Proof of WP

4.1   Soundness

Our main example is the WP micro-protocol for Cachet. This follows the outlines we have described, but it also involves a version of the "derived rule" example. The main optimization in this protocol is that it allows reconcile-on-clean as a single operation (without reference to the main memory, and thus avoiding all the overhead of queued messages and responses). In CRF this single operation becomes the triple <Purge, Reconcile, Cache>. So, as in the previous example, we must use stuttering variables to arrange that the single operation is preceded and followed by a stutter. Since there are different arrangements depending on whether the stutter precedes or follows the externally visible transition, we do this in two stages, using two stuttering variables; but the methodology for each stage is exactly as described above.

Our next task is to define the soundness invariant. Its principal clause asserts that a clean cache value is always equal to the value in the main memory—this is what is required to justify the reconcile-on-clean optimization. Other clauses (for example, that the messages in the queues are reasonable) are needed to guarantee that the abstraction function will behave as expected. Yet more clauses (for example, that various conditions are mutually exclusive) were added during early attempts at the proof—strengthening the hypothesis in order to prove the induction.

We prove that this invariant is preserved by any of the permissible transitions. (This proof is too big to be done monolithically, so it must be split into smaller sections. Since the clauses in this invariant are inter-related, it is best to split the proof by operation, so that each lemma says that the complete invariant is preserved by a particular operation. These lemmas are then used to prove that the invariant is preserved by any transition. This result, together with a straightforward proof that any state satisfying the initial predicate also satisfies the invariant, is then used to prove that the invariant always holds for any behavior satisfying the WP specification.

Next we define the abstraction function. This, as in the example above, provides a substitution for mem and cache; in fact, also as above, it never changes mem. As in the manual proof, the mapping is trivial when the queues are empty;

- For each site, the set of rules which complete processor operations (Load, Store, Reconcile, Commit) is strongly fair.
- For each site, the set which deals with stalled processor operations is weakly fair.
- For each site and address, the set which services the site's incoming queue is weakly fair.
- For each address, the set which services the memory's incoming queue is weakly fair.
- For each address in addition, the rule which services a CacheReq request when the memory is in its C state is strongly fair.
- For each address, the set of rules which deal with the memory's T state is weakly fair.

Fig. 13. The Fairness Constraints for WP

when there are queue entries, it is necessary to decide whether it is preferable to treat a particular entry as not having been issued or as having arrived at its destination. The abstraction function also has to handle the stuttering variables. So it does three things:

1. If either of the stuttering variables is non-null, it provides the appropriate intermediate state for the operation sequence;
2. it treats any WbAck or FlushAck command in the site queue as having arrived (but note that it ignores any Cache command in the site queue);
3. it translates the various cache states (Clean etc.) to their CRF equivalents.

The next stage is to prove, again operation by operation, that under this substitution each WP operation either simulates the appropriate CRF operation or is a CRF stutter (that is, a no-op). Finally, an argument manipulating the EXISTSV quantifiers, similar to that shown for the previous example, is required to complete the soundness proof.

4.2 Liveness

The liveness component of the WP protocol was, like its counterpart in CRF, simply

```
Cwp_fair : temporal_formula = LAMBDA b : FORALL i :
( []<>(op_is_ready(i)) )(b)
```

We now define a new version of this protocol Cwp_fair, in which this component is replaced by a formula asserting that various subsets of the transition rules are fair; the other components remain unchanged. The liveness proof consists of showing that this version is sufficient to imply the other; that is to say, that the fairness constraints are sufficient to guarantee that the original liveness criterion is satisfied.

The fairness constraints in Cwp_fair may be spelled out as in Figure 13. The various clauses sprung partly from intuition arising during the design of the protocol, and partly from the formal requirements of the TLA theorems used in the liveness proof. Note that the Cwp_fair specification is itself at only an intermediate stage in an implementation. Its terms may be regrouped into separate specifications of the various subcomponents of the system (the cache engines,

- The only commands in site queues are Cache, WbAck, FlushAck and PurgeReq.
- The only commands in home queues are CacheReq, Wb or Purged.
- The only non-empty cache states found are Clean, Dirty, CachePending and WbPending.
- If both a Cache and a WbAck or FlushAck command are in a site queue, the Cache command is later.
- If a stalled Wb command is in the sm component of a mem directory, the site concerned is not entered in the dir component.
- If a site is entered in the dir component, and mem is in a transient state, and the corresponding site queue is not empty, then its last entry is a PurgeReq command.
- If a site is entered in the dir component, and mem is in a transient state, then there is either a PurgeReq command in its site queue or a Wb or Purged command for that site in the home queue.
- If a site is in the CachePending state (for a given address), then any CacheReq command will be the latest entry for that site in the home queue.
- If a site is in the CachePending state (for a given address), then there is either a CacheReq message for that site in the home queue or in the queue for stalled CacheReq messages in mem, or a Cache command in its site queue.

Fig. 14. The Extra Invariants for the Liveness Proof

the queue-processing engines and so on), and these subcomponents then further refined. At this stage the fairness requirements of the separate subcomponents may be realized in various ways: using dedicated hardware, or scheduling resources in a way which guarantees service, or using queueing theory to show that the probability of denial of service tends to zero over time.

The liveness proof itself requires more invariants, in addition to those already required for the soundness proof. Unlike the latter, these involve directive messages as well as imperative ones. The extra clauses are shown in Figure 14. We must, as before, show that this invariant is preserved by the operations. (In this case, each new clause is independent of most of the others—sometimes they go in pairs. It is therefore possible to structure the proof differently from before, and to have each lemma prove a single clause across all the operations.)

After the invariant is shown always to hold, we must prove that (for each site) op is always eventually ready. For this it is enough to show that $op \neq$ Ready $\rightsquigarrow$ op = Ready. Since this transition is made by processor completion operations, which are strongly fair, this reduces to showing that such operations are continually being enabled. But these operations are enabled unless one of the following conditions holds:

1. The cache is in a transitory state (CachePending or WbPending).
2. The cache is empty, and a Load operation is requested.
3. The cache is dirty, and a Commit operation is requested.

So we must show that each of these conditions gets resolved. Since the stalling operations are weakly fair, conditions 2 and 3 eventually become 1; so we are left to show that the CachePending and WbPending states lead to the clean state or (for WbPending only) the empty state.

For WbPending, the invariant shows that there must be a message in the home queue or the site queue, or a stalled entry in the central memory's transient state. We show that each queue entry makes progress in its queue: this is a proof by well-founded induction to show that the entry eventually reaches the top of the queue, relying on the relevant fairness condition to show that any non-empty queue eventually receives attention. If the site is entered in the set of stalled sites at the main memory, we must show that it eventually leaves that state. This is another well-founded induction, to show that the cardinality of that set eventually decreases to zero; but a pre-condition for this is that the `dir` component of the `mem` state is empty. Showing that this eventually happens requires yet another well-founded induction: the invariant shows that for each element in this set there is a PurgeReq in the site queue or a Purged in the home queue, so two further inductions are required to show that these entries eventually have their effect.

The CachePending argument is similar, with the added complication of the possibility of stalling a CacheReq message and subsequently reinstating it in the original queue. This requires greater subtlety in the inductions, as the movement of the queue is no longer strictly FIFO.

It will be seen that this liveness proof itself is a complicated nest of cycles. While proving that there is progress in each cycle, it is always necessary to allow for the possibility of abandoning it because some outer cycle has been completed some other way (for example, a voluntary cache action may obviate further need to make progress with a CacheReq message). When dealing with an imperative message, we are usually concerned with the earliest occurrence in a queue; but in the case of a directive it is the latest one which is important—this leads to certain technical differences in treatment.

This proof is very complicated, and the corresponding proof for the complete, integrated Cachet protocol is still more complex. It is necessary to be very systematic in structuring the proof to avoid losing track: Lamport discusses this issue [Lam93] in the context of a manual proof. With Akhiani et al. [ADH+99] he has employed a hierarchical proof technique in a manual verification of sophisticated cache-coherence protocols for the Alpha memory model. The protocols are specified in TLA+ [Lam96,Lam97], a formal specification language based on TLA.

Plakal et al. [CHPS99,PSCH98] has also proposed a technique based on Lamport's logical clocks that can be used to reason about cache-coherence protocols. The method associates a counter with each host and provides a time-stamping scheme that totally orders all protocol events. The total order can then be used to verify that the requirements of specific memory models are satisfied.

5   Discussion

Our experience with the proof in the PVS system has convinced us that, at least in a context this complicated, the proof-assistant program needs detailed steering. It is naïve to think one can simply point a theorem prover at the problem and press "start". Choosing an appropriate invariant requires insight into why the implementation works as it does; and proving the various theorems requires insight into what are efficient strategies for the proof checker.

5.1 Model Checking

A more widely used approach to formal verification is model-checking [CGP99], which uses state enumeration [ID93a,ID93b], sometimes with symbolic techniques [CES86,McM92], to check the correctness of assertions by exhaustively exploring all reachable states of the system. For example, Stern and Dill [SD95] used the Murφ system to check that all reachable states satisfied certain properties attached to protocol specifications. Generally speaking, the major difference among these techniques is the representation of protocol states and the pruning method adopted in the state expansion process. Exponential state explosion has been a serious concern for model checking approaches, although various techniques have been proposed to reduce the state space. For example, Pong and Dubois [PD95] exploited the symmetry and homogeneity of the system states by keeping track of whether zero, one or multiple copies had been cached (this can reduce the state space and also makes the verification independent of the number of processors). Delzanno [Del00] extends this work, keeping a count of the number of processors in each state, and using integer-real relaxation techniques to handle the resulting model using real arithmetic.

The model-checking approach is attractive, since in principle it requires less detailed knowledge of the application being verified, and is more akin to testing. In particular, it can be used for initial sanity checking on small scale examples. Nevertheless, a theorem prover (or "proof assistant") is likely to be more successful for the verification of sophisticated protocols.

Many model-checking investigations of cache-coherence protocols are confined to verifying that the invariants hold. Some tools, however, are geared towards checking that an implementation is a faithful refinement of a specification. We have used one of these, FDR [Ros97,For], earlier in the present work, to verify a simpler protocol (see [Sto]), showing not only that the implementation was faithful to the specification, but also that it was free from deadlock or livelock. But we had to limit ourselves to considering one particular very simple configuration of caches, with an address space of size 1, and a storable-value space of size 2. Any increase in size caused a "state explosion" rendering the check infeasibly time-consuming.

The present protocol is much more complicated than this earlier one, and the dangers of a state explosion correspondingly greater. Moreover, some of the restrictions to small cases cause problems. The restriction to an address space of unit size is tolerable: we can show that each address is treated independently by both specification and implementation, so that the behavior of each can be viewed as an interleaving of the behaviors for each address considered separately. Thus if model-checking can show that a single-address implementation is faithful to a single-address specification, we can infer that the interleaved multi-address versions will be similarly faithful.

The restriction to a storable-value space of size two is also tolerable. Lazic [Laz99] has shown that in certain circumstances (satisfied in this case) a successful check for a small finite value space is sufficient to imply the correctness of the system for countably infinite spaces.

There remains the restriction to a simple configuration of just one or two caches. Lazic's current research suggests that it might be possible to prove the correctness of a system with arbitrarily many caches by means of an inductive argument, using model-checking to verify the inductive step. We await the outcome of this work with interest.

5.2   Model-Checking or Theorem-Proving

A problem with theorem-proving work in this area is that it is sometimes hard to convince practitioners of its importance. This may be partly because the mathematical nature of its techniques are far removed from the kind of testing more familiar to hardware engineers. This suggests that model-checking, more closely related to testing, has more intuitive appeal. But, as it stands, model-checking is applicable only to comparatively simple systems; and showing that a model-checking investigation suffices to show the correctness of an infinite class of systems is at present a task requiring considerable mathematical subtlety. It is to be hoped that this situation will improve, so that this mathematics can be to a large extent taken for granted. Meanwhile, however, from the point of view of a system designer, the mathematics of the theorem-proving approach may be more closely related to the design task itself, and therefore more likely to shed light on any design inadequacies.

5.3   The Structure of the Proof

The WP micro-protocol was originally designed in several stages [She00]. Although we have constructed the PVS proof for the final design only, it would have been possible to produce a proof of soundness (though not of liveness) structured in accordance with the design stages, as was done in the manual proof. Thus we could have considered a system containing only the imperative rules, with multi-set queues, and proved that it was faithful to the CRF specification. Then we could have made another simulation proof to show that the complete micro-protocol was faithful to that intermediate version.

In fact, however, the motivation for proceeding in this way is not as strong for the machine-assisted proof. The extra layer of simulation needs a good deal of new structure in the proof. It is easier to construct a single soundness proof for the complete protocol. We do this, however, by considering the imperative subset first (thus exploiting the modularity of the design methodology); then we add the directive messages and their operations. The presence of the new messages does not affect the validity of the soundness invariant (which does not refer to them). It is easy to adapt the soundness proof to accommodate these—it is principally a matter of showing that updating the queue by adding or removing a directive message does not affect the invariant. Similarly, specializing the non-deterministic choice in message retrieval to be FIFO has no effect on the soundness argument. The new operations are either equivalent to CRF no-ops (in the case of operations which issue directives) or are special cases of existing voluntary operations. In this latter situation the proofs for the two operations are very similar, and may be transferred by little more than cut-and-paste.

It should be emphasized that no such choice of approach is available for the liveness proof. The intermediate stages of the design do not satisfy the liveness criterion, and any proof of liveness has to be focussed on the final version of the protocol.

5.4   The Abstraction Function

In the manual proof the abstraction function was elegantly defined using the TRS mechanism, in terms of forward and reverse draining. In order to show that this produced a well-defined function, it was necessary to prove that the subsystem of draining rules always terminated and was strongly normalizing. This approach could also have been followed in the machine-assisted proof. The function could be defined[1]

as

$$f(s_0) = \epsilon(\lambda s.\forall b.b_0 = s_0 \wedge \Box[D]_{wp\_fp} \wedge WF_{wp\_fp}(D) \Rightarrow \Diamond\Box b = s),$$

where D defined the transition system for the draining. To prove that f was well defined, it would be necessary to prove that there was a unique state satisfying $\Diamond\Box b = s$. The proof that the behavior eventually achieved a constant state would be a well-founded induction, using the *LATTICE* rule of TLA and relying on the fairness premise; it would show that the total number of items in all the queues was decreasing, and would therefore need to invoke the finiteness of the system to show that the total number of queued items was itself well defined. To show that the state achieved was unique (and thus that f was a function, and not merely a relation), we might note that all its queues would be empty, and we might therefore define (and prove) an invariant of the state such that there was a unique empty-queue state satisfying it. When defining the invariant, we would have to resist any temptation to characterize the target state by means of an abstraction function, for this would beg the entire question.

The greater formality of the machine-assisted system, however, made all this more trouble than it was worth. It was much simpler to define the function explicitly, rather than in terms of draining operations, at the cost of the intuitive attraction to hardware people of the more operational approach.

In one detail the two functions are actually different. The function defined by draining Cache messages towards the cache; the function defined for PVS is as though those messages suffered reverse draining. This somewhat simplifies the treatment of the reconcile-on-clean operation, by ensuring that it is always simulated by a triplet of CRF operations.

---

[1]   The definition of the function ϵ is that for any predicate P, $\epsilon(P)$ is a value satisfying P, provided any such value exists.

5.5   A Comparison of the Proofs

Compared with a human mathematician, the machine is unforgiving; so employing machine assistance forces the human prover to give systematic attention to every area of the proof. This has advantages and disadvantages. It requires the explicit proof of results which might be thought "obvious" but lead to excessive formal detail in spelling it all out (an example is discussed in the previous section). On the other hand, such a systematic examination can bring to light aspects which were unnoticed before. For example, in our machine-assisted proof of WP, there was a place where we noticed we were relying on the queues being of unbounded length. This did not break the proof—the specification had no boundedness constraint—but it did not accord with the designer's intention, and the protocol definition was revised to avoid it.

5.6   Summary

It is difficult to gain confidence in the correctness of a complex protocol without some formal reasoning. We think that the first step in designing a robust protocol is to follow a methodology that keeps the correctness issue in the center of the whole design process. The Imperative-&-Directive methodology is one way of achieving this goal: it separates soundness and liveness, and lets the designer refine a simpler protocol into a more complex one by introducing pragmatic concerns one step at a time. But even after using such a methodology, if the resulting protocol is large or complex one needs to go the extra mile of using automatic tools for verification. Model checkers are unlikely to eliminate all doubts about correctness, because to avoid the state-space explosion one is forced to apply the model checker to a simpler or smaller version of the system. We think semi-automatic verification of the final protocol is the most promising approach to gain confidence in the correctness of a complex protocol; and even semi-automatic verification is possible only after the user has considerable insight into how the protocol works.

References

[ABM93]   Yehuda Afek, Geoffrey Brown, and Michael Merritt. Lazy Caching. *ACM Transactions on Programming Languages and Systems*, 15(1):182–205, January 1993.

[ADH+99] Homayoon Akhiani, Damien Doligez, Paul Harter, Leslie Lamport, Joshua Scheid, Mark Tuttle, and Yuan Yu. Cache coherence verification with TLA+. In *World Congress on Formal Methods in the Development of Computing Systems, Industrial Panel*, Toulouse, France, September 1999.

[AG96]   Sarita V. Adve and Kourosh Gharachorloo. Shared Memory Consistency Models: A Tutorial. *IEEE Computer*, pages 66–76, December 1996.

[Arc87]   James K. Archibald. The Cache Coherence Problem in Shared-Memory Multiprocessors. PhD Dissertation, Department of Computer Science, University of Washington, February 1987.

[Bro90]   Geoffrey M. Brown. Asynchronous Multicaches. *Distributed Computing*, 4:31–36, 1990.

[CES86]   E.M. Clarke, E.A. Emerson, and A.P. Sistla. Automatic Verification of Finite-State Concurrent Systems using Temporal Logic Specifications. *ACM Transactions on Programming Languages and Systems*, 8(2):244–263, April 1986.

[CGP99]   Edmund M. Clarke, Orna Grumberg, and Doron A. Peled. *Model Checking*. MIT Press, 1999.

[CHPS99]   Anne E. Condon, Mark D. Hill, Manoj Plakal, and Daniel J. Sorin. Using Lamport Clocks to Reason About Relaxed Memory Models. In *Proceedings of the 5th International Symposium on High-Performance Computer Architecture*, 1999.

[COR⁺95]   Judy Crow, Sam Owre, John Rushby, Natarajan Shankar, and Mandayam Srivas. A tutorial introduction to PVS. Presented at WIFT '95: Workshop on Industrial-Strength Formal Specification Techniques, Boca Raton, Florida, April 1995. Available, with specification files, at http://www.csl.sri.com/wift-tutorial.html.

[Del00]   Giorgio Delzanno. Automatic Verification of Parameterized Cache Coherence Protocols. Technical Report DISI-TR-00-1, DISI, University of Genoa, January 2000. Available at http://www.disi.unige.it/person/DelzannoG/papers.

[For]   Formal Systems (Europe) Limited. Fdr2. Web site. See http://www.formal.demon.co.uk/FDR2.html.

[HQR99]   Thomas A. Henzinger, Shaz Qadeer, and Sriram K. Rajamani. Verifying Sequential Consistency on Shared-Memory Multiprocessor Systems. In *Proceedings of the 11th International Conference on Computer-aided Verification (CAV)*, pages 301–315. Springer-Verlag, 1999. Lecture Notes in Computer Science 1633.

[ID93a]   C.N. Ip and D.L. Dill. Better Verification Through Symmetry. In *Proceedings of the 11th International Symposium on Computer Hardware Description Languages and Their Applications*, pages 87–100, April 1993.

[ID93b]   C.N. Ip and D.L. Dill. Efficient Verification of Symmetric Concurrent Systems. In *International Conference on Computer Design: VLSI in Computers and Processors*, October 1993.

[KPS93]   David R. Kaeli, Nancy K. Perugini, and Janice M. Stone. Literature Survey of Memory Consistency Models. Research Report 18843 (82385), IBM Research Devision, 1993.

[Lam93]   Leslie Lamport. How to write a proof. In *Global Analysis in Modern Mathematics*, pages 311–321. Publish or Perish, Houston, Texas, U.S.A., February 1993. A symposium in honor of Richard Palais' sixtieth birthday.

[Lam94]   Leslie Lamport. The temporal logic of actions. *ACM Transactions on Programming Languages and Systems*, 16(3):872–923, May 1994.

[Lam96]   Leslie Lamport. The Module Structure of TLA+. Technical Note 1996-002a, Compaq Systems Research Center, September 1996.

[Lam97]   Leslie Lamport. The Operators of TLA+. Technical Note 1997-006a, Compaq Systems Research Center, June 1997.

[Laz99]   Ranko Lazic. *A Semantic Study of Data Independence with Applications to Model Checking*. PhD thesis, Oxford University Computing Laboratory, 1999.

[McM92]   K.L. McMillan. Symbolic Model Checking: An Approach to the State Explosion Problem. PhD Dissertation, Carnegie Mellon University, May 1992.

[PD95]   Fong Pong and Michel Dubois. A New Approach for the Verification of Cache Coherence Protocols. *IEEE Transactions on Parallel and Distributed Systems*, 6, August 1995.

[PD96a]   Seungjoon Park and David L. Dill. Protocol Verification by Aggregation of Distributed Transactions. In *International Conference on Computer-Aided Verification*, July 1996.

[PD96b]   Seungjoon Park and David L. Dill. Verification of FLASH Cache Coherence Protocol by Aggregation of Distributed Transactions. In *Proceedings of the 8th ACM Symposium on Parallel Algorithms and Architectures*, June 1996.

[PD96c]   Fong Pong and Michel Dubois. Formal Verification of Delayed Consistency Protocols. In *Proceedings of the 10th International Parallel Processing Symposium*, April 1996.

[PNAD95]   Fong Pong, Andreas Nowatzyk, Gunes Aybay, and Michel Dubois. Verifying Distributed Directory-based Cache Coherence Protocols: S3.mp, a Case Study. In *Proceedings of the European Conference on Parallel Computing*, 1995.

[PSCH98]   Manoj Plakal, Daniel J. Sorin, Anne E. Condon, and Mark D. Hill. Lamport Clocks: Verifying a Directory Cache-Coherence Protocol. In *Proceedings of the 10th ACM Symposium on Parallel Algorithms and Architectures*, 1998.

[Ros97]   A.W. Roscoe. *The Theory and Practice of Concurrency*. Prentice Hall, 1997.

[SAR99a]   Xiaowei Shen, Arvind, and Larry Rodolph. CACHET: An Adaptive Cache Coherence Protocol for Distributed Shared-Memory Systems. In *Proceedings of the 13th ACM International Conference on Supercomputing*, June 1999.

[SAR99b]   Xiaowei Shen, Arvind, and Larry Rudolph. Commit-Reconcile & Fences (CRF): A New Memory Model for Architects and Compiler Writers. In *Proceedings of the 26th International Symposium on Computer Architecture*, May 1999.

[SD95]   Ulrich Stern and David L. Dill. Automatic Verification of the SCI Cache Coherence Protocol. In *Correct Hardware Design and Verification Methods: IFIP WG10.5 Advanced Research Working Conference Proceedings*, 1995.

[She00]   Xiaowei Shen. *Design and Verification of Adaptive Cache Coherence Protocols*. PhD thesis, Massachusetts Institute of Technology, February 2000.

[Sto]   Joseph E. Stoy. Web sites concerning Cachet, TLA in PVS, and cache protocol verification using FDR. See
           http://web.comlab.ox.ac.uk/oucl/work/joe.stoy/.

Model-Checking over Multi-valued Logics

Marsha Chechik, Steve Easterbrook, and Victor Petrovykh

Department of Computer Science, University of Toronto
Toronto ON M5S 3G4, Canada
{chechik,sme,victor}@cs.toronto.edu

Abstract. Classical logic cannot be used to effectively reason about systems with *uncertainty* (lack of essential information) or *inconsistency* (contradictory information often occurring when information is gathered from multiple sources). In this paper we propose the use of *quasi-boolean* multi-valued logics for reasoning about such systems. We also give semantics to a multi-valued extension of CTL, describe an implementation of a symbolic multi-valued CTL model-checker called Xchek, and analyze its correctness and running time.

1 Introduction

In the last few years, *model checking* [10] has become established as one of the most effective automated techniques for analyzing correctness of software artifacts. Given a system and a property, a model checker builds the reachability graph (explicitly or symbolically) by exhaustively exploring the state-space of the system. Model-checking has been effectively applied to reasoning about correctness of hardware, communication protocols, software requirements and code, etc. A number of industrial model checkers have been developed, including SPIN [19], SMV [24], and Murϕ [12]. Despite their variety, existing model-checkers are typically limited to reasoning in classical logic. However, there are a number of problems in software engineering for which classical logic is insufficient. One of these is reasoning under *uncertainty*, or when essential information is not available. This can occur either when complete information is not known or cannot be obtained (e.g., during requirements analysis), or when this information has been removed (abstraction). Classical model-checkers typically deal with uncertainty by creating extra states, one for each value of the unknown variable and each feasible combination of values of known variables. However, this approach adds significant extra complexity to the analysis.

Classical reasoning is also insufficient for models that contain *inconsistency*. Inconsistency arises frequently in software engineering [15]. In requirements engineering, models are frequently inconsistent because they combine conflicting points of view. During design and implementation, inconsistency arises when integrating components developed by different people. Conventional reasoning systems cannot cope with inconsistency; the presence of a single contradiction results in trivialization — anything follows from $A \wedge \neg A$. Hence, faced with an inconsistent description and the need to perform automated reasoning, we must either discard information until consistency is achieved again, or adopt a non-classical logic. The problem with the former approach is that we may be forced to make premature decisions about which information to discard [20]. Although inconsistency in software engineering occurs very frequently, there

J.N. Oliveira and P. Zave (Eds.): FME 2001, LNCS 2021, pp. 72–98, 2001.

have been relatively few attempts to develop automated reasoning tools for inconsistent models. Two notable exceptions are Hunter and Nuseibeh [21], who use a Quasi-Classical (QC) logic to reason about evolving specifications, and Menzies et al. [25], who use a paraconsistent form of abductive inference to reason about information from multiple points of view.

Paraconsistent logics are a promising alternative to classical reasoning — they permit some contradictions to be true, without the resulting trivialization of classical logic. The development of paraconsistent logics has been driven largely by the need for automated reasoning systems that do not give spurious answers if their databases become inconsistent. They are also of interest to mathematicians as a way of addressing the paradoxes in semantics and set theory. A number of different types of paraconsistent logic have been studied [26]. For example, relevance logics use an alternative form of entailment that requires a "relevant" connection between the antecedents and the consequents. Non-truth functional logics use a weaker form of negation so that proof rules such as disjunctive syllogism (i.e., $(A \vee B, \neg B) \vdash A$) fail. Multi-valued logics use additional truth values to represent different types of contradiction.

Multi-valued logics provide a solution to both reasoning under uncertainty and under inconsistency. For example, we can use "no information available" and "no agreement" as logic values. In fact, model-checkers based on three-valued and four-valued logics have already been studied. For example, [8] used a three-valued logic for interpreting results of model-checking with abstract interpretation, whereas [16,17] used four-valued logics for reasoning about abstractions of detailed gate or switch-level designs of circuits.

Different multi-valued logics are useful for different purposes. For example, we may wish to have several levels of uncertainty. We may wish to use different multi-valued logics to support different ways of merging information from multiple sources: keeping track of the origin of each piece of information, doing a majority vote, giving priority to one information source, etc. Thus, rather than restricting ourselves to any particular multi-valued logic, we are interested in extending the classical symbolic model-checking procedure to enable reasoning about arbitrary multi-valued logics, as long as conjunction, disjunction and negation of the logical values are specified.

This work is part of the χbel[1] (the Multi-Valued Belief Exploration Logics) project, outlined in [14]. The description of the system together with the description of the desired multi-valued logic and the set of correctness criteria expressed in CTL become input to our model-checker, called χchek, which returns a value of the logic best characterizing the validity of the formula in each initial state.

The rest of this paper is organized as follows: Section 2 describes a simple thermostat system which is used as a running example throughout the paper. Section 3 gives background on CTL model-checking. Section 4 describes the types of logics that we can analyze and the ways to represent them. Section 5 describes the multi-valued transition structures and extends CTL to reasoning over them. Section 6 discusses the implementation of χchek, whereas Section 7 contains the analysis of its correctness and running time. We conclude the paper with a summary of results and outline of future work in Section 8.

---

[1] pronounced "Chibel"

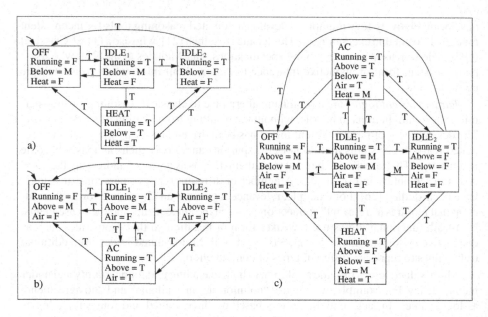

Fig. 1. Models of the thermostat. (a) Heat only; (b) AC only; (c) combined model.

2   Example

Consider three models of the thermostat given in Figure 1. Figure 1(a) describes a very simple thermostat that can run a heater if the temperature falls below desired. The system has one indicator (Below), a switch to turn it off and on (Running) and a variable indicating whether the heater is running (Heat). The system starts in state OFF[2] and transitions into IDLE$_1$ when it is turned on, where it awaits the reading of the temperature indicator. Once the temperature is determined, the system transitions either into IDLE$_2$ or into HEAT. The value of the temperature indicator is unknown in states OFF and IDLE$_1$. To model this, we could duplicate the states, assigning Below the value T in one copy and F in the other — the route typically taken by conventional model-checkers. Alternatively, we can model the system using the three-valued logic: T, F and M (Maybe), assigning Below the value M, as depicted in Figure 1(a)[3].

We can ask this thermostat model a number of questions:

Prop. 1. Can the system transition into IDLE$_1$ from everywhere?
Prop. 2. Can the heater be turned on when the temperature becomes below desired?
Prop. 3. Can the system be turned off in every computation?

Figure 1(b) describes another aspect of the thermostat system – running the air conditioner. The behavior of this system is similar to that of the heater, with one difference:

---

[2] Throughout this paper state labels are capitalized. Thus, HEAT is a state and Heat is a variable name.

[3] Each state in this and the other two systems in Figure 1 contains a self-loop with the value T which we omitted to avoid clutter.

this system handles the failure of the temperature indicator. If the temperature reading cannot be obtained in states AC or IDLE$_2$, the system transitions into state IDLE$_1$.

Finally, Figure 1(c) contains a merged model, describing the behavior of the thermostat that can run both the heater and the air conditioner. In this merge, we used the same three-valued logic, for simplicity. When the individual descriptions agree that the value of a variable or transition is T (F), it is mapped into T (F) in the combined model; all other values are mapped into M. During the merge, we used the simple invariants describing the behavior of the environment (Below $\rightarrow$ ¬Above, Above $\rightarrow$ ¬Below). Thus, the value of Below in state AC is inferred to be F. Note that the individual descriptions disagree on some states and transitions. For example, they disagree on a transition between IDLE$_2$ and IDLE$_1$; thus it receives the value M. Also, it is possible that the heater is on while the air conditioner is running.

Further details on the merge procedure are outside the scope of this paper, except to note that we could have chosen any of a number of different multi-valued logics to handle different combinations of values in the individual models. For example, we could have used a 9-valued logic where each value is a tuple formed from the values of the two individual models.

We can ask the combined model a number of questions that cannot be answered by either individual model, e.g.

Prop. 4. Is heat on only if air conditioning is off?
Prop. 5. Can heat be on when the temperature is above desired?

3   CTL Model-Checking

CTL model-checking is an automatic technique for verifying properties expressed in a propositional branching-time temporal logic called *Computational Tree Logic* (CTL) [10]. The system is defined by a Kripke structure, and properties are evaluated on a tree of infinite computations produced by the model of the system. The standard notation $M, s \models P$ indicates that a formula P holds in a state s of a model M. If a formula holds in the initial state, it is considered to hold in the model. A Kripke structure consists of a set of states S, a transition relation $R \subseteq S \times S$, an initial state $s_0 \in S$, a set of atomic propositions A, and a labeling function $L : S \rightarrow \mathcal{P}(A)$. R must be total, i.e, $\forall s \in S$, $\exists t \in S$, s.t, $(s, t) \in R$. If a state s_n has no successors, we add a self-loop to it, so that $(s_n, s_n) \in R$. For each $s \in S$, the labeling function provides a list of atomic propositions which are *True* in this state.

CTL is defined as follows:

1. Every atomic proposition $a \in A$ is a CTL formula.
2. If φ and ψ are CTL formulas, then so are $\neg\varphi, \varphi \wedge \psi, \varphi \vee \psi, EX\varphi, AX\varphi, EF\varphi,$ $AF\varphi, E[\varphi U \psi], A[\varphi U \psi]$.

The logic connectives ¬, ∧ and ∨ have their usual meanings. The existential (universal) quantifier E (A) is used to quantify over paths. The operator X means "at the next step", F represents "sometime in the future", and U is "until". Therefore, $EX\varphi$ ($AX\varphi$) means that φ holds in some (every) immediate successor of the current program state; $EF\varphi$ ($AF\varphi$) means that φ holds in the future along some (every) path emanating from the current state; $E[\varphi U \psi]$ ($A[\varphi U \psi]$) means that for some (every) computation path starting from the current state, φ continuously holds until ψ becomes true. Finally, we use $EG(\varphi)$ and $AG(\varphi)$ to represent the property that φ holds at every state for some (every) path emanating from s_0. Formally,

$$M, s_0 \models a \text{ iff } a \in L(s_0)$$
$$M, s_0 \models \neg\varphi \text{ iff } M, s_0 \not\models \varphi$$
$$M, s_0 \models \varphi \wedge \psi \text{ iff } M, s_0 \models \varphi \wedge M, s_0 \models \psi$$
$$M, s_0 \models \varphi \vee \psi \text{ iff } M, s_0 \models \varphi \vee M, s_0 \models \psi$$
$$M, s_0 \models EX\varphi \text{ iff } \exists t \in S, (s_0, t) \in R \wedge M, t \models \varphi$$
$$M, s_0 \models AX\varphi \text{ iff } \forall t \in S, (s_0, t) \in R \to M, t \models \varphi$$

$$M, s_0 \models E[\varphi U \psi] \text{ iff there exists some path } s_0, s_1, ..., \text{ s.t.}$$
$$\exists i, \, i \geq 0 \wedge M, s_i \models \psi \wedge$$
$$\forall j, \, 0 \leq j < i \to M, s_j \models \varphi$$
$$M, s_0 \models A[\varphi U \psi] \text{ iff for every path } s_0, s_1, ...,$$
$$\exists i, \, i \geq 0 \wedge M, s_i \models \psi \wedge$$
$$\forall j, \, 0 \leq j < i \to M, s_j \models \varphi.$$

where the remaining operators are defined as follows:

$$AF(\varphi) \equiv A[\top U \varphi] \quad \text{(def. of } AF)$$
$$EF(\varphi) \equiv E[\top U \varphi] \quad \text{(def. of } EF)$$
$$AG(\varphi) \equiv \neg EF(\neg\varphi) \quad \text{(def. of } AG)$$
$$EG(\varphi) \equiv \neg AF(\neg\varphi) \quad \text{(def. of } EG)$$

Definitions of AF and EF indicate that we are using a "strong until", that is, $E[\varphi U \psi]$ and $A[\varphi U \psi]$ are true only if ψ eventually occurs.

4   Specifying the Logic

Since our model checker works for different multi-valued logics, we need a way to specify the particular logic we wish to use. We can specify a logic by giving its inference rules or by defining conjunction, disjunction and negation operations on the elements of the logic. Since our goal is model-checking as opposed to theorem proving, we chose the latter approach. Further, the logic should be as close to classical as possible; in particular, the defined operations should be idempotent, commutative, etc. Such properties can be easily guaranteed if we ensure that the values of the logic form a lattice. Indeed, lattices are a natural way to specify our logics. In this section we give a brief introduction to lattice theory and describe the types of lattices used by our model-checker.

4.1   Lattice Theory

We introduce lattice theory here following the presentation in [2].

Definition 1 Lattice *is a partial order* $(\mathcal{L}, \sqsubseteq)$ *for which a unique greatest lower bound and least upper bound, denoted* $a \sqcap b$ *and* $a \sqcup b$ *exist for each pair of elements* (a, b).

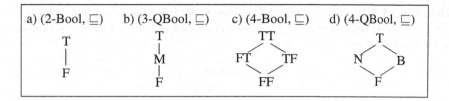

a) (2-Bool, $\sqsubseteq$)	b) (3-QBool, $\sqsubseteq$)	c) (4-Bool, $\sqsubseteq$)	d) (4-QBool, $\sqsubseteq$)

Fig. 2. Examples of logic lattices: (a) a two-valued lattice representing classical logic; (b) a three-valued lattice reflecting uncertainty; (c) a four-valued boolean lattice, a product of two (2-Bool, $\sqsubseteq$) lattices; (d) a four-valued quasi-boolean lattice.

	$\sqcap$	T	M	F		$\sqcup$	T	M	F		$\neg$	
	T	T	M	F		T	T	T	T		T	F
(a)	M	M	M	F	(b)	M	T	M	M	(c)	M	M
	F	F	F	F		F	T	M	F		F	F

Fig. 3. Tables of logic operations for (3-QBool, $\sqsubseteq$): (a) conjunction table; (b) disjunction table; (c) negation table.

The following are the properties of lattices:

$$a \sqcup a = a \qquad \text{(idempotence)}$$
$$a \sqcap a = a$$
$$a \sqcup b = b \sqcup a \qquad \text{(commutativity)}$$
$$a \sqcap b = b \sqcap a$$
$$a \sqcup (b \sqcup c) = (a \sqcup b) \sqcup c \qquad \text{(associativity)}$$
$$a \sqcap (b \sqcap c) = (a \sqcap b) \sqcap c$$
$$a \sqcup (a \sqcap b) = a \qquad \text{(absorption)}$$
$$a \sqcap (a \sqcup b) = a$$
$$a \sqsubseteq a' \wedge b \sqsubseteq b' \Rightarrow a \sqcap b \sqsubseteq a' \sqcap b' \qquad \text{(monotonicity)}$$
$$a \sqsubseteq a' \wedge b \sqsubseteq b' \Rightarrow a \sqcup b \sqsubseteq a' \sqcup b'$$

$a \sqcap b$ and $a \sqcup b$ are referred to as *meet* and *join,* representing for us conjunction and disjunction operations, respectively. Figure 2 gives examples of a few logic lattices. Conjunction and disjunction tables for the lattice in Figure 2(b) is shown in Figure 3(a)-(b). Our partial order operation $a \sqsubseteq b$ means that "b is more true than a".

Definition 2 *A lattice is* distributive *if*

$$a \sqcup (b \sqcap c) = (a \sqcup b) \sqcap (a \sqcup c) \qquad \text{(distributivity)}$$
$$a \sqcap (b \sqcup c) = (a \sqcap b) \sqcup (a \sqcap c)$$

All lattices in Figure 2 are distributive.

Definition 3 *A lattice is* complete *if the least upper bound and the greatest lower bound for each subset of elements of the lattice is an element of the lattice. Every complete lattice has a top and bottom.*

$$\bot = \sqcap \mathcal{L} \quad (\bot \text{ characterization})$$
$$\top = \sqcup \mathcal{L} \quad (\top \text{ characterization})$$

In this paper we use T to indicate $\top$ of the lattice, and F to indicate its $\bot$, although in principle $\top$ and $\bot$ might be labelled differently.

Finite lattices are complete by definition. Thus, all lattices representing finite-valued logics are complete.

Definition 4 *A complete distributive lattice is called a* complete Boolean lattice *if every element $a \in \mathcal{L}$ has a unique complement $\neg a \in \mathcal{L}$ satisfying the following conditions:*

$\neg\neg a = a$	($\neg$ involution)	$a \sqsubseteq b \Leftrightarrow \neg a \sqsupseteq \neg b$	($\neg$ antimonotonic)
$\neg(a \sqcap b) = \neg a \sqcup \neg b$	(de Morgan)	$a \sqcap \neg a = \bot$	($\neg$ contradiction)
$\neg(a \sqcup b) = \neg a \sqcap \neg b$	(de Morgan)	$a \sqcup \neg a = \top$	($\neg$ exhaustiveness)

In fact, $\neg$ involution, de Morgan and antimonotonic laws follow from $\neg$ contradiction and $\neg$ exhaustiveness.

Definition 5 *A* product *of two lattices $(\mathcal{L}_1, \sqsubseteq)$, $(\mathcal{L}_2, \sqsubseteq)$ is a lattice $(\mathcal{L}_1 \times \mathcal{L}_2)$, with the ordering $\sqsubseteq$ holding between two pairs iff it holds for each component separately, i.e.*

$$(a, b) \sqsubseteq (a', b') \Leftrightarrow a \sqsubseteq a' \wedge b \sqsubseteq b' \quad (\sqsubseteq \text{ of pairs})$$

Bottom, top, complement, meet and join in the product lattice are component-wise extensions of the corresponding operations of the component lattices. Product of two lattices preserves their distributivity, completeness and boolean properties. For example, out of the four lattices in Figure 2, only (2-Bool, $\sqsubseteq$) and (4-Bool, $\sqsubseteq$) are boolean. The former is boolean because $\neg$ T = F, $\neg$ F = T. The latter is a product of two (2-Bool, $\sqsubseteq$) lattices and thus is complete, distributive and boolean. The lattice (3-QBool, $\sqsubseteq$) is not boolean because $\neg$ M = M, and M $\sqcap \neg$ M $\neq \bot$.

4.2   Quasi-Boolean Lattices

Definition 6 *A distributive lattice $(\mathcal{L}, \sqsubseteq)$ is* quasi-boolean *[4] (also called* de Morgan *[13]) if there exists a unary operator $\neg$ defined for it, with the following properties $(a, b$ are elements of $(\mathcal{L}, \sqsubseteq))$:*

$\neg(a \sqcap b) = \neg a \sqcup \neg b$	(de Morgan)	$\neg\neg a = a$	($\neg$ involution)
$\neg(a \sqcup b) = \neg a \sqcap \neg b$		$a \sqsubseteq b \Leftrightarrow \neg a \sqsupseteq \neg b$	($\neg$ antimonotonic)

Thus, $\neg a$ is a quasi-complement *of a.*

Therefore, all boolean lattices are also quasi-boolean, whereas the converse is not true. Logics represented by quasi-boolean lattices will be referred to as *quasi-boolean logics*.

Theorem 1 *A product of two quasi-boolean lattices is quasi-boolean.*

Proof:
Refer to the Appendix for proof of this and other theorems of this paper.   □

For example, the lattice (3-QBool, $\sqsubseteq$), first defined in [23], and all its products are quasi-boolean. We refer to n-valued boolean lattices as (n-Bool, $\sqsubseteq$) and to n-valued quasi-boolean lattices as (n-QBool, $\sqsubseteq$). (4-QBool, $\sqsubseteq$) is a lattice for a logic proposed by Belnap for reasoning about inconsistent databases [3,1]. This lattice is quasi-boolean ($\neg N = N$; $\neg B = B$) and thus not isomorphic to (4-Bool, $\sqsubseteq$).

In the rest of this paper we assume that the negation operator given for our logic makes the lattice quasi-boolean. Figure 3(c) gives the negation function for lattice (3-QBool, $\sqsubseteq$).

What do quasi-boolean lattices look like? Below we define lattices which are (geometrically) horizontally-symmetric and show that, with negation defined by the horizontal symmetry, this is a sufficient condition for quasi-booleanness. We define:

Definition 7 *A lattice ($\mathcal{L}, \sqsubseteq$) is* horizontally-symmetric *if there exists a bijective function H such that for every pair a, b $\in$ $\mathcal{L}$,*

$$a \sqsubseteq b \Leftrightarrow H(a) \sqsupseteq H(b) \quad \text{(order } - \text{ embedding)}$$
$$H(H(a)) = a \quad \text{(H involution)}$$

Theorem 2 *Let ($\mathcal{L}, \sqsubseteq$) be a horizontally-symmetric lattice. Then the following hold for any two elements a, b $\in$ $\mathcal{L}$:*

$$H(a \sqcap b) = H(a) \sqcup H(b)$$
$$H(a \sqcup b) = H(a) \sqcap H(b)$$

Thus, horizontal symmetry is a sufficient condition for the corresponding lattice to be quasi-boolean, with $\neg a = H(a)$ for each element of the lattice, since it guarantees antimonotonicity and involution by definition, and de Morgan laws via Theorem 2.

5   Multi-valued CTL Model-Checking

In this section we extend the notion of boolean model-checking described in Section 3 by defining multi-valued Kripke structures and multi-valued CTL.

5.1   Defining the Model

A state machine M is a *multi-valued Kripke (XKripke) structure* if $M = (S, S_0, R, I, A, L)$, where

- L is a quasi-boolean logic represented by a lattice ($\mathcal{L}, \sqsubseteq$).
- A is a (finite) set of atomic propositions, otherwise referred to as variables (e.g. Running, Below, Heat in Figure 1(a)). For simplicity, we assume that all variables are of the same type, ranging over the values of the logic.

$$\neg AX\varphi = EX(\neg\varphi) \qquad \text{(negation of "next")}$$
$$A[\bot U\varphi] = E[\bot U\varphi] = \varphi \qquad (\bot \text{ "until"})$$
$$A[\varphi U\psi] = \psi \vee (\varphi \wedge AXA[\varphi U\psi] \wedge EXA[\varphi U\psi]) \qquad (AU \text{ fixpoint})$$
$$E[\varphi U\psi] = \psi \vee (\varphi \wedge EXE[\varphi U\psi]) \qquad (EU \text{ fixpoint})$$

Fig. 4. Properties of CTL operators (from [22,6]).

- S is a (finite) set of states. States are not explicitly labeled – each state is uniquely identified by its variable/value mapping. Thus, two states cannot have the same mapping. However, we sometimes use state labels as a shorthand for the respective vector of values, as we did in the thermostat example.
- $S_0 \subseteq S$ is the non-empty set of initial states.
- Each transition (s, t) in M has a logical value in $\mathcal{L}$. Thus, $R\colon S \times S \to \mathcal{L}$ is a total function assigning a truth value from the logic L to each possible transition between states. The value of (s, t) in M is thus referred to as $R^M(s, t)$, or, when M is clear from the context, simply as $R(s, t)$. Note that a $\mathcal{X}$Kripke structure is a completely connected graph. We also ensure that there is at least one non-false transition out of each state, extending the classical notion of Kripke structures. Formally,

$$\forall s \in S, \exists t \in S, \text{ s.t. } R(s, t) \neq \bot$$

To avoid clutter, we follow the convention of finite-state machines of not drawing F transitions. Thus, in Figure 1(a), transition between $IDLE_2$ and $IDLE_1$ is F, whereas in Figure 1(c) this transition is M.

- $I\colon S \times A \to \mathcal{L}$ is a total function that maps a state s and an atomic proposition (variable) a to a truth value v of the logic. For a given variable a, we will write I as $I_a\colon S \to \mathcal{L}$. Central to the rest of the paper will be a notion of *partitions* of the state space w.r.t. a variable a, referred to as $I_a^{-1}\colon \mathcal{L} \to 2^S$. A partition has the following properties:

$$\forall a \in A, \forall v_1, v_2 \in \mathcal{L} : v_1 \neq v_2 \Rightarrow (I_a^{-1}(v_1) \cap I_a^{-1}(v_2) = \emptyset) \quad \text{(disjointness)}$$
$$\forall a \in A, \forall s \in S, \exists v \in \mathcal{L} : s \in I_a^{-1}(v) \qquad\qquad\qquad \text{(cover)}$$

Finally, we refer to a value that a variable a takes in state s as $s[\![a]\!]^M$, or, when M is clear from context, simply as $s[\![a]\!]$.

5.2   Multi-valued CTL

Here we give semantics of CTL operators on a $\mathcal{X}$Kripke structure M over a quasi-boolean logic L. We will refer to this language as *multi-valued CTL, or $\mathcal{X}CTL$*. L is described by a finite, quasi-boolean lattice $(\mathcal{L}, \sqsubseteq)$, and thus the conjunction $\wedge$ ($\sqcap$ operation of the lattice), disjunction $\vee$ ($\sqcup$ operation of the lattice) and negation $\neg$ operations are available. We also define the material implication $\to$ as follows:

$$a \to b \equiv \neg a \vee b \quad \text{(definition of } \to)$$

In extending the CTL operators, we want to ensure that the expected CTL properties, given in Figure 4, are still preserved. Note that the AU fixpoint is somewhat unusual because it includes an additional conjunct, $EXA[fUg]$. The reason for this term is to preserve a "strong until" semantics for states that have no outgoing T transitions. This term was introduced by [6] for reasoning about non-Kripke structures.

We start defining $\mathcal{X}$CTL by giving the semantics of propositional operators. Here, s is a state and $v \in \mathcal{L}$ is a logic value:

$$s[\![a]\!] = I_a(s)$$
$$s[\![\neg\varphi]\!] = \neg s[\![\varphi]\!]$$
$$s[\![\varphi \wedge \psi]\!] = s[\![\varphi]\!] \wedge s[\![\psi]\!]$$
$$s[\![\varphi \vee \psi]\!] = s[\![\varphi]\!] \vee s[\![\psi]\!]$$

We proceed by defining EX and AX operators. Recall from Section 3 that these operators were defined using existential and universal quantification over next states. We extend the notion of quantification for multi-valued reasoning by using conjunction and disjunction operators. This treatment of quantification is standard [3,27]. The semantics of EX and AX operators is given below:

$$s[\![EX\varphi]\!] = \bigvee\nolimits_{t \in S}(R(s,t) \wedge t[\![\varphi]\!])$$
$$s[\![AX\varphi]\!] = \bigwedge\nolimits_{t \in S}(R(s,t) \rightarrow t[\![\varphi]\!])$$

Theorem 3 *Definitions of $s[\![EX\varphi]\!]$ and $s[\![AX\varphi]\!]$ preserve the negation of "next" property, i.e.*

$$\forall s \in S, \ \neg s[\![AX\varphi]\!] = s[\![EX\neg\varphi]\!]$$

Finally, we define AU and EU operators using the AU and EU fixpoint properties:

$$s[\![E[\varphi U\psi]]\!] = s[\![\psi]\!] \vee (s[\![\varphi]\!] \ \wedge \ s[\![EXE[\varphi U\psi]]\!])$$
$$s[\![A[\varphi U\psi]]\!] = s[\![\psi]\!] \vee (s[\![\varphi]\!] \ \wedge \ s[\![AXA[\varphi U\psi]]\!] \ \wedge \ s[\![EXA[\varphi U\psi]]\!])$$

The remaining CTL operators, $AF(\varphi)$, $EF(\varphi)$, $AG(\varphi)$, $EG(\varphi)$ are the abbreviations for $A[\top U\varphi]$, $E[\top U\varphi]$, $\neg EF(\neg\varphi)$, $\neg AF(\neg\varphi)$, respectively.

6 $\mathcal{X}$Chek: A Multi-valued Model-Checker

In this section we describe our implementation of a multi-valued CTL model-checker. This symbolic model-checker, called $\mathcal{X}$chek, is written in Java, and its architecture is depicted in Figure 5. The checking engine receives the $\mathcal{X}$CTL formulas to verify, the model of the system represented as an $\mathcal{X}$Kripke structure, and a lattice of logic values, and checks whether the specified property holds, returning an answer (one of the values of the passed lattice) and a counter-example, if appropriate. $\mathcal{X}$chek uses four supplementary libraries: $\mathcal{X}$DDs (a multi-valued extension of binary decision diagrams [5], described in [9]), a library for handling quasi-boolean lattices, a partition handler and a table inverter. The functionality of the latter two libraries is described below.

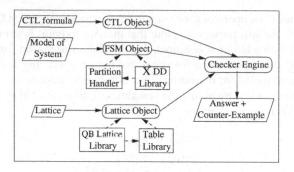

Fig. 5. Architecture of $\mathcal{X}$chek.

6.1   Table Library

The Table library contains several tables, indexed by the elements of the lattice, that give quick access to a variety of operations on lattice elements. In order to enable this indexing, we define $\text{Ord} : \mathcal{L} \to \mathbf{N}$ — a total order on the elements of our lattice $(\mathcal{L}, \sqsubseteq)$. Ord is a bijection, mapping each element $v \in \mathcal{L}$ onto the set $\{1...|\mathcal{L}|\}$. For example, we can order the elements of the lattice (3-QBool, $\sqsubseteq$) as follows:

$$\text{Ord(T)} = 1 \qquad \text{Ord(M)} = 2 \qquad \text{Ord(F)} = 3$$

This ordering is referred to as $\text{T} < \text{M} < \text{F}$.

Using Ord and the primitive lattice operations, we compute *inverted tables*: given a value, these tables give pairs of elements yielding this value when the corresponding operation is performed on them. Three inverted tables, $\text{InvTable}_\wedge$, $\text{InvTable}_\to$ and $\text{InvTable}_\vee$ are computed, one for each operator. For a table T and a value v, we use notation T_v to indicate an element associated with value v. $\text{InvTable}_\vee$ is defined as

$$\forall v \in \mathcal{L}, \; \text{InvTable}_{\vee,v} = \{(v_1, v_2) \mid v_1, v_2 \in \mathcal{L} \vee v_1 \wedge v_2 = v\}$$

For example, for the lattice (3-QBool, $\sqsubseteq$), $\text{InvTable}_{\vee,M} = \{(M, M), (F, M), (M, F)\}$. $\text{InvTable}_\wedge$ and $\text{InvTable}_\to$ are defined similarly.

Afterwards, we build generalized versions of the inverted tables for conjunction and disjunction over more than two operands. We call them $\text{BigOPTable}_\wedge$ and $\text{BigOPTable}_\vee$. Given a logic value v, $\text{BigOPTable}_{op,v}$ gives sets of logic values, where the corresponding operation op over the elements of the set yields v. For example, for the lattice (3-QBool, $\sqsubseteq$), $\text{BigOPTable}_{\vee,T}$ is $\{\{T\}, \{T, M\}, \{T, F\}, \{T, M, F\}\}$. $\text{BigOPTable}_\vee$ is defined as

$$\forall v \in \mathcal{L}, \; \text{BigOPTable}_{\vee,v} = \{V \mid V \in \mathcal{P}(\mathcal{L}) \wedge \bigvee V = v\}$$

$\text{BigOPTable}_\wedge$ is defined similarly. Since the generalized tables will be used only for computing commutative operations, we will not need to define $\text{BigOPTable}_\to$.

6.2   The Partition Handler

Central to the design of $\mathcal{X}$chek is the notion of *partition* and *cover*. A cover (satisfying the cover property given in Section 5.1) separates the states of the model into subsets corresponding to the different values of the logic for a proposition φ. If sets of states in a cover are mutually disjoint, we call it a partition. Disjointness property is also given in Section 5.1).

More formally, a cover $[\![\varphi]\!]^M$ for a property φ and a machine M is a tuple of sets such that the ith element of the tuple is a set of states where φ has the value $\mathrm{Ord}^{-1}(i)$ in M. When the choice of M is clear, we omit it, referring to the above as $[\![\varphi]\!]$. For a value $v \in \mathcal{L}$, we write $[\![\varphi]\!]v$ to indicate the set of states associated with v. Note that if φ is an arbitrary $\mathcal{X}$CTL property, then $[\![\varphi]\!]$ is a partition. For an example in Figure 1(a) and ordering $T < M < F$, $[\![\texttt{Below}]\!] = (\{\texttt{HEAT}\}, \{\texttt{OFF}, \texttt{IDLE}_1\}, \{\texttt{IDLE}_2\})$.

Further, we define a *predecessor function* pred which receives a cover $[\![\varphi]\!]$ and an operator $op \in \{\wedge, \rightarrow\}$ and returns a cover: a state s is associated with value v_1 in $\mathrm{pred}([\![\varphi]\!], op)$ iff s has a successor state t where φ has value v_2, and $R(s,t)\ op\ v_2 = v_1$. The function is given in Figure 6. For the lattice (3-QBool, $\sqsubseteq$), its ordering $T < M < F$ and the model in Figure 1(c), $\mathrm{pred}([\![\texttt{Running}]\!], \wedge)$ returns $(\{\texttt{IDLE}_1, \texttt{IDLE}_2, \texttt{AC}, \texttt{HEAT}\}, \{\texttt{IDLE}_2\}, \{\texttt{IDLE}_1, \texttt{IDLE}_2, \texttt{AC}, \texttt{HEAT}, \texttt{OFF}\})$.

We further define functions doOp and doBigOp, described in Figure 6. These functions evaluate the expression using the appropriate table ($\mathrm{InvTable}_{op}$ or $\mathrm{BigOPTable}_{op}$). Given covers $[\![\varphi]\!]$ and $[\![\psi]\!]$, doOP returns a cover for $\varphi\ op\ \psi$. If $[\![\varphi]\!]$ and $[\![\psi]\!]$ are partitions, then so is $\varphi\ op\ \psi$. For the lattice (3-QBool, $\sqsubseteq$) and the model in Figure 1(c), $[\![\mathrm{doOP}([\![\texttt{Above}]\!], \vee, [\![\texttt{Below}]\!])]\!]T$ returns a set of states in which Above $\vee$ Below is T, namely, $\{\texttt{AC}, \texttt{HEAT}\}$.

$\mathrm{doBigOP}(op, [\![\varphi]\!])$ computes a conjunction or a disjunction over a set of states. Recall that $\mathrm{BigOPTable}_{op,v}$ computes sets of logic values such that the operation op performed on them yields v. An operation $op\ \varphi$ over a set of states should yield v if the value of φ is in $\mathrm{BigOPTable}_{op,v}$ in *each* state in the set. Thus, for each V in $\mathrm{BigOPTable}_{op,v}$, we compute the intersection of states for which φ has a value in V and subtract the union of states in which φ does not have a value in V. $[\![\text{result}]\!]v$ is the union of all states computed via the above process for all V in $\mathrm{BigOPTable}_{op,v}$. For the model in Figure 1(c), $[\![\mathrm{doBigOP}(\vee, [\![\texttt{Heat}]\!])]\!]T$ returns $\{\texttt{HEAT}\}$. Note that if $[\![\varphi]\!]$ is a partition, $\mathrm{doBigOP}(op, [\![\varphi]\!])$ simply returns a partition $[\![\psi]\!]$, where $[\![\psi]\!]v = [\![\varphi]\!]v$ for each $v \in \mathcal{L}$.

6.3   Algorithm for $\mathcal{X}$Chek

The high-level algorithm, inspired by Bultan's symbolic model checker for infinite-state systems [6,7] and an abstract model-checker of [8], is given in procedure Check in Figure 6.

The algorithm recursively goes through the structure of the property under the analysis, associating each subproperty φ with a partition $[\![\varphi]\!]$. In fact, Check always returns partitions on the state-space (see Theorem 5). For the example in Figure 1(c) and the lattice ordering $T < M < F$,

$$
\begin{aligned}
\mathrm{Check}(\neg\texttt{Running}) &= (\{\texttt{OFF}\}, \{\}, \{\texttt{IDLE}_1, \texttt{IDLE}_2, \texttt{AC}, \texttt{HEAT}\}) \\
\mathrm{Check}(\texttt{Above} \vee \texttt{Below}) &= (\{\texttt{AC}, \texttt{HEAT}\}, \{\texttt{OFF}, \texttt{IDLE}_1\}, \{\texttt{IDLE}_2\}) \\
\mathrm{Check}(AX\ \neg\texttt{Heat}) &= (\{\texttt{OFF}, \texttt{AC}\}, \{\}, \{\texttt{IDLE}_1, \texttt{IDLE}_2, \texttt{HEAT}\})
\end{aligned}
$$

Function QUntil determines the value of $E[\varphi U \psi]$ and $A[\varphi U \psi]$ using a fixpoint algorithm given in Figure 6. The lowest ("most false") value that $A[\varphi U \psi]/E[\varphi U \psi]$ can have in each state s is $s[\![\psi]\!]$. Thus, QU_0 is equal to $[\![\psi]\!]$. At each iteration, the algorithm computes EXTerm_{i+1}, equal to $EXQU_i$. If the function is called with the universal quantifier, then it also computes AXTerm_{i+1}, equal to $AXQU_i$. Otherwise, AXTerm_{i+1} is not necessary, and thus we let AXTerm_{i+1} be $[\![\varphi]\!]$. $AXQU_i$ and $EXQU_i$ are computed by invoking the function doBigOP and passing it the result of the appropriate pred call. Then, for each state s, the algorithm determines where this state should be by computing dest $:= s[\![\psi]\!] \vee (s[\![\varphi]\!] \wedge s[\![\text{AXTerm}_{i+1}]\!] \wedge s[\![\text{EXTerm}_{i+1}]\!])$. If dest value is different from the one s had in QU_i, then it has to be moved to the appropriate place in QU_{i+1}. The algorithm proceeds until no further changes to QU_i can be made.

For example, suppose we are computing $E[\neg\text{Below } U \text{ Heat}]$ for our model in Figure 1(c) under the ordering $T < M < F$. QU_0 is initialized to $(\{\text{HEAT}\}, \{\text{AC}\}, \{\text{OFF}, \text{IDLE}_1, \text{IDLE}_2\})$. IDLE_2 has HEAT among its successors, so $\text{IDLE}_2[\![\text{EXTerm}_1]\!]$ is T. Thus,

$$\text{IDLE}_2[\![\text{Heat}]\!] \vee (\text{IDLE}_2[\![\neg\text{Below}]\!] \wedge \text{IDLE}_2[\![\text{EXTerm}_1]\!]) = F \vee (T \wedge T) = T$$

and so IDLE_2 should move to T. Using a similar process, we decide that dest for IDLE_1 in QU_1 is M, and that dest for AC and OFF in QU_2 are T and M, respectively. The next iteration does not change QU_2, and thus the algorithm terminates returning $(\{\text{HEAT}, \text{AC}, \text{IDLE}_2\}, \{\text{OFF}, \text{IDLE}_1\}, \{\})$.

Table 1. Results of verifying properties of the thermostat system.

Property	$\mathcal{X}$CTL formulation	Heater Model	AC Model	Combined Model
Prop. 1.	$AG\ EX\text{IDLE}_1$	F	T	F
Prop. 2.	$A\,[\neg\text{Heat } U \text{ Below}]$	T	–	T
Prop. 3.	$AG\ AF\neg\text{Running}$	F	F	F
Prop. 4.	$AG\ (\text{Heat} \leftrightarrow \text{Air})$	–	–	F
Prop. 5.	$AG\ (\text{Above} \rightarrow \neg\text{Heat})$	–	–	M

The properties of the thermostat system that we identified in Section 2 can be translated into $\mathcal{X}$CTL as described in Table 1. The table also lists the values of these properties in each of the models given in Figure 1. We use "–" to indicate that the result cannot be obtained from this model. For example, the two individual models disagree on the question of reachability of state IDLE_1 from every state in the model, whereas the combined model concludes that it is F.

7   Correctness and Termination of $\mathcal{X}$Chek

In this section, we analyze running time of $\mathcal{X}$chek and prove its correctness and termination.

7.1   Complexity

Theorem 4 *Procedure* Check(p) *terminates on every* $\mathcal{X}$CTL *formula p.*

Computation of Until takes the longest time. Each state can change its position in $[\![QU_i]\!]$ at most h times, where h is the height of the lattice $(\mathcal{L}, \sqsubseteq)$. Thus, the maximum number of iterations of the loop in QUntil is $|S| \times h$. Each iteration takes the time to compute doBigOP on pred: $O(|\mathcal{L}| \times 2^{|\mathcal{L}|} \times |S| + |\mathcal{L}|^2 \times |S|^2)$, plus the time to compute toMove and dest sets: $|\mathcal{L}|^4 \times O(|S|)$. Therefore, the running time of QUntil is

$$O(2^{|\mathcal{L}|} \times |S|^2 \times |S| \times h) = O(2^{|\mathcal{L}|} \times |S|^3)$$

and the running time of the entire model-checking algorithm on a property p is

$$O(2^{|\mathcal{L}|} \times |S|^3 \times |p|)$$

Note that in reality the running time is likely to be much smaller, because BigOPTable can be optimized and because set operations are BDD-based [9].

7.2 Correctness

In this section we prove correctness of $\mathcal{X}$chek by showing that it always returns exactly one answer (well-foundness) and that this answer is correct, i.e., it preserves the properties of $\mathcal{X}$CTL. We also show that multi-valued model-checking reduces to well-known boolean model-checking [24] if $(\mathcal{L}, \sqsubseteq)$ is the two-valued lattice representing classical logic.

We start by determining that procedure Check associates each state s with exactly one logical value for each $\mathcal{X}$CTL property p.

Theorem 5 *Procedure* Check *always returns a partition. Let p be an arbitrary $\mathcal{X}$CTL formula. Then,*

$$(a) \; \forall s \in S, \exists v_i \in \mathcal{L}, \text{s.t. } s \in [\![\text{Check}(p)]\!]v_i \qquad \text{(cover)}$$
$$(b) \; \forall s \in S, \exists v_i, v_j \in \mathcal{L}, \text{s.t.}$$
$$(s \in [\![\text{Check}(p)]\!]v_i \; \wedge \; s \in [\![\text{Check}(p)]\!]v_j) \to v_i = v_j \; \text{(disjointness)}$$

Now we show that our algorithm preserves the expected properties of $\mathcal{X}$CTL formulas given in Figure 4.

Theorem 6 *$\mathcal{X}$chek preserves the negation of "next" property, i.e.*

$$\forall s \in S, s \in [\![\text{Check}(AX\varphi)]\!]v \Leftrightarrow s \in [\![\text{Check}(EX\neg\varphi)]\!]\neg v$$

Theorem 7 *$\mathcal{X}$chek preserves fixpoint properties of AU and EU, i.e.*

$(1) \forall s \in S, s[\![\text{Check}(A[\varphi U\psi])]\!] = s[\![\text{Check}(\psi)]\!]\vee$
$\qquad (s[\![\text{Check}(\varphi)]\!] \wedge s[\![\text{Check}(AXA[\varphi U\psi])]\!] \; \wedge \; s[\![\text{Check}(EXA[\varphi U\psi])]\!])$
$(2) \forall s \in S, s[\![\text{Check}(E[\varphi U\psi])]\!] =$
$\qquad s[\![\text{Check}(\psi)]\!] \vee (s[\![\text{Check}(\varphi)]\!] \wedge s[\![\text{Check}(EXE[\varphi U\psi])]\!])$

($\perp$ "until") follows easily from AU and EU fixpoints.

```
function pred ([[φ]], op){
    foreach v ∈ L
        [[pred]]v := {s | ∃t ∈ S, ∃(v₁, v₂) ∈ InvTable_{op,v}, s.t. (t[[φ]] = v₂)}
    return pred
}
function doOP([[φ]], op, [[ψ]]) {
    foreach v ∈ L
        [[result]]v := {[[φ]]a ∩ [[ψ]]b | (a, b) ∈ InvTable_{op,v}}
    return result
}
function doBigOP(op, [[φ]]) {
    foreach v ∈ L
        [[result]]v := ∅
        foreach V ∈ BigOPTable_{op,v}
            [[result]]v := {⋂_{vᵢ∈V} [[φ]]vᵢ − ⋃_{vᵢ∈(L−V)} [[φ]]vᵢ} ∪ [[result]]v
    return result
}
function QUntil(quantifier, [[φ]], [[ψ]]) {
    QU₀ = [[ψ]]
    repeat
        EXTerm_{i+1} := doBigOP(∨, pred(QUᵢ, ∧))
        if (quantifier is A)
            AXTerm_{i+1} := doBigOP(∧, pred(QUᵢ, →))
        else
            AXTerm_{i+1} := [[φ]]
        foreach v₁, v₂, v₃, v₄ ∈ L
            toMove := [[φ]]v₁ ∩ [[ψ]]v₂ ∩ [[AXTerm_{i+1}]]v₃ ∩ [[EXTerm_{i+1}]]v₄
            dest := (v₁ ∧ v₃ ∧ v₄) ∨ v₂
            move all the states in toMove to [[QU_{i+1}]]dest
    until QU_{i+1} = QUᵢ
    return QUₙ
}
procedure Check(p){
    Case
        p ∈ A:        return [[p]] where
                      ∀v ∈ L, [[p]]v := I_p⁻¹(v)
        p = ¬φ:       return [[p]] where
                      ∀v ∈ L, [[p]]v := [[φ]]¬v
        p = φ ∧ ψ:    return doOp([[φ]], ∧, [[ψ]])
        p = φ ∨ ψ:    return doOp([[φ]], ∨, [[ψ]])
        p = EXφ:      return doBigOP(∨, pred([[φ]], ∧))
        p = AXφ:      return doBigOP(∧, pred([[φ]], →))
        p = E[φUψ]:   return QUntil(E, [[φ]], [[ψ]])
        p = A[φUψ]:   return QUntil(A, [[φ]], [[ψ]])
}
```

Fig. 6. Algorithm for $\mathcal{X}$chek.

Procedure BooleanCheck(p)
Case
$p \in A$: **return** $I_p^{-1}(\top)$
$p = \neg\varphi$: **return** $(S - \varphi)$
$p = \varphi \wedge \psi$: **return** $(\varphi \cap \psi)$
$p = \varphi \vee \psi$: **return** $(\varphi \cup \psi)$
$p = EX\varphi$: **return** pre(φ)
$p = AX\varphi$: **return** $(S - \text{pre}(S - \varphi))$
$p = E[\varphi U \psi]$: $Q_0 = \emptyset$
                   $Q_{i+1} = Q_i \cup (\psi \vee (\varphi \wedge EXQ_i))$
                   return Q_n when $Q_n = Q_{n+1}$
$p = A[\varphi U \psi]$: $Q_0 = \emptyset$
                   $Q_{i+1} = Q_i \cup (\psi \vee (\varphi \wedge EXQ_i \wedge AXQ_i))$
                   return Q_n when $Q_n = Q_{n+1}$

Fig. 7. Boolean Model-Checking Algorithm(adapted from [6]).

Our last correctness criterium is that the answers given by $\mathcal{X}$chek on (2-Bool, $\sqsubseteq$), a two-valued boolean lattice representing classical logic, are the same as given by a regular symbolic model-checker. We start by defining a "boolean symbolic model-checker" on Kripke structures, following [6] and changing some notation to make it closer to the one used in this paper. In particular, labeling functions used in boolean model-checking typically map a formula into a set of states where it is true, with the assumption that it is false in all other states. Thus, φ maps into $[\![\varphi]\!]\top$ in our notation. The algorithm is given in Figure 7, with pre defined as follows:

$$\text{pre}(Q) \equiv \{s \mid t \in Q \wedge (s, t) \in R\}$$

That is, pre(Q) computes all the states that can reach elements in Q in one step.

Theorem 8 $\mathcal{X}$chek, called on (2-Bool, $\sqsubseteq$), returns the same answers as a boolean model-checker BooleanCheck, given in Figure 7. That is, for each $\mathcal{X}$CTL property p and each state $s \in S$,

$$(1) \ s \in [\![\text{Check}(p)]\!]\top \Rightarrow s \in \text{BooleanCheck}(p)$$
$$(2) \ s \in [\![\text{Check}(p)]\!]\bot \Rightarrow s \notin \text{BooleanCheck}(p)$$

8   Conclusion and Future Work

Multi-valued logics are a useful tool for describing models that contain incomplete information or inconsistency. In this paper we presented an extension of classical CTL model-checking to reasoning about arbitrary quasi-boolean logics. We also described an implementation of a symbolic multi-valued model-checker $\mathcal{X}$chek and proved its termination and correctness. We plan to extend the work presented here in a number of directions to ensure that $\mathcal{X}$chek can effectively reason about non-trivial systems. We will start by addressing some of the limitations of our $\mathcal{X}$Kripke structures. In particular, so far we have assumed that our variables are of the same type, with elements described by values of the lattice associated with that machine. We need to generalize this approach to variables of different types.

Further, in this work we have only addressed single-processor models. We believe that synchronous systems can be easily handled by our framework, and it is essential to extend our model-checking engine to reasoning about synchronous as well as asynchronous systems.

We are also in the process of defining and studying a number of optimizations for storage and retrieval of logic tables. These optimizations and the use of the χDD library do not change the worst-case running-time of χchek, computed in Section 7. However, they significantly affect average-case running time. Once the implementation of the model-checker is complete, we intend to conduct a series of case studies to ensure that it scales up to reasoning about non-trivial systems.

Finally, we are interested in studying the properties of χchek in the overall framework of χbel. This framework involves reasoning about multiple inconsistent descriptions of a system. We are interested in characterizing the relationship between the types of merge of individual descriptions and the interpretation of answers given by χchek on the merged model.

Acknowledgments. We thank members of University of Toronto formal methods reading group, and in particular Ric Hehner, Albert Lai, Benet Devereux, Arie Gurfinkel, and Christopher Thompson-Walsh for numerous interesting and useful discussions and for careful readings of earlier drafts of this paper. We are also indebted to Albert and Benet for the proof of Theorem 2. Finally, we thank the anonymous referees for helping improve the presentation of this paper.

We gratefully acknowledge the financial support provided by NSERC and CITO.

References

1. A.R. Anderson and N.D. Belnap. *Entailment. Vol. 1*. Princeton University Press, 1975.
2. R.-J. Back and J. von Wright. *Refinement Calculus: A Systematic Approach*. Springer-Verlag, 1998.
3. N.D. Belnap. "A Useful Four-Valued Logic". In Dunn and Epstein, editors, *Modern Uses of Multiple-Valued Logic*, pages 30–56. Reidel, 1977.
4. L. Bolc and P. Borowik. *Many-Valued Logics*. Springer-Verlag, 1992.
5. R. E. Bryant. "Symbolic Boolean manipulation with ordered binary-decision diagrams". *Computing Surveys*, 24(3):293–318, September 1992.
6. T. Bultan, R. Gerber, and C. League. "Composite Model Checking: Verification with Type-Specific Symbolic Representations". *ACM Transactions on Software Engineering and Methodology*, 9(1):3–50, January 2000.
7. T. Bultan, R. Gerber, and W. Pugh. "Symbolic Model Checking of Infinite State Programs Using Presburger Arithmetic". In *Proceedings of International Conference on Computer-Aided Verification*, Haifa, Israel, 1997.
8. M. Chechik. "On Interpreting Results of Model-Checking with Abstraction". CSRG Technical Report 417, University of Toronto, Department of Computer Science, September 2000.
9. M. Chechik, B. Devereux, and S. Easterbrook. "Implementing a Multi-Valued Symbolic Model-Checker". In *Proceedings of TACAS'01*, April 2001.
10. E.M. Clarke, E.A. Emerson, and A.P. Sistla. "Automatic Verification of Finite-State Concurrent Systems Using Temporal Logic Specifications". *ACM Transactions on Programming Languages and Systems*, 8(2):244–263, April 1986.

11. E.W. Dijkstra and C.S. Scholten. *Predicate Calculus and Program Semantics*. Springer, 1990.
12. D.L. Dill. "The Murφ Verification System". In R. Alur and T.A. Henzinger, editors, *Computer-Aided Verification Computer*, volume 1102 of *Lecture Notes in Computer Science*, pages 390–393, New York, N.Y., 1996. Springer-Verlag.
13. J.M. Dunn. "A Comparative Study of Various Model-Theoretic Treatments of Negation: A History of Formal Negation". In Dov Gabbay and Heinrich Wansing, editors, *What is Negation*. Kluwer Academic Publishers, 1999.
14. S. Easterbrook and M. Chechik. "A Framework for Multi-Valued Reasoning over Inconsistent Viewpoints". In *Proceedings of International Conference on Software Engineering (ICSE'01)*, May 2001.
15. C. Ghezzi and B. A. Nuseibeh. "Introduction to the Special Issue on Managing Inconsistency in Software Development". *IEEE Transactions on Software Engineering*, 24(11):906–1001, November 1998.
16. S. Hazelhurst. *Compositional Model Checking of Partially Ordered State Spaces*. PhD thesis, Department of Computer Science, University of British Columbia, 1996.
17. S. Hazelhurst. "Generating and Model Checking a Hierarchy of Abstract Models". Technical Report TR-Wits-CS-1999-0, Department of Computer Science University of the Witwatersrand, Johannesburg, South Africa, March 1999.
18. E.C.R. Hehner. *A Practical Theory of Programming*. Texts and Monographs in Computer Science. Springer-Verlag, New York, 1993.
19. G.J. Holzmann. "The Model Checker SPIN". *IEEE Transactions on Software Engineering*, 23(5):279–295, May 1997.
20. A. Hunter. "Paraconsistent Logics". In D. Gabbay and Ph. Smets, editors, *Handbook of Defeasible Reasoning and Uncertain Information*, volume 2. Kluwer, 1998.
21. A. Hunter and B. Nuseibeh. "Managing Inconsistent Specifications: Reasoning, Analysis and Action". *ACM Transactions on Software Engineering and Methodology*, 7(4):335–367, October 1998.
22. M. Huth and M. Ryan. *Logic in Computer Science: Modeling and Reasoning About Systems*. Cambridge University Press, 2000.
23. S. C. Kleene. *Introduction to Metamathematics*. New York: Van Nostrand, 1952.
24. K.L. McMillan. *Symbolic Model Checking*. Kluwer Academic, 1993.
25. T.J. Menzies, S. Easterbrook, B. Nuseibeh, and S. Waugh. "An Empirical Investigation of Multiple Viewpoint Reasoning in Requirements Engineering". In *Proceedings of the Fourth International Symposium on Requirements Engineering (RE'99)*, Limerick, Ireland, June 7-11 1999. IEEE Computer Society Press.
26. G. Priest and K. Tanaka. "Paraconsistent Logic". In *The Stanford Encyclopedia of Philosophy*. Stanford University, 1996.
27. H. Rasiowa. *An Algebraic Approach to Non-Classical Logics. Studies in Logic and the Foundations of Mathematics*. Amsterdam: North-Holland, 1978.

A   Appendix

In this appendix we give proofs for the theorems appearing in the main body of the paper. The proofs follow the calculational style of [11]. Section A.1 presents proofs of theorems of lattice theory; Section A.2 gives proofs of correctness of the definition of $\mathcal{X}$CTL operators; Section A.3 lists properties of logic tables computed for $\mathcal{X}$chek; finally, Section A.4 uses the properties given in Section A.3 to prove correctness and termination of the implementation of $\mathcal{X}$chek.

A.1 Lattice Theory

Lattices have a number of properties that hold for them. We list several of them here, without proof.

$$
\begin{aligned}
a \sqsubseteq b &\Leftrightarrow \forall c,\ c \sqsubseteq a \Rightarrow c \sqsubseteq b && (\sqsubseteq \text{ introduction}) \\
a \sqsubseteq b &\Leftrightarrow \forall c,\ a \sqsubseteq c \Leftarrow b \sqsubseteq c && (\sqsubseteq \text{ introduction}) \\
&a \sqcap b \sqsubseteq b \text{ and } a \sqcap b \sqsubseteq a && (\sqcap \text{ elimination}) \\
u \sqsubseteq b \wedge a \sqsubseteq c &\Rightarrow a \sqsubseteq b \sqcap c && (\sqcap \text{ introduction}) \\
&a \sqsubseteq a \sqcup b \text{ and } b \sqsubseteq a \sqcup b && (\sqcup \text{ introduction}) \\
a \sqsubseteq c \wedge b \sqsubseteq c &\Rightarrow a \sqcup b \sqsubseteq c && (\sqcup \text{ elimination}) \\
a \sqsubseteq b &\Leftrightarrow a \sqcup b = b && (\text{correspondence}) \\
a \sqsubseteq b &\Leftrightarrow a \sqcap b = a && (\text{correspondence})
\end{aligned}
$$

The following are the properties of the product of two lattices $(\mathcal{L}_1, \sqsubseteq)$ and $(\mathcal{L}_2, \sqsubseteq)$:

$$
\begin{aligned}
\bot_{\mathcal{L}_1 \times \mathcal{L}_2} &= (\bot_{\mathcal{L}_1}, \bot_{\mathcal{L}_2}) && (\bot \text{ of pairs}) \\
\top_{\mathcal{L}_1 \times \mathcal{L}_2} &= (\top_{\mathcal{L}_1}, \top_{\mathcal{L}_2}) && (\top \text{ of pairs}) \\
\neg(a, b) &= (\neg a, \neg b) && (\neg \text{ of pairs}) \\
(a, b) \sqcap (a', b') &= (a \sqcap a', b \sqcap b') && (\sqcap \text{ of pairs}) \\
(a, b) \sqcup (a', b') &= (a \sqcup a', b \sqcup b') && (\sqcup \text{ of pairs})
\end{aligned}
$$

Theorem 1. *A product of two quasi-boolean lattices is quasi-boolean, that is,*

$$
\begin{aligned}
&(1) && \neg\neg(a, b) = (a, b) \\
&(2) && \neg((a_1, b_1) \sqcap (a_2, b_2)) = (\neg a_1, \neg b_1) \sqcup (\neg a_2, \neg b_2) \\
&(3) && \neg((a_1, b_1) \sqcup (a_2, b_2)) = (\neg a_1, \neg b_1) \sqcap (\neg a_2, \neg b_2) \\
&(4) && (a_1, b_1) \sqsubseteq (s_2, b_2) \Leftrightarrow \neg(a_1, b_1) \sqsupseteq \neg(a_2, b_2)
\end{aligned}
$$

Proof:

(1) $\neg\neg(a, b)$
$\Leftrightarrow$ ($\neg$ of pairs)
$\neg(\neg a, \neg b)$
$\Leftrightarrow$ ($\neg$ of pairs)
$(\neg\neg a, \neg\neg b)$
$\Leftrightarrow$ ($\neg$ involution)
(a, b)

(2) $\neg((a_1, b_1) \sqcap (a_2, b_2))$
$\Leftrightarrow$ ($\sqcap$ of pairs)
$\neg((a_1 \sqcap a_2), (b_1 \sqcap b_2))$
$\Leftrightarrow$ ($\neg$ of pairs)
$(\neg(a_1 \sqcap a_2), \neg(b_1 \sqcap b_2))$
$\Leftrightarrow$ (de Morgan)
$(\neg a_1 \sqcup \neg a_2, \neg b_1 \sqcup \neg b_2)$
$\Leftrightarrow$ ($\sqcup$ of pairs)
$(\neg a_1, \neg b_1) \sqcup (\neg a_2, \neg b_2)$

(4) $(a_1, b_1) \sqsubseteq (a_2, b_2)$
$\Leftrightarrow$ ($\sqsubseteq$ of pairs)
$a_1 \sqsubseteq a_2 \wedge b_1 \sqsubseteq b_2$
$\Leftrightarrow$ ($\neg$ antimonotonic)
$\neg a_1 \sqsupseteq \neg a_2 \wedge \neg b_1 \sqsupseteq \neg b_2$
$\Leftrightarrow$ ($\sqsupseteq$ of pairs)
$(\neg a_1, \neg b_1) \sqsupseteq (\neg a_2, \neg b_2)$
$\Leftrightarrow$ ($\neg$ of pairs)
$\neg(a_1, b_1) \sqsupseteq (\neg(a_2, b_2))$

The proof of (3) is similar to that of (2). $\qquad\qquad\qquad\qquad\qquad\qquad$ □

Theorem 2. *Let* $(\mathcal{L}, \sqsubseteq)$ *be a horizontally-symmetric lattice. Then the following hold for any two elements* $a, b \in \mathcal{L}$:

$$
\begin{aligned}
H(a \sqcap b) &= H(a) \sqcup H(b) \\
H(a \sqcup b) &= H(a) \sqcap H(b)
\end{aligned}
$$

Proof:
We will prove the first of these equations here, using the proof notation of [18]. The second one is a dual. We show

$$(1)\ H(a \sqcap b) \sqsubseteq H(a) \sqcup H(b)\ (1)$$
$$(2)\ H(a \sqcap b) \sqsupseteq H(a) \sqcup H(b)\ (2)$$

(1) $H(a \sqcap b) \sqsubseteq H(a) \sqcup H(b)$
$\Leftarrow$ ($\sqsubseteq$ introduction)
   $\forall z,\ (H(a \sqcap b) \sqsubseteq H(z)) \Leftarrow (H(a) \sqcup H(b) \sqsubseteq H(z))$
$\Leftarrow$ (H is order-embedding)
   $\forall z, (z \sqsubseteq a \sqcap b) \Leftarrow (H(a) \sqcup H(b) \sqsubseteq H(z))$
$\Leftarrow$ ($\sqcap$ elimination)
   $\forall z,\ (z \sqsubseteq a \wedge z \sqsubseteq b) \Leftarrow (H(a) \sqcup H(b) \sqsubseteq H(z))$
$\Leftarrow$ (H is order-embedding)
   $\forall z,\ (H(a) \sqsubseteq H(z) \wedge H(b) \sqsubseteq H(z)) \Leftarrow (H(a) \sqcup H(b) \sqsubseteq H(z))$
$\Leftarrow$ (rewriting $\Leftarrow$), ($\sqcup$ introduction)
   $\forall x,\ ((H(a) \sqcup H(b) \sqsubseteq H(z)) \wedge (H(a) \sqsubseteq H(a) \sqcup H(b)) \wedge (H(b) \sqsubseteq H(a) \sqcup H(b)))$
$\Leftarrow$ (transitivity)
   $\top$
(2) $H(a) \sqcup H(b) \sqsubseteq H(a \sqcap b)$
$\Leftarrow$ ($\sqcup$ elimination)
   $H(a) \sqsubseteq H(a \sqcap b) \wedge H(b) \sqsubseteq H(a \sqcap b)$
$\Leftarrow$ (H is order-embedding)
   $a \sqcap b \sqsubseteq a \wedge a \sqcap b \sqsubseteq b$
$\Leftarrow$ ($\sqcap$ elimination)
   $\top$

□

A.2 $\mathcal{X}$CTL

Theorem 3. *Definitions of $s[\![EX\varphi]\!]$ and $s[\![AX\varphi]\!]$ preserve the negation of "next" property, i.e.*

$$\forall s \in S,\ \neg s[\![AX\varphi]\!] = s[\![EX\neg\varphi]\!]$$

Proof:
Let $s \in S$ be an arbitrary state. Then,

   $\neg s[\![AX\varphi]\!]$
$=$ (definition of AX)
   $\neg(\bigwedge_{t \in S}(R(s,t) \rightarrow t[\![\varphi]\!]))$
$=$ (de Morgan), because $\neg$ is a quasi-boolean operator
   $\bigvee_{t \in S} \neg(R(s,t) \rightarrow t[\![\varphi]\!])$
$=$ (definition of $\rightarrow$), (de Morgan)
   $\bigvee_{t \in S}(\neg\neg R(s,t) \wedge \neg t[\![\varphi]\!])$
$=$ ($\neg$ involution), because $\neg$ is a quasi-boolean operator
   $\bigvee_{t \in S}(R(s,t) \wedge \neg t[\![\varphi]\!])$
$=$ (definition of $s[\![\neg\varphi]\!]$)
   $\bigvee_{t \in S}(R(s,t) \wedge t[\![\neg\varphi]\!])$
$=$ (definition of EX)
   $s[\![EX\neg\varphi]\!]$

□

A.3   Table Library

Here we give properties of inverse and BigOP tables defined in Section 6.1.

Lemma 1. *The following are properties of inverse tables, with* $op \in \{\wedge, \vee, \rightarrow\}$:

$$\forall v \in \mathcal{L}, \; (a, b) \in \texttt{InvTable}_{\rightarrow, v} \Leftrightarrow (a, \neg b) \in \texttt{InvTable}_{\wedge, \neg v}$$
($\rightarrow$ of $\texttt{InvTable}$)
$$\forall v \in \mathcal{L}, \; (a, b) \in \texttt{InvTable}_{\wedge, v} \leftrightarrow (\neg a, \neg b) \in \texttt{InvTable}_{\vee, \neg v}$$
(de Morgan of $\texttt{InvTable}$)
$$\forall v \in \mathcal{L}, \texttt{InvTable}_{op, v} \neq \emptyset$$
(non $-$ emptiness of $\texttt{InvTable}$)
$$\forall v_1, v_2 \in \mathcal{L}, \exists v_3 \in \mathcal{L}, \text{s.t. } (v_1, v_2) \in \texttt{InvTable}_{op, v_3}$$
(completeness *of* $\texttt{InvTable}$)
$$\forall v_1, v_2, v_3, v_4 \in \mathcal{L}, \; ((v_1, v_2) \in \texttt{InvTable}_{op, v_3} \wedge$$
$$(v_1, v_2) \in \texttt{InvTable}_{op, v_4}) \rightarrow (v_3 = v_4)$$
(uniqueness *of* $\texttt{InvTable}$)

Proof:
From the definition of inverse tables, negation properties, the definition of $\rightarrow$ and lattice properties. □

Lemma 2. *The following are the properties of BigOP tables, with* $op \in \{\wedge, \vee\}$:

$$\forall v \in \mathcal{L}, \quad (\emptyset \in \texttt{BigOPTable}_{\vee, v} \Leftrightarrow \mathcal{L} \in \texttt{BigOPTable}_{\wedge, \neg v}) \wedge$$
$$(\forall V \in \mathcal{P}(\mathcal{L}) - \emptyset, \; V \in \texttt{BigOPTable}_{\vee, v} \Leftrightarrow$$
$$\{\neg v \mid v \in V\} \in \texttt{BigOPTable}_{\wedge, \neg v})$$
(negation of $\texttt{BigOPTable}$)
$$\forall v \in \mathcal{L}, \quad (\emptyset \in \texttt{BigOPTable}_{\wedge, v} \Leftrightarrow \mathcal{L} \in \texttt{BigOPTable}_{\vee, \neg v}) \wedge$$
$$(\forall V \in \mathcal{P}(\mathcal{L}) - \emptyset, \; V \in \texttt{BigOPTable}_{\wedge, v} \Leftrightarrow$$
$$\{\neg v \mid v \in V\} \in \texttt{BigOPTable}_{\vee, \neg v})$$
(negation of $\texttt{BigOPTable}$)
$$\forall v \in \mathcal{L}, \quad \texttt{BigOPTable}_{op, v} \neq \emptyset$$
(non-emptiness of $\texttt{BigOPTable}$)
$$\forall V \in \mathcal{P}(\mathcal{L}), \exists v \in \mathcal{L}, \text{s.t. } V \in \texttt{BigOPTable}_{op, v}$$
(completeness of $\texttt{BigOPTable}$)
$$\forall V \in \mathcal{P}(\mathcal{L}), \forall v_1, v_2 \in \mathcal{L}, \; (V \in \texttt{BigOPTable}_{op, v_1} \wedge$$
$$V \in \texttt{BigOPTable}_{op, v_2}) \rightarrow (v_1 = v_2)$$
(uniqueness of $\texttt{BigOPTable}$)

Proof:
By construction of BigOP tables and by the idempotency property of lattices. □

Lemma 3. *The following are the properties of predecessor relations:*

$$\forall \varphi, \forall s \in S, \exists v \in \mathcal{L}, \text{s.t. } s \in [\![\texttt{pred}([\![\varphi]\!], op)]\!] v \; (\text{completeness of } \texttt{pred})$$
$$[\![\texttt{pred}([\![\varphi]\!], \wedge)]\!] v = [\![\texttt{pred}([\![\neg \varphi]\!], \rightarrow)]\!] \neg v \quad (\text{implication of } \texttt{pred})$$

Proof:

(completeness of pred)

Pick φ, pick a state s, pick a state t. Then, let $v_1 = R(s,t)$ and $v_2 = t[\![\varphi]\!]$. Further, let $v = v_1 \ op \ v_2$. Then, by the completeness of InvTable property, $s \in [\![\mathrm{pred}([\![\varphi]\!], op)]\!]v$.

(implication of pred)

Let $s \in S$ be an arbitrary state. Then,

$\quad s \in [\![\mathrm{pred}([\![\varphi]\!], \wedge]\!]v)$
$\Leftrightarrow$ (definition of pred)
$\quad \exists t \in S, \exists (v_1, v_2) \in \mathrm{InvTable}_{\wedge,v}, \text{s.t. } t[\![\varphi]\!] = v_2$
$\Leftrightarrow$ ($\rightarrow$ of InvTable)
$\quad \exists t \in S, \exists (v_1, \neg v_2) \in \mathrm{InvTable}_{\rightarrow,\neg v}, \text{s.t. } t[\![\varphi]\!] = \neg v_2$
$\Leftrightarrow$ (definition of pred)
$\quad s \in [\![\mathrm{pred}([\![\neg\varphi]\!], \rightarrow]\!]\neg v)$

$\square$

A.4 Correctness and Termination

Theorem 4. *Procedure* Check(p) *terminates on every $\mathcal{X}$CTL formula p.*

Proof:

Proof is on the structure of property p. Obviously, for all operators except "until", Check(p) terminates. We give proof for computing AU here. To prove that the execution of QUntil terminates, it suffices to show that $\forall s \in S, \forall i, s[\![QU_i]\!] \sqsubseteq s[\![QU_{i+1}]\!]$. Then, QU_i can change value at most h times, where h is the height of lattice $(\mathcal{L}, \sqsubseteq)$.

The proof goes by induction on i. Pick $s \in S$. Then,

Base case: $\quad s[\![QU_0]\!]$
$= $ (definition of QUntil)
$\quad s[\![\psi]\!]$
$\sqsubseteq$ (monotonicity of $\wedge$ (since it is $\sqcap$) and $\vee$ (since it is $\sqcup$))
$\quad s[\![\psi]\!] \vee (s[\![\varphi]\!] \wedge s[\![\mathrm{AXTerm}_1]\!] \wedge s[\![\mathrm{EXTerm}_1]\!])$
$= $ (definition of QUntil)
$\quad s[\![QU_1]\!]$

IH: $\quad s[\![QU_i]\!] \sqsubseteq s[\![QU_{i+1}]\!]$
Prove: $\quad s[\![QU_{i+1}]\!] \sqsubseteq s[\![QU_{i+2}]\!]$
Proof: $\quad s[\![QU_{i+1}]\!]$
$= $ (definition of QUntil)
$\quad s[\![\psi]\!] \vee (s[\![\varphi]\!] \wedge s[\![\mathrm{AXTerm}_{i+1}]\!] \wedge s[\![\mathrm{EXTerm}_{i+1}]\!])$
$= $ (definition of QUntil)
$\quad s[\![\psi]\!] \vee (s[\![\varphi]\!] \wedge \bigwedge_{t \in S}(\neg R(s,t) \vee s[\![QU_i]\!]) \wedge \bigvee_{t \in S}(R(s,t) \wedge s[\![QU_i]\!]))$
$\sqsubseteq$ (IH), (monotonicity)
$\quad s[\![\psi]\!] \vee (s[\![\varphi]\!] \wedge \bigwedge_{t \in S}(\neg R(s,t) \vee s[\![QU_{i+1}]\!]) \wedge \bigvee_{t \in S}(R(s,t) \wedge s[\![QU_{i+1}]\!]))$
$= $ (definition of QUntil)
$\quad s[\![\psi]\!] \vee (s[\![\varphi]\!] \wedge s[\![\mathrm{AXTerm}_{i+2}]\!] \wedge s[\![\mathrm{EXTerm}_{i+2}]\!])$
$= $ (definition of QUntil)
$\quad s[\![QU_{i+2}]\!]$

$\square$

Theorem 5. *Procedure* Check *always returns a partition. Let p be an arbitrary* χCTL *formula. Then,*

$$(a)\ \forall s \in S, \exists v_i \in \mathcal{L}, \text{s.t. } s \in [\![\text{Check}(p)]\!]v_i \qquad\qquad \text{(cover)}$$
$$(b)\ \forall s \in S, \exists v_i, v_j \in \mathcal{L}, \text{s.t.}$$
$$(s \in [\![\text{Check}(p)]\!]v_i \ \wedge \ s \in [\![\text{Check}(p)]\!]v_j) \to v_i = v_j \ \text{(disjointness)}$$

Proof:
The proof is by induction on the length of p.

Base case:$p \in A$. Check(p) uses I which is guaranteed to return a partition by deɒnition.
IH: Assume Check(p) returns a partition when $|p| \leq n$.
Prove: Check(p) returns a partition when $|p| = n+1$.
Proof:

$p = \neg\varphi$ Then, $[\![\varphi]\!]$ is a partition by IH, and negation is onto by $\neg$ involution.
$p = \varphi \wedge \psi$ Pick state $s \in S$. Since $[\![\varphi]\!]$ and $[\![\psi]\!]$ are partitions, $\exists v_1, v_2 \in \mathcal{L}$ s.t.
              $s \in [\![\varphi]\!]v_1$ and $s \in [\![\psi]\!]v_2$.
              (a) By completeness of InvTable, $\exists v_3$, s.t. $(v_1, v_2) \in \text{InvTable}_{\wedge,v_3}$,
                 so $s \in [\![p]\!]v_3$.
              (b) By uniqueness of InvTable.
$p = \varphi \vee \psi$ The proof is similar to the one above.
$p = EX\varphi$.   Pick a state $s \in S$.
              Create a set $V = \{v \mid s \in [\![\text{pred}([\![\varphi]\!], \wedge)]\!]v\}$
              (a) By completeness of BigOPTable, $\exists v_i \in \mathcal{L}$, s.t. $s \in [\![\text{doBigOP}$
              $(\vee, \text{pred}([\![\varphi]\!], \wedge))]\!]v_i$.
              (b) By uniqueness of BigOPTable, the above-found v_i is unique.
$p = AX\varphi$.   The proof is similar to the one above.
$p = E[\varphi U\psi]$ Partitionness is maintained as an invariant of QUntil:
              QUntil starts of with a partition, and move preserves partition.
$p = A[\varphi U\psi]$ Same as above.

$\square$

Theorem 6. χchek *preserves the negation of "next" property, i.e.*

$$\forall s \in S, s \in [\![\text{Check}(AX\varphi)]\!]v \Leftrightarrow s \in [\![\text{Check}(EX\neg\varphi)]\!]\neg v$$

Proof:
We prove

$$(1)\ s \in [\![\text{Check}(AX\varphi)]\!]v \quad \Rightarrow s \in [\![\text{Check}(EX\neg\varphi)]\!]\neg v$$
$$(2)\ s \in [\![\text{Check}(EX\neg\varphi)]\!]\neg v \Rightarrow s \in [\![\text{Check}(AX\varphi)]\!]v$$

(1) $s \in [\![\text{Check}(AX\varphi)]\!]v$
$\Rightarrow$ (deɒnition of Check)
$s \in [\![\text{doBigOP}(\wedge, \text{pred}([\![\varphi]\!], \to))]\!]v$
$\Rightarrow$ (deɒnition of doBigOP)
$\exists V \in \text{BigOPTable}_{\wedge,v}$, s.t. $(s \in \bigcap_{v_i \in V}[\![\text{pred}([\![\varphi]\!], \to)]\!]v_i) \wedge$
$\qquad\qquad\qquad\qquad\qquad\qquad (s \notin \bigcup_{v_i \in (\mathcal{L}-V)}[\![\text{pred}([\![\varphi]\!], \to)]\!]v_i)$
$\Rightarrow$ (negation of BigOPTable)
$\exists V_1 \in \text{BigOPTable}_{\vee,\neg v}$, s.t. $(s \in \bigcap_{\neg v_i \in V_1}[\![\text{pred}([\![\varphi]\!], \to)]\!]v_i) \wedge$
$\qquad\qquad\qquad\qquad\qquad\qquad (s \notin \bigcup_{\neg v_i \in (\mathcal{L}-V_1)}[\![\text{pred}([\![\varphi]\!], \to)]\!]v_i)$

$\Rightarrow$ (implication of pred)
$$\exists V_1 \in \texttt{BigOPTable}_{\vee, \neg v}, \text{s.t.} \quad (s \in \bigcap\nolimits_{\neg v_i \in V_1} [\![\texttt{pred}([\![\neg\varphi]\!], \wedge)]\!]\neg v_i) \wedge$$
$$(s \notin \bigcup\nolimits_{\neg v_i \in (\mathcal{L} - V_1)} [\![\texttt{pred}([\![\neg\varphi]\!], \wedge)]\!]\neg v_i)$$

$\Rightarrow$ (deﬁnition of doBigOP)
$$s \in [\![\texttt{doBigOP}(\vee, \texttt{pred}([\![\neg\varphi]\!], \wedge))]\!]\neg v$$

$\Rightarrow$ (deﬁnition of Check)
$$s \in [\![\texttt{Check}(EX[\![\neg\varphi]\!])]\!]\neg v$$

Proof of (2) is similar, and is based on implication of pred and negation of BigOPTable. $\square$

Theorem 7. $\mathcal{X}$*chek preserves fixpoint properties of AU and EU, i.e.*

$(1) \; \forall s \in S, s[\![\texttt{Check}(A[\varphi U \psi])]\!] = s[\![\texttt{Check}(\psi)]\!] \vee (s[\![\texttt{Check}(\varphi)]\!]$
$\qquad \wedge s[\![\texttt{Check}(AXA[\varphi U \psi])]\!] \wedge \; s[\![\texttt{Check}(EXA[\varphi U \psi])]\!])$

$(2) \; \forall s \in S, s[\![\texttt{Check}(E[\varphi U \psi])]\!] = s[\![\texttt{Check}(\psi)]\!] \vee (s[\![\texttt{Check}(\varphi)]\!]$
$\qquad \wedge s[\![\texttt{Check}(EXE[\varphi U \psi])]\!])$

Proof:
Pick a state s.

$(1) \; s \in [\![\texttt{Check}(A[\varphi U \psi])]\!]v$
$\Leftrightarrow$ (deﬁnition of Check)
$s \in [\![\texttt{QUntil}(A, [\![\varphi]\!], [\![\psi]\!])]\!]v$
$\Leftrightarrow$ (deﬁnition of QUntil)
$\qquad \exists n > 0, \text{s.t.,} \; QU_{n+1} = QU_n$
$\wedge \; s \in [\![QU_{n+1}]\!]v \Leftrightarrow (v = s[\![\texttt{Check}(\psi)]\!] \vee (s[\![\texttt{Check}(\varphi)]\!] \wedge s[\![\text{AXTerm}_{n+1}]\!]$
$\wedge s[\![\text{EXTerm}_{n+1}]\!]))$
$\Leftrightarrow$ (deﬁnition of AXTerm), (deﬁnition of EXTerm), (deﬁnition of AX in Check)
$\qquad \exists n > 0, \text{s.t.,} \; QU_{n+1} = QU_n$
$\wedge \; s \in [\![QU_{n+1}]\!]v \Leftrightarrow (v = s[\![\texttt{Check}(\psi)]\!] \vee (s[\![\texttt{Check}(\varphi)]\!] \wedge s[\![\texttt{Check}(AXQU_n)]\!]$
$\wedge s[\![\texttt{Check}(EXQU_n)]\!]))$
$\Leftrightarrow$ (combining the two conjuncts)
$s \in [\![QU_n]\!]v \Leftrightarrow (v = s[\![\texttt{Check}(\psi)]\!] \vee (s[\![\texttt{Check}(\varphi)]\!] \wedge s[\![\texttt{Check}(AXQU_n)]\!]$
$\wedge s[\![\texttt{Check}(EXQU_n)]\!]))$
$\Leftrightarrow$ ($A[\varphi U \psi] = QU_n$)
$s[\![\texttt{Check}(A[\varphi U \psi])]\!] = s[\![\texttt{Check}(\psi)]\!] \vee$
$\qquad (s[\![\texttt{Check}(\varphi)]\!] \wedge s[\![\texttt{Check}(AXA[\varphi U \psi])]\!] \wedge s[\![\texttt{Check}(EXE[\varphi U \psi])]\!])$

Proof of (2) is similar. $\qquad\qquad\qquad\qquad\qquad\qquad\qquad\qquad\qquad\qquad\qquad\qquad \square$

In our last theorem we want to prove that the result of calling $\mathcal{X}$chek with (2-Bool, $\sqsubseteq$), a lattice representing classical logic, is the same as the result of the boolean CTL model-checker.

We start by deﬁning inverse and BigOP tables for a boolean lattice:

$\texttt{InvTable}_{\wedge, \top} = \{(\top, \top)\}$ $\qquad\qquad$ $\texttt{BigOPTable}_{\wedge, \top} = \{\{\top\}, \emptyset\}$
$\texttt{InvTable}_{\wedge, \bot} = \{(\top, \bot), (\bot, \bot), (\bot, \top)\}$ $\quad$ $\texttt{BigOPTable}_{\wedge, \bot} = \{\{\bot\}, \{\bot, \top\}\}$
$\texttt{InvTable}_{\vee, \top} = \{(\top, \bot), (\top, \top), (\bot, \top)\}$ $\quad$ $\texttt{BigOPTable}_{\vee, \top} = \{\{\top\}, \{\top, \bot\}\}$
$\texttt{InvTable}_{\vee, \bot} = \{(\bot, \bot)\}$ $\qquad\qquad$ $\texttt{BigOPTable}_{\vee, \bot} = \{\{\bot\}, \emptyset\}$
$\texttt{InvTable}_{\rightarrow, \top} = \{(\bot, \bot), (\bot, \top), (\top, \top)\}$
$\texttt{InvTable}_{\rightarrow, \bot} = \{(\top, \bot)\}$

Lemma 4. *The following relations hold for each* $s \in S$ *when multi-valued model-checking is called on (2-Bool, $\sqsubseteq$):*

$$\forall s \in S, s \in [\![\mathrm{pred}([\![\varphi]\!], \wedge)]\!]\top \;\Rightarrow\; s \in \mathrm{pre}(\varphi) \quad \text{(property of } [\![\mathrm{pred}([\![\varphi]\!], \wedge)]\!]\top)$$
$$\forall s \in S, s \in [\![\mathrm{pred}([\![\varphi]\!], \rightarrow)]\!]\top \;\Rightarrow\; s \in \neg\mathrm{pre}(\neg\varphi) \quad \text{(property of } [\![\mathrm{pred}([\![\varphi]\!], \rightarrow)]\!]\top)$$
$$\forall s \in S, s \in [\![\mathrm{pred}([\![\varphi]\!], \wedge)]\!]\bot \;\Rightarrow\; s \in \neg\mathrm{pre}(\varphi) \quad \text{(property of } [\![\mathrm{pred}([\![\varphi]\!], \wedge)]\!]\bot)$$
$$\forall s \in S, s \in [\![\mathrm{pred}([\![\varphi]\!], \rightarrow)]\!]\bot \;\Rightarrow\; s \in \mathrm{pre}(\neg\varphi) \quad \text{(property of } [\![\mathrm{pred}([\![\varphi]\!], \rightarrow)]\!]\bot)$$

Proof:
We prove properties of $[\![\mathrm{pred}([\![\varphi]\!], \wedge)]\!]\top$ and $[\![\mathrm{pred}([\![\varphi]\!], \rightarrow)]\!]\top$. The others follow from (implication of pred). For an arbitrary state $s \in S$,

property of $[\![\mathrm{pred}([\![\varphi]\!], \wedge)]\!]\top$:
$\quad s \in [\![\mathrm{pred}([\![\varphi]\!], \wedge)]\!]\top$
$\Rightarrow$ (deдnition of pred)
$\quad \exists t \in S, \exists (v_1, v_2) \in \mathrm{InvTable}_{\wedge, \top}, \text{s.t. } t[\![\varphi]\!] = v_2$
$\Rightarrow$ (value of $\mathrm{InvTable}_{\wedge, \top}$)
$\quad \exists t \in S, \text{ s.t. } t[\![\varphi]\!] = \top$
$\Rightarrow$ (deдnition of pre)
$\quad s \in \mathrm{pre}(\varphi)$
property of $[\![\mathrm{pred}([\![\varphi]\!], \rightarrow)]\!]\top$:
$\quad s \in [\![\mathrm{pred}([\![\varphi]\!], \rightarrow)]\!]\top$
$\Rightarrow$ (deдnition of pred)
$\quad \exists t \in S, \exists (v_1, v_2) \in \mathrm{InvTable}_{\rightarrow, \top}, \text{s.t. } t[\![\varphi]\!] = v_2$
$\Rightarrow$ (value of $\mathrm{InvTable}_{\rightarrow, \top}$)
$\quad \exists t \in S, \neg((R(s, t) = \top) \wedge (t[\![\neg\varphi]\!] = \top))$
$\Rightarrow$ (deдnition of pre)
$\quad s \notin \mathrm{pre}(\neg\varphi)$

$\square$

Theorem 8. $\mathcal{X}\mathit{chek}$, *called on (2-Bool, $\sqsubseteq$), returns the same answers as a boolean model-checker. That is, for each* $\mathcal{X}$CTL *property p and each state* $s \in S$,

$$(1) \; s \in [\![\mathrm{Check}(p)]\!]\top \;\Rightarrow\; s \in \mathrm{BooleanCheck}(p)$$
$$(2) \; s \in [\![\mathrm{Check}(p)]\!]\bot \;\Rightarrow\; s \notin \mathrm{BooleanCheck}(p)$$

Proof:
The proof is by induction on the structure of property p.

Base Case:
$\quad p \in A :$ Check(p) and BooleanCheck(p) give the same answers by deдnition.
IH: Assume (1) and (2) hold for properties of length $\leq n$.
Prove: (1) and (2) hold for properties of length $n + 1$.
Proof:

$p = \neg\varphi :$ (1): $s \in [\![\mathrm{Check}(p)]\!]\top$
$\qquad\qquad\quad \Rightarrow$ (deдnition of Check)
$\qquad\qquad\qquad s \in [\![\varphi]\!]\bot$
$\qquad\qquad\quad \Rightarrow$ (deдnition of Check)
$\qquad\qquad\qquad s \in [\![\mathrm{Check}(\varphi)]\!]\bot$

$\Rightarrow$ (IH)

$s \notin \text{BooleanCheck}(\varphi)$

$\Rightarrow$ (definition of BooleanCheck)

$s \in \text{BooleanCheck}(p)$

Proof for (2) is similar

$p = \varphi \wedge \psi :$ (1): $s \in [\![\text{Check}(p)]\!]\top$

$\Rightarrow$ (definition of doOp)

$s \in [\![\varphi]\!]a \wedge s \in [\![\psi]\!]b \wedge (a,b) \in \text{InvTable}_{\wedge,\top}$

$\Rightarrow$ (value of InvTable$_{\wedge,\top}$)

$s \in [\![\varphi]\!]\top \wedge s \in [\![\psi]\!]\top$

$\Rightarrow$ (changing notation)

$s \in (\varphi \cap \psi)$

$\Rightarrow$ (definition of BooleanCheck)

$s \in \text{BooleanCheck}(p)$

Proof for (2) is similar. Because of the value of InvTable$_{\wedge,\perp}$, $s \in [\![\varphi]\!]a \wedge s \in [\![\psi]\!]b \wedge (a,b) \in \text{InvTable}_{\wedge,\perp}$ implies that $s \notin [\![\varphi]\!]\top \vee s \notin [\![\psi]\!]\top$.

$p = \varphi \vee \psi :$ Proofs are similar to the ones above and are based on values of InvTable$_{\vee,\top}$ and InvTable$_{\vee,\perp}$.

$p = EX\varphi :$ (1): $s \in [\![\text{Check}(p)]\!]\top$

$\Rightarrow$ (definition of Check)

$s \in [\![\text{doBigOP}(\vee, \text{pred}([\![\varphi]\!], \wedge))]\!]\top$

$\Rightarrow$ (definition of doBigOP), (value of BigOPTable$_{\vee,\top}$)

$[\![\text{result}]\!]\top = \emptyset \cup ([\![\text{pred}(\varphi, \wedge)]\!]\top - [\![\text{pred}(\varphi, \wedge)]\!]\perp)$
$\qquad\qquad \cup ([\![\text{pred}(\varphi, \wedge)]\!]\top \cap [\![\text{pred}(\varphi, \wedge)]\!]\perp)$

$\Rightarrow$ (properties of $[\![\text{pred}([\![\varphi]\!], \wedge)]\!]\top$ and $[\![\text{pred}([\![\varphi]\!], \wedge)]\!]\perp$)

$[\![\text{result}]\!]\top = (\text{pre}(\varphi) - (S - \text{pre}(\varphi))) \cup (\text{pre}(\varphi) \cap (S - \text{pre}(\varphi)))$

$=$ (set theory)

$s \in \text{pre}(\varphi)$

$\Rightarrow$ (definition of BooleanCheck)

$s \in \text{BooleanCheck}(p)$

(2): $s \in [\![\text{Check}(p)]\!]\perp$

$\Rightarrow$ (definition of Check), (definition of doBigOP), (value of BigOPTable$_{\vee,\perp}$)

$[\![\text{result}]\!]\perp = \emptyset \cup ([\![\text{pred}(\varphi, \wedge)]\!]\perp - [\![\text{pred}(\varphi, \wedge)]\!]\top)$

$\Rightarrow$ (properties of $[\![\text{pred}([\![\varphi]\!], \wedge)]\!]\top$ and $[\![\text{pred}([\![\varphi]\!], \wedge)]\!]\perp$), (logic)

$s \notin \text{pre}(\varphi)$

$\Rightarrow$ (definition of BooleanCheck)

$s \notin \text{BooleanCheck}(p)$

$p = AX\varphi :$ The proof of (1) and (2) is similar to the one above and is based on properties of $[\![\text{pred}([\![\varphi]\!], \wedge)]\!]\top$ and $[\![\text{pred}([\![\varphi]\!], \wedge)]\!]\perp$, values of BigOPTable$_{\wedge,\top}$ and BigOPTable$_{\wedge,\perp}$.

$p = A[\varphi U \psi]$ Since Check(p) expands into computing QU_n in QUntil$(A, [\![\varphi]\!], [\![\psi]\!])$, the proof for (1) goes by induction on n — the length of the path from s to a state where ψ holds.

Base case: $n = 0$.

$QU_1 = QU_0 \wedge s \in [\![Q_0]\!]\top$

$s \in [\![\psi]\!]\top$

$\Rightarrow$ (definition of BooleanCheck)

$s \in Q_1$

$\Rightarrow$ (de□nition of `BooleanCheck`)

$s \in \texttt{BooleanCheck}(p)$

IH: Assume (1) holds for all $n \le k$.

Prove: (1) holds for $n = k + 1$.

Proof: $s \in [\![\texttt{Check}(p)]\!]\bot$

$\Rightarrow$ (de□nition of `QUntil`), (de□nition of EXTerm), (de□nition of AXTerm)

$(QU_{k+2} = QU_{k+1}) \wedge (s[\![\psi]\!] \vee (s[\![\varphi]\!] \wedge s[\![AXQU_{k+1}]\!] \wedge s[\![EXQU_{k+1}]\!]) = \top)$

$\Rightarrow$ (boolean lattice rules)

$(QU_{k+2} = QU_{k+1}) \wedge$

$\quad (s[\![\psi]\!] = \top \vee (s[\![\varphi]\!] = \top \wedge s[\![AXQU_{k+1}]\!] = \top \wedge s[\![EXQU_{k+1}]\!] = \top))$

$\Rightarrow$ (Theorem 8 for $p = AX\varphi$), (Theorem 8 for $p = EX\varphi$), (IH)

$s \in \texttt{BooleanCheck}(\psi) \vee (s \in \texttt{BooleanCheck}(\varphi) \wedge$

$\quad s \in \texttt{BooleanCheck}(AXQ_k) \wedge s \in \texttt{BooleanCheck}(EXQ_k))$

$\Rightarrow$ (de□nition of `BooleanCheck`)

$s \in \texttt{BooleanCheck}(p)$

$(2)\, s \in [\![\texttt{Check}(p)]\!]\bot$

$\Rightarrow$ (de□nition of `Check`), (de□nition of AXTerm), (de□nition of EXTerm)

$\forall i, s[\![\psi]\!] \vee (s[\![\varphi]\!] \wedge s[\![AXQU_i]\!] \wedge s[\![AXQU_i]\!]) = \bot$

$\Rightarrow$ (boolean lattice laws)

$\forall i, s[\![\psi]\!] = \bot \wedge (s[\![\varphi]\!] = \bot \vee s[\![AXQU_i]\!] = \bot \vee s[\![EXQU_i]\!] = \bot)$

$\Rightarrow$ (Theorem 8 for $p = AX\varphi$), (Theorem 8 for $p = EX\varphi$), (Base Case)

$\forall i, s \notin \texttt{BooleanCheck}(\psi) \wedge (s \notin \texttt{BooleanCheck}(\varphi) \vee$

$\quad s \notin \texttt{BooleanCheck}(AXQ_i) \vee s \notin \texttt{BooleanCheck}(EXQ_i))$

$\Rightarrow$ (de□nition of `BooleanCheck`)

$\forall i, s \notin Q_i \Leftrightarrow s \notin \texttt{BooleanCheck}$

$p = E[\varphi U \psi]$: The proof of (1) and (2) is similar to the one above.

$\square$

How to Make FDR Spin
LTL Model Checking of CSP by Refinement

Michael Leuschel[1], Thierry Massart[2], and Andrew Currie[1]

[1] Department of Electronics and Computer Science
University of Southampton
Highfield, Southampton, SO17 1BJ, UK
{mal,ajc}@ecs.soton.ac.uk

[2] Computer Science Department
University of Brussels ULB - CP 212
Bld du Triomphe, B-1050 Brussels, Belgium
tmassart@ulb.ac.be

Abstract. We study the possibility of doing LTL model checking on CSP specifications in the context of refinement. We present evidence that the refinement-based approach to verification does not seem to be very well suited for verifying certain temporal properties. To remedy this problem, we show how to (and how not to) perform LTL model checking of CSP processes using refinement checking in general and the FDR tool in particular. We show how one can handle (potentially) deadlocking systems, discuss the validity of our approach for infinite state systems, and shed light on the relationship between "classical" model checking and refinement checking.

1 Introduction

Recent years have seen dramatic growth [8] in the application of model checking [7,4] techniques to the validation and verification of correctness properties of hardware, and more recently software systems.

One of the methods is to model a hardware or software system as a finite, labelled transition system (LTS) which is then exhaustively explored to decide whether a given temporal logic specification ϕ holds, i.e., *checking* whether the system is a *model* of the formula ϕ. This approach has lead to various implementations, such as SPIN [15] for model checking of formulas in LTL [3] or SMV [18] for CTL [7] model checking.

Another, quite different, approach is based on the notion of *refinement* and is used by tools such as FDR [19,12]. Here, the idea is to model *both* the system and the property in the *same* formalism, e.g., as CSP [14] processes. A system is said to satisfy a property ϕ if it is a refinement of ϕ. In CSP, refinement can be defined as language containment, failures containment, or failures and divergences containment.

The refinement-based approach suits itself very nicely to the stepwise development of systems, while the temporal logic approach often allows for more

J.N. Oliveira and P. Zave (Eds.): FME 2001, LNCS 2021, pp. 99–118, 2001.
© Springer-Verlag Berlin Heidelberg 2001

natural or succinct temporal specifications. It is quite surprising that the relationship between these two approaches appears not to have been studied. For instance, on the practical side, one might be interested in using tools such as FDR to do classical temporal logic model checking of CSP processes. In that context it would be interesting to know how (subclasses of) LTL or CTL temporal logic formulas can be translated into refinement tests. On the theoretical side, one might be interested in studying the expressive power of full LTL or CTL compared to refinement based model checking.

In this paper, we study the possibility of doing LTL model checking on CSP specifications in the context of refinement in general and using the FDR tool in particular. We discuss some unfruitful attempts at this translation, which show that it is surprisingly difficult to find intuitive formulations of classical model checking tasks as refinement checks. In particular, this means that a tool such as FDR can currently not be used by ordinary users to perform LTL or CTL model checking. This is a pity, as FDR can handle full CSP extended with functions and advanced datatypes (such as lists, integers, sets), thus providing a powerful specification and prototyping language, and it would be extremely valuable to apply "classical" model checking to such specifications (e.g., to validate the initial specification). To remedy this problem, we then present a translation from LTL to refinement (based on Büchi automaton) which *does* work and (once automated) allows one to easily perform "classical" model checking in a CSP setting with refinement.

The remaining part of this paper contains the following. Sect. 2 contains basic definitions concerning CSP and LTL. Sections 3 and 4 describe our (unsuccessful and successful) attempts at translating LTL model checks into refinement checks. In particular, we discuss the semantics of finite versus infinite traces and define LTL^Δ which can express properties both on infinite and deadlocking traces. We give our construction for a tester which allows us to achieve the model-checking using refinement. Section 6 contains discussions and future work.

2   Preliminaries

Let us first briefly recall main definitions concerning CSP and LTL. A more complete and motivated definition can be found in [19] for CSP and in [6] for LTL.

CSP and Refinement. CSP is a process algebra defined by Hoare [14]. The first semantics associated with CSP was a denotational semantics in terms of traces, failures and (failure and) divergences. An important notion is refinement: P refines Q denoted by $P \sqsupseteq Q$, iff $\|P\| \subseteq \|Q\|$, where $\|P\|$ stands for the (particular) semantics of P, thus trace refinement is no more than language containment. Also, P is said to be *equivalent* to Q *iff* P refines Q and Q refines P. CSP also has an operational semantics defined, e.g., in [19].

Let us now give the syntax and semantics of the subset of CSP we want to handle. This subset will be sufficient to illustrate the problems as well as the possible solutions for doing LTL model checking using refinement.

Given Σ, a finite or enumerable set of actions (which we will henceforth denote by lower case letters $a, b, c, \ldots$), and $\mathcal{X}$, an enumerable set of variables or processes (which we henceforth denote by identifiers such as $Q, R, \ldots$, or *MYPROCESS* starting with an uppercase letter), the syntax of a basic CSP expression is defined by the following grammar (where A denotes a set of actions):

$P ::=$

STOP (deadlock)	$a \rightarrow P$ (prefix)	
$P \sqcap P$ (internal choice)	$P \square P$ (external choice)	
$P \,\|A\|\, P$ (parallel composition)	$P \backslash A$ (hiding)	
Q (instantiation of a process)		

Moreover, each process Q used must have a (possibly recursive) definition $Q = P$. We suppose that all used processes are defined by at least one recursive definition (if there is more than one definition this is seen to be like an external choice of all the right-hand sides). In the following, we also suppose the alphabet Σ to be finite.

Intuitively, $a \rightarrow P$ means that the system proposes the action a to its environment, which can decide to execute it. The external choice is resolved by the environment (except when two branches propose the same action, where a nondeterministic choice is taken in case the environment chooses that action). Internal choice is made by the system without any control from the environment. $P \,\|A\|\, Q$ is the generalized parallel operator of [19], and means that the process P synchronizes with Q on any action in the set of actions A. If an action outside A is enabled in P or Q, it can occur without synchronization of both processes. Pure interleaving $P \,\|\emptyset\|\, Q$ is denoted by $P \,|||\, Q$. Pure synchronization $P \,\|\Sigma\|\, Q$ is denoted by $P \,||\, Q$. The hiding operator $P \backslash A$ replaces any visible action $a \in A$ of P by the internal action τ.

Note that the internal action τ is a particular action distinct from any action of Σ (called visible actions). Intuitively this internal action allows to denote a transition of the system from one state to another without any visible result to the outside world. In CSP, we handle *visible traces*, i.e. traces where τ actions have been removed.

In the trace semantics, the meaning $|P|$ of a process P is the prefix closed set of all the visible *finite* traces of P. The failure semantics additionally assigns to a process P the set *failures*(P) of couples: the first element is a visible finite trace t of the process P and the second component is a set R of refusals, i.e. the set of all sets of actions the process P can refuse after having performed the finite trace t. The divergence semantics of CSP also assigns to a process P the set *divergences*(P) of traces after which the process can diverge, i.e., perform an infinite number of invisible actions τ in sequence.

We shall denote $P \sqsupseteq_T Q$ and $P \sqsupseteq_F Q$ if the process P is resp. a trace or a failure refinement of Q. Note that these semantics are slightly different from classical CSP. In classical CSP, an immediately diverging process is equivalent to *CHAOS*, which can perform any sequence of actions and refuse any set of actions at any point. In our context, a diverging process cannot perform all possible traces and failures, which conforms to the traces-refinement and failure-refinement implemented in the FDR tool. A formal definition of the various semantics of CSP can be found in [19,14].

Example 1. Take $\Sigma = \{a, b\}$, $P_1 = a \rightarrow STOP$, and $P_2 = (a \rightarrow STOP) \sqcap (b \rightarrow STOP)$. Then $P_1 \sqsupseteq_{\mathcal{F}} P_2$ because $failures(P_1) = \{(\epsilon, \{b\}), (\epsilon, \emptyset), (a, \Sigma), (a, \{a\}), (a, \{b\}), (a, \emptyset)\}$ and $failures(P_2) = \{(\epsilon, \{b\}), (\epsilon, \emptyset), (\epsilon, \{a\}), (a, \Sigma), (a, \{a\}), (a, \{b\}), (a, \emptyset), (b, \Sigma), (b, \{a\}), (b, \{b\}), (b, \emptyset)\}$. Observe that $(\epsilon, \{a, b\}) \notin failures(P_2)$, i.e., P_2 cannot refuse both a and b (but it will refuse either a or b depending on the internal choice).

Also, for $P_3 = (a \rightarrow STOP) \square (b \rightarrow STOP)$ we have $P_1 \sqsupseteq_{\mathcal{T}} P_3$ but $P_1 \not\sqsupseteq_{\mathcal{F}} P_3$ because $failures(P_3)$ does not contain neither $(\epsilon, \{a\})$ nor $(\epsilon, \{b\})$.

LTL. LTL [3] is a linear-time temporal logic, in the sense that it uses a trace semantics. Given an alphabet Π of elementary propositions (which we denote by lower-case letters such as $a, b, c, \ldots$), the syntax of LTL is given by the following grammar:

$$\phi ::= false | true | a | \neg a | \phi \wedge \phi | \phi \vee \phi | \bigcirc \phi | \phi \, \mathcal{U} \, \phi | \phi \, \mathcal{R} \, \phi$$

Note that LTL is usually defined for state based models (i.e., Kripke structures) while the operational semantics of CSP provides a labelled transition system where transitions rather than states carry labels, and some of the transitions are labelled by the invisible action τ. We thus have to be very careful about what the meaning of an elementary formula a is and what the concept of a successor state (in light of τ) is[1].

First, we will set Π to be identical to the set of actions Σ used within CSP processes. Second, as usual in LTL, we will define the meaning of formulas on individual traces of a system, and a system is a model for a formula iff all its traces satisfy the formula. This definition means that the LTL formula a is true for a system iff the system can perform a visible action (possibly after a sequence of invisible ones) and that in all cases this *visible action must* be a. Also, the system is a model for $\neg a$ iff the action a can not be fired as first visible action.

Conjunction and disjunction have the usual meaning. $\bigcirc$ is the next operator; e.g. $\bigcirc \phi$ means that the system can always perform a visible action, and that after this action, the formula ϕ must be true. Notice that various invisible actions may occur before the first visible action i.e., in our context this operator is not a "next state" operator but a "next after visible action" operator. $\phi \, \mathcal{U} \, \psi$ means that for every execution of the system the formula ψ must eventually become true and furthermore the formula ϕ must be true until (but not necessarily including) the first point at which ψ becomes true. $\mathcal{R}$ is the release operator which is the dual of the $\mathcal{U}$ operator; $\phi \, \mathcal{R} \, \psi$ intuitively means that ψ must be true up until and including the first point at which ϕ becomes true (but ϕ need not necessarily ever become true).

---

[1] We do not have to handle "tick" to mark the termination of a process as we do not treat $SKIP$ or sequential composition.

Formal semantics: The truth value of an LTL formula is first defined individually for each valid trace of the system (rather than on the whole labelled transition system). Usually, these traces are supposed to be infinite, i.e., deadlocking is not allowed. Later in the paper, we will remove this limitation by extending the finite, deadlocking traces with an infinite number of special "Δ" actions.

First, given an infinite trace $\pi = \pi_0, \pi_1, \ldots$ we define π^i to be the trace $\pi_i, \pi_{i+1}, \ldots$. We now define $\pi \models \phi$ (a trace π satisfies or is a model of a formula ϕ) as follows:

- $\pi \not\models false$
- $\pi \models true$
- $\pi \models a$ iff $\pi_0 = a$
- $\pi \models \neg a$ iff $\pi_0 \neq a$
- $\pi \models \phi \wedge \psi$ iff $\pi \models \phi$ and $\pi \models \psi$
- $\pi \models \phi \vee \psi$ iff $\pi \models \phi$ or $\pi \models \psi$
- $\pi \models \bigcirc \phi$ iff $\pi^1 \models \phi$
- $\pi \models \phi \, \mathcal{U} \, \psi$ iff there exists a $k \geq 0$ such that $\pi^k \models \psi$ and $\pi^i \models \phi$ for all $0 \leq i < k$
- $\pi \models \phi \, \mathcal{R} \, \psi$ iff for all $k \geq 0$ such that $\pi^k \models \neg\psi$ there exists an $i, 0 \leq i < k$ such that $\pi^i \models \phi$

Moreover, two additional (derived) operators are usually defined: the always ($\square$) and the *eventually* ($\diamond$) operators: $\diamond\phi \equiv true \, \mathcal{U} \, \phi$ and $\square\phi \equiv \neg\diamond\neg\phi$.

As is well known, any LTL formula $\neg\phi$ can be normalized into a form where negation is only applied to elementary propositions.

A non-deadlocking system S satisfies a formula ϕ, denoted by $S \models \phi$, if all its infinite traces satisfy ϕ: $S \models \phi$ iff $\forall \pi \in \llbracket S \rrbracket_\omega, \pi \models \phi$, where $\llbracket S \rrbracket_\omega$ is the set of the infinite traces of S. Note that in LTL $S \not\models \phi$ does *not* imply $S \models \neg\phi$ (although for each individual trace we have $\pi \not\models \phi$ iff $\pi \models \neg\phi$).

One can characterise two important classes of LTL formulas as follows [2]:

Definition 1 (safety, liveness). *Given a set S of traces in $\Sigma^\omega \cup \Sigma^*$ we define:* $pre(S) = \{\gamma \in \Sigma^* \mid \exists\sigma \text{ with } \gamma\sigma \in S\}$. *The LTL formula ϕ is a liveness property over an alphabet Σ iff $pre(\llbracket\phi\rrbracket_\omega) = \Sigma^*$. ϕ is a safety property over Σ iff $\forall\gamma \in \Sigma^\omega$ we have $\gamma \not\models \phi \Rightarrow \exists\sigma \in pre(\{\gamma\})$ such that $\forall\delta \; \sigma\delta \not\models \phi$.*

Any LTL property can be represented as the intersection of a liveness and a safety property [2].

3 Model Checking Using a Specification and Refinement

We report on our first attempts to do LTL model checking using the classical refinement based approach, i.e., writing a *specification* describing all admissible behaviours and then checking that our system is a valid *refinement* of that specification. As we will show below this turns out to be surprisingly difficult; it might even be impossible in general.

Let us first try to solve the problem for systems S which do not deadlock. If we denote by $\|\phi\|_\omega$ the set of infinite traces which satisfy the formula ϕ, we have $S \models \phi$ iff $\|S\|_\omega \subseteq \|\phi\|_\omega$. The link between LTL model checking and trace refinement is thus obvious and model checking corresponds to language containment. If we succeed in building a process $Spec_\phi$ which generates all the traces that satisfy ϕ, we could try to use trace refinement to do LTL model checking. Unfortunately, refinement in FDR and CSP[2] is based on *finite* traces only and a simple example suffices to show that a finite traces refinement test $S \sqsupseteq_T Spec_\phi$ is, in general, not adequate to model check $S \models \phi$.

Example 2. Indeed, $S \sqsupseteq_T Spec_\phi$ iff $\|S\| \subseteq \|\phi\|$, where we denote by $\|S\|$, resp. $\|\phi\|$, the prefix closed set of all finite traces of S, resp. $Spec_\phi$. Thus, since any trace $\langle a^i b...\rangle$ with any finite number of actions a followed by an action b satisfies $\Diamond b$, the prefix closed set $\|\Diamond b\|$ includes all the traces $\langle a^i \rangle$ with any number of actions a. Thus, we unavoidably have that a process S defined by $S = a \rightarrow S$ will satisfy $\|S\| \sqsupseteq_T \|\Diamond b\|$ even though $S \not\models \Diamond b$ and $\|S\|_\omega \not\subseteq \|\phi\|_\omega$ (because $\langle a, a, a, ...\rangle \in \|S\|_\omega$ and $\langle a, a, a, ...\rangle \notin \|\Diamond b\|_\omega$). Similarly, for Q defined by $Q = a \rightarrow STOP$, we would have that $\|Q\| \sqsupseteq_T \|\Diamond b\|$, even though $Q \not\models \Diamond b$. If we look at failure refinement with the same process $S = a \rightarrow S$ and formula $\|\Diamond b\|$ where obviously $S \not\models \Diamond b$, we can see, as for trace refinement that $\|S\| \sqsupseteq_{\mathcal{F}} \|\Diamond b\|$

This leads us to the following proposition:

Proposition 1.

1. $S \models \phi \Rightarrow \|S\| \sqsupseteq_T \|\phi\|$ *(and thus $S \not\models \phi \Leftarrow \|S\| \not\sqsupseteq_T \|\phi\|$)*   *but*
2. $S \models \phi \not\Leftarrow \|S\| \sqsupseteq_T \|\phi\|$
3. $S \models \phi \not\Leftarrow \|S\| \sqsupseteq_{\mathcal{F}} \|\phi\|$

It is thus *impossible* to achieve our goal in this manner, using the finite traces or failures refinements provided by CSP or FDR. The following corollary pinpoints exactly when this approach fails (and when it actually succeeds):

Corollary 1. *Let ϕ be a liveness property. Then $\|S\| \sqsupseteq_T \|\phi\|$ for any CSP process S and there exists a CSP process P such that $\|P\| \sqsupseteq_{\mathcal{F}} \|\phi\|$ and $P \not\models \phi$. Let ψ be a safety property and S a non-deadlocking CSP process. Then $S \models \psi$ iff $\|S\| \sqsupseteq_T \|\psi\|$*

Since as we mentioned earlier, any LTL property can be represented as the intersection of a liveness and a safety property [2], our approach will therefore fail for any LTL property which is not a pure safety property.

An interesting question is now whether it might be possible to do LTL model checking by using more sophisticated tests, e.g., using the full failure-divergence refinement and some other CSP operators? Indeed, sometimes it is definitely possible to find clever solutions (using hiding, relational renaming, and divergence checking).

---

[2] [19] defines a theory of infinite traces for CSP, but to our knowledge this has not been implemented in any tool for CSP. But even if FDR could handle such a theory of infinite traces, a proper encoding of $\|\phi\|_\omega$ in CSP will in general be infinitely-branching (cf., Section 5), putting LTL model checking out of reach in practice.

For example, to check whether a system S without divergent states, satisfies $\Diamond b$ we can
- define $S' = S\backslash(\Sigma \setminus \{b\})$, i.e., hide all but the action b from S,
- then check whether $|b \to STOP| \sqsupseteq_T |S'|$, i.e., check that S' can perform b,
- and finally check that S' cannot diverge in the initial state, i.e., ensuring that b must eventually happen (this divergence test can be done using FDR).

It is thus possible, using hiding, traces refinement, and divergence testing to check whether a (divergence-free) system S satisfies $\Diamond b$.

Unfortunately, this approach (of using hiding plus divergence testing to test for eventuality $\Diamond$) does not scale up to more complicated formulas. For example, when checking $\Box(a \Rightarrow \Diamond b)$, we can no longer systematically hide a; we would need to hide a (and check for divergence) after each occurrence of a so as to check whether $\Diamond b$ holds at that state. Bill Roscoe came up with a clever solution to the above problem, using relational renaming [19]. Other formulas, however, are much more difficult to tame, and we are still unsure whether there exists a general solution. Anyway, the solutions seem to get more and more complex and are definitely outside the reach of an average user.

In summary, using existing features, it seems extremely difficult (maybe even impossible) for a normal FDR user to achieve LTL model checking using the classical specification-based approach. In other words, the specification-based approach to verification, i.e., writing specifications and then checking whether your system is a valid refinement of that specification, does not seem to be very well suited for verifying some temporal properties. (Maybe this situation will change if infinite traces [19] can be integrated into FDR. Also, some temporal properties related to the distinction between external and internal choice are easy to express in FDR but impossible to express in temporal logics such as LTL or CTL.)

4 Model Checking Using a Tester and Composition

The unfruitful attempts in the previous section have led us to develop an alternative approach. Indeed, instead of checking whether a system S under consideration is a refinement of some specification ϕ, we can build, from ϕ, a tester T_ϕ, then *compose* it with the system S, and finally check whether the composition satisfies some properties which ensure that $S \models \phi$.

If we look at the possible LTL formulas, for some of them a success or failure can be declared after having looked at a finite prefix of an infinite trace, such as $a, a \wedge b, \bigcirc a$. However, in general, entire infinite traces must be tested either to infer that a formula is satisfied (as in $\Box a$) or that it is not satisfied (as in $\Diamond a$). Therefore, a general solution is to build a tester which produces infinitely many *successes* iff a trace is accepted. A classical procedure defined by Vardi and Wolper [24] consists in verifying that $|S|_\omega \cap |\neg\phi|_\omega = \emptyset$ by building a so-called *Büchi automaton* able to do all the traces of $|\neg\phi|_\omega$, composing it with S and verifying the emptiness of the resulting process using the Büchi acceptance condition. In brief, a Büchi automaton, is a finite automaton whose corresponding language is the set of all infinite words which have a path going infinitely often through an accepting state.

We will try to pursue this avenue to solve our problem. We can already use tools such as SPIN [15] to obtain the Büchi automaton corresponding to an LTL formula ϕ. We will use parallel composition to compose the system with a tester CSP process derived from the Büchi automaton of $\neg\phi$.

However, we must take special care of deadlocking traces. Classically, when a system deadlocks, finite traces are extended by a special "Δ" (deadlock) action different from any others, so as to produce infinite traces only. Unfortunately, even though we can easily replace, in any CSP specification, $STOP$ by a process which loops on "Δ" actions, this is not possible in general. Take for example the process $(a \rightarrow b \rightarrow STOP) \,|\{a,b\}|\, (a \rightarrow a \rightarrow STOP)$, where after the first a action, a deadlock occurs. No static analysis (not doing some kind of reachability analysis) is, for arbitrary CSP expressions, able to detect all such deadlocks. Moreover, since the system may be infinite state, in general this problem is clearly undecidable.

Therefore, since we do not want to (or cannot, e.g., wrt FDR) change the semantics of CSP (e.g., stipulating that when a process deadlocks it can perform Δ actions), we must consider a method which leaves the process S unchanged and build a tester which accepts both infinite traces (using Büchi acceptance condition) and deadlocking traces which satisfy the formula $\neg\phi$. The precise meaning of satisfaction of a formula by a deadlocking trace will be given later.

Therefore, in our setting 3 main problems arise:
1. how can we tackle deadlocking traces,
2. how can we translate the tester into CSP, and
3. how can we check emptiness using FDR.

We address all of these issues below.

4.1   Tackling Deadlocking Traces

To handle deadlocking traces we use LTL^Δ simply defined as LTL over $\Sigma \cup \{\Delta\}$ where $\Delta \notin \Sigma$ and where a valid trace π is either an infinite trace over Σ or a finite trace over Σ terminated with an infinite number of Δ's.

We have to be careful that the semantics of this extension is in agreement with our intuition. For example, intuitively a system S should satisfy $\neg a$ iff S can not perform an a as next visible action. Hence S may either perform only actions b different from a or it may deadlock. Similarly a system which satisfies $\neg \bigcirc a$ can either deadlock immediately or perform some visible action and then satisfy $\neg a$.

To capture our intuition about when a deadlocking trace satisfies an ordinary LTL formula over Σ, we can do a translation from LTL into LTL^Δ, e.g., as follows:

- $\bigcirc \phi \quad \rightsquigarrow \quad \neg\Delta \wedge \bigcirc \phi$
- $\neg \bigcirc \phi \quad \rightsquigarrow \quad \Delta \vee \bigcirc \neg \phi$

The definition of $S \models \phi$ is very similar to the one for LTL:
$S \models \phi$ iff $\forall \pi \in \lfloor S \rfloor_\Delta,\, \pi \models \phi$

where $\|S\|_\Delta = \|S\|_\omega \cup \{\gamma\Delta^\omega \mid (\gamma, \Sigma) \in failures(S)\}$, i.e., all the infinite traces of S plus all finite traces which can lead to a deadlock, then extended by an infinite sequence ofΔs.

However, recall that even if satisfaction of LTL formulas by deadlocking traces is defined by extending these traces, in practice we have seen that we cannot modify the CSP system S to do the same. Therefore, we must build a tester which tests both infinite traces and deadlocking traces.

For that, we first use the classical construction of a Büchi automaton $\mathcal{B}$ for ψ, where ψ is the translation in LTL$^\Delta$ of $\neg\phi$ and ϕ is the LTL formula to check. This automaton $\mathcal{B}$ handles infinite traces from Σ^ω, but also (infinite) traces containing Δ actions. Now, we know that the system S can only perform traces in $\Sigma^* \cup \Sigma^\omega$ and thus it is impossible to get traces which contain actions from Σ after an action Δ. We can use this to simplify $\mathcal{B}$. On the other hand, if $\mathcal{B}$ accepts a trace $\gamma\Delta^\omega$ where $\gamma \in \Sigma^*$, our tester should accept the finite trace γ if it is a deadlocking trace of S. To achieve this, we translate the Büchi automaton $\mathcal{B}$ into an extended automaton $\mathcal{B}_\Delta$ with *two* acceptance conditions:

- the classical Büchi acceptance condition for infinite traces
- another acceptance condition, based on a set of *deadlock monitor states*: a deadlocking trace γ will be accepted by $\mathcal{B}_\Delta$ if $\mathcal{B}_\Delta$ has a run taking the trace t which ends up in a so-called *deadlock monitor state*.

Definition 2. *A Büchi Δ-automaton is a six tuple $\mathcal{B} = (\Sigma, Q, T, Q^0, F, D)$ where Σ is the alphabet, Q is the set of states, $T \subseteq Q \times \Sigma \times Q$ is the transition relation, $Q^0 \subseteq Q$ is a set of initial states, $F \subseteq Q$ is a set of infinite trace accepting states, and $D \subseteq Q$ is a set of deadlock monitor states.*

Büchi Δ-automata include acceptance conditions both from finite automata and Büchi automata:

Definition 3. *Given a Büchi Δ-automaton $\mathcal{B} = (\Sigma, Q, T, Q^0, F, D)$, the language associated to $\mathcal{B}$ is $L(\mathcal{B}) = L_\omega(\mathcal{B}) \cup L_\Delta(\mathcal{B})$ with $L_\omega(\mathcal{B}) = \{\sigma \mid \sigma \in \Sigma^\omega$ and there are $s_0, s_1, s_2, \ldots \in Q$ and $\sigma = a_1, a_2, a_3, \ldots$ such that $s_0 \in Q^0$ and $s_0 \xrightarrow{a_1} s_1 \xrightarrow{a_2} s_2 \ldots$ and $s_i \in F$ for infinitely many values of $i\}$ and $L_\Delta(\mathcal{B}) = \{\sigma \mid \sigma \in \Sigma^*$ and there are $s_0, s_1, s_2, \ldots s_n \in Q$ with $s_n \in D$ and $\sigma = a_1, a_2, a_3, \ldots a_n$ such that $s_0 \in Q^0$ and $s_0 \xrightarrow{a_1} s_1 \xrightarrow{a_2} s_2 \ldots \xrightarrow{a_n} s_n\}$*

In practice, we will modify a classical Büchi automaton $\mathcal{B}$ (over the alphabet $\Sigma \cup \{\Delta\}$) into a Büchi Δ-automaton $\mathcal{B}_\Delta$ (over the alphabet Σ)as follows

1. states, reachable from an initial state through transitions labelled by actions in Σ, which accept (with the classical Büchi condition) the string Δ^ω are defined to be *deadlock monitor states*,
2. all Δ transitions are now removed from $\mathcal{B}$,
3. transitions (and states) which cannot lead to the acceptance of a trace are removed.

Observe that $L_\omega(\mathcal{B})$ is the language of $\mathcal{B}$ viewed as a classical Büchi automaton. Also note that in [23] Valmari defines a similar (though more sophisticated) tester.

One can easily see that the construction of $\mathcal{B}_\Delta$ from $\mathcal{B}$ can be done by an algorithm inspired from the Tarjan's search of strongly connected components (see, e.g., [21]): this algorithm does a linear parse of $\mathcal{B}$ (which defines the set of deadlock monitor states). The algorithm can be found in [10]. This translation from $\mathcal{B}$ to $\mathcal{B}_\Delta$ is correct in the following sense:

Proposition 2. $L(\mathcal{B}_\Delta) = L_\omega(\mathcal{B}) \cap (\Sigma^\omega \cup \Sigma^*.\Delta^\omega)$.

The two following subsections discuss how to translate $\mathcal{B}_\Delta$ into CSP and how to check our two accepting conditions using FDR.

4.2   Translation of the Tester into CSP

We now present the translation of our Büchi Δ-automaton into a CSP process, which translates every state of Q into a CSP process and where

- an accepting state process produces a special *success* action (*success* $\notin \Sigma$),
- for every deadlock monitor state a special "Δ" transition is added to the corresponding CSP process which leads to the special process $DEADLOCK$ defined below.

Definition 4. *Formally, we define our translation* $csp(\mathcal{B})$ *of a Büchi Δ-automaton into a CSP process as follows:*

- *we map every* $q \in Q$ *to a CSP process name* $NAME(q)$
- *for every* $q \in Q^0$ *we add the CSP definition:* $TESTER = NAME(q)$
- *for every non-accepting state* $q \in Q \backslash F$ *and for all outgoing edges* $(q, a, q') \in T$ *we add the definition:*
  $NAME(q) = a \rightarrow NAME(q')$
- *for every accepting state* $q \in F$ *where* $\{(q, a_1, q_1), \dots, (q, a_n, q_n)\} \subseteq T$ *are all the outgoing edges of* q *add the definition:*
  $NAME(q) = success \rightarrow (a_1 \rightarrow NAME(q_1) \; \square \; \dots \; \square \; a_n \rightarrow NAME(q_n))$
- *For every state* $q \in D$, *we add a definition (this is equivalent to adding an external choice to the above definition):*
  $NAME(q) = deadlock \rightarrow DEADLOCK$
- *We add a single definition of* $DEADLOCK$ *(where* $\Sigma = \{a_1, \dots, a_n\}$*):*
  $DEADLOCK = a_1 \rightarrow ko \rightarrow STOP \; \square \; \dots \; \square \; a_n \rightarrow ko \rightarrow STOP$

The idea behind the special $DEADLOCK$ process is that if the system to be verified (with which it will run in parallel, synchronised on Σ) is not deadlocked then the $DEADLOCK$ process will be able to perform the special ko action (with $ko \notin \Sigma$). Hence, the existence of an accepted "really" deadlocking trace corresponds to a CSP failure trace $(deadlock, \{ko\})$ of $(S \; |\!|\Sigma|\!| \; TESTER)) \backslash (\Sigma \cup \{success\})$, i.e., we can perform *deadlock* and then *refuse* to perform the ko action.

Example 3. For $\phi = \neg \Diamond b$ and $\Sigma = \{a, b, c\}$ we would produce

$$\mathcal{B}: \quad a, c, \Delta \downarrow \bigcirc \xrightarrow{\;b\;} \bigcirc \qquad\qquad \mathcal{B}_\Delta: \quad a, c \downarrow \textcircled{\in D}$$

and $csp(\mathcal{B}_\Delta) =$

$TESTER = State1$
$State1 = success \to ((a \to State1) \;\square\; (c \to State1))$
$State1 = deadlock \to DEADLOCK$
$DEADLOCK = (a \to ko \to STOP) \;\square\; (b \to ko \to STOP) \;\square\; (c \to ko \to STOP)$

The above approach can easily be extended to CSP with datatypes, as provided by FDR. For example, if a is a channel of type *Int.Bool* and c a channel of type *Bool* we would produce:

$State1 = success \to ((a?i?b \to State1) \;\square\; (c?b \to State1))$

One can also easily extend the basic propositions of LTL to enable more sophisticated pattern matching on actions. For example, one might want to check a formula $\Diamond a?i!true$ or $\square(reqtoks?c?o \Rightarrow \Diamond colltoks!c!o?t)$ (see Appendix B).

4.3   Testing Emptiness in CSP/FDR

Let us summarise our approach so far. Given a CSP process S to be verified and an LTL formula ϕ to be checked, we do the following to construct a CSP process which will be used to verify $S \models \phi$:

1. negate the formula and translate it into LTL$^\Delta$, yielding ψ,
2. construct a Büchi automaton $\mathcal{B}$ for ψ using a classical construction,
3. translate $\mathcal{B}$ into a Büchi Δ-automaton $\mathcal{B}_\Delta$, to properly handle deadlocking traces,
4. translate $\mathcal{B}_\Delta$ into a CSP process $csp(\mathcal{B}_\Delta)$ (defining the $TESTER$ process).

We now want to check whether there exists an infinite or a finite deadlocking trace of the system under consideration which satisfies $\neg \phi$. If no such a trace exists, then the formula ϕ is verified and the system is a model for ϕ. We conduct this test, using FDR, via two refinement checks: one for traces which generate an infinite number of successes and one to verify success due to deadlocks.

For the latter, as already discussed in Sect. 4.2, the existence of an accepted deadlocking trace corresponds to a CSP failure trace $(deadlock, \{ko\})$ of $D = (S \;|\Sigma|\; TESTER)) \backslash (\Sigma \cup \{success\})$. To check this condition we thus use FDR to check whether $deadlock \to STOP \sqsupseteq_{\mathcal{F}} D$ holds.

The procedure to check the acceptance condition on infinite traces without deadlocks, looks like the one given in [24], except that our tester synchronised with the system will produce infinitely many *success actions* when it accepts a trace. More precisely, we have to check whether $S \;|\Sigma|\; TESTER$ can produce a trace containing infinitely many *success* actions. This can be simplified into checking whether $C = (S \, [\![\Sigma]\!] \, TESTER) \backslash \Sigma$ can produce the infinite trace $success^\omega$. Now, as our environment (FDR) cannot analyse infinite traces, we resort to the following "trick": check using FDR whether $SUC \sqsupseteq_T C$, where $SUC = success \to SUC$, i.e., checking whether for all i, $success^i$ can be done by C.

For non-deadlocking systems, we would like to have $SUC \sqsupseteq_T C$ iff $S \not\models \phi$. We will see that this depends on whether the system S is finite state or not.

Finite state processes. Suppose that the system to be verified is finite state. Since the tester can also be defined as a finite state process, C will be finite state, and if C produces an unbounded number of success actions, it means that there must be a cyclic path, reachable from the initial state and including a *success* action. This is therefore equivalent to verifying that $success^\omega$ is a trace of C and we thus have the following proposition:

Proposition 3. *Let S be a finite state, non-deadlocking CSP process and ϕ a LTL formula. Let $TESTER$ be obtained by Def. 4. Then $S \models \phi$ iff $SUC \not\sqsupseteq_T$ $(S \, [\![\Sigma]\!] \, TESTER) \backslash \Sigma$.*

Note that one can put syntactic restrictions on the CSP processes to ensure that they are finite state (see, e.g., [17]): in our case it is sufficient to forbid any parallel operator in a recursive process.

Infinite state processes. Let us show now an example which proves the *incompleteness* of our procedure (which is still sound to conclude that the property indeed holds). Take the following CSP process definitions:

$$S = (P \, [\![\{a, c\}]\!] \, Q) \, ||| \, R, \text{ with}$$
$$P = a \to P \sqcap T$$
$$T = c \to T$$
$$Q = a \to (c \to STOP \, ||| \, Q)$$
$$R = b \to R$$

The process R has been added to produce a non-deadlocking process. We can see that $S \models \neg \Box \Diamond c$, i.e. that S can never perform a c action forever, since in each branch of S, after a finite number of actions a and c, only b actions are possible. However, for each integer n, there is a branch (trace) which does n actions c. If we want to check if $S \models \neg \Box \Diamond c$ holds, the tester will produce a *success* action after each c action, and our test will conclude, since $SUC \sqsupseteq_T C$, that $S \not\models \neg \Box \Diamond c$, which is wrong!

Notes:
- The previous example can also be used as a counter example to show that neither failure nor divergence will be able, in general, to discriminate an infinite trace from an unbounded one.

- The procedure given in [24] detects reachable loops. In general, this method will not be sufficient for infinite state systems. For example,. $S = a \rightarrow (S \,|\{a\}|\, S)$ satisfies $\Box a$ but never loops! We suspect this problem to be undecidable.

4.4 Summary

To check $S \models \phi$ we perform the following 2 checks using FDR, where $TESTER$ be obtained by Def. 4:

1. $SUC \sqsupseteq_{\mathcal{T}} (S \,|\Sigma|\, TESTER)\backslash(\Sigma \cup \{deadlock, ko\})$

2. $deadlock \rightarrow STOP \sqsupseteq_{\mathcal{F}} (S \,|\Sigma|\, TESTER)\backslash(\Sigma \cup \{success\})$

If the first test succeeds, then we know, *if S is finite*, that $S \not\models \phi$ (there exists an infinite trace in S accepted by $csp(\mathcal{B}_\Delta)$). Otherwise, if the second test succeeds (there exists a deadlocking trace in S accepted by $csp(\mathcal{B}_\Delta)$), then $S \not\models \phi$. If both refinement checks fail, then we know that $S \models \phi$.

Observe that the first test uses the traces-refinement while the second one uses failures-refinement. This is because in the second test we have to check whether an "alleged" deadlock is a real deadlock.

A fully worked-out example in CSP (and FDR), checking whether a *System* satisfies $\neg\Diamond b$ is given in Appendix A. A more complicated and realistic example can be found in Appendix B, and the alternating-bit protocol is treated in [10].

5   Preservation of LTL under Refinement

Despite the failure of refinement to capture temporal properties in Section 3, we can still derive some positive results. Suppose that for some LTL formula ϕ and CSP process P, we know that $Q \models \phi$ by applying the technique just presented. In addition, suppose that we derive a new CSP process Q which refines P, i.e., $P \sqsupseteq Q$: are there circumstances where we are assured that $P \models \phi$? A positive answer would allow us, in a design process where the consecutive specifications $S_0, S_1, \ldots, S_{n-1}, S_n$ satisfy $S_n \sqsupseteq S_{n-1} \ldots S_1 \sqsupseteq S_0$ and where we have checked $S_0 \models \phi$, to be sure that at the end $S_n \models \phi$; i.e., we would only have to model check the initial specification and not all the successive refinements. As we have already seen in Sect. 3, traces refinement alone is not sufficient to achieve this goal:

Proposition 4. *Traces refinement does not preserve satisfaction of LTL formulas.*

Proof. Using the following counter-example: $S_0 = a \rightarrow (b \rightarrow STOP \sqcap c \rightarrow STOP)$, $S_1 = a \rightarrow STOP \sqcap S_0$, $\phi \equiv \Diamond(b \vee c)$, we have $S_1 \sqsupseteq_{\mathcal{T}} S_0$, $S_0 \models \phi$ and $S_1 \not\models \phi$.

Unfortunately, the same holds for failures refinement in general:

Proposition 5. *Failures refinement does not preserve satisfaction of LTL formulas.*

Proof. Again, let us show that on a counter-example. In the paragraph 4.3 discussing infinite state processes, we have seen that for the formula $\phi \equiv \neg\Box\Diamond c$ and the infinite state process S, $S\backslash\{a,b\} \models \phi$ and $T = c \to T \sqsupseteq_\mathcal{F} S\backslash\{a,b\}$, but $T \not\models \phi$ (in fact $T \models \neg\phi$).

Fortunately, if we restrict ourselves to finite state processes or even finitely-branching processes (using visible a-transition relations[3]), failures refinement does preserve LTL.

Proposition 6. *Failures refinement of finitely-branching CSP processes (using the* visible *transition relations) preserves satisfaction of LTL formula.*

Proof. Suppose that P and Q are finitely-branching CSP processes such that $P \sqsupseteq_\mathcal{F} Q$. We have to prove that for any LTL formula ϕ, $P \models \phi \Rightarrow Q \models \phi$, i.e. $\langle P \rangle_\Delta \subseteq \langle Q \rangle_\Delta$. Suppose $\gamma \in \langle P \rangle_\Delta$ but $\gamma \notin \langle Q \rangle_\Delta$. Either $\gamma \in \Sigma^\omega$ or $\gamma \in \Sigma^* \Delta^\omega$.
1. First, suppose $\gamma \in \Sigma^\omega$. Let τ be the tree representing the labelled transition systems of Q. We know that this tree is finitely-branching. Now, let us derive τ' from τ by removing from τ any node n (and its descendants) such that the path from the root of τ to n is not a prefix of γ. Trivially τ' is still finitely branching. We also know that τ' is infinite: suppose that τ' was finite then there must be maximum depth m of τ', which contradicts the fact that any prefix of γ (in particular the prefix of length $m+1$) can be generated by Q (because $P \sqsupseteq_\mathcal{F} Q$). Hence, by Königs lemma we know that there is an infinite branch in τ', i.e., $\gamma \in \langle Q \rangle_\Delta$ which contradicts our hypothesis.
2. If $\gamma \in \Sigma^* \Delta^\omega$, then $\gamma = t\Delta^\omega$ and $(t, \Sigma) \in \langle P \rangle$ and since $P \sqsupseteq_\mathcal{F} Q$, $(t, \Sigma) \in \langle Q \rangle$. Therefore, $\gamma \in \langle Q \rangle_\Delta$, which again contradicts our hypothesis.

Thus, if we manage to write a finite state specification S_0 and model check a formula ϕ, then we do not have to check ϕ for refinements of S_0. Observe that this result, does not contradict Section 3 and does not enable us to solve the model checking problem itself more naturally using failures refinement! Indeed, a specification generating all traces and failures of an LTL formula ϕ will in general be infinitely branching (e.g., for $\Diamond b$) and we cannot apply Proposition 6. In fact, it will be finitely branching for safety properties but infinitely branching for liveness properties (cf. Corollary 1). So, even if the theory of infinite traces [19] were to be added to FDR, classical LTL model checking of finite systems, using refinement, will require the treatment of infinitely branching systems.

6   Complexity, Future Work, and Conclusion

At the complexity level, the difference between classical LTL model checking and our approach is due to the test of emptiness. For the method of Vardi and Wolper, it is exponential in the size of the formula ϕ, but linear in the size of the composition of the tester with the system and this composition can be done on-the fly [13]. Our procedure uses FDR to check language containment, whose complexity is PSPACE-complete (checking full failures/divergences refinement is even PSPACE-hard, even though "real" processes do not behave as badly [19]).

---

[3] Which link two processes (states) P and Q when Q is reachable from P using one visible action a and possibly invisible actions τ before and after this a-transition.

Furthermore, from an efficiency point of view, our system to be verified is on the wrong side of the FDR refinement check (i.e., on the side which FDR normalises). On the other hand, using FDR means that optimisations such as hierarchical compression, data-independence and induction [20,19,9] can be applied. This will allow us to handle some infinite state systems, but the overall effect on the complexity is unclear (all the examples in the appendices were handled without any problem).

Fortunately, there might a way to get the best of both worlds, by adding a special check for refinement problems of the form $a^\omega \sqsupseteq_T S$ into FDR, thus achieving the same linear complexity as Vardi and Wolper. Obviously, we cannot add this improvement ourselves to FDR, but we will try to convince the FDR implementors to do exactly that.

Another issue that needs to be resolved is the following: when a formula is *not* satisfied by a system, one of the interests of model checking is the production of a counter example. However, FDR only provides a counter example if a refinement check fails and not if the check succeeds; unfortunately the latter is what we would require! Fortunately, it seems possible to feed the result of the refinement checker into an animator (such as PROBE). Further work and cooperation with the FDR implementors is needed to establish this. Another interesting further research, is to study and apply our techniques within the context of other refinement-based formalisms such as action systems or B [1] and the associated tools B-TOOL and ATELIER-B. In fact, the refinement notion within these approaches connects more tightly with the infinite traces model of CSP than with the finite traces model [5], and so the relationship and needs will be somewhat different.

Other issues that should be studied further are the performance of (suitably extended) FDR on realistic benchmarks, and the study of other temporal logics such as CTL or CTL*. One possible approach to achieve CTL model checking of finite and infinite state CSP systems, is to write an interpreter for CSP in logic programming and then use the approach of [16]. Finally, we intend to find a semi-algorithm (using abstractions), to determine when an infinite state system does *not* satisfy a property.

History of the paper: This paper arouse out of discussions with proponents of refinement (and CSP) who proclaimed that "One does *not* need LTL model checking (for CSP or FDR), one can always write a specification describing all admissible behaviours and then checking that the system under consideration is a valid *refinement* of that specification." As we have shown in Section 3 this turns out to be extremely difficult (or even impossible in general). We have thus developed another, tester based approach, which can be fully automated. This paper thus underlines that "One *does* need LTL model checking, as one can *not* always (easily) write a specification describing all admissible behaviours and then checking that our system is a valid refinement of that specification."

In conclusion, we hope that we have shed light on the relationship between model checking and refinement checking. We have unveiled shortcomings of the specification/refinement based approach to model checking, but have shown how to overcome them. Indeed, we have shown how to do LTL model checking of finite state CSP processes using refinement in general and the FDR environment in particular. We have also shown that our method is sound (but not complete) for processes which have an infinite number of states.

Acknowledgements. We want to thank Michael Butler, Marielle Doche, Javier Esparza, Andy Gravell, Ranko Lazic, Ulrich Ultes-Nitsche, Jean-François Raskin and Moshe Vardi as well as the anonymous referees for extremely useful comments, feedback, and explanations about CSP and LTL. We also would like to thank David Jackson for some insightful comments about FDR. Finally, we are grateful for the comments and constructive criticisms of the anonymous referees of VCL'2000 (a preliminary version of this paper appeared in the proceedings of VCL'2000).

References

1. J.-R. Abrial. *The B-Book*. Cambridge University Press, 1996.
2. B. Alpern and F. B. Schneider. Defining liveness. *Information Processing Letters*, 21(4):181–185, October 1985.
3. A.Pnueli. The temporal logic of concurrent programs. *Theoretical Computer Science*, 13:45–60, 1981.
4. R. Bryant. Symbolic boolean manipulation with ordered binary-decision diagrams. *ACM Computing Surveys*, 24(3):293–318, September 1992.
5. M. Butler and C. Morgan. Action systems, unbounded nondeterminism, and infinite traces. *Formal Aspects of Computing*, 7:37–53, 1995.
6. E. Clarke, O. Grumberg, and D. Peled. *Model Checking*. MIT Press, 1999.
7. E. M. Clarke, E. A. Emerson, and A. P. Sistla. Automatic verification of finite-state concurrent systems using temporal logic specifications. *ACM Transactions on Programming Languages and Systems*, 8(2):244–263, 1986.
8. E. M. Clarke and J. M. Wing. Formal methods: State of the art and future directions. *ACM Computing Surveys*, 28(4):626–643, Dec. 1996.
9. S. J. Creese and A. W. Roscoe. Data independent induction over structured networks. In *International Conference on Parallel and Distributed Processing Techniques and Applications (PDPTA '00)*, Las Vegas, USA, June 2000.
10. M. Leuschel, T. Massart, and A. Currie. How to make FDR spin: LTL model checking of CSP by refinement. Technical Report DSSE-TR-2000-10, Department of Electronics and Computer Science, University of Southampton, September 2000.
11. J. Esparza. Decidability of model-checking for infinite-state concurrent systems. *Acta Informatica*, 34:85–107, 1997.
12. Formal Systems (Europe) Ltd. *Failures-Divergence Refinement — FDR2 User Manual*.
13. R. Gerth, D. Peled, M. Y. Vardi, and P. Wolper. Simple on-the-fly automatic verification of linear temporal logic. In *Proc. 15th Workshop on Protocol Specification, Testing, and Verification*, Warsaw, June 1995. North-Holland.
14. C. Hoare. *Communicating Sequential Processes*. Prentice Hall, 1985.
15. G. Holzmann. *Design and Validation of Computer Protocols*. Prentice Hall, 1991.
16. M. Leuschel and T. Massart. Infinite state model checking by abstract interpretation and program specialisation. In A. Bossi, editor, *Proceedings of LOPSTR'99*, LNCS 1817, pages 63–82, Venice, Italy, September 1999.

17. J. Magee and J. Kramer. *Concurrency: State Models & Java Programs*. Wiley, 1999.
18. K. L. McMillan. *Symbolic Model Checking*. PhD thesis, Boston, 1993.
19. A. Roscoe. *The Theory and Practice of Concurrency*. Prentice Hall, 1997.
20. A. W. Roscoe and R. S. Lazic. Using logical relations for automated verification of data-independent CSP. In *Proceedings of Oxford Workshop on Automated Formal Methods ENTCS*, 1996.
21. R. Sedgewick. *Algorithms in C++*. Addison-Wesley, 1992.
22. A. P. Sistla and E. M. Clarke. The complexity of propositional linear temporal logics. *Journal of the ACM*, 32(3):733–749, July 1985.
23. A. Valmari. On-the-fly verification with stubborn sets. In C. Courcoubetis, editor, *Proceedings of CAV'93*, LNCS 697, pages 397–408. Springer-Verlag, 1993.
24. M. Y. Vardi and P. Wolper. An automata-theoretic approach to automatic program verification. In *Proceedings of LICS'86*, pages 332–344, 1986.

A   A Simple Example in FDR 2.28

Here is an original System to verify, using the machine-readable CSP syntax employed by FDR:

```
channel a,b,c,d
System =  (b->System) []  (b->c->a->SKIP)
```

Suppose we wanted to establish whether the system satisfied $\Diamond b$ using $\Sigma = \{a, b, c, d\}$. We would then construct the extended Büchi automaton $\mathcal{B}$ for $\neg \Diamond b$ (see Ex. 3) and apply our translation (Def. 4) to obtain $csp(\mathcal{B})$:

```
channel success, deadlock,ko
TESTER = State1
State1 = (success->((a->State1) [] (c->State1) [] (d->State1))) [] deadlock -> Deadlock
Deadlock = (a->ko->STOP) [] (b->ko->STOP) [] (c->ko->STOP) [] (d->ko->STOP)
```

We now compose $csp(\mathcal{B})$ with the system to be verified:

```
Composition = (System [| {a,b,c,d} |] TESTER) \{a,b,c,d,deadlock,ko}
```

and then check whether this composition can generate an infinite number of success actions:

```
SUC = success -> SUC
assert Composition [T= SUC
```

In our case, this refinement test fails. However, for *System2* defined below, it succeeds, meaning that *System2* does not satisfy $\Diamond b$ (as it is finite state):

```
System2 =  (a->System2) []  (b->c->a->SKIP) [] STOP
```

To test whether there is, in our *System*, a deadlocking trace that accepts the formula $\neg\phi$ we do the following composition:

```
CompositionRD = (System [| {a,b,c,d} |] TESTER) \{a,b,c,d,success}
```

and check whether this can generate a real deadlock:

```
RealDeadlock = deadlock -> STOP
assert CompositionRD [F= RealDeadlock
```

In our case, this refinement test fails and we have thus established $System \models \Diamond b$. However, for *System3* defined below, it succeeds, meaning that the system does not satisfy $\Diamond b$. For *System4* the refinement check fails, i.e., when checking for deadlocks, there is a distinction between internal and external choice.

```
System3 =  (b->c->STOP) |~| (a->c->STOP)
System4 =  (b->System4) [] (b->c->a->SKIP) [] STOP
```

B   A More Complicated Example in FDR

The following is a more complicated CSP specification, which models distributed system for pension (i.e., tokens) distribution via postoffices. Customers have a preferred postoffice, but they can collect their pension from any postoffice. In the latter case, the authority to distribute the pension must be requested from the Home-postoffice. (This case study grew out of interaction with one of the industrial partners of the EPSRC-funded critical systems project "ABCD", currently ongoing at the University of Southampton.)

```
-- ==========================================================
-- A distributed pension distribution scheme via Postoffices
-- by Marielle Doche, University of Southampton
-- ==========================================================
nametype Tokens = {0..5}
nametype Cust = {1,2,3}  -- 3 customers
nametype Home = {0,1,2}  -- 0 = centre; 1,2 = offices
nametype Office = diff(Home, {0})
home(1) = 1
home(2) = 2
home(3) = 0
channel reqtoks : Cust.Office
channel colltoks : Cust.Office.Tokens

-- This process gives a global specification from a Customer point of view
CUST(c,n) = reqtoks.c?o -> colltoks.c!o!n -> CUST(c,0)

-- abstract spec of the system with 3 customers
SPEC = ||| c : Cust @ CUST(c,4)
-------------------------------------------------------------------------
-- This specification describes the centre, which communicates with the offices
channel disthome, sendoff, rechome : Cust.Office.Tokens
channel reqoff, queryhome : Cust.Office
CENTRE(c,n) =
      n>0  and home(c)!=0 & disthome.c?o:{home(c)}!n -> CENTRE(c,0)
   [] reqoff.c?o:Office ->
         (if n>0 or home(c)==0 or home(c)==o
            then sendoff.c!o!n -> CENTRE(c,0)
            else queryhome.c?o1:{home(c)} -> rechome.c.home(c)?a:Tokens
                     -> sendoff.c!o!a -> CENTRE(c,n) )
-------------------------------------------------------------------------
-- This specification describes an office which communicates with the centre
-- about a customer
channel sendcentre, reccentre, recdist : Cust.Office.Tokens
channel reqcentre, querycentre : Cust.Office
OFF(c,o,n) =  n==0 & recdist.c.o?a:Tokens -> OFF(c,o,a)
   []    reqcentre.c.o -> sendcentre.c.o!n -> OFF(c,o,0)
   [] reqtoks.c.o ->
         (n > 0 & colltoks.c.o!n -> OFF(c,o,0)
         []
         n ==0 & (
            (querycentre.c.o -> (
               reccentre.c.o?a:Tokens -> colltoks.c.o!a -> OFF(c,o,0)
```

```
         []     -- (+)
            recdist.c.o?a:Tokens ->
            reccentre.c.o?b:Tokens ->        -- ($)
            -- colltoks.c.o!a -> OFF(c,o,0)    -- (+)
            colltoks.c.o!a -> OFF(c,o,b)    -- (+) ($)     ) )
         []
          (o == home(c) & recdist.c.o?a:Tokens
                -> colltoks.c.o!a -> OFF(c,o,0))    ) )
----------------------------------------------------------------------------
-- This process describe for a given customer a synchronous communication
-- between the centre and the offices
SYNCHCOM(c,n) =
    CENTRE(c,n)
    [disthome.c.o.a <-> recdist.c.o.a, sendoff.c.o.a <-> reccentre.c.o.a,
  rechome.c.o.a <-> sendcentre.c.o.a, reqoff.c.o <-> querycentre.c.o,
  queryhome.c.o <-> reqcentre.c.o | o <- Office, a <- Tokens]
    (|||o: Office @ OFF(c,o,0))
----------------------------------------------------------------------------
SYNCHTRANS(c,n) =
    CUST(c,n)[|{|reqtoks.c, colltoks.c |}|]
    (SYNCHCOM(c,n)\{|disthome.c, recdist.c, sendoff.c,
                reccentre.c, rechome.c, sendcentre.c,
                reqoff.c, querycentre.c, queryhome.c, reqcentre.c|})
SYNCH = ||| c : Cust @ SYNCHTRANS(c,4)
```

In the remainder of this appendix, we will assume that any channel or action stands for all its "completions". For example, *reqtoks* stands for *reqtoks*.1.0, *reqtoks*.1.1, ...

Let us now try to verify the LTL formula $\Box(reqtoks \Rightarrow \Diamond colltoks)$, i.e., whenever a token (i.e., pension) is requested by a user a token will eventually be collected. For this we first negate the formula, i.e., we get $\neg\Box(reqtoks \Rightarrow \Diamond colltoks)$ $= \Diamond(reqtoks \wedge \neg\Diamond colltoks) = \Diamond(reqtoks \wedge \Box\neg colltoks)$. We now translate this into a Büchi automaton, and simplify for deadlocks, giving us Figure 1. (Observe that this automaton is non-deterministic; there is no equivalent deterministic automaton for that property.) We now translate Figure 1 into CSP as described in the paper:

```
channel success,deadlock,ko
TESTER = STATE1
STATE1 = reqtoks?c?o -> STATE1 [] colltoks?c2?o2?t -> STATE1 [] reqtoks?c?o -> STATE2
STATE2 = ((success -> (reqtoks?c?o -> STATE2)) [] deadlock -> Deadlock)
Deadlock = (reqtoks?c?o->ko->STOP [] colltoks?c?o?t->ko->STOP)
```

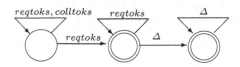

Fig. 1. A Büchi automaton for $\Diamond(reqtoks \wedge \Box\neg colltoks)$

We now encode our refinement checks as described in the paper:

```
SComposition = (SPEC [| {|reqtoks,colltoks|} |] TESTER) \{| reqtoks,colltoks,deadlock,ko|}
SComposition2 = (SPEC [| {|reqtoks,colltoks|} |] TESTER)\{| reqtoks,colltoks,success |}
Composition = (SYNCH [| {|reqtoks,colltoks|} |] TESTER) \{| reqtoks,colltoks,deadlock,ko |}
Composition2 = (SYNCH [| {|reqtoks,colltoks|} |] TESTER)\{| reqtoks,colltoks,success |}
SUC = success->SUC
RealDeadlock = deadlock->STOP
assert SComposition [T= SUC
-- refinement fails => no infinite trace violates formula => OK
assert SComposition2 [F= RealDeadlock
-- refinement fails => no deadlocking trace violates formula => OK
assert Composition [T= SUC
-- refinement fails => no infinite trace violates formula => OK
assert Composition2 [F= RealDeadlock
-- refinement fails => no deadlocking trace violates formula => OK
```

So, both the very high-level specification $SPEC$ and the more detailed specification $SYNCH$ satisfy the LTL formula $\Box(reqtoks \Rightarrow \Diamond colltoks)$.

We can actually try to verify a more complicated property, namely $\Box(reqtoks?c?o \Rightarrow \Diamond colltoks!c!o?t)$, by re-defining STATE1 as follows:

```
STATE1 =  reqtoks?c?o -> STATE1 [] colltoks?c2?o2?t -> STATE1 [] reqtoks?c?o -> STATE2(c,o)
STATE2(c,o) = ((success -> ((reqtoks?c2?o2 -> STATE2(c,o))
                    [] (colltoks?c2?o2?t -> STATE3(c,o,c2,o2)))) [] deadlock -> Deadlock)
STATE3(c,o,c2,o2) = if ((c==c2) and (o==o2)) then STOP else STATE2(c,o)
```

We are now checking that if a customer c request a token (at office o) that he will eventually get a token (at that same office o).

Now the refinement checks look as follows:

```
assert SComposition [T= SUC
-- refinement succeeds => infinite trace violates formula => NOT OK !!
assert SComposition2 [F= RealDeadlock
-- refinement fails => no deadlocking trace violates formula => OK

assert Composition [T= SUC
-- refinement succeeds => infinite trace violates formula => NOT OK !!
assert Composition2 [F= RealDeadlock
-- refinement fails =>  no deadlocking trace violates formula => OK
```

This is essentially due to possible starvation of a customer because other customers can repeatedly ask for and always collect a token before he gets his token. However, if we change the specification of the behaviour of customers to:

```
CUST(c,n) = reqtoks.c?o -> colltoks.c!o!n -> STOP
```

i.e., the customers do not repeatedly ask for tokens (pensions), then all refinement checks fail and the formula is actually satisfied.

Avoiding State Explosion for Distributed Systems with Timestamps

Fabrice Derepas[1], Paul Gastin[2], and David Plainfossé[1]

[1] Nortel Networks, 1, Place des frères Montgolfier,
78928 Yvelines Cedex 09, France.
fderepas|plaindav@nortelnetworks.com
[2] LIAFA, UMR 7089 Université Paris 7, 2 place Jussieu,
F-75251 Paris Cedex 05, France.
Paul.Gastin@liafa.jussieu.fr

Abstract. This paper describes a reduction technique which is very useful against the state explosion problem which occurs when model checking many distributed systems. Timestamps are often used to keep track of the relative order of events. They are usually implemented with very large counters and therefore they generate state explosion. The aim of this paper is to present a very efficient reduction of the state space generated by a model checker when using timestamps. The basic idea is to map the timestamps values to the smallest possible range. This is done dynamically and on-the-fly by adding to the model checker a call to a reduction function after each newly generated state. Our reduction works for model checkers using explicit state enumeration and does not require any change in the model. Our method has been applied to an industrial example and the reduction obtained was spectacular.

1 Introduction

Now days there are more and mode critical systems which need to be verified. In this paper we focus on the use of timestamps to ensure causality between events. This kind of mechanism can be found in many distributed systems. We had to face this problem during the verification of an industrial protocol designed to resynchronize a telecommunication system after some fault.

Distributed systems are difficult to verify using model checkers due to the state explosion problem. For n independent components, with S states and T transitions the number of states and transitions of the system may be as large as $S_n = S^n$ and $T_n = nTS^{n-1}$.

To reduce the state explosion, a number of formal methods and tools have been applied including SDL and LOTOS [2]. However, many attempts end up compromising either the level of abstraction [3], the number of processes in a network [4,5] or complete exploration of the state space [6].

In Spin, partial oder reductions were implemented and used with a great success [7,8]. In Murφ, symmetry was exploited thanks to a special data structure

J.N. Oliveira and P. Zave (Eds.): FME 2001, LNCS 2021, pp. 119–134, 2001.
© Springer-Verlag Berlin Heidelberg 2001

named scalarset [9] resulting again in a substantial reduction in the sate space generated. But these techniques have no effect on the state explosion generated by the very large range required by timestamps in a lot of protocols. Note that timestamps cannot usually be implemented using a scalarset since we need to compare their values.

Another way to validate a protocol is to use a proof checker [10,11]. Systems can be modeled using I/O automata [12], and then a manual proof is performed for these automata. This proof can then be checked using a theorem prover like Larch [13], but this method is highly time-consuming for both manual proof and verification with the theorem prover. In [10] a protocol using timestamps is verified this way.

Using a natural model of our system, we were not able to use a model checker due to the state explosion problem. Then, we have implemented the reduction presented in this paper and thanks to the huge reduction of the state space, we were able to verify our system using the model checker Spin [1].

More precisely, this paper is based on a case study of a real time fault tolerant distributed algorithm used in a telecommunication platform. Our protocol uses timestamps to keep track of the relative order of messages and to be able to get back to a coherent state after some fault. The easiest way to implement timestamp variables is to use unbounded counters, or in practice, 32 bits or 64 bits counters. Indeed, this results in the state explosion problem when trying to verify our protocol with a model checker using explicit state enumeration. Actually, there are only a small number of different values of timestamps simultaneously stored in the variables of the system. Using the fact that we are only interested in the relative order of the timestamps, we have implemented a function which changes the timestamps contained in each newly generated state so that the smallest possible range for timestamps is used.

Our technique does not require any change of the model. Instead, it adds a call to our function in the model checker itself. The result is a huge reduction of the state space generated by the model checker. To implement this reduction, a library of approximately a hundred lines of C code has been linked with the existing model checker source code.

This work can be useful to anyone willing to fine tune model checkers targeted at validating distributed systems with some causal dependencies.

In section 2 we detail the kind of system we are verifying, as well as the way we use timestamps. This enable to understand the reusability of our work. Section 3 details our reduction on timestamps.

2   High Availability and Distributed Systems

This section presents the application we are verifying. It is not our purpose to describe in details this application. We describe the general context, stressing those points which make the application complex. Then we describe in more details the part of the application we want to verify.

2.1 Managing Resources in a Distributed System

We are interested in the software managing a cellular phone network. When a call is established several links are reserved for the communication. These resources will be released afterwards. During these phases, several "users" ask some "allocators" for resources. Once they are granted the right to use them, they can perform operations, such as connection for a new incoming call for instance. We are in a distributed system and there is no global clock.

Automata for a user and an allocator are represented in figure 1. A question mark '?' denotes the fact that a message is received, and '!' denotes the sending of a message.

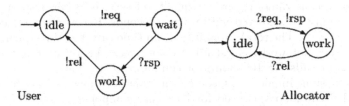

Fig. 1. Automata for user and allocator

The type of system previously described is named three tier systems. A simple execution is shown in figure 2. The user sends a request for a resource. The resource is then given to the user which can afterwards request the operator to perform operations on the resource. After some time the user releases the resource and informs the allocator.

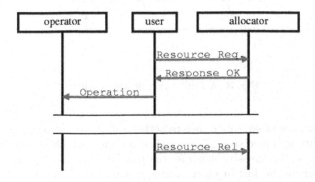

Fig. 2. Simple three tier model

This kind of model is very common. For instance on the world wide web, a browser is the user, the allocator is the web server, and transaction can lead to modification of a data base, which is the operator (in this case the `operation` request of figure 2 can be sent from the allocator instead of the user).

Our protocol uses this notion at different level simultaneously. A single actor might have several different roles (server, client or operator) regarding the same resource. It might also have different roles for different resources. Since we use it in a mobile environment, resources are allowed to move from one actor to another, e.g. when a mobile subscriber moves from one cell to another. In the protocol we want to verify, we have approximatively 100 actors in our network, running on 16 hosts. This gives an idea of the description of our system.

2.2   Quality of Service and Fault Tolerance

There are some constraints regarding quality of service in our system. For instance a fault must be detected within three seconds. Recovery must then take at most two seconds. The total capability down time (average time during which the network does not work) is 0.4 minutes per year. There must not be more than 10^4 loss of calls for 10^9 hours of communication. These strong requirements of the system implies that some fault tolerance mechanisms have to be implemented. Redundancy is used for hardware components. We will focus on software aspects.

An active/passive replication scheme has been chosen [14]. In order to cope with real time constraints no group membership techniques have been implemented [15]. This means that every software application is duplicated. It has an active form which performs the regular work and a passive form which asynchronously receives messages to update its state. The passive form consumes much less resource than the active one. This allows to save hardware resources when we have a lot of applications running.

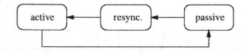

Fig. 3. A fault tolerant application

After a fault, the passive switches to active and starts from the latest state for which an update was received. This is called a swact, which stands for switch of activity. In this active/passive scheme, the passive process only knows the state of its active when the last update message was sent. Therefore a swact may cause some loss of information, typically the passive is not aware of the latest transactions. Before resuming its nominal activities, it must be resynchronized with other active entities. Figure 3 shows the high level states of each application.

Alloc(a)	*User (u)*
Active	**Idle** (*state ← idle*)
when receiving $req(u)$	Environment send $a \in [0, n-1]$
if $\exists r$ such that $busy[r] = False$	$alloc[a]!req(u)$ goto Wait
$date[r] \leftarrow newValue$	**Wait** (*state ← wait*)
$user[u]!rsp(r, date[r])$	when receiving rsp_nack from a
$busy[r] \leftarrow True$	goto Idle
update passive	when receiving $rsp(r, d)$
else	update passive
$user[u]!rsp\_nack$	goto Work
goto Active	**Work** (*state ← work*)
when receiving $rel(r, d)$	Environment decides to finish the call.
if $date[r] \leq d$	send $alloc[a]!rel(r, d)$
$busy[r] \leftarrow False$	update passive
update passive	goto Idle
goto Active	

Allocator resynchro.	**Response to allocator resynchro.**
For all r $busy[r] \leftarrow False$	when receiving $resync\_req(a')$
For all $u \in [0, m-1]$	if $a = a' \wedge state = work$
$user[u]!resync\_req(a)$	$alloc[a']!resync\_rsp(r, d)$
For all $u \in [0, m-1]$ receive	goto work
$resync\_rsp(r, d)$ or $resync\_req(r, d)$	else
if $\neg busy[r] \vee date[r] \leq d$	if $a \neq a$
$date[r] \leftarrow d$	$alloc[a']!resync\_rsp\_empty$
$busy[r] \leftarrow True$	goto *state*
$resync\_rsp\_empty$ and do nothing.	else $alloc[a']!resync\_rsp\_empty$
update passive	goto *idle*
goto Active	

Response to user resynchro.	**User resynchronization**
when receiving $resync\_req(r, d)$ from u	if $state = work$
if $\neg busy[r]$	$alloc[a]!resync\_req(r, d)$
$user[u]!resync\_rsp\_nack$	if receive $resync\_rsp\_ack$
else	goto work
if $date[r] = d$	if receive $resync\_rsp\_nack$
$user[u]!resync\_rsp\_ack$	update passive with an idle
else $user[u]!resync\_rsp\_nack$	state
$busy[r] \leftarrow False$	goto idle
update passive	else
	goto idle

Fig. 4. Resynchronization for allocators and users

In order to allow the resynchronization, timestamps are used to order the causality of events in our system. This is shown in figure 4. In this figure unspecified reception are dropped. And for both entities the passive form is:

Passive   for $Alloc(a)$ or $User(u)$
when receiving $update(m)$ store m,
    goto Passive
when receiving $swact$ from environment
    goto Resync.

The $newValue$ function in figure 4 denotes the creation of a new timestamps more recent than all existing ones. The response to the swact of an allocator can be in any of the following state for users $Idle$, $Wait$ or $Work$. The response to the swact of a user can be in the $Active$ state of an allocator.

There are two kinds of properties we want to check:

- safety: current context of applications should not be corrupted after the resynchronization.
- liveness: unused resources should be released eventually.

3   Abstraction on Timestamps

Clocks and timestamps are often used in distributed systems. They provide a way to record causal relationships between events [16,17]. Systems which use timestamps [10] often lead to state explosion. More precisely, the easiest way to implement a local clock is to use a counter which is large enough (e.g. 32 or 64 bits). This causes a major problem for automatic model checking using explicit state enumeration because the number of states of the system is then much too large. Since there are often a rather small number of values (timestamps) simultaneously present in the variables of the system, one would like to take advantage of this fact to reduce the number of states reached in the analysis of the model. This is precisely the aim of this section.

A classical abstraction to tackle the state explosion is to assume a relatively small bound on the counter, but this is not satisfactory in most cases. If the bound is small enough to avoid state explosion then it usually yields to counter overflows and the actual system is not faithfully described by the model.

If one knows a bound on the number of values simultaneously present for a clock, one may use sophisticated algorithms to keep the number of timestamps bounded (see e.g. [18,19]). But again this is not a solution to our problem. First because it is not used in practice and therefore one should not use this in the model, and second because the bound needed by these algorithms is still much too large [20].

Our technique is very simple but proved to be highly efficient. It is designed to work with a model checker using explicit state vectors. The idea is to link a small library with the model checker whose aim is to reduce the timestamps contained in each newly generated state vector to a smaller range. This allows to dynamically use the smallest possible range for the timestamps. Also, our method does not require any change in the model, which is a major advantage.

3.1   Timestamps in State Vector

The state vector of the system is the vector composed of all the parameters which describe the global state of the system: automaton states, variable values, message queue contents. Figure 5 shows a state vector with a single timestamp t_1 associated with some clock c. Then another timestamp t_2 for the same clock c appears in the system, it can be in some message queue or some local variable. These two timestamps can be different since they reflect the value of the clock c at different moments.

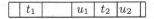

Fig. 5. A timestamp appearing

Actually in our system, each allocator has its own clock, and we have several families of timestamps as shown on figure 6. For instance two users have timestamps t_1 and t_2 from a clock c in an allocator, and two other have u_1 and u_2 from another allocator.

Fig. 6. Several families of timestamps

3.2   Principle

As explained above, implementing timestamps as a counter over bytes results in a huge number of global states for the system. We propose to map these timestamps to a smaller domain. This is done directly at the level of the model checker. More precisely, since we are only interested in the relative values of timestamps attached to some clock x, we can map n timestamps $t_1, ..., t_n$ to the interval $0, \dots , n-1$. Timestamps may also disappear leaving holes in the integer range $0, \dots , n-1$. We then have to map these values so that they again form an integer interval. For instance if we have timestamps 0, 1, 2, 2, 3, 4 and during the next step the values 1 and 3 disappear and 8 is inserted then we get 0, 1, 1, 2, 3.

Using suitable data structures, we will show how to implement these operations with a complexity of $n \log n$, n being the number of timestamps in the system. The result is that for each clock, all of its timestamps are consecutive integers. This dramatically reduces the state space.

3.3   Formal Description

The way we use timestamps is very important. For timestamps t_i and t_j, we do not need to check properties such as $t_i < 4$ or perform operation such as $t_i := t_j^2$, or verify a property like "sometimes in the future t_i will be greater than 5".

We only perform the following operations: $t_i := t_j$ (set to an old value), $t_i := 0$ (reset to the original value) or $t_i := \text{newValue}$ (get a new value for this timestamp, the new value is positive and strictly greater than all other existing values). And we can only perform the following tests $t_i \sharp t_j$ or $t_i \sharp 0$ where $\sharp$ is one of $<, >, \leq, \geq, =$.

In order to give formal results, we assume that all timestamps are kept into variables and we denote by V the set of those variables. All other variables that the system may use are abstracted in the state of the automaton. This leads to the following definition.

Definition 1. *An automaton $\mathcal{A}$ is a tuple (Q, S, V, T), where:*

- *Q is the set of states,*
- *$S \subseteq Q$ is the set of initial states,*
- *V is the set of integer valued variables holding timestamps, they are initialized to 0,*
- *T is the set of transitions of our system. A transition is a quadruple (q, g, a, q') where p and q are states, g is a guard which is a boolean combination of atomic conditions such as $x \sharp 0$ or $x \sharp y$ with $x, y \in V$ and $\sharp \in \{=, <, >, \leq, \geq\}$, and a is an action which is a sequence of atomic actions such as $x := 0$, $x := y$ or $x := \text{newValue}$.*

Examples previously shown in figure 1 and 4 can be encoded this way.

Definition 2. *A concrete state of the automaton $\mathcal{A}$ is a pair $(q, \sigma) \in Q \times \mathbb{N}^V$, where σ gives the value of each variable in V. The concrete initial states are $S \times \{0\}^V$. A transition (q, g, a, q') is enabled in state (q, σ) if $\sigma \models g$ (the guard is true) and when fired the resulting state is (q', σ') where σ' is obtained by applying the action a to σ, denoted by $\sigma' = a(\sigma)$.*

An execution of $\mathcal{A}$ is a sequence $(q_0, \sigma_0), (g_1, a_1), (q_1, \sigma_1), \dots$ where for all i, $\sigma_i \models g_{i+1}$, $\sigma_{i+1} = a_{i+1}(\sigma_i)$ and $(q_i, g_{i+1}, a_{i+1}, q_{i+1})$ is a transition of $\mathcal{A}$.

In order to define the reduced automaton, we introduce the reduction $\rho : \mathbb{N}^V \to \{0, ..., |V|\}^V$. This corresponds to the remapping of timestamps. The implementation of function ρ will be described in figure 7. It maps 0 to 0, positive integers to positive integers and it is such that for all $\sigma \in \mathbb{N}^V$ we have

- $\rho \circ \sigma(V) \cup \{0\}$ is an initial interval of $\mathbb{N}$,
- for all $x, y \in V$, $\sigma(x) \leq \sigma(y)$ if and only if $\rho \circ \sigma(x) \leq \rho \circ \sigma(y)$.

Note that the reduction ρ is idempotent.

For instance the following sequence of timestamps $(1, 1, 3, 13, 13)$ will be mapped to $(1, 1, 2, 3, 3)$ by ρ. If 2 is removed, we have the sequence $(1, 1, 3, 3)$ which is mapped by ρ to $(1, 1, 2, 2)$.

The reduced automaton $\mathcal{A}' = \rho(\mathcal{A})$ is then defined as the quadruple (Q, S, V, T') where $T' = \{(q, g, a; \rho, q') \mid (q, g, a, q') \in T\}$. As above, the transition $(q, g, a; \rho, q')$ is enabled in state (q, σ) if $\sigma \models g$ and applying the transition results in the state $(q', \rho(a(\sigma)))$.

The basic result is that ρ defines a bisimulation between the automata $\mathcal{A}$ and $\mathcal{A}'$. In order to prove this, we need the following two lemmas.

Lemma 1. *Let g be a guard and $\sigma \in \mathbb{N}^V$ a valuation of variables. Then, $\sigma \models g$ if and only if $\rho \circ \sigma \models g$.*

Proof. Let $\sigma \in \mathbb{N}^V$ a valuation of variables and $x \sharp y$ be an atomic guard. Since ρ preserves the ordering we have:

$$\sigma \models x \sharp y \quad \Leftrightarrow \quad \sigma(x) \sharp \sigma(y) \quad \Leftrightarrow \quad \rho \circ \sigma(x) \sharp \rho \circ \sigma(y) \quad \Leftrightarrow \quad \rho \circ \sigma \models x \sharp y.$$

Similarly, $\sigma \models x \sharp 0$ if and only if $\rho \circ \sigma \models x \sharp 0$ since the reduction ρ maps 0 to 0, and positive integers to positive integers.

Now we can easily conclude using the fact that an arbitrary guard is a boolean combination of atomic guards.

Lemma 2. *Let a be an action and $\sigma \in \mathbb{N}^V$ a valuation of variables. Then,*

$$(a; \rho)(\rho \circ \sigma) = \rho(a(\rho \circ \sigma))) = \rho(a(\sigma)).$$

Proof. We first introduce some notations. Let $\sigma_1 = \rho \circ \sigma$, $\sigma' = a(\sigma)$ and $\sigma_1' = a(\sigma_1)$. We have to show that $\rho \circ \sigma' = \rho \circ \sigma_1'$, that is that the following diagram commutes.

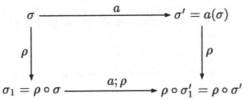

Since an arbitrary action is just a sequence of atomic actions, we can easily conclude by induction once we have shown the lemma for atomic actions.

Assume that a is one of the atomic action $x := 0$, $x := y$ or $x := \text{newValue}$. We first show that $\rho \circ \sigma'(z) = \rho \circ \sigma_1'(z)$ for all $z \neq x$. There are two cases.

- If $\sigma(x') = \sigma(x)$ for some $x' \neq x$ (including $x' = y$ when a is the atomic action $x := y$). Then, we also have $\sigma_1(x') = \sigma_1(x)$ for the same x'. We deduce that for all $z \neq x$ it holds

$$\rho \circ \sigma'(z) = \rho \circ \sigma(z) = \rho \circ \rho \circ \sigma(z) = \rho \circ \sigma_1(z) = \rho \circ \sigma_1'(z).$$

- If $\sigma(x') \neq \sigma(x)$ for all $x' \neq x$. Then, $\sigma_1(x') \neq \sigma_1(x)$ for all $x' \neq x$ and we deduce that for all $z \neq x$ it holds
  - If $\sigma(z) < \sigma(x)$ then also $\sigma_1(z) < \sigma_1(x)$ and we have

$$\rho \circ \sigma'(z) = \rho \circ \sigma(z) = \rho \circ \rho \circ \sigma(z) = \rho \circ \sigma_1(z) = \rho \circ \sigma_1'(z).$$

– If $\sigma(z) > \sigma(x) > 0$ then also $\sigma_1(z) > \sigma_1(x) > 0$ and we have

$$\rho \circ \sigma'(z) = \rho \circ \sigma(z) - 1 = \rho \circ \rho \circ \sigma(z) - 1 = \rho \circ \sigma_1(z) - 1 = \rho \circ \sigma'_1(z).$$

– If $\sigma(x) = 0$ then for all $z \neq x$, $\sigma(z) > 0$ and $\sigma_1(z) > 0$. It follows
$$\rho \circ \sigma'(z) = \rho \circ \sigma(z) = \rho \circ \rho \circ \sigma(z) = \rho \circ \sigma_1(z) = \rho \circ \sigma'_1(z).$$

It remains to show that $\rho \circ \sigma'(x) = \rho \circ \sigma'_1(x)$. The proof depends on the specific atomic action.

– Assume that a is the atomic action $x := 0$. Then, $\sigma'(x) = 0$ and $\sigma'_1(x) = 0$. The result follows since ρ maps 0 to 0.
– Assume that a is the atomic action $x := y$. If $x = y$ then the action a has no effect and we can conclude since ρ is idempotent. Hence we can assume that $y \neq x$ and use the result above. We have

$$\rho \circ \sigma'(x) = \rho \circ \sigma'(y) = \rho \circ \sigma'_1(y) = \rho \circ \sigma'_1(x).$$

– Finally, assume that a is the atomic action $x := \text{newValue}$. We have

$$\rho \circ \sigma'(x) = 1 + \max_{z \neq x} \rho \circ \sigma'(z) = 1 + \max_{z \neq x} \rho \circ \sigma'_1(z) = \rho \circ \sigma'_1(x).$$

Proposition 1. *The reduction ρ defines a bisimulation between the automata $\mathcal{A}$ and $\mathcal{A}'$. More precisely,*

1. *If $(q, \sigma) \xrightarrow{g,a} (q', \sigma')$ is a transition in $\mathcal{A}$, then, $(q, \rho \circ \sigma) \xrightarrow{g,a;\rho} (q', \rho \circ \sigma')$ is a transition in $\mathcal{A}'$.*

2. *If $(q, \sigma_1) \xrightarrow{g,a;\rho} (q', \sigma'_1)$ is a transition in $\mathcal{A}'$, then $(q, \sigma) \xrightarrow{g,a} (q', \sigma')$ is a transition in $\mathcal{A}$ for some σ, σ' such that $\sigma_1 = \rho \circ \sigma$ and $\sigma'_1 = \rho \circ \sigma'$.*

Proof. First, if $(q, \sigma) \xrightarrow{g,a} (q', \sigma')$ is a transition in $\mathcal{A}$ then $\sigma \models g$ and $\sigma' = a(\sigma)$. Using Lemmas 1 and 2 we deduce that $\rho \circ \sigma \models g$ and that $(a; \rho)(\rho \circ \sigma) = \rho(a(\sigma))$. Therefore, $(q, \rho \circ \sigma) \xrightarrow{g,a;\rho} (q', \rho \circ \sigma')$ is a transition in $\mathcal{A}'$.

Second, if $(q, \sigma_1) \xrightarrow{g,a;\rho} (q', \sigma'_1)$ is a transition in $\mathcal{A}'$ then $\sigma_1 \models g$ and $\sigma'_1 = (a; \rho)(\sigma_1)$. If in addition we have $\sigma_1 = \rho \circ \sigma$ then using Lemma 1 we deduce that $\sigma \models g$. Therefore, $(q, \sigma) \xrightarrow{g,a} (q', a(\sigma))$ is a transition in $\mathcal{A}$. We can conclude using Lemma 2 that $(a; \rho)(\rho \circ \sigma) = \rho(a(\sigma))$.

From Proposition 1 we deduce immediately that

Proposition 2.

1. *If the state (q, σ) is reachable in $\mathcal{A}$ then the state $(q, \rho \circ \sigma)$ is reachable in $\mathcal{A}'$.*
2. *If the state (q, σ') is reachable in $\mathcal{A}'$ then there exists a valuation $\sigma \in \mathbb{N}^V$ such that (q, σ) is reachable in $\mathcal{A}$ and $\sigma' = \rho \circ \sigma$.*
3. *If $(q_0, \sigma_0), (g_1, a_1), (q_1, \sigma_1), \ldots$ is an execution of $\mathcal{A}$ then $(q_0, \rho \circ \sigma_0), (g_1, a_1; \rho), (q_1, \rho \circ \sigma_1), \ldots$ is an execution of $\mathcal{A}'$.*
4. *If $(q_0, \sigma'_0), (g_1, a_1; \rho), (q_1, \sigma'_1), \ldots$ is an execution of $\mathcal{A}'$ and $\rho \circ \sigma'_0 = \sigma'_0$ then, for all i there exists σ_i such that $\sigma'_i = \rho \circ \sigma_i$ and $(q_0, \sigma_0), (g_1, a_1), (q_1, \sigma_1), \ldots$ is an execution of $\mathcal{A}$.*

Let us now pay attention to model checking for linear temporal logic (LTL [21]) or computation tree logic (CTL or CTL* [22]).

Proposition 3. *Let* Prop *be a set of atomic propositions and let $\ell : Q \to 2^{\mathrm{Prop}}$ be a mapping which associates with each state q the set of atomic propositions which are satisfied in state q. If φ is a CTL* formula build over the propositions of* Prop *and the atomic predicates $x \sharp 0$ and $x \sharp y$ where $x, y \in V$ and $\sharp \in \{=, <, >, \leq, \geq\}$. Then $\mathcal{A}, \ell \models \varphi$ if and only if $\mathcal{A}', \ell \models \varphi$.*

This proposition in another consequence of Proposition 1. The key point is that the bisimulation between $\mathcal{A}$ and $\mathcal{A}'$ defined by ρ preserves the atomic formulas. Indeed, let (q, σ) and $(q, \rho \circ \sigma)$ be two bisimilar states. The atomic propositions from Prop satisfied by the two states are given by $\ell(q)$. Using Lemma 1, we also deduce that the two states satisfy the same atomic predicates. The proposition follows then easily using classical results concerning bisimilar systems.

We could also define an equivalence on the concrete states of $\mathcal{A}$ by setting $(q, \sigma) \equiv (q, \sigma')$ if and only if $\rho \circ \sigma = \rho \circ \sigma'$. We could then show this equivalence is a bisimulation. The automaton $\mathcal{A}'$ is then isomorphic to the quotient of $\mathcal{A}$ by this equivalence.

3.4   Implementation

We are using the model checker Spin and its associated modeling language Promela. Using a small library in C-code of approximately a hundred lines we managed to achieve the timestamps reduction described in section 3.3. The library is linked with the C code (named pan) generated by the Spin model checker. The outline of the treatment which is done at each step is given in figure 7.

If m is the state vector size, and n_i the number of timestamps for clock i then the complexity at each step is $O(m + \sum_i n_i \log(n_i))$. Let us denote by n the maximum number of timestamps in the system, then $\sum_i n_i \leq n$ and the complexity for each step is smaller than $O(m + n \log n)$.

```
Empty all l_i lists.
Read state vector:
      when a timestamp from process i
      is encountered add a pointer to
      it in l_i.
for all processes i
      sort the list l_i according to the
      value pointed to.
      read the list l_i and change values
      to have a consecutive range
      of integers.
endfor
```

Fig. 7. Timestamps mapping

This implementation is done simply by adding one line of code to the Spin model checker: a call to our function which performs the reduction of timestamps described in figure 7.

3.5   Experimental Results

We performed the test with a system consisting of two allocators and two users as described in figure 4. In order to verify this protocol, we used Spin version 3.3.6 on a Sun Sparc Ultra 10 workstation running Solaris with 512Mb of RAM and a clock speed of 300 MHz.

Figure 8 presents some experimental results showing the difference between a naive implementation and the abstraction described in section 3.2.

The first column *timestamp range* shows how many different values are used for timestamps. As explained above, in order to avoid overlaps between timestamps, *timestamp range* should be large enough. Here we start at 5 because in our system we have at most 5 different timestamps which can be compared. Notice that this is not enough for the basic (without timestamp reduction) implementation because it would cause timestamp overlaps.

The second column shows the number of states, transitions and memory in megabytes used for the basic model. The third column shows results for the abstraction described in this section. N/A denotes the fact that the computation required more memory than was available. Using swap memory dramatically increases the time and has to be avoided in practice.

timestamp range	without reduction	with reduction	
5	3.3×10^6 4.9×10^6 438	7.5×10^4 1.1×10^5 375	states transitions Mb. of memory
6	5.9×10^6 8.7×10^6 488	*as above*	st. tr. Mb.
7	9.8×10^6 1.1×10^7 563	*as above*	st. tr. Mb.
128	N/A	*as above*	st. tr. Mb.

Fig. 8. Results for timestamps mapping

One can notice that timestamp reduction gives the same results regardless of the timestamp range. So if a timestamp stays a long time in the system there will be no problem with the abstraction of section 3.2, whereas the basic implementation will require a timestamp range which will be much too large to allow automatic verification.

This idea of modifying the state vector generated by the model checker in order to get a bisimilar transition system can be used in other systems using vector of timestamps, like the Fidge-Mattern protocol [23,24]. Reduction in the number of states can be less significant for protocols which store a lot of causal information like the Raynal-Schiper-Toueg protocol [16].

3.6   Some Results

This section gives two examples of some errors which were found in the protocol. This was possible due to the previous abstraction.

Let us consider a dialog between two actors A and B. If B switches from active to passive then messages sent by the old active entity and the new one may not be in FIFO order. Such an error is shown in figure 9: user sends a requests to obtain a resource. This requests is successful, and a Resource Response is sent. Unfortunately the allocator switches its activity (swacts), before its passive instance has been updated.

A resynchronization request issued by the newly active allocator is read by the user. Since this is a third actor it may be treated before the response from the old active allocator. This leads to a system state where the allocator has an unused resource but this resource is used by the user.

We found a solution to this problem, by adding a timestamp verification when receiving `Resource Rsp`.

Here is a more subtle error. A Message Sequence Chart (MSC) is shown in figure 10. There are two levels of allocation: a pure allocator named *Allocator* on

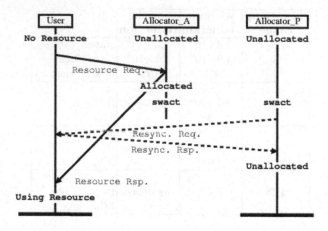

Fig. 9. Stream scheduling

figure 10 allocates resources for another actor named *User/All*. Theses resources are then again allocated for actors *User1* or *User2* by *User/All*. This enables the system to handle user mobility.

Let us have a closer look at the MSC: *User1* sends a message to *User/All* which is forwarded to *Allocator*. *User/All* swacts, forgets its state. Then *User/All* understands the Rsc. Ack. message from allocator as the response to the resource request message from *User2*.

In order to have a correct protocol we had to add an identifier (which was missing) to the request response in order to check it corresponds to the desired request.

4   Conclusion and Future Work

We managed to reduce the combinatorial explosion by mapping timestamps onto a list of consecutive integers. This reduction enabled us to formally model check the untimed properties of an industrial protocol and to exhibit some unknown errors. Hence the work was very helpful for the designers of the protocol.

Our reduction technique can also be applied to other structures which memorize a small number of causal events.

Our method is efficient and simple. It does not require any change of the model. It can cope with some kind of infinite state systems. It is not tailored to any special kind of property to be checked but instead works for all CTL* formulae since it gives a reduced system which is bisimilar to the original one.

On the other hand the process is not automatic yet, and it seems difficult to use it with symbolic model checking.

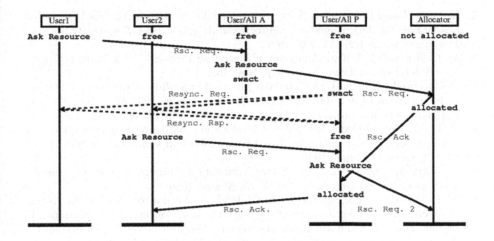

Fig. 10. Checking timestamps upon request response

Two main axes can be considered for future work:

– The work described in this paper has been done manually. We think it would be interesting to add some extensions to the Promela language to describe distributed system, in a way that the reduction described in this paper could be performed automatically.
– Our method has been designed to work with model checker using an explicit state enumeration. Though it does not seem clear how to extend this to symbolic model checking, this would be a very interesting track of research.

Acknowledgments. we would like to thank Xavier Lasne designer of resynchronization protocol, for his continuous interests in our activities. We would like to thank Gawain Bolton for comments and suggestions on the paper.

References

1. G. J. Holzmann. The Spin Model Checker. *IEEE Trans. on Software Engineering*, 23(5):279–295, May 1997.
2. T. Bolognesi and E. Brinksma. Introduction to the ISO Specification Language lotos. *Computer Networks and ISDN Systems*, pages 25–59, 1987.
3. M. Plath and M. Ryan. Plug and Play Features. *Fifth International Workshop on Feature Interactions in Telecommunications and Software Systems*, 1998. IOS Press.
4. C. Pecheur. Advanced Modeling and Verification Techniques Applied to a Cluster File System. *Proc. of the 14th IEEE International Conference on Automated Software Engineering ASE-99*, October 1999.

5. H. Garavel and L. Mounier. Specification and Verification of Various Distributed Leader Election Algorithms for Unidirectional Ring Networks. *Science of Computer Programming*, 29(1-2):171–197, 1997.
6. M. Calder and A. Miller. Analyzing a Basic Call Protocol Using Promela/Xspin. *Fourth International Spin Workshop*, Nov. 1998.
7. P. Godefroid. "*Partial-Order Methods for the Verification of Concurrent Systems – An Approach to the State-Explosion Problem*, volume 1032 of *Lecture Notes in Computer Science*. Springer-Verlag, January 1996. ISBN 3-540-60761-7.
8. D. Peled. Partial-Order Reductions: Model Checking Using Representatives. In *Proc. of MFCS'96*, number 1113 in Lecture Notes in Computer Science, pages 93–112. Springer-Verlag, 1996.
9. C. Norris Ip and D. L. Dill. Better Verification Through Symmetry. *Formal Methods in System Design*, 9(1/2):41–75, August 1996.
10. T. P. Petrov, A. Pogosyants, S. J. Garland, V. Luchangco, and N. A. Lynch. Computer-Assisted Verification of an Algorithm for Concurrent Timestamps. In Reinhard Gotzhein and Jan Bredereke, editors, *Formal Description Techniques IX: Theory, Applications, and Tools*, pages 29–44. Chapman & Hall, 1996.
11. R. Khazan, A. Fekete, and N. A. Lynch. Multicast Group Communication as a Base for a Load-Balancing Replicated Data Service. *DISC '98(formerly WDAG) 12th International Symposium on DIStributed Computing*, 1998.
12. N. A. Lynch and M. R. Tuttle. An Introduction to Input/Output Automata. *CWI-Quaterly*, 2(3):219–246, September 1989.
13. S. Garland and J. Guttag. A Guide to lp, the Larch Prover. Technical Report 82, DEC Systems Research Center, 1991.
14. R. Guerraoui and A. Schiper. Fault-Tolerance by Replication in Distributed Systems. *Reliable Software Technologies - Ada Europe '96. Lecture Notes in Computer Science*, 1088, 1996.
15. D. R. Cheriton and D. Skeen. Understanding the Limitations of Causally and Totally Ordered Communication. *Proc. of the 14th Symposium on Operating Systems Principles*, December 1993.
16. M. Raynal, A. Schiper, and S. Toueg. The Causal Ordering Abstraction and a Simple Way to Implement It. *IPL*, 39(6):343–350, 1991.
17. K. Birman, A. Schiper, and P. Stephenson. Lightweight Causal and Atomic Group Multicast. *ACM Trans. on Computer Systems*, pages 272–314, August 1991.
18. A. Israëli and M. Li. Bounded Time-Stamps. *Proc 28th IEE Symposium on Foundations of Computer Science*, pages 371–382, 1987.
19. D. Dolev and N. Shavit. Bounded Concurrent Time-Stamping. *SIAM Journal on Computing*, 26(2):418–455, April 1997.
20. R. Cori and E. Sopena. Some Combinatorial Aspects of Time-Stamp Systems. *European Journal of Combinatorics*, pages 95–102, 1993.
21. A. Pnueli. The Temporal Logic of Programs. *Proc 18th IEEE Symp. Foundations of Computer Science*, pages 46–57, 1977.
22. E.A. Emerson. Temporal and Modal Logic. In J. van Leeuwen, editor, *Handbook of Theoretical Computer Science, chapter 16*, pages 995–1072. Elsevier Publ. Co., Amsterdam, 1990.
23. C. J. Fidge. Timestamps in Message-Passing Systems that Preserve the Partial Ordering. *Australian Computer Science Communications*, 10(1):56–66, February 1988.
24. F. Mattern. Virtual Time and Global States of Distributed Systems. In M. Cosnard et al., editor, *Parallel and Distributed Algorithms*, pages 215–226. North-Holland, 1989.

Secrecy-Preserving Refinement

Jan Jürjens*

Computing Laboratory, University of Oxford, GB

Abstract. A useful paradigm of system development is that of *stepwise refinement*. In contrast to other system properties, many security properties proposed in the literature are not preserved under refinement (*refinement paradox*).

We present work towards a framework for stepwise development of secure systems by showing a notion of secrecy (that follows a standard approach) to be preserved by standard refinement operators in the specification framework Focus (extended with cryptographic primitives). We also give a rely/guarantee version of the secrecy property and show preservation by refinement. We use the secrecy property to uncover a previously unpublished flaw in a proposed variant of TLS, propose a correction and prove it secure. We give an abstract specification of a secure channel satisfying secrecy and refine it to a more concrete specification that by the preservation result thus also satisfies secrecy.

1 Introduction

A useful paradigm of system development is that of *stepwise refinement*: One starts with an abstract specification and refines it in several steps to a concrete specification which is implemented. Advantage of this approach is that mistakes may be detected rather early in the development cycle, which leads to considerable savings (late correction of requirements errors costs up to 200 times as much as early correction [Boe81]).

Clearly, the concrete specification must have all relevant properties of the initial specification. This is indeed the case for system properties that can be expressed as properties on traces (taking refinement to be reverse inclusion on trace sets). A classical example is the Alpern-Schneider framework of safety and liveness properties.

However, many security properties proposed in the literature are properties on trace sets rather than traces and give rise to the *refinement paradox* which means that these properties are not preserved under refinement (for noninterference this is pointed out in [McL94,McL96]; the same observation applies to equivalence-based notions of secrecy explained e. g. in [Aba00]).

For such properties, developing secure systems in a stepwise manner requires to redo security proofs at each refinement step. More worryingly, since an implementation is necessarily a refinement of its specification, an implementation

---

* Internet: http://www.jurjens.de/jan – e-mail: jan@comlab.ox.ac.uk – This work was supported by the Studienstiftung des deutschen Volkes and Lucent Technologies.

J.N. Oliveira and P. Zave (Eds.): FME 2001, LNCS 2021, pp. 135–152, 2001.

of a secure specification may not be secure. Thus the results of verifying such properties on the level of specifications needs to be applied with care, as pointed out in [RS98].

In this work, we seek to address this problem. In the specification framework Focus [Bro99,BS00] (extended by cryptographic operations including symmetric and asymmetric encryption and signing) we consider a secrecy property following the approach of [DY83] and show that it is preserved by the various refinements of the framework. We also give a rely/guarantee version of the secrecy property and show preservation by refinement. We demonstrate adequacy of the proposed secrecy notion by using it to uncover a previously unpublished flaw in a variant of the handshake protocol of TLS[1] proposed in [APS99], to propose a correction and to prove it secure. As an example for the stepwise development of a secure system we then give an abstract specification of a secure channel and refine it to a more concrete specification. The abstract specification satisfies secrecy, and by our preservation result the concrete one does as well.

In the next subsection we put our work into context and refer to related work on the subject of this paper. In Section 2, we introduce the specification framework Focus with the cryptographic extension. In Section 3 we give the secrecy properties considered in this work. In Section 4 we define the notions of refinement provided in Focus and show that they preserve the secrecy properties. In Section 5 we specify the variant of the TLS handshake protocol in our language, demonstrate the flaw, give a corrected version and prove it secure. In Section 6 we develop a specification of a secure channel in a stepwise manner. After that, we conclude.

Some of the proofs have to be omitted for lack of space; they are to be found in the long version of this paper to be published.

1.1   Security and Refinement

In the specification of systems one may employ nondeterminism in different ways, including the following:

under-specification: to simplify design or verification of systems. Certain details may be left open in the early phases of system development or when verifying system properties, to simplify matters or because they may not be known (for example the particular scheduler used to resolve concurrency).
unpredictability: to provide security. For example, keys or nonces are chosen in a way that should make them unguessable.

While the first kind of nondeterminism is merely a tool during development or verification, the second is a vital part of the functionality of a system. When one identifies the two kinds of nondeterminism one faces the refinement paradox mentioned above.

We separate the two kinds of nondeterminism in the following way: The nondeterminism of functional importance for the system is *only* modelled by specific primitives (such as key generation), possibly making use of syntax. Thus

---

[1] TLS is the successor of the Internet security protocol SSL.

the security of a system does *not* rely on nondeterministic choice in the formal model. Providing unpredictability through under-specification may be compared to providing *security by obscurity*. It has been argued that this is inferior to open design [SS75].

It is quite common in the formal modelling of security to provide special primitives for operations such as key generation, encryption etc.. However, security properties for nondeterministic specifications often also use the nondeterministic choice operators to provide unpredictability (since they generally do not seek to provide a security-preserving refinement). Our security property rules this out. This should not be seen as a restriction: Nondeterministic choice playing a functional role can always be modelled by explicitly generating coins and branching on them.

Many secrecy properties follow one of the following two approaches (discussed in [RS99,Aba00]; an example for a different approach can be found in [Sch96]). One is based on equivalences: Suppose a process specification P is parameterised over a variable x representing a piece of data whose secrecy should be preserved. The idea is that P preserves the secrecy of this data if for any two data values d_0, d_1 substituted for x, the resulting processes $P(d_0)$ and $P(d_1)$ are equivalent, i. e. indistinguishable to any adversary, (this appears e. g. in [AG99]). This kind of secrecy property ensures a rather high degree of security. However, if it should be preserved by the usual refinement, it seems to require a rather fine-grained model: The equivalence may only relate those traces in the trace sets of $P(d_0)$ and $P(d_1)$ that originate from the same nondeterministic component of P, because otherwise dropping nondeterministic components during refinement may not preserve the equivalence. Such a model can be constructed (e. g. using ideas from [Jür00a]), but it seems to be necessarily relatively complicated.

The secrecy property considered in this paper relies on the idea that a process specification preserves the secrecy of a piece of data d if the process never sends out any information from which d could be derived, even in interaction with an adversary (this is attributed to [DY83] and used e. g. in [CGG00]; a similar notion is used in [SV00]). In general, it is slightly coarser than the first kind in that it may not prevent implicit information flow, but both kinds of security properties seem to be roughly equivalent in practice [Aba00]. But even a secrecy property that uncovers only *most* flaws but is preserved under standard refinements is useful enough, especially since more fine-grained security properties may be hard to ensure in practice, as pointed out in [RS99].

With a secrecy-preserving refinement, one can also address situations where implementations of formally verified security protocols turn out to be insecure, because the cryptographic primitive chosen in the implementation introduces new equalities between terms (as pointed out in [RS98]) by proving the nondeterministic sum of the protocol behaviour each with the different primitives, and thus deriving the security wrt. to each primitive separately.

Related Work. For results on the use of formal methods in the development of secure systems cf. [FBGL94]. The survey article [Mea96] identifies the idea of security by design as a major area for future research.

In [Lot00], threat scenarios are used to formally develop secure systems using Focus. The considered security properties do not seem to be preserved under refinement and issues of refinement are left for further work.

[Sch96] gives a confidentiality property preserved under refinement. However, cryptographic primitives are not considered and it is pointed out that their treatment may be less straightforward.

For a discussion on refinement of secure information flow properties cf. [Mea92,McL94,McL96]. [RWW94] avoids the "refinement paradox" by giving a security property that requires systems to appear deterministic to the untrusted environment. Special refinement operators that preserve information flow security are considered e. g. in [Man00].

A related problem is that formal specifications involving cryptographic operations usually assume unconditional security while implementations generally provide security only against adversaries with bounded resources. This problem is addressed in [AR00,AJ00] (the second article considers our model here).

2   Specification Language

In this work, we view specifications as nondeterministic programs in the specification framework Focus [BS00]. Note that in addition to these executable specifications, Focus also allows the use of non-executable specifications ((non-)executability of security specifications is discussed in [LFBG95]). Executable specifications allow a rather straightforward modelling of cryptographic aspects such as encryption.

Specifically, we consider concurrently executing processes interacting by transmitting sequences of data values over unidirectional FIFO communication channels. Communication is asynchronous in the sense that transmission of a value cannot be prevented by the receiver (note that one may model synchronous communication using handshake [BS00]).

Focus provides mechanical assistance in form of the CASE tool Autofocus [HMR$^+$98].

Processes are collections of programs that communicate synchronously (in rounds) through channels, with the constraint that for each of its output channels c the process contains exactly one program p_c that outputs on c. This program p_c may take input from any of P's input channels. Intuitively, the program is a description of a value to be output on the channel c in round $n + 1$, computed from values found on channels in round n. Local state can be maintained through the use of feedback channels, and used for iteration (for instance, for coding *while* loops).

To be able to reason inductively on syntax, we use a simple specification language from [AJ00,Jür01]. We assume disjoint sets $\mathcal{D}$ of data values, **Secret** of unguessable values, **Keys** of keys, **Channels** of channels and **Var** of variables. Write **Enc** $\overset{\text{def}}{=}$ **Keys**∪**Channels**∪**Var** for the set of *encryptors* that may be used for encryption or decryption. The values communicated over channels are formal *expressions* built from the error value $\perp$, variables, values on input channels, and data values using concatenation. Precisely, the set **Exp** of expressions contains the empty expression ε and the non-empty expressions generated by the grammar

$E ::=$	expression
d	data value $(d \in \mathcal{D})$
N	unguessable value $(N \in \textbf{Secret})$
K	key $(K \in \textbf{Keys})$
c	input on channel c $(c \in \textbf{Channels})$
x	variable $(x \in \textbf{Var})$
$E_1 :: E_2$	concatenation
$\{E\}_e$	encryption $(e \in \textbf{Enc})$
$\mathcal{D}ec_e(E)$	decryption $(e \in \textbf{Enc})$

An occurrence of a channel name c refers to the value found on c at the previous instant. The empty expression ε denotes absence of output on a channel at a given point in time. We write **CExp** for the set of *closed* expressions (those containing no subterms in **Var** $\cup$ **Channels**). We write the decryption key corresponding to an encryption key K as K^{-1}. In the case of asymmetric encryption, the encryption key K is public, and K^{-1} secret. For symmetric encryption, K and K^{-1} may coincide. We assume $\mathcal{D}ec_{K^{-1}}(\{E\}_K) = E$ for all $E \in \textbf{Exp}, K, K^{-1} \in \textbf{Keys}$ (and we assume that no other equations except those following from these hold, unless stated otherwise).

(Non-deterministic) programs are defined by the grammar:

$p ::=$	programs
E	output expression $(E \in \textbf{Exp})$
either p or p'	nondeterministic branching
if $E = E'$ then p else p'	conditional $(E, E' \in \textbf{Exp})$
case E of key do p else p'	determine if E is a key $(E \in \textbf{Exp})$
case E of $x :: y$ do p else p'	break up list into head::tail $(E \in \textbf{Exp})$

Variables are introduced in case constructs, which determine their values. The first case construct tests whether E is a key; if so, p is executed, otherwise p'. The second case construct tests whether E is a list with head x and tail y; if so, p is evaluated, using the actual values of x, y; if not, p' is evaluated. In the second case construct, x and y are bound variables. A program is *closed* if it contains no unbound variables. *while* loops can be coded using feedback channels.

From each assignment of expressions to channel names $c \in \textbf{Channels}$ appearing in a program p (called its *input channels*), p computes an output expression.

For simplification we assume that in the following all programs are *well-formed* in the sense that each encryption $\{E\}_e$ and decryption $\mathcal{D}ec_e(E)$ appears as part of p in a *case E' of key do p else p'* construct (unless $e \in \textbf{Keys}$), to ensure that only keys are used to encrypt or decrypt. It is straightforward to enforce this using a type system.

Example. The program *case c of key do $\{d\}_c$ else ε* outputs the value received at channel d encrypted under the value received on channel c if that value is a key, otherwise it outputs ε.

A *process* is of the form $P = (I, O, L, (p_c)_{c \in \tilde{O} \cup L})$ where

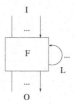

- $I \subseteq$ **Channels** is called the set of its *input channels* and

- $O \subseteq$ **Channels** the set of its *output channels*,

and where for each $c \in \tilde{O} \overset{\text{def}}{=} O \cup L$, p_c is a closed program with input channels in $\tilde{I} \overset{\text{def}}{=} I \cup L$ (where $L \subseteq$ **Channels** is called the set of *local channels*). From inputs on the channels in $\tilde{I}$ at a given point in time, p_c computes the output on the channel c.

We write I_P, O_P and L_P for the sets of input, output and local channels of P, $K_P \subseteq$ **Keys** for the set of keys and $S_P \subseteq$ **Secret** for the set of unguessable values (such as nonces) occurring in P. We assume that different processes have disjoint sets of local channels, keys and secrets. Local channels are used to store local state between the execution rounds.

2.1   Stream-Processing Functions

In this subsection we recall the definitions of streams and stream-processing functions from [Bro99,BS00].

We write $\textbf{Stream}_C \overset{\text{def}}{=} (\textbf{CExp}^\omega)^C$ (where $C \subseteq$ **Channels**) for the set of C-indexed tuples of (finite or infinite) sequences of closed expressions. The elements of this set are called *streams*, specifically *input streams* (resp. *output streams*) if C denotes the set of non-local input (resp. output) channels of a process P. Each stream $s \in \textbf{Stream}_C$ consists of components $s(c)$ (for each $c \in C$) that denote the sequence of expressions appearing at the channel c. The nth element in this sequence is the expression appearing at time $t = n$.

A function $f : \textbf{Stream}_I \to \mathcal{P}(\textbf{Stream}_O)$ from streams to sets of streams is called a *stream-processing function*.

The composition of two stream-processing functions $f_i : \textbf{Stream}_{I_i} \to \mathcal{P}(\textbf{Stream}_{O_i})$ $(i = 1, 2)$ with $O_1 \cap O_2 = \emptyset$ is defined as

$$f_1 \otimes f_2 : \textbf{Stream}_I \to \mathcal{P}(\textbf{Stream}_O)$$
(with $I = (I_1 \cup I_2) \setminus (O_1 \cup O_2)$, $O = (O_1 \cup O_2) \setminus (I_1 \cup I_2)$).

where $f_1 \otimes f_2(s) \overset{\text{def}}{=} \{t \mid_O : t \mid_I = s \mid_I \wedge t \mid_{O_i} \in f_i(s \mid_{I_i})(i = 1, 2)\}$ (where t ranges over $\textbf{Stream}_{I \cup O}$). For $t \in \textbf{Stream}_C$ and $C' \subseteq C$, the restriction $t \mid_{C'} \in \textbf{Stream}_{C'}$ is defined by $t \mid_{C'} (c) = t(c)$ for each $c \in C'$. Since the operator $\otimes$ is associative and commutative [BS00], we can define a generalised composition operator $\bigotimes_{i \in I} f_i$ for a set $\{f_i : i \in I\}$ of stream-processing functions.

Example. If $f : \textbf{Stream}_{\{a\}} \to \mathcal{P}(\textbf{Stream}_{\{b\}})$, $f(s) \overset{\text{def}}{=} \{0.s, 1.s\}$, is the stream-processing function with input channel a and output channel b that outputs the input stream prefixed with either 0 or 1, and $g : \textbf{Stream}_{\{b\}} \to$

$[E](M) = \{E(M)\}$ $\qquad\qquad$ where $E \in \mathbf{Exp}$

$[either\ p\ or\ p'](M) = [p](M) \cup [p'](M)$

$[if\ E = E'\ then\ p\ else\ p'](M) = [p](M)$ $\qquad$ if $[E](M) = [E'](M)$

$[if\ E = E'\ then\ p\ else\ p'](M) = [p'](M)$ $\qquad$ if $[E](M) \neq [E'](M)$

$[case\ E\ of\ key\ do\ p\ else\ p'](M) = [p](M)$ $\qquad$ if $[E](M) \in \mathbf{Keys}$

$[case\ E\ of\ key\ do\ p\ else\ p'](M) = [p'](M)$ $\qquad$ if $[E](M) \notin \mathbf{Keys}$

$[case\ E\ of\ x :: y\ do\ p\ else\ p'](M) = [p[h/x, t/y]](M)$ $\qquad$ if $[E](M) = h :: t$

$\qquad\qquad$ where $h \neq \varepsilon$ and h is not of the form $h_1 :: h_2$ for $h_1, h_2 \neq \varepsilon$

$[case\ E\ of\ x :: y\ do\ p\ else\ p'](M) = [p'](M)$ $\qquad$ if $[E](M) = \varepsilon$

Fig. 1. Definition of $[p](M)$.

$\mathcal{P}(\mathbf{Stream}_{\{c\}})$, $g(s) \overset{\text{def}}{=} \{0.s, 1.s\}$, the function with input (resp. output) channel b (resp. c) that does the same, then the composition $f \otimes g : \mathbf{Stream}_{\{a\}} \to \mathcal{P}(\mathbf{Stream}_{\{c\}})$, $f \otimes g(s) = \{0.0.s, 0.1.s, 1.0.s, 1.1.s\}$, outputs the input stream prefixed with either of the 2-element streams 0.0, 0.1, 1.0 or 1.1.

2.2 Associating a Stream-Processing Function to a Process

A process $P = (I, O, L, (p_c)_{c \in O})$ is modelled by a stream-processing function $[\![P]\!] : \mathbf{Stream}_I \to \mathcal{P}(\mathbf{Stream}_O)$ from input streams to sets of output streams.

For honest processes P, $[\![P]\!]$ is by construction *causal*, which means that the $n + 1^{st}$ expression in any output sequence depends only on the first n input expressions. As pointed out in [Pfi98], adversaries can not be assumed to behave causally, therefore for an adversary A we need a slightly different interpretation $[\![A]\!]_r$ (called *sometimes rushing adversaries* in [Pfi98]).

For any closed program p with input channels in $\tilde{I}$ and any $\tilde{I}$-indexed tuple of closed expressions $M \in \mathbf{CExp}^{\tilde{I}}$ we define a set of expressions $[p](M) \in \mathcal{P}(\mathbf{CExp})$ in Figure 1, so that $[p](M)$ is the expression that results from running p once, when the channels have the initial values given in M.

We write $E(M)$ for the result of substituting each occurrence of $c \in \tilde{I}$ in E by $M(c)$ and $p[E/x]$ for the outcome of replacing each free occurrence of x in process P with the term E, renaming variables to avoid capture.

Then any program p_c (for $c \in \mathbf{Channels}$) defines a causal stream-processing function $[p_c] : \mathbf{Stream}_{\tilde{I}} \to \mathcal{P}(\mathbf{Stream}_{\{c\}})$ as follows. Given $s \in \mathbf{Stream}_{\tilde{I}}$, let $[p_c](s)$ consist of those $t \in \mathbf{Stream}_{\{c\}}$ such that

- $t_0 \in [p_c](\varepsilon, \ldots, \varepsilon)$
- $t_{n+1} \in [p_c](s_n)$ for each $n \in \mathbb{N}$.

Finally, a process $P = (I, O, L, (p_c)_{c \in \tilde{O}})$ is interpreted as the composition $[\![P]\!] \overset{\text{def}}{=} \bigotimes_{c \in \tilde{O}} [p_c]$.

Similarly, any p_c (with $c \in \mathbf{Channels}$) defines a non-causal stream-processing function $[p_c]_r : \mathbf{Stream}_{\tilde{I}} \to \mathcal{P}(\mathbf{Stream}_{\{c\}})$ as follows. Given $s \in \mathbf{Stream}_{\tilde{I}}$, let $[p_c]_r(s)$ consist of those $t \in \mathbf{Stream}_{\{c\}}$ such that $t_n \in [p_c]_r(s_n)$ for each $n \in \mathbb{N}$.

An adversary $A = (I, O, L, (p_c)_{c \in \bar{O}})$ is interpreted as the composition $[\![A]\!]_r \stackrel{\text{def}}{=} \bigotimes_{c \in O} [p_c]_r \otimes \bigotimes_{l \in \bar{O} \setminus O} [p_l]$. Thus the programs with outputs on the non-local channels are defined to be *rushing* (note that using the local channels an adversary can still show causal behaviour).

Examples

- $[\textit{if } \mathcal{D}ec_{K'}(\{0\}_K) = 0 \textit{ then } 0 \textit{ else } 1](s) = (0, 0, 0, \ldots)$ iff $K = K'$
- For the process P with $I_P = \{i\}$, $O_P = \{o\}$ and $L_P = \{l\}$ and with $p_l \stackrel{\text{def}}{=} l :: i$ and $p_o \stackrel{\text{def}}{=} l :: i$ we have $[\![P]\!](s) = \{(\varepsilon, s_0, s_0 :: s_1, s_0 :: s_1 :: s_2, \ldots)\}$ and $[\![P]\!]_r(s) = \{(s_0, s_0 :: s_1, s_0 :: s_1 :: s_2, \ldots)\}$.

3   Secrecy

We say that a stream-processing function $f : \mathbf{Stream}_I \to \mathcal{P}(\mathbf{Stream}_O)$ *may eventually output* an expression $E \in \mathbf{Exp}_c$ if there exist streams $s \in \mathbf{Stream}_I$ and $t \in f(s)$, a channel $c \in O$ and an index $j \in \mathbb{N}$ such that $(t(c))_j = E$.

Definition 1. *We say that a process P leaks a secret $m \in \mathbf{Secret} \cup \mathbf{Keys}$ if there is a process A with $m \notin S_A \cup K_A$ such that $[\![P]\!] \otimes [\![A]\!]_r$ may eventually output m. Otherwise we say that P preserves the secrecy of m.*

The idea of this definition is that P preserves the secrecy of m if no adversary can find out m in interaction with P. In our formulation m is either an unguessable value or a key; this is seen to be sufficient in practice, since the secrecy of a compound expression can usually be derived from that of a key or unguessable value [Aba00].

For a comparison with other secrecy properties cf. Section 1.

Examples

- $p \stackrel{\text{def}}{=} \{m\}_K :: K$ does not preserve the secrecy of m or K, but $p \stackrel{\text{def}}{=} \{m\}_K$ does.
- $p_l \stackrel{\text{def}}{=}$ case c of key do $\{m\}_c$ else ε (where $c \in \mathbf{Channels}$) does not preserve the secrecy of m, but $P \stackrel{\text{def}}{=} (\{c\}, \{e\}, (p_d, p_e))$ (where $p_e \stackrel{\text{def}}{=} \{l\}_K$) does.

We also define a rely-guarantee condition for secrecy.

Given a relation $C \subseteq \mathbf{Stream}_O \times \mathbf{Stream}_I$ and a process A with $O \subseteq I_A$ and $I \subseteq O_A$ we say that A *fulfils* C if for every $s \in \mathbf{Stream}_{I_A}$ and every $t \in [\![A]\!](s)$, we have $(s \downharpoonright_O, t \downharpoonright_I) \in C$.

Definition 2. *Given a   relation $C \subseteq \mathbf{Stream}_{O_P} \times \mathbf{Stream}_{I_P}$ from output streams of a process P to input streams of P, we say that P leaks m assuming C (for $m \in \mathbf{Secret} \cup \mathbf{Keys}$) if there exists a process A with $m \notin S_A \cup K_A$ that fulfils C and such that $[\![P]\!] \otimes [\![A]\!]_r$ may eventually output m. Otherwise P preserves the secrecy of m assuming C.*

This definition is useful if P is a component of a larger system S that is assumed to fulfil the rely-condition, or if the adversary is assumed to be unable to violate it.

Example $p \stackrel{\text{def}}{=} if\ c = \textbf{password}\ then\ \textbf{secret}\ else\ \varepsilon$ preserves the secrecy of *secret* assuming $C = \{(\boldsymbol{t}, \boldsymbol{s}) : \forall n.\boldsymbol{s}_n \neq \textbf{password}\}$.

4 Refinement

We define various notions of refinement given in [BS00] and exhibit conditions under which they preserve our proposed secrecy properties.

4.1 Property Refinement

Definition 3. *For processes P and P' with $I_P = I_{P'}$ and $O_P = O_{P'}$ we define $P \rightsquigarrow P'$ if for each $\boldsymbol{s} \in \textbf{Stream}_{I_P}$, $[\![P]\!](\boldsymbol{s}) \supseteq [\![P']\!](\boldsymbol{s})$.*

Example (either p or q) $\rightsquigarrow$ p and (either p or q) $\rightsquigarrow$ q for any programs p, q.

Theorem 1.
  - *If P preserves the secrecy of m and $P \rightsquigarrow P'$ then P' preserves the secrecy of m.*
  - *If P preserves the secrecy of m assuming C (for any $C \subseteq \textbf{Stream}_{O_P} \times \textbf{Stream}_{I_P}$) and $P \rightsquigarrow P'$ then P' preserves the secrecy of m assuming C.*

4.2 Interface Refinement

Definition 4. *Let P_1, P_2, D and U be processes with $I_{P_1} = I_D$, $O_D = I_{P_2}$, $O_{P_2} = I_U$ and $O_U = O_{P_1}$. We define $P_1 \stackrel{(D,U)}{\rightsquigarrow} P_2$ to hold if $P_1 \rightsquigarrow D \otimes P_2 \otimes U$.*

Example. Suppose we have

  - $P_1 = (\{c\}, \{d\}, p_d \stackrel{\text{def}}{=} if\ c = 1\ then\ 2\ else\ 3)$,
  - $P_2 = (\{c'\}, \{d'\}, p_{d'} \stackrel{\text{def}}{=} if\ c' = 4\ then\ 5\ else\ 6)$,
  - $D = (\{c\}, \{c'\}, p_{c'} \stackrel{\text{def}}{=} if\ c = 1\ then\ 4\ else\ \varepsilon)$ and
  - $U = (\{d'\}, \{d\}, p_d \stackrel{\text{def}}{=} if\ d' = 5\ then\ 2\ else\ 3)$.

Then we have $P_1 \stackrel{(D,U)}{\rightsquigarrow} P_2$.

For the preservation result we need the following concepts.

Given a stream $\boldsymbol{s} \in \textbf{Stream}_X$ and a bijection $\iota : Y \rightarrow X$ we write $\boldsymbol{s}_\iota$ for the stream in $\textbf{Stream}_Y$ obtained from $\boldsymbol{s}$ by renaming the channel names using ι: $\boldsymbol{s}_\iota(y) = \boldsymbol{s}(\iota(y))$.

Given processes D, D' with $O_D = I_{D'}$ and $O_{D'} \cap I_D = \emptyset$ and a bijection $\iota : O_{D'} \rightarrow I_D$ such that $[\![D]\!] \otimes [\![D']\!](\boldsymbol{s}) = \{\boldsymbol{s}_\iota\}$ for each $\boldsymbol{s} \in \textbf{Stream}_{I_D}$, we say that D is a *left inverse* of D' and D' is a *right inverse* of D.

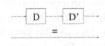

Example. $p_d \overset{\text{def}}{=} 0 :: c$ is a left inverse of $p_e \overset{\text{def}}{=}$ *case c of h :: t do t else ε.*

We write $S \circ R \overset{\text{def}}{=} \{(x, z) : \exists y.(x, y) \in R \wedge (y, z) \in S\}$ for the usual composition of relations R, S and generalize this to functions $f : X \to \mathcal{P}(Y)$ by viewing them as relations $f \subseteq X \times Y$.

Theorem 1 *Let P_1, P_2, D and U be processes with $I_{P_1} = I_D$, $O_D = I_{P_2}$, $O_{P_2} = I_U$ and $O_U = O_{P_1}$ and such that D has a left inverse D' and U a right inverse U'. Let $m \in (\textbf{Secret} \cup \textbf{Keys}) \setminus \bigcup_{Q \in \{D', U'\}} (S_Q \cup K_Q)$.*

  − *If P_1 preserves the secrecy of m and $P_1 \overset{(D,U)}{\leadsto} P_2$ then P_2 preserves the secrecy of m.*
  − *If P_1 preserves the secrecy of m assuming $C \subseteq \textbf{Stream}_{O_{P_1}} \times \textbf{Stream}_{I_{P_1}}$ and $P_1 \overset{(D,U)}{\leadsto} P_2$ then P_2 preserves the secrecy of m assuming $[\![U']\!] \circ C \circ [\![D']\!]$.*

4.3   Conditional Refinement

Definition 5. *Let P_1 and P_2 be processes with $I_{P_1} = I_{P_2}$ and $O_{P_1} = O_{P_2}$. We define $P_1 \leadsto_C P_2$ for a total relation $C \subseteq \textbf{Stream}_{O_{P_1}} \times \textbf{Stream}_{I_{P_1}}$ to hold if for each $s \in \textbf{Stream}_{I_{P_1}}$ and each $t \in [\![P_2]\!]$, $(t, s) \in C$ implies $t \in [\![P_1]\!]$.*

Example. $p \leadsto_C$ (*if $c = $ **emergency** then q else p*) *for $C = \{(t, s) : \forall n.s_n \neq$* **emergency**$\}$.

Theorem 2
Given total relations $C, D \subseteq \textbf{Stream}_{O_P} \times \textbf{Stream}_{I_P}$ with $C \subseteq D$, if P preserves the secrecy of m assuming C and $P \leadsto_D P'$ then P' preserves the secrecy of m assuming C.

5   A Variant of TLS

To demonstrate usability of our specification framework we specify a variant of the handshake protocol of TLS as proposed in [APS99] and demonstrate a previously unpublished weakness.

5.1   The Handshake Protocol

The goal is to let a client C send a master secret $m \in \textbf{Secret}$ to a server S in a way that provides confidentiality and server authentication.

The protocol uses both RSA encryption and signing. Thus in this and the following section we assume also the equation $\{\mathcal{D}ec_{K^{-1}}(E)\}_K = E$ to hold (for each $E \in \textbf{Exp}$ and $K \in \textbf{Keys}$). We also assume that the set of data values $\mathcal{D}$ includes process names such as $C, S, Y, \ldots$ and a message *abort*.

The protocol assumes that there is a secure (wrt. integrity) way for C to obtain the public key K_{CA} of the certification authority, and for S to obtain a certificate $\mathcal{D}ec_{K_{CA}^{-1}}(S :: K_S)$ signed by the certification authority that contains its name and public key. The adversary may also have access to K_{CA}, $\mathcal{D}ec_{K_{CA}^{-1}}(S ::$ $K_S)$ and $\mathcal{D}ec_{K_{CA}^{-1}}(Z :: K_Z)$ for an arbitrary process Z.

The channels between the participants are thus as follows.

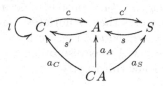

The following is the message flow diagram for the protocol that we present to aid understanding. Note that this kind of notation is merely short-hand for the more explicit specification given below and needs to be interpreted with care [Aba00].

$$C \xrightarrow{\quad N_C :: K_C :: \mathcal{D}ec_{K_C^{-1}}(C :: K_C) \quad} S$$

$$C \xleftarrow{\quad N_S :: \{\mathcal{D}ec_{K_S^{-1}}(K_{CS} :: N_C)\}_{K_C} :: \mathcal{D}ec_{K_{CA}^{-1}}(S :: K_S) \quad} S$$

$$C \xrightarrow{\quad \{m\}_{K_{CS}} \quad} S$$

Now we specify the protocol in our specification framework (here and in the following we denote a program with output channel c simply as c for readability).

$$c \stackrel{\text{def}}{=} \textit{if } l = \varepsilon \textit{ then } N_C :: K_C :: \mathcal{D}ec_{K_C^{-1}}(C :: K_C)$$
$$\textit{else case } s' \textit{ of } s_1 :: s_2 :: s_3$$
$$\textit{do case } \{s_3\}_{a_C} \textit{ of } S :: x$$
$$\textit{do if } \{\mathcal{D}ec_{K_C^{-1}}(s_2)\}_x = y :: N_C \textit{ then } \{m\}_y$$
$$\textit{else abort}$$
$$\textit{else abort}$$
$$\textit{else } \varepsilon$$
$$l \stackrel{\text{def}}{=} 0$$
$$s \stackrel{\text{def}}{=} \textit{case } c' \textit{ of } c_1 :: c_2 :: c_3$$
$$\textit{do case } \{c_3\}_{c_2} \textit{of } x :: c_2 \textit{ do } N_S :: \{\mathcal{D}ec_{K_S^{-1}}(K_{CS} :: c_1)\}_{c_2} :: a_S$$
$$\textit{else abort}$$
$$\textit{else } \varepsilon$$
$$a_C \stackrel{\text{def}}{=} K_{CA}$$
$$a_A \stackrel{\text{def}}{=} K_{CA} :: \mathcal{D}ec_{K_{CA}^{-1}}(S :: K_S) :: \mathcal{D}ec_{K_{CA}^{-1}}(Z :: K_Z)$$
$$a_S \stackrel{\text{def}}{=} \mathcal{D}ec_{K_{CA}^{-1}}(S :: K_S)$$

For readability we leave out a time-stamp, a session id, the choice of cipher suite and compression method and the use of a temporary key by S since these are not relevant for the weakness. We use syntactic sugar by extending the case list construct to lists of finite length and by using pattern matching, and we also leave out some *case of key do else* constructs to avoid cluttering. Here the local channel l of C only ensures that C initiates the handshake protocol only once. The exchanged key is symmetric, i. e. we have $K_{CS}^{-1} = K_{CS}$. The values sent on a_A signify that we allow A to eavesdrop on a_C and a_S and to obtain the certificate issued by CA of some third party.

5.2   The Flaw

Theorem 3 $P \stackrel{\text{def}}{=} C \otimes S \otimes CA$ *does not preserve the secrecy of* m.

We specify an attacker A and show that it is successful.

$$c' \stackrel{\text{def}}{=} \textit{case } c \textit{ of } c_1 :: c_2 :: c_3$$
$$\textit{do } c_1 :: K_A :: \mathcal{D}ec_{K_A^{-1}}(C :: K_A)$$
$$\textit{else } \varepsilon$$
$$s' \stackrel{\text{def}}{=} \textit{case } s \textit{ of } s_1 :: s_2 :: s_3$$
$$\textit{do } s_1 :: \{\mathcal{D}ec_{K_A^{-1}}(s_2)\}_{K_C} :: s_3$$
$$\textit{else } \varepsilon$$
$$l_A \stackrel{\text{def}}{=} \textit{if } l_A = \varepsilon \textit{ then case } s \textit{ of } s_1 :: s_2 :: s_3$$
$$\textit{do case } \{\mathcal{D}ec_{K_A^{-1}}(s_2)\}_{K_S} \textit{ of } x_1 :: x_2 \textit{ do } x_1 \textit{ else } l_A$$
$$\textit{else } l_A$$
$$c_0 \stackrel{\text{def}}{=} \textit{case } l_A \textit{ of key do if } \mathcal{D}ec_{l_A}(c) = \perp \textit{ then } \varepsilon \textit{ else } \mathcal{D}ec_{l_A}(c) \textit{ else } \varepsilon$$

Proposition 1 $\llbracket P \rrbracket \otimes \llbracket A \rrbracket_r$ *eventually outputs* m.

The message flow diagram corresponding to this man-in-the-middle attack follows.

5.3   The Fix

Let S' be the process derived from S by substituting $K_{CS} :: c_1$ in the second line of the definition of s by $K_{CS} :: c_1 :: c_2$. Change C to C' by substituting $y :: N_C$ in the fourth line of the definition of c by $y :: N_C :: K_C$.

$$C \xrightarrow{\quad N_C::K_C::\mathcal{D}ec_{K_C^{-1}}(C::K_C) \quad} S$$

$$C \xleftarrow{\quad N_S::\{\mathcal{D}ec_{K_S^{-1}}(K_{CS}::N_C::\underline{K_C})\}_{K_C}::\mathcal{D}ec_{K_{CA}^{-1}}(S::K_S) \quad} S$$

$$C \xrightarrow{\quad \{m\}_{K_{CS}} \quad} S$$

Theorem 4 $P' \overset{\text{def}}{=} C' \otimes S' \otimes CA$ *preserves the secrecy of* m.

Proof. For lack of space we only give an informal (but mathematically precise) sketch of the proof.

Given an adversary A with $n \notin S_A \cup K_A$, we need to show that $[\![P']\!] \otimes [\![A]\!]_r$ does not eventually output m. We proceed by execution rounds, making use of the fact that the adversary may let its output depend on the output from the honest participants at the same time.

In every round, 0 is output on l, K_{CA} on a_C and a_A, and $\mathcal{D}ec_{K_{CA}^{-1}}(S :: K_S)$ on a_S. After the first round, the local storage of C remains unchanged whatever happens, and S and CA do not have a local storage. Thus we only need to consider those actions of A that immediately increase its knowledge (i. e. we need not consider outputs of A that prompt C or S to output ε or *abort* in the following round.

In the first round, $N_C :: K_C :: \mathcal{D}ec_{K_C^{-1}}(C :: K_C)$ is output on c and ε on s. Since A is not in possession of any message containing S's name and signed by CA at this point, any output on s' will prompt C to output ε or *abort* in the next round, so the output on s' is irrelevant. Similarly, the only relevant output on c' is of the form $c_1 :: K_X :: \mathcal{D}ec_{K_X^{-1}}(Y :: K_X)$, where K_X is a public key with corresponding private key K_X^{-1} and Y a name of a process.

In the second round, the output on c is ε or *abort*, and that on s is ε or *abort* or $N_S :: \{\mathcal{D}ec_{K_S^{-1}}(K_{CS} :: c_1 :: K_X)\}_{K_X} :: a_S$. The only possibility to cause C in the following round to produce a relevant output would be for A now to output a message of the form $N_Z :: \{\mathcal{D}ec_{K_Z^{-1}}(K_{CS} :: c_1 :: K_X)\}_{K_X} :: \mathcal{D}ec_{K_{CA}^{-1}}(S :: K_Z)$. Firstly, the only certificate from CA containing S in possession of A is $\mathcal{D}ec_{K_{CA}^{-1}}(S :: K_S)$. Secondly, the only message containing a message signed using K_S in possession of A is $\{\mathcal{D}ec_{K_S^{-1}}(K_{CS} :: c_1 :: K_X)\}_{K_X}$. In case $K_X \neq K_C$ the message signed by S is of the form $\mathcal{D}ec_{K_S^{-1}}(K_{CS} :: c_1 :: K_X)$ for $K_X \neq K_C$, so that C outputs *abort* on receipt of this message anyhow. In case $K_X = K_C$, A cannot decrypt or alter the message $\{\mathcal{D}ec_{K_S^{-1}}(K_{CS} :: c_1 :: K_C)\}_{K_C}$ by assumptions on cryptography and since A does not possess K_C^{-1}. A may forward the message on s'. In this case, C outputs $\{m\}_{K_{CS}}$ in the following round, which A cannot decrypt.

Since the internal state of C, S and CA does not change after the first round, further interaction does not bring any change whatsoever (since it makes no difference if A successively tries different keys K_X or names Y).

Thus P' preserves the secrecy of x.

Note that the nonce N_S is in fact superfluous.

6   Implementing Secure Channels

As an example for a stepwise development of a secure system from an abstract specification to a concrete one, we consider the implementation of a secure channel W from a client C to a server S using the handshake protocol considered in Section 5.

The initial requirement is that a client C should be able to send a message n on W with intended destination a server S so that n is not leaked to A. Before a security risk analysis the situation may simply be pictured as follows:

$$\boxed{C} \xrightarrow[c_i]{c_o} \boxed{W} \xrightarrow[s_o]{s_i} \boxed{S}$$

Since there are no unconnected output channels, the composition $C \otimes W \otimes S$ obviously does not leak m.

Suppose that the risk analysis indicates that the transport layer over which W is to be implemented is vulnerable against active attacks. This leads to the following model.

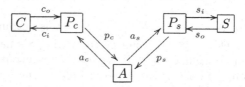

We would like to implement the secure channel using the (corrected) variant of the TLS handshake protocol considered in Section 5. Thus P_c resp. P_s are implemented by making use of the client resp. server side of the handshake protocol. Here we only consider the client side:

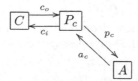

We would like to provide an implementation P_c such that for each C with $n \in S_C$, $C \otimes P_c$ preserves the secrecy of n (where n represents the message that should be sent to S). Of course, P_c should also provide functionality: perform the initial handshake and then encrypt data from C under the negotiated key $K \in \mathbf{Keys}$ and sent it out onto the network. As a first step, we may formulate the possible outputs of P_c as nondeterministic choices (in order to constrain the overall behaviour of P_c). We also allow the possibility for P_c to signal to C the readiness to receive data to be sent over the network, by sending ok on c_i.

$$p_c \stackrel{\mathrm{def}}{=} \textit{either if } c_o = \varepsilon \textit{ then } \varepsilon \textit{ else } \{c_o\}_K$$
$$\textit{or } c_K$$
$$c_i \stackrel{\mathrm{def}}{=} \textit{either } \varepsilon \textit{ or ok}$$

Here c_K denotes the following adaption of the (corrected) program c defined in Section 5 (for readability, we allow to use syntactic "macros" here, the resulting program is obtained by "pasting" the following program text in the place of $c(K)$ in the definition of p_c). For simplicity, we assume that P_c has already received the public key K_{CA} of the certification authority. We leave out the definition of c_i since at the moment we only consider the case where C wants to sent data to S.

$$c_K \stackrel{\mathrm{def}}{=} \textit{either } N_C :: K_C :: \mathcal{D}ec_{K_C^{-1}}(C :: K_C)$$
$$\textit{or case } a_c \textit{ of } s_1 :: s_2 :: s_3$$
$$\textit{do case } \mathcal{D}ec_{K_{AC}}(s_3) \textit{ of } S :: x$$
$$\textit{do if } \{\mathcal{D}ec_{K_C}(s_2)\}_x = y :: N_C :: K_C \textit{ then } \{K\}_y$$
$$\textit{else abort}$$
$$\textit{else abort}$$
$$\textit{else abort}$$

One can show that for any C, the composition $C \otimes P_c$ preserves the secrecy of n.

As a next step, we may split P_c into two components: the client side H of the handshake protocol (as part of the security layer) and program P (in the application layer) that receives data from C, encrypts it using the key received from H and sends it out on the network:

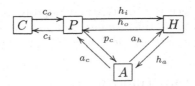

$$h_a \stackrel{def}{=} if\ h_i = \varepsilon\ then\ N_C :: K_C :: Dec_{K_C^{-1}}(C :: K_C)$$

$$else\ case\ a_h\ of\ s_1 :: s_2 :: s_3$$

$$do\ case\ Dec_{K_{AC}}(s_3)\ of\ S :: x$$

$$do\ if\ \{Dec_{K_C}(s_2)\}_x = y :: N_C :: K_C\ then\ \{m\}_y$$

$$else\ abort$$

$$else\ abort$$

$$else\ abort$$

$$h_o \stackrel{def}{=} if\ h_i = \varepsilon\ then\ \varepsilon$$

$$else\ case\ a_h\ of\ s_1 :: s_2 :: s_3$$

$$do\ case\ Dec_{K_{AC}}(s_3)\ of\ S :: x$$

$$do\ if\ \{Dec_{K_C}(s_2)\}_x = y :: N_C :: K_C\ then\ finished$$

$$else\ \varepsilon$$

$$else\ \varepsilon$$

$$else\ \varepsilon$$

$$h_i \stackrel{def}{=} 0$$

$$p_c \stackrel{def}{=} if\ c_o = \varepsilon\ then\ \varepsilon\ else\ \{c_o\}_K$$

$$c_i \stackrel{def}{=} if\ h_o = finished\ then\ ok\ else\ \varepsilon$$

We have the conditional interface refinement $P_c \stackrel{(D,U)}{\rightsquigarrow_T} P \otimes H$ where

- $T \subseteq \mathbf{Stream}_{O_{P_c}} \times \mathbf{Stream}_{I_{P_c}}$ consists of those (s, t) such that for any n, if $(s(\tilde{c}_i)) \mid_i \neq finished$ for all $i \leq n$ then $(s(\tilde{c}_o)) \mid_i = \varepsilon$ for all $i \leq n + 1$
- and D and U have channel sets $I_D = \{\tilde{c}_o, \tilde{a}_c\}$, $O_D = \{c_o, a_c, a_h\}$, $I_U = \{c_i, p_c, h_a\}$ and $O_U = \{\tilde{c}_i, \tilde{p}_c\}$ and are specified by

$$c_o \stackrel{def}{=} \tilde{c}_o, \qquad a_c \stackrel{def}{=} \tilde{a}_c, \qquad a_h \stackrel{def}{=} \tilde{a}_c,$$

$$\tilde{c}_i \stackrel{def}{=} c_i, \qquad \tilde{p}_c \stackrel{def}{=} h_a$$

(after renaming the channels of P_c to $\tilde{c}_o, \tilde{c}_i, \tilde{p}_c, \tilde{a}_c$).

Therefore, for any C with $[\![C]\!] \subseteq T$, we have an interface refinement $C \otimes P_c \stackrel{(D,U)}{\rightsquigarrow} C \otimes P \otimes H$. Since for any C, the composition $C \otimes P_c$ preserves the secrecy of n, as noted above, this implies that for any C with $[\![C]\!] \subseteq T$, the composition $C \otimes P \otimes H$ preserves the secrecy of n by Theorem 1 (since D and U clearly have inverses).

7 Conclusion and Further Work

We presented work towards a framework for stepwise development of secure systems by showing a notion of secrecy (that follows a standard approach) to be preserved by standard refinement operators in the specification framework Focus. We gave a rely/guarantee version of the secrecy property and showed preservation by refinement. We used the secrecy property to uncover a previously unpublished flaw in a proposed variant of TLS, proposed a correction and proved it secure. We gave an abstract specification of a secure channel satisfying secrecy and refined it to a concrete specification, thus satisfying secrecy by the preservation result.

In further work [Jür00b] we exhibit conditions for the compositionality of secrecy using ideas from [Jür00c].

Future work will give internal characterisations for the notion of secrecy (that do not directly refer to adversaries and therefore are easier to check) and address other security properties such as integrity and authenticity and the integration into current work towards using the Unified Modeling Language to develop secure systems [Jür01].

Acknowledgements. Many thanks go to Martín Abadi for interesting discussions and to Zhenyu Qian for providing the opportunity to give a talk on this work at Kestrel Institute (Palo Alto) and to the members of the institute for useful feedback. Many thanks also to G. Wimmel and the anonymous referees for comments on the draft.

This work was performed during a visit at Bell Labs Research at Silicon Valley / Lucent Technologies (Palo Alto) whose hospitality is gratefully acknowledged.

References

[Aba00]   M. Abadi. Security protocols and their properties. In F.L. Bauer and R. Steinbrueggen, editors, *Foundations of Secure Computation*, pages 39–60. IOS Press, 2000. 20th Int. Summer School, Marktoberdorf, Germany.

[AG99]   M. Abadi and Andrew D. Gordon. A calculus for cryptographic protocols: The spi calculus. *Information and Computation*, 148(1):1–70, January 1999.

[AJ00]   M. Abadi and Jan Jürjens. Formal eavesdropping and its computational interpretation, 2000. submitted.

[APS99]   V. Apostolopoulos, V. Peris, and D. Saha. Transport layer security: How much does it really cost ? In *Conference on Computer Communications (IEEE Infocom)*, New York, March 1999.

[AR00]   M. Abadi and P. Rogaway. Reconciling two views of cryptography (invited lecture). In *TCS 2000 (IFIP conference)*, Japan, August 2000.

[Boe81]   B.W. Boehm. *Software Engineering Economics*. Prentice-Hall, 1981.

[Bro99]   M. Broy. A logical basis for component-based systems engineering. In M. Broy and R. Steinbrüggen, editors, *Calculational System Design*. IOS Press, 1999.

[BS00]   M. Broy and K. Stølen. *Specification and Development of Interactive Systems*. Springer, 2000. (to be published).

[CGG00]   L. Cardelli, G. Ghelli, and A. Gordon. Secrecy and group creation. In *CONCUR 2000*, pages 365–379, 2000.

[DY83]   D. Dolev and A. Yao. On the security of public key protocols. *IEEE Transactions on Information Theory*, 29(2):198–208, 1983.

[FBGL94]   S. Fitzgerald, T. M. Brookes, M. A. Green, and P. G. Larsen. Formal and informal specifications of a secure system component: first results in a comparative study. In M. Naftalin, B. T. Denvir, and M. Bertran, editors, *FME'94: Industrial Benefit of Formal Methods*, pages 35–44. Springer, 1994.

[HMR+98]   F. Huber, S. Molterer, A. Rausch, B. Schätz, M. Sihling, and O. Slotosch. Tool supported Specification and Simulation of Distributed Systems. In *International Symposium on Software Engineering for Parallel and Distributed Systems*, pages 155–164, 1998.

[Jür00a]   Jan Jürjens. Abstracting from failure probabilities, 2000. submitted.

[Jür00b]   Jan Jürjens. Composability of secrecy, 2000. submitted.

[Jür00c]   Jan Jürjens. Secure information flow for concurrent processes. In C. Palamidessi, editor, *CONCUR 2000 (11th International Conference on Concurrency Theory)*, volume 1877 of *LNCS*, pages 395–409, Pennsylvania, 2000. Springer.

[Jür01]   Jan Jürjens. Towards development of secure systems using UML. In H. Hußmann, editor, *Fundamental Approaches to Software Engineering*, LNCS. Springer, 2001. to be published.

[LFBG95]   P. G. Larsen, S. Fitzgerald, T. M. Brookes, and M. A. Green. Formal modelling and simulation in the development of a security-critical message processing system. In *Formal Methods, Modelling and Simulation for Systems Engineering*, 1995.

[Lot00]   V. Lotz. Formally defining security properties with relations on streams. *Electronic Notes in Theoretical Computer Science*, 32, 2000.

[Man00]   H. Mantel. Possibilistic definitions of security - an assembly kit. In *IEEE Computer Security Foundations Workshop*, 2000.

[McL94]   J. McLean. Security models. In John Marciniak, editor, *Encyclopedia of Software Engineering*. Wiley & Sons, Inc., 1994.

[McL96]   J. McLean. A general theory of composition for a class of "possibilistic" properties. *IEEE Transactions on Software Engineering*, 22(1):53–67, 1996.

[Mea92]   C. Meadows. Using traces based on procedure calls to reason about composability. In *IEEE Symposium on Security and Privacy*, pages 177–188, 1992.

[Mea96]   C. Meadows. Formal verification of cryptographic protocols: A survey. In *Asiacrypt 96*, 1996.

[Pfi98]   B. Pfitzmann. Higher cryptographic protocols, 1998. Lecture Notes, Universität des Saarlandes.

[RS98]   P. Ryan and S. Schneider. An attack on a recursive authentication protocol. *Inform. Proc. Letters*, 65:7–10, 1998.

[RS99]   P. Ryan and S. Schneider. Process algebra and non-interference. In *IEEE Computer Security Foundations Workshop*, 1999.

[RWW94]   A. Roscoe, J. Woodcock, and L. Wulf. Non-interference through determinism. In *ESORICS 94*, volume 875 of *LNCS*. Springer, 1994.

[Sch96]   S. Schneider. Security properties and CSP. In *IEEE Symposium on Security and Privacy*, pages 174–187, 1996.

[SS75]   J. Saltzer and M. Schroeder. The protection of information in computer systems. *Proceedings of the IEEE*, 63(9):1278–1308, September 1975.

[SV00]   P. Sewell and J. Vitek. Secure composition of untrusted code: Wrappers and causality types. In *CSFW*, 2000.

Information Flow Control and Applications
– Bridging a Gap –

Heiko Mantel

German Research Center for Artificial Intelligence (DFKI)
Stuhlsatzenhausweg 3, 66123 Saarbrücken, Germany
mantel@dfki.de

Abstract. The development of formal security models is a difficult, time consuming, and expensive task. This development burden can be considerably reduced by using generic security models. In a security model, confidentiality as well as integrity requirements can be expressed by restrictions on the information flow. Generic models for controling information flow in distributed systems have been thoroughly investigated. Nevertheless, the known approaches cannot cope with common features of secure distributed systems like channel control, information filters, or explicit downgrading. This limitation caused a major gap which has prevented the migration of a large body of research into practice. To bridge this gap is the main goal of this article.

1 Introduction

With the growing popularity of e-commerce the security of networked information systems becomes an increasingly important issue. Since such distributed systems are usually quite complex, the application of formal methods in their development appears to be most appropriate in order to ensure security. In this process, the desired security properties are specified in a formal security model. This becomes a necessary task if the system shall be evaluated according to criteria like ITSEC or CC (level E4/EAL5 or higher). However, the development of security models is a difficult, time consuming, and expensive task. Therefore it is highly desirable to have *generic security models* which are well suited for certain application domains and which only need to be instantiated (rather than being constructed from scratch) for each application. In a security model, confidentiality as well as integrity requirements can be expressed by restrictions on the information flow. Generic security models for information flow control like [GM82,Sut86,McL96] are well-known. However, the use of such models for distributed systems has been quite limited in practice. The main reason is that the known models cannot cope with intransitive flow policies which are necessary in order to express common features like channel control, information filters, or explicit downgrading. In this article, we propose a solution to this problem.

In information flow control one first identifies different domains within a system and then decides if information may flow between these domains or not. This results in a *flow policy*. Next, a *definition of information flow* must be

J.N. Oliveira and P. Zave (Eds.): FME 2001, LNCS 2021, pp. 153–172, 2001.
© Springer-Verlag Berlin Heidelberg 2001

chosen. The common intuition underlying such definitions is that information flows from a domain D_1 to a domain D_2 if the behaviour of D_2 can be affected by actions of D_1. However, this intuition can be formalized in different ways and at least for non-deterministic systems no agreement on an optimal definition of information flow has been reached. Rather a collection of definitions co-exist. Frameworks like [McL96,ZL97,Man00a] provide a suitable basis for choosing an appropriate definition for a given application since they allow one to investigate the various definitions in a uniform way and to compare them to each other.

To achieve confidentiality or integrity by restricting the flow of information within a system is a very elegant and thus appealing approach. However, the assumptions underlying the existing approaches for information flow control are often too restrictive for real applications. Even though information flow shall be restricted in such applications, it must be possible to allow for *exceptions* to these restrictions. Typical examples for such exceptions are that two domains *should not* communicate with each other *unless* they use a particular communication channel which contains an information filter, that a domain which has access to sensitive data *should not* communicate with an open network *unless* the data has been properly encrypted, or that data *should not* be publicly accessible *unless* the data has been downgraded because a certain period of time has passed or a particular event has occurred. In information flow control, such exceptions can be expressed by *intransitive flow policies*. Intransitive policies indeed are necessary for real applications as can be seen at case studies like [SRS+00]. However, all known approaches (e.g. [Rus92,Pin95,RG99]) which are compatible with intransitive flow are limited to deterministic systems ([RG99] can deal with some, but severely limited non-determinism). Hence, they are not applicable to distributed systems which are certainly the most interesting ones in the presence of the Internet. The unsolved problem of how to cope with intransitive policies created a major gap which has prevented the application of a large body of work on information flow control in practice. To *bridge this gap* is the main goal of this article in which we extend our previously proposed framework [Man00a] to cope also with intransitive policies. We are confident that this is a major step for bringing information flow control into practice.

The overall structure of a security model based on information flow control is depicted in Figure 1. As usual, such a model consists of three main components: a formal specification of the system under consideration, a specification of one or more security properties, and a proof that the system satisfies these security properties. In information flow control, a security property again consists of two parts: a flow policy which defines where information flow is permissible or restricted, and a formal definition of what information flow means.

In this article, we focus on definitions of information flow. Our main contributions are novel definitions which can cope with a class of flow policies, namely intransitive policies, which, for non-deterministic systems, has been outside the scope of the existing approaches (cf. Section 3). Moreover, we present an unwinding theorem (cf. Section 4) which simplifies the proof that a system satisfies a security property. How to develop system specifications, however, is *not* dis-

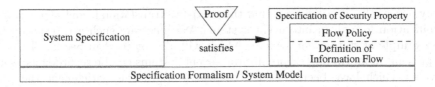

Fig. 1. Structure of a security model based on information flow control

cussed in this article. Nevertheless, we have to choose a specification formalism in order to refer to the underlying concepts in the specification of security properties. In Section 2 we introduce such a formalism and also give an introduction to security properties. We conclude this article by discussing related work in Section 5 and summarizing our results in Section 6.

2   Information Flow Control

In this section, we give an introduction to the basic concepts of information flow control before we turn our attention to intransitive information flow in subsequent sections. In Section 2.1 we define a specification formalism, or more precisely a system model on which such a formalism can be based. In Section 2.2 we introduce flow policies and provide various examples. Existing definitions of information flow are investigated in Section 2.3.

2.1   Specification Formalism / System Model

For the formal specification of distributed systems one has a choice among many different formalisms, like process algebras, temporal logics, or non-deterministic state machines. Rather than choosing a specific syntactic formalism we use a system model which is semantically motivated. This trace based model has already a tradition in the context of information flow control [McC87,JT88,ZL97, Man00a].

An *event* is an atomic action with no duration. Examples are sending or receiving a message on a communication channel, or writing data into a file. We distinguish *input events* which cannot be enforced by the system from *internal* and *output events* which are controlled by the system. However, we do *not* make the restricting assumption that input events are always enabled. At the interface, input as well as output events can be observed while internal events cannot. The possible behaviours of a system are modeled as sequences of events.

Definition 1. *An* event system *ES is a tuple* (E, I, O, Tr) *where E is a set of events, $I, O \subseteq E$ respectively are the input and output events, and $Tr \subseteq E^*$ is the set of traces, i.e. finite sequences over E. Tr must be closed under prefixes.*

Although event systems are used as system model throughout this article, our results are not limited to systems which are specified using event systems. To apply our results, it is sufficient that there exists a translation from the particular specification formalism into event systems. We illustrate such a translation by the example of state-event systems which will also be used in Section 4 where we present an unwinding theorem. State-event systems can be regarded as event systems which have been enriched by states. With this enrichment the pre-condition of an event e is the set of states in which e possibly can occur. The post-condition is a function from states to the set of possible states after the event has occurred in the respective state. The notion of state is transparent. Note that the occurrence of events can be observed while states are not observable.

Definition 2. *A state-event system SES is a tuple (S, S_I, E, I, O, T) where S is a set of states, $S_I \subseteq S$ are the initial states, E is a set of events, $I, O \subseteq E$ are the input and output events, and $T \subseteq S \times E \times S$ is a transition relation.*

A *history* of a state-event system SES is a sequence $s_1.e_1.s_2 \dots s_n$ of states and events. The set of histories $Hist(SES) \subseteq S \times (E \times S)^*$ for SES is defined inductively. If $s \in S_I$ then $s \in Hist(SES)$. If $s_1.e_1.s_2 \dots s_n \in Hist(SES)$ and $(s_n, e_n, s_{n+1}) \in T$ then $s_1.e_1.s_2 \dots s_n.e_n.s_{n+1} \in Hist(SES)$. Each state-event system $SES = (S, S_I, E, I, O, T)$ can be translated into an event system $ES_{SES} = (E, I, O, Tr_{SES})$ where the set of traces $Tr_{SES} \subseteq E^*$ results from $Hist(SES)$ by deleting states from the histories.

2.2   Flow Policies

Flow policies specify restrictions on the information flow within a system. They are defined with the help of a set $\mathcal{D}$ of *security domains*. Typical domains are e.g. groups of users, collections of files, or memory sections. We associate such a security domain $dom(e) \in \mathcal{D}$ to each event $e \in E$.

Definition 3. *A flow policy FP is a tuple $(\mathcal{D}, \leadsto_V, \leadsto_N, \not\leadsto)$ where $\leadsto_V, \leadsto_N, \not\leadsto \subseteq \mathcal{D} \times \mathcal{D}$ form a disjoint partition of $\mathcal{D} \times \mathcal{D}$ and $\leadsto_V$ is reflexive. FP is called transitive if $\leadsto_V$ is transitive and, otherwise, intransitive.*

$\not\leadsto$ is the *non-interference relation* of FP and $D_1 \not\leadsto D_2$ expresses that there must be no information flow from D_1 to D_2. Rather than having only a single interference relation $\leadsto$ to specify allowed information flow we distinguish two relations $\leadsto_V$ and $\leadsto_N$. While $D_1 \leadsto_V D_2$ expresses that events in D_1 are visible for D_2, $D_1 \leadsto_N D_2$ expresses that events from D_1 may be deducible for D_2 but must not reveal any information about other domains.

We depict flow policies as graphs where each node corresponds to a security domain. The relations $\leadsto_V$, $\leadsto_N$, and $\not\leadsto$ are respectively depicted as solid, dashed, and crossed arrows. For the sake of readability, the reflexive subrelation of $\leadsto_V$ is usually omitted. This graphical representation is shown on the left hand side of Figure 2 for the flow policy $FP1$ which consists of three domains HI (high-level input events), L (low-level events), and $H \backslash HI$ (high-level internal and output events). According to $FP1$, low-level events are visible for both high-level domains ($L \leadsto_V HI$, $L \leadsto_V H \backslash HI$). High-level inputs must not be

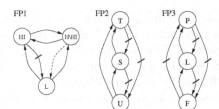

	$\mathcal{V}_{HI}$	$\mathcal{V}_L$	$\mathcal{V}_{H\backslash HI}$
$FP1$	$(H\cup L,\emptyset,\emptyset)$	$(L,H\backslash HI,HI)$	$(H\cup L,\emptyset,\emptyset)$

	$\mathcal{V}_U$	$\mathcal{V}_S$	$\mathcal{V}_T$
$FP2$	$(U,\emptyset,S\cup T)$	$(U\cup S,\emptyset,T)$	$(U\cup S\cup T,\emptyset,\emptyset)$

	$\mathcal{V}_F$	$\mathcal{V}_L$	$\mathcal{V}_P$
$FP3$	$(F,\emptyset,L\cup P)$	$(L\cup F,\emptyset,P)$	$(P\cup L,\emptyset,F)$

Fig. 2. Example flow policies and corresponding basic scenes

deducible for the low-level ($HI \not\leadsto L$). Other high-level events may be deduced (due to $H\backslash HI \leadsto_N L$). However, such deductions must not reveal any information about (confidential) high-level inputs. E.g. if each occurrence of an event $ho \in H\backslash HI$ is directly preceeded by a high-level input $hi \in HI$ then an adversary should not learn that ho has occurred because, otherwise, he could deduce that hi has occurred. Thus, if an event $e \in H\backslash HI$ closely depends on events in HI then nothing about e must be deducible for L. However, if e does not depend on confidential events from HI then everything about e may be deducible.

Traditionally, $FP1$ would be defined as a policy with two domains L, H and the policy $H \not\leadsto L$, $L \leadsto H$. This leaves it implicit that high-level internal and output events may be deducible for the low-level. Our novel distinction between $\leadsto_V$ and $\leadsto_N$ allows one to make such assumptions explicit in the flow policy.

I, O specifies the interface of a system when it is used in a non-malicious environment. This intended interface should be used when properties apart from security are specified. However, in the context of security other interfaces must be considered as well since usually not all internal events are protected against malicious access. Making a worst case assumption, we assume that internal events are observable. The view of a given domain expresses which events are visible or confidential for that domain. Formally, a *view* $\mathcal{V}$ is a triple (V, N, C) of sets of events such that the sets V, N, C form a disjoint partition of E.

Definition 4. *The view* $\mathcal{V}_D = (V, N, C)$ *for a domain* $D \in \mathcal{D}$ *in FP is defined by* $V = \bigcup\{D' \in \mathcal{D} \mid D' \leadsto_V D\}$, $N = \bigcup\{D' \in \mathcal{D} \mid D' \leadsto_N D\}$, *and* $C = \bigcup\{D' \in \mathcal{D} \mid D' \not\leadsto D\}$. *The* basic scene $\mathcal{BS} = \{\mathcal{V}_D \mid D \in \mathcal{D}\}$ *for FP contains views for all domains in* $\mathcal{D}$.

We call V the *visible*, C the *confidential*, and N the *non-confidential events* of $\mathcal{V}_D$. Only events in V are directly observable from a given view. Among the non-observable events we distinguish events in C which must be kept confidential and events in N which need not. While events in C must not be deducible, events in N may be deducible, however, such deductions must not reveal any information about confidential events in C. Note that in Definition 4 each of the sets V, N, C is constructed using one of $\leadsto_V$, $\leadsto_N$, $\not\leadsto$ (hence the indices).

Example 1. The basic scene for flow policy $FP1$ is depicted in the table on the right hand side of Figure 2. Most interesting is the view of domain L. For this domain, events in L are visible, events in HI confidential, and events in $H\backslash HI$

may be deduced (but must not reveal information about events in HI). The flow policy $FP2$ defines a multi-level security policy. $FP2$ could be used, for example, to express the security requirements of a file system with files of three different classifications: T (top secret), S (secret), and U (unclassified). While events which involve files must not be deducible for domains which have a lower classification than these files, there is no such requirement for higher classifications. E.g. a user with clearance secret must not be able to learn anything about events on top secret files but may learn about unclassified files.

Notational Conventions. Throughout this article we assume that ES denotes the event system (E, I, O, Tr), that SES denotes the state-event system (S, S_I, E, I, O, T), and that FP denotes the flow policy $(\mathcal{D}, \rightsquigarrow_V, \rightsquigarrow_N, \not\rightsquigarrow)$. The projection $\alpha|_{E'}$ of a sequence $\alpha \in E^*$ to the events in $E' \subseteq E$ results from α by deleting all events *not* in E'. We denote the set of all events in a given domain D also by the name D of the security domain and use that name in lower case, possibly with indices or primes, e.g. $d, d_1, \ldots$, to denote events in the domain. For a given view $\mathcal{V}$, we denote the components by $V_\mathcal{V}$, $N_\mathcal{V}$, and $C_\mathcal{V}$.

2.3   Formal Definitions of Information Flow

Various formal definitions of information flow have been proposed in the literature. Such a definition should accept a system as secure if and only if intuitively there is *no* information flow which violates the flow policy under consideration. The definitions of information flow which we investigate in this article follow the *possibilistic* approach. This is already implied by our choice of a system model in which only the possibility of behaviours is specified (in contrast to more complicated *probabilistic* models, e.g. [WJ90]). The possibilistic approach is compatible with non-determinism and allows us to abstract from probabilities and time.

When defining what information flow from a domain D_1 to a domain D_2 means, it is helpful to distinguish direct flow from indirect flow. *Direct flow* results from the observability of occurrences of events in D_1 from the perspective of D_2. For a given view $\mathcal{V} = (V, N, C)$ all occurrences of events in V are directly observable, i.e. for a given behaviour $\tau \in E^*$, the projection $\tau|_V$ of τ to the visible events, is observed. *Indirect information flow* results from deductions about given observations. We assume that an adversary has complete knowledge of the static system, i.e. knows the possible behaviours in Tr. This is a worst case assumption which follows the 'no security by obscurity paradigm'. From this knowledge an adversary can deduce the set $\{\tau \in Tr \mid \tau|_V = \overline{\tau}\}$ of all traces which might have caused a given observation $\overline{\tau} \in V^*$. Confidentiality can be expressed as the requirement that this *equivalence set* is big enough in order to avoid leakage of confidential information. However, the various definitions of information flow formalize this requirement by different closure conditions.

Non-inference [O'H90], for example, demands that for any trace τ the sequence $\tau|_V$ must also be a trace, i.e. $\forall \tau \in Tr.\tau|_V \in Tr$. Thus, for non-inference, all equivalence sets must be closed under projections to events in V. For a system which fulfills non-inference, an adversary cannot deduce that confidential events have occurred because every observation could have been generated by a trace in which no such events have occurred. Another possibilistic definition is *separability* [McL96]. For any two traces τ_1, τ_2 it requires that any interleaving of the confidential subsequence of τ_1 with the visible subsequence of τ_2 must, again, be a trace. Thus, every confidential behaviour is compatible with every observation. Besides non-inference and separability, many other possibilistic definitions of information flow have been proposed (e.g. [Sut86,McC87,JT88,ZL97, FM99]) which correspond to different closure conditions on the equivalence sets. In order to simplify the investigation and comparison of such definitions, uniform frameworks have been developed [McL96,ZL97,Man00a].

Our assembly kit [Man00a] allows for the uniform and modular representation of possibilistic definitions of information flow. Each such definition is expressed as a *security predicate* which is assembled from *basic security predicates* (abbreviated by BSP in the sequel) by conjunction. BSPs can be classified in two dimensions. In the first dimension, it is required that the possible observations for a given view are *not increased* by the occurrence of confidential events. Otherwise, additional observations would be possible and one could deduce from such an observation that these confidential events must have occurred. In the second dimension the occurrence of confidential events must *not decrease* the possible observations. Otherwise, any of the observations which become impossible after these events, would lead to the conclusion that the confidential events have not occurred. In applications it can be sensible to emphasize one of these dimensions more than the other one. E.g. if a system is equipped with an alarm system then taking the alarm system off line must be kept confidential for possible intruders. However, it might be less important to keep it confidential that the alarm system has not been taken off-line because this is the default situation.

For the purposes of this paper it suffices to investigate two specific BSPs, one for each dimension. <u>B</u>ackwards <u>s</u>trict <u>d</u>eletion of confidential events ($BSD_{\mathcal{V}}$) demands for a given view $\mathcal{V} = (V, N, C)$ that the occurrence of an event from C does *not add* possible observations. Considering the system after a trace β has occurred, any observation $\overline{\alpha} \in V^*$ which is possible after $c \in C$ must also be possible if c has not occurred. If the observation $\overline{\alpha}$ results from $\alpha \in (V \cup N)^*$, i.e. $\alpha|_V = \overline{\alpha}$, after c has occurred then some $\alpha' \in (V \cup N)^*$ must be possible after c has not occurred where α' may differ from α only in events from N. For a given view $\mathcal{V} = (V, N, C)$, $BSD_{\mathcal{V}}$ is formally defined as follows:

$$BSD_{V,N,C}(Tr) \equiv \forall \alpha, \beta \in E^*.\forall c \in C.((\beta.c.\alpha \in Tr \wedge \alpha|_C = \langle \rangle)$$
$$\Rightarrow \exists \alpha' \in E^*.(\alpha'|_V = \alpha|_V \wedge \alpha'|_C = \langle \rangle \wedge \beta.\alpha' \in Tr)) .$$

Note that the definition of $BSD_{\mathcal{V}}$ becomes much simpler if $N = \emptyset$, i.e.

$$BSD_{V,\emptyset,C}(Tr) \equiv \forall \alpha, \beta \in E^*.\forall c \in C.((\beta.c.\alpha \in Tr \wedge \alpha|_C = \langle \rangle) \Rightarrow \beta.\alpha \in Tr) .$$

If N is non-empty then the general definition of BSD is required for a correct handling of events in N. To allow such events in α and to allow their adaption in α' opens the spectrum from being deducible (but independent from confidential events) to being closely dependent on confidential events (but not deducible).

Backwards strict insertion of admissible confidential events ($BSIA_\mathcal{V}$) requires that the occurrence of an event from C does *not remove* possible low-level observations. α and α' are related like in BSD. The additional premise $\beta.c \in Tr$ ensures that the event c is admissible after β which is a necessary condition for dependencies of confidential events on visible events [ZL97,Man00a].

$$BSIA_{V,N,C}(Tr) \equiv \forall \alpha, \beta \in E^*.\forall c \in C.((\beta.\alpha \in Tr \wedge \alpha|_C = \langle\rangle \wedge \beta.c \in Tr)$$
$$\Rightarrow \exists \alpha' \in E^*.(\alpha'|_V = \alpha|_V \wedge \alpha'|_C = \langle\rangle \wedge \beta.c.\alpha' \in Tr))$$

Inductive definitions of BSPs like BSD and $BSIA$ were helpful to identify the two dimensions and simplified the development of unwinding conditions [Man00b]. They also provide a basis for handling intransitive policies in Section 3.

Recall that security predicates are constructed by conjoining BSPs. Each security predicate SP is a conjunction of BSPs. Often, one BSP from each dimension is taken. For example constructions of security predicates we refer to [Man00a]. Security predicates are parametric in the event system and in the flow policy. Fixing the flow policy yields a *security property* $\mathcal{SP} = (SP, FP)$.

Definition 5. *Let* $SP_\mathcal{V} \equiv BSP_\mathcal{V}^1 \wedge \ldots \wedge BSP_\mathcal{V}^n$ *be a security predicate and FP be a transitive flow policy. The event system ES satisfies* (SP, FP) *iff* $BSP_\mathcal{V}^i(Tr)$ *holds for each* $i \in \{1, \ldots, n\}$ *and for each view* $\mathcal{V}$ *in the basic scene* $\mathcal{BS}_{FP}$.

Example 2. Let $ES = (E, I, O, Tr)$ be an event system which specifies a three-level file system and $FP2$ (cf. Figure 2) be the flow policy for ES. Assume that information flow is defined by the security predicate $SP_\mathcal{V} \equiv BSD_\mathcal{V} \wedge BSIA_\mathcal{V}$. This, together with $\mathcal{D} = \{U, S, T\}$ implies that the following theorems must be proved: $BSD_{\mathcal{V}_U}(Tr)$, $BSD_{\mathcal{V}_S}(Tr)$, $BSD_{\mathcal{V}_T}(Tr)$, $BSIA_{\mathcal{V}_U}(Tr)$, $BSIA_{\mathcal{V}_S}(Tr)$, and $BSIA_{\mathcal{V}_T}(Tr)$. The indices can be instantiated according to the table in Figure 2.

3   Intransitive Information Flow

Transitive flow policies, like the ones discussed in Example 1, are very restrictive. If $F \not\leadsto P$ is required for two domains F and P then *absolutely no* information must flow from F to P. However, in practical applications it is often necessary to allow exceptions to such restrictions. Exceptions can be described by intransitive flow policies like $FP3$ (cf. Figure 2). In $FP3$, $F \not\leadsto P$ only requires that there is no information flow from F *directly* to P. Although direct information flow is forbidden, information flow via the domain L is permitted. Thus, $F \leadsto_V L$ and $L \leadsto_V P$ provide an exception to the requirement $F \not\leadsto P$. Events in F may become deducible for P if they are followed by events in L. An application for $FP3$ could be a system which consists of a printer (domain P), a labeller (L) and a file system (F). In $FP3$, $F \not\leadsto P$, $F \leadsto_V L$, and $L \leadsto_V P$ ensure that all files must be labelled before being printed. Note, that such a requirement could not be properly formalized with a transitive flow policy.

Unfortunately, intransitive flow policies have been outside the scope of definitions of information flow for non-deterministic systems. This includes the definitions investigated in [Sut86,McC87,JT88,O'H90,WJ90,McL96,ZL97] and also the BSPs which we discussed in Section 2.3 of this article. To the best of our knowledge, intransitive flow policies are outside the scope of all definitions of information flow which have been previously proposed for non-deterministic systems. The underlying problem is that these definitions cannot deal with exceptions. If a flow policy (like $FP3$) requires $F \not\leadsto P$ then these definitions require that there is *no* information flow from F to P (without exceptions).

In Section 3.1 we present further applications in which intransitive information flow is required. We illustrate the problems of previously proposed definitions of information flow with intransitive flow policies in Section 3.2 at the example of BSD. For one application we derive a specialized solution in Section 3.3 and then integrate a generalized solution into our assembly kit in Section 3.4. This allows us to represent BSPs which can cope with intransitive flow in the same uniform way as other BSPs. We evaluate our approach in Section 3.5.

3.1   More Applications of Intransitive Information Flow

Before we discuss the existing problems with intransitive flow policies we want to emphasize their practical importance by presenting typical applications for which intransitive information flow is necessary. The example of the printer/labeller/file system has already been investigated at the beginning of this section.

Another application is a communication component for connecting a system which contains classified data to an open network. In the component, a red side which has direct access to classified data and a black side which is connected to an open network are distinguished. Before a message which contains classified data may be passed from the red to the black side, the message body must be encrypted. The message header, however, may be transmitted in plaintext. This is expressed by the flow policy $FP4$ (cf. Figure 3). Events which involve the protected system are assigned domain R (red), events which model encryption domain CR (crypto), events which involve passing the header information domain BP (bypass), and events which involve the open network domain B (black). $FP4$ is an intransitive flow policy because the domains BP and CR provide exceptions to the requirement $R \not\leadsto B$.

Another application which requires an intransitive flow policy results from a modification of the three-level file system in Example 1. According to policy $FP2$ the classification of data cannot be lowered. However, the need to protect the confidentiality of data may disappear over time. For example, in order to execute

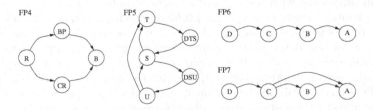

Fig. 3. More example flow policies ($\not\leadsto$ and reflexive subrelation of $\leadsto_V$ omitted)

a plan for a top secret mission, usually orders must be passed to people with lower clearance. Each of these orders reveals information about the mission plan. However, until the decision to execute the mission has been made no information about the corresponding mission plan must be revealed. This can be regarded as an example of downgrading. Policy $FP5$ in Figure 3 extends the policy $FP2$ for a three-level file system by two additional domains DTS and DSU. These domains allow for the downgrading of information from top secret to secret (domain DTS) and from secret to unclassified (DSU).

3.2   The Problem

In order to illustrate the problems which are caused by intransitive policies, we use the printer/labeller/file system as a running example. Let $ES = (E, I, O, Tr)$ be the specification of such a system and $FP3$ (cf. Figure 2) be the flow policy which shall be enforced. Hence, files may only be passed to the printer if they have been labelled before. As definition of information flow we investigate BSD.

If we pretend that intransitive flow policies could be handled like transitive ones then we had to prove $BSD_{\mathcal{V}_P}(Tr)$, $BSD_{\mathcal{V}_L}(Tr)$, and $BSD_{\mathcal{V}_F}(Tr)$ (according to Definition 5). The view of the printer illustrates the problems with intransitivity. For this view we have to prove $BSD_{\mathcal{V}_P}(Tr)$, i.e.

$$\forall \alpha, \beta \in E^*.\forall f \in F.((\beta.f.\alpha \in Tr \wedge \alpha|_F = \langle\rangle) \Rightarrow \beta.\alpha \in Tr) \ . \tag{1}$$

This requirement is too strong as the following example illustrates. Let $write(f, d)$ denote an event in which the contents of file f is replaced by data d, $label(f, d, ld)$ denote an event in which the contents d of file f is labelled with result ld, and $print(ld)$ denote an event in which the data ld is sent to the printer. Then

$$write(f_1, d_1).write(f_1, d_2).label(f_1, d_2, lab(d_2)).print(lab(d_2)) \tag{2}$$

is a possible trace of the system. We assign domains by $dom(write(\_,\_)) = F$, $dom(label(\_,\_,\_)) = L$, and $dom(print(\_)) = P$. Thus, $BSD_{\mathcal{V}_P}(Tr)$ requires

$$write(f_1, d_1).label(f_1, d_2, lab(d_2)).print(lab(d_2)) \in Tr \ . \tag{3}$$

The conclusion is (with $d_1 \neq d_2$) that the labeller must not depend on any changes to the contents of files but rather has to invent the data which it labels. This restriction is caused by the use of BSD and not by the flow policy according to which $F \rightsquigarrow_V L$ holds. In any sensible implementation of such a system the labeller would depend on the file system and, thus, the implementation would be rejected by BSD as being insecure, even if it intuitively respects $FP3$. Hence BSD is incompatible with the intransitive flow in policy $FP3$.

This example points to a general problem which is neither a peculiarity of BSD nor of this particular example. All previously proposed definitions of information flow for non-deterministic systems exclude intransitive information flow. Any system with intransitive flow would be rejected by these definitions as being insecure, even if it intuitively complies with the respective (intransitive) flow policy. This incompatibility has made it impossible to apply information flow control to non-deterministic systems when intransitive policies shall be enforced. However, intransitive flow is required by many applications (cf. the examples in Section 3.1). Thus, a limitation to transitive flow policies would be rather severe.

3.3   Towards a Solution

What is the reason for this problem? Let us revisit the printer/labeller/file system in which, according to $FP3$, events from domain F *may* become deducible through events from domain L. However, $BSD_{\mathcal{V}_P}$ (cf. formula (1)) requires that deleting the last event with domain F from a trace *must* again yield a trace, no matter whether an event with domain L occurs or not. This is the reason why BSD is too restrictive for intransitive flow policies. Formally this problem is caused by the assumption $\alpha|_F = \langle\rangle$ in formula (1). Thus, the first step towards a solution is to replace it by the stronger assumption $\alpha|_{F \cup L} = \langle\rangle$. This results in

$$\forall \alpha, \beta \in E^*.\forall f \in F.((\beta.f.\alpha \in Tr \wedge \alpha|_{F \cup L} = \langle\rangle) \Rightarrow \beta.\alpha \in Tr) . \qquad (4)$$

This modification of $BSD_{\mathcal{V}_P}$ requires that deleting events with domain F must yield a trace only if these events are not followed by any events with domain L, e.g. deleting $write(f_1, d_2)$ from trace (2) need not yield a trace. This precisely reflects the requirements of the flow policy $FP3$. According to $FP3$, events in domain F may be deduced by domain P if they are followed by events in domain L. Thus, events in L *extend* the view of P.

We now generalize this idea to arbitrary flow policies and define the notion of an *extension set*. For a given domain D, the extension set X_D contains all events which are visible to D and which possibly extend the view of D. Formally, X_D is defined by $X_D = \bigcup\{D' \in \mathcal{D} \mid D' \leadsto_{\mathcal{V}_D} D \wedge D' \neq D\}$. Generalizing formula (4) to an arbitrary view $\mathcal{V} = (V, N, C)$ and extension set X results in

$$\forall \alpha, \beta \in E^*.\forall c \in C.((\beta.c.\alpha \in Tr \wedge \alpha|_{C \cup X} = \langle\rangle)$$
$$\Rightarrow \exists \alpha' \in E^*.(\alpha'|_V = \alpha|_V \wedge \alpha'|_{C \cup X} = \langle\rangle \wedge \beta.\alpha' \in Tr)). \qquad (5)$$

If $X \cap N = \emptyset$ (which will hold in this article) then formula (5) is weaker than $BSD_{\mathcal{V}}(Tr)$. In fact, it is too weak as we will now illustrate at the flow policy $FP6$ in Figure 3 (The problem does not occur with $FP3$.). Let a, b, c, d be events respectively with domain A, B, C, D, and $Tr = \{\langle\rangle, d, b, d.b, d.b.a\}$ be a set of traces. According to Tr, a is only enabled if $d.b$ has previously occurred. Thus, an observer with view A can conclude from the observation a that d has occurred. Such deductions result in information flow from D to A through B which does not comply with the policy ($D \not\leadsto A$, $D \not\leadsto B$). Intuitively, Tr violates $FP6$. Nevertheless, formula (5) is fulfilled for each of the views $\mathcal{V}_A$, $\mathcal{V}_B$, $\mathcal{V}_C$, $\mathcal{V}_D$ and the extension sets X_A, X_B, X_C, and X_D. The reason is that the assumptions of formula (5) are not fulfilled for a trace which contains an event $x \in X$ which is not followed by any events from C. Thus, formula (5) enforces no restrictions for such a trace. However, rather than making no restrictions, it should enforce $FP7$ (cf. Fig. 3) for such traces which compared to $FP6$ additionally permits information flow from C to A. Note that information flow from D to A is *not* permitted by $FP7$. $FP7$ results from $FP6$ by combining the views of A and B.

Consequently, BSPs should be enforced for a larger set of views. Additional views result from the combination of domains. Such combinations are constructed along $\leadsto_V$, e.g. AB denotes the combination of A and B in $FP6$ which we discussed above. Other combinations are BC, CD, ABC, BCD, and $ABCD$. The resulting views which must be investigated for $FP6$ are depicted in Figure 4. Note that there are six additional views, $\mathcal{V}_{AB}$, $\mathcal{V}_{BC}$, $\mathcal{V}_{CD}$, $\mathcal{V}_{ABC}$, $\mathcal{V}_{BCD}$, and $\mathcal{V}_{ABCD}$ which are not contained in the basic scene. We will refer to the extension of basic scenes by these views as *scene*.

3.4   A Solution

The solution for intransitive information flow which we have derived for our running example can now be generalized to arbitrary systems and flow policies. The example showed that definitions of information flow like the basic security predicate *BSD* rule out intransitive flow. In order to be able to cope with intransitive policies in formula (5) we had to introduce the extension set X as additional parameter. We now present two novel BSPs: *IBSD* (*intransitive backwards strict deletion of confidential events*) and *IBSIA* (*intransitive backwards strict insertion of admissible confidential events*) which are respectively derived from *BSD* and *BSIA* but which are compatible with intransitive flow. Let $\mathcal{V} = (V, N, C)$.

$$IBSD_{\mathcal{V}}^{X}(Tr) \equiv \forall \alpha, \beta \in E^*.\forall c \in C.((\beta.c.\alpha \in Tr \wedge \alpha|_{C \cup X} = \langle\rangle)$$
$$\Rightarrow \exists \alpha' \in E^*.(\alpha'|_V = \alpha|_V \wedge \alpha'|_{C \cup X} = \langle\rangle \wedge \beta.\alpha' \in Tr))$$

$$IBSIA_{\mathcal{V}}^{X}(Tr) \equiv \forall \alpha, \beta \in E^*.\forall c \in C.((\beta.\alpha \in Tr \wedge \alpha|_{C \cup X} = \langle\rangle \wedge \beta.c \in Tr)$$
$$\Rightarrow \exists \alpha' \in E^*.(\alpha'|_V = \alpha|_V \wedge \alpha'|_{C \cup X} = \langle\rangle \wedge \beta.c.\alpha' \in Tr))$$

Apparently, *IBSD* and *IBSIA* are very similar respectively to *BSD* and *BSIA*. The only differences are that $\alpha|_C = \langle\rangle$ is replaced by $\alpha|_{C \cup X} = \langle\rangle$ and $\alpha'|_C = \langle\rangle$ by $\alpha'|_{C \cup X} = \langle\rangle$. We now state some simple facts about the validity of these new BSPs and relate them to the existing ones.

Fact 1. *Let* $\mathcal{V} = (V, N, C)$ *be a view and* $X \subseteq E$.

1. $IBSD_{\mathcal{V}}^{\emptyset}(Tr)$ $[IBSIA_{\mathcal{V}}^{\emptyset}(Tr)]$ *if and only if* $BSD_{\mathcal{V}}(Tr)$ $[BSIA_{\mathcal{V}}(Tr)]$
2. *If* $IBSD_{\mathcal{V}}^{\emptyset}(Tr)$ $[IBSIA_{\mathcal{V}}^{\emptyset}(Tr)]$ *and* $X \subseteq V$ *then* $IBSD_{\mathcal{V}}^{X}(Tr)$ $[IBSIA_{\mathcal{V}}^{X}(Tr)]$.
3. $IBSD_{V,N,\emptyset}^{X}(Tr)$ *and* $IBSIA_{V,N,\emptyset}^{X}(Tr)$ *hold.*

For intransitive policies it does not suffice to investigate the views of single domains. Rather the views of combinations of domains along $\leadsto_V$ must be considered as well. The need for the investigation of such views arises from the fact that events which are not deducible for a given domain can become deducible if they are followed by certain other events. E.g. in $FP6$, which we discussed at the

	A	B	C	D	AB	BC	CD	ABC	BCD	ABCD
V	$A \cup B$	$B \cup C$	$C \cup D$	D	$A \cup B \cup C$	$B \cup C \cup D$	$C \cup D$	$A \cup B \cup C$	$B \cup C \cup D$	$A \cup B \cup C \cup D$
N	$\emptyset$	$\emptyset$	$\emptyset$	$\emptyset$	$\emptyset$	$\emptyset$	$\emptyset$	$\emptyset$	$\emptyset$	$\emptyset$
C	$C \cup D$	$A \cup D$	$A \cup B$	$A \cup B \cup C$	D	A	$A \cup B$	$\emptyset$	A	$\emptyset$
X	B	C	D	$\emptyset$	C	D	$\emptyset$	D	$\emptyset$	$\emptyset$

Fig. 4. Basic scene and scene for $FP6$

end of the previous subsection, events in C may become deducible for A if they are followed by events in B. Events in D may also become deducible for A but this requires that they are followed by events in C *and* events in B. The following definition expresses which combinations of domains must be considered.

Definition 6. *Let $FP = (\mathcal{D}, \rightsquigarrow_V, \rightsquigarrow_N, \not\rightsquigarrow)$ be a flow policy. The set of combined domains $\mathcal{C}_{FP} \subseteq \mathcal{P}(\mathcal{D})$ for FP is the minimal set which is closed under*

1. *If $D \in \mathcal{D}$ then $\{D\} \in \mathcal{C}_{FP}$ and*
2. *if $\mathcal{D}' \in \mathcal{C}_{FP}$, $D \in \mathcal{D}$, and $\exists D' \in \mathcal{D}'.D \rightsquigarrow_V D'$ then $\mathcal{D}' \cup \{D\} \in \mathcal{C}_{FP}$.*

For intransitive policies, extended views must be considered. An *extended view* $\mathcal{X}$ is a pair $(\mathcal{V}, X)$ consisting of a view $\mathcal{V}$ and a set X of events, the *extension set*. Since extended views for combined domains must be considered, we define the extended view for sets $\mathcal{D}'$ of domains rather than for single domains.

Definition 7. *The* extended view *$\mathcal{X}_{\mathcal{D}'} = ((V, N, C), X)$ for $\mathcal{D}' \subseteq \mathcal{D}$ is defined by*

$$V = \{e \in E \mid \exists D' \in \mathcal{D}'.dom(e) \rightsquigarrow_V D'\}$$
$$N = \{e \in E \mid \not\exists D' \in \mathcal{D}'.dom(e) \rightsquigarrow_V D' \wedge \exists D' \in \mathcal{D}'.dom(e) \rightsquigarrow_N D'\}$$
$$C = \{e \in E \mid \forall D' \in \mathcal{D}'.dom(e) \not\rightsquigarrow D'\}$$
$$X = \bigcup\{D \in \mathcal{D} \mid \exists D' \in \mathcal{D}'.D \rightsquigarrow_V D' \wedge D \notin \mathcal{D}'\}$$

The scene $\mathcal{S}_{FP}$ for FP contains the extended view $\mathcal{X}$ for each $\mathcal{D}' \in \mathcal{C}_{FP}$.

We now state some facts about scenes which directly follow from Definition 7.

Fact 2. *Let $\mathcal{V} = (V, N, C)$ be a view and $X \subseteq E$.*

1. *If $(\mathcal{V}, X) \in \mathcal{S}_{FP}$ then $X \subseteq V$.*
2. *If FP is transitive then $(\mathcal{V}, X) \in \mathcal{S}_{FP} \Rightarrow (\mathcal{V}, \emptyset) \in \mathcal{S}_{FP}$.*

We now define when a security property with an arbitrary flow policy is satisfied.

Definition 8. *Let $ISP_{\mathcal{V}}^X \equiv IBSP_{\mathcal{V}}^{X,1} \wedge \ldots \wedge IBSP_{\mathcal{V}}^{X,n}$ be an intransitive security predicate and FP be a flow policy. An event system ES satisfies (ISP, FP) iff $IBSP_{\mathcal{V}}^{X,i}(Tr)$ holds for each $i \in \{1, \ldots, n\}$ and for each $\mathcal{X}$ in the scene $\mathcal{S}_{FP}$.*

Definition 5 stated when an event system satisfies a given security property with a transitive flow policy. Clearly, Definition 5 and Definition 8 should be equivalent for the special case of transitive flow policies. The following theorem ensures that this, indeed, holds for *IBSD* and *IBSIA*.

Theorem 1. *Let FP be a transitive flow policy.*

1. *$BSD_{\mathcal{V}}(Tr)$ holds for each view $\mathcal{V}$ in the basic scene $\mathcal{BS}_{FP}$ if and only if $IBSD_{\mathcal{V}}^X(Tr)$ holds for each extended view $(\mathcal{V}, X)$ in the scene $\mathcal{S}_{FP}$.*
2. *$BSIA_{\mathcal{V}}(Tr)$ holds for each view $\mathcal{V}$ in the basic scene $\mathcal{BS}_{FP}$ if and only if $IBSIA_{\mathcal{V}}^X(Tr)$ holds for each extended view $(\mathcal{V}, X)$ in the scene $\mathcal{S}_{FP}$.*

Proof. We prove the first proposition. The second can be proved analogously.

$\Rightarrow$) Assume that $BSD_{\mathcal{V}}(Tr)$ holds for each $\mathcal{V} \in \mathcal{BS}_{FP}$. With Fact 1.1 we receive $IBSD_{\mathcal{V}}^{\emptyset}(Tr)$. Fact 1.2 implies $IBSD_{\mathcal{V}}^{X}(Tr)$ for all $X \subseteq V_{\mathcal{V}}$. From Fact 2.1 we conclude that $IBSD_{\mathcal{V}}^{X}(Tr)$ holds for all $(\mathcal{V}, X) \in \mathcal{S}_{FP}$.

$\Leftarrow$) Assume that $IBSD_{\mathcal{V}}^{X}(Tr)$ holds for each $(\mathcal{V}, X) \in \mathcal{S}_{FP}$. Fact 2.2 implies that if $IBSD_{\mathcal{V}}^{X}(Tr)$ then $IBSD_{\mathcal{V}}^{\emptyset}(Tr)$. From Fact 1.1 we conclude that $BSD_{\mathcal{V}}(Tr)$ holds for each $\mathcal{V} \in \mathcal{BS}_{FP}$. $\qquad\square$

3.5   The Solution Revisited

Theorem 1 demonstrates that *IBSD* and *IBSIA* are, respectively, extensions of *BSD* and *BSIA* to the intransitive case. For the special case of transitive flow policies the corresponding BSPs are equivalent. However, in the intransitive case the new BSPs are less restrictive. E.g. *IBSD* accepts systems with intransitive flow as secure wrt. a given (intransitive) flow policy if they intuitively comply with this policy while *BSD* rejects any system with intransitive flow as insecure. It remains to be shown that *IBSD* (and *IBSIA*) rejects systems with intransitive flows as insecure if they intuitively violate the (intransitive) policy under consideration. We demonstrate this by several examples. Note that a formal proof of such a statement is impossible since the point of reference is our intuition.

We use the 3-level file system with 2 downgraders from Section 3.1 and flow policy $FP5$ from Figure 3 as running example. For each case, which we investigate, we assume that the system is intuitively insecure in a certain sense and then argue that *IBSD* indeed rejects the system as insecure.

Example 3. Let us first assume that downgrading events never occur. Thus there should not be any intransitive information flow in the system even though the flow policy is intransitive. Moreover, assume that domain U can deduce that events from T have occurred. Thus, the system is intuitively insecure. However, since events from $DSU \cup DTS$ do not occur in traces, *IBSD* enforces the same restrictions (for the extended views $\mathcal{X}_{TSU}$, $\mathcal{X}_{SU}$, $\mathcal{X}_{U}$ in $\mathcal{S}_{FP5}$) as *BSD* does for the views $\mathcal{V}_{T}$, $\mathcal{V}_{S}$, $\mathcal{V}_{U}$ in the basic scene of $FP2$. Thus, *IBSD* rejects such a system as insecure wrt. $FP5$ because *BSD* would reject the system for $FP2$.

Let us next assume that only downgrading events in DSU never occur. Thus, there should not be any information flow from T or S to U and information may flow from T to S only via DTS. Firstly, assume that the system is intuitively insecure because U can deduce the occurrence of events from $T \cup S$. *IBSD* rejects such a system as insecure. The reason is that *BSD* would reject such a system for the (transitive) flow policy which is defined by $U \rightsquigarrow_{V} S$, $U \rightsquigarrow_{V} DTS$, $U \rightsquigarrow_{V} T$, $S \rightsquigarrow_{V} DTS$, $S \rightsquigarrow_{V} T$, $DTS \rightsquigarrow_{V} S$, $DTS \rightsquigarrow_{V} T$, $T \rightsquigarrow_{V} S$, $T \rightsquigarrow_{V} DTS$, $S \not\rightsquigarrow U$, $DTS \not\rightsquigarrow U$, and $T \not\rightsquigarrow U$. Secondly, assume that the system is intuitively insecure because S can deduce the occurrence of events from T which are not followed by any events from DTS. Thus, there must be a sequence $\beta.t.\alpha \in Tr$ with $t \in T$, $\alpha|_{DTS \cup U} = \langle\rangle$ such that $\beta.\alpha \notin Tr$. However, this would violate $IBSD_{\mathcal{X}}$ for the extended view $\mathcal{X} = ((DTS \cup S \cup DSU \cup U, \emptyset, T), DTS)$.

Let us now assume that no downgrading events in DTS occur. If such a system is intuitively insecure then it is rejected by *IBSD* as insecure. The argument can be carried out along the same lines as in the previously discussed case where no events in *DSU* occurred. The case which remains to be discussed is the general case in which events from all domains may occur. In this case more kinds of (intuitive) insecurity must be investigated. However, for each of these insecurities one can argue along the same lines as before that *IBSD* correctly rejects any corresponding (intuitively insecure) system.

4   Verification Conditions

Unwinding conditions simplify the proof that a system satisfies a given security property. While BSPs like *IBSD* or *IBSIA* are expressed in terms of *sequences of events*, unwinding conditions are stated in terms of the pre- and postconditions of *single events*. In [Man00b], we have presented such unwinding conditions for a large class of BSPs which can be applied for transitive flow policies. By an *unwinding theorem* we have guaranteed that these unwinding conditions are correct. The development of unwinding conditions for *IBSD* and *IBSIA* along the same lines is a straightforward task. However, in general, the unwinding conditions must be proved for all combinations of domains (cf. Definition 6) rather than only for single domains (as in [Man00b]). Interestingly, this can be optimized for the special case of flow policies with $\leadsto_N = \emptyset$. In this section we demonstrate that it suffices for such policies to prove the unwinding conditions for single domains only, thus, reducing the verification burden considerably.

In order to express unwinding conditions we use state-event systems (cf. Definition 2) and make the same assumptions as in [Man00b], i.e. there is only one initial state s_I and the effect of events is deterministic (the transition relation T is functional). However, state-event systems are still non-deterministic because of the choice between different events and since internal events may cause effects.

The *successor set* for $s_1 \in S$ and $e \in E$ is $succ(s_1, e) = \{s_2 \in S \mid (s_1, e, s_2) \in T\}$. According to our simplification, $succ(s_1, e)$ has at most one element. We extend $succ$ to sets $S_1 \subseteq S$ of states and sequences $\alpha \in E^*$ of events:

$$succ(S_1, \alpha) \equiv \text{if } \alpha = \langle \rangle \text{ then } S_1 \text{ else let } e.\alpha' = \alpha \text{ in } succ(\bigcup_{s \in S_1} succ(s, e), \alpha') .$$

A sequence α of events is *enabled*, denoted by $enabled(\alpha, s)$, in a state s if and only if $succ(s, \alpha) \neq \emptyset$. A state s is *reachable*, denoted by $reachable(s)$, if and only if there is a sequence α of events such that $s \in succ(s_I, \alpha)$.

Our unwinding conditions are based on preorders (unlike most other approaches which are based on equivalence relations, e.g. [RS99]). For a discussion of the advantage of using preorders we refer to [Man00b]. A *domain possibility preorder* for a domain $D \in \mathcal{D}$ is a reflexive and transitive relation $\ltimes_D \subseteq S \times S$. Our intuition is that $s_1 \ltimes_D s_2$ should imply that every D-observation which is possible in s_1 should also be possible in s_2. We now construct a relation $\sqsubseteq_{\mathcal{D}'}$ with a corresponding idea for combined domains, i.e. $s_1 \sqsubseteq_{\mathcal{D}'} s_2$ should imply that every $\mathcal{D}'$-observation which is possible in s_1 should also be possible in s_2.

Definition 9. *Let $\mathcal{D}' \subseteq \mathcal{D}$ be a set of domains and $(\ltimes_D)_{D \in \mathcal{D}}$ be a family of domain possibility preorders on S. We define a relation $\sqsubseteq_{\mathcal{D}'} \subseteq S \times S$ by*

$$s_1 \sqsubseteq_{\mathcal{D}'} s_2 \equiv \forall D \in \mathcal{D}'.s_1 \ltimes_D s_2 .$$

Each of our unwinding conditions $wosc_D$, lrf_D, and lrb_D is defined in terms of single events. $wosc_D$ (weak output step consistency) demands that $s_1 \ltimes_D s_1'$ implies that any event $e' \in D$ which is enabled in s_1 is also enabled in s_1'. Moreover, if $s_1 \ltimes_D s_1'$, $s_1 \ltimes_{dom(e)} s_1'$, and an event $e \in E$ is enabled in s_1 then e is also enabled in s_1' and the preorder is preserved after the occurrence of e, i.e. $s_2 \ltimes_D s_2'$ holds for the successor states. If an event $e \in E$ is enabled in a state s with resulting state s' then $s' \ltimes_D s$ is required for all domains D with $dom(e) \not\leadsto D$ by lrf_D (locally respects forwards). Similarly, lrb_D (locally respects backwards) requires $s \ltimes_D s'$.

$$wosc_D : \forall s_1, s_2, s_1' \in S.\forall e \in E.((s_1 \ltimes_D s_1' \wedge (s_1, e, s_2) \in T \wedge s_1 \ltimes_{dom(e)} s_1')$$
$$\Rightarrow \exists s_2' \in S.(s_2' \in succ(s_1', e) \wedge s_2 \ltimes_D s_2')$$

$$lrf_D: \forall s, s' \in S.\forall e \in E.((dom(e) \not\leadsto D \wedge reachable(s) \wedge (s, e, s') \in T) \Rightarrow s' \ltimes_D s)$$

$$lrb_D: \forall s \in S.\forall e \in E.((dom(e) \not\leadsto D \wedge reachable(s) \wedge enabled(e, s))$$
$$\Rightarrow (\exists s' \in S.(s, e, s') \in T \wedge s \ltimes_D s'))$$

The following lemma shows that $\ltimes_D$ and $\sqsubseteq_{D'}$ respectively are orderings on D- and D'-observations of arbitrary length when $wosc_D$ holds for all $D \in \mathcal{D}$.

Lemma 1. *If SES fulfills $wosc_D$ for $\ltimes_D$ for all $D \in \mathcal{D}$ then*

$$\forall s_1, s_1' \in S.\forall \mathcal{D}' \subseteq \mathcal{D}.\forall \alpha \in (\textstyle\bigcup_{D \in \mathcal{D}'} D)^*.((s_1 \sqsubseteq_{\mathcal{D}'} s_1' \wedge enabled(\alpha, s_1))$$
$$\Rightarrow \exists s_n \in succ(s_1, \alpha), s_n' \in succ(s_1', \alpha).s_n \sqsubseteq_{\mathcal{D}'} s_n').$$

Proof. We prove the lemma by induction on the length of α. In the base case, i.e. for $\alpha = \langle \rangle$, the proposition holds trivially. In the step case, i.e. for $\alpha = e_1.\alpha'$, we assume $s_1 \sqsubseteq_{\mathcal{D}'} s_1'$ and $enabled(\alpha, s_1)$. Thus, there is a state $s_2 \in succ(s_1, e_1)$ with $enabled(\alpha', s_2)$. Let $D \in \mathcal{D}'$ be arbitrary. $s_1 \ltimes_D s_1'$, $(s_1, e, s_2) \in T$, $s_1 \ltimes_{dom(e)} s_1'$, and $wosc_D$ imply that there is a $s_2' \in S$ with $(s_1', e, s_2') \in T$ and $s_2 \ltimes_D s_2'$. Since D is arbitrary, we receive $s_2 \sqsubseteq_{\mathcal{D}'} s_2'$. $s_2 \sqsubseteq_{\mathcal{D}'} s_2'$, $enabled(\alpha', s_2)$, and the induction hypothesis imply the lemma. $\square$

Theorem 2 (Unwinding Theorem). *Let FP be a security policy with a finite set $\mathcal{D}$ of disjoint domains and $\leadsto_N = \emptyset$.*

1. $\forall D \in \mathcal{D}.(wosc_D \wedge lrf_D) \Rightarrow \forall \mathcal{D}' \in \mathcal{C}_{FP}.IBSD_{\mathcal{V}_{\mathcal{D}'}}^{\mathcal{X}_{\mathcal{D}'}}(Tr)$
2. $\forall D \in \mathcal{D}.(wosc_D \wedge lrb_D) \Rightarrow \forall \mathcal{D}' \in \mathcal{C}_{FP}.IBSIA_{\mathcal{V}_{\mathcal{D}'}}^{\mathcal{X}_{\mathcal{D}'}}(Tr)$

Proof. We prove the first proposition. The second can be proved analogously.

Let $\mathcal{D}' \in \mathcal{C}_{FP}$ and $\mathcal{X}_{\mathcal{D}'} = ((V, N, C), X)$. Let $\beta.c.\alpha \in Tr$ be arbitrary with $c \in C$ and $\alpha|_{C \cup X} = \langle \rangle$. We have to show that $\beta.\alpha \in Tr$ holds. $\beta.c.\alpha \in Tr$ implies that there are states $s_1, s_2 \in S$ with $s_1 \in succ(s_I, \beta)$, $(s_1, c, s_2) \in T$, and $enabled(\alpha, s_2)$. We choose $D' \in \mathcal{D}'$ arbitrarily. $dom(c) \not\leadsto D'$ because of $c \in C$ (cf. Definition 7). From $lrf_{D'}$ we conclude $s_2 \ltimes_{D'} s_1$. This implies $s_2 \sqsubseteq_{\mathcal{D}'} s_1$ because D' was chosen arbitrarily. Finally, Lemma 1 implies that $enabled(\alpha, s_1)$, i.e. $\beta.\alpha \in Tr$. $\square$

The unwinding theorem ensures that a proof of the unwinding conditions implies that the flow policy is respected, i.e. the unwinding conditions are correct. Interestingly, it suffices to prove the unwinding conditions *for single domains* (rather than for combined domains) for policies with $\leadsto_N = \emptyset$. In order to show that the unwinding conditions are not too restrictive a completeness result would be desirable. In the transitive case such a completeness result can be achieved if $\leadsto_N = \emptyset$ holds (cf. [Man00b]). For the intransitive case no general completeness result holds unless one makes the additional (quite artificial) assumption that different sequences of events always result in different states. However, we plan to investigate these issues more closely in future research.

5   Related Work

The approach to information flow control in non-deterministic systems which we have proposed in this article is compatible with intransitive information flow. All previously proposed approaches are either restricted to deterministic systems or cannot cope with intransitive information flow.

Information flow control based on non-interference was first introduced by Goguen and Meseguer in [GM82]. This original version of non-interference was incompatible with intransitive information flow. In order to overcome this shortcoming for channel control policies, a special case of intransitive flow policies, an *unless* construct was introduced in [GM84]. However, this *unless* construct did not capture the intuition of intransitive flow. It accepted many intuitively insecure systems as being secure. This weakness of the *unless* construct has some similarities to the weakness which would result from using basic scenes (rather than scenes) together with *IBSD* and *IBSIA* in our approach (cf. Section 3.3). The first satisfactory formal account of intransitive information flow was proposed by Rushby [Rus92]. The key for the compatibility with intransitive flow in his solution was the use of an *ipurge* function instead of the traditional *purge* function. A similar notion of non-interference was proposed by Pinsky [Pin95]. All work discussed so far in this section uses deterministic state machines as system model and, thus, is not directly applicable to non-deterministic systems. Another approach (based on determinism in CSP) which is more restrictive than Rushby's approach has been proposed by Roscoe and Goldsmith [RG99]. It detects some insecurities which are not detected by Rushby's approach but, since it is based on determinism, an extension to distributed systems will be difficult.

The first generalization of non-interference to non-deterministic systems was non-deducibility as proposed by Sutherland [Sut86]. Subsequently, various other generalizations (e.g. [McC87,O'H90,McL96,ZL97]) have been proposed and there seems not to be one single optimal generalization of non-interference for non-deterministic systems. To our knowledge, none of these generalizations can cope with intransitive information flow. The system models underlying the different approaches are either state based, like non-deterministic state machines, or event based, like event systems or the process algebras CSP or CCS. The various event based models differ in which specifications they consider as semantically equivalent. While event systems use trace semantics, i.e. specifications are equivalent if they describe the same set of traces, CSP uses failure divergence semantics (early versions used trace semantics), and CCS uses weak bisimulation. Trace semantics identify more specifications than failure divergence or weak bisimulation semantics, however, none of these semantics is in general superior to one of the others. For an overview on these and other semantics we refer to [vG90, Sch00].

Today, Rushby's approach to information flow control with intransitive policies seems to be the most popular one for deterministic systems. It is feasible for real applications as has been demonstrated by case studies like [SRS+00]. However, Roscoe and Goldsmith [RG99] recently identified a shortcoming of Rushby's solution which we explain at the example of the flow policy $FP5$ (cf. Figure 3). Let us assume that the file system has two files f_{t1} and f_{t2} which are both assigned the security domain T and that there are two downgrading events dts_1 and dts_2 with domain DTS which should respectively downgrade information only about either f_{t1} or f_{t2}. Note, however, that no such requirement is expressed in $FP5$. Consequently, certain insecurities, e.g that dts_1 downgrades information about f_{t1} as well as f_{t2}, cannot be detected by applying Rushby's intransitive non-interference. Roscoe and Goldsmith argued that this would be a shortcoming of Rushby's definition of information flow. However, we do not fully agree with this critique (although it points to an important problem) because it does not identify a problem which is specific to this definition of information flow. Either a security requirement can be expressed by a flow policy (e.g. by assigning different domains $T1$ and $T2$ respectively to f_{t1} and f_{t2}) or the concept of flow policies alone is not adequate and, hence should be combined with some other concept which further restricts possible downgrading of information. In the first case, Rushby's intransitive non-interference can be applied but, in the second case, flow policies are insufficient, in general. Intransitive flow policies restrict *where* downgrading can occur but do not allow further restrictions on *what* may be downgraded. How to specify *good downgrading* is an important question which, however, is unresolved for deterministic as well as for non-deterministic systems. In our opinion the contribution of [Rus92] has been to allow information flow control to be applied for restricting *where* downgrading can occur.

Unwinding conditions for information flow control (in the intransitive case) have been proposed by Rushby [Rus92] and Pinsky [Pin95]. While Rushby's unwinding conditions are based on equivalence relations, Pinsky's unwinding conditions are based on equivalence classes (β-families in his terminology). Both authors proved unwinding theorems which ensure the correctness of their unwinding conditions and also present completeness results. However, the completeness results are limited to the special case of transitive policies (in [Pin95] this restriction results from the assumption $SA(\text{basis}_\pi(z), \alpha) \subseteq \text{view}(\text{state\_action}(z, \alpha))$ in the proof of the corollary on page 110).

6   Conclusion

When using information flow control in real applications it is often necessary to allow for certain exceptions to the restrictions of information flow. Such exception can be expressed by intransitive flow policies. The incompatibility of all previously proposed approaches for information flow control in *non-deterministic systems* with intransitive policies created a major gap which has prevented the migration of research results on information flow control into practice. In this article, we have constructed a bridge over this gap by proposing an approach to information flow control which is compatible with intransitive flow and which can be applied to non-deterministic systems. We have argued that our approach only accepts systems as secure if they are intuitively *secure wrt. a given flow policy* (cf. Section 3.5). Thus, the same kind of insecurities are detected as in Rushby's approach for *deterministic systems*. Consequently, our approach also suffers from the limitations identified in [RG99]. However, these are limitations of flow policies in general (cf. Section 5). Although the properties of our solution are similar to the ones of Rushby's solution, our formalization differs considerably. This is a necessary difference because our work is based on a different system model, i.e. event systems, which is compatible with non-determinism while Rushby's state machines are deterministic.

We have integrated our approach to information flow control for intransitive flow policies into our previously proposed assembly kit [Man00a]. To us it was very appealing that this did not require major changes to the assembly kit but only the definition of novel BSPs. The unwinding conditions we have presented are also similar to the ones for the transitive case [Man00b]. We are confident that the presented approach provides a suitable basis for applying information flow control to distributed systems. Our approach is the first proposal which can be used for such systems in the context of intransitive information flow. However, we neither claim that this is the only solution nor that it is the optimal one. In order to improve this solution further research will be useful which, in our opinion, should be driven by experiences from case studies. We plan to experiment with our approach in case studies in future work.

Acknowledgments. This work benefited from discussions with Dieter Hutter and Axel Schairer. The author would like to thank Serge Autexier and Alexandra Heidger for many valuable comments on the presentation.

References

[FM99]   Riccardo Focardi and Fabio Martinelli. A Uniform Approach to the Definition of Security Properties. In *FM'99 – Formal Methods (vol. 1)*, LNCS 1708, pages 794–813. Springer, 1999.

[GM82]   J. A. Goguen and J. Meseguer. Security Policies and Security Models. In *Proceedings of the IEEE Symposium on Security and Privacy*, pages 11–20, Oakland, CA, April 26–28 1982.

[GM84]   J. A. Goguen and J. Meseguer. Inference Control and Unwinding. In *Proceedings of the IEEE Symposium on Security and Privacy*, pages 75–86, Oakland, CA, April 29–May 2 1984.

[JT88]   Dale M. Johnson and F. Javier Thayer. Security and the Composition of Machines. In *Proceedings of the Computer Security Foundations Workshop*, pages 72–89, Franconia, NH, June 1988.

[Man00a]   Heiko Mantel. Possibilistic Definitions of Security – An Assembly Kit –. In *Proceedings of the IEEE Computer Security Foundations Workshop*, pages 185–199, Cambridge, UK, July 3–5 2000. IEEE Computer Society.

[Man00b]   Heiko Mantel. Unwinding Possibilistic Security Properties. In *European Symposium on Research in Computer Security (ESORICS)*, pages 238–254, LNCS 1895, Toulouse, France, October 4–6 2000. Springer.

[McC87]   Daryl McCullough. Specifications for Multi-Level Security and a Hook-Up Property. In *Proceedings of the IEEE Symposium on Security and Privacy*, pages 161–166, Oakland, CA, April 27–29 1987.

[McL96]   John McLean. A General Theory of Composition for a Class of "Possibilistic" Security Properties. *IEEE Transaction on Software Engineering*, 22(1):53–67, January 1996.

[O'H90]   Colin O'Halloran. A Calculus of Information Flow. In *Proceedings of the European Symposium on Research in Computer Security (ESORICS)*, pages 147–159, Toulouse, France, October 24–26 1990.

[Pin95]   Sylvan Pinsky. Absorbing Covers and Intransitive Non-Interference. In *Proceedings of the IEEE Symposium on Security and Privacy*, pages 102–113, Oakland, CA, May 8–10 1995.

[RG99]   A.W. Roscoe and M.H. Goldsmith. What is intransitive noninterference? In *Proceedings of the 12th IEEE Computer Security Foundations Workshop*, pages 228–238, Mordano, Italy, June 28–30 1999.

[RS99]   P.Y.A. Ryan and S.A. Schneider. Process Algebra and Non-interference. In *Proceedings of the 12th IEEE Computer Security Foundations Workshop*, pages 214–227, Mordano, Italy, June 28–30 1999.

[Rus92]   John Rushby. Noninterference, Transitivity, and Channel-Control Security Policies. Technical Report CSL-92-02, SRI International, 1992.

[Sch00]   Steve Schneider. *Concurrent and real-time systems : the CSP approach.* John Wiley, Chichester, England ; New York, 2000.

[SRS+00]   G. Schellhorn, W. Reif, A. Schairer, P. Karger, V. Austel, and D. Toll. Verification of a Formal Security Model for Multiapplicative Smart Cards. In *European Symposium on Research in Computer Security (ESORICS)*, pages 17–36, LNCS 1895, Toulouse, France, October 4–6 2000. Springer.

[Sut86]   D. Sutherland. A Model of Information. In *9th National Computer Security Conference*, September 1986.

[vG90]   R.J. van Glabbeek. The Linear Time – Branching Time Spectrum. In *Proceedings of CONCUR'90, Theories of Concurrency: Unification and Extensions*, pages 278–297, LNCS 458. Springer, 1990.

[WJ90]   J. Todd Wittbold and Dale M. Johnson. Information Flow in Nondeterministic Systems. In *Proceedings of the IEEE Symposium on Research in Security and Privacy*, pages 144–161, Oakland, CA, May 1990.

[ZL97]   Aris Zakinthinos and E.S. Lee. A General Theory of Security Properties. In *Proceedings of the IEEE Symposium on Security and Privacy*, pages 94–102, Oakland, CA, May 4–7 1997.

A Rigorous Approach to
Modeling and Analyzing E-Commerce Architectures*

Vasu S. Alagar and Zheng Xi

Department of Computer Science
Concordia University
Montreal, Quebec H3G 1M8, Canada
alagar@cs.concordia.ca

Abstract. The main issue in the development of agent-based architectures for E-Commerce applications is to produce specifications that describe precisely the functional and temporal properties of agents and their roles. An agent should be able to dynamically change its behavior according to the context of its collaboration. Interactions among agents must remain secure and consistent with E-Commerce business rules. Formal modeling, and analysis of agent-based architectures promote understanding and reasoning on these issues. This paper presents a theory of agents, and a formal description of an E-Commerce architecture. The visual and formal descriptions are complementary, leading to validation and verification prior to committing to an implementation.

1 Introduction

This paper focuses on a formal basis for architectural descriptions for E-Commerce automation. E-Commerce is a distributed environment in which a large number of participants, who can be classified as customers, brokers, and service providers, collaborate to conduct transactions. Dependability and security are two major concerns for the developers and participants of an E-Commerce system. A sound architecture that simplifies the construction of large complex E-Commerce system and withstands the design changes forced by a steady stream of new requirements can serve as a testbed for simulating E-Commerce games, and evaluating evolving business strategies. Griss and Letsinger [8] suggest game theory approach as a means of complementing formal analysis and simulation to understand E-Commerce systems. However, formal analysis cannot be done on the current architectural descriptions for E-Commerce applications because they are typically expressed only informally, in terms such as "client-server organization", "layered systems", and "blackboard architecture". Diagrammatic representations, in terms of box-and-line drawings showing the global organization of computational components and their interactions lack the semantics for a formal analysis. More detailed descriptions that accompany diagrammatic descriptions are traditionally provided by Module Interconnection Languages (MILs) and Interface Definition Languages (IDLs). which focus on *implementation* relationships among parts of the system. Although such descriptions

---

* This work is supported by grants from Natural Sciences and Engineering Research Council, Canada

J.N. Oliveira and P. Zave (Eds.): FME 2001, LNCS 2021, pp. 173–196, 2001.
© Springer-Verlag Berlin Heidelberg 2001

are essential, neither of them is suitable for analyzing the internal consistency, communication patterns, and the behavior of business strategies in an architecture. The distinction between abstract architectural descriptions and implementation-dependent descriptions, and the need to describe architectures at a level above their implementation details are clearly brought out in [5]. This is the primary motivation for our work.

1.1   Basic Concepts

Three distinct building blocks of a software architecture are *components*, *connectors*, and *configurations*. The term *agent* is used in E-Commerce community to refer to software components that run continuously, exist as semi-autonomous entitities, and render various services in fulfilling a transaction. Although there is no consensus definition of an agent, Chen etal [7] gives the definition: "Software agents are personalized, continuously running and semi-autonomous, driven by a set of beliefs, desires, and intentions (BDI)." For us, an agent is an encapsulated system with the following properties:

1. an agent is a software component designed to achieve certain *goals*;
2. an agent is either autonomous or always responds to a stimulus from its environment, which is a collection of agents;
3. an agent has sufficient computational power, *resources*, and *knowledge* to complete the *tasks* assigned to it and deliver results within specified time bounds;
4. an agent communicates with other agents in its environment through messages at its *ports*, where a port is an abstraction of an access point for a bidirectional communication.
5. an agent can dynamically change its behavior whenever the context changes.

We define an E-Commerce architecture as the triple ⟨ *agents, connectors, configurations* ⟩. A connector is a communication link between two agents and is characterized by the protocols of message exchange along that connector. A configuration defines the interaction among a finite number of agents with connectors established for communication. That is, agents in an architectural configuration communicate along connectors and collaboratively achieve a task. Each configuration models a role. An agent may participate in different roles. A configuration might also include sub-configurations, where each sub-configuration is an architectural configuration. The system of interacting agents in a role is secure if every message is responded within the specified time bound; if no time bound is specified, the response should take effect instantaneously. A system is safe if every role in the system is secure. An important goal of formalizing E-Commerce architecture is to enable a rigorous analysis of the high-level view of the system to ensure that the desired properties of the specified business models and strategies are not violated.

The architecture proposed in this paper is quite generic and can be adapted to a broader application domain. For instance, in [2,3] real-time reactive systems are specified using this architecture.

2   A Theory of Agent-Based Systems

The *global context* for an E-Commerce system is a tuple $GC = \langle \mathcal{A}, \mathcal{R}, \mathcal{P} \rangle$, where

- $\mathcal{A}$ is a finite set of agent-types, where each agent type is parameterized with a finite set of port types,
- $\mathcal{R} = M \cup m$, where M is a set of messages for interactions among agents, $m = \{create, dispatch, engage, disengage, dispose, (silent)\}$ is the set of *control messages*, $M \cap m = \emptyset$, and
- $\mathcal{P}$ is a finite set of applications.

A port type defines a set of messages that can occur at a port of that type. The symbol @ is used to introduce port types. An agent of the agent type $A[L] \in \mathcal{A}$, where L is the list of port types, is created by instantiating each port type in L by a finite number of ports and assigining the ports to the agent. Any message defined for a port type can be received or sent through any port of that type. For instance, $A_1[p_1, p_2 : @P; q_1, q_2, q_3 : @Q]$, and $A_2[r_1 : @P; s_1, s_2 : @Q]$ are two agents of the agent type $A[@P, @Q]$. The agent A_1 has two ports p_1 and p_2 of type $@P$, and three ports q_1, q_2, q_3 of type $@Q$. Both p_1 and p_2 can receive or send messages of type $@P$; the ports q_1, q_2, and q_3 can receive and send messages of type $@Q$. Sometimes the port parameters of agents are omitted in our discussion below. Messages may have parameters.

An E-Commerce system based on GC consists of a finite set A of agents $A_1, \ldots A_n$, where each A_i is an instance of some agent type in $\mathcal{A}$. An *incarnation* of an agent A_i is a copy of A_i with a name different from the name of any other agent in the system, and with its port types renamed, if necessary. Several incarnations of the same agent can be created and distinguished by their *id*s. Letting ids to be positive integers, $A_1[1]$, $A_1[2]$ are two distinct incarnations of the agent A_1. Every incarnation of an agent retains the same port interfaces. For instance $A_1[1][a_1, a_2 : @P; b_1, b_2, b_3 : @Q]$ and $A_1[2][p_1, p_2 : @P; q_1, q_2, q_3 : @Q]$ are two distinct incarnations of the agent $A_1[p_1, p_2 : @P; q_1, q_2, q_3 : @Q]$. The contexts and behavior of incarnations of an agent A_i are in general independent. The context for the incarnation $A_i[k]$ is defined by the set of applications in which it can participate. Hence the context of an incarnation effectively determines the agents with whom it can interact and the messages it can use in such an interaction. For instance, the incarnations $A_1[1][a_1, a_2 : @P; b_1, b_2, b_3 : @Q]$ and $A_1[2][p_1, p_2 : @P; q_1, q_2, q_3 : @Q]$ can be plugged into two distinct configurations for two distinct applications in a system. In the rest of the paper we use the term agent to mean incarnation as well.

2.1   Modes of Agents

All agents share the *modes* shown in Fig. 1 (a) and have identical mode change behavior. When an agent is created its ports, id, and attributes are initialized and is in mode initial. This mode is the result of the *create* message. An internal (silent) transition takes the agent to the mode wait, where it is waiting to act. An agent can be in wait mode either at "home" or in a remote site. In either case it can be sent to another site through the message *dispatch*, where it is in mode dispatched. When the message *engage* is received the mode of the agent changes from dispatched to remote_run, where it performs the remote task. After completing the task it automatically returns to **pause** mode. If there are no more tasks to be performed at that site, it will receive the message *disengage* and subsequently the mode is changed to **wait**. An agent in **wait** mode in a remote site may be reclaimed by the message *recall*. Upon receiving this message the agent changes its mode to **retract**. The message *engage* changes the mode from **retract** to **local_run**. After completing the task the agent automatically goes into the **pause** mode. When an agent in mode **wait** receives the message *dispose* it changes its mode to **disposed**. The set $Modes$ includes all the modes shown in Fig. 1 (a). The transition function $next\_mode : Modes \times m \rightarrow Modes$ is a partial function providing the new mode for a given mode and a control message.

The function $which\_mode? : A \rightarrow Modes$ provides the mode of an agent at any time in the system. The inverse relation $which\_mode^{-1}$ provides a set of tuples tu for a given mode $v \in Modes$ such that $dom(tu) \subset A$ is the set of agents that are in mode v. The *situation* of an agent A_i is the pair $\langle A_i, which\_mode?(A_i) \rangle$. The *setting* of a system is a collection of situations:

$$setting \triangleq \{ \langle A_i, which\_mode?(A_i) \rangle \mid A_i \in A \}$$

A set $INI \subset \{ s \mid s \in \mathbb{P} setting \}$ defines several possible initializations of systems with agents from A, and modes and control messages as defined in Fig. 1(a).

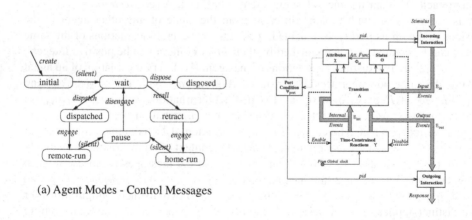

(a) Agent Modes - Control Messages

(b) Anatomy of an Agent

Fig. 1. Agent Modes and Agent Behavior

2.2   Anatomy of an Agent

The resources in possession of an agent are formalized by *abstract data types*. We have chosen Larch traits [9] to specify resources. The main advantage in using Larch is that the traits can be developed independently and incrementally and can be imported to different agents participating in different applications. The functional and time constrained behavior of an agent is modeled by a state machine, extended with ports, hierarchical states, and transitions governed by clocks and guards. The state machine of an agent imports the traits that specify the resources for the agent. The traits and other attributes that can be modified in a state of the state machine is defined by an attribute function, which for a given state provides the attributes that can be modified in that state.

Figure 1(b) shows the running behavior of an agent when it is activated by a message. The running behavior depends on the context, defined by the set of messages that can be received from or sent to other agents in a specific application. The filled arrows in the Fig. indicate flow of events. A message is either an input event or an output event. An internal event corresponds to a task that the agent has to perform by itself. Messages are received and sent at the ports. All ports of a specific type can receive or send only those messages associated with that type. Every agent has a finite set of attributes. The static attributes are the resources at its disposal, tables of information and rules for encoding knowledge, and functions to fulfill the tasks that it has to perform. The dynamic attributes are those that are required for its interaction in different contexts. When an agent is created, a finite number of ports for each port type defined for it are created and attributes are initialized. The states (Θ), transitions (Λ), and time constraints (Υ) in Fig. 1 (b) describe the behavior of a running agent in fulfilling a task in a specific context. A message from the context is received only when the internal state of the running agent, and the port-condition where the message is received satisfy the specification for state change. When the incoming message causes a state transition it may also involve a computation. A computation updates the agent's state and attributes, shown by the arrow labeled with 'Att.Func.' The dotted arrow connecting the block of computation to that of time-constrained reaction signifies the enabling of one or more future actions due to a computation. Based on the clock, an outstanding event is fired by the agent, thereby generating either an internal event or a message (interaction message or control message).

The significant features of the abstraction are the following:

1. An agent can be specified individually.
2. Several agent instances and incarnations can be created from an agent type. Each agent owns the resources inherited from the agent type.
3. The specification hides information and promotes controlled refinement. Two types of refinements are possible:
   a) New modes and messages may be added. An existing mode can be refined into submodes.
   b) The anatomy that describes the behavior of an agent can be refined by adding more resources, or by refining states, or strengthening time constraints.
4. Timing constraints are encapsulated, thereby precluding an input event from being a time constrained event. That is, an agent has no control over the times of occurrences of input events since they are under the control of its environment.
5. In a collaborative multi-tasking environment an agent has complete choice over selecting the port (and hence the external agent) to communicate.

2.3 Formal Notation for Agents

Each agent $A_i \in A$ is an extended finite state machine given in the form of a 8-tuple ($\mathcal{E}$, Θ, $\mathcal{X}$, $\mathcal{L}$, Φ, Λ, Υ, $\circ$) such that:

1. $\mathcal{E}$ is a finite set of messages (events) and includes the silent-event tick. The set $\mathcal{E} - \{\text{tick}\}$ is partitioned into three disjoint subsets: the set $\mathcal{E}_{int}$ is the set of events internal to the agent; the set $\mathcal{R} - \mathcal{E}_{int}$ is the disjoint union of $\mathcal{E}_{in}$, the set of input messages, and $\mathcal{E}_{out}$, the set of output messages. Each $e \in (\mathcal{E}_{in} \cup \mathcal{E}_{out})$, is associated with a unique port-type. Every input event is decorated with the symbol '?' and every output message is decorated with '!'.

2. Θ is a finite set of states. $\theta_0 \in \Theta$, is the *initial* state.

3. $\mathcal{X}$ is a finite set of typed attributes. The attributes can be of one of the following two types: i) an abstract data type specification of a data model; ii) a port reference type.

4. $\mathcal{L}$ is a finite set of LSL traits introducing the abstract data types used in $\mathcal{X}$.

5. Φ is a function-vector (Φ_s, Φ_{at}) where,

   a) $\Phi_s : \Theta \to 2^\Theta$ associates with each state θ a set of states, possibly empty, called *substates*. A state θ is called *atomic*, if $\Phi_s(\theta) = \emptyset$. By definition, the initial state θ_0 is atomic. For each non-atomic state θ, there exists a unique atomic state $\theta^* \in \Phi_s(\theta)$, called the entry-state.

   b) $\Phi_{at} : \Theta \to 2^\mathcal{X}$ associates with each state θ a set of attributes, possibly empty, called the *active* attribute set.

6. Λ is a finite set of *transition specifications*. A transition specification $\lambda \in \Lambda$, is a three-tuple $\langle (\theta, \theta') ; e(\varphi_{port}); \varphi_{en} \Longrightarrow \varphi_{post} \rangle$; where:

   a) $\theta, \theta' \in \Theta$ are the source and destination states of the transition;

   b) event $e \in \mathcal{E}$ labels the transition; φ_{port} is an assertion on the attributes in $\mathcal{X}$ and a reserved variable pid, which signifies the identifier of the port at which an interaction associated with the transition can occur. If $e \in \mathcal{E}_{int} \cup \{\text{tick}\}$, then the assertion φ_{port} is absent and e is assumed to occur at the null-port $\circ$.

   c) φ_{en} is the enabling condition and φ_{post} is the postcondition of the transition. φ_{en} is an assertion on the attributes in $\mathcal{X}$ specifying the condition under which the transition is enabled. φ_{post} is an assertion on the attributes in $\mathcal{X}$, primed attributes in $\Phi_{at}(\theta')$ and the variable pid and it implicitly specifies the data computation associated with the transition.

7. Υ is a finite set of *time-constraints*. A timing constraint $\upsilon_i \in \Upsilon$ is a tuple $(\lambda_i, e'_i, [l, u], \Theta_i)$ where,

   a) $\lambda_i \neq \lambda_s$ is a transition specification.

   b) $e'_i \in (\mathcal{E}_{out} \cup \mathcal{E}_{int})$ is the *constrained event*.

   c) $[l, u]$ defines the minimum and maximum response times.

   d) $\Theta_i \subseteq \Theta$ is the set of states wherein the timing constraint υ_i will be ignored.

The language for describing an agent is shown in Fig. 2. The functions *Ports*, *Events*, and *States* are defined for A, the set of agents in the system, which for a given agent $A_i \in A$ respectively provide the ports, events, and states defined in the state machine description of the agent A_i.

2.4   Operational Semantics of an Agent

An agent responds to every message it receives. Every message is a triple of the form $\langle e, p_i, t \rangle$, denoting that the message e occurs at time t, at a port p_i. The *status* of an agent at any instant t is a tuple $\mathcal{OS} = (\theta; a; \mathcal{R})$, where the current state θ is a simple state of the agent, a is the assignment vector (showing the values for the attributes), and $\mathcal{R}$

Agent $< identifier >$ [$< porttypes >$]
    Events:
    States:
    Attributes:
    Traits:
    Attribute-Function:
    Transition-Specifications:
    Time-Constraints:
end

Subsystem $< identifier >$
    Include:
    Instantiate:
    Configure:
end

Fig. 3. Template for System Configuration Specification

Fig. 2. Template for Specifying Agent Types

is the vector of triggered requests not yet fulfilled. A *computational step* occurs when the agent with status $(\theta; a; \mathcal{R})$, receives a message $\langle e, p_i, t \rangle$ and there exists a transition specification that can change the status of the agent. A computation c of an agent A_i is a sequence of alternating statuses and messages, $\mathcal{OS}_0 \overset{\langle e_0, p_0, t_0 \rangle}{\rightarrow} \mathcal{OS}_1 \overset{\langle e_1, p_1, t_1 \rangle}{\rightarrow} \dots$. We denote by $\mathcal{SS}$ the set of statuses of agents in A, and define the function $what\_status?$: $A \rightarrow \mathcal{SS}$ which for a given agent A_i provides the status of the agent at the time of invoking the function $what\_status?$.

Two agents communicate through events which differ only in their decorations: that is, the message $e!$ sent by one agent is received as $e!$ by the other agent engaged in the communication. For simplicity in design, we assume that message exchanges *synchronize*, causing a simultaneous status change in the two agents interacting through the message. Hence, the behavior of two agents that collaborate to complete a transaction is given by the synchronous product machine of the state machines corresponding to the agents.

2.5 Connectors and Configurations

A configuration is an active setting with communication links between compatible ports of interacting objects. Two ports p and q are compatible, written $compatible(p, q)$, if the set of input messages at one port is equal to the set of output messages at the other port:

$$\mathcal{E}_{in}(p) = \mathcal{E}_{out}(q); \mathcal{E}_{in}(q) = \mathcal{E}_{out}(p)$$

The composition operator $\leftrightarrow$ is a symmetric and irreflexive binary relation on the ports of agents, serving as the connector for ports associated with the agents. If the port p of agent A_i is connected to one of its compatible port q of agent A_j then $A_i.@p \leftrightarrow A_j.@q$ or equivalently $\langle A_i.@p, A_j.@q \rangle \in \leftrightarrow$. When a message is exchanged through the link connecting two agents, the agents change their statuses simultaneously.

The syntax for *System Configuration Specification* is shown in Fig. 3. The Include section lists imported subsystems. Agents with a finite number of ports for each port type are listed in the Instantiate section. The Configure section defines port links between interacting objects; it contains every entry in the relation $\leftrightarrow$.

At any instant, a configuration $\mathbb{C}$ is a 4-tuple $\langle X, \leftrightarrow, what\_status?, which\_mode? \rangle$ where X is a set of agents, $\leftrightarrow$ is the connector relation on the ports of agents in X, $what\_status?$ gives the status for every agent in X, and the function $which\_mode?$ gives the mode for each agent in X. The configuration changes due to message interactions. So, we denote the set of agents in a configuration $\mathbb{C}$ by $agents(\mathbb{C})$.

An initial configuration $\mathbb{C}_0$ is one for which $\{\langle A_i, which\_mode?(A_i) \rangle \mid A_i \in agents(\mathbb{C}_0)\} \in INI$ is true. We assume that every agent in the initial configuration $\mathbb{C}_0$ is in its initial mode and initial status; that is, every agent is in its initial state, with its attribute vector initialized, and the list of outstanding requests is empty. A system, starting from the initial configuration undergoes changes due to message requests, resulting in a sequence of configurations. Whenever a computational step in an agent is completed causing the status change of that agent, the configuration changes. Similarly, whenever the mode of an agent changes, the configuration changes.

Let $e(\mathbb{C}_{j-1}) \in \mathcal{R}$ denote the set of messages that can possibly happen in configuration $\mathbb{C}_{j-1}$. A request in $e(\mathbb{C}_{j-1})$ can be regarded as a vector $\boldsymbol{\sigma}$ of messages of length $k > 0$, where each entry in the vector is a triple of the form $\langle A_u, A_i, \sigma \rangle$ representing the message σ from agent A_u to A_i. A valid request should satisfying the following conditions:

$\forall v, 1 \leq v \leq k, \boldsymbol{\sigma}[v] = \langle A_u, A_i, \sigma \rangle$ satisfies only one of the following conditions:

1. internal message:

$$u = i \wedge \sigma = \langle e, p, t \rangle \wedge e \in M \Rightarrow A_i \in agents(\mathbb{C}_{j-1}) \wedge e \in \mathcal{E}_{int}(A_i) \wedge p = \circ$$

2. external message or control message:

$$u \neq i \wedge \sigma = \langle e, p, t \rangle \wedge e \in \mathcal{R} \Rightarrow A_i \in agents(\mathbb{C}_{j-1}) \wedge A_u \in agents(\mathbb{C}_{j-1})$$

$$\wedge\, p \in ports(A_i) \wedge \neg(e \in \mathcal{E}_{int}(A_i) \wedge e \in \mathcal{E}_{int}(A_u))$$

$$\wedge\, e \in \mathcal{E}_{in}(p) \wedge \exists q \in ports(A_u) \bullet (e \in \mathcal{E}_{in}(q) \wedge \langle A_u.@q, A_i.p \rangle \in \leftrightarrow)$$

Every message in a request $\boldsymbol{\sigma}$ is uniquely utilized by only one agent in $\mathbb{C}_{j-1}$. After the tasks involved in the request $\boldsymbol{\sigma}$ are completed, the configuration $\mathbb{C}_{j-1}$ changes to its successor configuration $\mathbb{C}_j = \langle agents(\mathbb{C}_j), \leftrightarrow', what\_status', which\_status' \rangle$. That is,

$$\mathbb{C}_{j-1} \xrightarrow{\sigma} \mathbb{C}_j$$

$\forall w, 1 \leq w \leq k$, the components of the tuple $\mathbb{C}_j$ are calculated as follows: let $\boldsymbol{\sigma}[w] = \langle A_u, A_i, \sigma \rangle$, where $\sigma = \langle e, p, t \rangle$.

1. $i = u \wedge e \in (M \wedge \mathcal{E}_{int}(A_i))$. The status change for the agent A_i is

$$(\boldsymbol{\theta}[i], \bar{X}[i], \bar{R}[i]) \xrightarrow{\sigma} (\boldsymbol{\theta}'[i], \bar{X}'[i], \bar{R}'[i])$$

as defined by the operational semantics of A_i; there is no change in other components of $\mathbb{C}_{j-1}$:

$$what\_status?' = what\_status? \oplus \{A_i \rightarrow (\boldsymbol{\theta}'[i], \bar{X}'[i], \bar{R}'[i])\}$$

$$which\_mode?' = which\_mode?$$

$$agents(\mathbb{C}_j) = agents(\mathbb{C}_{j-1})$$

$$\leftrightarrow' = \leftrightarrow$$

2. $i = u \wedge e = (silent) \in m$. Only the mode of A_i changes:

$$what\_status?' = what\_status?$$

$$which\_mode?' = which\_mode? \oplus \{A_i \rightarrow next\_mode(which\_mode(A_i), \boldsymbol{\sigma}[i])\}$$

$$agents(\mathbb{C}_j) = agents(\mathbb{C}_{j-1})$$

$$\leftrightarrow' = \leftrightarrow$$

3. $i \neq u$ and e is an external message. The status change occurs simultaneously for the agents A_i and A_u, where $A_i.@p_l \leftrightarrow A_u.@q_l$ holds in configuration $\mathbb{C}_{j-1}$. The status changes are defined by the operational semantics:

$$(\boldsymbol{\theta}[i], \bar{X}[i], \bar{R}[i]) \xrightarrow{\sigma} (\boldsymbol{\theta}'[i], \bar{X}'[i], \bar{R}'[i])$$

as defined in the transition specification of the agent A_i labelled by σ;

$$(\boldsymbol{\theta}[u], \bar{X}[u], \bar{R}[u]) \xrightarrow{\sigma} (\boldsymbol{\theta}'[u], \bar{X}'[u], \bar{R}'[u])$$

as defined in the transition specification of the agent A_u labelled by σ; the modes of A_i and A_u do not change:

$$what\_status?' = what\_status? \oplus \{A_i \rightarrow (\boldsymbol{\theta}'[i], \bar{X}'[i], \bar{R}'[i])\}$$

$$\oplus \{A_u \rightarrow (\boldsymbol{\theta}'[u], \bar{X}'[u], \bar{R}'[u])\}$$

$$which\_mode?' = which\_mode?$$

$$agents(\mathbb{C}_j) = agents(\mathbb{C}_{j-1})$$

$$\leftrightarrow' = \leftrightarrow$$

4. $i \neq u$ and $e \in m$ is not a silent transition.
   4.1 $e = create$: An incarnation $A_i[id]$ of the agent A_i is created, and its mode is set to initial. The new agent is added to the set of agents for the next configuration:

$$\mathbb{C}_j = \mathbb{C}_{j-1} \cup \{A_i[id]\}$$

$$which\_mode?' = which\_mode? \oplus \{A_i[id] \rightarrow initial\}$$

$$what\_status?' = what\_status? \oplus \{A_i[id] \rightarrow (\theta_0; \boldsymbol{a}_0; \emptyset)\}$$

$$\leftrightarrow' = \leftrightarrow$$

4.2 $e = dispatch$: The message has no effect if $which\_mode?(A_i) \neq wait$. If $which\_mode?(A_i) = wait$, $\mathbb{C}_j$ is defined as follows:

$$\mathbb{C}_j = \mathbb{C}_{j-1} \setminus \{A_i\}$$

A_i is attached to the configuration in the remote site - see [3.3] below for calculating $\leftrightarrow'$.

$$which\_mode?' = which\_mode? \oplus \{A_i \rightarrow dispatched\}$$

$$what\_status?' = what\_status?$$

4.3 $e = recall$: The message has no effect if $whic\_mode?(A_i) \neq wait$. If $whic\_mode?(A_i) = wait$, $\mathbb{C}_j$ is defined as follows:

$$\mathbb{C}_j = \mathbb{C}_{j-1} \cup \{A_i\}$$

A_i is attached to the configuration in the home site:

$$ports\_to\_attach = \{p_l \mid p_l \in ports(A_k) \wedge A_k \in agents(\mathbb{C}_{j-1})\}$$

$$\leftrightarrow' = \leftrightarrow \oplus \{\langle p_l, q_k \rangle \mid p_l \in ports\_to\_attach \wedge q_k \in ports(A_i)$$

$$\wedge compatible(p_l, q_k)\}$$

$$what\_status?' = what\_status?$$

$$which\_mode?' = which\_mode? \oplus \{A_i \rightarrow retract\}$$

4.4 $e = disengage$: The message has no effect if $which\_mode(A_i) \neq pause$. If $which\_mode(A_i) = pause$, $\mathbb{C}_j$ is defined as follows:

$$\mathbb{C}_j = \mathbb{C}_{j-1} \setminus \{A_i\}$$

A_i is removed from the current configuration:

$$ports\_to\_remove = \{p_l \mid p_l \in ports(A_k) \wedge A_k \in agents(\mathbb{C}_{j-1})$$

$$\wedge (\exists q_k \in ports(A_i) \bullet \langle p_l, q_k \rangle \in \leftrightarrow)\}$$

$$\leftrightarrow' = \leftrightarrow \setminus ports\_to\_remove$$

$$what\_status?' = what\_status? \oplus \{A_i \rightarrow (\theta_0; a_0; \emptyset)\}$$

$$which\_mode?' = which\_mode? \oplus \{A_i \rightarrow wait\}$$

4.5 $e = dispose$; The message has no effect if $which\_mode(A_i) \neq wait$. If $which\_mode(A_i) = wait$, then $\mathbb{C}_j$ is defined as follows:

$$\mathbb{C}_j = \mathbb{C}_{j-1} \setminus \{A_i\}$$

$$which\_mode?' = which\_mode? \oplus \{A_i \rightarrow disposed\}$$

$$\leftrightarrow' = \leftrightarrow$$

$$what\_status?' = what\_status?$$

3   Specification of an E-Commerce Architecture - An Example

We develop the formal specification of an E-Commerce system consisting of four agents User, EBroker, Merchant, and Bank who collaborate in negotiated on-line transactions. Many other specific applications can be obtained by adapting business rules and strategies on the high-level architecture shown in Fig. 4(a). We assume the following business pattern of event-driven transactions in this model:

> The user provides the address of a webpage to an electronic broker(E-broker), who in turn contacts the respective merchant, receives a confirmation from the merchant and gives the message that the webpage is available for the user to view. The user can browse the page for product information, select the products and for each selected product enter the quantity needed and the price per unit that he is willing to pay. The user submits this offer for negotiation to the E-broker. The E-broker executes a risk analysis to determine whether or not the proposed price is acceptable. The E-broker's negotiation strategy depends upon the total number of a particular item requested by several clients at that stage of negotiation, the extent of risk to profit ratio involved in bidding a price to the clients. The E-broker gives the order form to the user if the bidding proposed by the E-broker is accepted. The user may still decide not to buy the product. However, if the user completes the order form and provides the credit card information, he is bound to buy the product in the total quantity entered in the order form. The E-broker submits the order form and credit card information of the user to the merchant whose webpage was used in the transaction, and requests the merchant for an invoice. The merchant gives the client information to the bank, who processes the credit card payment. After receiving a confirmation from the bank the merchant ships the product to the user.

Table 1. Knowledge, Goals and Tasks of Agents

Agent Name	Knowledge	Goal	Task
User	Products	Best Buy	Interact with E-Brokers
EBroker	Products Negotiation Strategies	Service Provider Profit Making Timely Response to clients Client Satisfaction	Interact with Users Interact with Merchants
Merchant	Products	Service Provider Generate Invoice	Interact with EBrokers Interact with Bank
Bank	Accounts	Service Provider Check Credits Charge Account	Interact with Merchant

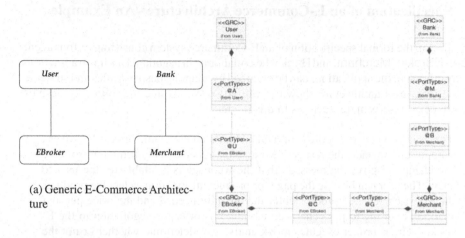

(a) Generic E-Commerce Architecture

(b) Agent Types and Port Types

Fig. 4. High-Level Architecture Diagrams

Table 2. EBroker Events with Port Type @U (User)

Events	Meaning	Parameters
BrowseAdd? (idle → getProduct)	Receives the request from user with web address to browse product information	(uid, url)
AddressError! (browseFailed → idle)	Sends the message to user that the product is not found.	
Page! (browseSucceed → idle)	Sends the product information to requested user.	(uid, productName, description, unitPrice, mid, pid)
Item? (idle → startNegotiation)	Receives desired price for the products and the quantity user wants to buy.	(uid, quantity, negoUnitPrice)
Confirmed! (negoResult→ idle)	Sends the message to user that the proposed price is accepted.	(uid, quantity, negoUnitPrice)
NotConfirmed! (negoResult → idle)	Sends the message to user that the proposed price is not accepted.	
Purchase? (idle → startInvoice)	Receives the account information and shipping information from user when user decides to buy the products.	(uid, userName, SIN, userAddress, bankName, creditCard, shippingInfo)
InvoiceFailed! (failure → idle)	Sends the message to user that the invoice is not generated successfully.	
ReceiveInvoice! (negoResult→ idle)	Sends the message to user that the invoice is generated successfully and the final purchase is made.	(uid, invoiceID)

3.1 Visual Models

Visual UML models are constructed following the methodology outlined in [3]. A formal justification for UML extensions is given in [10]. From the architecture shown in Fig. 4(a) we determine the agent types and port types for each agent type. From the description of the problem we extract the messages for communication, and partition the messages, creating port-types. For instance, the EBroker agent type requires two port types: one for communication with the User agent and the other for communication with the Merchant

Table 3. EBroker Events with Port Type @C (Merchant)

Events	Meaning	Parameters
GetProductInfo! (getProduct → waitProduct)	Sends the request to merchant to get product information.	(uid, url)
ProductNotFind? (getProduct → browseFailed)	Receives the message from merchant that the requested product is not found.	
ProductInfo? (getProduct → browseSucceed)	Receives the message that the product is found and its information.	(uid, productName, description, unitPrice, mid, pid)
GenerateInvoice! (startInvoice → askMerchant)	Sends the customer's account and shipping information to mechant to generate invoice.	(uid, quantity, negoUnitPrice, userName, SIN, userAddress, bankName, creditCard, shippingInfo)
Unsuccessful? (askMerchant → failure)	Receives the message that the invoice is not generated successfully.	
Successful? (askMerchant → succeed)	Receives the message that the invoice is generated successfully.	(uid, invoiceID)

agent. The agents' knowledge, goals, and tasks are next determined from the application domain and problem description. These are shown in Table 1.

We refine the high-level architecture shown in Fig. 4(a) by adding the port-type information to each agent. The refined model is shown in Fig. 4(b). We further refine the model of each agent by including abstract attributes that model the resources, and knowledge-base for the agent. Table 2 and Table 3 describe the meaning of events and their parameters.

The state machine description of an agent gives its behavior when the mode is either local-run or remote-run. Fig. 5 shows the state machines for the agents. To illustrate the usefulness of time constraints we have specified time constraints for **EBroker** actions. In general **Merchant** and **Bank** agents should also respect timeliness, and appropriate time constraints can be introduced in their specifications.

A successful transaction is conducted by the agents in the following manner. The E-Commerce system is initiated with the message *BrowseAdd* from a user to the broker. Both **User** and **EBroker** agents synchronize on this event: the agent **User** goes to *active* state, the agent **EBroker** goes to the state *getProduct*. The other agents do not change their states. The agent **EBroker** sends the message *GetProductInfo* to the **Merchant** agent within 2 units of time from the instant of receiving the message *BrowseAdd*, and they both simultaneously change their states to *waitProduct*, and *product* respectively. The **Merchant** agent responds to the agent **EBroker** with the message *ProductInfo* which cause them to simultaneously change their states to *idle*, and *browseSucceed*. Within 2 units of time of receiving the webpage from the merchant the **EBroker** communicates to the **User** agent with the message *page*, causing them to simulataneously change their states to *idle* and *readPage*. This completes the first phase of a successful user interaction, where the user has received a web page for browsing.

The user may decide to exit or may enter the next phase of transaction by initiating the message *Item* to the agent **EBroker**. In the later case, they synchronize and change their states to *wait* and *startNegotiation*. The user continues to wait until the **EBro-ker** agent completes a sequence of internal computations triggered by the internal events ⟨*AddStatistic, TotalQuantity, GetMinPrice, GetRiskBalance, CalculateAcceptablePrice*⟩. All brokers share a table of information on user requests. Each entry in the table is a tuple containing *userid, merchantid, productid, quantity_requested* and *priceofferred*. Based on this table of information and a formula for risk-profit analysis, the broker determines a price of a product. We have included Larch traits and introduced variables of the types corresponding to the Larch traits to abstractly specify the above functionalities. Appendix I shows the LSL traits used by EBroker.

After completing the risk-profit analysis, the offer made by the user is either accepted or rejected by the agent EBroker. The decision to accept or reject the price offer is communicated to the user within the time interval [t+5, t+8], where t is the time at which the message *item* was received by the broker. For a successful transaction, the message *Confirmed* is exchanged between the User and EBroker agents, causing their simultaneous transitions to the states conﬁrmation and *idle*. This completes the second phase of successful transaction. At this instance, the User agent is in state *confirmation* and the other agents are in idle states.

The user can exit from the system without making a purchase at this stage. The product is purchased by the user and the invoice is received in the next and final phase of the transaction. The message *Purchase* is sent by the agent User to the agent EBroker, and the User agent goes to *waitinvoice* state where it waits until receiving the message *ReceiveInvoice* from the agent EBroker. The EBroker agent communicates with Merchant agent through the message *GenerateInvoice* and they simultaneously change their states to *askMerchant* and *getInvoice*. At this instant, the User is in state *waitinvoice*, the agent EBroker is in state *askMerchant*, the agent Merchant is in state *getinvoice*, and the agent Bank is in state *idle*. The states of User and EBroker do not change until the agents Merchant and Bank collaborate to produce the invoice.

To produce the invoice, the agent Merchant sends the message *GetMerchantAcc* to the agent Bank, receives back the reply *SucceedMerchantAcc*, and then responds through the message *Charge*. At the end of this sequence of message exchanges, they reach the states *startCharge* and *chargeAcc*. The Merchant agent waits in state *startCharge* until the Bank agent completes a sequence of internal computations and sends the message *SucceedAtCharge* to it. Upon receiving this message, the Bank agent goes to *idle* state, the Merchant agent goes to *succeed* state. After completing the internal computation to record the invoice, the *Merchant* agent communicates to EBroker through the message *Successful* and their states to *idle*, and *succeed*. At this instance, the agents Bank and Merchant are in their *idle* states, the agent EBroker is in state *succeed*, and the agent User is in state *waitinvoice*. The agent EBroker records the commission earned in this transaction within 2 time units of receiving the message *ReceiveInvoice* and sends the invoice to the User. Having sent the invoice, the agent EBroker goes to its *idle* state. The agent User executes the internal message *Exit* and goes into its *idle* state.

Figure 6 shows the architecture of an e-commerce subsystem with three users, one E-broker, two merchants and three banks. Each instance of User type models a user with one port of type @A to communicate with an agent of EBroker type. The E-broker agent in the subsystem is an instance of EBroker agent type having three ports of type @U, one port for each user; the two ports of type @M are for communication with the merchants in the system. Each merchant agent in the system is an instance of Merchant agent type with a port of type @G for communicating with the broker agent, and three ports of type @B to communicate with the banks in the system. The agents are linked through connectors at their respective compatible ports for communication. For instance, the port @$A1$ of user $U1$ is linked to the port @$U1$ of the E-broker $E1$. That link is not shared by any other agent. Consequently, the architecture specification ensures secure communication.

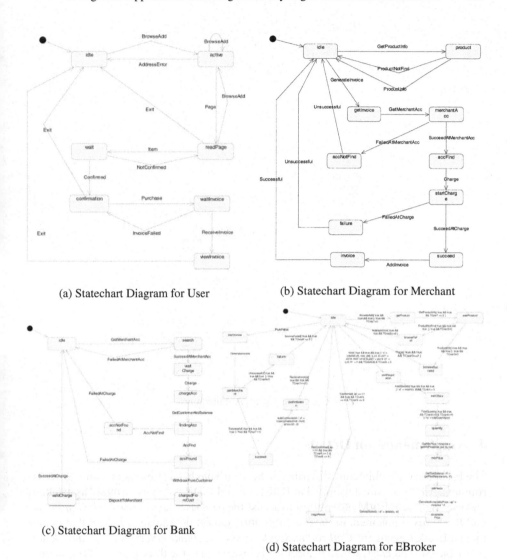

(a) Statechart Diagram for User

(b) Statechart Diagram for Merchant

(c) Statechart Diagram for Bank

(d) Statechart Diagram for EBroker

Fig. 5. Class Diagrams

3.2   Formal Specifications

Formal specifications conforming to the syntax in Fig. 2 can be composed directly from the class diagrams and state machine descriptions of the agents. Alternately, one can use the tool developed recently [11]. This tool translates the visual models into formal specifications, in the syntax described in Section 2. The translator is designed in such a way as to emphasize the correct information flow between the corresponding visual and formal components. The textual specifications can be type checked and analyzed for semantic consistency using the interpreter [12]. Appendix II shows the formal specifications generated by the translator from the state machine diagrams of the agents, and from the subsystem architecture shown in Fig. 6.

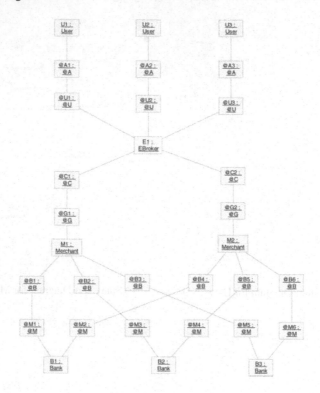

Fig. 6. Subsystem Architecture

4   Implementation Details

The E-commerce architecture described in Section 3 has been implemented in Unix environment. All classes are developed in JDK 1.1.6 and JSDK 2.0. It uses mysql as database and uses twz1jdbcForMysql library to access the database. Java classes *Merchant.class* and *Bank.class* implement the agents Merchant and Bank. The three classes that implement EBroker agent are *GetProductServlet.class*, *NegotiationServlet.class* and *GenerateInvoiceServlet.class*, which respectively correspond to the three phases of transaction described in Section 3.

1. *GetProductServlet.class* gets the product information requested by the user and displays the product information to the user.
2. *NegotiationServlet.class* gets the negotiation request from the user, executes the negotiation process and gives the negotiation results to the user.
3. *GenerateInvoiceServlet.class* gets the final purchase request from user, requests the merchant to generate invoice and sends the final invoice to the user in success.

The implementation of agents strictly conforms to their state machine descriptions.

A user chooses a product name through the HTML file, *Main.htmln* and submits the request to view detailed product information, such as, product description and unit price. When the request is submitted, the system loads *GetProductServlet.class*, one of the EBroker classes, and runs it. Several copies of this program may run at one time when prompted by different user requests. *GetProductServlet.class* will parse the parameters passed by user and search for the product by calling *Product.class*. *Product.class* will establish a mysql database connection and execute the sql statement to get the complete product information from the database. If the product information is found, *Product.class* will pass it to *GetProductServlet.class*, which in turn displays it to the user.

The user starts negotiation with E-broker after viewing the product information by entering the desired unit price and quantity of the product. E-broker loads *Negotiation-Servlet.class* and executes it. The class *NegotiationServlet.class* parses the parameters sent by user, establishs a mysql database connection and saves the request in a database table using *Statistic.class*. *NegotiationServlet.class* waits for a certain time interval(as specified), then it will call *Statistic.class* again to get the total quantity of the product requested by all the users who are negotiating with the EBroker system. *Negotiation-Servlet.class* takes the total quantity and product ID to *Rule.class* to get the minimum acceptable price. *NegotiationServlet.class* divides the user requested quantity by the total quantity, call it as risk-percentage, then it calls *Risk.class* to get risk factor. The higher risk-percentage implies a lower risk factor. Then, the *NegotiationServlet.class* calculates the acceptable price as product ($minimum price \times risk factor$). Then, the entry for this user is deleted from the database. Finally, it compares the user's requested price with the acceptable price. If the former one is less than the later one, the EBroker informs the user that the price offerred is not acceptable. Otherwise, it informs the user that the offer is accepted and gives the order form to user to fill out.

After viewing the result of the negotiation, the user may or may not submit the order form. If the user submits the order form with personal information and bank information filled out, it means that the user wishes to make the final purchase. After the user submits the order form, EBroker loads *GenerateInvoiceServlet.class* and executes it. It sends the information to *Merchant.class*, which sends part of information, such as, total amount charged and customer's account ID, to the bank. *Bank.class* searches the database to validate the customer's account. If the customer's account is valid and has enough credit, *Bank.class* will charge the amount from customer's account, deposit it into merchant's account and send the confirmation to the merchant. After *Merchant.class* receives the confirmation from bank, it records the information in the invoice table of the database, and sends the successful message to EBroker. In the case of successful transaction, *GenerateInvoiceServlet.class* records the commission for agent in the commission table of the database by calling *Commisssion.class*. Finally, it displays the invoice to the user. Appendix III shows the Java Servelet code that parses parameters received, and JDBC codes for establishing the database connection and query processing.

5 Conclusion

Architecture-based software development offers great potentials for software reuse. Formal descriptions of architectures are necessary for understanding a high-level view of the system and the properties implied in it. Such an understanding promotes the reuse of agents in different contexts, as well as the reuse of agent architectures as a whole. To allow reuse at different levels of abstraction we have used a two-tier notation, adapted from [3,10] studied for real-time reactive systems. The translator [11] mechanically translates the visual models into a formal notation. We have an animation tool [6] to simulate and validate real-time reactive systems, and currently adapting it to animate and debug the E-Commerce architectural specifications. An important future goal is to model user characteristics as knowledge owned by broker agents, and simulate E-Commerce games using the animator. In particular, simulated experiments may be conducted on the formal model to explore and reason about many of the issues raised in [8]:

1. **Effectiveness** For a given set of customer characteristics what business strategy is most effective, in the sense of optimal service time and cost for the seller?
2. **Stability** Which business strategy is least affected by small variations in customer characteristics? What is the impact on effectiveness due to small changes in business rules?
3. **Timeliness** Does every customer get service within a reasonable amount of waiting time under realistic load variations and business rules?

Agent specifications can be refined in two tiers: in one tier modes and messages can be added; in another tier, states and events may be added, timing constraints may be strengthened, datatype abstractions can be refined, and new port types can be added. The two-tier refinement provides flexibility and controlled design of E-Commerce system from its initial architural design. In addition, reuse is enhanced which in turn promotes software productivity. These issues need deeper study and experimentation.

Ensuring specific properties at the architecture level is of little value unless they are also ensured in the resulting implementation. The current Java implementation does not handle control messages, and allows only single threads of computation. Although the program can be run simultaneously at different stations, lack of concurrency in the computation models imposes some limitations.

References

1. R. Achuthan.: *A Formal Model for Object-Oriented Development of Real-Time Reactive Systems*. Ph.D. thesis, Concordia University, Montreal, Canada, October 1995
2. V.S. Alagar, R. Achuthan, and D. Muthiayen.: TROMLAB: An Object-Oriented Framework for Real-Time Reactive Systems Development, (Revised Version November 2000), submitted for publication. December 2000
3. V.S. Alagar and D. Muthiayen.: A Formal Approach to UML Modeling of Complex Real-Time Reactive Systems, submitted for publication. November 1999
4. V.S. Alagar, V. Bhaskar and Z. Xi.: Visual Modeling of e-Commerce Architectures. Technical Report, Department of Computer Science, Concordia University, Montreal, Canada, August 1999
5. R. Allen and D. Garlan.: A Formal Basis for Architectural Connection. *ACM Transactions on Software Engineering and Methodology*. July 1997
6. V. S. Alagar. D. Muthiayen, and R. Achuthan.: Animating Real-Time Reactive Systems. In *Proceedings of Second IEEE International Conference on Engineering of Complex Computer Systems*. ICECCS'96, Montreal, Canada, October 1996
7. Q. Chen, M. Hsu, U. Dayal, M. Griss.: Multi–Agent Cooperation, Dynamic Workflow and XML for E-Commerce Automation. in Proceedings Autonomous Agents 2000, June, Barcelona, Spain, June 2000
8. M.L. Griss and R. Letsinger.: Games at Work:Agent–Mediated E-commerce Simulation. Workshop Proceedings, Autonomous Agents 2000, Barcelona, Spain, June 2000

9. J.V. Guttag and J.J. Horning.: *Larch: Languages and Tools for Formal Specifications*. Springer-Verlag, 1993

10. D. Muthiayen.: *Real-Time Reactive System Development – A Formal Approach Approach Based on UML and PVS*. Ph.D. Thesis, Concordia University, Montreal, Canada, January 2000

11. O. Popistas.: *Rose–GRC translator: Mapping UML visual models onto formal specifications*. M.S. Thesis, Department of Computer Science, Concordia University, April 1999

12. H. Tao.: Static Analyzer: A Design Tool for TROM. M.S. Thesis, Concordia University, Montreal, Canada, August 1996

A   Appendix I - Larch Traits

Rule(R) : trait
  introduces
      first: R → Int
      second: R → Int
      third: R → Int
      fourth: R → Int
      fifth: R → Int
      create: Int, Int, Int, Int, Int → R
  asserts
      t: R, mid, pid, min, max, u :Int
      first(t) > 0 ∧ second(t) > 0
      ∧ third(t) > 0 ∧ fourth(t) > 0
      ∧ fifth(t) > 0
      first(create(mid, pid, min, max, u))
          == mid
      second(create(mid, pid, min, max, u))
          == pid
      third(create(mid, pid, min, max, u))
          == min
      fourth(create(mid, pid, min, max, u))
          == max
      fifth(create(mid, pid, min, max, u))
          == u
      third(t) < fourth(t)
RuleList(R,T) : trait
  includes
      Rule(R)
      BasicList(R for E, Tfor L)
  introduces
      getMinPrice: Int, Int, Int, T → Int
  asserts
      ll :T, mid, pid, q :Int
      getMinPrice(mid, pid, q, ll) == if mid = first(head(ll))
      ∧ pid = second(head(ll)) ∧ q ≥ third(head(ll))
      ∧ q ≤ fourth(head(ll)) then fifth(head(ll))
          else getMinPrice(mid, pid, q, tail(ll))

Fig. 7. Traits for Rule and Rule List

Risk(R) : trait
  includes
      FloatingPoint(F)
  introduces
      first: R → F
      second: R → F
      third: R → F
      create: Int, Int, Int → R
  asserts
      t: R, min, max, f: F
      first(t) ≥ 0
      first(t) < 1
      second(t) > 0
      second(t) ≤ 1
      third(t) ≥ 1
      first(create(min, max, f)) == min
      second(create(min, max, f)) == max
      third(create(min, max, f)) == f
      first(t) < second(t)
RiskList(R,T) : trait
  includes
      Risk(R)
      BasicList(R for E, T for L)
  introduces
      getRiskBalance: Int, T → Int
  asserts
      ll :T, p :Int
      getRiskBalance(p, ll) == if p ≥
      first(head(ll))
      ∧ p ≤ second(head(ll))
          then third(head(ll))
          else getRiskBalance(p, tail(ll))

Fig. 8. Traits for Risk and RiskList

B   Appendix II - Formal Specifications for E-Commerce System

SCS ECommerce
  Includes:
  Instantiate:
     U1::User[@A:1];
     U2::User[@A:1];
     U3::User[@A:1];
     E1::EBroker[@U:3, @C:2];
     M1::Merchant[@G:1, @B:3];
     M2::Merchant[@G:1, @B:3];
     B1::Bank[@M:2];
     B2::Bank[@M:2];
     B3::Bank[@M:2];
  Configure:
     E1.@U1:@U ↔ U1.@A1:@A;
     E1.@U2:@U ↔ U2.@A2:@A;
     E1.@U3:@U ↔ U3.@A3:@A;
     B1.@M1:@M ↔ M1.@B1:@B;
     B2.@M3:@M ↔ M1.@B2:@B;
     B3.@M5:@M ↔ M1.@B3:@B;
     B1.@M2:@M ↔ M2.@B4:@B;
     B2.@M4:@M ↔ M2.@B5:@B;
     B3.@M6:@M ↔ M2.@B6:@B;
     M1.@G1:@G ↔ E1.@C1:@C;
     M2.@G2:@G ↔ E1.@C2:@C;
end

Agent Bank [@M]
Events: GetMerchantAcc?@M, FailedAtMerchantAcc!@M, SucceedAtMerchantAcc!@M, GetCustomerAccBalance,
    AccNotFind, AccFind, FailedAtCharge!@M, WithdrawFromCustomer, DepositToMerchant, SucceedAtCharge!@M,
    Charge?@M
States: *idle, search, chargeAcc, findingAcc, accNotFound, accFound, chargedFromCust, validCharge, waitCharge
Attributes:
Traits:
Attribute-Function: idle → {};search → {};chargeAcc → {};findingAcc → {};accNotFound → {};accFound → {};
    chargedFromCust → {};validCharge → {};waitCharge → {};
Transition-Specifications:
    R1: ⟨idle,search⟩; GetMerchantAcc(true); true ⇒ true;
    R2: ⟨search,idle⟩; FailedAtMerchantAcc(true); true ⇒ true;
    R3: ⟨search,waitCharge⟩; SucceedAtMerchantAcc(true); true ⇒ true;
    R4: ⟨chargeAcc,findingAcc⟩; GetCustomerAccBalance(true); true ⇒ true;
    R5: ⟨findingAcc,accNotFound⟩; AccNotFind(true); true ⇒ true;
    R6: ⟨findingAcc,accFound⟩; AccFind(true); true ⇒ true;
    R7: ⟨accNotFound,idle⟩; FailedAtCharge(true); true ⇒ true;
    R8: ⟨accFound,chargedFromCust⟩; WithdrawFromCustomer(true); true ⇒ true;
    R9: ⟨accFound,idle⟩; FailedAtCharge(true); true ⇒ true;
    R10: ⟨chargedFromCust,validCharge⟩; DepositToMerchant(true); true ⇒ true;
    R11: ⟨validCharge,idle⟩; SucceedAtCharge(true); true ⇒ true;
    R12: ⟨waitCharge,chargeAcc⟩; Charge(true); true ⇒ true;
Time-Constraints:
end

Fig. 9. Formal specifications - Subsystem Architecture and Bank Agent

Agent User [@A]
Events: BrowseAdd!@A, Page?@A, AddressError?@A, NotConfirmed?@A, Confirmed?@A, Exit, Item!@A,
    Purchase!@A, ReceiveInvoice?@A, InvoiceFailed?@A
States: *idle, active, wait, readPage, confirmation, waitInvoice, viewInvoice
Attributes:
Traits:
Attribute-Function: idle → {};active → {};wait → {};readPage → {};confirmation → {};waitInvoice → {};
    viewInvoice → {};
Transition-Specifications:
    R1: ⟨idle,active⟩; BrowseAdd(true); true ⇒ true;
    R2: ⟨active,readPage⟩; Page(true); true ⇒ true;
    R3: ⟨active,active⟩; BrowseAdd(true); true ⇒ true;
    R4: ⟨active,idle⟩; AddressError(true); true ⇒ true;
    R5: ⟨wait,readPage⟩; NotConfirmed(true); true ⇒ true;
    R6: ⟨wait,confirmation⟩; Confirmed(true); true ⇒ true;
    R7: ⟨readPage,active⟩; BrowseAdd(true); true ⇒ true;
    R8: ⟨readPage,idle⟩; Exit(true); true ⇒ true;
    R9: ⟨readPage,wait⟩; Item(true); true ⇒ true;
    R10: ⟨confirmation,idle⟩; Exit(true); true ⇒ true;
    R11: ⟨confirmation,waitInvoice⟩; Purchase(true); true ⇒ true;
    R12: ⟨waitInvoice,viewInvoice⟩; ReceiveInvoice(true); true ⇒ true;
    R13: ⟨waitInvoice,confirmation⟩; InvoiceFailed(true); true ⇒ true;
    R14: ⟨viewInvoice,idle⟩; Exit(true); true ⇒ true;
Time-Constraints:
end

Agent Merchant [@G, @B]
Events: GetProductInfo?@G, GenerateInvoice?@G, ProductNotFind!@G, ProductInfo!@G, GetMerchantAcc!@B,
    SucceedAtMerchantAcc?@B, FailedAtMerchantAcc?@B, Charge!@B, SucceedAtCharge?@B, FailedAtCharge!@B,
    Unsuccessful!@G, AddInvoice, Successful!@G
States: *idle, product, getInvoice, merchantAcc, accFind, startCharge, accNotFind, succeed, failure, invoice
Attributes:
Traits:
Attribute-Function: idle → {};product → {};getInvoice → {};merchantAcc → {};accFind → {};startCharge → {};
    accNotFind → {};succeed → {};failure → {};invoice → {};
Transition-Specifications:
    R1: ⟨idle,product⟩; GetProductInfo(true); true ⇒ true;
    R2: ⟨idle,getInvoice⟩; GenerateInvoice(true); true ⇒ true;
    R3: ⟨product,idle⟩; ProductNotFind(true); true ⇒ true;
    R4: ⟨product,idle⟩; ProductInfo(true); true ⇒ true;
    R5: ⟨getInvoice,merchantAcc⟩; GetMerchantAcc(true); true ⇒ true;
    R6: ⟨merchantAcc,accFind⟩; SucceedAtMerchantAcc(true); true ⇒ true;
    R7: ⟨merchantAcc,accNotFind⟩; FailedAtMerchantAcc(true); true ⇒ true;
    R8: ⟨accFind,startCharge⟩; Charge(true); true ⇒ true;
    R9: ⟨startCharge,succeed⟩; SucceedAtCharge(true); true ⇒ true;
    R10: ⟨startCharge,failure⟩; FailedAtCharge(true); true ⇒ true;
    R11: ⟨accNotFind,idle⟩; Unsuccessful(true); true ⇒ true;
    R12: ⟨succeed,invoice⟩; AddInvoice(true); true ⇒ true;
    R13: ⟨failure,idle⟩; Unsuccessful(true); true ⇒ true;
    R14: ⟨invoice,idle⟩; Successful(true); true ⇒ true;
Time-Constraints:
end

Fig. 10. Formal specification of User and Merchant Agents

Agent EBroker [@U, @C]
Events: BrowseAdd?@U, Item?@U, Purchase?@U, GetProductInfo!@C, ProductNotFind?@C, ProductInfo?@C,
  AddressError!@U, Page!@U, AddStatistic, TotalQuantity, GetMinPrice, GetRiskBalance,
  CalculateAcceptablePrice, DeleteStatistic, Confirmed!@U, NotConfirmed!@U, GenerateInvoice!@C,
  Unsuccessful?@C, Successful?@C, AddCommission, InvoiceFailed!@U, ReceiveInvoice!@U
States: *idle, getProduct, waitProduct, browseFailed, browseSucceed, startNegotiation, waitOthers, quantity, minPrice,
  riskFactor, acceptablePrice, negoResult, startInvoice, askMerchant, succeed, failure, commission
Attributes: q:Integer;tq:Integer;minprice:Integer;rf:Integer;ap:Integer;uid1:Integer;mid1:Integer;pid1:Integer;q1:Integer;
  n1:Integer;s: ST;sl:SL;ru: RT;rul:RL;ri:R;ril:TL;c:C;cl: CL
Traits: Statistic[Integer, ST],StatisticList[ST,SL],Rule[Integer, RT],RuleList[RT,RL],Risk[Integer,R],RiskList[R,TL],
  Commission[Integer,C],CommissionList[C, CL]
Attribute-Function: idle → {};getProduct → {};waitProduct → {};browseFailed → {};browseSucceed → {};
  startNegotiation → {s, uid1, mid1, pid1, q1, n1};waitOthers → {sl};quantity → {tq};minPrice → {minprice};
  riskFactor → {rf}; acceptablePrice → {ap};negoResult → {sl};startInvoice → {};askMerchant → {};succeed → {};
  failure → {};commission → {cl};
Transition-Specifications:
  R1: ⟨idle,getProduct⟩; BrowseAdd(true); true ⇒ true;
  R2: ⟨idle,startNegotiation⟩; Item(true); true ⇒ s'=create(uid,mid,pid,q,n) ∧ uid1'=uid ∧ mid1'=mid ∧ pid1'=pid∧
    q1'=q ∧ n1'=n;
  R3: ⟨idle,startInvoice⟩; Purchase(true); true ⇒ true;
  R4: ⟨getProduct,waitProduct⟩; GetProductInfo(true); true ⇒ true;
  R5: ⟨waitProduct,browseFailed⟩; ProductNotFind(true); true ⇒ true;
  R6: ⟨waitProduct,browseSucceed⟩; ProductInfo(true); true ⇒ true;
  R7: ⟨browseFailed,idle⟩; AddressError(true); true ⇒ true;
  R8: ⟨browseSucceed,idle⟩; Page(true); true ⇒ true;
  R9: ⟨startNegotiation,waitOthers⟩; AddStatistic(true); true ⇒ sl'=insert(s,sl);
  R10: ⟨waitOthers,quantity⟩; TotalQuantity(true); true ⇒ tq'=totalQuantity(sl);
  R11: ⟨quantity,minPrice⟩; GetMinPrice(true); true ⇒ minprice=getMinPrice(mid,pid,tq,rul);
  R12: ⟨minPrice,riskFactor⟩; GetRiskBalance(true); true ⇒ rf'=getRiskBalance(q/tq,ril);
  R13: ⟨riskFactor,acceptablePrice⟩; CalculateAcceptablePrice(true); true ⇒ ap'=minprice*rf;
  R14: ⟨acceptablePrice,negoResult⟩; DeleteStatistic(true); true ⇒ sl'=delete(s,sl);
  R15: ⟨negoResult,idle⟩; Confirmed(ap⟨=n1); true ⇒ true;
  R16: ⟨negoResult,idle⟩; NotConfirmed(ap¿n1); true ⇒ true;
  R17: ⟨startInvoice,askMerchant⟩; GenerateInvoice(true); true ⇒ true;
  R18: ⟨askMerchant,failure⟩; Unsuccessful(true); true ⇒ true;
  R19: ⟨askMerchant,succeed⟩; Successful(true); true ⇒ true;
  R20: ⟨succeed,commission⟩; AddCommission(true); true ⇒ cl'=insert(create(mid,invid,amount),cl);
  R21: ⟨failure,idle⟩; InvoiceFailed(true); true ⇒ true;
  R22: ⟨commission,idle⟩; ReceiveInvoice(true); true ⇒ true;
Time-Constraints:
  TCvar1: R1, GetProductInfo, [0, 2], {};
  TCvar2: R5, AddressError, [0, 2], {};
  TCvar3: R6, Page, [0, 2], {};
  TCvar4: R9, TotalQuantity, [3, 6], {};
  TCvar5: R2, Confirmed, [5, 8], {};
  TCvar6: R2, NotConfirmed, [5, 8], {};
  TCvar8: R18, InvoiceFailed, [0, 2], {};
  TCvar7: R19, ReceiveInvoice, [0, 2], {};
end

Fig. 11. Formal specification of EBroker Agent

C Appendix III - Java Code

```
String unitPrice[];//the price proposed by user
String quantity[];//the quantity proposed by user

HttpSession session = request.getSession(true);
ServletInputStream in = request.getInputStream();
int len = request.getContentLength();
Hashtable data = HttpUtils.parsePostData(len,in);

//get value passed by browser
unitPrice = (String[]) (data.get("Price"));
quantity = (String[]) (data.get("Quantity"));
```

Parse Parameters

```
String JDBCDriver = "twz1.jdbc.mysql.jdbcMysqlDriver";
Connection con;
try {
  Class.forName(JDBCDriver);
} catch (Exception e) {
  System.err.println("Unable to load driver.");
  e.printStackTrace();
}
+try {
  con = DriverManager.getConnection( "jdbc:z1MySQL://arachne.cs.
    concordia.ca/cs49003?user=username", "databasename", "password");
} catch(SQLException ex) {
  System.err.println("SQLException: " + ex.getMessage());
}
```

Establish Database Connection

```
String query;
query = "INSERT INTO Statistic VALUES(" + userID + "," + merchantID
  + "," + productID + "," + quantity + "," + price +")" ;
Statement stmt;
try {
  stmt = con.createStatement();
  try {
      stmt.executeUpdate(query);
  } catch (Exception et) {
      et.printStackTrace();
  }
  stmt.close();
} catch(SQLException ex) {
  System.err.println("SQLException: " + ex.getMessage());
}
```

SQL Query Execution

Fig. 12. Java Implementation - Sample Code

A Formal Model for Reasoning about Adaptive QoS-Enabled Middleware

Nalini Venkatasubramanian[1], Carolyn Talcott[2], and Gul Agha[3]

[1] Univ. of California Irvine, Irvine, CA 92697-3425, USA,
nalini@ics.uci.edu
[2] Stanford University, Stanford, CA 94305, USA,
clt@cs.stanford.edu
[3] University of Illinois at Urbana-Champaign, Urbana, IL 61801, USA,
agha@cs.uiuc.edu

Abstract. Systems that provide QoS-enabled services such as multimedia are subject to constant evolution - customizable middleware
is required to effectively manage this change. Middleware services for
resource management such as scheduling, protocols providing security
and reliability, load balancing and stream synchronization, execute
concurrently with each other and with application activities and can
therefore potentially interfere with each other. To ensure cost-effective
QoS in distributed systems, safe composability of resource management
services is essential. In this paper we present a meta-architectural
framework for customizable QoS-based middleware based on the actor
model of concurrent active objects. Using TLAM, a semantic model
for specifying and reasoning about components of open distributed
systems, we show how a QoS brokerage service can be used to coordi-
nate multimedia resource management services in a safe, flexible and
efficient manner. In particular, we show that a system in which the
multimedia actor behaviors satisfy the specified requirements, provides
the required multimedia service. The behavior specification leaves open
the possibility of a variety of algorithms for resource management as
well as adding additional resource management activities by providing
constraints to ensure their non-interference.

Keywords: meta-object models, distributed systems, theoretical foundations, object-oriented applications, multimedia

1 Introduction

In the coming years, QoS-enabled distributed servers will be deployed to deliver a
variety of interactive services. Applications such as telemedicine, distance learning and electronic commerce exhibit varying requirements such as timeliness,
security, reliability and availability. The set of servers, clients, user requirements,
network and system conditions, in a wide area infrastructure are changing continuously. Future applications will require dynamic invocation and revocation of
services distributed in the network without violating QoS constraints of ongoing

J.N. Oliveira and P. Zave (Eds.): FME 2001, LNCS 2021, pp. 197–221, 2001.

applications. To assure safe adaptation to dynamically changing requirements it is important to have a rigorous semantic model of the system: the resources, middleware that provides system management, the application activities, and the sharing and interactions among these. Using such a model, designs can be analyzed to clarify assumptions that must be met for correct operation, and to establish criteria for non-interference. In [29,25], we presented the TLAM(Two Level Actor Machine) semantic framework for specifying, composing and reasoning about resource management services in open distributed systems. The TLAM is based on the actor model of computation, a natural model for dynamic object-based distributed systems. In the TLAM, a system is composed of two kinds of actors (active objects), base actors and meta actors, distributed over a network of processing nodes. *Base-actors* carry out application level computation, while *meta-actors* are part of the runtime system which manages system resources and controls the runtime behavior of the base level. The two levels provide a clean separation of concerns and a natural basis for modeling and reasoning about customizable middleware and its integration with application activity. Based on the two-level architecture, a customizable and safe distributed systems middleware infrastructure, called **CompOSE|Q** (Composable Open Software Environment with QoS) [26] is being developed at the University of California, Irvine, that has the ability to provide cost-effective and safe QoS-based distributed resource management.

Our general approach to modeling systems using a TLAM framework is to develop a family of specifications at from different points of view and at different levels of abstraction. We begin with the abstract notion of end-to-end service provided by a system in response to a request. This high-level view can be refined (here we use the word informally) by expressing system wide properties in terms of of abstract properties of the underlying network. Another point of view specifies constraints on the behavior and distribution of a group of actors. This local behavior point of view can be further refined by specifying protocols and algorithms for the actions of individual actors. The two points of view are related by the notion of a group of meta actors providing a service, in a system satisfying suitable initialization and non-interference conditions. The staging and refinement of specifications provides a form of modularity, scalability, and reusability by reducing the task of implementation to that of implementing individual abstract behaviors. Behavior level specifications can be used to guide or check implementations or even serve as executable prototypes.

In previous applications of the TLAM [28,29] we have focused on defining core services such as remote creation and snapshots, understanding their potential interactions, and composing services built up such core services. Of particular concern were constraints on meta-level behavior needed to maintain a consistent view of the actor acquaintance topology. In this paper, we use the TLAM framework to develop a formal model for customizable, cost-effective middleware to enforce QoS requirements in multimedia applications. Here we explicitly model resources of the network infrastructure and constraints on the proper management of these resources. We begin by informally describing the notion of a system providing *QoS-based MM Service*.We then map QoS requirements to resource requirements and focus on modeling and reasoning about the resource management underlying a QoS-based service. For this purpose we define, in a rigorous manner, the notions of a system providing *Resource-based MM Service*, of a system having *Resource-based MM Behavior*, and finally refining the system with an *Adaptive Request Scheduling Policy*. The Resource-based MM Service specification reflects the chosen system resource architecture and allows us to reason about the availability and use of resources. The Resource-based MM Behavior specification models the QoS broker software architecture presented in [25,27] and places constraints on the actions of the QoS meta actors. Such a behavior specification can serve as a first stage in refining a service specification into an implementation. The *Adaptive Request Scheduling Policy* illustrates such refinement. It specifies one of the resource management policies developed in [25] by giving high-level algorithms for determining meta actor behavior. The main results are:

(1) if a system provides Resource-based MM Service, then (under the assumptions on the mapping from QoS requirements to Resource requirements) it provides QoS-based MM Service;
(2) if a system has Resource-based MM Behavior, and meets certain initialization and non-interference conditions, it provides Resource-based MM Service;
(3) if a system is refined with the Adaptive Request Scheduling Policy, then it implements Resource-based MM Behavior.

A consequence of (2) is that new broker policies can be safely installed as long as they satisfy the behavior constraints. (3) is an example of such a policy.

The rest of this paper is organized as follows. Section 2 reviews the TLAM framework concepts needed to understand the formal model of the QoS Broker. Section 3 recalls the QoS Broker multimedia server meta-architecture of [25]: its physical and software architectures, and a mapping of the software architecture onto the physical architecture. Section 4 describes several resource management policies that we have used in realizing the software architecture. Section 5 shows how we use the TLAM framework to formally model and reason about systems such as QoS Broker. Section 6 discusses related work and outlines areas for future research.

2 The Two Level Meta-architecture

In this section we briefly summarize the main concepts of the TLAM semantic framework. More detail can be found in [29,25]. The Actor model is a model of concurrent active objects that has a built-in notion of encapsulation and inter-action and is thus well-suited to represent evolution and co-ordination among interacting components in distributed multimedia applications. Traditional passive objects encapsulate state and a set of procedures that manipulate the state;

actors extend this by encapsulating a thread of control as well. Each actor potentially executes in parallel with other actors and interacts only by sending and receiving messages. (See [1,2] for more discussion of the actor model, and for many examples of programming with actors.) As mentioned earlier, in a TLAM model, a system is composed of two kinds of actors, base actors and meta actors, distributed over a network of processing nodes. *Base-actors* carry out application level computation, while *meta-actors* are part of the runtime system which manages system resources and controls the runtime behavior of the base level. A TLAM model provides an abstract characterization of actor identity, state, messages, and computation, and of the connection between base- and meta-level computation. Meta-actors communicate with each other via message passing as do base-actors, and meta-actors may also examine and modify the state of the base actors located on the same node. Base-level actors and messages have associated runtime annotations that can be set and read by meta actors, but are invisible to base-level computation. Actions which result in a change of base-level state are called events. Meta-actors may react to events occurring on their node.

A TLAM is a structure of the form

$$TLAM = <Net, TLAS, loc>$$

where Net is the underlying computer network with processor nodes and communication links; and $TLAS$ is a two-level actor system distributed over the network by the map, loc. The semantics of a TLAM model is given by a labeled transition relation on configurations. A TLAM *configuration*, C, has sets of base- and meta-level actors, and a set of undelivered messages. Each actor has a unique name (address) and the configuration associates a current state $getS(C,a)$ to each actor name, a. $Cast(C)$ is the set of names of actors in C. $getA(C,a,t)$ is the value, in C, of the annotation of base-actor a with tag t; $setA(C,a,t,v)$ sets the value of the annotation of a with tag t, returning the updated configuration. Thus $getA(setA(C,a,t,v),a,t) = v$. The undelivered messages are distributed over the network – some are traveling along communication links and others are held in node buffers. There are two kinds of transition: communication and execution. Communication transitions move undelivered messages from node buffers to links and links to node buffers and are the same in every TLAM. An execution transition consists of a computation step taken by a base- or meta-level actor, by applying an enabled *step rule*, followed by application of all enabled *event handling rules* (in some order). *Step rules* specify messages delivered to and sent by the stepping actor, change of the stepping actors state, and possibly newly created actors. In addition meta-level step rules may specify changes in the state of base-level actors, base-level messages to be sent, and base-level actors to be created. A step that delivers or sends base-level messages, changes base-level state, or creates new base-level actors signals corresponding events. *Event handling rules* specify the response of meta-level actors to signalled events. Note that no message is delivered and the only base-level modifications that can be specified are annotation modifications. In particular no events are signaled. All actors modified or created in an execution transition reside on the node of the stepping actor.

A *computation path* for initial configuration C_0 is an infinite sequence of labeled transitions:

$$\pi = [\ C_i \xrightarrow{l_i} C_{i+1} \mid i \in \mathbf{Nat}\ ]$$

where l_i is the transition, indicating the transition rule applied. The semantics of a configuration is the set of fair computation paths starting with that configuration, where fairness means that any enabled communication transition will eventually happen, and enabled reaction rules will either fire or become permanently disabled.

A *system* is a set of configurations closed under the transition relation. We say that π is a computation path of a system S if it is a computation path with initial configuration some configuration C of S. Properties of a system modeled in the TLAM are specified as properties of computation paths. A property can be a simple invariant that must hold for all configurations of a path, a requirement that a configuration satisfying some condition eventually arise, or a requirement involving the transitions themselves. Properties are checked using the properties of the building blocks for configurations – message contents and actor state descriptions – and of the TLAM reaction rules that determine the behavior of actors in the system.

3   The QoS Broker Meta-architecture for QoS-Based Services

Using the TLAM framework, we develop a meta-architectural model of a multimedia server that provides QoS based services to applications. The physical architecture of the MM server consists of:

- a set of data sources (DS) that provide high bandwidth streaming MM access to multiple clients. Each independent data source includes high capacity storage devices (e.g. hard-disks), a processor, buffer memory, and high-speed network interfaces for real-time multimedia retrieval and transmission;
- a specific node designated as the distribution controller (DC) that coordinates the execution of requests on the data sources; and
- a tertiary storage server that contains the MM objects—replicas of these MM objects are placed on the data source nodes.

All the above components are interconnected via an external distribution network that also transports multimedia information to clients.

The software architecture of a multimedia server consists of two subsystems - the base level and meta-level subsystems corresponding to the application and system level resource management components respectively. The base level component represents the functionality of the MM application: *replica actors* models both MM data objects and their replicas (e.g. video and audio files), and *request actors* model MM requests to access this data. The meta-level component deals with the coordination of multiple requests, sharing of existing resources among multiple requests, and ensuring that the resources needed by requests being serviced at any given time do not exceed the system capacity. To provide co-ordination at the highest level we introduce, the *QoS Broker* meta-actor, *QB*. The two main functions of the QoS Broker are data management and request management. The *data management* component decides the placement of data in the distributed system, i.e., it decides when and where to create additional replicas of data. It also determines when replicas of data actors are no longer needed and can be dereplicated. The *request management* component performs the task of admission control for incoming requests, i.e., it decides whether or not a request can be admitted for service. It must ensure the satisfaction of QoS constraints for requests that are ongoing in the system. The multimedia data and request management functions of the QoS broker in turn require a number of services. The organization of the QoS Broker services is shown in Figure 1. Each of these services in turn can be based on one or more of the core services integrated into the metaarchitecture - remote creation, distributed snapshot and directory services.

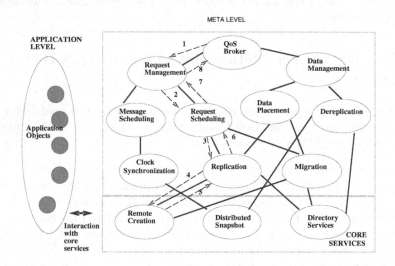

Fig. 1. Detailed architecture of the QoS meta-architecture system.

We model both *adaptive* and *predictive* resource management services. An adaptive service makes decisions based on the state of the system at the time a service is requested. A predictive service has a model of expected request arrival times and attempts to arrange system parameters (e.g. replication state) to maximize some measure, e.g. number of requests served. In this paper we restrict attention to the services related to replication and dereplication. Issues such as message synchronization and migration are topics for future work.

•*Replication:* creates copies of media objects on data sources. Issues to consider include where and when to replicate and object. The rate at which replication proceeds also has a direct impact on system performance.

•*Dereplication:* marks some replicas as removable – the objective being to optimize utilization of storage space by removing replicas that are not needed to make room for ones that are. A dereplication service may base its decisions on current load in the system as well as on expected future demands for an object. Dereplication does not immediately remove a marked copy, this can only happen after all requests that are currently being serviced by that copy have completed.

In order to map the QoS meta-architecture to the physical system architecture, we distinguish between local and global components and define interactions between local resource managers on nodes and the global resource management component. The global component includes the QoS broker and associated meta-actors which reside on the distribution controller node. The node local components include, for each DS node:

• a DS meta-actor for load-management on that node. The DS meta-actor contains state information regarding the current state of the node in terms of available resources, replicas, ongoing requests and replication processes etc.

• Request base actors corresponding to the requests assigned to that node.

• Replica base actors that correspond to the replicas of data objects currently available on that node.

4   Resource Management Policies for MM Servers

Apart from the QoS broker, QB, the MM system contains a number of meta-actors whose behaviors are coordinated by QB to provide the resource management services discussed above. In this section, we describe some of the load management policies that have been treated in the formal model. The policies are implemented as meta-level actors and provide a modular and integrated approach to managing the individual resources of a MM server so as to effectively utilize all of the resources such as disks, CPU, memory and network resources. A MM request specifies a client, one or more multi-media objects, and a required QoS. The QoS requirement in turn is translated into resource allocation requirements. The ability of a data source to support additional requests is dependent not only on the resources that it has available, but also on the MM object requested and the characteristics of the request (e.g., playback rate, resolution). We characterize the degree of loading of a data source DS with respect to request R in terms of its load factor, $LF(R, DS)$, as:

$$LF(R, DS) = max(\frac{DB^R}{DB^{DS}}, \frac{Mem^R}{Mem^{DS}}, \frac{CPU^R}{CPU^{DS}}, \frac{NetBW^R}{NetBW^{DS}})$$

where DB^R, Mem^R, CPU^R, and $NetBW^R$ denote the disk bandwidth, memory buffer space, CPU cycles, and network transfer bandwidth, respectively, that are necessary for supporting request R and similarly Res^{DS} denotes the amount of resource *Res* available on data source *DS*. The load factor helps identify the critical resource in a data source, i.e., the resource that limits the capability of the data source to service additional requests. By comparing the load factor values for different servers, load management decisions can be taken by the QoS brokerage service. Below we briefly describe the QoS meta-actors coordintaed by the QoS broker for scheduling of MM requests and placement of MM data.

Scheduling of Multimedia Requests: The Request Scheduling meta-actor (RS) implements an adaptive scheduling policy that compares the relative utilization of resources at different data sources to generate an assignment of requests to replicas, so as to maximize the number of requests serviced. The data source that contains a copy of the MM object requested and which entails the least overhead (as determined by the computed load factor) is chosen as the candidate source for an incoming request. If no candidate data source can be found for servicing request R, then the meta-actor RS can either reject the incoming request or initiate *replication on demand* - implemented via a replication on demand meta-actor (ROD). The QoS broker also analyzes the rejections over time and triggers appropriate placement policies, implemented via predictive placement and dereplication meta-actors (PP and DR) to reduce the rate of rejection. The replication on demand meta-actor ROD attempts to create a new replica of a requested MM object on the fly. The source DS on which the new replica is to be made is one that has minimum load-factor with respect to the request, R, i.e., with the minimum value of $LF(R, DS)$. By doing so, ROD attempts to maximize the possibility of the QoS broker servicing additional requests from the same replica. In order for this approach to be feasible and attractive, the replication must proceed at a very high rate, thereby consuming vital server resources for replication.

Placement of MM Objects: The predictive placement and dereplication meta-actors (PP and DR) implement a placement policy that determines in advance when, where and how many replicas of each MM object should be placed in a MM server, and when to dereplicate an existing replica. In particular, the goal of the predictive placement procedure is to facilitate the task of the adaptive scheduler meta-actor, by allocating MM objects in such a way as to maximize system-wide revenue, by permitting a maximum number of requests to be admitted and scheduled for service.

Placement mechanisms must be designed to work effectively with request scheduling. For example replication and derpelicatation activities should not simply cancel each others effects. One way of coordinating these activities is to run dereplication before replication. Another potential for interference arises with the concurrent execution of the ROD and PP processes. The current PP process that initiates replica creation is based on a current snapshot of available systems resources, e.g. disk space. Without proper constraints, this snapshot will not account for replicas being created dynamically by the ROD process. A simple solution is to disable ROD when the PP process is initiated. Achieving more concurrency requires more complex coordination and synchronization.

Some Performance Results: Performance studies show that application objects can be managed effectively by composing multiple resource management activities managed at the metalevel [27]. Figure 2 illustrates the performance, measured by request rejection rate, of various policies for load management - (a) purely adaptive (on-the-fly) scheduling and placement(P1), (b) purely predictive (decided a priori) scheduling and placement(P2), (c) composite policies that provide adaptive scheduling and predictive placement(P3 and P4, an optimized version of policy P3). The left hand side graph illustrates the request rejection rate under purely adaptive policies for placement and scheduling. *Startup latency* is a QoS factor that indicates how long the user is willing to wait for a replica to be created adaptively. The graph demonstrates that when the startup latency is below a threshold value (2 min), the purely adaptive mechanisms, represented by P1 force a very large fraction of the requests received to be rejected. Assuming that startup latency is sufficiently large, the right hand side depicts the inadequacy of P2, that relies on only predictive policies for scheduling and placement. In comparison, the other 3 policies (P1, P3 and P4), show hardly any rejects (indicated by the overlapping lines in the graph). As can be observed from the performance results, the ability to run multiple policies simultaneously (as in cases P3 and P4) reduced the total number of rejected requests in the overall system. In this paper, we study complex interactions that can arise due to the simultaneous execution of multiple system policies.

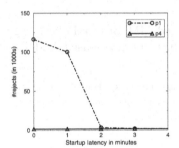 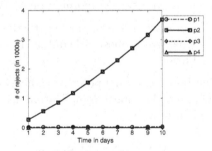

Fig. 2. Comparison of the performance of load management policies for request scheduling and video placement in a distributed video server.

5   Reasoning about QoS-Based MM Services

Assuring safe composability of resource management services is essential for efficient management of distributed systems with widely varying and dynamically changing requirements. In this section we show how the TLAM framework is used to model and reason about the multimedia meta-architecture and resource management policies presented above. Following our basic approach to modeling systems in the TLAM framework we specify the QoS broker from different points of view (end-to-end services and individual behaviors) and at different levels of abstraction and establish theorems relating the different specifications.

In § 5.1 we informally describe the notion of a system providing *QoS-based MM Service*. This is the high-level system wide request based service that the customer sees. In § 5.2 we define the notion of a system providing *Resource-based MM Service*. This reflects the relevant system resources and expresses high-level resource management requirements that must be met in order to provide the QoS-based MM Service. We postulate a function that translates QoS requirements to resource requirements and argue that:

- if a system provides Resource-based MM Service, then under the given assumptions on the mapping from QoS requirements to Resource requirements, the system provides QoS-based MM Service.

In § 5.3 we define the notion of a system having *Resource Based MM Behavior*. This specification reflects the QoS broker software architecture and places constraints on the actions of the QoS meta actors. We define initial and non-interference conditions, and show that

- if a system has Resource-based MM Behavior, then if the initial and non-interference conditions hold, the system provides Resource-based MM Service.

In § 5.4 we refine the behavior by requiring the system to act according to given *Resource Based MM Broker Policies*. Here we focus on one specific policy, the *Adaptive Request Scheduling* Policy. We show that

- if a system acts according to the Resource-based MM Broker Policy, (e.g. Adaptive request Scheduling Policy), then it has Resource-based MM Behavior.

The Resource-based policy specifications include algorithms for request scheduling and replication / dereplication decisions. Thus they constitute a step towards implementation.

5.1   QoS Based MM Service

We assume that there is a fixed set, *MMObjects*, of MM objects available in the system and let *MM* range over *MMObjects*. We also assume given a set *MMreqset* of MM requests—messages used to request MM service—and let *MMreq* range over *MMreqset*. A MM request message *MMreq* determines a triple (α_{cl}, MM, qs). This is interpreted as a request to initiate a MM streaming service from the server receiving the request to the client α_{cl}, using the MM object *MM*, and obeying the QoS requirement *qs*.

Definition 1 (QoS-based MM Service).   A system S provides a QoS-based MM Service over the set of MM objects, *MMObjects*, and request messages *MMreqset* iff for every configuration C of S, if there is an undelivered request message *MMreq* in C, then along any path π from C exactly one of the following properties hold:

(1) there is a unique transition in π where *MMreq* is accepted for service, and service is provided with the required QoS until complete, or

(2) there is a unique transition in π where *MMreq* is rejected, and for this to happen it must be the case that the requested QoS cannot be provided at the time that *MMreq* arrives.

A more advanced QoS-based service that negotiates with the client for lower QoS or delayed service in the case that the request can not be served as presented could be built on top of the simple QoS-based MM Service specified above. That is outside the scope of the current work.

5.2   Specifying a Resource Based MM Service

We assume given a function *QoSTranslate* that maps MM requests to resource requirements which, if met, will ensure the requested QoS. Thus real-time requirements typical of MM applications, for example required bit-rate of video, are translated into corresponding resource requirements, for example a bandwidth requirement. (See [18] for examples of such QoS translation functions). For the purposes of this specification, we assume that if resource are allocated for a request, then they are used (as needed) to provide the requested QoS.

Definition 2 (Managed Resources). We consider four managed resources: network bandwidth (*NetBW*), CPU cycles (*CPU*), disk bandwidth (*DB*), and memory buffer (*Mem*). We let *Resources* denote this set of resources and let *Res* range over *Resources*. We use the notation $Unit_{Res}$ for the units in which we measure the resource *Res*, and let $QoSTuple = Unit_{DB} \times Unit_{CPU} \times Unit_{NetBW} \times Unit_{Mem}$. For an element qt of *QoSTuple* we write qt_{Res} to select the component associated to *Res*.

Definition 3 (QoSTranslate requirements). The function *QoSTranslate* maps MM requests to 4-tuples representing resource allocation requirements for the four managed resources: $QoSTranslate : MMreqset \rightarrow QoSTuple$. For request *MMreq*, we require that $QoSTranslate(MMreq)$ be such that the QoS requirement of *MMreq* is met if

(a) the resources allocated to *MMreq* are at least those specified by $QoSTranslate(MMreq)$ together with access to a copy of the MM object of *MMreq*, and

(b) the allocated resources are continuously available during the service phase for *MMreq*.

Availability means that the MM object replica is not deleted (or overwritten) and that the total allocation never exceeds capacity, since over-allocation implies that resources must be taken from some already admitted request thereby possibly violating the QoS constraints for that request.

MM System Architecture. The physical layer of Section 3 is represented as a TLAM network by mapping nodes in the MM server to TLAM nodes. Recall that there are several kinds of nodes: a set of data source nodes that hold replicas and provide the actual MM streaming, a distribution controller node responsible for coordinating the data source nodes, and a set of client nodes from which MM requests arise. (There are also a tertiary storage nodes that contain the MM objects which we omit here to simplify the presentation.) We let *DSnodes* be the set of data source nodes and let *DS* range over *DSnodes*. We assume, given, a function *capacity* such that $capacity(DS, Res) \in Unit_{Res}$ for any data source node *DS* and resource *Res*.

The MM state of the system is modeled by functions characterizing the state of replicas on each data source node and functions characterizing the state of each request that has arrived. The resource based MM service is then specified in terms of constraints on the values of these given functions and the way the values may change, such that if the MM request scheduling and replication processes obey these constraints, then the QoS-based service requirements will be met and the underlying streaming mechanisms will be able to provide the desired QoS-based service. In particular, any policies that entail these constraints can be used to implement the MM service.

Definition 4 (Functions characterizing replicas). There is at most one replica of a given MM object on any DS node, and thus it can be uniquely identified by the node and object. There are three functions characterizing the state of the replica of a MM object *MM* on a DS node *DS* in system configuration *C*:

- $replState(C, DS, MM) \in ReplStates = \{InQueue, InProgress, replCompleted\}$ is the replication status of the multimedia object *MM* on node *DS*. *InQueue* indicates that replication has been requested but not initiated, *InProgress* indicates that replication is in progress, and *replCompleted* indicates that replication is complete.
- $replnBW(C, DS, MM) \in Unit_{NetBW}$ is the minimum bandwidth available to complete a replication, meaningful only if replication is in progress or in queue.
- $replClass(C, DS, MM) \in \{0, 1, 2, 3\}$ is the replication class of the multimedia object *MM* on node *DS*. Class 0 indicates that the replica is not present on the node. A replica of class 1 is guaranteed to be available. A replica of class 2 is considered marked as dereplicable but remains available until all requests assigned to it have completed. A replica of class 3 exists on the node in the sense that it has not been overwritten, but there is no guarantee it will remain that way and can not be considered available until its class is changed.

The constraints, $\phi_{\text{repl}}(S)$, on the replica functions require that as the system evolves, the replication state of a replica moves from *InQueue* to *InProgress* to *replCompleted* and that the *replClass* function satisfies the constraints specified by the transition diagram given in Figure 3. For example the diagram specifies that if $replClass(C, DS, MM) = 0$, and $C \to C'$, then $replClass(C', DS, MM) \in$

$\{0, 1, 3\}$. Also, if $replClass(C, DS, MM) = 2$, and $replClass(C', DS, MM) = 3$, then there are no active requests assigned to this replica.

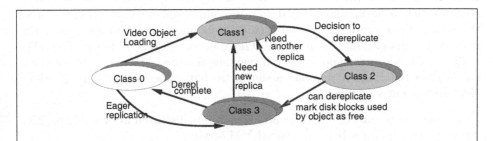

Fig. 3. State transition diagram specifying the allowed changes in the class of a MM object replica. States are labelled by values of the class values and the arrows indicate allowed changes in the value as the system evolves. Class 0 indicates that the replica is not present on the node. A replica of class 1 is guaranteed to be available. A replica of class 2 is considered marked as dereplicable but remains available until all requests assigned to it have completed. The Class2 to Class3 transition is allowed only when there are no active(ongoing) requests assigned to the replica. A replica of class 3 cannot be assigned until it is changed to a 1 replica.

Definition 5 (Functions characterizing requests). Each MM request that has been delivered in a system has a uniquely associated base actor that represents the request during admission control and servicing. We let *ReqActors* be a subset of the base actor identifiers set aside for association with MM requests and let α^{req} range over *ReqActors*. We assume given, the following functions characterizing requests:

- $reqClientId(C, \alpha^{req})$ – identifies the client making the request.
- $reqObjId(C, \alpha^{req})$ – the MM object requested.
- $reqQoS(C, \alpha^{req})$ – the 4-tuple returned by *QoSTranslate*.
- $reqState(C, \alpha^{req}) \in ReqStates = \{Waiting, Granted, Denied, Servicing, reqCompleted\}$
- $reqReplica(C, \alpha^{req}) \in DSnodes + \{\texttt{nil}\}$ – the DS node to which the request has been assigned if any.

The constraints, $\phi_{req}(S)$, on the request functions require that as a system evolves, the values of *reqClientId*, *reqObjId*, and *reqQoS* are constant throughout the life of a request actor, and once defined, the replica associated to a request actor remains constant. Furthermore, the state of request actor must move from *Waiting* to *Granted* or *Denied*, and from *Granted* to *Servicing* to *reqCompleted*, and if the state is *Servicing*, then the replication of the associated replica is competed.

The final definition needed before we state the full specification deals with the use of resources as determined for a given configuration by the replica and request functions.

Definition 6 (TotalResource Property ($\phi_{res}(S)$)). $\phi_{res}(S)$ states that for every configuration in the system, every data source node, and every managed resource, the sum of the resource allocation over requests on the node do not exceed the nodes total capacity for that resource. The resources currently allocated on a DS node include resources allocated to streaming accepted MM requests, as given the *reqQoS* function for requests assigned to that node, as well as replications that are currently ongoing.

Using the characterizing functions and constraints discussed above, we now give the requirements for a Resource-based MM service.

Definition 7 (Resource-Based MM Service). A system S provides Resource-based MM service with respect to requests in *MMreqset*, functions *QoSTranslate*, *capacity*, and the functions characterizing replica and request state as specified above iff

- S satisfies the constraints $\phi_{req}(S)$ (Definition 5), $\phi_{repl}(S)$ (Definition 4), and $\phi_{res}(S)$ (Definition 6), and
- for $C \in S$, if there is an undelivered message, *MMreq*, with parameters (α_{cl}, MM, qs), then along any computation path from C there is a (unique) transition which delivers *MMreq* and creates a new request actor, α^{req}, such that in the resulting configuration C': $reqClientId(C', \alpha^{req}) = \alpha_{cl}$, $reqObjId(C', \alpha^{req}) = MM$, $reqQoS(C', \alpha^{req}) = QoSTranslate(qs)$, $reqState(C', \alpha^{req}) = Waiting$, and $reqReplica(C', \alpha^{req}) = \texttt{nil}$.

Theorem 1 (QoS2Resource). If a system S provides Resource-based MM service as defined in 7 and the function *QoSTranslate* satisfies the requirements of definition 3, then S provides QoS Based Service according to definition 1.

5.3   A Resource Based MM Behavior

At the behavior level we make explicit the QoS meta actors that cooperate to provide the Resource-based MM service. Constraints on their behavior are expressed in terms of abstract meta-actor states and reaction rules specifying allowed actions.

Representing Request and Replica Functions (MM Resource State)

The actual MM resource state of a configuration, modeled previously by the request and replica functions, is recorded in annotations of base-level actors implementing the MM streaming service. We partition the MM base actors of a configuration into three groups. *ReqActors* correspond to delivered MM requests and are located on the control node. *DSReqActors* are request actors representing granted requests, each located on the DS node to which the request is assigned. We define $NodeReq(C, \alpha^{req})$ to be α^{req}_{ds} if α^{req} represents a granted request with DS representative α^{req}_{ds}, and `nil` if the request status is waiting or denied. *DSReplActors* correspond to the replica actors on the DS nodes. We define $NodeRepl(C, DS, MM)$ to be the replica base actor corresponding to the replica of MM on DS, if a replica is present, and `nil` otherwise.

Definition 8 (Replica and request functions).   For each replica function *replX*, X one of *State*, *BW*, *Class*, there is an annotation tag X to represent that function: $replX(C, DS, MM)$ is the value of the X annotation of $NodeRepl(C, DS, MM)$ in C. Similarly, for each request function *reqX* (for X one of *ClientId*, *ObjId*, *QoS*, *State*, *Replica*) there is an annotation tag X and $replX(C, \alpha^{req})$ is defined to be the value of the X annotation of $NodeReq(C, \alpha^{req})$ in C for a granted request, and to be the X annotation of α^{req} in C otherwise.

Representing MM Meta-actor Behavior

Following the QoS Broker software architecture discussed in section 3 there are five broker meta actors residing on the DC node. In addition there is a DSNode meta actor $DSma(DS)$ on each DS node DS. The QoS meta actors, their services and their possible states are summarized in figure 4. We represent the QoS meta actors knowledge of the MM state as a function from requests (represented by actors in *ReqActors*) and replicas (represented by pairs (DS, MM)) to a function from annotation tags to corresponding values or `nil` if undefined. We let *MMState* denote this set of functions, and we let $mms, mms', mmsU$ range over *MMState*.

The QoS broker QB coordinates the QoS resource management services: scheduling, replication, predictive placement, and dereplication. Since these activities use and modify the actual MM state, care must be taken to avoid interference among these activities. The QoS broker uses a function, *status*, to

Service(ActorName)	States
QoS Broker (QB)	$QBB(MMState, Status)$
Request Scheduler(RS)	$IdleB_{rs}, WaitB_{rs}(MMState, ReqActors, MMState)$
Replication on Demand (ROD)	$IdleB_{rod}, WaitB_{rod}(MMState)$
DeReplication(DR)	$IdleB_{dr}, WaitB_{dr}(MMState, \mathbf{P}_\omega(()DSnodes))$
Predictive Placement(PP)	$IdleB_{pp}, WaitB_{pp}(MMState, \mathbf{P}_\omega(()DSnodes))$
DSnode QoS mgr($DSma(DS)$)	$DSB(DS)$

Fig. 4. QoS meta actors, services and states.

keep track of which processes are ongoing. $status(RS) = (\alpha^{req}, rod)$ for rod a boolean, indicates that RS has been requested to schedule α^{req} and scheduling is in progress, with RS allowed to invoke ROD only if rod is true, $status(RS) = \texttt{nil}$ indicates that there is no outstanding request from QB to RS and consequently no undelivered messages to or from RS. For $X \in \{PP, DR\}$, $status(X) = \texttt{true}$ indicates the process X is ongoing and $status(X) = \texttt{false}$ indicates the process X is not active and there are no outstanding requests from QB to X. We let $Status$ denote the set of status functions and let $status$ range over $Status$. The rules for QB behavior assure non-interference amongst the QoS broker services, by not allowing two replication services to run concurrently or a dereplication service to run concurrently with either scheduling or replication.

Meta-level Messages

The QoS meta-actor rules specify the reaction of a meta-actor upon receiving a QoS message. Figure 5 summarizes the internal QoS messages. In addition to the

request	reply
$RS \lhd \texttt{schedule}(\alpha^{req}, mms, b) \; @ \; QB$	$QB \lhd \texttt{scheduleReply}(mmsU) \; @ \; RS$
$DR \lhd \texttt{derepl}(mms) \; @ \; QB$	$QB \lhd \texttt{dereplReply}(replU) \; @ \; DR$
$PP \lhd \texttt{place}(mms) \; @ \; QB$	$QB \lhd \texttt{placeReply}(replU) \; @ \; PP$
$DSma(DS) \lhd \texttt{assign}(reqU) \; @ \; RS$	$RS \lhd \texttt{assignAck}() \; @ \; DSma(DS)$
$ROD \lhd \texttt{repl}(mms, MM, qt) \; @ \; RS$	$RS \lhd \texttt{replAck}(replU) \; @ \; ROD$
$DSma(DS) \lhd \texttt{repl}(replU) \; @ \; X$	$X \lhd \texttt{replAck}() \; @ \; DSma(DS)$
for $X \in \{ROD, DR, PP\} \wedge DS \in DSnodes$	

notifications
$QB \lhd \texttt{notify}([(DS, MM) = [State = replCompleted]]) \; @ \; DSma(DS)$
$QB \lhd \texttt{notify}([\alpha^{req} = [State = reqCompleted]]) \; @ \; DSma(DS)$

Fig. 5. Internal QoS Messages. These are classified either as requests with corresponding reply messages, or as notifications, which need no reply. The general form of a message is $X \lhd \texttt{mid}(\dots) \; @ \; Y$ where X is the intended receiver of the message, Y is the sender, $\texttt{mid}$ is the message type, and $(\dots)$ contains parameters.

internal QoS messages there are the messages used to communicate with clients, and transition rules for these messages. A client α_{cl} may send MM requests to QB of the form $QB \lhd \texttt{mmReq}(\alpha_{cl}, MM, qs)$ and the reply has one of the following forms:

$$\alpha_{cl} \lhd \texttt{granted}(MM, qs) \; @ \; QB \quad \text{or} \quad \alpha_{cl} \lhd \texttt{denied}(MM, qs) \; @ \; QB.$$

The Transition Rules

In the following we briefly summarize the behavior specified by QoS Broker transition rules. The complete set of rules appears in the full paper.

QB rules. The transition rules for the QoS broker, QB, provide the overall organization of the QoS service activities. If neither dereplication nor request scheduling are in progress then an MM request, $QB \lhd \mathtt{mmReq}(\alpha_{cl}, MM, qs)$, can be processed. A message $RS \lhd \mathtt{schedule}(mms', \alpha^{req}, rod)$ is sent, where mms' is QBs current model of the MM state augmented with request information associated to the new request actor α^{req}, and rod indicates whether replication-on-demand is enabled for the scheduler.

QB may invoke predictive placement if dereplication is not in progress and replication-on-demand is not enabled, by sending a message of the form $PP \lhd \mathtt{place}(mms) @ QB$. The firing of this rule depends only on the state of QB and, unlike most of the other rules, does not consume a message. Initiation of dereplication is analogous.

When a reply to an outstanding scheduling, placement or dereplication request arrives, QB updates its state using the update MM state contained in the reply message. In the case of a scheduling request, QB also sends a reply to the requesting client indicating whether the request has been granted or denied. Similarly, when a DS notification arrives the QoS broker uses the contained MM state to update its MM state. The $\mathtt{notify}$ messages are just to inform QB that some resources have been released. Notification is needed because the resources can not be considered available for reuse until such a notification is received by QB.

DS manager rules. When a DS node manager $DSma(DS)$ receives an assignment request with MM state $mmsU$ it creates a new request actor, sets the annotations of this actor and of the replica actor for the requested MM object using $mmsU$ (which contains the MM request information, and name of the associated request actor), and sends an $\mathtt{assignAck}$ reply to RS. When a DS node manager $DSma(DS)$ receives a replication request it uses the MM state replica information to update the annotations of its replica actors and then sends a $\mathtt{replAck}$ reply to the requester (which could be ROD, PP, or DR).

When servicing of a request with request actor α_{ds}^{req} completes on a DS node, an event $\mathtt{reqCompletes}(\alpha_{ds}^{req})$ is signaled. The DS node manager then updates the annotations of α_{ds}^{req} to record the completion, and sends a notification to QB with the state update for the request actor associated to this request.

Similarly, when replication of an MM object on a DS nodes completes the replica actor annotations are updated, and a notification is sent to QB. Also, if any requests are waiting for this completion they are moved from *Granted* state to *Servicing* state.

Rules for RS, PP, ROD, DR. **RS.** Suppose RS receives a scheduling request, $RS \lhd \mathtt{schedule}(mms, \alpha^{req}, rod)$. If there is some DS node to which the request represented by α^{req} in *mms* can be assigned without violating resource constraints, then *RS* picks one and sends an assignment request to the DS manager of that node. If there is no such DS node and ROD is disabled (*rod* is false), then *RS* sends the broker a denied update. If there is no DS suitable node to which the request can be assigned but *rod* is true, then *RS* sends a replication-on-demand request to *ROD* containing *mms*, along with the requested MM object and QoS requirement. If *RS* receives an acknowledgment to an outstanding assignment request to a DS node, then it sends a granted reply to the broker with MM state that contains the update information for α^{req} representing the request along with any replication update that has been done. If *RS* receives a replication update from an outstanding request to *ROD* that allows the request it is attempting to schedule to be granted, then *RS* picks a suitable DS node and sends a corresponding assign request to the nodes DS manager. If the replication update from *ROD* does not allow the request to be granted, then *RS* sends a denied reply to *QB*.

ROD. When *ROD* receives a request, $ROD \vartriangleleft \mathtt{repl}(mms, MM, qt) @ RS$ for replication of MM object, MM, with QoS resource requirements qt, it looks, using *mms*, for a DS node that doesn't have the needed MM object and that has the required resources available. If one is found, a replication request is sent to that DS node and *ROD* waits for an acknowledgment. When the acknowledgment message is received, a reply is sent to *RS* with MM state containing the replica update information. If no such DS node is found, then a failure reply is sent to *RS*.

PP, DR. Based on the information in the MM state of a `place` request, *PP* may decide to reclassify some replicas from 0, 2, or 3 to 1, and in the case of moving from 0 to 1 initiate replication. It then notifies each DS node of any changes on that node, waits for acknowledgments from these DS nodes, and then sends a reply to *QB* containing the updated replica state. Similarly, upon receiving a dereplication request, *DR* may decide to reclassify some replicas from 1 to 2. It then notifies each DS node of any changes on that node, waits for acknowledgments, and then sends a reply *QB* containing the replica state update. (Note that in practice, *PP* and *DR* also use other information for predicting requests which we do not model at this level of abstraction.)

Definition 9 (Resource-Based MM Behavior). A system S has *Resource-Based MM Behavior* with respect to the underlying system architecture (DS Nodes and capacity function), the QoS meta actors *QB*, *RS*, *ROD*, *DR*, *PP*, and the DS node managers *DSma(DSnodes)*, if

- for each configuration C in S, the state of X in C is appropriate for X according to Figure 4, for X one of *QB*, *RS*, *ROD*, *DR*, *PP*, or *DSma(DS))* for $DS \in DSnodes$;
- every computation π of S obeys the transition rules for QoS meta-actors discussed above and guarantees termination of servicing and replication-in-progress states;
- for any transition $\tau = C \longrightarrow C'$ of S $\mathtt{replCompletes}(\alpha)$ is an event of τ only if $getA(C, \alpha, State) = InProgress$, for any replica actor α, and

reqCompletes(α_{ds}^{req}) is an event of τ only if $getA(C, \alpha_{ds}^{req}, State) = Servicing$ for any DS request actor α_{ds}^{req}.

To state the "Resource-based MM Behavior provides QoS-based MM Service" theorem it is necessary to specify the conditions under which this in fact holds. For this purpose we define the requirements for QoS Initial configurations and QoS NonInterference. QoS Initial configurations are those in which no QoS meta activity is going on. QoS NonInterference expresses constraints on the environments in which the QoS system can operate correctly.

Definition 10 (QoS Initial). $QoSInitial(C)$ holds for a configuration C just if: QB's status function says there has no active processes; RS, ROD, DR, PP are Idle; and there are no undelivered internal QoS messages in C.

Definition 11 (NonInterference Requirement). S satisfies the $QoSBroker\ Non$-$Interference\ Requirement$ iff transitions that do not involve a QoS meta actor as the principle actor obey the following constraints

- Neither QoS annotations nor the state of actors in $ReqActors$, $DSReqActors$, or $DSReplActors$ are modified.
- No resource dedicated to QoS is used.
- No internal QoS messages (Definition 5) are sent.

Theorem 2 (Resource-based MM Behavior implies Resource-based MM Service). If a system S satisfies

- S has Resource-based MM behavior (Definition 9)
- S satisfies the QoS NonInterference Requirement (Definition 11)
- Every configuration C in S is reachable from a configuration satisfying the QoSInitial conditions (Definition 10)
- $QoSTranslate$ satisfies the QoSTranslate requirements (Definition 3)

then S provides Resource-based MM Service (Definition 7) with respect to the given functions $QoSTranslate$ and $capacity$, with $MMreqset$ being messages of the form $QB \triangleleft \mathtt{mmReq}(\alpha_{cl}, MM, qs)$, and replica and request functions defined in terms of annotations according to Definition 8.

The proof of this theorem (which appears in the full paper) is organized as follows. First the possible system configurations are characterized in terms of combinations of meta actor states and undelivered messages is established. Then a notion of pending update for the broker model of the MM state is defined and it is shown that the broker MM state model modified by the pending updates is an accurate model of the actual MM state, and that the pending updates preserve the QoS replica, request, and resource constraints (with MM states in place of configurations). Finally, fairness of the actor model and the definition of QoS reaction rules are used to establish that the QoS broker meta actor, QB is always eventually able to receive a MM request.

Theorem 3 (Resource-based MM Behavior implies QoS-based MM Service). If a system S satisfies the premises of Theorem 2, then S provides QoS-based MM Service (Definition 1) with respect to the given functions *QoSTranslate* and *capacity*, with *MMreqset* being messages of the form $QB \triangleleft \mathtt{mmReq}(\alpha_{cl}, MM, qs)$.

Proof: By Theorem 2 and Theorem 1.   □

5.4   Specifying an Adaptive Resource Scheduling Policy for a QoS Broker

In this section, we illustrate how we refine the Resource-Based MM Behavior specification, by introducing the load-factor based adaptive scheduling algorithm to constrain the behavior of the request scheduler meta-actor. To show this is correct we need only show that the resource-based behavior requirements are met. This follows from the fact that the algorithm meets the constraints implicit in the request scheduler transition rules.

The adaptive scheduling algorithm is used to select a data source to serve a request. The algorithm takes as input a MM request and returns the best data source on which to schedule that request based on the current load and the minimal load-factor criteria.

Recall that the request scheduler receives scheduling requests of the form $RS \triangleleft \mathtt{schedule}(mms, \alpha^{req}, rod)$ from the QoS broker, where mms is the QoS brokers perception of the current MM state. In particular mms contains information about existing replicas and request assignments that reflects the availability of resources at each data source. We adapt the load-factor function (Section 4) to take an MM state, a request actor and a DS node as arguments, using correspondingly adapted functions for calculating the resource allocation in a given configuration. This is then used to define the *Candidates* function that determines the best candidate DS node(s) for assignment of the request according to the load factor criteria.

Definition 12 (Candidates function).   We calculate the available resources on each node for the load factor calculation by subtracting the resources currently allocated from the total capacity of a data source.

$$Available(mms, DS, Res) = capacity(DS, Res) - ResAlloc(mms, DS, Res)$$

where $ResAlloc(mms, DS, Res)$ is amount of resource Res allocated to requests on DS, according to the information in mms. The adaptive load factor calculation is then defined as follows.

$$LF(mms, \alpha^{req}, DS) = max(\frac{qt_{DB}}{DB^{DS}}, \frac{qt_{Mem}}{Mem^{DS}}, \frac{qt_{CPU}}{CPU^{DS}}, \frac{qt_{NetBW}}{NetBW^{DS}})$$

where

$$qt = mms(\alpha^{req}, QoS)$$

$$R^{DS} = Available(mms, DS, R) \quad \text{for} \quad R \in Resources$$

The candidate data sources, $Candidates(mms, \alpha^{req})$ are those such that the load factor is minimal and not infinite, and a replica of the requested MM object exists on the data source.

We define Adaptive Request Scheduling MM Behavior by modifying the RS rules for scheduling requests (§ 5.3) to pick a data source for assignment from the candidates set rather than from the set of all data sources that have the required resources available. The rules for *ROD* are similarly modified to use the load factor calculation to find a candidate node for replication.

Definition 13 (Adaptive RS MM Behavior). A system S has *Adaptive Request Scheduling MM Behavior* with respect to the underlying system architecture, the QoS meta actors *QB*, *RS*, *ROD*, *DR*, *PP*, and the DS node managers *DSma(DSnodes)*, if it satisfies the conditions for Resource-based MM behavior, modified by replacing the request scheduler and replication-on-demand rules as discussed above.

The correctness theorem for Adaptive Resource Scheduling MM Behavior is the following.

Theorem 4 (Adaptive RS MM Behavior implies QoS-based MM Service). If

- S has Adaptive Resource Scheduling MM behavior (Definition 13)
- S satisfies the QoS NonInterference Requirement (Definition 11)
- every $C \in S$ is reachable from a configuration satisfying the QoSInitial conditions (Definition 10)
- *QoSTranslate* satisfies the QoSTranslate requirements (Definition 3)

then S provides QoS-based MM Service (Definition 1).

Proof: By Theorem 3 we only need to show that under the QoS-Initial and QoS-NonInterference assumptions a system that has Adaptive RS MM Behavior also has Resource-based MM Behavior. For this, it is sufficient to check that the each transition arising from an Adaptive RS or ROD rule is a transition allowed by the corresponding generic Resource-based rule. This holds because (1) every DS node in $Candidates(mms, \alpha^{req})$ can be assigned the request associated to α^{req} in mms by the generic rules, and (2) if $Candidates(mms, \alpha^{req}) = \emptyset$ then there is no DS node that can be assigned the request associated to α^{req} in mms by the generic rules.   □

6   Related Work and Future Research Directions

Commercially available object-based middleware infrastructures such as CORBA and DCOM represent a step toward compositional software architectures but do not deal with interactions of multiple object services executing at the same time, or the implication of composing object services. Architectures that provide real-time extensions to CORBA [22,32] necessary to support timing-based

QoS requirements [35] have been proposed and used to study performance optimizations [12]. In the Java Development Environment, the ability to deal with real-time thread management is dependent on the underlying threads implementation, making QoS support complicated to achieve. Various systems such as the Infospheres Infrastructure [7] and the Globe System [24] explore the construction of large scale distributed systems using the paradigm of distributed objects. Globus, a metacomputing framework, defines a QoS component called Related work in the area of multimedia QoS management includes projects such as *QualMan* [19] and systems that implement a variety of algorithms for MM server management [33,30,10,31,9].

Reflection allows application objects to customize the system behavior as in Apertos [13] and 2K [15]. The Aspect Oriented Programming paradigm [14] makes it possible to express programs where design decisions can be appropriately isolated permitting composition and re-use. Some of the more recent research on actors has focused on coordination structures, meta-architectures and runtime systems [2,23]. In other reflective models for distributed object computation [20,8,4], an object is represented by multiple models allowing behavior to be described at different levels of abstraction and from different points of view. Many of the middleware systems described focus heavily on implementation issues while the focus of the work presented in this paper is on developing formal semantics and reasoning for a QoS-based middleware environment.

Much of the work on formal models for QoS has been in the context of QoS specification mechanisms and constructs. In some implementation driven methods of QoS specification, the specification of QoS requirements is intermixed with the service specification [16,17]. Other approaches address the representation of QoS via multiparadigm specification techniques that specify functional behavior and performance ' constraints distinctly using multiple languages [3,34,5,6]. Synchronizers and RtSynchronizers [11,21] allow us to express QoS constraints via coordination constraints in the actor model.

We are actively working on extending the existing meta-architecture to support more services. Specifying and reasoning about enforcement of timing-based QoS requirements of multiple sessions involves a more thorough treatment of time and synchronization. For end-to-end QoS, it is necessary to determine how *real-time scheduling* strategies for time constrained task management interact with strategies for other tasks such as CPU intensive calculations, or network communication with clients. We are currently working on formalizing other components of the MM meta-architecture such as message scheduling and synchronization. Supporting requirements such as fault-tolerance, availability and hard real-time QoS will require further extensions of the existing MM metaarchitecture. We are currently studying the composability of multiple protocols and mechanisms to address these requirements in the MM metaarchitecture.

In general, the dynamic nature of applications such as those of multimedia under varying network conditions, request traffic, etc. imply that resource management policies must be dynamic and customizable. Current mechanisms, which allow arbitrary objects to be plugged together, are not sufficient to capture the richness of interactions between resource managers and application components. For example, they do not allow customization of execution protocols for scheduling, replication, etc. This implies that the components must be redefined to incorporate the different protocols representing such interaction. In this paper we have shown, using the QoS broker MM architecture, how a meta-architectural framework, such as the TLAM, can be used to specify and reason about distributed middleware services and their composition, and have also indicated how specifications in the framework can lead to implementations. We believe that a cleanly defined meta-architecture which supports customization and composition of protocols and services is needed to support the flexible use of component based software.[1]

References

1. G. Agha. *Actors: A Model of Concurrent Computation in Distributed Systems.* MIT Press, Cambridge, Mass., 1986.
2. G. Agha, S. Frølund, W. Kim, R. Panwar, A. Patterson, and D. Sturman. Abstraction and Modularity Mechanisms for Concurrent Computing. *IEEE Parallel and Distributed Technology: Systems and Applications,* 1(2):3–14, May 1993.
3. G. Blair, L. Blair, H. Bowman, and A. Chetwynd. *Formal Specifications of Distributed Multimedia Systems.* UCL Press, 1988.
4. G. Blair, G. Coulson, P.Robin, and M. Papathomas. An architecture for next generation middleware. In *Middleware '98,* 1998.
5. L. Blair and G. Blair. Composition in multiparadigm specification techniques. In *ECOOP Workshop on Aspect Oriented Programming,* July 1999.
6. L. Blair and G. Blair. Composition in multiparadigm specification techniques. In *IFIP Workshop on Formal Methods for Open Object-based Distributed Systems, FMOODS'99,* Feb. 1999.
7. K. Chandy, A. Rifkin, P. A. Sivilotti, J. Mandelson, M. Richardson, W. Tanaka, and L. Weisman. A world-wide distributed system using java and the internet. In *Proceedings of IEEE International Symposium on High Performance Distributed Computing (HPDC-5), Syracuse, New York,* Aug. 1996.
8. F. Costa, G. Blair, and G. Coulson. Experiments with reflective middleware. In *European Workshop on Reflective Object-Oriented Programming and Systems, ECOOP'98.* Springer-Verlag, 1998.
9. A. Dan and D. Sitaram. An online video placement policy based on bandwidth to space ratio (bsr). In *SIGMOD '95,* pages 376–385, 1995.
10. A. Dan, D. Sitaram, and P. Shahabuddin. Dynamic batching policies for an on-demand video server. *ACM Multimedia Systems,* 4:112–121, 1996.
11. S. Frølund. *Coordinating Distributed Objects: An Actor-Based Approach to Synchronization.* MIT Press, 1996.
12. A. Gokhale and D. C. Schmidt. Evaluating the Performance of Demultiplexing Strategies for Real-time CORBA. In *Proceedings of GLOBECOM '97,* Phoenix, AZ, 1997.

[1] Acknowledgements: The authors would like to thank the anonymous referees for valuable suggestions for improving previous versions of this paper. This research was partially supported by DARPA/NASA NAS2-98073, ONR N00012-99-C-0198, ARPA/SRI subcontract 17-000042, NSF CCR-9900326.

13. J. ichiro Itoh, R. Lea, and Y. Yokote. Using meta-objects to support optimization in the Apertos operating system. In *USENIX COOTS (Conference on Object-Oriented Technologies*, June 1995.
14. G. Kiczales, J. Lamping, A. Mendhekar, C. Maeda, C. V. Lopes, J.-M. Loingtier, and J. Irwin. Aspect-Oriented Programming. In *Proceedings of ECOOP'97 European Conference on Object-Oriented Programming*, June 1997.
15. F. Kon, A. Singhai, R. H. Campbell, D. Carvalho, R. Moore, and F. J. Ballesteros. 2K: A Reflective, Component-Based Operating System for Rapidly Changing Environments . In *Proceedings of ECOOP'98 Workshop on Reflective Object-Oriented Programming and Systems*, Brussels, Belgium, July 1998.
16. P. Leydekkers and V. Gay. Odp view on qos for open distributed mm environments. In J. d. Meer and A. Vogel, editors, *4th International IFIP Workshop on Quality of Service, IwQos96 Paris, France*, pages 45–55, Mar. 1996.
17. F. H. d. S. Lima and E. R. M. Madeira. Odp based qos specification for the multiware platform. In J. d. Meer and A. Vogel, editors, *4th International IFIP Workshop on Quality of Service, IwQos96 Paris, France*, pages 45–55, Mar. 1996.
18. K. Nahrstedt. *Network Service Customization: End-Point Perspective*. PhD thesis, University of Pennsylvannia, 1995.
19. K. Nahrstedt, H.-H. Chu, and S. Narayan. Qos-aware resource management for distributed multimedia applications.
20. H. Okamura, Y. Ishikawa, and M. Tokoro. Al-1/d: A distributed programming system with multi-model reflection framework. In A. Yonezawa and B. C. Smith, editors, *Reflection and Meta-Level Architetures*, pages 36–47. ACM SIGPLAN, 1992.
21. S. Ren, G. Agha, and M. Saito. A modular approach for programming distributed real-time systems. *Journal of Parallel and Distributed Computing*, 36(1), July 1996.
22. D. C. Schmidt, D. Levine, and S. Mungee. The design of the tao real-time object request broker. *Computer Communications Special Issue on Building Quality of Service into Distributed System*, 1997.
23. D. Sturman. *Modular Specification of Interaction Policies in Distributed Computing*. PhD thesis, University of Illinois at Urbana-Champaign, May 1996. TR UIUCDCS-R-96-1950.
24. M. van Steen, A. Tanenbaum, I. Kuz, and H. Sip. A scalable middleware solution for advanced wide-area web services. In *Proc.Middleware '98, The Lake District, UK*, 1998.
25. N. Venkatasubramanian. *An Adaptive Resource Management Architecture for Global Distributed Computing.* PhD thesis, University of Illinois, Urbana-Champaign, 1998.
26. N. Venkatasubramanian. Compose—q - a qos-enabled customizable middleware framework for distributed computing. In *Proceedings of the Middleware Workshop, International Conference on Distributed Computing Systems (ICDCS99)*, June 1999.
27. N. Venkatasubramanian and S. Ramanathan. Effective load management for scalable video servers. In *Proceedings of the International Conference on Distributed Computing Systems (ICDCS97)*, May 1997.
28. N. Venkatasubramanian and C. L. Talcott. A metaarchitecture for distributed resource management. In *Hawaii International Conference on System Sciences, HICSS-26*, Jan. 1993.
29. N. Venkatasubramanian and C. L. Talcott. Reasoning about Meta Level Activities in Open Distributed Systems. In *14th ACM Symposium on Principles of Distributed Computing*, pages 144–152, 1995.

30. H. M. Vin and P. V. Rangan. Designing a multi-user hdtv storage server. *IEEE Journal on Selected Areas in Communications*, 11(1):153–164, Jan. 1993.
31. J. L. Wolf, P. S. Yu, and H. Shachnai. Dasd dancing: A disk load balancing optimization scheme for video-on-demand computer systems. In *Proceedings of ACM SIGMETRICS '95, Performance Evaluation Review*, pages 157–166, May 1995.
32. V. F. Wolfe, J. K. Black, B. Thuraisingham, and P. Krupp. Real-time method invocations in distributed environments. In *Proceedings of the HiPC'95 Intl. Conference on High Performance COmputing*, 1995.
33. P. Yu, M. Chen, and D. Kandlur. Design and analysis of a grouped sweeping scheme for multimedia storage management. *Proceedings of Third International Workshop on Network and Operating System Support for Digital Audio and Video, San Diego*, pages 38–49, November 1992.
34. P. Zave and M. Jackson. Requirements for telecommunications services: An attack on complexity. In *IEEE International Symposium on Requirements Engineering*, 1997.
35. J. Zinky, D. Bakken, and R. Schantz. Architectural support of quality of service. *Theory and Practice of Object Systems*, 3(1), 1997.

A Programming Model for Wide-Area Computing

Jayadev Misra

Department of Computer Sciences
University of Texas
Austin, Texas, USA
misra@cs.utexas.edu

Abstract. During the last decade there have been great strides in broadband communication, and the World Wide Web provides a giant repository of information. This combination promises development of a new generation of distributed applications, ranging from mundane office tasks — e.g., planning a meeting by reading the calendars of the participants — to real-time distributed control and coordination of hundreds of machines —e.g., as would be required in a recovery effort from an earthquake.

The distributed applications we envisage have the structure that they collect data from a number of sources, compute for a while and then distribute the results to certain destinations. This simple paradigm hides a multitude of issues. When should an application start executing: when invoked by a human, by another application, periodically say, at midnight, or triggered by an event, say, upon detection of the failure of a communication link? How does an application ensure that the data it accesses during a computation is not altered by another concurrently executing application? How do communicating parties agree on the structure of the data being communicated? And, how are conflicts in a concurrent computation arbitrated? In short, the basic issues of concurrent computing such as, exclusive access to resources, deadlock and starvation, and maintaining consistent copies of data, have to be revisited in the wide-area context.

There seems to be an obvious methodology for designing distributed applications: represent each device (computer, robot, a site in the World Wide Web) by an object and have the objects communicate by messages or by calling each others' methods. This representation maps conveniently to the underlying hardware, and it induces a natural partition on the problem that is amenable to step-wise refinement. We start with this model as our basis, simplify and enhance it so that it is possible to address the concurrent programming issues. In this talk, I discuss the programming model and some of our experience in building distributed applications.

J.N. Oliveira and P. Zave (Eds.): FME 2001, LNCS 2021, p. 222, 2001.

A Formal Model of Object-Oriented Design and GoF Design Patterns

Andres Flores[1], Richard Moore[2], and Luis Reynoso[1]

[1] Department of Informatics and Statistics - University of Comahue
Buenos Aires 1400, 8300 Neuquen, Argentina
E-mail: {aflores, lreynoso}@uncoma.edu.ar
[2] United Nations University - International Institute for Software Technology
P.O. Box 3058, Macau
E-mail: rm@iist.unu.edu

Abstract. Particularly in object-oriented design methods, design patterns are becoming increasingly popular as a way of identifying and abstracting the key aspects of commonly occurring design structures. The abstractness of the patterns means that they can be applied in many different domains, which makes them a valuable basis for reusable object-oriented design and hence for helping designers achieve more effective results. However, the standard literature on patterns invariably describes them informally, generally using natural language together with some sort of graphical notation, which makes it very difficult to give any meaningful certification that the patterns have been applied consistently and correctly in a design. In this paper, we describe a formal model of object-oriented design and design patterns which can be used to demonstrate that a particular design conforms to a given pattern, and we illustrate using an example how this can be done. The formality of the model can also help to resolve ambiguities and incompletenesses in the informal descriptions of the patterns.

1 Introduction

Design patterns offer designers a way of reusing proven solutions to particular aspects of design rather than having to start each new design from scratch. Patterns are generic and abstract and embody "best practice" solutions to design problems which recur in a range of different contexts [1], although these solutions are not necessarily the simplest or most efficient for any given problem [11]. Patterns are also useful because they provide designers with an effective "shorthand" for communicating with each other about complex concepts [3]: the name of the pattern serves as a precise and concise way of referring to a design technique which is well-documented and which is known to work well.

One specific and popular set of software design patterns, which are independent of any specific application domain, are the so-called "GoF"[1] patterns which are described in the catalogue of Gamma et al. [10]. The GoF catalogue

---

[1] "Gang of Four"

J.N. Oliveira and P. Zave (Eds.): FME 2001, LNCS 2021, pp. 223–241, 2001.
© Springer-Verlag Berlin Heidelberg 2001

is thus a description of the know-how of expert designers in problems appearing in various different domains.

Although there is nothing in design patterns that makes them inherently object-oriented [3], the GoF catalogue uses object-oriented concepts to describe twenty three patterns which capture and compact the essential parts of corresponding design solutions. Each GoF pattern thus identifies a group of classes, together with the key aspects of their functionality and interactions, which commonly occur in a range of different object-oriented design problems.

The descriptions of the GoF patterns in [10] are largely informal, consisting of a combination of a graphical notation based on an extension of OMT (Object Modelling Technique [16]) together with natural language and sample code. This gives a very good intuitive picture of the patterns, but is not sufficiently precise to allow a designer to demonstrate conclusively that a particular problem matches a particular pattern or that a proposed solution is consistent with a particular pattern. The notation also makes it difficult to be certain that the patterns used are meaningful and contain no inconsistencies.

A formal model of patterns can help to alleviate these problems. One existing approach to this [6] represents patterns as formulae in LePUS, a language defined as a fragment of higher order monadic logic [7]. A second [13] formalises the temporal behaviour of patterns using the DisCo specification method, which is based on the Temporal Logic of Actions [12]. Another [5,4] specifies the essential elements of GoF patterns using RSL (the RAISE Specification Language; [14]).

Our approach is based on the last of these, though it significantly extends the scope of the model used therein in several ways. First, we generalise the model so that it describes an arbitrary object-oriented design and not just the patterns. Second, we formally specify how to match a design against a pattern. And third we include in our model specifications of the behavioural properties of the design, specifically the actions that are to be performed by the methods, which was omitted from the model described in [5,4]. In this way, we can formally model all the components of an generic object-oriented design and also formally check that a given subset of that design matches a given pattern. Indeed, the model has been used as the basis for a thorough analysis and formal specification of the properties of the majority of the patterns in the GoF catalogue, as a result of which a number of ambiguities and incompletenesses in the informal descriptions of several of the GoF patterns have been identified and extended pattern structures have been proposed [15,8,2].

We begin by giving an overview of the extended OMT notation and of our formal model of a generic object-oriented design based upon it in Section 2. Then we discuss how to formally link a design with a pattern in Section 3. Section 4 then shows how the properties of individual patterns are specified in our model, using the State pattern from the GoF catalogue [10] as an example, and Section 5 gives an example of the whole process of specifying a design and verifying that it matches a pattern, again using an example of a design based on the State pattern. We conclude with a summary of our work and an indication of future work we plan in this field.

2   A Formal Model of Object-Oriented Design

Since we are primarily interested in using our general model to specify properties of object-oriented design patterns, in particular the GoF patterns [10], we base it on the extended OMT [16] notation which is used in [10] to describe the structure of GoF patterns and which has to a large extent been used as a standard notation for describing patterns. An example of this notation is shown in Figure 1, which represents the structure of the State pattern.

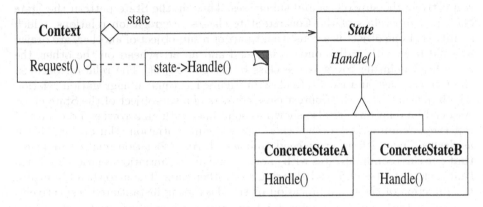

Fig. 1. State Pattern Structure

We begin by giving an informal overview of this notation in Section 2.1, then introduce our formal model in Section 2.2.

2.1   An Overview of Extended OMT Notation

In the extended OMT notation, a design consists essentially of a collection of classes and a collection of relations linking the classes. Each class is depicted as a rectangle containing the name of the class, the signatures (i.e. names and parameters) of the operations or methods which objects of the class can perform, and the state variables or instance variables which represent the internal data stored by instances of the class. Every class in a design has a unique name.

Classes and methods are designated as *abstract* or *concrete* by writing their name in italic or upright script respectively in the OMT diagram. No instances (objects) may be created from an abstract class, and an abstract method cannot be executed (often because the method is only completely defined in subclasses).

Concrete methods, which can be executed, may additionally have *annotations* in the OMT diagram which indicate what actions the method should perform. These annotations appear within rectangles with a "folded" corner which are attached to a method within the class description rectangle by a dashed line ending in a small circle.

Thus, for example, the structure in Figure 1 indicates that the class Context in the State pattern is a concrete class which contains a concrete method called Request, while the class State is an abstract class which contains an abstract method called Handle. In addition, the annotation attached to the Request method in the Context class indicates that the action of this method is to invoke the Handle method on the variable called state.

Relations specify connections or communications between classes and are represented as lines linking classes in the OMT diagram. Four different types of relations are used – *inheritance, aggregation, association* and *instantiation* – and these are distinguished in the diagram using different types of lines. Inheritance relations have a triangle in the middle of the line whose point and base indicate respectively the superclass and subclasses. Thus, in the State pattern the State class is a superclass of the ConcreteState classes. Aggregation relations, which signify that one object is a constituent part or a sub-object of another, are drawn as solid lines with a diamond on one end and an arrowhead on the other, the arrowhead pointing towards the class of the sub-object. The relation between the Context class and the State class in Figure 1 is thus an aggregation relation which indicates that the Context class consists of a sub-object of the State class. Association relations are also shown as solid lines with an arrowhead on one end but they are unmarked at the other end, while instantiation relations are shown as dashed lines with an arrowhead on one end. An association relation indicates that one class communicates with another, and an instantiation relation indicates that a class creates objects belonging to another class. The arrowhead indicates the direction of the communication or the class being instantiated respectively.

Association and aggregation relations also have an associated *arity*, which may be one or many according to whether each object of one class communicates with or is composed of a single object or a collection of objects of the other class. Relations of arity many are indicated by adding a solid black circle to the front of the arrowhead.

2.2   The Formal Model

From the patterns and examples in [10] it can be seen that the various actions that can appear as annotations to methods in a design basically correspond to the different types of relations that can link the classes, except that at the level of the actions there is no distinction between aggregation and association relations. Thus, in our formal model we define three types of actions – invocation, instantiation, and self or super invocation – which we use to model these actions.

An invocation represents an interaction that corresponds to an association or aggregation relation: objects of one class request objects of another class to perform some action by executing some method. Some variable (generally the "name" of the relation) in the first class represents the object that receives the request, while the request itself consists of the name of the method which should be executed together with appropriate parameters for that method. In the RSL specification variables are represented by the type 'Variable_Name' and the parameters of a request by the type 'Actual_Parameters', which is basically just a list of variables which does not include the reserved variable name super which is used exclusively in super invocations (described below). Then the request as a whole is modelled using the type 'Actual_Signature' and the whole invocation by the type 'Invocation'.

> Invocation ::
>   call_vble : Variable_Name   call_sig : Actual_Signature,
> Actual_Signature ::
>   meth_name : Method_Name   a_params : Actual_Parameters,
> Actual_Parameters = Wf_Variable_Name*

An instantiation of course represents an interaction which corresponds to an instantiation relation: one class requests another class to create a new object. In most object-oriented programming languages there are essentially two ways in which this sort of object creation can be performed. First, the class might create a "default" instance of itself (for example in Smalltalk by using the basic creation method *new* which is available in every class) and then set the state variables of this instance appropriately using other methods. Or second, the class may have other local creation methods which create customised instances directly using parameters to the methods (as, for example, in the parameterised method *new:* in Smalltalk which uses its parameter to additionally set the state of the instance it creates). We cover both of these situations in our model by defining an instantiation (the type 'Instantiation') to consist of the name of the class to be instantiated together with a possibly empty list of parameters.

> Instantiation ::
>   class_name : Class_Name   a_params : Actual_Parameters

Self and super invocations are analogous to invocations except that the invocation is to the same class or to a superclass respectively. Super invocations therefore correspond in some sense to inheritance relations, but there is no such correspondence with relations in the case of self invocations because relations between a class and itself are generally not shown explicitly in an OMT diagram. In our formal model we use the type 'Invocation' to model both self and super invocations, except that in these cases the call variable of the invocation is the specific variable name 'self' or 'super' respectively.

> self, super : Variable_Name

In general, an annotation can contain one or more instantiations or invocations, the order of which is generally important. We model this as a list of *requests*, where a request can be either an invocation or an instantiation. Annotations can also indicate assignments to variables, including both state variables and local (dummy) variables. Two forms of assignment are used: one where the results of some request are assigned to variables, generally for use in a later request, and the second where the parameters of the method are assigned to variables, generally state variables. These assignments are modelled using the type 'Variable_Change', which maps sets of variables to either requests or sets of variables. These correspond to the two forms of assignment described above.

The predicate defining the subtype here ensures that the empty set is not in the domain of the map and that no two sets in the domain have variables in common[2].

> Variables = Wf_Variable_Name-**set**,
> Request = Invocation | Instantiation | _,
> Request_or_Var = Request | Variables,
> Variable_Change =
>   {| m : Wf_Vble_Name-**set** $\xrightarrow{m}$ Request_or_Var •
>   is_wf_vchange(m)
> |}

The requests and the variable assignments constitute the *body* of a concrete or *implemented* method. The actions performed by abstract or *defined* methods are unspecified, however, so these methods basically have no body. And some patterns (e.g. the Composite pattern in [10]), and hence of course designs, can include methods which are defined in a superclass but which should not be implemented in all subclasses and indeed do not make sense in some subclasses. Such methods, which we call *error* methods, also have no body. Our formal definition of the body of a method then takes the form of a variant type which defines each of the three different types of method, the bodies of defined and error methods being represented simply as the constants of the same names.

> Method_Body ==
>   defined |
>   error |
>   implemented
>   (variable_change : Variable_Change, request_list : Request*)

The other important components of a method are its result, which we model as a set of variables, its formal parameters, which is a list of parameters, each of which is a variable (which cannot be 'self' or 'super'; the type 'Wf_Vble_Name') with optionally the name of a class indicating the type of that variable, and its name. The well-formedness condition 'is_wf_formal_parameters' on the formal parameters ensures that all the variables representing the formal parameters are distinct (so that they can be distinguished in the body of the method). There are also consistency conditions on the components of the method, for example that every set of variables to which the result of an instantiation is assigned can contain only one variable, and these are similarly embodied in the function 'is_wf_method' and hence in the definition of a *well-formed* method.

The method names are included in the form of a map from method names to well-formed methods since the names of the methods in a particular class must all be different. The constraint 'is_wf_class_method' simply states that certain reserved method names cannot be used.

---

[2] Although this latter condition might at first sight seem to be too restrictive, our model is an abstract one in which we only model the final value of each particular variable.

Method ::
    f_params : Wf_Formal_Parameters
    meth_res : Result
       body : Method_Body,
Result = Variables,
Parameter ==
    var(Wf_Vble_Name) |
    paramTyped(paramName : Wf_Vble_Name, className : Class_Name),
Wf_Formal_Parameters =
    {| p : Parameter* • is_wf_formal_parameters(p) |}
Wf_Method = {| m : Method • is_wf_method(m) |},
Map_Methods = Method_Name $\xrightarrow{m}$ Wf_Method,
Class_Method = {| m : Map_Methods • is_wf_class_method(m) |}

The state of a class is similarly defined as a set of variables, which also may not include the reserved variables 'self' and 'super. This, together with the methods and the class type, which is simply either of the two values 'abstract' or 'concrete', then forms all the important components of a class definition except its name. We again include the class names using a map from class names to *well-formed* classes because the names of all classes in a design must be distinct. The well-formedness condition on a class requires that state variables cannot be used as formal parameters to methods.

        State = Wf_Vble_Name-**set**,
        Class_Type == abstract | concrete,
        Design_Class ::
           class_state : State
           class_methods : Class_Method
           class_type : Class_Type,
        Wf_Class = {| c : Design_Class • is_wf_class(c) |},
        Classes = Class_Name $\xrightarrow{m}$ Wf_Class

A relation is basically determined by the classes it links and its type, which may be inheritance, association, aggregation, or instantiation. All relations except inheritance relations are binary, linking a single *source* class to a single *sink* class. We in fact also model inheritance relations as binary relations by considering the case in which a class has several subclasses as many inheritance relations, one linking the superclass to each individual subclass. Thus, our basic definition of a relation is embodied in the record type 'Design_Relation'.

In the case of instantiation and inheritance relations, there can be at most one such relation between any pair of classes. The type together with the source and sink classes is thus sufficient to identify the relation uniquely. However, it is possible to have more than one association or aggregation relation between the same two classes, and furthermore the arity of these relations can be indicated, at least to the extent that it is either one or many. We therefore introduce the type 'Card' to represent the arity and use the names of the relations to distinguish between them. In this way, for example, the aggregation relation between the

Context and State classes in the State pattern (see Figure 1) has arity one-one and is identified uniquely by its name state.

The well-formedness condition 'wf_relation' states that instantiation relations are not explicitly shown between a class and itself and that there cannot be inheritance relations between a class and itself.

> Card == one | many,
> Ref ::
>   relation_name : Wf_Vble_Name
>   sink_card : Card
>   source_card : Card,
> Relation_Type ==
>   inheritance |
>   association(as_ref : Ref) |
>   aggregation(ag_ref : Ref) |
>   instantiation,
> Design_Relation ::
>   relation_type : Relation_Type
>   source_class : Class_Name
>   sink_class : Class_Name,
> Wf_Relation = {| r : Design_Relation • wf_relation(r) |}

An object-oriented design, which is represented in our model by the type 'Design_Structure', then simply consists of a collection of classes and a collection of relations, together with appropriate consistency conditions (for example that there are no circularities in inheritance relations, that an abstract class cannot be the sink of an instantiation relation because creating instances of abstract classes is not allowed, that an abstract class must have subclasses, etc. Full details of these consistency conditions can be found in [9]).

> Design_Structure = Classes × Wf_Relations,
> Wf_Design_Structure =
>   {| ds : Design_Structure • is_wf_design_structure(ds) |}

3 Matching Designs to Patterns

We now go on to explain how to link our model of a design to the design patterns in such a way that it is possible to determine whether or not the two match.

We make this link using a *renaming map*, which associates the names of entities (classes, methods, state variables and parameters) in the design with the names of corresponding entities in the pattern. Thus, the correspondences between state variables and between parameters are modelled using the type 'VariableRenaming', which simply maps variables in the design to variables in the pattern. The type 'Method_and_Parameter_Renaming' relates methods in the design to methods in the pattern. It consists of two parts: the first simply defines the correspondence between the names of the methods and the second relates their parameters. This nested structure is necessary because two different methods may have parameters with the same name.

The renaming of a class has a similarly nested structure, the type 'Class-Renaming' consisting of the name of the class in the pattern together with one renaming map for the methods in the class and another for the state variables. However, in this case it is possible for a single class in the design to play several *roles* in the pattern (for instance, in the example illustrating the Command pattern in [10] the class Application in the design plays both the Client and the Receiver roles in the pattern). We therefore map each design class to a set of class renamings in the renaming map, and the full renaming map is represented by the type 'Renaming'. The well-formedness condition requires that no design class can have an empty set of renamings and that the renamings of any one design class must all refer to different pattern classes.

VariableRenaming = Variable_Name $\xrightarrow{m}$ Variable_Name,
Method_and_Parameter_Renaming = Method_Name $\xrightarrow{m}$ Method_Renaming,
Method_Renaming ::
    method_name : Method_Name   parameterRenaming : VariableRenaming,
ClassRenaming ::
    classname : Class_Name
    methodRenaming : Method_and_Parameter_Renaming
    varRenaming : VariableRenaming,
Renaming = Class_Name $\xrightarrow{m}$ ClassRenaming-**set**,
Wf_Renaming = {| r : Renaming • is_wf_Renaming(r) |}

Finally, we link the design with the renaming map through the type 'Design_Renaming'. Its well-formedness condition is quite complicated so we refer the reader to [9] for the details.

Design_Renaming = Wf_Design_Structure × Wf_Renaming,
Wf_Design_Renaming =
    {| pr : Design_Renaming • is_wf_design_renaming(pr) |}

4   Specifying the Properties of the Patterns

In order to check whether a particular (subset of a) design matches a particular pattern, we formally specify functions which embody all the properties that the entities in the pattern must exhibit, then we require that every entity in the design which has a renaming under the renaming map to an entity in the pattern satisfies the properties of that entity in the pattern. We illustrate how the properties of the patterns are specified by considering the specification of the State pattern in [10] (see Figure 1).

The structure of the State pattern comprises a single hierarchy of classes rooted at the State class, together with a single Context class. The Context class basically defines a common interface which clients can use to interact with the various ConcreteState subclasses, and essentially it simply forwards requests appropriately via its state variable. This is represented by the single aggregation relation between these classes in the pattern structure.

We define the function 'hierarchy' to specify the first of these properties. This is a generic function which checks that a hierarchy of classes in the design has as its root a class which plays a given role in the pattern and which is unique in the design, has leaf classes which play any of a given set of roles in the pattern[3], and has no classes which play roles from a given set of roles (in this case Context and Client). The specific property of the State pattern that we require is then embodied in the function 'State_hierarchy' which simply instantiates the function 'hierarchy' with the required roles. We omit the specification of the function 'hierarchy', which is rather long, for brevity and refer the reader to [9] for the details.

$$\text{State\_hierarchy} : \text{Wf\_Design\_Renaming} \rightarrow \textbf{Bool}$$
$$\text{State\_hierarchy}(dr) \equiv$$
$$\text{hierarchy}(\text{State}, \{\text{ConcreteState}\}, \{\text{Context, Client}\}, dr)$$

Another property of the State pattern is that there is a single class which plays the Context role, and this is a concrete class. This is specified using the functions 'exists_one' and 'is_concrete_class' from [9]. The function 'exists_one' checks that a single class in the design plays a given role in the pattern, and the function 'is_concrete_class' checks that all classes that play a given role are concrete. Again, the specifications of the required property of the State pattern, which are represented by the functions 'exists_one_Context' and 'is_concrete_Context', are obtained by instantiating these functions with the appropriate roles from the State pattern.

$$\text{exists\_one} : \text{Class\_Name} \times \text{Wf\_Design\_Renaming} \rightarrow \textbf{Bool}$$
$$\text{exists\_one}(cp, (ds, r)) \equiv$$
$$(\exists ! \; cd : \text{Class\_Name} \bullet \text{renaming\_class\_name}(cd, cp, r)),$$

$$\text{is\_concrete\_class} : \text{Class\_Name} \times \text{Wf\_Design\_Renaming} \rightarrow \textbf{Bool}$$
$$\text{is\_concrete\_class}(cp, ((dsc, dsr), r)) \equiv$$
$$($$
$$\forall \; cd : \text{Class\_Name} \bullet$$
$$\text{renaming\_class\_name}(cd, cp, r) \Rightarrow \text{is\_concrete\_class}(dsc(cd))$$
$$),$$

$$\text{exists\_one\_Context} : \text{Wf\_Design\_Renaming} \rightarrow \textbf{Bool}$$
$$\text{exists\_one\_Context}(dr) \equiv \text{exists\_one}(\text{Context}, dr),$$

$$\text{is\_concrete\_Context} : \text{Wf\_Design\_Renaming} \rightarrow \textbf{Bool}$$
$$\text{is\_concrete\_Context}(dr) \equiv \text{is\_concrete\_class}(\text{Context}, dr)$$

---

[3] In this case there is only one class in this set, namely ConcreteState, but it is possible to have more than one class as, for example, in the Command pattern in [10].

Other properties of the State pattern are specified similarly. These include, for example, that the class which plays the Context role contains a single state variable which plays the state role and that it also contains at least one method which plays the Request role, all such methods being implemented and containing an invocation to the state variable of a method which plays the Handle role. Together with the properties specified above, these lead us to the definition of the function 'is_state_pattern' which embodies all the essential properties of the elements of the State pattern. Again, full details can be found in [9].

$$
\begin{aligned}
&\text{is\_state\_pattern} : \text{Wf\_Design\_Renaming} \rightarrow \textbf{Bool} \\
&\text{is\_state\_pattern}(dr) \equiv \\
&\quad \text{State\_hierarchy}(dr) \wedge \\
&\quad \text{exists\_one\_Context}(dr) \wedge \\
&\quad \text{is\_concrete\_Context}(dr) \wedge \dots
\end{aligned}
$$

In fact we have already completed specifications of this form for almost all of the patterns in the GoF catalogue. Full details of these specifications can be found in [15,8,2].

5 An Example: Checking an Instantiation of the State Pattern

In this section we give an example of how an object-oriented design is represented in our model and how we relate this to a pattern using the renaming map. As the basis for this, we use the example which is used in [10] to illustrate the motivation and sample code of the State pattern.

This example is a model of a TCP network connection. This connection can be in one of several states – closed, established, listening, etc. – and different operations can be applied to these states to manipulate the connection.

The OMT-extended diagram of this design, where we only include classes representing the three states mentioned above, is shown in Figure 2.

We give only a representative sample of the specification of the design here, defining only the class TCPConnection and the relations in detail. The complete specification can be found in [9].

We begin by defining RSL constants which represent the names of the classes, methods, state variables and parameters which are used in the design. Those used in the class TCPConnection and the relations are:

> TCPConnection : Class_Name,
> TCPState : Class_Name,
> TCPEstablished : Class_Name,
> Client : Class_Name,
> ActiveOpen : Method_Name,
> PassiveOpen : Method_Name,
> Close : Method_Name,
> Send : Method_Name,

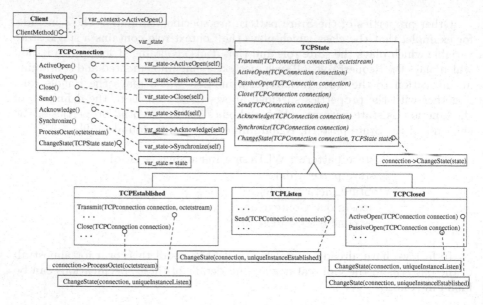

Fig. 2. Design for a TCP Network Connection

Acknowledge : Method_Name,
Synchronize : Method_Name,
ProcessOctet : Method_Name,
ChangeState : Method_Name,
var_state : Variable_Name,
var_context : Variable_Name,
state : Variable_Name,
octetstream : Variable_Name

Next we define the other parts of the methods – their bodies, results and parameters – and the collection of all methods in the class.

Although there are eight methods in the class TCPConnection, the forms of ActiveOpen, PassiveOpen, Close, Send, Acknowledge and Synchronize are essentially the same: each has no parameters, returns no result, causes no variable changes, and has a body which consists of a single invocation to the var_state variable of the corresponding method (i.e. the method with the same name) in the TCPState class, the parameter of each invocation being self. The specifications of these six methods are therefore all identical up to the names involved. Therefore we only show the specification of one of them, ActiveOpen, here together with the specifications of ProcessOctet and ChangeState.

We first define constants representing the bodies of the methods.

Because there are many cases in which different methods in the design have essentially the same structure as, for example, with the six methods described above, we introduce generic parameterised functions to represent these common structures and then define the individual methods in terms of these. An additional advantage of this approach is that the generic functions are likely to be reusable across many different designs.

We therefore begin by defining the function 'one_inv_meth_body' which describes in parameterised form the bodies of the first six methods in TCPConnection. This function then basically describes the body of any method in the design which consists of a single invocation to a given variable of a given method, the invocation having a single given parameter and the method involving no variable changes. Note that the invoked method and its parameter form an actual signature (see Section 2.2) in the specification. Then the body of the ActiveOpen method is represented by a constant, 'meth_body_AOctn', which is constructed by instantiating the function 'one_inv_meth_body' appropriately, in this case with the values var_state, ActiveOpen and self.

> one_inv_meth_body :
>   Variable_Name × Method_Name × Wf_Variable_Name →
>   Method_Body
> one_inv_meth_body(v, m, p) ≡
>   implemented
>   ([ ], ⟨mk_Invocation(v, mk_Actual_Signature(m, ⟨p⟩))⟩),
>
> meth_body_AOctn : Method_Body =
>   one_inv_meth_body(var_state, ActiveOpen, self)

The ProcessOctet and ChangeState methods are treated similarly. The first of these, like several other methods in the design, has no explicit body, so we introduce a generic constant 'empty_method_body' to represent the body of all such methods. The second simply assigns its parameter to a particular state variable, so its body is empty apart from a single variable change which represents this assignment. This type of body is modelled generically using the function 'assign_param_meth_body' and the body of the ChangeState method is again obtained by instantiating this function appropriately, in this case with the variables var_state and state.

> empty_method_body : Method_Body = implemented([ ], ⟨⟩),
>
> assign_param_meth_body :
>   Variable_Name × Wf_Variable_Name → Method_Body
> assign_param_meth_body(v, p) ≡
>   implemented([{v} ↦ Request_or_Var_from_Variable(p)], ⟨⟩),
>
> meth_body_ChgSt : Method_Body =
>   assign_param_meth_body(var_state, state)

Having defined the bodies of the methods, we now proceed to define the methods as a whole.

Again there are similarities in the structure of the methods: the first six methods in the TCPConnection class all have no parameters and no result, though

they have different bodies; the method ProcessOctet has a single untyped parameter and no result; and the method ChangeState, in common with the majority
of the methods in the other classes, has a single typed parameter and no result. We therefore introduce the two generic functions 'method_with_body' and
'method_with_body_param' to describe each of these forms in an appropriately
parameterised way.

$$\text{method\_with\_body : Method\_Body} \rightarrow \text{Method}$$
$$\text{method\_with\_body(b)} \equiv \text{mk\_Method}(\langle\rangle, \{\}, b),$$

$$\text{method\_with\_body\_param :}$$
$$\quad \text{Method\_Body} \times \text{Wf\_Formal\_Parameters} \rightarrow \text{Method}$$
$$\text{method\_with\_body\_param(b, p)} \equiv \text{mk\_Method}(p, \{\}, b)$$

Then the specifications of the individual methods in the class TCPConnection are obtained by appropriately instantiating these generic functions, and
the collection of all methods in the class, which is represented by the RSL
constant 'Ctn_Class_Methods', is formed by constructing a map from each
method name to the appropriate method. However, the methods constructed by
these generic functions do not necessarily satisfy the well-formedness condition
'is_wf_method' (the result type of the functions is 'Method' not 'Wf_Method').
Similarly, the collection of methods must satisfy the well-formedness condition
'is_wf_class_method'. We must therefore check that these conditions are satisfied
in order to be certain that the design is well-formed and the definition below is
correctly typed.

Ctn_Class_Methods : Class_Method =
    [
        ActiveOpen $\mapsto$ method_with_body(meth_body_AOctn),
        PassiveOpen $\mapsto$ method_with_body(meth_body_POctn),
        Close $\mapsto$ method_with_body(meth_body_Cctn),
        Send $\mapsto$ method_with_body(meth_body_Sctn),
        Acknowledge $\mapsto$ method_with_body(meth_body_Akctn),
        Synchronize $\mapsto$ method_with_body(meth_body_Syctn),
        ProcessOctet $\mapsto$
          method_with_body_param
            (empty_method_body, $\langle$var(octetstream)$\rangle$),
        ChangeState $\mapsto$
          method_with_body_param
            (meth_body_ChgSt, $\langle$paramTyped(state, TCPState)$\rangle$)
    ]

The sets of methods for the other classes are defined similarly.

The next step is to incorporate the definitions of the methods in the class
into a definition of the class as a whole. For this we need to additionally define
the class state and its type.

In the design, the class TCPConnection has a single state variable var_state and is a concrete class. The specification of this class, which we must again check for well-formedness (the function 'is_wf_class') is therefore:

Ctn_Class : Wf_Class =
   mk_Design_Class({var_state}, Ctn_Class_Methods, concrete)

Next we turn to the relations in the design. There are in fact one aggregation relation, one association relation and three inheritance relations (one between TCPState and each of its subclasses) included. Here we only show the specification of one of the inheritance relations because the others are entirely analogous up to the names of the classes involved.

The aggregation and association relations are both one-one, so their specifications (the constants 'agg_rel' and 'ass_rel' respectively) are similar apart from their types and the names of the classes and variables involved. The inheritance relations are simply specified as inheritance relations between the appropriate pair of classes. Each must of course be shown to satisfy the well-formedness condition 'wf_relation'.

agg_rel : Wf_Relation =
  mk_Design_Relation
    (
        aggregation(mk_Ref(var_state, one, one)),
        TCPConnection,
        TCPState
    ),

ass_rel : Wf_Relation =
  mk_Design_Relation
    (
        association(mk_Ref(var_context, one, one)),
        Client,
        TCPConnection
    ),

inh1_rel : Wf_Relation =
   mk_Design_Relation(inheritance, TCPState, TCPEstablished)

The other classes and relations in the design are specified in a similar way, then the specification of the design as a whole is obtained by combining them together. To do this, we construct a map which associates each class name in the design with its definition and a set containing all the relations in the design. The design as a whole is then represented by the pair constructed from these two components. Checking the remaining well-formedness conditions then ensures that the design as a whole is well-formed.

Class_Map : Classes =
[
    Client $\mapsto$ Cli_Class,
    TCPConnection $\mapsto$ Ctn_Class,
    TCPState $\mapsto$ Sta_Class,
    TCPEstablished $\mapsto$ Est_Class,
    TCPListen $\mapsto$ Lis_Class,
    TCPClosed $\mapsto$ Clo_Class
],

Rel_set : Wf_Relation-**set** =
    {agg_rel, inh1_rel, inh2_rel, inh3_rel, ass_rel},

State_DS : Wf_Design_Structure = (Class_Map, Rel_set)

This completes the specification of the design and we must now link the design to the pattern by defining a renaming mapping from the names of the classes, methods, state variables and parameters in the design to the corresponding entities which represent their roles in the pattern (see Figure 1). Again we concentrate on the class TCPConnection here.

The class TCPConnection corresponds to the Context class in the pattern, and the first six methods (ActiveOpen, PassiveOpen, Close, Send, Acknowledge, and Synchronize) in TCPConnection all correspond to the Request operation in the pattern. Thus, in this example there are many elements of the design which play a single role in the pattern.

Since all the above methods play the same role in the pattern and have no explicit parameters, they all have the same renaming. We therefore simplify our specification by introducing a constant 'Ctn_req_mtd' which represents this renaming. Then we construct a renaming map 'Ctn_mtd' for the methods (and their parameters) by mapping each of the methods at the design level to this constant.

Note that the methods ProcessOctet and ChangeState have no counterparts in the pattern so are simply omitted from the method renaming map.

Ctn_req_mtd : Method_Renaming = mk_Method_Renaming(S.Request, [ ]),

Ctn_mtd : Method_and_Parameter_Renaming =
[
    ActiveOpen $\mapsto$ Ctn_req_mtd,
    PassiveOpen $\mapsto$ Ctn_req_mtd,
    Close $\mapsto$ Ctn_req_mtd,
    Send $\mapsto$ Ctn_req_mtd,
    Acknowledge $\mapsto$ Ctn_req_mtd,
    Synchronize $\mapsto$ Ctn_req_mtd
]

We similarly build a variable renaming map to associate the state variables in the TCPConnection class with those in the Context class. This is then combined with the method renaming to yield the renaming for the whole class.

$$\text{Ctn\_vbles} : \text{VariableRenaming} = [\,\text{var\_state} \mapsto \text{S.state}\,],$$

$$\text{Ctn\_Class\_Renaming} : \text{ClassRenaming} =$$
$$\text{mk\_ClassRenaming}(\text{S.Context}, \text{Ctn\_mtd}, \text{Ctn\_vbles})$$

We follow the same procedure for the other classes in the design to obtain the renaming for the whole design, which simply associates the names of the classes in the design with the appropriate class renaming. Note that each design class plays a single role in the pattern so there is only a single class renaming for each design class. Again, we must check that the well-formedness condition 'is_wf_Renaming' is satisfied.

$$\text{State\_Renaming} : \text{Wf\_Renaming} =$$
$$[$$
$$\quad \text{TCPConnection} \mapsto \{\text{Ctn\_Class\_Renaming}\},$$
$$\quad \text{TCPState} \mapsto \{\text{Sta\_Class\_Renaming}\},$$
$$\quad \text{TCPEstablished} \mapsto \{\text{Con\_Class\_Renaming}\},$$
$$\quad \text{TCPListen} \mapsto \{\text{Con\_Class\_Renaming}\},$$
$$\quad \text{TCPClosed} \mapsto \{\text{Con\_Class\_Renaming}\},$$
$$\quad \text{Client} \mapsto \{\text{Cli\_Class\_Renaming}\}$$
$$]$$

The final step is to combine the specifications of the design and the renaming and to check that these together satisfy the well-formedness condition 'is_wf_design_renaming'.

$$\text{State\_Pat\_Ren} : \text{Wf\_Design\_Renaming} = (\text{State\_DS}, \text{State\_Renaming})$$

This value is then used as input to the function 'is_state_pattern' defined in Section 4 to check whether or not the TCP network connection design is an instance of the State pattern.

6   Conclusions

We have described a formal model of a generic object-oriented design based on the extended OMT notation and we have shown how a design in this model can be linked to a GoF pattern using the renaming map. We have furthermore shown how the specific properties of individual GoF patterns can be specified in this model, and we have illustrated using an example design how the specifications can be used to determine whether or not a given design matches a given pattern. This allows designers to be sure, as well as to demonstrate to others that they are using the patterns correctly and consistently. The model can also help designers to understand the properties of the GoF patterns clearly, and indeed our analysis of the various GoF patterns using the model has identified a number of inconsistencies and incompletenesses in the informal descriptions of a number of patterns and has led us to propose modified pattern structures which resolve these problems [15,8,2].

The work presented here concentrates on matching a subset of a design to a single pattern at a time, whereas in practice a design is of course likely to be based around several different patterns and may even comprise several instances of the same pattern. We have in fact considered the possibility of extending the model to deal with multiple patterns and it turns out that this can easily be done by simply redefining the renaming map slightly. In future work we plan to investigate this extension further with a view to describing so-called "compound" patterns [17].

Although we have limited our attention to GoF patterns in our current work, we believe that our basic model is in fact sufficiently general that it could be applied in a similar way to give formal descriptions of other design patterns based on the extended OMT notation. We also believe that our work could form a strong basis for a similar model of an object-oriented design based on the UML notation (http://www.omg.org/uml), and we propose to investigate this in the future.

Finally, we believe that the formality of our general model and of our specifications of the individual GoF patterns makes them a useful basis for tool support for GoF patterns and we plan to investigate this possibility in the future.

References

1. Brad Appleton. Patterns and Software: Essential Concepts and Terminology. http://www.enteract.com/~bradapp, November 1997.
2. Gabriela Aranda and Richard Moore. GoF Creational Patterns: A Formal Specification. Technical Report 224, UNU/IIST, P.O. Box 3058, Macau, December 2000.
3. Kent Beck, James O. Coplien, Ron Crocker, Lutz Dominick, Gerard Meszaros, Frances Paulisch, and John Vlissides. Industrial Experience with Design Patterns. Technical report, First Class Software, AT&T, Motorola Inc, Siemens AG, Bell Northern Research, Siemens AG, and IBM Research. http://www1.bell-labs.com/user/cope/Patterns/ICSE96/icse.html.
4. Alejandra Cechich and Richard Moore. A Formal Specification of GoF Design Patterns. Technical Report 151, UNU/IIST, P.O.Box 3058, Macau, January 1999.
5. S. Alejandra Cechich and Richard Moore. A Formal Specification of GoF Design Patterns. In Proceedings of the Asia Pacific Software Engineering Conference: APSEC'99, Takamatsu, Japan, December 1999.
6. A. Eden, J. Gil, Y. Hirshfeld, and A. Yehudai. Towards a Mathematical Foundation for Design Patterns. http://www.math.tau.ac.il/~eden/bibliography.html.
7. A. Eden, Y. Hirshfeld, and A. Yehudai. LePUS - A Declarative Pattern Specification Language. http://www.math.tau.ac.il/~eden/bibliography.html.
8. Andres Flores and Richard Moore. GoF Structural Patterns: A Formal Specification. Technical Report 207, UNU/IIST, P.O. Box 3058, Macau, August 2000.
9. Andres Flores, Luis Reynoso, and Richard Moore. A Formal Model of Object-Oriented Design and GoF Design Patterns. Technical Report 200, UNU/IIST, P.O. Box 3058, Macau, July 2000.

10. Erich Gamma, Richard Helm, Ralph Johnson, and John Vlissides. *Design Patterns: Elements of Reusable Object-Oriented Software*. Addison Wesley, 1995.
11. Ralph Johnson. Design Patterns in the Standard Java Libraries. In *Proceedings of the Asia Pacific Software Engineering Conference: Keynote Materials, Tutorial Notes*, pages 66–101, 1999.
12. L. Lamport. The Temporal Logic of Actions. *ACM Transactions on Programming Languages and Systems*, 16(3):872–923, May 1994.
13. Tommi Mikkonen. Formalizing Design Patterns. In *Proceedings of the International Conference on Software Engineering ICSE'98*, pages 115–124. IEEE Computer Society Press, 1998.
14. The RAISE Language Group. *The RAISE Specification Language*. BCS Practitioner Series. Prentice Hall, 1992.
15. Luis Reynoso and Richard Moore. GoF Behavioural Patterns: A Formal Specification. Technical Report 201, UNU/IIST, P.O. Box 3058, Macau, May 2000.
16. J. Rumbaugh. *Object-Oriented Modeling and Design*. Prentice Hall, 1991.
17. John Vlissides. Pluggable Factory, Part I. C++ Report, November-December 1998. http://www.research.ibm.com/people/v/vlis/pubs.html.

Validation of UML Models Thanks to Z and Lustre

Sophie Dupuy-Chessa[1] and Lydie du Bousquet[2]

[1] CUI, University of Geneva, 24 rue Général Dufour, 1211 Genève 4, Suisse
`Sophie.Chessa@cui.unige.ch`
[2] Laboratoire LSR-IMAG, BP 72, 38402 Saint Martin d'Hères cedex, France
`Lydie.du-Bousquet@imag`

Abstract. Graphical notations such as UML are very popular thanks to their simplicity and their intuitive aspect. Nevertheless their lack of precise semantics limits the possibility of the specification validation. So we propose here to translate some of the UML models into Z and Lustre formal specifications in order to use a theorem prover and a test generator to validate the models. This approach is presented on the "cash-point" service case study proposed during the world Formal Method congress 1999 tool contest.

1 Introduction

Generally, software engineers use graphical models like those of the *Unified Modeling Language* (UML [3]) to describe a system. These models offer intuitive notations which favor the communication within the specification team and with the customers. As the semantics of these notations are not always precise, their use can lead to ambiguities and misunderstandings of the specifications. They also limit the potential and the tools to validate the models.

In order to offer a more efficient framework to validate system specifications, it has been proposed to integrate semi-formal graphical notations with formal ones [21,12,18, 20,16]. Formal methods offer mathematical notations which have a precise semantics that removes ambiguities and offers a potential for reasoning and automation. Formal reasoning can be used to detect inconsistencies in specifications and tools can take advantage of the formal semantics not only to support the reasoning process but also to help to synthesize efficient implementation or test suites.

To integrate semi-formal and formal notations, we choose an approach that takes advantage of the benefits of each ones: the graphical methods serve for the development of the system specification while the formal notations and their tools are used for the system validation. Our approach is based on the translation of the semi-formal specifications into formal ones and on the use of the tool support of formal notations. So the system is first described by a graphical intuitive model before being made precise and validated thanks to a formal specification. We have chosen to develop this approach with UML which is now a standard for object-oriented modeling notations. It enables designers to express models from different points of view, their data structures and operations (static part of the model) as well as their behaviors (dynamic part). For the validation of both static and dynamic parts of UML models, we translate the UML description into appropriate formal languages and use their tools to process the validation (Fig. 1).

J.N. Oliveira and P. Zave (Eds.): FME 2001, LNCS 2021, pp. 242–258, 2001.
© Springer-Verlag Berlin Heidelberg 2001

The static part of a UML model is composed of the class diagram. In knowledge systems and data base systems, it is frequent to express some constraints on the classes and relations, and then to check them. To do that, languages such as Z [24], B [1] or VDM [2] are quite appropriate because their concepts are close to the UML class diagram ones and they have tool support both for proving and animating specifications. Among these languages, we choose Z for its visibility and its adequacy to the constraint language OCL [25], proposed to complete UML models. To validate the static part, we generate Z formal specification with proof obligations. *This is done automatically* thanks to one of our tool RoZ [9]. Then we use the Z-EVES theorem prover [22].

To validate the dynamic part of the model, several methods are classically used (animation/testing, model-checking, theorem proving). The animation and test techniques can be used if the system is executable ; model-checking and theorem proving require the model to be small enough so that the verification can be done in a limited space or time. We decided to extract an executable specification from the dynamic part of the model, so that animation or testing techniques can be applied. We translate statecharts diagrams into Lustre specifications [4], which are validated by our testing environment, Lutess [6].

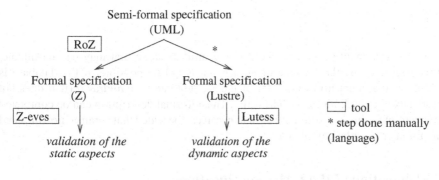

Fig. 1. The approach

In the paper, we illustrate this approach for modeling and validation on a case study, and we underline the kinds of help that formal specifications can bring to validate the system models. The case study is the world Formal Method 1999 congress contest where exhibitors were invited to specify a "cash-point" service with their own formalism(s), and to process that specification with their tool(s). In the following, we detail our approach and we illustrate it with the contest example [8].

2 The "Cash-Point" Service

We present here a brief summary of the "cash-point" service. A complete description can be found in [8].

For the "cash-point" service, there are tills which can access a central resource containing the detailed records of customers'bank accounts (Fig. 2). A till is used by inserting a card and typing in a personal identification number (PIN) which is encoded by the till and compared with the code stored on the card.

After successfully identifying themselves to the system, customers may try to view the balance of their account, make a withdrawal of cash, or ask for a statement of their account to be sent by post. The "illegal" cards are kept by the till. A card can be "illegal" if it has been stolen or if it has a defect.

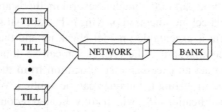

Fig. 2. Physical architecture of the system

Information about accounts is held in a central database that may be unavailable. In this case, viewing the balance of an account is not be possible. If the database is available, any amount up to the total of the account can be withdrawn (if it does not exceed a fixed daily limit on withdrawals). This informal description can be completed by concurrent or time constraints. For instance, it can be added that a transaction initiated by a customer must be completed.

3   Elaboration of the UML Specification

The UML specification is the central point of our approach. First it permits to better understand requirements and to propose a model of the system to be built. Secondly, it is the starting point for the generation of more formal specifications. This section provides an overview of the UML models developed for the cash-point service. We focus on the statement clarifications and on the choices made during the development.

3.1   Requirement Capture

We start the requirement capture by identifying the functionalities of the system. According to the problem statement, the cash-point offers at least three functionalities:

1. viewing of the balance of an account,
2. making a withdrawal of cash,
3. asking for a statement of the account to be sent by post.

We add to these functionalities the possibility to cancel the "customer session" (i.e. to stop any actions). In UML, the functionalities are represented by use cases which interact with the system actors. In the cash-point service, the customer is the only actor. Moreover all the functionalities start by an identification step. We choose to express this by a use case "Identification" which is used by the other functionalities. So the use case diagram of figure 3 represents the requirements for the cash-point service.

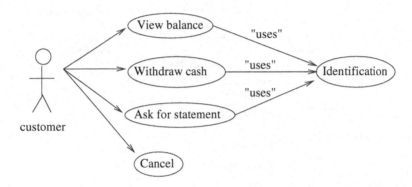

Fig. 3. Use cases for the cash-point service

In order to describe each use case, we develop activity diagrams which express what activities are undertaken (by which object) to realize a use case. For brevity sake, we present here only one activity diagram (Fig. 4). The other diagrams can be found in [8]. The description of the activity diagrams helps us to clarify the following points:

1. Is a card always readable?
   No, a card can be damaged and then become unreadable.
2. What happens if the card is damaged?
   The card is kept by the till and a message informs the customer about this.
3. What should be done if the database is unavailable?
   A message informs the customer that the database is unavailable and his/her card is given back by the till.
4. What should be done to avoid the use of stolen cards?
   The till checks if the card is stolen before asking to the customer the card PIN. This was decided so as to reduce the use of stolen cards and to gain access to the account.
5. How many times is the code tested?
   The customer has three attempts to enter the correct code of his/her card.
6. Can the identification be cancelled after the entry of a wrong code?
   Yes.
7. What happens if the till does not have enough cash for the withdrawal or if the maximum daily withdrawal is reached?
   The till gives the card back to the customer.
8. Is the cash given with the card?
   No, the customer must get his/her card to have the cash.

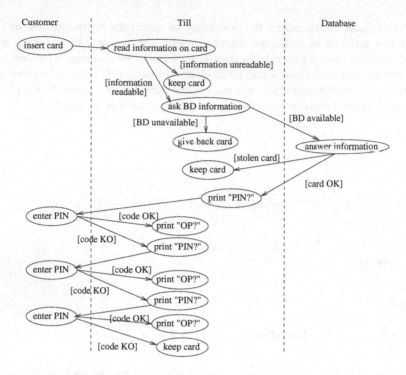

Fig. 4. Activity diagram for the customer identification

The requirements being better understood, we develop UML models to describe the system structure and its behavior.

3.2 The Static Part of the Cash-Point Service

From requirements capture, we produce UML models representing the static and the dynamic parts of the cash-point service. The static part is described by an UML class diagram which is composed of four classes:

– "BANK" which represents the database of the bank,
– "TILL" which represents the bank tills,
– "ACCOUNT" which represents the customer accounts,
– "CARD" which represents the customer cards.

The bank is composed of accounts, tills and cards. Moreover the association "BankInvalidCardsRel" describes the invalids cards. An account can have zero or many cards and a card is linked to one account or zero if the card is stolen. A card can be inserted in at most one till at a given moment.

This model does not express the full specification of the application data: to be complete the data structure must satisfy more than the static constraints of the class diagram. So we add to the graphical model the following constraints:

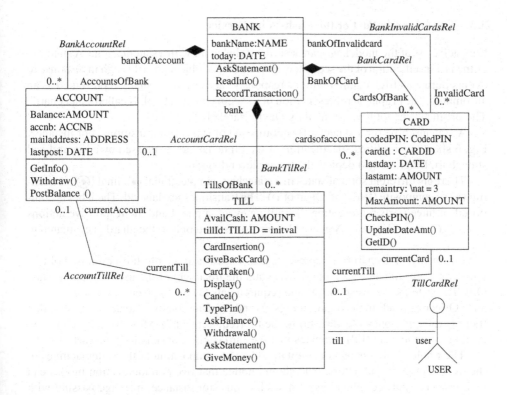

Fig. 5. Class diagram for the cash-point service

1. The amount withdrawn during a day must be greater than zero but less than the maximum amount permitted.
2. The PIN must be coded/decoded by a given function.
3. The balance of an account must be greater or equal to zero.
4. The attribute "cardid" is a key of "CARD".
5. The last day of a card (which represents the last date the card was used) must be less or equal to today.
6. If the till is linked to a card and an account, the account must the one corresponding to the card.

Then to describe the static part of the cash-point service, we have created a class diagram completed by static constraints. We have chosen to express these constraints in Z in order to make them unambiguous. Nevertheless, we cannot know if the annotations are mutually inconsistent or inconsistent with the model. For instance, does the operation to update the amount withdrawn preserve the constraint that the amount must not exceed a daily limit?

3.3   The Dynamic Part of the Cash-Point Service

For each class of the model, we can describe its behavior with a statemachine. A statemachine is a specification of the sequence of states that an object goes through in response to events during its life, together with its responsive actions. It is usually represented as an automaton. The graphical representation of a statemachine in UML is called "statechart". The original concept was invented by David Harel [15].

A statemachine (or a statechart) is composed of states and transitions. For instance, Fig. 6 shows a simplified specification of the till behaviors, expressed by a hierarchical statechart. Diagram 6(a) depicts the higher level diagram.

There are different sorts of states in a statechart: simple, initial (•), final (◉), branching (◇) or composite (INIT and OP in 6(a)). The transitions are labeled. The label is composed of three parts representing the calling event, a guard and the responsive actions (*Event [Guard] / Actions*). A guarded transition is fired only if the guard is evaluated to true.

Informally, statechart 6(a) represents a user session at the till. It is composed of two parts: the user authentication (state INIT) and the treatment of the user operation (state OP). The state INIT corresponds to the requirements (1) to (6) given in section 3.1. The state OP corresponds to the requirements (7) and (8). One condition to deliver cash is that there is enough money (AvailCash) in the till (requirement 7). Moreover, the transition exiting from the state $W21$ indicates that the card is given back before the cash.

The whole system behavior is obtained by the composition of the statemachines of the system objects and actors. One should notice that two communication modes can be considered between the objects: asynchronous (for instance, message passing with queue) or synchronous (for instance, call of a method). At the specification level, it is not necessary (and probably dangerous) to specify the communication modes between the objects. This choice should be done at the implementation level, when the system architecture is definitely fixed.

The development of the UML models permit to better understand the cash-point requirements and to propose a first specification of the system. To validate this specification, we translate it into formal specification: the class diagram is automatically mapped into a Z specification that is used with a theorem prover while the statechart diagram gives rise to a Lustre model which is validated with a test tool.

4   Validation of the Static Part

To validate the static part of the cash-point service system, we first use a tool, RoZ [9], to generate the Z specification corresponding to the class diagram and its static constraints. Then RoZ generates proof obligations that are used in the ORA theorem prover, Z-EVES, to check the mutual consistency of the diagram and its constraints.

4.1   Generating Z Specifications

The generation of the Z specification corresponding to the static description of the cash-point service is realized in two steps: first the class diagram gives rise to Z specification

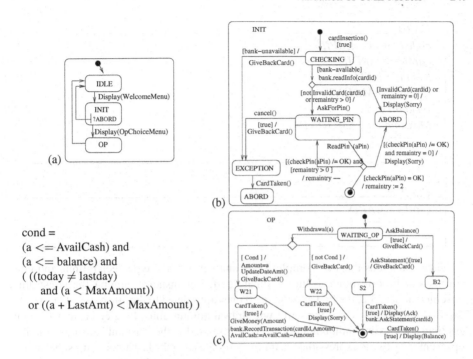

cond =
(a <= AvailCash) and
(a <= balance) and
((((today ≠ lastday)
    and (a < MaxAmount))
    or ((a + LastAmt) < MaxAmount))

Fig. 6. Till behaviors depicted by statecharts

skeletons which are completed by annotations in a second step. The Z specification skeletons are produced according to some translation rules described in [10]. These rules consider the main concepts (class, attribute, operation, association, inheritance, aggregation and composition) of the UML class diagram except multiple inheritance which cannot be represented correctly in Z. Such rules have also be proposed to translate UML into Object-Z [7]. But even if Object-Z is more appropriate to represent object notions, it does not provide powerful tools in order to exploit its specifications. Thus we chose to work with Z to be able to use tools such as theorem provers.

Let us consider the rule for translating the class concept for example. In UML, a class has two aspects: it is an object factory and an object tank (i.e. the collection of objects of the class present in the system). So a formal representation of a class must distinguish object existence and class attributes. A class is mapped into two Z schemas. Each is a data specification structure composed of two parts: the declarations which constitute the local variable lexicon and the predicates expressing constraints on these variables. For the "CARD" class, the factory aspect is represented by the "CARD" schema which contains the declaration of the attributes while the "CardExt" schema introduces the "Card" variable describing the set of existing cards. The attributes of "CARD" are "codedpin" which is the pin number of the card, "cardid" that represents the card identity, "lastday" which is the last date where the card was used, "lastamt" which is the total amount withdrawn during the last day and "remaintry" which is a counter for the number of code attempts.

```
┌─ CARD ─────────────────────────────────────────────────
│ codedpin : CodedPIN
│ cardid : CARDID
│ lastday : DATE
│ lastamt : AMOUNT
│ remaintry : ℕ
│ MaxAmount : AMOUNT
├─────────────────
│
│ ...
└─────────────────────────────────────────────────────────
```

```
┌─ CardExt ──────────────────────────────────────────────
│ Card : 𝔽 CARD
├─────────────────
│
│ ...
└─────────────────────────────────────────────────────────
```

These skeletons must be completed by annotations like type declarations and constraints which correspond to the predicate part. For instance, among the constraints presented in Sec. 3.2, the first and the third ones are related to the attributes of "CARD". The first one specifies that the daily withdrawal amount must be greater than zero but less than the maximal amount authorized. It is related to the "lastamt" attribute and it is represented by two Z expressions: $lastamt \geq 0$ states that the last amount must be greater than zero and $lastamt < MaxAmount$ expresses that it must be inferior to the maximal amount. For the constraint on the codedpin, let us call "codefct2" a function between a pin and a coded one. Then the second constraint "the PIN must be coded/decoded by a given function" is expressed in Z by $codedpin \in (\text{ran}\,codefct2)$. The three Z expressions representing the constraints on the "CARD" attributes complete the Z skeleton of "CARD":

```
┌─ CARD ─────────────────────────────────────────────────
│ codedpin : CodedPIN
│ cardid : CARDID
│ lastday : DATE
│ lastamt : AMOUNT
│ remaintry : ℕ
│ MaxAmount : AMOUNT
├─────────────────
│ lastamt ≥ 0
│ lastamt < MaxAmount
│ codedpin ∈ (ran codefct2)
└─────────────────────────────────────────────────────────
```

Constraint 4 which specifies that cardid is a key of CARD is a comparison between existing cards. So it is expressed in the "CardExt" schema.

```
┌─ CardExt ──────────────────────────────────────────────
│ Card : 𝔽 CARD
├─────────────────
│ ∀ c1, c2 : CARD | c1 ≠ c2 @ c1.cardid ≠ c2.cardid
└─────────────────────────────────────────────────────────
```

Following the same principle of constraints, a complete specification of the class operations can be produced. This permits to fully automate the production of Z specifications from an annotated class diagram. This is realized by our tool, RoZ [9] which is an extension of the Rational Rose$^{(TM)}$ environment to integrate UML and Z notations. It translates the UML constructs and merges them with the diagram annotations (constraints and operation specification) expressed in Z. The Rose environment is used to build the UML models which are completed by formal annotations in Z. The annotations are expressed into forms. A form should contain all the information mandatory to complete Z skeletons. So each form corresponds to a kind of annotation and it is attached to the class diagram element that it complets. The use of forms make our tool different from any other translators to Z [23,11] or VDM++ [17]. As a matter of fact, these tools generate formal skeletons, but the designer has to fulfil them. In RoZ, all the modeling work (diagram and annotations) is realized in the same standard environment, Rose.

For the cash point service, the class diagram is edited in the usual Rose environment (Fig. 7). The constraints related to the attributes of "CARD" are expressed in Z style in the forms corresponding to these attributes. For instance, the constraint specifying that the amount withdrawn during a day must be greater than zero and inferior to the maximal amount authorized is expressed in the form related to the "lastamt" attribute.

The class diagram gives us the structure of the corresponding Z specification while the constraints in the forms add the details. So the "CARD" class is translated into a Z schema which contains the attribute declarations. This schema is complemented by the constraints on the amount and on the coded pin. So RoZ automatically produces the "CARD" schema given previously. Similarly, RoZ proposes forms to write the predicates corresponding to the operation pre and post-conditions so that it can also produce automatically the operation specifications. We would like to also use forms for type or function declarations. But we did not find a satisfying place in the actual Rose forms. So for the moment, this information is registered in a file which is included during the generation of the Z specifications.

So for the FM'99 contest, RoZ generated the complete Z specification corresponding to the information contained in the cash-point service class diagram and its forms. This specification is composed of:

- eight Z schemas for the four classes "BANK", "ACCOUNT", "CARD" and "TILL";
- seven schemas for the seven associations;
- twenty operation schemas corresponding to the twenty operations.

4.2   Using a Prover to Validate the Static Part

At this point, we have produced a Z specification and we can start to investigate the properties of our model. In particular we want to check that the class diagram and its constraints are not inconsistent or that the constraints are not mutually inconsistent. Then to validate the specification, we propose to prove that the operations do not violate the data integrity imposed by the class diagram and its added constraints. So the designer can identify guards which will be evaluated before the operation execution and which can avoid the execution an operation violating the constraints. Each guard is validated by proving that it is actually a pre-condition of the operation.

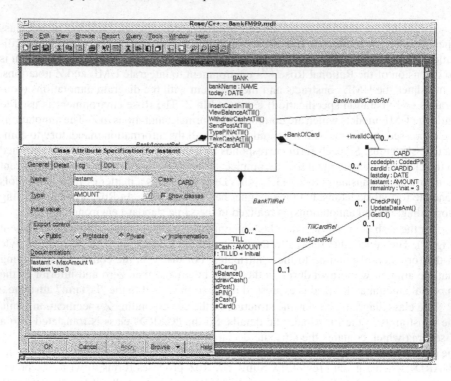

Fig. 7. Rose interface

Let us consider the operation which updates the amount withdrawn during the current day. "CARDUpdateDateAmt" has as input parameters the date ("d?") and the amount to withdraw ("a?"). The first predicate states that the amount "a?" must be greater than zero. The two following ones express the modification of the amount withdrawn at the date "d?". If "d?" is the day of the last withdrawal, "a?" is added to the last amount. Otherwise no withdrawal has been realized during the day ; the last amount takes the values of "a?" and the date of the last withdrawal becomes "d?" . The other attributes of "CARD" keep their values.

$$
\begin{array}{l}
\rule{5cm}{0.4pt}\ CARDUpdateDateAmt\ \rule{5cm}{0.4pt} \\
\Delta CARD \\
d? : DATE \\
a? : AMOUNT \\
\hline
a? > 0 \\
d? = lastday \Rightarrow lastamt' = lastamt + a? \wedge lastday' = lastday \\
d? \neq lastday \Rightarrow lastamt' = a? \wedge lastday' = d? \\
codedpin' = codedpin \\
cardid' = cardid \\
remaintry' = remaintry
\end{array}
$$

"CARDUpdateDateAmt" changes the amount withdrawn during a day, but it does not guarantee that the constraint on the maximal amount to withdraw daily. In Z, this constraint is implicitly included in the operation by $\Delta CARD$. In order to avoid executing "CARDUpdateDateAmt" when the last amount is greater than the limit authorized, we propose to identify a guard for this operation. Here the chosen guard is composed of several conditions. If some withdrawal has already by done at the date "d?", the total amount of this day must be less than the maximal amount ($lastamt + a? < MaxAmount$); otherwise no amount has been withdrawn yet and the amount to withdraw must be inferior to the maximal amount ($d? \neq lastday \wedge a? < MaxAmount$). The theorem "CARDUpdateDateAmt_Pre" states that this guard is a condition strong enough to logically imply the weakest pre-condition of "CARDUpdateDateAmt", given by the Z operator "pre".

theorem CARDUpdateDateAmt_Pre
$$\forall CARD;\ d? : DATE;\ a? : AMOUNT$$
$$|\ (lastamt + a? < MaxAmount \vee (d? \neq lastday \wedge a? < MaxAmount))$$
$$@\ pre\ CARDUpdateDateAmt$$

In fact, the proof obligations to validate operation guards are constructed according to the following form [19]:

theorem
$$\forall State, i? : IN\ |\ guard(State, i?)\ @\ pre\ Op$$

This theorem expresses that for an operation "Op" which modifies the schema "State" and has "i?" as input parameter, the proposed guard "guard(State,i?)" implies the weakest pre-condition of "Op" (pre Op). Using this framework, the RoZ tool can generate the proof obligation to validate each operation guard. Actually it allows the designer to record a guard for each operation and produce the corresponding proof obligation. For the "UpdateDateAmt" operation, its specification is contained into Rose forms as we have shown previously for the constraints. For instance, its guard is registered in RoZ in the "Pre conditions" field of its form (Fig. 8). This allows RoZ to produce the "CARDUpdateDateAmt" schema and the "CARDUpdateDateAmt_Pre" theorem given above.

Finally the Z-EVES prover (from ORA [22]) is used to discharge the proof obligations. Z-EVES features both interactive and automatic modes, automatic mode being used for simple theorems. Actually the automatic mode can also be used as a help to simplify theorems. For the "cash-point" service, we used Z-EVES to validate the guards of fifteen operations. The use of Z-EVES helped us to correct our specification by finding mistakes or by improving some annotations.

The tools helped in three different ways. First, RoZ made precise the semantics of the class diagram. Second, when constraints were difficult to write, the use of Z-EVES helped in writing the formulae. For the operation specifications, Z-Eves helped us to identify the two cases (whether or not the day of the withdrawal is the current date) of the "CARDUpdateDateAmt" operation and of its guard. Finally, we discovered some mistakes. For instance, we forgot that the balance of account can be equal to zero, and we also have forgotten to specify the case in which the last amount of a card must be equal or greater to zero.

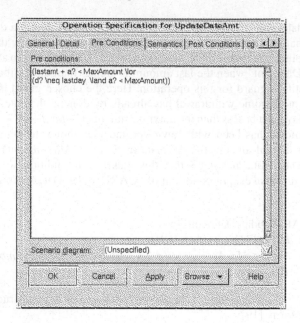

Fig. 8. The"UpdateDateAmt" form

5 Validation of the Dynamic Part of UML Model

The validation of the dynamic part must help the user to decide whether his UML model behaves according to his hopes. In order to do that, we propose to animate the statechart views of the model. The animation technique consists in considering the system under test as a black box, to simulate its environment behavior, and to check if its reactions are the ones that are expected.

As an example, let us study the validation of a system composed of the bank and one till (Fig. 9(a)). The system environment is composed of one user.

To simulate the environment behavior, one has to determine what are the possible user actions, and when it is possible to do them. Basically, the user actions are: insert a card or take the card off, type a cancel order, type a pin, and ask for a withdrawal, for an account balance, or for a statement of the account to be sent by post. Let us consider that it is always possible to type a command on the keyboard. The till is responsible for determining when a command should be taken into account. For the actions "insert card" and "take the card off", it is a little bit different, because "physically", it is not possible to realize them whenever one wants. If there are no stolen or damaged cards, it is only possible to take the card off after one has been introduced, and after the till has given it back. In this case, it is also possible to introduce a new card in the till, only after a "sorry" message. Figure 10 describes a model for such an environment (for improved readability, the connections between the user and the till statechart are not fully described).

The validation activity consists in firing the transitions of the user statechart, and observing whether the till reactions are those which were expected. For instance, let us fire the transition "OpWithdrawal" at the initial state of the user statechart. If the till specification reaction is to give some money, then there is clearly a problem.

During the contest, we used the Lutess testing tool to automatically animate the UML model. Lutess is a tool which produces automatically and dynamically test data with respect to some environment constraints of the program under test [6]. Lutess requires an executable program under test and a description of the environment in Lustre. Lustre is a programming language, which can be seen also as a past temporal logic [4].

To obtain an executable program from the UML model, several solutions can be studied. During the FM contest, we choose to translate UML statecharts in a Lustre program. This step was done manually but systematically. This was long and error prone. Currently, we study some solutions to automate the translation.

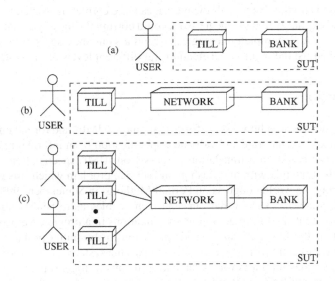

Fig. 9. Example of test configuration for incremental validation

To validate a system, it is generally possible to proceed in an incremental way (see Fig. 9). This approach facilitates the error diagnosis. For the "cash-point" service , we validate first a system composed of one till and the bank (Fig. 9(a)). Next, we introduced the network (Fig. 9(b)), and then several other Tills (Fig. 9(c)).

During the contest, the testing phase allowed us to discover several incorrect or missing behaviors. For instance, we detected that in the statechart depicted figure 6(c), it is not possible to cancel the choice of an operation (contrary to the informal requirements).

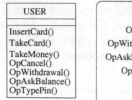
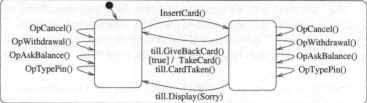

Fig. 10. An environment model

The validation phase also showed that our first UML model was not robust enough at the database level: the database took all messages from a till into account even those corrupted by the network. This point was due to incompatible implicit assumptions which were done during the statechart conception. When the bank statechart was built, it was supposed (implicitly) that all the messages were correct. However, the validation phase showed explicitly that (1) the network could corrupt the messages, and (2) that the tills could generate incomplete messages, or send a same message several times. This allowed us to adjust the security verifications (at different levels of the system).

6   Conclusion

In this paper, we describe how a semi-formal language (UML) and formal ones (Z, Lustre) can be mixed to elaborate and validate a specification from informal requirements. Our approach is based on a translation process from UML specifications into Z and Lustre. We illustrate this with the "cash point" service problem which was proposed as a contest during the world congress on Formal Methods, in September 1999.

This case study has shown that our approach enables us to better understand the system requirements and to improve our specifications in a progressive way. First, the development of UML specifications adds precision to the initial problem statement. Then the translation into formal specification makes the system specification even more precise and provides the basis for its validation thanks to tools supporting the formal notations. The use of RoZ and the Z-EVES prover helps to validate the static part of the system by checking the consistency of the UML class diagram and its annotations. For the dynamic part, test or animation (here with Lutess tool) allows to discover erroneous or missing cases of behaviors. The main help provided by our tools concerns the writing of correct specifications which could also be used to find mistakes in the requirements document. So UML specifications give rise to translations into various formal languages whose choice depends on the properties to check.

The contest has shown the interest of the approach by showing us its benefits. Nevertheless the validation of the models still requires a deep knowledge into formal languages and their tools. Then a first perspective of our work could be to develop a domain knowledge that could help in using formal tools. For example, we have noticed that proofs have often the same forms for the same kind of constraints. So it seems possible to propose some standard proofs for standard operations like attribute modification or add/suppression of an object, and to add them as proof strategies in RoZ (like in PVS [5]).

We could also try to take advantage of the formalization in Z or Lustre by exploiting other tools supporting these languages. For example, we could simulate Z specifications or use a model checker such as Lesar [14] to prove Lustre ones. The use of such a model-checker helps to prove that with the specified behavior, the model can never do forbidden actions. And if it is possible, the model-checker returns a counter-example.

Finally considering the usefulness of the translation of UML models into Z or Lustre specifications, it could be interesting to extend it to other UML models. In particular, it could be interesting to exploit the information given by UML scenarii to propose test series. This could be another way of considering and validating the information given informally in UML.

Following the principle of doing partial translation into the more appropriate formal language, we could also try to exploit other formal languages or other tools to validate UML models. For instance, UMLAUT is interesting for the validation of the dynamic part. It is a UML model editor and transformation framework, developed by IRISA [16]. It allows to produce automatically an executable program. Moreover, it is connected to the CADP library [13], which provides several validation tools (animating tool, testing environment, model-checker...). So our future work could be to connect RoZ (for the validation of the static part of a UML model) and UMLAUT (for the validation of the dynamic part).

References

1. J.R. Abrial. *The B-Book.* Cambridge University Press, 1996.
2. D.J. Andrews, H. Bruun, B.S. Hansen, P.G. Larsen, N. Plat, et al. *Information Technology — Programming Languages, their environments and system software interfaces — Vienna Development Method-Specification Language Part 1: Base language.* ISO, 1995.
3. G. Booch, I. Jacobson, and J. Rumbaugh. *The Unified Modeling Language- User Guide.* Addison-Wesley, 1998.
4. P. Caspi, N. Halbwachs, D. Pilaud, and J. Plaice. LUSTRE, a declarative language for programming synchronous systems. In *14th Symposium on Principles of Programming Languages (POPL 87), Munich*, pages 178–188. ACM Press, 1987.
5. J. Crow, S. Owre, J. Rushby, N. Shankar, and M. Srivas. A tutorial introduction to PVS. In *Workshop on Industrial-Strength Formal Specification Techniques*, Boca Raton, Florida, USA, April 1995.
6. L. du Bousquet, F. Ouabdesselam, J.-L. Richier, and N. Zuanon. Lutess: a specification-driven testing environment for synchronous software. In *21st International Conference on Software Engineering*, pages 267–276. ACM Press, May 1999.
7. S. Dupuy. *Couplage de notations semi-formelles et formelles pour la spécification des Systèmes d'Informations.* PhD thesis, Université Joseph Fourier, Grenoble, 2000.
8. S. Dupuy and L. du Bousquet. "Cash-Point service": a multi-formalism approach for specification. technical report PFL, IMAG - LSR, Grenoble, France, 1999.
9. S. Dupuy, Y. Ledru, and M. Chabre-Peccoud. An Overview of RoZ : a Tool for Integrating UML and Z Specifications. In *12th Conference on Advanced information Systems Engineering-CAiSE'2000*, volume 1789 of *Lecture Notes in Computer Science*, Stockholm, Sweden, 2000. Springer-Verlag.

258   S. Dupuy-Chessa and L. du Bousquet

10. S. Dupuy, Y. Ledru, and M. Chabre-Peccoud. Vers une intégration utile de notations semi-formelles et formelles : une expérience en UML et Z. *L'Objet, numéro thématique Méthodes formelles pour les objets*, 6(1), 2000.
11. R. France, J.-M. Bruel, and M. Larrondo-Petri. An Integrated Object-Oriented and Formal Modeling Environment. *Journal of Object Oriented Programming*, pages 25–34, November/Decembrer 1997.
12. R. France, J.-M. Bruel, M. Larrondo-Petrie, and M. Shroff. Exploring the Semantics of UML type structures with Z. In H. Bowman and J. Derrick, editors, *Proc. 2nd IFIP Workshop on Formal Methods for Open Object-Based Distributed Systems (FMOODS)*, pages 247–260, Canterbury, UK, 1997. Chapman and Hall, London.
13. Hubert Garavel. Open/cæsar: An open software architecture for verification, simulation, and testing. In *Proceedings of the First Int. Conference on Tools and Algorithms for the Construction and Analysis of Systems (TACAS)*. LNCS 1384, Springer Verlag, 1998.
14. N. Halbwachs, F. Lagnier, and C. Ratel. Programming and Verifying Real-Time Systems by Means of the Synchronous Data-Flow Programming Language LUSTRE. *IEEE Transactions on Software Engineering*, pages 785–793, September 1992.
15. D. Harel. Statecharts: A visual formalism for complex systems. *Science of Computer Programming*, 8(3):231–274, 1987.
16. W.-M. Ho, J.-M. Jézéquel, A. LeGuennec, and F. Pennaneac'h. Umlaut: an extensible uml transformation framework. In *Proceedings of Automated Software Engineering (ASE)*, Florida, USA, October 1999. IEEE.
17. IFAD. The Rose-VDM++ Link. http://www.ifad.dk/Products/rose-vdmpp.htm.
18. K Lano and S. Goldsack. Intregrated Formal and Object-Oriented Methods: The VDM++ Approach. In A. Bryant and L. Semmens, editors, *Proceedings of Method Integration Workshop, Electronic Workshop in Computing*, Leeds, March 1996. Springer-Verlag.
19. Y. Ledru. Identifying pre-conditions with the Z/EVES theorem prover. In *Proc. of the 13th Int. Conf. on Automated Software Engineering*. IEEE, 1998.
20. E. Meyer and J. Souquières. A systematic approach to transform OMT diagrams to a B specification. In J. Wing, J. Woodcock, and J. Davies, editors, *World Congress on Formal Methods in the Development of Computing Systems - FM'99*, volume 1708 of *Lecture Notes in Computer Science*, pages 875–896, Toulouse, France, 1999. Springer-Verlag.
21. F. Polack, M. Whiston, and K. Mander. The SAZ Project: Integrating SSADM and Z. In *Intenational Symposium Formal Methods Europe*, Odense, Danemark, Avril 1993.
22. M. Saaltink. The Z/EVES system. In J. Bowen, M. Hinchey, and D. Till, editors, *Proc. 10th Int. Conf. on the Z Formal Method (ZUM)*, volume 1212 of *Lecture Notes in Computer Science*, pages 72–88, Reading, UK, april 1997. Springer-Verlag, Berlin.
23. Headway Software. The RoZeLink 1.0. http://www.calgary.shaw.wave.ca/headway/index.htm.
24. J.M. Spivey. *The Z notation*. Prentice-Hall International, 1992.
25. J. Warmer and A. Kleppe. *The Object Constraint Language*. Addison-Wesley, 1998.

Components, Contracts, and Connectors for the Unified Modelling Language UML

Claus Pahl

Dublin City University, School of Computer Applications
Dublin 9, Ireland
cpahl@compapp.dcu.ie

Abstract. The lack of a component concept for the UML is widely acknowledged. Contracts between components can be the starting point for introducing components and component interconnections. Contracts between service providers and service users are formulated based on abstractions of action and operation behaviour using the pre- and postcondition technique. A valid contract allows to establish an interconnection - a connector - between the provider and the user. The contract concept supports the re-use of components by providing means to establish and modify component interconnections. A flexible contract concept shall be based on a refinement relation for operations and classes, derived from operation abstractions. Abstract behaviour, expressed by pre- and postconditions, and refinement are the key elements in the definition of a formal and flexible component and component interconnection approach.

1 Introduction

Contracts formulate an agreement between two (or more) components: a user needs additional functionality in order to fulfill his/her duties, a provider offers services which might help the user. A contract specifies obligations. The provider guarantees a certain functionality if the user guarantees a certain environment. The obligations can be expressed using the pre- and postcondition technique [1,2]. A *connector* realises a *contract* between a service provider and a service user, i.e. it establishes an interconnection between both of them. The contract states which semantic requirements (or expectations) these services should match. The *re-usability* of components depends on the support of component abstraction in order to make components available through libraries and on the support of adaptation techniques in order to adapt library components to actual requirements, i.e. to glue service provider and user together [3,4,5].

The package concept of the Unified Modelling Language UML is a grouping mechanism which allows a designer to assemble classes (or other elements) into components. The need to improve the notion of packages in the UML has been clearly identified. Two reasons are usually given [6]. Firstly, packages themselves should be developed into components in order to integrate component-based development into the UML-notation. Secondly, packages are the main element of

J.N. Oliveira and P. Zave (Eds.): FME 2001, LNCS 2021, pp. 259–277, 2001.
© Springer-Verlag Berlin Heidelberg 2001

the meta-notation used to describe the semantics of UML. Packages should help to develop a modular definition and to provide a flexible language architecture.

We propose to improve the interfaces of packages by providing import and export interfaces based on abstract semantical information. Packages shall be composed based on these interfaces. An import interface states which services from other packages shall be used and how they are expected to work. An export interface describes the services in abstract terms which are provided. The export states the properties of services that are available to prospective users. Contracts are formed based on the services required and the services provided.

We will use the UML context to motivate and present a flexible re-use oriented component composition framework. Interaction is the composition mechanism. Two components are composed by establishing an interaction infrastructure between them. The flexibility of the composition mechanism is crucial. Two issues have to be addressed: firstly, the contracts shall be formulated using a powerful constraint language, and, secondly, the connectors shall allow a flexible establishment and re-configuration of connections between components.

We believe that a refinement relation is important for the rigorous development of software artifacts, and that a powerful refinement notion can also form the glue needed to adapt services provided by some package to the requirements stated in a contract. Refinements of operation and action abstractions based on pre- and postconditions will forms the basis of a refinement relation between classes and components. The essential advantage of the pre- and postcondition technique is that it is suitable for abstracting internal object behaviour, but can also be used to constrain the interaction between objects via contracts. In [6] semantics for the UML is suggested as a combination of denotational semantics and proof rules. We will follow this suggestion. We will in particular focus on a framework which allows us to establish a proof system. Modal logics [7] – and its constructive variants such as TLA [8,9] – have motivated our formal framework for the specification and reasoning of properties of dynamic systems. The semantics of actions – and other model elements – can be given in terms of modal logics. Modal logic provides therefore the opportunity to express a more precise semantics of refinement and other forms of abstractions in terms of abstract dynamic behaviour. The way to semantical package interfaces and connectors leads via abstraction of actions.

Formulating contracts between components and formalising the infrastructure for the interaction between these components based on the contracts needs particular attention. An extension of the π-calculus [10,11,12] shall be used to define contracts and establish connectors between components. The π-calculus is combined with first-order modal reasoning, which is integrated into the calculus via a constraint language. A composition calculus for contracts and connectors is developed. Both contracts and connectors for the dynamic interaction are defined in the calculus. The extended calculus including the modal calculus can be interpreted in state-based algebraic structures (called objects). The π-calculus has been designed to deal with *mobility*, i.e. the capacity to change the connectivity of a network. We apply this idea to the space of connected (or composed) components. We use the *polyadic π-calculus* as the underlying framework to define contracts for component composition and interaction. The calculus is in particular suitable since it models the establishment of connections and also their maintenance (changing compositions due to evolving requirements). It provides the basis for a flexible re-use based concept for component composition and interaction.

Section 2 introduces behaviour abstraction, abstract interfaces and a notion of components. Their interconnection based on contracts and connectors is dealt with in Section 3. In Section 4, we present a semantical framework for behaviour abstractions, interfaces and components. Reasoning about component composition is the content of Section 5. This involves a formalisation and generalisation of the refinement and their properties. We end with related work and conclusions.

2 Abstract Behaviour, Interfaces, and Components

Among the requirements for an improved UML package concept stated by the *precise UML group* in their *Response to the UML 2.0 Request for Information* [6] are *multiple imports* (a package can import several services from several packages at the same time – this means that possibly a number of contracts are formed), *renaming* (syntactical adjustment should be possible, names of service in export and import interface might not be the same, even though they might realise the same service), and *adding elements* to imported elements (it should be possible to add elements to imported elements in the importing package, thus refining the import). Formality and rigour are two general requirements which shall be added to the list. In this section, we will outline the concepts to tackle these requirements.

The case study from which excerpts shall be used to motivate and illustrate our ideas is a Web-based document authoring and management system consisting of:

- Interfaces for authors and users `UserInterface`: the operations `followLink` and `inputURL` are available to the user, whereas `sendRequest` is an internal operation which contacts the server.
- Servers for authors `AuthoringServer` and users `ContentServer`: The content server is located at a particular `address`. It requests a document (identified by a URL) from the database and returns the document. The authoring server works on a particular current document, which can be loaded, modified, and checked syntactically with respect to its internal structure.
- A shared database for documents `Document`. A document can be updated with some text at a particular document position.

Some of the class signatures are presented in Figure 1. We narrow our interpretation of a component to classes in this example. We can identify two instantiations of the same pattern in our example – a 3-tiered architecture for database-supported, Web-interfaced systems with the same database part. The

Class UserInterface
  attributes
    XML_enabled:boolean
  operations
    followLink(url:URL)
    inputURL(url:URL)
    sendRequest(url:URL)

Class ContentServer
  attributes
    address:URL
  operations
    request(url:URL):Document

Class Document
  attributes
    content:Text
    author:String
  operations
    edit(pos:Position,update:Text)

Class AuthoringServer
  attributes
    currentDoc:Document
    parseDoc():boolean
  operations
    loadDoc(url:URL)
    modifyDoc(pos:Position,update:Text)

Fig. 1. Classes for the Document Management System

operations in the system are rather simplistic, an in-depth modelling with substates and subactions is in general not necessary. This simplicity makes it an ideal candidate for illustration.

2.1 Actions, Operations, and Their Abstraction

The *internal dynamics* of an object, i.e. which states it can have, can be described by statechart diagrams. Activities of a state can be specified. An activity consists of an event and the action which is triggered by the event (possibly guarded):

$$\textit{event-signature} \; [\; \textit{guard-condition} \;] \; / \; \textit{action-expression} \qquad (1)$$

Events cause transitions between states. Each state is described by a name and internal (state) transitions. The UML definition includes an explicit *send-clause*, a special action, which shall be subsumed here as an action for simplicity. We associate *event signatures* and *action expressions* obtaining *operation definitions* in order to simplify the notion of actions and operations for this investigation:

$$e(p_1 : t_1, \ldots , p_n : t_n) \stackrel{\text{def}}{=} \textit{action-expression} \qquad (2)$$

Action expressions can be assignments to state variables $x := t$, operation calls $op(x_1, \ldots , x_n)$, send clauses $obj.op(x_1, \ldots , x_n)$ and action sequences combined using the sequence combinator ';'.

Objects interact dynamically via message exchange, realised by operation calls. *Object interaction* can be described using sequence, collaboration and activity diagrams. We have already introduced object interaction through the *send*-action. The sequence diagram allows us to describe sequences of object interactions considering several objects at the same time. It describes the interaction protocol.

An action expression or an operation definition can be *abstracted* by *pre- and postconditions* in order to express abstract dynamic behaviour. The *Object Constraint Language OCL* [13] supports *pre- and postconditions* for the specification of operations. Abstract specifications are essential to built declarative, possibly under-determined models – an important feature for the formal development of software systems. Preconditions associate constraints with parameters and the postcondition constrains the operation result.

$$operationName(p_1 : t_1, \ldots, p_n : t_n) \ returns \ rt$$
$$pre : p_1 > \ldots \tag{3}$$
$$post : result = \ldots$$

An **abstract specification** or an **abstract interface** is a collection of abstract operation specifications using pre- and postconditions. An example shall illustrate the pre- and postconditions:

```
request ( url: URL ) returns Document
      pre   url > checkURL(url)        -- URL is well-formed
      post  result = DocForURL(url)    -- Doc corresponds to URL
```

The `request` operation is provided by the `ContentServer` which can act as a service provider. The service user might be the `UserInterface`. It might call `request` within its `sendRequest` operation. This functionality request would be stated in its import interface. A library of re-usable components could include a content server component. Its export interface has to satisfy the user's requirements, which are formulated in a contract between both parties. A semantical adaptation might be necessary, if e.g. the library component is too general (a generic component can be instantiated).

2.2 The Specification of Interfaces and Components

We will apply the component-notion to UML packages. Packages allow us to group semantically related model elements. Packages do not provide much semantics currently [13], except that packages 'own' their constituent elements, i.e. these elements can only be part of one package. There is one important relationship between packages: import (from other packages that own the desired element). Import expresses a dependency. An import section specifies what services are needed, but not where these services might come from. Packages, and classes in UML can have interfaces. An interface is described by a set of operation signatures. Other packages might relate to these interfaces. Their purpose is to support well-structured system architectures, providing contracts between participating model elements.

Let us define a **component** (or package – we shall use both terms synonymously) as a triple $C = \langle Imp, Class, Exp \rangle$ where[1]

---

[1] Sometimes we use projections $Imp(C)$, $Class(C)$, or $Exp(C)$ to refer to the respective elements.

```
Contract Contr
        provider    ContentServer
        user        UserInterface
    attributes
        currentURL : URL
    operations
        myRequest(url:URL) : Document
            pre   checkURL(url)
            post  resultDoc = DocForURL(url)
        mySearch(term:Text) : Document
            pre   ..
            post  ..
    syntactic match
        myRequest is matched by request
        ..
```

Fig. 2. A Contract – an Abstract Interface

- *Imp* is called the *import interface* (importing requested functionality described by pre- and postcondition-based constraints),
- *Class* is the class or package implementation (e.g. in terms of actions),
- *Exp* is called the *export interface* (abstracting the services provided by the component in terms of pre- and postconditions).

An abstract interface is decribed by a signature, pre- and postconditions for each operation, and invariants. A notion of *correctness* shall be introduced: the export *Exp* has to be an abstraction of the implementation *Class*. Each abstract operation in an interface is specified by pre- and postconditions in a form that generalises the OCL here (cf. (3)):

$$operationName(p_1 : t_1, \ldots , p_n : t_n) : rt$$
$$pre : F \qquad\qquad (4)$$
$$post : G$$

F and G can be arbitrary first-order formulas. Each class, interface or operation has an associated *signature*. A signature assembles the sorts of the constituent elements of the particular element. Figure 1 contains class and operation signatures.

Figure 2 contains an example of a (rather incomplete) abstract interface – the attribute and operation parts. Attributes are also part of the interface since they implement observations on the current state, but do not change the state. Attributes can be accessible to other users. This abstract interface is wrapped up by a contract between two components. The export interface of a suitable reusable library component has to satisfy the requirements stated in the contract. *Contracts* are extensions of abstract interfaces that will specify the requirements of the prospective service user which a service provider is supposed to satisfy. Additionally, a contract includes syntactic matching information, here that the myRequest operation – as the operation might be called in the user interface – is matched by request of the service provider. A component can import from various other components, i.e. it can make separate contracts with each of these components. Contracts are formulated in the customer's (service user's) terminology. This is sensible because names in the library components might be too generic and thus not suitable for the application context.

Contracts between components might be designed before the components itself are realised. A contract is an abstract interface describing a set of operations through pre- and postconditions. Both service provider and service user have to relate to the contract description. The provider must satisfy the contract constraints. The service user might be satisfied with less than what is described in the connector. The contract is instantiated into a *connector* for object interactions between service provider and service user.

3   Component Composition

The composition mechanism is interaction: functionality is requested by one component and provided by another via a communication channel. Two components are composed by establishing an interconnection – a connector – between them. Contracts constrain the composition. We propose a two-tiered approach for the composition of components. The *upper*, more abstract *tier* defines contracts between components, i.e. a service provider and a service user. Technically, a contract establishes a communication infrastructure on which the components can interact. A private interaction channel between provider and user is created, if the contract constraints are satisfied. The *lower*, more implementation-oriented *tier* realises a connector, an interaction channel, between provider and user. Messages can be passed along that channel, i.e. provider services can be invoked and results can be transferred back.

We assume a collection of re-usable library components (service providers) and a collection of components part of a system to be developed. The latter ones (service users) require functionality in order to be executable. These requirements are formulated in form of an import interface. A contract establishes a relationship between the import requirements and provided services.

All components shall initially be connected via a **select channel** sC of sort *selectChan* which shall help us to formulate the interconnection of two components related by a contract. A suitable service provider has to be selected based on a component's import requirements. The most suitable should be selected among the available ones. Technically, a request from the component C

$$C \stackrel{\text{def}}{=} \text{SELECT } \overline{sC}\langle cC \rangle.cC(x).C' \tag{5}$$

should be answered by the most suited service provider P_i from the library

$$P_i \stackrel{\text{def}}{=} \text{CHOOSE } sC(y).\overline{y}\langle \epsilon \rangle.P_i' \tag{6}$$

using the **contract channel** $cC : contractChan$ between C and P_i (supplied by C and bound to the formal parameter y in P_i). $\overline{sC}\langle cC \rangle$ denotes the output of

cC on channel sC and $sC(y)$ denotes input of parameter y via the same channel. The provider replies to the user by sending an empty data token via the contract channel cC, which is bound to its formal parameter y.

3.1 Contracts

The situation before establishing the contract shall be described as follows: the component C (the user) requires a service (an operation) m and the provider P offers a service (an operation) n. Both operations m and n are described by pre- and postconditions, e.g. $pre(m)$ and $post(m)$.

Several constraints have to be considered. The *first syntactical issue* to be considered is the proper use of names in interactions. This shall be captured in a variant of the standard REACT-rule which describes the state transformation triggered by an interaction realising a *sorting discipline* [12].

$$\text{REACT}_S : \ \overline{z}\langle x \rangle.C|z(y).P \longrightarrow C|P \ \text{ iff } \ \text{if } z : \sigma \text{ then } x : ob(\sigma) \text{ and } y : ob(\sigma) \quad (7)$$

This expresses that an interaction can only take place using channel z if the parameters x and y are of the same sort $ob(\sigma)$ which characterises the sort of names allowed on channel z. The sorting ob applied to a channel name is a mapping which characterises the sorts of elements that can be passed along a channel. The sorting is preserved by the interaction rule [12]. The *second syntactical issue* relates to the *syntactical matching* between service user and service provider, see e.g. Figure 2. The syntactical constraint can be formally expressed by the existence of a signature morphism $\rho : C \to P$. The signature morphism ρ has to be applied to show that all elements required are actually provided in the correct form. The *semantical condition* is the existence of a refinement relation between m and $\rho(m)$, expressed as $m \xrightarrow{R} \rho(m)$ or m is refined by $\rho(m)$ (or $\rho(m)$ satisfies m). We define the refinement using pre- and postconditions.

$$m \xrightarrow{R} \rho(m) \ \text{ iff } \ pre(m) \to pre(\rho(m)) \wedge post(\rho(m)) \to post(m) \quad (8)$$

Preconditions can be weakened – the refinement is more likely to be applicable – and postconditions can be strengthened – the result is better. $\rho(m)$ describes the provided service, reachable via the provider's in-port. Here, $\rho(m)$ shall refer to n. m describes the required service. It will be accessed via the user's out-port.

We shall illustrate the refinement now. `modifyDoc` is an operation which is provided by the `AuthoringServer` class and might be requested by an `Interface` class. The `UserInterface` is the service user and the `AuthoringServer` is the service provider, see Figure 3. The library may provide an XML-Update method, which works for well-formed XML documents, i.e. documents with correct tag-nesting. The operation updates the document and acknowledges success to the user. The user has specified an operation, which is only required to work on valid XML-documents, i.e. documents that are well-formed and conform to a document type definition (DTD). Additionally, an acknowledgement shall not be required. A contract would state the user's require-

Requirements specification - service user:

```
myModifyDoc ( myDoc:Document, myUpdate:Text ) returns Document
       pre   isValid()
       post  updated()
```

Service specification - library component:

```
modifyDoc ( doc:Document, update:Text ) returns Document
       pre   isWellFormed()
       post  updated() and acknowledged()
```

Fig. 3. Service Request and Service Provider

ments. Syntactically, $\rho(\texttt{myModifyDoc}) = \texttt{modifyDoc}$ matches. The contract requires semantically a refinement $\texttt{myModifyDoc} \stackrel{\mathcal{R}}{\longrightarrow} \texttt{modifyDoc}$, which means $pre(\texttt{myModifyDoc}) \rightarrow pre(\texttt{modifyDoc})$ or $\texttt{isValid()} \rightarrow \texttt{isWellFormed()}$, and that $post(\texttt{modifyDoc}) \rightarrow post(\texttt{myModifyDoc})$, which is true since $\texttt{updated()}$ and $\texttt{acknowledged()}$ implies $\texttt{updated()}$. This shows that the library operation matches the requirements. The contract is satisfied and an interconnection between the components can be established.

A contract between a single import m of component C and a provider P providing $\rho(m)$ should result in an interconnection between both. We assume that the contract channel cC exists with sorting $sort(cC) = interactChan$ (i.e. $sort(sC)$ equals $contractChan$). For a user C' defined by REQUEST $\overline{cC}\langle m \rangle.C''$ and a provider P' defined by PROVIDE $cC(n).P''$ we define the **contract rule** CONTRACT:

$$\text{REQUEST } \overline{cC}\langle m \rangle.C' | \text{PROVIDE } cC(n).P' \longrightarrow \texttt{private } m{:}iC \ (C'|P'\{^m/_n\}) \quad (9)$$

constrained by the sorting constraints and the refinement, i.e. iff $m \stackrel{\mathcal{R}}{\longrightarrow} n$. Channel $m{:}interactChan$ is the **interaction channel**, or the **connector**, between C and P. The **restriction private** $m{:}iC$ creates a private channel m of sort iC between C and P (by introducing a scope). The sorting of m should correspond to m's signature. The CONTRACT-rule is a variation of the π-calculus REACT-rule, which formulates the basic interaction between two agents. In addition to the interaction, we have introduced a private channel as well.

We illustrate this again using the $\texttt{modifyDoc}$-operation, see Figure 4. The user $\texttt{Interface}$ requests the service $\texttt{myModifyDoc}$ which is provided by the $\texttt{AuthoringServer}$. Applying the CONTRACT-rule results in a parallel composition of $\texttt{Interface}$ and $\texttt{AuthoringServer}$ objects where $\texttt{modifyDoc}$ replaces $\texttt{myModifyDoc}$ in the provider $\texttt{AuthoringServer}$.

We shall briefly address a contract between a component and two providers illustrating multiple imports. Allowing a component to import functionality from several providers was one of the reasons to choose the π-calculus because of its ability to express the concurrent existence of service providers. Otherwise, a variant of the λ-calculus might have been another suitable formalism

Specifications for the contract:

$$\text{Interface}' \overset{\text{def}}{=} \text{REQUEST } \overline{cC}\langle\text{myModifyDoc}\rangle.\text{Interface}''$$
$$\text{AuthoringServer}' \overset{\text{def}}{=} \text{PROVIDE } cC(\text{modifyDoc}).\text{AuthoringServer}''$$

Fig. 4. Contract between Service Requester and Service Provider

$$\text{Interface}'' \overset{\text{def}}{=} \text{WRITE } \overline{\text{myModifyDoc}}\langle\text{doc}, \text{update}\rangle.\text{Interface}'''$$
$$\text{AuthoringServer}'' \overset{\text{def}}{=} \text{READ } \overline{\text{modifyDoc}}\langle x_1, x_2\rangle.\text{AuthoringServer}'''$$

Fig. 5. Interaction between Service Requester and Service Provider

(see [14]). Let $C' \overset{\text{def}}{=} \text{REQUEST } \overline{cC_1}\langle m_1\rangle.\overline{cC_2}\langle m_2\rangle.C''$ be the user, and $P_1' \overset{\text{def}}{=}$ PROVIDE $cC_1(n).P_1''$ and $P_2' \overset{\text{def}}{=}$ PROVIDE $cC_2(n).P_2''$ two service providers. The channel m_1 is local to C and P_1; m_2 is local to C and P_2.

3.2 Connectors

We look at single connectors first, i.e. connectors for a single contract. A private interaction channel $m : iC$, the connector, is established between provider and user. The provider has an input-port (called n) and the user has an output-port m (by default the name of the connector). The interaction between the user

$$C'' \overset{\text{def}}{=} \text{WRITE } \overline{m}\langle a\rangle.C''' \tag{10}$$

and the provider

$$P'' \overset{\text{def}}{=} \text{READ } m(x).P''' \tag{11}$$

can happen if permitted by the sorted REACT_S-rule. Here a is a single parameter (we could have used a parameter list in the polyadic π-calculus).

We use again the interface and the authoring server interaction for illustration, see Figure 5. The user interface requests a document modification using the private channel myModifyDoc, which has been established as the interconnection between **Interface** and **AuthoringServer** for this particular service. Parameters are passed along that channel. The authoring server carries out its modifyDoc-operation (which is linked to myModifyDoc).

If multiple contracts – and, thus, multiple connectors m_i – exist, the behaviour of C can be abstracted by:

$$C'' \overset{\text{def}}{=} \text{WRITE } \overline{m_1}\langle a_1\rangle.C'' + \text{WRITE } \overline{m_2}\langle a_2\rangle.C'' + \tau.C'' \tag{12}$$

The computation is either a call of m_1 with value a_1 or a call of m_2 with value a_2 or an empty action τ (representing some internal computation). This is executed repeatedly. The interaction channels are scoped as follows in this example: **private** $m_1:iC$ $(C|P_1)$ and **private** $m_2:iC$ $(C|P_2)$.

We could introduce a *reply* construct using the same interaction channel:

$$C'' \stackrel{\text{def}}{=} \text{WRITE } \overline{m}\langle a\rangle.\text{READREPLY } m(x).C'''$$

and

$$P'' \stackrel{\text{def}}{=} \text{READ } mx.\text{WRITEREPLY } \overline{m}\langle b\rangle.P'''$$

for an operation m with a return value. We will not investigate this further, see e.g. [15] for a suitable concept.

4   Semantics for Components

In this section, we will give semantics to the previous constructs. It shall make some of the notions introduced only intuitively in the previous sections more precise. We will interpret entities in state-based structures, called objects. Constraints are embedded into a modal state-based logic over these structures.

4.1   Semantics of Actions and Operations

The OMG *Request For Proposals on Action Semantics for the UML* [16] requests semantics for actions essentially for two reasons: formality and abstractness. System analysis and proof of correctness are possible within an abstract and formal framework. Abstractness enables interoperability and platform-independence. Object behaviour is essentially based on state transitions expressed by actions. These actions shall be formalised in a denotational style and abstracted by pre- and postconditions. Using dynamic logic as a framework allows us to establish a development calculus centered around proof rules.

A *labelled transition system* consists of a set of states $State$, a set of transition labels $Tran$ and a relation on $State \times Tran \times State$. One state shall be distinguished as an initial state. Behaviour is modelled as a traversal of the transition system. A *state machine* executes the actions associated with the transitions. *Objects* shall be state machines with structured states and relations on states which form functions. An object state is a binding between state variables and their values. Each transition label denotes an operation definition, characterised by a signature and an implementation consisting of actions. Operations are interpreted by functions on states,possibly producing a result value. The signature of these functions is $State \times S_1 \times \ldots \times S_n \rightarrow State \times S_0$. The S_i are value domains. Projections onto the resulting pair select the appropriate component of an operation instance. An **object** is an algebraic structure with:

- a carrier set S for each sort s,
- a function of type $S_1 \times \ldots \times S_n \rightarrow S$ for each attribute with signature $s_1 \times \ldots \times s_n \rightarrow s$,
- a carrier set $State$ for sort $state$ containing total assignments $Id \rightarrow F$ where Id is a set of function identifiers and F is the set of functions that match the signatures of attributes,
- a function of type $(State \times S_1 \times \ldots \times S_m) \rightarrow (State \times S)$ for each operation symbol with the corresponding signature.

Objects are hidden algebras for a signature with state [17,18,19]. An object consists of a **state** that maintains bindings between identifiers and functions, **attributes**, i.e. functions of the state which allow observations of the state, and **operations**, i.e. state transitions which modify the state by modifying its attributes. *Actions* can be *interpreted* by transitions on objects:

- The *assignment* modifies the state binding between state variables and values, i.c. assigns a new value to the state variable.
- The *operation call* invokes a local operation of the object, which might result in a new state.
- The *sequence* is executed by executing the second action in the resulting state of the first action execution.

Entities that we have used in the definition of contract and connector channels also have denotations in this semantical structure. The semantics of a component C is an object. That of a channel z is an operation of an object: an output $\overline{x}\langle y \rangle$ is an interaction (or send-activity) which invokes an operation at the other object, an input $x(y)$ is an operation invocation at the current object itself.

4.2   Abstraction of Actions and Operations

The *Action Semantics RFP* [16] requests a framework to carry out formal analysis and proofs of correctness. *Modal logic* – a logic with a notion of state or time – is a suitable framework for reasoning about concurrent and reactive systems. In order to express abstract constraints on states and transitions (operations), we propose an extension of the OCL-notion of pre- and postconditions based on a simplified *dynamic logic*:

$$opName(p_1 : t_1, \ldots , p_n : t_n) : rt$$
$$pre : F \qquad (13)$$
$$post : G$$

where F and G are arbitrary first-order formulas. We have simplified the modal calculus in order to avoid reasoning about nested modal combinators in the context of UML. As usual, the name *self* can be used, and values of state variables in the previous state can be accessed by the @*pre*-postfix. Pre- and postconditions are *observations on states*, they describe properties of states. Additionally, using the reserved name *result* we can specify the return value of the operation in a postcondition. The precondition F corresponds to the guard from transition descriptions in statechart diagrams.

The *semantics of constraints* shall be given in form of a *satisfaction* relation. *State properties* can be specified using **equations** based on expressions involving state variables and attributes. An equation $x = y$ is *satisfied* in a state if the interpretations of both sides are the same (x and y are expressions consisting of values, operators, and operation applications). The **implication** $f \rightarrow g$ holds iff f and not g holds. The **formula** $\square(F \rightarrow [P]G)$ shall abbreviate the pre- and postcondition specification in (13) with $P \equiv opName(x_1, \ldots , x_n)$. The formula

$\Box([P]G)$ holds iff the execution of P terminates in a state satisfying G. The UML definition assumes a non-partial (terminating) behaviour[2].

An **abstract specification** or **abstract interface** $S = \langle \Sigma, E \rangle$ consists of a signature and well-formed axioms in dynamic logic describing operations on objects in abstract terms. An axiomatic specification and the interpretation of elements in semantic structures gives rise to a *notion of model classes*, here the class of objects which satisfy some specification. The semantics of a specification S is a model class $Mod(S)$.

5   Reasoning about Composition and Contracts

We will extend our formal framework in order to allow reasoning about component composition and contracts. We generalise the refinement relation into a general abstraction/implementation relation. The relations play an important role in the definition of a flexible composition mechanism.

UML offers several ways of relating classes statically. The main relationships are association, generalisation, dependency and refinement. We will concentrate on the *abstraction* relations, in particular *refinement* and *implementation*. A refinement relates two elements describing the same on different levels of abstraction. The name indicates that structure, knowledge, or properties are added in a refinement. It also suggests that properties of the more abstract description should be preserved. The refinement is particulary important since it can form the basis of a formally supported stepwise development method. Refinement is defined for the UML [13] as the description of something on a lower level of abstraction. Lowering the level of abstraction means to make a description more concrete by adding details. These can be details about the underlying structure or can be details about the behaviour of operations. Certainly, we expect that *properties* specified on the abstract level are *preserved* in a refinement.

5.1   Implementing and Refining Abstract Specifications

We can distinguish two dimensions of development: horizontal and vertical development. Horizontal development refers to the composition of packages, vertical development means using refinement, realisation, implementation or any other construct which lowers the level of abstraction.

Implementation captures the idea of making design decisions, i.e. lowering the level of abstraction. Formally, this can be expressed by model class inclusion

$$S \rightsquigarrow S' \quad \text{iff} \quad Mod(S') \subseteq Mod(S) \tag{14}$$

for two specifications S and S'. The inverse of an implementation is an **abstraction**. We now formalise the **correctness** condition on components $C = \langle Imp, Class, Exp \rangle$ – Exp is an abstraction of $Class$:

$$sig(Exp) \subseteq sig(Class) \ \land \ Exp \rightsquigarrow Class \tag{15}$$

---

[2] If we would extend our approach to partial correctness (the above is a total correctness assertion), we would add a *liberal* variant of the formula involving an undefinedness predicate, see [2].

We require that only a subset of attributes and operations is exported (or visible) and that *Exp* abstracts *Class*, or *Class* implements *Exp*.

The **refinement** is a constructive support for the implementation only based on pre- and postconditions: preconditions are weakened and/or postconditions are strengthened. *Implication* is the formal basis of the refinement [20], relating behavioural abstractions of operations in terms of pre- and postconditions. We reformulate the refinement in terms of the box-operator notation:

$$\frac{F \to F', \; \Box(F \to [P]G), \; G' \to G}{\Box(F' \to [P]G')} \qquad (16)$$

Proving an implication between pre- or postconditions is usually less complex compared to proper modal formulas. In modal logics, the rule above is known as the *consequence rule*. In refinement calculi, it is known as a combination of the *weaken precondition-* and *strengthen postcondition*-rule [21,22,23]. Ideas from refinement calculi can be used to provide a *constructive calculus of derivations*. The refinement here is only basic definition and needs to be accompanied by an appropriate calculus to *support the modelling process*.

We need to distinguish two forms of implementation and refinement: $\overset{\leadsto}{op}$ and $\overset{R}{\underset{op}{\leadsto}}$ are relations between operations, and $\overset{\leadsto}{}$ and $\overset{R}{\leadsto}$ are relations between abstract specifications. The derivation rule above defines a notion of *refinement* for *operations*. *Refinement between interfaces* shall now be addressed. Ideally, we would find a notion which is *compositional*; a notion which defines the refinement of interfaces based on the refinement of its constituent operation specifications. That requires that invariants and other constraints can be dealt with as part of operation specifications. Implementation and refinement are **compositional**: $S \leadsto S'$ iff $P \leadsto P'$ for all constituent procedures P. A corresponding definition can be found in [14].

We can show that our refinement is a close approximation to an inclusion of model classes for a concrete and an abstract specification, see [14] for details. The following theorem formalises this important property. It shows that the implementation generalises the refinement. For two specifications S and S': refinement implies implementation, or

$$S \overset{R}{\leadsto} S' \text{ implies } S \overset{\leadsto}{} S' \qquad (17)$$

This proposition is based on some assumptions. Invariants *inv* are added to pre- and postconditions $\Box(F \land inv \to [P] \; G \land inv)$. Attribute definitions do not change and can, thus, be specified as invariants. These assumptions do not restrict the approach, however, they simplify proofs. The implication $S_1 \overset{\leadsto}{} S_2$ *implies* $S_1 \overset{R}{\leadsto} S_2$ can *not* be established – the notions of refinement and model class inclusion are different – if states are involved which are not reachable from any initial state or formulas specify states which are not satisfiable.

We see implementation as a fundamental relation since it captures property-preservation. Property-preservation can also be the foundation of the various UML abstraction relations. These relations are important for the *development of software components*. This can include the implementation, but also the composition of components where the implementation (or the refinement) can play the role of a *correctness* criterion – e.g. the glue between a service provider and a service user. The refinement has already been used to define the notion of *contracts* between provider and user. A service provided needs to satisfy requirements formulated by a service user, i.e. the provided service refines or implements – we can generalise the definition – the user's import requirements, see [14]. These results can be used in the definition of an extension and improvement of the UML package concept.

The refinement relation is based on the operation specification in OCL. The implementation is a generalisation, which captures property-preservation. Both notions can serve as a basis for a practical development method.

An example shall illustrate a contract between two components matched by strengthening postconditions. The refinement is the tool to prove the correctness constraint for semantical matching. The contract might specify a postcondition `updated()` for an operation `myModifyDoc` and a library version `modifyDoc` might provide `updated()` ∧ `acknowledged` as the postcondition. We get for the corresponding interfaces in the implementation

$$Imp(\texttt{myModifyDoc}) \overset{\downarrow}{\leadsto} Exp(\texttt{modifyDoc})$$

since the implication $post(\texttt{myModifyDoc}) \rightarrow post(\texttt{modifyDoc})$ holds. We can easily show the refinement. With the proposition (17) we can deduce the more general implementation from the refinement. The refinement is used here as a proof tool to prove the correctness of a component composition with respect to a contract.

5.2 Composition of Components

A **composition** between two components can be formulated **syntactically** by

$$compose\ U = \langle Imp, Class, Exp\rangle\ with\ P = \langle Imp', Class', Exp'\rangle\ via\ \rho \quad (18)$$

expressing that a component U uses services provided by P. A contract C can be derived from the abstract interface Imp, which is the requirements specification of the service user. The **correctness constraint** for composition based on a contract C with provider P and user U is the following:

$$\rho(sig(Imp(U))) = sig(Exp'(P))\ and\ Imp(U) \overset{\downarrow}{\leadsto} Exp'(P)_{|\rho} \quad (19)$$

This criterion is based on syntactical and semantical properties of the abstract interfaces of the components involved. With $Exp'(P)_{|\rho}$ we denote the restriction of P to elements in the range of $\rho(sig(Imp))$. Technically, the composition results in the establishment of an interaction infrastructure between components so that services requested by a user can actually be accessed. A component can import from several library components. Each import is defined in a separate contract and results in a separate connector. The **composition** of service requester and service provider can be defined **semantically** by

$$compose\ \langle Imp, Class, Exp\rangle\ with\ \langle Imp', Class', Exp'\rangle\ via\ \rho\ :=$$
$$\langle Imp', Class|Class', Exp\rangle \quad (20)$$

where ρ shall be a signature morphism $\rho : sig(Imp) \rightarrow sig(Exp')$. The correctness constraint for composition needs to be applied. The composed component forms again a component with the parallel composition $Class|Class'$ of the component implementations at its core. The new import is that of the provider and the export is that of the user.

The composition of the two components user interface and authoring server *compose* Interface *with* AuthoringServer *via* ρ is defined as as a component with the import $imp($Interface$)$, body Interface | AuthoringServer and export $exp($AuthoringServer$)$. The internal communication between both is captured by the CONTRACT-rule.

In the π-calculus, the interaction between two processes in a parallel composition is considered as not being observable from the outside. We have followed this idea, and defined the composition of two components as a new component, which hides the parallel composition of its interacting objects inside.

6   Related Work

Catalysis is a development approach building up on the UML incorporating formal aspects such as the pre- and postcondition technique [24]. Catalysis uses ideas from formal languages such as OBJ, CLEAR or EML. The concept of the connector that we have used here is motivated by the Catalysis approach. There, connectors allow the communication between ports of two objects. A connector defines a protocol between the ports. Several other authors also address contracts based on pre- and postconditions for the UML, including [25] and [26]. The combination of the pre- and postcondition technique and refinement calculi is explored in e.g. [27] or [26].

KobrA [28] is another approach which combines the UML with the component paradigm. The basic structuring mechanism is the *is-component-of* hierarchy, forming a tree-structured hierarchy of components, i.e. sub-components. Each component is described by a suite of UML diagrams. A component consists of a specification (an abstract export interface) and a realisation.

In earlier work [14], we have used a variant of the λ-calculus to define a single import using reduction as the mechanism for import actualisation. The variant is called $\lambda\pi$-calculus, and has been developed by L. Feijs [29]. The calculus has been used to define module parameterisation for the state-based specification language COLD [30]. This $\lambda\pi$-calculus can be interpreted in semantic structures, as we have done it here for the constrained interaction calculus. We have used a π-calculus variant here, because it offers multiple (concurrent) connections and it allows to model two layers: contracts and connectors.

A composition language for components which is also based on the π-calculus is presented in [15]. A variation of the π-calculus is used to realise a composition language which supports various forms of components, and, thus, various composition mechanisms.

Walker [31] introduces object intercommunication into the π-calculus. The difference between our approach and Walker's approach is that in our approach the user is the active entity which initiates the establishment of the connections. In Walker's formalisation, the service provider also provides the communication channels. The service user acquires the contract channel, then acquires the interaction channels via the appropriate contract channels and finally uses the interaction channels to invoke methods of the service providers.

7   Conclusions

A composition mechanism for component-based software development has been developed and illustrated in the UML-context. Components are specifications with abstract import and export interfaces which encapsulate and abstract (possibly complex) objects. We have addressed the *abstraction of behaviour* and formalised *notions of refinement and implementation*. The internal behaviour of operations is specified by actions. Pre- and postconditions specify the abstract behaviour of operations. Their specifications can be related through pre- and postcondition-based implementation and refinement relations, whereby the refinement can be used to prove implementations. These relations capture the idea of property preservation.

The basis of component composition is interaction. One component interacts with another component if it requires services of the latter. The user's requirements – or expectations how the required services will work – are the basis on which a contract between both parties is formulated. These constraints formulated by the contract are based on the refinement relation.

The essential result here is that the pre- and postcondition technique extended to a refinement approach solves two problems. Firstly, the internal behaviour of operations on objects can be abstracted by pre- and postconditions, and the refinement relation based on this can form the foundation of a stepwise development calculus. Secondly, pre- and postconditions formalise conditions necessary to constrain interactions between objects. The refinement is the tool to prove these constraints. We have addressed both the interaction infrastructure and the constraint language necessary to control the composition. The result is a composition approach which allows re-use of existing components and reasoning about composition contracts.

One future research focus concerns the maintainability of systems and the evolution of contracts in these systems. Changing requirements make it necessary to re-negotiate contracts, i.e. to either adapt the existing partners to the new requirements or to involve other components. Assessing the suitablity of contracts in an evolving environment might be supported by the bisimilarity concept of the π-calculus. Another direction in which the adaptability of re-usable components could be investigated is the deployment of matching approaches, as presented in [32] for the Larch language family.

A further direction concerns the extension of the constraint language. In *reactive systems*, *liveness* is the second important property besides *safety* (which has been addressed only so far). Liveness can be expressed using the eventually-operator: $\Diamond([P]F)$ expresses that by executing P a state described by F will eventually be reached. Formally, the eventually-operator can be defined via the always operator: $\Diamond([P]F) := \neg\Box([P]\neg F)$. A modal logic framework was chosen in order to be able to extend the approach to reactive systems modelling.

References

1. Bertrand Meyer. Applying Design by Contract. *Computer*, pages 40–51, October 1992.
2. G.T. Leavens and A.L. Baker. Enhancing the Pre- and Postcondition Technique for More Expressive Specifications. In R. France and B. Rumpe, editors, *Proceedings 2nd Int. Conference UML'99 - The Unified Modeling Language.* Springer Verlag, LNCS 1723, 1999.
3. W. Weck. Inheritance Using Contracts & Object Composition. In *Proceedings 2nd International Workshop on Component-Oriented Programming WCOP '97.* Turku Center for Computer Science, General Publication No.5-97, Turku University, Finland, 1997.
4. E.K. Nordhagen. *A Computational Framework for Verifying Object Component Substitutability.* PhD thesis, University of Oslo, November 1998.
5. G.T. Leavens and M. Sitamaran. *Foundations of Component-Based Systems.* Cambridge University Press, 2000.
6. precise UML Group. Response to UML 2.0 Request for Information, 1999. http://www.cs.york.ac.uk/puml.
7. C. Stirling. Modal and Temporal Logics. In S. Abramsky, D. Gabbay, and T. Maibaum, editors, *Handbook of Logic in Computer Science, Vol. II*, pages 477–563. Oxford University Press, 1992.
8. L. Lamport. The Temporal Logic of Actions. *ACM Transactions on Programming Languages and Systems*, 16(3):872–923, May 1994.
9. L. Lamport. Specifying Concurrent Systems with TLA$^+$. In M. Broy and R. Steinbrüggen, editors, *Calculational System Design.* IOS Press, Amsterdam, 1999.
10. R. Milner, J. Parrow, and D. Walker. A calculus of Mobile Processes, part I. *Information and Computation*, 100(1):1–40, 1992.
11. R. Milner, J. Parrow, and D. Walker. A calculus of Mobile Processes, part II. *Information and Computation*, 100(1):41–77, 1992.
12. R. Milner. *Communicating and Mobile Systems: the π-Calculus.* Cambridge University Press, 1999.
13. Object Management Group. UML 1.3 Specification, 1999. http://www.omg.org/technology/uml.
14. C. Pahl. Modal Logics for Reasoning about Object-based Component Composition. In *Proc. 4rd Irish Workshop on Formal Methods, July 2000, Maynooth, Ireland.* BCS, eWiC series, 2000. (to appear).
15. M. Lumpe, F. Achermann, and O. Nierstrasz. A Formal Language for Composition. In G.T. Leavens and M. Sitamaran, editors, *Foundations of Component-Based Systems.* Cambridge University Press, 2000.
16. Object Management Group. Action Semantics for the UML – RFP, 1998. http://www.omg.org/technology/uml.
17. C. Pahl. A Model for Dynamic State-based Systems. In A.S. Evans and D.J. Duke, editors, *Proc. Northern Formal Methods Workshop, Sept.'96, Bradford, UK.* Springer-Verlag, 1997.
18. J. Goguen. Hidden Algebra for Software Engineering. In *Proceedings Conference on Discrete Mathematics and Theoretical Computer Science, Auckland, New Zealand*, pages 35–59. Australian Computer Science Communications, Volume 21, Number 3, 1999.

19. J. Goguen and G. Malcolm. A Hidden Agenda. *Theoretical Computer Science*, 2000. Special Issue on Algebraic Engineering – to appear.
20. L. Lamport. Refinement in State-based Formalisms. SRC Technical Note 1996-001, Digital Equipment Corporation, Systems Research Center, 1996.
21. R.J.R. Back. A Calculus of Refinements for Program Derivations. *Acta Informatica*, 25:593–624, 1988.
22. J.M. Morris. Programs from Specifications. In E.D. Dijkstra, editor, *Formal Development of Programs and Proofs*. Addison-Wesley, 1990.
23. C. Morgan. *Programming from Specification 2e*. Addison-Wesley, 1994.
24. D. D'Souza and A.C. Wills. *Objects, Components and Frameworks in UML: the Catalysis approach*. Addison-Wesley, 1998.
25. L.F. Andrade and J.L. Fiadero. Interconnecting Objects via Contracts. In R. France and B. Rumpe, editors, *Proceedings 2nd Int. Conference UML'99 - The Unified Modeling Language*. Springer Verlag, LNCS 1723, 1999.
26. R.-J. Back, L. Petre, and I.P. Paltor. Analysing UML Use Cases as Contracts. In R. France and B. Rumpe, editors, *Proceedings 2nd Int. Conference UML'99 - The Unified Modeling Language*. Springer Verlag, LNCS 1723, 1999.
27. M. Büchi and E. Sekerinski. Formal Methods for Component Software: The Refinement Calculus Perspective. In *Proceedings 2nd International Workshop on Component-Oriented Programming WCOP '97*. Turku Center for Computer Science, General Publication No.5-97, Turku University, Finland, 1997.
28. C. Atkinson, J. Bayer, O. Laitenberger, and J. Zettel. Component-Based Software Engineering: The KobrA Approach. In *Proc. Internal Workshop on Component-Based Software Engineering, Limerick, Ireland*. 2000. ICSE (International Conference on Software Engineering) Workshop.
29. L.M.G. Feijs. The calculus $\lambda\pi$. In *Algebraic Methods: Theory, Tools and Applications*, pages 307–328. Springer-Verlag, 1989.
30. L.M.G Feijs and H.B.M Jonkers. *Formal Specification and Design*. Cambridge University Press, 1992.
31. D. Walker. Objects in the π-Calculus. *Information and Computation*, 115:253–271, 1995.
32. A. Moormann Zaremski and J.M. Wing. Specification Matching of Software Components. In Gail E. Kaiser, editor, *Proc. ACM SIGSOFT Symposium on Foundations of Software Engineering*, pages 6–17. ACM Software Engineering Notes 20(4), October 1995.

An Integrated Approach to Specification and Validation of Real-Time Systems

Adnan Sherif, Augusto Sampaio, and Sérgio Cavalcante

Federal University of Pernambuco
Center of Informatics
P.O. BOX 7851 Cidade Universitaria
50740-540 Recife - PE Brazil
{ams,acas,svc}@cin.ufpe.br

Abstract. This work presents an integrated approach which covers from the formal specification to the analysis and use of tools to prove properties about real-time systems. The proposed language to specify the system behaviour is Timed-CSP-Z, a combination of Timed CSP and Z. We propose a rule-based strategy for converting a Timed-CSP-Z specification to TER Nets, a high level Petri Net based formalism with time. The conversion enables us to use the CABERNET tool to analyse desired properties. As a practical case study we discuss the application of this approach to the specification and analysis of an On-board Computer of a Brazilian microsatellite.

1 Introduction

Real-time computer systems differ from general-purpose computer systems in that they introduce the time notion to the computational requirements of the system. Real-time systems must not only provide logically correct and adequate results but these results also have to be provided within a certain period of time.

First generation real-time applications were relatively simple and did not involve sophisticated algorithms or extensive computational complexity. However, things have changed in the last decades towards more complex and more safety critical applications such as aerospace navigation and control, monitoring factories and nuclear power plants, among others. The use of real-time systems in safety critical applications makes them a serious candidate for the use of formal methods concerning their specification and validation.

The choice of the language to be used in the specification of a software system is an important factor concerning the success of the entire development. The language should cover the several facets of the system requirements and it should have a suitable observation model. The model is used to study the behaviour of the system and to establish the validity of desired properties. Another important factor to be considered is the popularity of the language.

During the last years, the software engineering researchers have developed a large number of formal specification languages. However, each of these languages is suitable for expressing a particular characteristic and lacks the power

J.N. Oliveira and P. Zave (Eds.): FME 2001, LNCS 2021, pp. 278–299, 2001.

of expressing others. For example, Z [Spi88] is a formal language used to define data types and to show the effect of operations on these types. But lacks tools to express the order in which the operations are executed [Eva94]. On the other hand, CSP [Hoa85,BHR84,Ros98] is a language suitable for showing the order of the events occurrence but lacks abstract data types and facilities to express (in a natural way) the effect of the events on data. Formalisms like temporal logic [BH81] concentrates on time aspects.

There are many proposals to extending existing languages as well as merging two or more languages and giving a new semantics to the integrated language. For example, CSP-Z, the solution proposed by Fischer [Fis96,Fis00], combines CSP and Z. CSP-Z is based on the Failure Divergence model of CSP [Ros98]. The adaptation of the model was proposed by Fischer in [Fis96,Fis00].

In this work we propose an approach to the specification and validation of real time systems. This approach was applied in the specification of the On-board Computer of the first Brazilian satellite for scientific applications (SACI-1) [SN95,dPJ95]. The language (Timed-CSP-Z) extends CSP-Z with facilities to specify real-time systems. The extension was achieved by substituting the CSP part of the language by Timed CSP [RR86,DS95] (a version of CSP capable of expressing timed behaviour). Timed-CSP-Z is based on an observation model different from the one used by CSP-Z, as explained in Section 2.3

The main advantage of using formal methods in system specifications is the ability of studying a specification with the aim of assuring the presence and/or absence of properties in the system behaviour. One approach to achieving this objective is to use model checking to compare different observed behaviours of a system. Model checking is an automatic tool that helps to compare different specifications based on an observation model.

Ideally, we should use a model-checking tool like FDR [For96] to carry out such analysis, since FDR handles CSP specifications. But, unfortunately, FDR deals only with pure CSP (without time operations) and there are no tools available for the proposed language (Timed-CSP-Z).

Based on recent work in the literature related to process algebra, we adopted the solution of translating Timed-CSP-Z to a Petri Net formalism called Timed Environment Relational Nets (TER Nets)[GMMP91]. We developed rules to convert a specification written in Timed-CSP-Z to TER Nets. We then used a tool (CABERNET) to analyse the resulting Petri Nets.

The remainder of this paper is organised as follows. The proposed integrated language for the specification of real-time systems is introduced in Section 2, through the specification of the Watchdog Timer (which is part of the SACI-1 satellite). In Section 3 we focus on the approach to analysis, where we describe both a strategy to convert a Timed-CSP-Z specification into TER Nets and the use of the CABERNET tool to conduct the analysis automatically. In Section 4 we summarise the results of our research and discuss topics for future work.

2   Timed-CSP-Z

Timed-CSP-Z is based on CSP-Z [Fis96], which is itself a combination of CSP and Z. CSP-Z encapsulates the process description in a specification unit containing two main blocks: a CSP block containing the CSP equations that show the sequential and concurrent behaviour of the events, and a Z block which defines a state and an operation associated with each event of the CSP part. An operation defines the precondition for an event to occur and the effect of the event occurrence on the state space. The language also permits combining the behaviour of specification units using the CSP operators.

CSP-Z is based on the Failure Divergence model of CSP [Ros98]. The adaptation of the model was proposed by Fisher in [Fis96]. In [MS00] Mota and Sampaio show the use of FDR [For96] as a model checking tool for CSP-Z.

In this section we intend to show how time aspects are added to the language in order to allow one to use the language for the specification of real-time systems. To achieve this, the CSP part of the specification is substituted by Timed CSP. A new semantic model is used as a semantic basis for the extended language (Timed-CSP-Z). In what follows we will introduce the syntax and briefly discuss the semantics of this new language.

The syntax of Timed-CSP-Z is not much different from the one of CSP-Z. The original syntax is conserved, as Timed CSP is a superset of CSP and the Z part of the language is not affected by this extension. To better express the syntax of the language we will use an example for illustration: the Watchdog Timer (WDT) process which is part of the SACI-1 On-board Computer (OBC), the first of a series of microsatellites developed by the Brazilian National Institute for Space Research (INPE). The approach was used to formally specify and analyse the satellite behaviour. A complete specification of the satellite OBC and the application of this approach to the case study can be found in [She00].

2.1   Formal Specification of the WDT

The task of the WDT is to monitor the Fault Tolerant Router (FTR) and make sure it is functioning properly. The WDT achieves this by waiting for a reset signal from the FTR within a given amount of time. If the time elapses and the reset signal is not received, the WDT sends an interrupt signal to the observed FTR and waits again for a new reset signal. If it does not receive this signal within a predefined amount of time it will consider the monitored FTR to be out of order. First the WDT will try to recover the FTR by resetting it and then returns to function normally as before. If the FTR does not respond for more than seven consecutive times then it is considered to be failed and so should be cut off from the rest of the system. If this happens then the WDT process itself will stop (behaving like the canonical deadlock process).

A process specification in Timed-CSP-Z starts with the keyword *Spec* followed by the process name.

Spec WDT$_i$

Observe that the process name *WDT* is indexed, which indicates that the process is parameterised by this variable. We can parameterise a process for modularity. In our case we will specify *WDT$_i$* to represent the behaviour of the *WDT* processes. When defining the complete system we will have three copies of the process, namely *WDT$_1$*, *WDT$_2$* and *WDT$_3$*. Each occurrence of *i* in the process specification will be replaced by the corresponding number. The numbers in our case study represent the three different CPUs of the Satellite.

The next step is to declare the channels used by the process. The channels can be divided into external channels, prefixed by the keyword *channel*, and internal channels, prefixed by the keyword *local channel*. Channels can represent events when they have no type. If a channel is declared of an appropriate type then the channel is used for communication between processes: the information exchanged will be of the declared type. In the case of our WDT process only external event channels are declared.

channel resetWDT$_i$, failed$_i$, WDTint$_i$, resetFTR$_i$

All Timed-CSP-Z processes as previously mentioned have two main blocks. The first is the specification of the control part (in Timed CSP), and the other is the specification of the data part (in Z). The Timed CSP part starts by defining the *main* process. This process is the starting point of the Timed CSP specification.

$$main_i = (resetWDT_i \rightarrow main_i) \overset{WDTPeriod}{\triangleright} Interrupt_i$$
$$Interrupt_i = WDTint_i \rightarrow (resetWDT_i \rightarrow main_i) \overset{WDTIntPeriod}{\triangleright} InterruptFailed_i$$
$$InterruptFailed_i = (resetFTR_i \rightarrow main_i) \square (failed_i \rightarrow STOP)$$

The above specification ensures that the WDT will wait for a reset signal within the time period defined between the start of the process main and the elapse of the amount of *WDTPeriod*. In case the reset is not received then the WDT shall send a *WDTint* signal to call the attention of the monitored FTR. It then waits for the reset signal for a new amount of time. If the reset is not received, the WDT sends a *resetFTR* signal re-initialising the FTR or a failed signal indicating the failure of the FTR. The decision of considering the FTR to be failed or not is determined by the Z part of the specification, which begins by defining any constants and related axioms used in the specification of the process. In the case of the WDT process we will define *WDTPeriod* and *WDTIntPeriod* as being two constants of type natural.

$WDTPeriod : \mathbb{N}$	$WDTIntPeriod : \mathbb{N}$
$WDTPeriod = 100$	$WDTIntPeriod = 100$

Next we define the state affected by each event of the process. This is defined using a Z state declaration. A special schema *Init* is also defined as the initialisation of the process state. The operational view is that it will be executed as soon as the process starts and before any activity is carried out.

$$
\begin{array}{|l}
\hline \text{\_State} \rule{4cm}{0pt} \\
\text{FailCounter} : \mathbb{N} \\
\hline
\text{FailCounter} \le 7 \\
\hline
\end{array}
\qquad
\begin{array}{|l}
\hline \text{\_Init} \rule{3cm}{0pt} \\
\text{State}' \\
\hline
\text{FailCounter}' = 0 \\
\hline
\end{array}
$$

Observe that the only variable in the *state* schema is a natural variable which will hold the count of failures at any given instance. It is limited by the restriction that it should hold values less or equal to 7, which is the maximum number of times the CPU can fail. The *Init* schema initialises the *FailCounter* variable with 0. The next step is to define the Z schemas relative to the Timed CSP events. The schema has the same name as the event but prefixed with the keyword com_. Each Z schema will also define the preconditions of the event. It also shows the consequence of the event execution on the data variables of the process state.

$$
\begin{array}{|l}
\hline \text{\_com\_resetFTR}_i \rule{3cm}{0pt} \\
\Delta State \\
\hline
FailCounter < 7 \\
FailCounter' = FailCounter + 1 \\
\hline
\end{array}
\qquad
\begin{array}{|l}
\hline \text{\_com\_failed}_i \rule{2.5cm}{0pt} \\
\Xi State \\
\hline
FailCounter = 7 \\
\hline
\end{array}
$$

Observe that $com\_resetFTR_i$ is defined to have the precondition that *File-Counter* should be less than 7. The effect of executing this event will be to increment by one the value of the counter.

$$
\begin{array}{|l}
\hline \text{\_com\_resetWDT}_i \rule{6cm}{0pt} \\
\Delta State \\
\hline
FailCounter' = 0 \\
\hline
\end{array}
$$

$$com\_WDTint_i \ \widehat{=}\ [\Xi State]$$

Observe as well that $com\_resetWDT_i$ resets the counter to zero. This event is triggered by the FTR when the condition stated by com_failed is satisfied. *WDTint* is declared not to affect the state of the process. These events normally represent actions or external interrupts. With this we finish the body of the WDT_i unity. All process specifications in Timed-CSP-Z terminate with the keyword *end Spec*.

end Spec

2.2   Formal Specification of the OBC

As it was previously mentioned the OBC of the SCAI-1 is composed of three CPUs. The set of the satellite application processes are partioned in the sense that each CPU will have instances of all the application processes, but only one copy of the application processes will be active in a unique CPU at a given time. To achieve this a special process known as the Fault Tolerant Router (FTR) is used. This process acts as the operating system of the OBC. As we mentioned in the previous section the process is responsible for responding to the WDT process, while its main activity is to switch messages between the application processes. So a more abstract description of the OBC will be a network of processes exchanging messages which are routed by the FTRs which in turn are monitored by the WDTs.

Here we present the top level specification of the OBC system, in order to give an idea of its structure. To achieve this we will use the CSP operators to combine and join specification units. The first process defined below is the CPU_i' process which is the parallel composition of the WDT_i process (defined in the previous section) and the satellite Fault Tolerant Router (FTR). Next the resulting process of the first equation is executed in parallel with the rest of the application processes represented here by the APP process (Telecommand, Telemetry .....) in order to form the complete model of the CPU. Observe that each of the application processes is a separate specification unit. In [She00] a detailed specification of each of these specification units is presented.

$$CPU_i' = FTR_i \parallel WDT_i$$
$$\{resetWDT_i, resetFTR_i, WDTint_i, failed_i\}$$

$$APP_i = TC_i \parallel TM_i \parallel SGC_i \parallel EDAC_i \parallel EDA_i \parallel SRI_i \parallel SDC_i \parallel ADC_i \parallel DAC_i$$
$$\parallel HK_i$$
$$\parallel D_i \parallel EMM_i$$

$$CPU_i = APP_i \parallel CPU_i'$$
$$\{getMsg\_i, putMsg\_i\}$$

The set of events used as subscripts of the parallel operator describes the points of synchronisation of the processes running in parallel. Before we introduce the final equation that composes the three CPUs to form the OBC process we will define two sets that will be used in the equation.

$$INTERFACE_{12} = \{failed_1, failed_2\}$$
$$INTERFACE_{123} = INTERFACE_{12} \cup \{failed_3\}$$

Finally we define the equation that defines the complete on-board computer subsystem of the SACI-1.

$$OBC_i = (CPU_1 \parallel CPU_2) \parallel CPU_3$$
$$INTERFACE_{12} \quad INTERFACE_{123}$$

2.3   The Semantics of Timed-CSP-Z

The semantics of CSP-Z as defined in [Fis96] is the Failure Divergence model $\mathcal{M}_{\mathcal{FD}}$ of CSP [BR85]. An interesting aspect of the semantics of CSP-Z is that the Z part is given a semantics in $\mathcal{M}_{\mathcal{FD}}$. As CSP has already a semantics in the same model, a desired uniformity is achieved. Intuitively, a CSP-Z process can be understood as the parallel composition of its CSP part and a CSP process, say P, built from the Z part:

$$CSP\text{-}Block \parallel P(Z\text{-}Block)$$
$$\Sigma$$

where Σ is the alphabet of the process, and the process P is parameterised by the state space of the Z block which is basically the external choice of all the events of the original CSP-Z process. These events are actually guarded by the precondition of the corresponding Z schema.

Operationally, the CSP part acts like a master process which controls the execution and the Z part as a slave process. When an event occurs in the CSP part this will synchronise with the Z part, and the associated effect in the state space will happen. A more detailed definition of the semantic model of CSP-Z can be found in [Fis96,Fis00].

Timed-CSP-Z adopts the same principles used by CSP-Z except for the use of the Timed Failure Model $\mathcal{M}_{TF}$ of Timed CSP instead of the Failure Divergence model used by CSP-Z. A more detailed description about the semantic model of Timed-CSP-Z can be found in [She00].

3   The Specification Analysis: Strategy and Tools

The main advantage of using formal methods in system specifications is the ability of studying the specification with the aim of assuring the presence or the absence of properties in the system behaviour. To achieve this objective, model checking is used to compare different observed behaviours of a system. Model checking is usually performed by automatic tools, which help to compare different specifications based on an observation model.

An important observation that is studied about concurrent and parallel systems is the presence or absence of deadlock states in the system specification. This type of study will be the analysis goal of the SACI-1 OBC specification partially introduced in the previous section.

As mentioned before no analysis tools exist for Timed-CSP-Z to help in model checking. The language that gave origin to Timed-CSP-Z, CSP-Z, has no tools either. In [MS00] a method was introduced to adapt FDR (a tool used in the analysis of CSP processes) to the analysis of CSP-Z. This method uses parameterised processes to represent the state space of the specification and translates the Z part of the specification into a parametrised CSP process. This method works fine for CSP-Z as it uses the same observation models of CSP. Unfortunately, the same method cannot be adapted for Timed-CSP-Z as the observation model is different and FDR does not offer any analysis based on the timed models of CSP.

Based on recent work in the literature [MMR+98,Bal92] related to process algebra, we have adopted the solution of translating Timed-CSP-Z to a Petri Net formalism called environment relational nets (ER Net)[GMMP91] for which there exists an analysis tool. TER Nets were originally presented in [GMMP91] and consist of a high-level Petri Net where tokens are environments, i.e., functions associating values to variables. Furthermore, an action is associated with each transition describing which input tokens can participate in a transition firing and the possible tokens produced by the transition. A complete definition of TER Nets and time representation in TER Nets can be found in [GMMP91].

3.1   Converting Timed-CSP-Z to TER Nets

A method for converting a Timed-CSP-Z specification into a TER Net is proposed in this section. The conversion rules for CSP are taken from previous work related to converting CSP to Petri Nets [MMR+98,Bal92]. These conversion rules have been adapted to take into account the state space introduced by the Z part, and new rules have been added to cover the time aspects. These rules are presented below.

Rule 0. Basic elements

The basic element of a Timed-CSP-Z specification is an event, say e, in the CSP part of the specification and a corresponding Z schema representing the Z part of the specification. Each Z schema predicate is divided into two parts: the precondition for the event to occur which depend on the value of input variables and current value of the state space of the specification, and the post-condition or the effect of the event occurrence on the state space. The translation of this

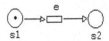

Fig. 1. The PN Representation of an Event e.

basic element is shown in Figure 1. Where S1 represents the input place to the basic element and holds the data space before the event occurrence, and S2 is the output place which holds the resulting state of the data space generated by the event occurrence. The event itself is represented by the transition that connects the input places to the output places. The transition firing represents the event occurrence.

To better illustrate the rule consider the following portion of a specification:

Spec ex1

      channel e

      main = $e \rightarrow main$

      ┌─ *State* ────────
      │ $x : Int$
      └─────────────

      ┌─ *Init* ──────────
      │ *State'*
      │ ─────────
      │ $x' = 0$
      └─────────────

┌─ *com_e* ────────────
│ $\Delta State$
│ ─────────────
│ $x < 10$
│ $x' = x + 1$
└─────────────────

end Spec

The example above can be translated to the TER Net shown in Figure 2. The initial token in place P_1 represents the starting point of the specification. The *Init* schema is represented in the initialisation value of the token. The value of the

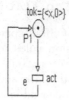

Fig. 2. An Example of Converting Timed-CSP-Z to TER Nets.

token *tok* at place P_1 represents the state space before the occurrence of the event e. The resulting token represents the result of the occurrence of the event e. The event is represented by the transition e in the Petri Net. The action associated to the transition is defined from the Z schema associated to the corresponding CSP event. The action is defined by specifying the sequence of input places to the transition and the sequence of output places to the transition. Then the action behaviour is defined using a logical predicate to state the conditions on the input places and the result of the transition firing on the tokens produced in the output place.

$\quad$ act_e $= \ <P_1, P_1' >| \ P_1.x < 10$ and $P_1'.x = P_1.x + 1$

All arcs have weight 1 meaning that for each transition firing there will be only one resulting token for each place.

STOP and SKIP, which are special processes of CSP, represent a failure and a successful termination, respectively. The similarity between these two processes is that both suspend the program execution and no events occur after these processes are reached. In Petri Nets we can represent both processes as a sink place.

Rule 1. Prefixing

Let P be a non-recursive process represented in CSP by:

$$P = e_1 \rightarrow e_2 \rightarrow STOP$$

Each event in P has its corresponding Z schema, in the Z part of the specification. Consider the following schemas.

com_e_1	com_e_2
$\Delta State$	$\Delta State$
$x > 10$ $x' = x + 10$	$x < 30$ $x' = x + 1$

The translation of each separate event can be done using rule 0. A sequential non-recursive composition of two events can be done simply by merging the output place of the first event with the input place of the next event. The result can be observed in Figure 3. The action statement for event e_1 and e_2 is described as follows:

$$\text{act\_}e_1 = <P_1, P_2 >| \ P_1.x > 10 \text{ and } P_2.x = P_1.x + 10$$
$$\text{act\_}e_2 = <P_2, P_3 >| \ P_2.x < 30 \text{ and } P_3.x = P_2.x + 1$$

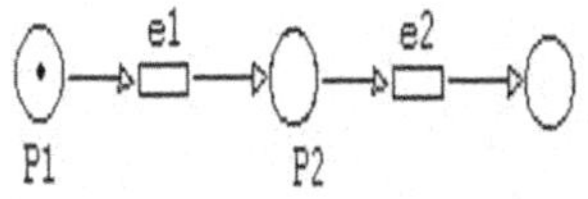

Fig. 3. Sequential Composition.

For recursive processes, the difference lies in the last event output place. The same rule applies to this case, except that the last place (sink place) in the previous example is removed and the output place of the last transition is the input place of the first transition. The new action statement for events e_1 and e_2 can be described as follows:

$$act\_e_1 =< P_1, P_2 >| P_1.x > 10 \text{ and } P_2.x = P_1.x + 10$$
$$act\_e_2 =< P_2, P_1 >| P_2.x < 30 \text{ and } P_1.x = P_2.x + 1$$

Rule 2. Choice

A deterministic choice in CSP-Z is not determined only by the CSP operator, but also by the value of the preconditions of the events involved in the branching. If all preconditions are true then the choice with respect to the Z part of the specification is nondeterministic. Consider the following example.

$$P = a \rightarrow b \rightarrow STOP$$
$$Q = c \rightarrow d \rightarrow STOP$$
$$main = P \square Q$$

com_a
$\Delta State$

$x > 10$
$x' = x - 1$

com_c
$\Delta State$

$x \le 10$
$x' = x + 1$

$$com\_b \cong com\_d \cong [\Xi State]$$

The example can be represented by the ER Net shown in Figure 4. Observe that the input place for a and c is shared. This permits that they use the same state space to validate the choice.

The actions associated with the transitions are:

$$act\_a =< P_1, P_2 >| P_1.x > 10 \text{ and } P_2.x = P_1.x - 1$$
$$act\_b =< P_2, P_3 >| P_3.x = P_2.x$$
$$act\_c =< P_1, P_4 >| P_1.x \le 10 \text{ and } P_4.x = P_1.x + 1$$
$$act\_d =< P_4, P_5 >| P_5.x = P_4.x$$

A non-deterministic choice can be clearly represented by simply ignoring the precondition associated with the first event. Figure 5 clearly represents this. Consider the same previous example except that this time the nondeterministic operator of CSP is used.

The actions associated with the transitions are:

$$act\_e1 =< P_1, P_2 >| true \text{ and } P_2.x = P_1.x$$
$$act\_e2 =< P_1, P_4 >| true \text{ and } P_4.x = P_1.x$$

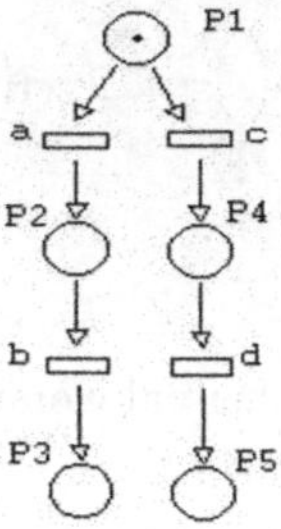

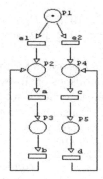

Fig. 4. A Non-Recursive Deterministic Choice Operation.

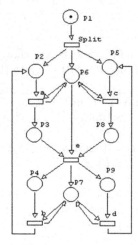

Fig. 5. A Non-deterministic Recursive Choice Operation.

Fig. 6. Synchronised Parallel Processes.

act_a=$< P_2, P_3 > | \ P_2.x > 10$ and $P_3.x = P_2.x - 1$
act_b=$< P_3, P_2 > | \ P_2.x = P_3.x$
act_c=$< P_4, P_5 > | \ P_4.x \leq 10$ and $P_5.x = P_4.x + 1$
act_d=$< P_5, P_4 > | \ P_4.x = P_5.x$

Rule 3. Parallel Composition

Parallel composition is the most difficult operation to convert. This again is due to the lack of modularity of Petri Nets. Consider the case of two processes, say P and Q, that synchronise without data exchange. This happens when the processes are running in the same specification unit they share the same data space.

$$P = a \rightarrow e \rightarrow b \rightarrow P$$
$$Q = c \rightarrow e \rightarrow d \rightarrow Q$$
$$R = P \parallel Q$$
$$\{e\}$$

Figure 6 presents the conversion result of the above example. Observe that the processes start in a common place, as the initialisation process is common to both of them. The transition *Split* is used to start the parallel composition. The firing of the transition *Split* results in three tokens. The first token passes control to the process P, the next passes control to process Q and the last simply carries the common data state between the running processes. This is because processes in the same specification unit share the same data space. So, even though the processes are independent of each other, and may not need to communicate, they still share the same data space. The places P_6 and P_7 act as a common storage between the processes executing in parallel. The other type of parallel composition is the operation involving different specification units. In this case the communication is performed with data typed channels and needs to be synchronised. ER-Nets does not have any operational semantics for modelling and grouping nets into processes or models. This makes our problem more difficult to resolve. The solution is to share data spaces and to share transitions between specification units. The communication is explicitly performed at the moment of the transition firing. Instead of communication channels, the shared transition simply exchange the data values between the data spaces of the two specification units simulating a communication. Figure 7 illustrates a sender/receiver problem.

The following three rules deal with the time operators. In TER Nets, it is assumed that each environment contains a variable, called *chronos* [GMMP91], whose value is of numerical type, representing the timestamp of the token. For example, timestamps would assume natural number values, when dealing with discrete time models; on the other hand, they assume real number values in order to deal with a continuous time model. The actions associated with the transitions are responsible for producing timestamps for the tokens that are inserted into the output places based on the values of the environments of the chosen input enabling tuples. The basic idea is that the timestamp represents the time when the token was produced. In order to capture the intuitive concept of time, however, *chronos* cannot be treated as an unconstrained variable and the following axioms must be satisfied [GMMP91].

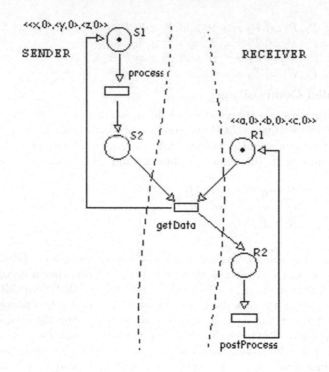

Fig. 7. Synchronised Parallel Specification Units.

- Axiom 1: Local monotonicity. For any firing, the value of *chronos* in the environments produced by the firing cannot be less than the value of *chronos* in any environment removed by the firing.
- Axiom 2: Constraint on timestamps. For any firing $x =< enab, t, prod >$, all elements of the tuple prod have the same value of *chronos*, called the time of the firing. We denote such value as time(x).
- Axiom 3: Firing sequence monotonicity. For any firing sequence s, the times of firing should be monotonically non-decreasing with respect to their occurrence in s.

Rule 4. Wait Operation

The time is represented in ER-Nets by means of a variable common to all processes that can be affected by the firing of any transition in the net. For this reason, we consider the preconditions of the time passing but do not study the actual increment operation as this is considered to be automatic. However the time variable can be changed by the action of a transition to reflect the duration of an event. To illustrate the WAIT operation, consider the following example.

$$P = a \rightarrow b \rightarrow P$$
$$main = Wait\ TimeDelay;\ P$$

$TimeDelay : \mathbb{N}$
$TimeDelay = 30$

$com\_b \mathrel{\widehat{=}} [\Xi State]$

$$\underline{\ com\_a\ }$$
$\Delta State$
$x > 10$
$x' = x - 1$

The process waits for 30 time units before performing process P. We can interpret the WAIT operation as a simple transition with a precondition based on the time the transition was armed to fire. The conversion is illustrated in Figure 8. The actions associated with the transitions are:

act_TimeOut=$< Wait, P_1 >|\ P_1.chronos \geq Wait.chronos + 30$
act_a=$< P_1, P_2 >|\ P_1.x > 10$ and $P_2.x = P_1.x - 1$
act_b=$< P_2, P_3 >|\ P_3.x = P_2.x$

Observe that the transition Wait was added to impose the time precondition.

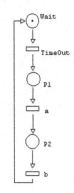

Fig. 8. Example of a Wait Operation.

Rule 5. TimeOut Operation

The time out operation uses two processes. It should offer the first process for a determined period of time. If within this time the first event occurs the operation executes the first process but if the event does not occur then the process will never be executed and the control passes to the second process. Consider the following example.

$$P = a \rightarrow b \rightarrow P$$
$$Q = c \rightarrow d \rightarrow Q$$
$$main = P \overset{TimeOut}{\triangleright} Q$$

$TimeOut : \mathbb{N}$
$TimeOut = 30$ $com\_b \mathrel{\widehat{=}} com\_d \mathrel{\widehat{=}} [\Xi State]$

com_a
$\Delta State$
$x > 10$ $x' = x - 1$

com_c
$\Delta State$
$x \le 10$ $x' = x + 1$

The conversion of the example above is similar to the conversion of the choice operator. In this case, as the processes are recursive we need to create a new event to show the difference between the first event, when it occurs in the timeout operation, and the normal behaviour of the event. The conversion can be seen in Figure 9. The actions associated to the net are:

$act\_a_1 = < P_1, P_2 > | \; P_2.chronos \le P_1.chronos + 30$ and $P_1.x > 10$ and $P_2.x = P_1.x$

$act\_c_1 = < P_1, P_4 > | \; P_4.chronos \ge P_1.chronos + 30$ and $P_1.x \le 10$ and $P_4.x = P_1.x$

$act\_a_2 = < P_2, P_3 > | \; P_2.x > 10$ and $P_3.x = P_2.x - 1$

$act\_b = < P_3, P_2 > | \; P_2.x = P_3.x$

$act\_c_2 = < P_4, P_5 > | \; P_4.x \le 10$ and $P_5.x = P_4.x + 1$

$act\_d = < P_5, P_4 > | \; P_4.x = P_5.x$

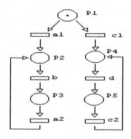

Fig. 9. Example of a Timeout Operation.

Observe that the transitions a_1 and c_1 are used in order to add a time precondition to the processes. The action associated with each transition imposes the timing restrictions. That is a_1 only executes within 30 time units from initialisation while c_1 only executes after 30 time units from the initialisation, but never after a_1. Observe as well that the time intervals used in the precondition overlap. If the time is within the overlapping period then the choice is nondeterministic as imposed by the description of the Timeout operation in Timed CSP.

Rule 6. Timed Interrupt Operation

The timed interrupt is similar to the interrupt operation, except that a time precondition is added to the start of the interrupting process. These preconditions normally represent the time at which the first process should terminate and the second should begin. The actions of the interrupted process should have a way to avoid their execution after been interrupted. Consider the following example. We omit the Z schemas associated with the events since they are the same as the in the previous example.

$$P = a \rightarrow b \rightarrow P$$
$$Q = c \rightarrow d \rightarrow Q$$
$$main = P \ _{IntTime} \diagup Q$$

The conversion of the example above is shown in Figure 10. The following represents the actions associated to the transitions.

$$act\_out_1 = << P_1, P_3, P_4 > | \ P_4.chronos \geq P_3.chronos + 30$$
$$act\_out_2 = << P_2, P_3 >, P_4 > | \ P_4.chronos \geq P_3.chronos + 30$$
$$act\_a = < P_1, P_2 > | \ P_1.x > 10 \text{ and } P_2.x = P_1.x - 1$$
$$act\_b = < P_2, P_1 > | \ P_1.x = P_2.x$$
$$act\_c = < P_4, P_5 > | \ P_4.x \leq 10 \text{ and } P_5.x = P_4.x + 1$$
$$act\_d = < P_5, P_4 > | \ P_4.x = P_5.x$$

The transitions a and b in this case are weak in the sense that they can only fire if there are no strong (normal) transitions enabled to fire. This condition avoids the transitions a and b from firing after the time out period.

3.2   An Analysis Example

As a conversion example we present the application of the conversion rules to the WDT process of the SACI-1 OBC. Figure 11 shows the Petri Net resulting from applying the conversion rules to the WDT specification previously described. The event $resetWDT$ is converted into two transitions as for each occurrence of an event in the CSP part a transition is added to the net.

The net starts by determining whether or not to fire the transition $ResetWDT1$ that represents the reception of the event $resetWDT$ before its deadline. If not, the transition $WDTint$ representing the timeout operation is fired. The actions associated to the transitions are:

$act\_ResetWDT1 \ =< \ WDT_1, WDT_1' \ >| \ WDT_1'.chronos \ \leq \ WDT_1.chronos + WDTPeriod$

$$and \, WDT_1'.FailCounter = WDT_1.FailCounter$$

$act\_WDTint =< WDT_1, WDT_2 >| \ WDT_2.chronos > WDT_1.chronos + WDTPeriod$
$$and \, WDT_2.FailCounter = WDT_1.FailCounter$$

If the process is not reset within the predetermined amount of time then the process sends an interrupt signal represented in our net by the transition $WDTint$. Afterwards the process makes the choice of waiting for another reset signal (represented by the net as the transition $ResetWDT2$) or whether it should reset the CPU (represented by the transition $ResetFTR$), or still whether

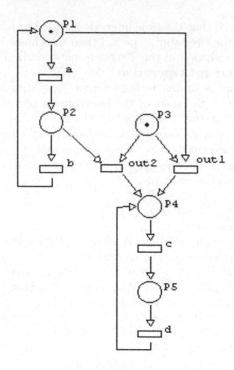

Fig. 10. Example of a Timed Interrupt Operation.

it should consider the CPU to have failed (represented in the net by the transition *Failed*). Once the process is considered failed it terminates. This is represented by the sink place *STOP*. The actions associated with the transitions are:

$act\_ResetWDT2 \; =< \; WDT_2, WDT_1 \; >| \; WDT_1.chronos \; \leq \; WDT_2.chronos +$ $WDTIntPeriod$

$$and\, WDT_1.FailCounter = WDT_2.FailCounter$$

$act\_ResetFTR \; = \; < \; WDT_2, WDT_1 \; >| \; WDT_1.chronos \; > \; WDT_2.chronos +$ $WDTIntPeriod$

$$and\, WDT_2.FailCounter < 7$$
$$and\, WDT_1.FailCounter = WDT_2.FailCounter + 1$$

$act\_Failed =< WDT_2, STOP >| STOP.chronos > WDT_2.chronos + WDTIntPeriod$
$$and\, WDT_2.FailCounter = 7$$
$$and \; STOP.FailCounter = WDT_2.FailCounter$$

The above example is a subset of the complete specification of the SACI-1 OBC. In [She00] a more detailed description of the conversion rules and their application to the rest of the SACI-1 OBC processes can be found.

The resulting nets serve as input to the CABERNET analysis tool. The tool uses Cab nets, a typed version of TER Nets where the actions are converted to C++ statements and the tokens are described using C++ classes. One of the limitations of CABERNET is the absence of abstract data types. During the

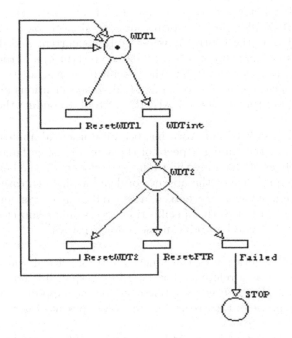

Fig. 11. The PN Representation of the WDT process.

specification we make use of many abstract data types to eliminate the need of details related to their implementation. As part of the conversion process, we need to carry out some data refinement to implement these abstract types as more concrete data types (available in C++).

Another limitation of CABERNET involves the specification size. The tool was unable to handle large nets and so some Petri Nets reduction rules were used and the specification was broken in parts to be analysed.

By applying the tool analyser upon the satellite OBC specification we observed that some subsystems of the satellite may lead to a deadlock state based upon the values of the systems timing variables. The analysis process carried out should serve as an important tool to the designer to predict consequences of any changes on the time requirements. See [She00] for further details.

4   Conclusion

We presented in this paper an approach to the specification and validation of real-time systems and discussed the application of this approach to the specification and analysis of an industrial case study: the microsatellite SACI-1 On-Board Computer (OBC). The proposed approach suggests the use of Timed-CSP-Z for specification and a Petri Net based formalism for analysis (specification valida-tion). Timed-CSP-Z allows us to capture the several facets of a real-time system in an integrated way: the control flow, possibly concurrent and distributed (in CSP), the data space in terms of abstract data types (in Z) and the time aspects (in Timed-CSP). In order to validate the specification, a strategy was suggested to allow a systematic conversion of Timed-CSP-Z specifications into TER Nets. Finally we single out the use of the CABERNET tool to conduct the specification analysis.

An important result of this work has been its practical application: the for-mal specification of the timing aspects of the satellite using Timed-CSP-Z, the analysis of the effect of changing the timing parameters on the behaviour of the satellite, and the presence or the absence of deadlock in such cases.

The application of formal methods to a real and complex system offers various potential benefits. Although the specification covers only a subset of the SACI-1 OBC we hope that it can be useful in the following ways.

- A precise documentation of the functionality of critical parts of the satel-lite can be used as a reference for the group responsible for developing the system. It can also be used as a reference for the support group during the maintenance phase of the project, or the development of new projects based on the SACI-1.
- The formal description is a solid basis for the verification of the satisfaction of desired properties and the absence of undesirable properties in the system specification. Especially because the system cannot run in its natural envi-ronment for testing, the tests need to cover all the possible combinations and under the different possible conditions. Simulating the occurrence of errors and tracing the specification behaviour with the CABERNET might be very helpful for achieving this goal.

The specification of the On-Board Computer (OBC) of the SACI-1 briefly illustrated here (and more completely in [She00]) is based on an untimed speci-fication which was developed using CSP-Z [Mot97]. We have not only developed a more detailed specification of each component of the OBC but also dealt with all the time aspects.

During the development of this work we observed that a similar work was carried out by Dong and Mahony [MD98], where they introduce a new language based on the combination of Timed CSP and Object-Z. The new language is named Timed Communicating Object-Z, which models objects as processes and gives the Object-Z objects predicates and operations based on the CSP syntax. This has the disadvantage of not having a clear separation between the different aspects of the process where the behaviour of the process is incorporated into the data state of the system, while in our approach the control state is totally independent of the data state and can be studied separately; this makes the specification more readable as well. Furthermore, to our knowledge, no significant specification of a case study has been developed using Timed Communication Object-Z. Concerning analysis, no approach has been suggested. In our work we have dealt with these aspects in an integrated way.

Another similar approach, Real-Time Z (RT-Z) was introduced in [Suh99]. Although the work is based on the same basic elements, the difference lies first in the syntax to integrate the Z part of the specification with the CSP part of the specification. In this approach, the use of special constructs tends to make it difficult to distinguish where the data part of the process starts and where it terminates. Another difference between this approach and ours is the use of bi-directional schemes and events to simulate the start of an operation and the end of the same operation. This approach makes it possible to describe actions and considers time operations on the start and end of a particular action. No strategy or tools were mentioned to be used to analyse specifications written in RT-Z, as well as no significant specification of a case study seems to have been developed using RT-Z.

Although we believe our approach is promising, it is important to justify the use of different formalisms for the specification and analysis, since this has required a conversion between them. The use of Petri Nets for analysis was a consequence of the lack of tools to validate the Timed-CSP-Z specification. The positive side is that the conversion was systematised by explicit conversion rules (although those rules have not been formally verified).

One might also claim that it would perhaps be more practical to have started with Petri Nets from the very beginning. Although this would avoid the need for a conversion between formalisms, we would lose the more abstract and modular presentation allowed by a Timed-CSP-Z specification.

To make the approach of more practical use, an alternative is to automate the proposed conversion strategy. From a more theoretical point of view it would also be necessary to prove the correctness of such conversion rules, based on the formal semantics of the two formalisms. Another alternative is to avoid the conversion and build an analysis tool for Timed-CSP-Z, possibly extending FDR [For96]. The advantage of developing an analysis tool for Timed-CSP-Z is that the conversion to a different formalism and all the related inconveniences are avoided.

On the other hand, converting to Petri Nets (as we have done here) might have some potential benefits towards an implementation of the specification. The converted specification can be introduced into a Petri Net based scheduler, for example into the scheduler introduced in [Cav97], to obtain the possible scheduling information regarding the system processes.

Acknowledgements. We would like to thank Alexandre Mota for his invaluable help with information regarding the SACI-1 OBC, and for the discussions related to this research.

References

[Bal92]   G. Balbo. Performance Issues in Parallel Programming. In *13th International Conference on Application and Theory pf Petri Nets*, volume 616, pages 1–23, Sheffield, UK, 1992. Lecture Notes in Computer Science.

[BH81]   A. Bernstein and P.K. Harter. Proving Real-time Properties of Programs with Temporal Logic. In *Proceedings 8thSymposium on Operating System Principles, ACM SIGOPS*, pages 1–11, 1981.

[BHR84]   S. D. Brookes, C. A. R. Hoare, and A. W. Roscoe. A Theory of Communicating Sequential Processes. *Journal of the Association for Computing Machinery*, 31(3):560–599, July 1984.

[BR85]   S. D. Brookes and A. W. Roscoe. An improved failures model for communicating processes. In *Lecture Notes on Computer Science*, volume 197, pages 281–305, 1985.

[Cav97]   S. V. Cavalcante. *A Hardware-Software Co-Design System for Embedded Real-Time Applications.* PhD thesis, Department of Electrical and Electronic Engineering, University of Newcastle upon Tyne, England, 1997.

[dPJ95]   A. R. de Paula Jr. Fault Tolerance Aspects of the SACI-1. *VI Simpósio de Computadores Tolerantes a Falhas*, 1995.

[DS95]   J. Davies and S. Schneider. A brief history of timed csp. *Theoretical Computer Science*, 138(2):243–271, 1995.

[Eva94]   A. S. Evans. Visualising Concurrent Z Specifications. In J. P. Bowen and J. A. Hall, editor, *Z User Workshop*, pages 269–281, Cambridge, June 1994. Proceedings of the 8th Z User Meeting, Springer-Verlag Workshop in Computing.

[Fis96]   C. Fischer. Combining CSP and Z. Technical report, University of Oldenburg, 1996.

[Fis00]   C. Fischer. *Combination and implementation of processes and data: from csp-oz to java.* PhD thesis, University of Oldenburg, 2000.

[For96]   Formal Systems (Europe) Ltd. *FDR: User Manual and Tutorial, version 2.01*, August 1996.

[GMMP91]   C. Ghezzi, D. Mandrioli, S. Morasca, and M. Pezze. A Unified High-level Petri Net Formalism for Time-Critical Systems. *IEEE Transactions on Software Engineering*, 17(2):160–172, 1991.

[Hoa85]   C. A. R. Hoare. *Communicating Sequential Processes.* Prentice-Hall, 1985.

[MD98]   B. Mahony and J. Song Dong. Blending Object-Z and Timed CSP: An introduction to TCOZ. In *Proceedings of the 1998 Internaltional Conference on Software Engineering*, pages 95–104, 1998.

[MMR+98]   A. Mazzeo, N. Mazzocca, S. Russo, C. Savy, and V. Vittorini. Formal Specification of Concurrent Systems: A Structured Approach. *The Computer Journal*, 41(3):145–162, 1998.

[Mot97]   A. Mota. Formalização e Análise do SACI-1 em CSP-Z. Master's thesis, Departamento de Informática, Centro de Ciências Exatas e da Natureza, UFPE, 1997.

[MS00]   A. Mota and A. Sampaio. Model-Checking CSP-Z, Strategy, Tool Support and Industrial Application. *Science of Computer Programing*, 39(1), 2000.

[Ros98]   A. W. Roscoe. *The Theory and Practice of Concurrency.* Prentice-Hall International, 1998.

[RR86]   G. M. Reed and A. W. Roscoe. A timed model for communication sequential processes. In *Proceedings of ICALP '86*, volume 226. Lecture Notes in Computer Science, 1986.

[She00]   A. Sherif. Formal Specification and Validation of Real-Time Systems. Master's thesis, Centro de Informática, UFPE, 2000. http://www.di.ufpe.br/~ams/thesis.html.

[SN95]   M. E. Saturno and J. B. Neto. Software Requirement Specification for the OBC/SACI-1 Application Programs. Technical report, Instituto Nacional de Pesquisas Espaciais - INPE, 1995.

[Spi88]   J. M. Spivey. *Understanding Z: a specification language and its formal semantics*. Cambridge Tracts in Theoretical Computer Science 3, 1988.

[Suh99]   C. Suhl. RT-Z: An Integration of Z and timed CSP. In *Proceedings of the 1st Internaltional Conference on Integrated Formal Methods*, 1999.

Real-Time Logic Revisited

Stephen E. Paynter

Matra BAe Dynamics (UK) Ltd, Filton, Bristol, UK

Abstract. This paper redefines RTL within classical many-sorted logic with natural number and real arithmetic. In doing so, RTL is generalised in a number of ways. In particular, functionality is handled through the use of timed variables. Various models of time for RTL are discussed, and it is argued that, providing events satisfy a countable occurrence property, time in RTL can be continuous. A number of useful RTL theorems are stated, and it is shown that RTL can naturally express all the usual temporal requirements that are placed on real-time systems. RTL is compared with other timed logics.

1 Introduction

Real-Time Logic (RTL) was one of the first logics proposed for the specification and description of real-time systems, [JaM86]. Since then RTL has been used in the definition of the semantics of a number of graphical notations for designing real-time systems, including: Modecharts, [JLM88], [JAM94], [MSJ96]; Statecharts, [ArB96], [Arm98]; Real-Time Mode-Machines, [Pay96], and ADL, [PAH00]; and in defining the semantics of a family of communication protocols, [Sim00], and Kernels, [FoW96] and [FoW97]. Various fragments of RTL have been investigated, [JaM87], [Mil92], and RTL has been integrated with untimed formalisms to form more expressive notations, [Fid92]. Extensions to RTL have been proposed to make it applicable to hybrid systems, [HaL96].

RTL was originally presented as classical unsorted first-order logic with Presburger arithmetic and an uninterpreted function symbol, [JaM86]. It used functions from state predicates to events to integrate functionality into the basic RTL timed event model. Here RTL is presented as many-sorted logic (MSL) with real and integer arithmetic, and functionality is handled by timed variables.

The main reasons for this reformulation are that it enables time to be modeled by the real numbers (as opposed to the natural numbers used in [JaM86]), and it enables a wider range of functional behaviour to be integrated into the RTL timed event model. In reformulating RTL, some of the restrictions adopted in previous definitions of RTL are removed and RTL is generalised. Table 1 summarises the main differences between the version of RTL presented here and previous presentations of RTL.

Briefly, the reasons for these changes are:

- Real-time is now usually understood to be continuous (or at least dense), and the use of dense time means that the problem of deciding *a priori* what the basic time unit should be is avoided;

J.N. Oliveira and P. Zave (Eds.): FME 2001, LNCS 2021, pp. 300–317, 2001.
© Springer-Verlag Berlin Heidelberg 2001

Table 1. RTL Generalisations

	RTL Previously	RTL in this Paper
Logic	First-Order	MSL with arithmetic
Time	Discrete	Continuous
Events	only event constants	quantified event variables
Occurrence Arithmetic	Decidable (Presburger)	Full (Peano)
Actions	Positive duration	May be instantaneous
Functionality	State predicates	Predicates over Timed Variables

- Quantification over events is often natural, for example, in defining the RTL axioms;
- Having real arithmetic for time undermines the point of restricting arithmetic for occurrences;
- Instantaneous actions are sometimes a useful fiction, see for example, [Sim00]; and
- Predicates over timed variables integrates the property being specified into the logic, allowing functionality to be reasoned about within RTL.

Each of these topics is treated more fully below.

Some of the restrictions in earlier presentations of RTL are hard to justify, because, in spite of them, RTL has been shown to be undecidable, [JMS88]. Hence, while acknowledging the usefulness of the fragments of RTL explored in [JaM87] and [Mil92], the position in this paper is that full RTL should be made as expressive as needed to support the natural specification and analysis of real-time systems[1].

The rest of the paper is organised as follows. Section 2 describes the basic RTL model. Section 3 discusses the model of time in RTL, and argues that time may be continuous, providing event occurrences are appropriately countable. Section 4 reviews how actions, states, and variables are handled in RTL. Section 5 defines RTL within many-sorted logic. Section 6 catalogues a number of RTL theorems which are invariably needed when performing proof in RTL. Section 7 shows how RTL can be used to formalise a typical temporal requirements on real-time systems. Section 8 shows a shallow embedding of RTL in the PVS logic, [OSR99a]. Section 9 compares RTL with other timed logics, including the DC and ERTL.

---

[1] Of course, expanding RTL to include, for example, full natural number arithmetic, entails the loss of completeness as well as decidability, and the inability to prove consistency, [Göd31]. However, using a result of Gentzen's, expanding RTL even further, such as by embedding it in a formal system which supports transfinite induction (up to ε_0, the first ordinal greater than $\omega^{\omega^{\cdots}}$), would make it possible to prove the consistency of RTL arithmetic, [Kle52]. Kleene hypothesises in [Kle52] that transfinite induction up to even higher ordinals might make it possible to prove the consistency of real analysis (i.e. second-order arithmetic, Z_2). Currently, the consistency of the $\prod_2^1 - CA$ fragment has been demonstrated, [Rat95].

2   The Basic RTL Model

The basic RTL concept is of *timed events*: RTL events occur at specific times and they have no duration. RTL events can re-occur at different times. An RTL event is therefore a *class* of actual event occurrences. Re-occurrences of an event must occur at later times than earlier occurrences. RTL therefore does not support the super-dense "micro-step" model described in [MaP93]. RTL has no concept of events which occur at an instant being ordered or causally related.

The RTL syntax associates together an event, a time, and the number of occurrences of that event up to that time. The original RTL syntax used an "@" function, which returned the time of a particular event occurrence.

$$@ : Event \times Occ \rightarrow Time$$

where *Event*, *Occ*, and *Time* are the types of events, occurrence numbers, and times, respectively. *Occ* is typically taken to be N^+, the set of all positive integers, although there are cases where N is more useful, either because it allows "0" to model a start-up "initial" occurrence of an event, e.g. in [Sim00], or because the theorem prover being used to support RTL makes induction over the naturals easier than induction over the positive naturals. In this paper N is used. A discussion of the type *Time* is postponed until the next section.

$@(e, i)$ is understood to return the time of the ith occurrence of e.

Although "@" has been used in some later RTL papers, e.g. [JaM94], a proposal in [JMS88] advocated the use of an occurrence relation, θ, instead. θ is a predicate with the following signature:

$$\theta : Event \times Occ \times Time \rightarrow \mathcal{B}$$

where $\mathcal{B}$ is the Boolean sort, and $\theta(e, i, t)$ is to be read as asserting that event e occurs for the ith time at time t.

A strong argument in favour of θ over @, is that $\theta(e, i, t)$ is a total function, unlike $@(e, i)$, which is undefined if there is not an ith occurrence of event e. The restriction to total functions significantly simplifies the logic, and allows classical theorems provers, such as PVS [OSR99b], to be used to reason about RTL. θ has been used in [ArB96], [Arm98], [PAH00] and [Sim00].

The basic properties of RTL events, namely, that occurrence numbers of an event increase monotonically over time, and later occurrences of an event occur at later times, are captured in the following two axioms:

Ax 1 $\forall e : Event, i : Occ, t_1, t_2 : Time \bullet \ \theta(e, i, t_1) \wedge \ \theta(e, i, t_2) \Rightarrow \ t_1 = t_2$

Ax 2 $\forall e : Event, i : Occ, t_1 : Time \bullet$
$$\theta(e, i + 1, t_1) \Rightarrow \exists t_2 : Time \bullet \ \theta(e, i, t_2) \wedge \ t_2 < t_1$$

The above axioms which distinguish events, occurrences, and times, and which involve arithmetic of occurrence numbers, and ordering relations over times, suggests that RTL can be naturally formalised in classical many-sorted logic (MSL) extended with arithmetic, [Man93], or in classical typed higher-order logic. The definition of RTL in many-sorted logic is pursued in Section 5.

3   Time in RTL

In earlier presentations of RTL, for example [JaM86] and [JMS88], time is taken to be discrete. More precisely, *Time* has been taken to be N^+, the set of positive integers. However, since RTL was defined in 1986, real-time formalisms have come to be understood to be those which use the real numbers to represent time. That is, "real-time" is now understood to be continuous.

It is argued here that RTL can be modified to use continuous time. However, it is not possible simply to set *Time* to be $R_{\geq 0}$, the positive reals including "0". This can be seen when an event which occurs at every time is considered. It would occur more often than could be counted by an occurrence number, the cardinality of N being strictly smaller than $R_{\geq 0}{}^2$.

The addition of a "countable occurrence" requirement to RTL overcomes this problem by forcing events in continuous time to have a natural number occurrence. This requirement is defined using a new occurrence predicate, ψ, which is true whenever a particular event occurs at a particular time. That is, $\psi(e, t)$ says event e occurs at time t.

The countable occurrence axiom is:

Ax 3 $\forall e : Event, t : Time \bullet \ \psi(e, t) \Rightarrow \exists i : Occ \bullet \ \theta(e, i, t)$

This ensures that there is always a finite number of occurrences of an event up to any (finite) time. There is hence no contradiction in assuming time is continuous if events obey this axiom.

Clearly, $\psi(e, t)$ will also satisfy the following property:

Ax 4 $\forall e : Event, i : Occ, t : Time \bullet \ \theta(e, i, t) \Rightarrow \psi(e, t)$

Another property that can cause problems in dense time formalisms is so-called "Zeno" behaviour, where time advances but is bounded. Since [AbL91] it has been widely recognised that it is not necessary to impose an *a priori* lower bound on the gap between time points to prohibit Zeno behaviour.

Zeno behaviour is excluded from RTL by adopting the following axiom, which asserts that an event may not occur at all, or it may only occur a finite number of times (i.e. it occurs for a last time), or there is no bound on the times when it will occur.

Ax 5 $\forall e : Event \bullet$
$(\neg \ \exists t : Time \bullet \ \psi(e, t)) \ \vee$
$(\exists t : Time \bullet \ \psi(e, t) \wedge \ \neg \ \exists t_1 : Time \bullet \ t_1 > t \wedge \ \psi(e, t_1)) \ \vee$
$(\neg \ \exists t_1 : Time \bullet \ \forall t : Time \bullet \ \psi(e, t) \Rightarrow \ t < t_1)$

---

[2] It is noted that dense time based on Q, the rationals, is also problematic, although Q is countable. The reason being that Q is not enumerable with the conventional ordering. (The author thanks a referee for bringing this to his attention.)

It is the last clause of this axiom which prohibits the Zeno behaviour of an infinite number of events prior to some time: events which occur a countable number of times occur at ever increasing and unbounded times.

It is noted that many finite event occurrence properties can be be expressed using ψ instead of θ. For example, the fact that an event e occurs for the third time at time t, i.e. $\theta(e, 3, t)$, would be:

$$\psi(e, t) \wedge \exists\, t_1, t_2 : Time \bullet$$
$$\psi(e, t_1) \wedge\ \psi(e, t_2) \wedge\ t_1 < t \wedge\ t_2 < t \wedge\ t_1 \neq\ t_2\ \wedge$$
$$\neg\,\exists\, t_3 : Time \bullet\ t_3 < t \wedge\ \psi(e, t_3) \wedge\ t_3 \neq\ t_1 \wedge\ t_3 \neq\ t_2.$$

Obviously, the use of occurrence numbers are more readable and succinct, especially for higher occurrence numbers. However, occurrence numbers are not redundant and a mere syntactic convenience. An infinite occurrence property that cannot be expressed using ψ in non-infinitary logics, like RTL, is that an event, e say, occurs an unbounded number of times. That is:

$$\forall\, i : Occ \bullet\ \exists\, t : Time \bullet\ \theta(e, i, t).$$

It is also not possible to express using ψ variable occurrence properties, such as:

$$\forall\, i : Occ \bullet\ \theta(e, i, t) \Rightarrow\ \theta(e, i+1, t+1)$$

It is noted that one implication of using $R_{\geq 0}$ for time is that time becomes totally ordered. Lamport, however, has argued convincingly that in some applications, this is a stronger property than is required, [Lam86]. However, the development of a weakly monotonic RTL is beyond the scope of this paper. Another implication of using $R_{\geq 0}$ is that the basic elements of time in RTL are point instances - the real numbers. This is in contrast with interval logics such as DC, [ZHR91], where the basic elements of time are intervals. See [Haj95] for a discussion of various ways point and interval temporal structures can be axiomatised.

In the author's experience, many proofs about systems described in RTL proceed by induction over the occurrence numbers of events, and make no use of the denseness or discreteness of time.

One property which only holds with discrete time is the following relationship between occurrence numbers and times, [Arm99], (assuming the type system allows occurrences and times to be compared):

$$\forall\, e : Event, i : Occ, t : Time \bullet\ \theta(e, i, t) \Rightarrow\ i \leq\ t$$

4   Actions, States, and Variables in RTL

In RTL actions are characterised by two events: a start and a stop event. Two functions, $\uparrow$ and $\downarrow$, from actions to events return start and stop events, respectively.

These functions return appropriately distinct events, as defined by the following two axioms:

Ax 6 $\forall a_1, a_2 : Action \bullet (\downarrow a_1 = \downarrow a_2 \Rightarrow a_1 = a_2) \wedge (\uparrow a_1 = \uparrow a_2 \Rightarrow a_1 = a_2)$

Ax 7 $\forall a_1 : Action \bullet \neg \exists a_2 : Action \bullet (\downarrow a_1 = \uparrow a_2) \vee (\uparrow a_1 = \downarrow a_2)$

In previous RTL papers, a property of actions which distinguished them from events was that they had duration. In particular, that:

$$\forall a : Action, i : Occ, t_2 : Time \bullet$$
$$\theta(\downarrow a, i, t_2) \Rightarrow \exists t_1 : Time \bullet \theta(\uparrow a, i, t_1) \wedge t_1 < t_2$$

A minor but important generalisation is to allow RTL actions to be instantaneous. It is occasionally useful to be able to exploit such actions, for example, when using actions to model parts of an algorithm which may not be executed, [Sim00].

Ax 8 $\forall a : Action, i : Occ, t_2 : Time \bullet$
$$\theta(\downarrow a, i, t_2) \Rightarrow \exists t_1 : Time \bullet \theta(\uparrow a, i, t_1) \wedge t_1 \leq t_2{}^3$$

In modeling actions which are only executed sequentially, the following property holds:

Ax 9 $\forall a : Action, i : Occ, t_2 : Time \bullet$
$$\theta(\uparrow a, i + 1, t_2) \Rightarrow \exists t_1 : Time \bullet \theta(\downarrow a, i, t_1) \wedge t_1 \leq t_2$$

It is noted that this does not prevent different types of actions from occurring concurrently.

States can be handled in a similar way to actions, using functions which return the entering and leaving of a state. Examples of the use of RTL to describe state-machines can be found in [Arm98] and [PAH00].

RTL, as described in [JaM86] and [JMS88], had functions from "state predicate" identifiers to events, denoted by ":= T" and ":= F". The events they returned were defined to occur when the state predicate became true or false. For example, $\theta(\alpha := T, i, t)$ asserts that state predicate α became true for the ith time at time t, where α is defined outside of RTL.

One limitation of an approach which fails to integrate the state predicate language into RTL can be seen when another state predicate, β say, is considered, such that, in an appropriate logic: $\alpha \vdash \beta$. Knowing $\psi(\alpha := T, t)$ one would wish to be prove within RTL that:

---

[3] It is noted that the second axiom prevents an action repeatedly executing instantaneously without some intervening delay.

$$\exists\, t_1 : Time \bullet\ t_1 \leq\ t \wedge\ \psi(\beta\ := T, t_1) \wedge$$
$$\neg\, \exists\, t_2 : Time \bullet\ t_1 \leq\ t_2 \leq\ t \wedge\ \psi(\beta\ := F, t_2).$$

This cannot be deduced within RTL as previously presented. Another problem arises with a (presumably) untimed state predicate language, namely, that it is not possible to describe the predicates over variables at multiple times, for example, to constrain a variable to values which increase monotonically over time.

An alternative approach advocated here is the direct use of predicates over timed variables. That is, variables should be modeled as functions from time to their value domain. For example, a variable v of type T becomes:

$$v : Time \rightarrow\ T$$

This enables single time predicates to be defined, such as "$v_1(t) = v_2(t)$", as well as multiple time predicates, such as, "$v_1(t_1) > v_2(t_2)$".

It is noted that a consequence of this use of timed variables is that variables can only have a single value at a particular time. Therefore, an RTL expression which asserts otherwise will be inconsistent. This is particularly important when the functionality of instantaneous and concurrent (coincident) actions are being defined[4].

A single time predicate (P say, over a set of variables, V) may be related to events when it becomes true and false. This is a common enough requirement that it is helpful to define the following "schemas":

$\nearrow$: $PREDICATE \times Event \times Time \rightarrow \mathcal{B}$
$\nearrow (P, e, t) \triangleq \psi(e, t) \Leftrightarrow$
$\quad (P(V(t)) \wedge\ (t = 0 \vee$
$\qquad \exists\, t_1 : Time \bullet\ t_1 < t \wedge\ \forall\, t_2 : Time \bullet\ t_1 < t_2 < t \Rightarrow\ \neg\ P(V(t_2))))) \vee$
$\quad (\neg\ P(V(t)) \wedge\ \exists\, t_1 : Time \bullet\ t_1 > t \wedge\ \forall\, t_2 : Time \bullet\ t < t_2 < t_1 \Rightarrow\ P(V(t_2)))$

$\searrow$: $PREDICATE \times Event \times Time \rightarrow \mathcal{B}$
$\searrow (P, e, t) \triangleq \psi(e, t) \Leftrightarrow$
$\quad (\neg\ P(V(t)) \wedge\ (t = 0 \vee$
$\qquad \exists\, t_1 : Time \bullet\ t_1 < t \wedge\ \forall\, t_2 : Time \bullet\ t_1 < t_2 < t \Rightarrow\ P(V(t_2))))) \vee$
$\quad (P(V(t)) \wedge\ \exists\, t_1 : Time \bullet\ t_1 > t \wedge\ \forall\, t_2 : Time \bullet\ t < t_2 < t_1 \Rightarrow\ \neg\ P(V(t_2)))$

Here $\nearrow$ ("becomes true") and $\searrow$ ("becomes false") are schemas, or templates which should be expanded when encountered. Turning them into functions or operators in the logic would require RTL to be made a full second or higher order logic, and not only one which exploits second order concepts in the definition of real and integer arithmetic. The definitions of $\nearrow$ and $\searrow$ are based on almost identical definitions in ERTL, [LeH95].

---

[4] Functionality will typically be defined by asserting that an action termination causes a particular (timed) predicate to hold at that moment.

Other helpful schemas for RTL are the ones which assert that:

- a predicate holds over a period;
- a predicate will hold until a particular time; and
- a predicate started to hold at a particular time.

The following are definitions of these schemas:

$hold\_over :\ PREDICATE \times Time \times Time \rightarrow \mathcal{B}$
$hold\_over(P, t_1, t_2) \triangleq \forall\, t : Time \bullet\ t_1 \leq t \leq t_2 \Rightarrow P(V(t)).$

$hold\_until :\ PREDICATE \times Time \times Time \rightarrow \mathcal{B}$
$hold\_until(P, now, then) \triangleq$
$\quad hold\_over(P, now, then) \wedge \exists\, e : Event \bullet\ \psi(e, then) \wedge \searrow (P, e, then)$

$hold\_since :\ PREDICATE \times Time \times Time \rightarrow \mathcal{B}$
$hold\_since(P, then, now) \triangleq$
$\quad hold\_over(P, then, now) \wedge \exists\, e : Event \bullet\ \psi(e, then) \wedge \nearrow (P, e, then).$

There are many other possible schemas, although two which are likely to be useful are schemas which assert:

- the time a predicate has held within a period; and
- the number of times a predicate has switched within a period.

An example definition of the first schema is given below:

$duration :\ PREDICATE \times Time \times Time \times Time \rightarrow \mathcal{B}$
$duration(P, begin, end, t) \triangleq$
$\quad (hold\_over(P, begin, end) \Rightarrow\ t = end - begin) \wedge$
$\quad (\exists\, t_1 : Time \bullet\ begin \leq t_1 < end \wedge\ hold\_over(P, begin, t_1) \Rightarrow$
$\qquad t = t_1 - begin + duration(P, t_1, end)) \wedge$
$\quad (\neg\, (\exists\, t_1 : Time \bullet\ begin \leq t_1 \wedge\ hold\_over(P, begin, t_1)) \wedge$
$\qquad \exists\, e : Event, t_2 : Time \bullet\ begin \leq t_2 < end \wedge\ \nearrow (P, e, t_2) \wedge$
$\qquad\quad \neg\, (\exists\, e_1 : Event, t_3 : Time \bullet$
$\qquad\qquad begin \leq t_3 < t_2 \wedge\ \nearrow (P, e_2, t_3))) \Rightarrow\ t = duration(P, t_2, end) \wedge$
$\quad (\neg\, (\exists\, t_1 : Time \bullet\ begin \leq t_1 \wedge\ hold\_over(P, begin, t_1)) \wedge$
$\qquad \neg\, \exists\, e : Event, t_2 : Time \bullet\ begin \leq t_1 < end \wedge\ \nearrow (P, e, t_2)) \Rightarrow\ t = 0$

It is noted the above definition is recursive, and hence termination depends upon predicates over variables obeying a "finite variability" condition. The DC, [ZHR91], for example, also requires a finite variability constraint to ensure integrability. It is further noted that "$duration(P,\ begin,\ end,\ t)$" is similar to the Duration Calculus expression: "$t = \int_{begin}^{end} P$". However, the use of this definition of "duration" means that RTL is not as expressive as MTL-$\int$, [LaH94].

5   Many-Sorted Logic

Many-Sorted Logic (MSL), [Man93], modifies classical first-order logic by:

- identifying sorts (or types) with each constant and variable;
- identifying sorted (typed) signatures with each function; and by
- requiring quantification to range over a particular sort.

MSL is strictly no more expressive than unsorted logic, but for many purposes the notation is more compact and readable. MSL has been advocated as a unifying logic in which other logics should be defined, [Man96].

5.1   The MSL Language

The basic symbols of the version of MSL used here are: $\{$ (,), $\neg$, $\wedge$, $\forall$, :, $\bullet$, $=$ $\}$, along with an infinite set of sort symbols, $\{\mathcal{B}, S_1, S_2, S_3, ...\}$, where $\mathcal{B}$ is the "Boolean" sort; an infinite set of variables, $\{$ x_1, x_2, x_3, ..., y_1, y_2, ... $\}$, where a sort is associated with each variable; and an infinite set of function symbols of each arity, from zero upwards, $\{F_1^0, F_2^0, F_3^0, ..., F_1^1, F_2^1, ... \}$, where F_j^n is the jth function F with arity n. Associated with each function symbol, F_j^n is its signature which defines the sorts of the parameters and result of the function, F_j : $S_1 \times S_2 \times ... \times S_n \to S$. The arity of a function is its number of parameters. Functions with an arity of zero are known as *constants*. Functions of result sort $\mathcal{B}$ are known as *predicates*.

The well-formed sentences of MSL are defined by the following grammar:

S_k-**Var** ::= v, where the sort of v is S_k;
S_k-**Term** ::= S_k-Var $\mid F_j^n(t_1, t_2, ..., t_n)$, where F_j^n is a function with signature:
     $S_1 \times S_2 \times ... \times S_n \to S_k$ and each t_i, i in 1..n, is an S_i-term;
S ::= '(' $S_\mathcal{B}$ -Term ')' $\mid$ '(''$\neg$' S ')' $\mid$ '('S '$\wedge$' S ')' $\mid$ '(' S_k-Term '=' S_k-Term ')'
     $\mid$ '(' '$\forall$' S_k-Var ':' 'S_k' '$\bullet$' S ')';

The usual abbreviations and conventions are typically used in MSL.

5.2   An MSL Proof System

A natural deduction proof system for MSL is given in Table 2.

5.3   MSL Models

The structure, St, in which MSL sentences are interpreted, contains a set of domains, D. There is a domain d_{S_i} of values for each sort, S_i, of the language. St also contains a set of functions, F, which contains a function, $f_{F_j^n}$, for each function in in the language, and a set of variable names, V. An assignment, A, is mapping from $V \to D$, where each v of each sort S_i gets assigned a value from d_{S_i}. An equality function Eq is defined as expected over values in the elements of D.

Table 2. A Natural Deduction System for MSL

Introduction Rules	Elimination Rules
$\wedge\text{-i} = \dfrac{\vdash \alpha;\ \vdash \beta}{\vdash \alpha \wedge \beta}$	$\wedge - e_1 = \dfrac{\vdash \alpha \wedge \beta}{\vdash \alpha}$ $\wedge - e_2 = \dfrac{\vdash \alpha \wedge \beta}{\vdash \beta}$
$\vee - i_1 = \dfrac{\vdash \alpha}{\vdash \alpha \vee \beta}$ $\vee - i_2 = \dfrac{\vdash \alpha}{\vdash \beta \vee \alpha}$	$\vee\text{-e} = \dfrac{\vdash \alpha \vee \beta;\ \alpha \vdash \gamma;\ \beta \vdash \gamma}{\vdash \gamma}$
$\neg\neg\text{-i} = \dfrac{\vdash \alpha}{\vdash \neg\neg\alpha}$	$\neg\neg\text{-e} = \dfrac{\vdash \neg\neg\alpha}{\vdash \alpha}$
$\Rightarrow\text{-i} = \dfrac{\alpha \vdash \beta}{\vdash \alpha \Rightarrow \beta}$	$\Rightarrow\text{-e} = \dfrac{\vdash \alpha;\ \vdash \alpha \Rightarrow \beta}{\vdash \beta}$
$\Leftrightarrow\text{-i} = \dfrac{\vdash \alpha \Rightarrow \beta \wedge \beta \Rightarrow \alpha}{\vdash \alpha \Leftrightarrow \beta}$	$\Leftrightarrow\text{-e} = \dfrac{\vdash \alpha \Leftrightarrow \beta}{\vdash \alpha \Rightarrow \beta \wedge \beta \Rightarrow \alpha}$
$\neg\text{-i} = \dfrac{\alpha \vdash \bot}{\vdash \neg\alpha}$	$\neg\text{-e} = \dfrac{\vdash \alpha;\ \vdash \neg\alpha}{\vdash \bot}$
$\bot\text{-i} = $ There is no such rule.	$\bot\text{-e} = \dfrac{\vdash \bot}{\vdash \alpha}$
$=\text{-i} = \dfrac{}{\vdash t_S = t_S}$	$=\text{-e} = \dfrac{\vdash t_{1_S} = t_{2_S};\ \vdash \alpha\,[t_{1_S}/x]}{\vdash \alpha\,[t_{2_S}/x]}$
$\forall\text{-i} = \dfrac{x_0 \in S \vdash \alpha\,[x_0/x]}{\vdash \forall\, x : S \bullet \alpha}$	$\forall\text{-e} = \dfrac{\vdash \forall\, x : S \bullet \alpha}{\vdash \alpha\,[t_S/x]}$
$\exists\text{-i} = \dfrac{\vdash \alpha\,[t_S/x]}{\vdash \exists\, x : S \bullet \alpha}$	$\exists\text{-e} = \dfrac{\vdash \exists\, x : S \bullet \alpha;\ x_0 \in S, \alpha\,[x_0/x] \vdash \beta,\ x_0\ \text{free in }\alpha}{\vdash \beta}$

The interpretation function for MSL, I, is defined by the following rules:

1. For every variable, v, $I(v) = A(v)$
2. For every function, F_j^n, $I(F_j^n(\alpha_1, ..., \alpha_n) = f_{F_j^n}(I(\alpha_1), ...I(\alpha_n))$.
3. For every sentence, s, $I(\neg s) = 1$ if $I(s) = 0$, otherwise $I(\neg s) = 0$.
4. For every pair of sentences, s_1 and s_2, $I(s_1 \wedge s_2) = 1$ if $I(s_1) = 1$ and $I(s_2) = 1$, otherwise $I(s_1 \wedge s_2) = 0$.
5. For every pair of expressions, e_1 and e_2, $I(e_1 = e_2) = 1$ if $Eq(I(e_1), I(e_2)) = 1$, otherwise $I(e_1 = e_2) = 0$.
6. $I(\forall\, v : S_i \bullet S) = 1$ if for every value, x, in d_{S_i}, $I(S[x/v]) = 1$, otherwise $I(\forall\, v : S_i \bullet S) = 0$

A model of MSL is a tuple: $[St, I]$.

5.4   RTL in MSL

RTL can be defined in MSL by adding sorts: *Events*, *Time*, *Occ* and *Action*, the functions θ, ψ, $\uparrow$, $\downarrow$ and the normal arithmetical operations, $+$, $-$, $*$, $/$, $<$, $>$,

$\leq$, and $\geq$. θ, ψ, $\uparrow$ and $\downarrow$ are axiomatised using the axioms given above. These axioms constrain the standard MSL model that the interpretation function I defines for RTL.

Clearly, embedding RTL in an 'MSL' requires the logic to be more expressive than first-order logic, if full natural number or real arithmetic is exploited. Therefore, although the RTL syntax does not explicitly support second-order predicates and quantification, it implicitly does by exploiting arithmetic: RTL is *not* a first-order logic.

6   RTL Theorems

This section includes a number of simple but useful RTL theorems, each of which the author has proven using the PVS theorem prover, [OSR99b], and the shallow embedding of RTL in PVS given in Section 8.

Earlier occurrences of events occur at earlier times.

Th 1 $\forall\, e : Event, i, j : Occ, t_1, t_2 : Time\,\bullet$
$\qquad \theta(e, i, t_1) \land\ \theta(e, j, t_2) \land\ i < j \Rightarrow\ t_1 < t_2$

Only one occurrence of an event occurs at a time.

Th 2 $\forall\, e : Event, i, j : Occ, t : Time\,\bullet\ \theta(e, i, t) \land\ \theta(e, j, t) \Rightarrow\ i = j$

If an event has occurred for the ith time, it has occurred for all earlier occurrences (at earlier times).

Th 3 $\forall\, e : Event, i : Occ, t_1 : Time\,\bullet$
$\qquad \theta(e, i, t_1) \land\ i > 0 \Rightarrow$
$\qquad\qquad (\forall\, j : Occ\,\bullet\ j < i \Rightarrow\ \exists\, t_2 : Time\,\bullet\ \theta(e, j, t_2) \land\ t_2 < t_1)$

An earlier occurrence of an event has an earlier occurrence number.

Th 4 $\forall\, e : Event, i, j : Occ, t_1, t_2 : Time\,\bullet$
$\qquad \theta(e, i, t_1) \land\ \theta(e, j, t_2) \land\ t_1 < t_2 \Rightarrow\ i < j$

An earlier or equal occurrence of an event has an earlier or equal occurrence number. (This is a simple corollary of theorems 2 and 4.)

Th 5 $\forall\, e : Event, i, j : Occ, t_1, t_2 : Time\,\bullet$
$\qquad \theta(e, i, t_1) \land\ \theta(e, j, t_2) \land\ t_1 \leq t_2 \Rightarrow\ i \leq j$

7   Typical Real-Time Requirements in RTL

This section has two aims: one, to provide a formal statement of a number of common real-time requirements, and two, to provide some validation of the RTL notation, by showing that it is capable of expressing simply and clearly these common requirements. The formalisation of these requirements have arisen out of work with the BAE SYSTEMS Dependable Computing System Centre on capturing real-time requirements using real-time transactions, [Hav97] and [Pay99].

One of the commonest properties of real-time systems (or assumptions about their environments) is that certain events occur periodically. Formally,

$periodic : Event \times Time \to \mathcal{B}$

$periodic(e, period) \; \triangle$

$\quad \exists \, t : Time \bullet \; \theta(e, 0, t) \; \wedge$

$\quad \forall \, i : Occ, t_1 : Time \bullet \; \theta(e, i, t_1) \Rightarrow \; \exists \, t_2 : Time \bullet \; \theta(e, i+1, t_2) \wedge \; t_2 = t_1 + period.$

Note, this definition requires periodic events to keep on occurring. In specifying particular systems it may be desirable to define the conditions under which such events may cease (e.g. when the system loses power).

Another common property is that an event is sporadic: that is, aperiodic, with a minimum inter-arrival time (miat). Formally,

$sporadic : Event \times Time \to \mathcal{B}$

$sporadic(e, miat) \; \triangle$

$\quad \forall \, i : Occ, t_1, t_2 : Time \bullet \; \theta(e, i, t_1) \wedge \; \theta(e, i+1, t_2) \Rightarrow \; t_2 \geq \; t_1 + miat.$

Note that sporadic events need not occur at all.

A common requirement of a real-time computation is that one event (typically an input or triggering event) causes another event (typically an output) within a lower and upper time bound of the first event occurring. Formally,

$deadline : Event \times Event \times Time \times Time \to \mathcal{B}$

$deadline(e_1, e_2, l, u) \; \triangle$

$\quad \forall \, i : Occ, t_1 : Time \bullet \; \theta(e_1, i, t_1) \Rightarrow \; \exists \, t_2 : Time \bullet \; \theta(e_2, i, t_2) \wedge \; t_1 + u \geq \; t_2 \geq \; t_1 + l.$

Another common requirement is that an (input or output) event must fall within a time window relative to a periodic event (such as a clock 'tick').

$window : Event \times Event \times Time \times Time \to \mathcal{B}$

$window(e, clock, l, u) \; \triangle$

$\quad \forall \, i : Occ, t_1 : Time \bullet \; \theta(e, i, t_1) \Rightarrow$

$\quad\quad \exists \, j : Occ, t_2 : Time \bullet \; \theta(clock, j, t_2) \wedge \; t_2 + u \geq \; t_1 \geq \; t_2 + l^5$

---

[5] It is noted that this does not require any event to occur within the window, nor does it prevent multiple occurrences of the event occurring within the same window. In the author's experience, this is compatible with the reason that windowed constraints are typically defined - for example, where the function is used to constrain the events which denote one process' access to a shared resource. The reader may need variants of this definition which do not have these properties on occasion.

A more interesting real-time requirement to formalise is *jitter*, because of the lack of consensus on its definition. Here a definition is given that the author has found useful. A jitter requirement is a positive and negative timing constraint on when one (nominally periodic) event may occur relative to a periodic clock event. To avoid the proliferation of events, it is helpful to allow the jitter constraints to be offset from the periodic event.

$$jitter : \ Event \times Event \times Time \times Time \times Time \to \mathcal{B}$$
$$jitter(e, clock, x_1, x_2, offset) \ \triangle$$
$$\forall \, i : Occ, t_2 : Time \bullet \ \theta(clock, i, t_2) \Rightarrow$$
$$\exists \, t_1 : Time \bullet \ \theta(e, i, t_1) \wedge \ t_2 + offset + x_2 \geq \ t_1 \geq \ t_2 + offset - x_1.$$

A related requirement to jitter, but one which it is necessary to distinguish, is a temporal constraint on consecutive occurrences of a (nominally periodic) event. The author refers to this as a *Consecutive Occurrence Bound* or COB.

$$COB : \ Event \times Time \times Time \to \mathcal{B}$$
$$COB(e, max, min) \ \triangle$$
$$\exists \, t : Time \bullet \ \theta(e, 0, t) \wedge$$
$$\forall \, i : Occ, t_1 : Time \bullet \ \theta(e, i, t_1) \Rightarrow$$
$$\exists \, t_2 : Time \bullet \ \theta(e, i + 1, t_2) \wedge \ t_1 + max \geq \ t_2 \geq \ t_1 + min.$$

8   A Shallow Embedding of RTL in PVS

This section presents an encoding of RTL events and actions in the PVS logic, [OSR99a]. It is similar to other encodings, e.g. [FoW97], and differs little from the axioms given above. It demonstrates how easy it is to embed RTL transparently in PVS, and it means that PVS' powerful decision procedures can be applied when reasoning about RTL expressions.

```
rtl : THEORY
BEGIN

  Event: NONEMPTY_TYPE
  Time: TYPE = real
  Occ: TYPE = nat
  Action : NONEMPTY_TYPE

  th : [Event, Occ, Time -> bool] %-- th = occurrence predicate
  psi : [Event, Time -> bool] %-- psi = second occurrence predicate
  start : [Action -> Event]
  stop : [Action -> Event]

  ------------ RTL Axioms
```

```
%-- The "event occurrences occur only once" axiom
RTLax1: AXIOM
  FORALL (e : Event, i : Occ, t1, t2 : Time):
    th(e, i, t1) AND th(e, i, t2) IMPLIES t1 = t2


%-- The "monotonically increasing event occurrences" axiom
RTLax2: AXIOM
  FORALL (e : Event, i : Occ, t1 : Time): th(e, i + 1, t1) IMPLIES
    EXISTS (t2 : Time): th(e, i, t2) AND t2 < t1


%-- The "countable event occurrences" axiom
RTLax3 : AXIOM
  FORALL (e : Event, t : Time):
    psi(e, t) IMPLIES EXISTS (i: Occ): th(e, i, t)


%-- The "occurrence predicates link" axiom
RTLax4 : AXIOM
  FORALL (e : Event, i : Occ, t : Time):
    th(e, i, t) IMPLIES psi(e, t)


%-- The "Non-Zeno behaviour" axiom
RTLax5 : AXIOM
  FORALL (e : Event):
    (NOT EXISTS (t : Time): psi(e, t)) OR
    (EXISTS (t : Time): psi(e, t) AND
      NOT EXISTS (t1 : Time): t1 > t AND psi(e, t1)) OR
    NOT EXISTS(t1 : Time): FORALL(t : Time):
          psi(e, t) IMPLIES t < t1)


%-- The "starts and stops of different actions are different" axiom
RTLax6 : AXIOM
  FORALL (a1, a2 : Action):
    (stop(a1) = stop(a2) IMPLIES a1 = a2) AND
    (start(a1) = start(a2) IMPLIES a1 = a2)


%-- The "no start and stop event are the same" axiom
RTLax7 : AXIOM
  FORALL (a1 : Action): NOT EXISTS (a2 : Action):
    stop(a1) = start(a2) OR start(a1) = stop(a2)


%-- The "actions start before they stop" axiom
RTLax8 : AXIOM
  FORALL (a : Action, i : Occ, t2 : Time):
    th(stop(a), i, t2) IMPLIES
      EXISTS(t1 : Time): th(start(a), i, t1) AND t1 <= t2
```

```
    %-- The "earlier actions finish before they restart" axiom
  RTLax9 : AXIOM
    FORALL (a : Action, i : Occ, t2 : Time):
      th(start(a), i + 1, t2) IMPLIES
        EXISTS(t1 : Time): th(stop(a), i, t1) AND t1 <= t2
```

```
END rtl
```

9   Conclusions and Related Work

This paper has represented RTL in classical many-sorted logic with real and integer arithmetic. In doing so, a countable occurrence axiom and a non-Zeno behaviour axiom have been added which allows RTL time to be continuous and which disallows infinite events to be bounded in time. Also, RTL actions have been modified to allow them to be instantaneous. It has been argued that functional behaviour should be handled in RTL using predicates over timed variables, and mappings between these predicates and events have been defined. RTL has been shown to be a natural formalism for expressing a wide range of typical requirements on real-time systems, and a shallow embedding of RTL has been given in the PVS logic.

One of the main logics discussed in the literature for specifying and modeling real-time systems is the Duration Calculus (DC). The basic duration calculus, [ZHR91], is a modal interval logic with a chop operator, extended with an integration operator that sums the time that a state predicate has been true over an interval. The DC has continuous time, although state predicates are constrained to have finite variability. Many variants of the DC has been proposed in the literature, including weakly monotonic time and probabilistic versions, [PaH98] and [Liu96]. The DC has been given a deeper embedding into PVS than the RTL embedding presented above, [SkS94].

It was illustrated in Section 4 how a "duration" schema could be used to handle predicates over timed variables in a similar style to the way durations are handled in the DC. However, without further syntactic changes, RTL would still refer to explicit times, something which the designers of the DC tried to avoid. The ability in RTL to refer to the number of occurrences of an event makes it relatively easy to specify properties such as, "the pump may be switched on or off no more than n times in any interval of x time units." It is not immediately obvious how to capture this in the DC, although it is a typical type of requirement for systems such as mine pumps and gas burners, which the DC has been developed to handle.

A variant of RTL has been proposed in the literature, *Extended RTL* or *ERTL*, [LeH95] and [Hal96]. ERTL adds a new predicate to RTL, the *holding* predicate, Φ. Φ asserts that a particular *untimed* predicate holds for a particular occasion at a particular time. That is, $\Phi(P, i, t)$ asserts that (untimed) predicate P holds for the ith time at time t (that is, has come to hold for the ith time).

ERTL stratifies the language into untimed and timed predicates to avoid making Φ a second-order predicate.

It is noted that RTL (as defined here) is already a second-order logic, thus presumably undermining one motivation for extending it with Φ. It is also noted that in ERTL it is not possible to define the value of a variable at one time as depending upon its value at an earlier time - for example, a monotonically increasing value over time cannot be defined because the predicate asserted to hold and which constraints the value, being untimed, cannot refer to earlier times[6]. This contrasts with multiple time predicates over timed variables discussed in Section 4.

RTL would benefit from better tool support, for example, by producing a deeper embedding of RTL into PVS, similar to the DC proof assistant described in [SkS94]. The author's main interest in RTL, however, is in using it to explicate the semantics of various informal concepts and notations used in the specification and design of real-time systems, [Pay96], [Pay99], [PAH00], and [Sim00]. RTL has proved to be a simple yet expressive logic for such work.

Acknowledgements. Matra BAe Dynamics (UK) Ltd. funded this research. My ideas about RTL have benefited from conversations with Drs. J.M. Armstrong and J.S. Fitzgerald, and Mr. N. Henderson. The author wishes to thank the reviewers for their many helpful comments.

References

[AbL91]   Abadi, M. and Lamport, L.: 'An Old Fashioned Recipe for Real-Time', *Proc. REX Workshop - Real-Time: Theory in Practice*, LNCS 600, Springer, 1991, pp. 1-27.

[ArB96]   Armstrong, J.M. and Barroca, L.: 'Specification and Verification of Reactive System Behaviour: The Railroad Crossing Example', *J. Real-Time Systems*, 10 (2), March 1996, pp. 143-178.

[Arm98]   Armstrong, J.M.: 'Industrial Integration of Graphical Formal Specifications', *J. Systems Software*, 40, 1998, pp. 211-225.

[Arm99]   Armstrong, J.M.: 'The Proofcharts-PVS Manual - Part II: The Proofcharts-PVS Theorem Library', BAE SYSTEMS DCSC Technical Report, DCSC/TR/1999/5, University of Newcastle, 1999.

[Fid92]   Fidge, C.J.: 'Specification and Verification of Real-Time Behaviour Using Z and RTL', *Proc. 2nd Int. Symp. on Formal Techniques in Real-Time and Fault-Tolerant Systems*, LNCS 571, Springer, 1992.

[FoW96]   Fowler, S. and Wellings, A.J.: 'Formal Analysis of a Real-Time Kernel Specification', *Proc. 4th Int. Symp. on Formal Techniques in Real-Time and Fault-Tolerant Systems*, LNCS 1135, Springer, 1996.

[FoW97]   Fowler, S. and Wellings, A.J.: 'Formal Development of a Real-Time Kernel', *Proc. 18th IEEE Real-Time Systems Symp.*, San Francisco, December 1997.

---

[6] This limitation is overcome to some extent in the ERTL literature by defining one "untimed" predicate to be the derivative of another.

[Göd31]   Gödel, K.: 'Über formal unentscheidbare Sätze der Principia Mathematica and verwandter Systeme I', In Monatshefte für Mathematik and Physik, Vol. 38, pp. 173-198, 1931. Reprinted in Translation in 'On Formally Undecidable Propositions of Principia Mathematica and Related Systems', Dover Publications, 1992.

[HaL96]   Hall, J.G. and Lemos, R. de.: 'ERTL: An Extension to RTL for the Specification, Analysis and Verification of Hybrid Systems', *Proc. of the IEEE EuroMirco'96 Conf.*, 1996.

[Haj95]   Hajnicz, E.: 'An Analysis of Structure of Time in the First Order Predicate Calculus', In L. Bolc and A. Szalas (Editors): 'Time and Logic: A Computational Approach', UCL Press (London), 1995, pp. 279-322.

[Hav97]   Haveman, J.: 'Transaction Decomposition: Refinement of Timing Constraints', *Proc. of the South Pacific Conf. on Formal Methods*, 1997.

[JaM86]   Jahanian, F., and Mok, A.K.: 'Safety Analysis of Timing Properties in Real-Time Systems', *IEEE Trans. on Soft. Eng.*, 12(9), 1986, pp. 890-904.

[JaM87]   Jahanian, F., and Mok, A.K.: 'A Graph-Theoretic Approach for Timing Analysis and its Implementation', *IEEE Trans. on Comp.*, 36(18), 1987, pp. 961-975.

[JaM94]   Jahanian, F., and Mok, A.K.: 'Modechart: A Specification Language for Real-Time Systems', *IEEE Trans. on Soft. Eng.*, 20(12), 1994, pp. 933-947.

[JLM88]   Jahanian, F., Lee, R. and Mok, A.K.: 'Semantics of Modechart in Real-Time Logic', *IEEE Proc. of the 21st Annual Hawaiian Int. Conf. on System Science*, 1988.

[JMS88]   Jahanian, F., Mok, A.K., and Stuart, D.A.: 'Formal Specification of Real-time Systems', Technical Report TR-88-25, Department of Computer Science, University of Texas at Austin, June 1988.

[Kee52]   Kleene, S.C.: 'Introduction to Metamathematics', North-Holland Publishing Company, 1952.

[LaH94]   Lakhneche, Y. and Hooman, J.: 'Reasoning about Durations in Metric Temporal Logic', *Proc. 3rd Int. Symp. on Formal Techniques in Real-Time and Fault-Tolerant Systems*, LNCS 863, Springer-Verlag, 1994, pp. 488-510.

[Lam86]   Lamport, L.: 'On Interprocess Communication - Part 1: Basic Formalism', *Distributed Comp.* 1, 1986, pp. 77-85.

[LeH95]   Lemos, R. de. and Hall, J.G. : 'Extended RTL in the Specification and Verification of an Industrial Press', *Proc. of DIMAC'95 Conf.*, 1995.

[Liu96]   Liu, Z.: 'Specification and Verification in the Duration Calculus', Chapter 7 of M. Joseph (Editor): 'Real-Time Systems: Specification, Verification, and Analysis', Prentice-Hall International Series in Computer Science, 1996.

[MaP93]   Manna, Z. and Pnueli, A.: 'Models of Reactivity', *Acta Informatica*, 30(7), 1993, pp. 609-678.

[Man93]   Manzano, M.: 'Introduction to Many-Sorted Logic', in 'Many-Sorted Logic and its Applications', Edited by K. Meinke and J.V. Tucker, Wiley Professional Computing, 1993

[Man96]   Manzano, M.: 'Extensions of First-Order Logic', Tracts in Theoretical Computer Science, Cambridge University Press, 1996

[Mil92]   Millet, O.: 'Multicycles and RTL Logic Satisfiability', *Proc. 2nd Int. Symp. on Formal Techniques in Real-Time and Fault-Tolerant Systems*, LNCS 571, Springer, 1992.

[MSJ96]   Mok, A.K., Stuart, D.A., and Jahanian, F.: 'Specification and Analysis of Real-Time Systems: Modechart Language and Toolset', Chapter in Heitmeyer, C. and Mandrioli, D. (Editors): 'Formal Methods for Real-Time Computing', Trends in Software 5, Wiley, 1996.

[OSR99a]   Owre, S., Shanker, N., Rushby, J.M., and Stringer-Calvert, D.W.J.: 'PVS Language: Version 2.3', Computer Science Laboratory, SRI International, September 1999.

[OSR99b]   Owre, S., Shanker, N., Rushby, J.M., and Stringer-Calvert, D.W.J.: 'PVS System Guide: Version 2.3', Computer Science Laboratory, SRI International, September 1999.

[PaH98]   Pandya, P.K. and Hung, D.V.: 'Duration Calculus of Weakly Monotonic Time', *Proc. 5th Int. Symp. on Formal Techniques in Real-Time and Fault-Tolerant Systems*, LNCS 1486, Springer, 1998.

[Pay96]   Paynter, S.E.: 'Real-Time Mode-Machines', *Proc. 4th Int. Symp. on Formal Techniques in Real-Time and Fault-Tolerant Systems*, LNCS 1135, Springer, 1996, pp. 90-109.

[Pay99]   Paynter, S.E.: 'Real-Time Transactions Revisited', Unclassified MBD(UK) Technical Report, DR16972, 1999.

[PAH00]   Paynter, S.E., Armstrong, J.M., and Haveman, J.: 'ADL: An Activity Description Language for Real-Time Networks', *Formal Aspects of Comp.*, 12(2), 2000, pp. 120-144.

[Rat95]   Rathjen, M.: 'Recent Advances in Ordinal Analysis: $\prod_2^1 - CA$ and Related Systems', *Bulletin of Symbolic Logic*, 1, 1995, pp. 468-485.

[SkS94]   Skakkebaek, J.U. and Shankar, N.: 'Towards a Duration Calculus Proof Assistant in PVS', *Proc. 3rd Int. Symp. on Formal Techniques in Real-Time and Fault-Tolerant Systems*, LNCS 863, Springer-Verlag, 1994.

[Sim00]   Simpson, H.R.: 'Protocols for Process Interaction', Submitted to *IEE Proc. on Soft. Eng.*, Also three MBD(UK) Technical Reports, 2000.

[ZHR91]   Zhou, C. Hoare, C.A.R., and Ravn, A.P.: 'A Calculus of Durations', *Inform. Proc. Letters*, 40, 1991, pp. 269-276.

Improvements in BDD-Based Reachability Analysis of Timed Automata

Dirk Beyer

Software Systems Engineering Research Group,
Technical University Cottbus,
D 03013 Cottbus, Postfach 10 13 44, Germany,
Tel. +49 (3 55) 69 - 38 02, Fax. 69 - 38 10,
db@informatik.tu-cottbus.de

Abstract. To develop efficient algorithms for the reachability analysis of timed automata, a promising approach is to use binary decision diagrams (BDDs) as data structure for the representation of the explored state space. The size of a BDD is very sensitive to the ordering of the variables. We use the communication structure to deduce an estimation for the BDD size. In our experiments, this guides the choice of good variable orderings, which leads to an efficient reachability analysis. We develop a discrete semantics for closed timed automata to get a finite state space required by the BDD-based representation and we prove the equivalence to the continuous semantics regarding the set of reachable locations. An upper bound for the size of the BDD representing the transition relation and an estimation for the set of reachable configurations based on the communication structure is given. We implemented these concepts in the verification tool Rabbit [BR00]. Different case studies justify our conjecture: Polynomial reachability analysis seems to be possible for some classes of real-time models, which have a good-natured communication structure.

Keywords: Timed automata, Discretization, BDDs, Formal verification, Real-time systems

1 Introduction

The demand for correct controllers in reactive systems, especially in safety-critical systems, has more and more influence on the development process. Therefore, many developers use formal methods. Model checking, i.e. the process which checks whether a particular model satisfies a given specification or not, is commonly used for verification of automata-based models. It is very popular because the verification task is done full-automatically by tools.

In this paper we use timed automata as the formalism to describe the system and reachability analysis for the verification process. To ensure safety properties, the set of reachable configurations is computed and then it is checked whether unsafe states are reachable or not.

J.N. Oliveira and P. Zave (Eds.): FME 2001, LNCS 2021, pp. 318–343, 2001.

Reachability analysis of timed automata has been implemented in tools like Kronos [BDM+98] and Uppaal [LPY97] which represent the continuous part of the model (i.e. the clock valuations) as difference bound matrices. This technique has two main disadvantages: firstly, locations are enumerated explicitly, which often results in the state explosion problem, and secondly, that there is no canonical representation for (non-convex) clock valuations, which often hinders the construction of efficient algorithms.

Because binary decision diagrams became very popular as a data structure for model checking of automata-based models, it is obvious to use a symbolic representation based on BDDs for the discrete states in a first step. The second step towards an efficient reachability check is to use a discrete semantics for the timed automata. Using BDDs also for the representation of the continuous state space allows a uniform representation of the discrete as well as the continuous part of the model. There already exists some experience with tool implementations of this technique, e.g. using a BDD-based version of Kronos [BMPY97].

One of the most important demands for industrial use is the efficiency of the verification process. This means that our task is to find efficient algorithms and heuristics that solve the problem with good (desired polynomial) space and time complexity.

In this paper we introduce a third step leading to polynomial time and space complexity of the reachability analysis for some classes of models. We use the communication structure, and also the knowledge of the developer of the model (by providing a notation for structural modeling) to compute good variable orderings for the BDD representation. Using such variable orderings compresses the BDD representation of the reachable configurations dramatically and thus, leads to more efficient verification.

Our paper is structured as follows: Section 2 introduces the formal definition of timed automata and their continuous semantics. We also explain our notation for modular modeling. Section 3 illustrates a modular model of a MOS circuit and the timed automaton for Fischer's protocol. Section 4 introduces a discrete semantics for closed timed automata and a proof of the equivalence of both semantics regarding the reachability problem. In Section 5 we explain the impact of the communication structure on the BDD representation, we introduce an estimation for the size of the BDD for the reachable set and its implications for finding good variable orderings. Section 6 explains the results of our experiments.

2   Cottbus Timed Automata

The main goal of our modeling formalism is to combine knowledge of software engineering, i.e. hierarchical structuring of large system descriptions, and the well-investigated theoretical basis of timed automata. Thus, we use compositional modules that have well-defined interfaces and contain timed automata to describe its behavior [BR98,BR99]. In this section we introduce timed automata informally using an example, then we introduce CTA modules which is a mod-

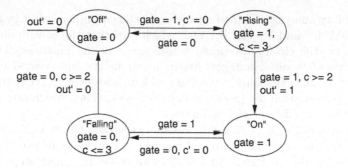

Fig. 1. Timed automaton for an nMOS transistor.

eling concept providing means for modular design. After this we give a formal definition of timed automata as used in this paper.

2.1   Example

Fig. 1 shows a timed automaton which models the behavior of an nMOS transistor. The automaton consists of four locations. Location Off is the initial location of the automaton and the initial value for out is 0. It models the situation that the transistor is non-conducting. The transistor can stay in this situation as long as the input gate is 0. When the gate becomes high the automaton takes the transition to location Rising and resets clock c. In this moment the transistor starts to open its channel. Location Rising as well as location Falling are called unstable, because in reality the output changes during this situation. If the gate is still high after at least 2 time units the channel of the transistor can be conducting and thus, the automaton can go to location On setting variable out to high. The variable out represents the state of the transistor. After at most 3 time units the automaton must leave location Rising. A transition to location On is possible, or if the gate is low meanwhile the automaton has to go to location Off immediately. The automaton has an analogous behavior for switching from conducting (out = 1) to non-conducting (out = 0).

2.2   Informal Introduction to CTA Modules

This section describes informally the formalism of Cottbus Timed Automata (CTA). A formal definition and the complete semantics of CTA are given in [BR99].

A CTA system description consists of a set of modules. One of them is designated as the top module. It models the whole system. The other modules are used as templates. They can be instantiated several times in different modules. Thus, it is possible to express a hierarchical structure of the system, and to define replicated components of a system just once.

Each module consists of the following components:

- An **identifier.** Identifiers are used to name the modules within the system description.
- An **interface.** The interface contains the declarations of clock variables, discrete variables and synchronization labels used by the components of the module.
  - **Synchronization labels.** Synchronization labels (shortly called signals) are used to synchronize transitions of automata contained in different modules. Synchronization labels follows the concepts of events in CSP.
  - **Variables.** Clock variables are used to model (predominantly) continuously changing components of a real-time system. Discrete variables are provided to store discrete values. The values are changed by an assignment in a transition of the automaton.
- A **timed automaton.** A module contains an automaton. This automaton consists of a finite set of states, a finite set of transitions between these states, and an alphabet of synchronization labels.
- **Initial condition.** This is a predicate over the module variables and the states of the module's automaton specifying the initial configuration.
- **Instances.** A module may contain instances of previously defined modules. This is used to model systems containing subsystems, and it is especially helpful if a subsystem occurs several times in a system. An instance consists of the following components:
  - An **identifier** is used to give a name to the instance.
  - A reference to a **module** defines which module is instantiated.
  - A **unification** of interface components of the instantiated module with declared components of the containing module defines how the instance is connected to the containing module. This may identify interface signals and interface variables of the instantiated module with signals and variables of the containing module.

In a CTA module each of the interface components has a **restriction type** to control the access to the component. There are four different restriction types for variables and signals:

- **INPUT** The declaration of a variable as input variable for a module means that this module can only read this variable: the value of an input variable may not be restricted within any value assignment of a transition. For a signal the declaration as input means the following: for each input signal and each state of the automaton, some transition labeled with the signal can always be taken. In this way the automaton does not restrict the input signal and thus it is not to blame for a timed deadlock. Thus, it is a guarantee for the environment that the module does not change that component.
- **OUTPUT** the declaration of a variable or signal as OUTPUT is an assumption, that the variable or signal is used only as INPUT in all other modules in the environment.

- **MULTREST** The multiply restricted components are available for all access modes. A module as well as the environment for which a signal or variable is declared as multiply restricted can restrict the component in any way.
- **LOCAL** The declaration of a variable or signal as LOCAL means that it is not visible outside the module and thus no other module can access such a variable or signal.

2.3   Timed Automata

This section gives a definition of timed automata and their continuous semantics. We use a formal definition of timed automata similar to that introduced by Alur and Dill [AD94], because it is commonly accepted and provides a good standard.

Definition. We define **clock constraints** allowed as invariants and guards in an automaton. Let X be a set of clocks. Clock constraints over X are conjunctions of comparisons of a clock with a time constant from $\mathbb{N}$, the set of natural numbers (including 0). Formally, the following grammar generates the set of clock constraints over X:

$$\varphi := x \leq c \mid x \geq c \mid x < c \mid x > c \mid \varphi \wedge \varphi,$$

with $x \in X$ and $c \in \mathbb{N}$.

A **clock assignment** v of X is a total function from X into the set of nonnegative real numbers $\mathbb{R}^+$. $Val(X)$ denotes the set of all clock assignments of X. For a clock constraint $\varphi \in \Phi(X)$, $[\![\varphi]\!]$ denotes the set of all clock assignments of X that satisfy φ.

The clock assignment which assigns the value 0 to all clocks is denoted by v^0. For $v \in Val(X)$ and $\delta \in \mathbb{R}^+$, $v + \delta$ is the clock assignment of X that assigns the value $v(x) + \delta$ to each clock x. For $v \in Val(X)$ and $Y \subseteq X$, $v[Y := 0]$ denotes the clock assignment of X that assigns the value 0 to each clock in Y and leaves the other clocks unchanged.

A **timed automaton** $\mathcal{A}$ is a tuple $(L, L^0, X, \Sigma, I, E)$, where

- L is a finite set of locations,
- $L^0 \subseteq L$ is a set of initial locations,
- X is a finite set of clocks,
- Σ is a finite set of synchronization labels,
- I is a total function that assigns an invariant from $\Phi(X)$ to each location in L,
- $E \subseteq L \times \Sigma \times \Phi(X) \times 2^X \times L$ is a set of switches. A switch (l, a, φ, Y, m) represents a transition from location l to location m labeled with synchronization label a. The guard φ has to be satisfied to enable the location switch. The switch resets all clocks in the set Y to the value 0.

A **configuration** of a timed automaton $\mathcal{A}$ is a pair (l, v) with $l \in L$ and $v \in Val(X)$.

For a more compact notation discrete variables (which have a finite subset of the natural numbers as domain) are introduced which change their value only by location switches. Discrete variables are not considered explicitly here because they can be considered as an abbreviating notation for automata. Our tool implementation allows for discrete variables because it does not matter whether a BDD variable represents the state of an automaton or the value of a discrete variable directly. We can apply the theoretical results by transforming discrete variables into automata where a location represents the value and a labeled transition represents a read/write operation for the value change of a discrete variable.

Semantics. The semantics of a timed automaton is defined by associating a labeled transition system with it. A **labeled transition system** $\mathcal{S}$ is a tuple $(Q, Q^0, \Sigma, \rightarrow)$ where Q is the set of configurations, $Q^0 \subseteq Q$ is a set of initial configurations, Σ is a set of labels, and $\rightarrow \subseteq Q \times \Sigma \times Q$ is a set of transitions. The system starts in an initial configuration and can change its configuration from q to q' on label a if $q \xrightarrow{a} q'$. $q \rightarrow q'$ is written if $q \xrightarrow{a} q'$ for some label a.

The **continuous semantics** $[\![\mathcal{A}]\!]_C$ of a timed automaton $\mathcal{A} = (L, L^0, X, \Sigma, I, E)$ is the labeled transition system $(L \times Val(X), L^0 \times \{v^0\}, \Sigma \cup \mathbb{R}^+, \rightarrow)$, with $\rightarrow$ containing two kinds of transitions:

- Time transitions:
  For $(l, v) \in L \times Val(X)$ and $\delta \in \mathbb{R}^+$, $(l, v) \xrightarrow{\delta} (l, v + \delta)$ if $v \in [\![I(l)]\!]$ and $v + \delta \in [\![I(l)]\!]$.
- Discrete transitions:
  For $(l, v) \in L \times Val(X)$ and $(l, a, \varphi, Y, m) \in E$, $(l, v) \xrightarrow{a} (m, v[Y := 0])$ if $v \in [\![\varphi]\!]$.

Note that for all clock constraints $\varphi \in \Phi(X)$ the statements "$v \in [\![\varphi]\!]$ and $v + \delta \in [\![\varphi]\!]$" and "for all $\delta' \in \mathbb{R}$ with $0 \leq \delta' \leq \delta, v + \delta' \in [\![\varphi]\!]$ holds" are equivalent. This is true because only conjunctions are allowed as clock constraints.

In the following we define the runs and the reachable locations for a timed automaton $\mathcal{A} = (L, L^0, X, \Sigma, I, E)$ and a labeled transition system $\mathcal{S} = (Q, Q^0, \Sigma_{\mathcal{S}}, \rightarrow)$. Let $(q_0, q_1, ..., q_k)$ be a finite sequence of configurations and $a_0, a_1, ..., a_{k-1} \in \Sigma_{\mathcal{S}}$, such that $q_0 \in Q^0$ and $q_i \xrightarrow{a_i} q_{i+1}$ holds for all $i \in \{0, 1, ..., k - 1\}$. Then $(q_0, q_1, ..., q_k)$ is a **run** of $\mathcal{A}$ with semantics $\mathcal{S}$. $Run_{\mathcal{A},\mathcal{S}}$ denotes the set of runs of $\mathcal{A}$ with semantics $\mathcal{S}$. The configuration q_k is called **reachable**. $Reach_{\mathcal{A},\mathcal{S}}$ denotes the set of reachable configurations of $\mathcal{A}$ with semantics $\mathcal{S}$. If $q_k = (l, v)$ with $l \in L$ and $v \in Val(X)$, then the location l is called **reachable**. $ReachLoc_{\mathcal{A},\mathcal{S}}$ denotes the set of reachable locations of $\mathcal{A}$ with semantics $\mathcal{S}$.

Two semantics $\mathcal{S}_1$ and $\mathcal{S}_2$ are **location-equivalent** for a timed automaton $\mathcal{A}$, iff $ReachLoc_{\mathcal{A},\mathcal{S}_1} = ReachLoc_{\mathcal{A},\mathcal{S}_2}$ holds.

The **reachability problem** for a timed automaton is the question whether for a given timed automaton $\mathcal{A}$ and a location l, $l \in ReachLoc_{\mathcal{A},[\![\mathcal{A}]\!]_C}$ holds.

Complex systems can be described as **parallel composition** of a set of timed automata which communicate through synchronization labels.

The semantics of a composition of two timed automata $\mathcal{A}_1$ and $\mathcal{A}_2$ with disjoint sets of clocks is defined to be the semantics of the product automaton $\mathcal{A}_1 \| \mathcal{A}_2$. The locations of the product automaton are pairs of component locations, and their invariants are conjunctions of the invariants of the corresponding component locations. Two switches of different components with the same synchronization label are synchronized. We define formally:

Let $\mathcal{A}_1 = (L_1, L_1^0, X_1, \Sigma_1, I_1, E_1)$ and $\mathcal{A}_2 = (L_2, L_2^0, X_2, \Sigma_2, I_2, E_2)$ be two timed automata, and assume that $X_1 \cap X_2 = \emptyset$. The product automaton $\mathcal{A}_1 \| \mathcal{A}_2$ is the timed automaton $(L_1 \times L_2, L_1^0 \times L_2^0, X_1 \cup X_2, \Sigma_1 \cup \Sigma_2, I, E)$ with $I(l_1, l_2) = I_1(l_1) \wedge I_2(l_2)$ and E defined as the set of the following switches:

- for $a \in \Sigma_1 \cap \Sigma_2$, for every $(l_1, a, \varphi_1, Y_1, m_1) \in E_1$ and $(l_2, a, \varphi_2, Y_2, m_2) \in E_2$ we have $((l_1, l_2), a, \varphi_1 \wedge \varphi_2, Y_1 \cup Y_2, (m_1, m_2)) \in E$,
- for $a \in \Sigma_1 \setminus \Sigma_2$, for every $(l_1, a, \varphi_1, Y_1, m_1) \in E_1$ and $l_2 \in L_2$ we have $((l_1, l_2), a, \varphi_1, Y_1, (m_1, l_2)) \in E$,
- for $a \in \Sigma_2 \setminus \Sigma_1$, for every $(l_2, a, \varphi_2, Y_2, m_2) \in E_2$ and $l_1 \in L_1$ we have $((l_1, l_2), a, \varphi_2, Y_2, (l_1, m_2)) \in E$,
- these are all transitions.

3   Examples: CTA Models of a Mutex Protocol and a MOS Circuit

In this section we introduce CTA models of two examples: Fischer's timing-based protocol for mutual exclusion for n processes [Lam87], which serves as benchmark in many publication and an AND circuit with 4 input lines. A model of this circuit using plain timed automata is used by [BMPY97] for the tool Kronos. At the end of the paper we use this example for verification and comparison with Kronos.

Fischer's protocol. The model is composed from n timed automata like the one depicted in Figure 2, each modeling one process. Each component automaton has four locations. Uncritical is the initial location and represents the uncritical region of the process. The shared discrete variable k is initialized with the value 0. From this location only one transition is possible: If the shared variable ensures that no other process tries to enter the critical region ($k = 0$), the process can move to the location Assign. This location expresses that a process needs at most a time units to complete the assignment $k := i$. Therefore, the clock x_i measures the staying time in this location, and the invariant forces the automaton to leave the location within a time units. Then the transition to the Wait location sets the variable k to process identifier i. In this location the process has to wait at least b time units to guarantee that all other processes completed the assignment.

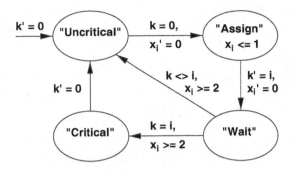

Fig. 2. Fischer's mutual exclusion protocol.

After b time units it is allowed to enter the critical region if $k = i$. Otherwise it goes back to the uncritical region. Leaving the critical region the automaton sets k to value 0 to signify that the resource is free again.

MOS circuit. How the model is built up by several module instances and automata is shown in Fig. 3. It illustrates the communication connections between different components in a manner something like data flow diagrams. An edge from a variable to a module instance indicates read only access, an edge from a module instance to a variable indicates an exclusive write access. The main module modeling the behavior of the logical AND gate with four inputs consists of two module instances of a NAND gate and one module instance of a NOR gate. The environment of the AND gate is modeled by a clock p for the time cycles and four variables to model the four input lines. The clock has the initial value 0, and when the value 15 is reached the automaton resetP resets the clock to 0. (Automata are drawn as graphs within a circle.) A module Input consists of an automaton which can change the value of one of the input variables once during the first five clock ticks of p. During the last ten clock ticks the input signals stay unchanged (they are stable). The binary variables o1 and o2 represent the output values of the two NAND gates and o models the output of the NOR gate and thus the output of the whole circuit.

Fig. 4 shows the structure of the module for NAND gates (named Nand in the figure). It consists of two pMOS transistors and two nMOS transistors. Reading the variable out (conducting or non-conducting) of the transistors (connected to this module as oP1, oN1, oP2 and oN2) the automaton (named nand in the figure) determines the output of the NAND gate. The behavior of the module for NOR gates is analogous.

A module for an nMOS transistor contains a clock c and an automaton. An nMOS transistor takes between 2 and 3 time units to change the output after a change of the gate is detected as shown in Fig. 1. The differences to pMOS transistors are the inverse output value and that the pMOS transistors have to react not earlier than 4 time units after a change at the gate.

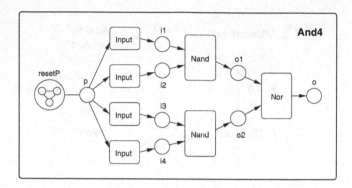

Fig. 3. Model of the AND circuit.

Interesting questions about the behavior of the AND gate are for example: How many transistors can switch their state together at the same point in time? (This number is proportional to the maximum of current needed by the gate.) Is it possible that a short circuit occurs in the AND gate? To answer these questions we have to compute the reachable configurations of the model. In Section 6 we show only results for the computation of reachable configurations because this is the bottleneck of the reachability analysis.

The real-valuedness of the clocks leads to an infinite state space. Therefore, we use a discretization of the continuous state space as a requirement to get a finite state space. We give a formal definition of a discrete semantics in the next section.

4   Discretization

The discretization of time is possible for all timed automata [GPV94]. However, in the following we restrict ourselves to the subclass of closed timed automata to permit a discretization which is particularly simple and which allows very efficient reachability analysis. **Closed timed automata** have only clock constraints φ generated by $\varphi := x \leq c \mid x \geq c \mid \varphi \wedge \varphi$ with $x \in X$ and $c \in \mathbb{N}$, i.e. the relations $<$ and $>$ are not allowed. The product automaton of two closed timed automata is closed again.

For closed timed automata it is sufficient to use integer clock values for the computation of reachable locations. For a set of clocks X the set of integer clock assignments $Val_I(X)$ is defined to be the set of total functions from X to $\mathbb{N}$. Let $C_{\mathcal{A}}(x)$ be the greatest constant occurring in some expression constraining the variable x. For $v \in Val_I(X)$ and $\delta \in \mathbb{N}$, $v \oplus \delta$ is the clock assignment of X that assigns the value $min\,(v(x) + \delta, C_{\mathcal{A}}(x) + 1)$ to each clock x. The definition of the discrete semantics is analogous to the continuous semantics previously defined.

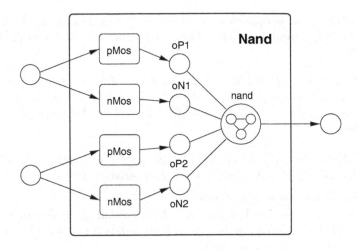

Fig. 4. Model of the logical NAND.

Let $\mathcal{A} = (L, L^0, X, \Sigma, I, E)$ be a closed timed automaton. The **discrete semantics** $[\![\mathcal{A}]\!]_I$ of $\mathcal{A}$ is the labeled transition system $(L \times Val_I(X), L^0 \times \{v^0\}, \Sigma \cup \mathbb{N}, \rightarrow_I)$ with the following transitions:

- For $(l, v) \in L \times Val_I(X)$ and $\delta \in \mathbb{N}$, $(l, v) \xrightarrow{\delta}_I (l, v \oplus \delta)$ if $v \in [\![I(l)]\!]$ and $v \oplus \delta \in [\![I(l)]\!]$.
- For $(l, v) \in L \times Val_I(X)$ and $(l, a, \varphi, Y, m) \in E$, $(l, v) \xrightarrow{a}_I (m, v[Y := 0])$ if $v \in [\![\varphi]\!]$.

To prove the *location equivalence* of discrete and continuous semantics, we define for a set of clocks X the relation $\succ \subseteq Val(X) \times Val_I(X)$ associating every continuous clock assignment with its possible discrete **representatives**. For $v \in Val(X)$ and $v' \in Val_I(X)$, $v \succ v'$ holds iff there exists some $\gamma \in \mathbb{R}$ with $0 \leq \gamma < 1$, such that for each clock $x \in X$:

a) $v'(x) - 1 + \gamma < v(x) \leq v'(x) + \gamma$, or
b) $v'(x) - 1 + \gamma < v(x)$ and $v'(x) = C_{\mathcal{A}}(x) + 1$.

Thus, v' is a representative of v if v' results from v by rounding off all clock values with fractional parts smaller than or equal to a certain bound and by rounding up all clock values with fractional parts greater than this bound in the first case. The second case restricts the range of the representatives to the greatest constant $C_{\mathcal{A}}(x) + 1$; this is sufficient to distinguish the interesting situations.

Theorem 1. *Let $\mathcal{A}$ be a closed timed automaton with the set of clocks X and let $v \in Val(X)$ and $w \in Val_I(X)$ be clock assignments with $v \succ w$.*

1. *If v satisfies a clock constraint φ of $\mathcal{A}$, then w also satisfies φ.*
2. *For all $Y \subseteq X$, $v[Y := 0] \succ w[Y := 0]$.*

Proofs of the *location equivalence* of the discrete semantics and the continuous semantics for other formalisms than timed automata can be found in [HMP92] and [AMP98].

Lemma 1. *Let* $\mathcal{A} = (L, L^0, X, \Sigma, I, E)$ *be a closed timed automaton with the continuous semantics* $[\![\mathcal{A}]\!]_C = (L \times Val(X), L^0 \times \{v^0\}, \Sigma \cup \mathbb{R}^+, \rightarrow_C)$ *and the discrete semantics* $[\![\mathcal{A}]\!]_I = (L \times Val_I(X), L^0 \times \{v^0\}, \Sigma \cup \mathbb{N}, \rightarrow_I)$. *Then the following holds:*

1. *Let* $(l, v'), (l, w') \in L \times Val_I(X), \delta' \in \mathbb{N}$, *such that* $(l, v') \xrightarrow{\delta'}_I (l, w')$ *holds. Then for all* $v \in Val(X)$ *with* $v \succ v'$ *there exists a* $w \in Val(X)$, *such that* $(l, v) \xrightarrow{\delta'}_C (l, w)$ *and* $w \succ w'$ *holds.*
2. *Let* $(l, v'), (m, w') \in L \times Val_I(X), a \in \Sigma$, *such that* $(l, v') \xrightarrow{a}_I (m, w')$ *holds. Then for all* $v \in Val(X)$ *with* $v \succ v'$ *there exists a* $w \in Val(X)$, *such that* $(l, v) \xrightarrow{a}_C (l, w)$ *and* $w \succ w'$ *holds.*
3. *Let* $(l, v), (l, w) \in L \times Val(X), \delta \in \mathbb{R}^+$, *such that* $(l, v) \xrightarrow{\delta}_C (l, w)$ *holds. Then for all* $v' \in Val_I(X)$ *with* $v \succ v'$ *there exists a* $\delta' \in \mathbb{N}$ *and a* $w' \in Val_I(X)$, *such that* $(l, v') \xrightarrow{\delta'}_I (l, w')$ *and* $w \succ w'$ *holds.*
4. *Let* $(l, v), (m, w) \in L \times Val(X), a \in \Sigma$, *such that* $(l, v) \xrightarrow{a}_C (m, w)$ *holds. Then for all* $v' \in Val_I(X)$ *with* $v \succ v'$ *there exists a* $w' \in Val_I(X)$ *such that* $(l, v') \xrightarrow{a}_I (m, w')$ *and* $w \succ w'$ *holds.*

Proof. The statements 1 and 2 follow from the definitions of the semantics.

Statement 3: We have to distinguish the two cases of the definition of $\succ$. Let $v' \in Val_I(X), v \succ v'$. Then according to the definition of the relation $\succ$ there exists some $\gamma \in \mathbb{R}$ with $0 \le \gamma < 1$, such that the following holds for all $x \in X$:

Case a) $v'(x) + \gamma + \delta < C_{\mathcal{A}}(x) + 1$:
$$v'(x) - 1 + \gamma < v(x) \le v'(x) + \gamma.$$
Because $w = v + \delta$, the following holds for all $x \in X$:
$$v'(x) - 1 + \gamma + \delta < w(x) \le v'(x) + \gamma + \delta.$$
Let $\delta' = \lfloor \delta + \gamma \rfloor$ and $w' = v' + \delta'$. Then for all $x \in X$ the following holds:
$$w'(x) - \delta' - 1 + \gamma + \delta < w(x) \le w'(x) - \delta' + \gamma + \delta.$$
Because $0 \le \gamma + \delta - \delta' < 1$, this implies $w \succ w'$.

Case b) $v'(x) + \gamma + \delta \ge C_{\mathcal{A}}(x) + 1$:
Using $\delta' = \lfloor \delta + \gamma \rfloor$ and $w' = v' \oplus \delta'$, analogously to Case 1 we obtain:
$$w'(x) - \delta' - 1 + \gamma + \delta < w(x),$$
and thus, $w \succ w'$.

Because v and w satisfy the invariant $I(l)$ and $v \succ v'$ and $w \succ w'$ hold, we can conclude from Theorem 1, statement 1 that v' and w' satisfy the invariant $I(l)$. Thus, we get $(l, v') \xrightarrow{\delta'}_I (l, w')$.

Statement 4 follows from Theorem 1.   □

Theorem 2. *For every closed timed automaton* $\mathcal{A}$, *ReachLoc*$_{\mathcal{A}, [\![\mathcal{A}]\!]_C}$ = *ReachLoc*$_{\mathcal{A}, [\![\mathcal{A}]\!]_I}$ *holds.*

Proof. Let $\mathcal{A} = (L, L^0, X, \Sigma, I, E)$ be a timed automaton with the continuous semantics $[\![\mathcal{A}]\!]_C = (L \times Val(X), L^0 \times \{v^0\}, \Sigma \cup \mathbb{R}^+, \rightarrow_C)$ and the discrete semantics $[\![\mathcal{A}]\!]_I = (L \times Val_I(X), L^0 \times \{v^0\}, \Sigma \cup \mathbb{N}, \rightarrow_I)$.

At first, we prove *ReachLoc*$_{\mathcal{A}, [\![\mathcal{A}]\!]_C} \subseteq$ *ReachLoc*$_{\mathcal{A}, [\![\mathcal{A}]\!]_I}$. We show per induction over k that for every run $((l_0, v_0), (l_1, v_1), ..., (l_k, v_k))$ in *Run*$_{\mathcal{A}, [\![\mathcal{A}]\!]_C}$ there exists a run $((l_0, v'_0), (l_1, v'_1), ..., (l_k, v'_k))$ in *Run*$_{\mathcal{A}, [\![\mathcal{A}]\!]_I}$, such that $v_i \succ v'_i$ holds for all $i \in \{0, 1, ..., k\}$.

Start of induction: According to the definition of run, $l_0 \in L^0$ and $v_0 = v^0$ hold. $((l_0, v^0))$ is also in *Run*$_{\mathcal{A}, [\![\mathcal{A}]\!]_I}$, and $v_0 \succ v^0$ holds.

Inductive step: We have to show that there exists some $a' \in \Sigma \cup \mathbb{N}$ and some v'_{i+1} with $v_{i+1} \succ v'_{i+1}$, such that $(l_i, v'_i) \xrightarrow{a'}_I (l_{i+1}, v'_{i+1})$. The inductive hypothesis ensures $v_i \succ v'_i$ and there exists some $a \in \Sigma \cup \mathbb{R}^+$ with $(l_i, v_i) \xrightarrow{a}_R (l_{i+1}, v_{i+1})$. The assertion of the theorem follows from the claim of Lemma 1, statement 3, if $a \in \mathbb{R}^+$, and of statement 4, if $a \in \Sigma$. This finishes the inductive proof.

Similarly, we can show using statements 1 and 2 of Lemma 1: *ReachLoc*$_{\mathcal{A}, [\![\mathcal{A}]\!]_I} \subseteq$ *ReachLoc*$_{\mathcal{A}, [\![\mathcal{A}]\!]_C}$. □

5   Efficient Verification Using the Structure of the Model

Because the number of states of a product automaton grows exponentially in the number of processes, the state explosion problem forces typically the use of symbolic representation of the state space. The technique of representing sets of states as binary decision diagrams is in widespread use and also implemented in our tool Rabbit. The second step to efficient verification is to use a finite set of configurations for the reachability analysis by introducing a discrete semantics. The discretization enables a unique representation of the set of configurations consisting of locations of the automata together with the discretized continuous state space of clocks. This technique is also examined in [BMPY97].

In this section we introduce an advanced technique for efficient verification of some classes of models. We use a variable ordering resulting from the communication structure of a system and we determined empirically the polynomial complexity of the reachability analysis of some classes of models. We prove an upper bound for the representation of the transition relation and that it is polynomial for Fischer's protocol. Because of our empirical studies we think that it is sound to infer from these results a size estimation for the representation of the set of reachable configurations. We use this estimation as a qualitative assessment of different variable orderings.

5.1   Communication Graph and Variable Ordering

Aziz et al. proved an upper bound for the size of BDDs for transition relations of communicating finite automata [ATB94]. On the basis of this upper bound

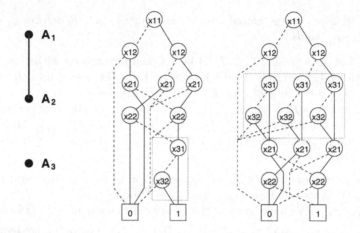

Fig. 5. Communication graph and variable ordering, example 1.

they determine good variable orderings for the set of reachable locations. In this section we use the results of that work to explain the characteristics of good variable orderings for timed automata.

The problem is to find a variable ordering for a given parallel composition of the timed automaton $\mathcal{A}$ such that the number of nodes of the BDD representation of $Reach_{\mathcal{A}, [\![\mathcal{A}]\!]_I}$ is as small as possible. For this purpose we investigate the communication between the components. Two components $\mathcal{A}_j$ and $\mathcal{A}_k$ with $j, k \in \{1, ..., n\}$, are **communicating**, symbolically $\mathcal{A}_j \rightleftharpoons \mathcal{A}_k$, iff $\Sigma_j \cap \Sigma_k \neq \emptyset$ and $j \neq k$. Considering the components as nodes and the communication relation $\rightleftharpoons$ as set of edges we get the **communication graph**.

We use simple examples to illustrate two general characteristics of good variable orderings:

1. Communicating components have successive positions within the ordering.
2. Components which communicate with many other components are at the beginning of the ordering.

We consider three finite automata (i.e. timed automata without clocks) $\mathcal{A}_1$, $\mathcal{A}_2$ and $\mathcal{A}_3$, each having the locations l_1, l_2 and l_3.

In the first example $\mathcal{A}_3$ communicates neither with $\mathcal{A}_1$ nor with $\mathcal{A}_2$. $\mathcal{A}_1$ and $\mathcal{A}_2$ ensure by communication that they stay in the same location every time. Let x_{i1} and x_{i2} encode the configuration of $\mathcal{A}_i$. Fig. 5 shows the communication graph and the BDDs of the reachable locations for the variable ordering $(x_{11}, x_{12}, x_{21}, x_{22}, x_{31}, x_{32})$ on the left side and $(x_{11}, x_{12}, x_{31}, x_{32}, x_{21}, x_{22})$ on the right side. It illustrates that respecting characteristic 1 leads to a better variable ordering.

In the second example $\mathcal{A}_1$ communicates with $\mathcal{A}_2$ and $\mathcal{A}_3$, and $\mathcal{A}_2$ does not communicate with $\mathcal{A}_3$. It is ensured by communication that $\mathcal{A}_1$ and $\mathcal{A}_2$ as well as $\mathcal{A}_1$ and $\mathcal{A}_3$ stay in different locations every time. Fig. 6 shows the commu-

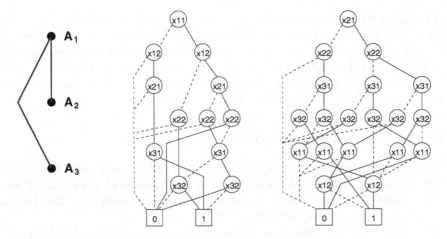

Fig. 6. Communication graph and variable ordering, example 2.

nication graph and the BDDs of the reachable locations for the variable orderings $(x_{11}, x_{12}, x_{21}, x_{22}, x_{31}, x_{32})$ and $(x_{21}, x_{22}, x_{31}, x_{32}, x_{11}, x_{12})$. Both orderings do not differ with respect to the first characteristic, but the sizes of their BDDs are different. We see that of two variable orderings the one respecting characteristic 2 is better.

To derive an algorithm for finding variable orderings we first show an upper bound of the BDD's size of a transition relation of the product automaton. The only bottleneck in our algorithms is the size of the BDD for the reachable configurations, because we do not compute the monolithic transition relation (instead we use partitioned transition relations represented by very small BDDs [RAB+95]). But we need the upper bound for the transition relation, because good variable orderings for the transition relation are often good for the set of reachable configurations. Therefore, we derive an estimation for the size of the set of reachable configurations from the upper bound for the size of the transition relation. An algorithm for finding a good variable ordering searches for a variable ordering having a low size estimation.

To justify this argumentation we refer to results of other research groups: The result of [ATB94] is that there is a good correlation between the BDD size predicted by the bound and the actual BDD size for the transition relation. Experiments in [YBO+98] show that good variable orderings for the transition relation are also good for the set of reachable locations. In [ATB94] as well as in this paper it is demonstrated by empirical studies that we actually find good variable orderings for the set of reachable configurations using this strategy. However, there are counterexamples with linear growth of BDDs for the transition relation but exponential growth of BDDs for the reachable configurations [McM92].

For the purpose of finding good variable orderings it is not necessary that the estimated size is absolutely close to the real size because the estimation should only reflect the relation between different variable orderings, i.e. good variable orderings should lead to better estimations than bad variable orderings. Last, but not least the upper bound for the BDD's size in the next section and algorithms using the estimation have the advantage that they behave according to both of the characteristics mentioned in this section, and these characteristics reflect the experience and intuition of many experts.

5.2   Upper Bound for the BDD's Size

In this section we prove the upper bound for the number of nodes of the BDD for the transition relation. We start with an introduction of some conventions and notations. In this section we adapt the notations introduced in Section 2.3 to be able to represent assignments by BDDs.

$Range(x)$ is used to denote the range of a discrete variable x. Boolean variables are special discrete variables with the range $\{0, 1\}$. Let X be a set of discrete variables. The set $\Phi(X)$ of **constraints** φ is generated by the following grammar: $\varphi := x_1 \sim c \mid x_1 \sim x_2 \mid \varphi \wedge \varphi$, with $x_1, x_2 \in X$, $\sim \ \in \{\leq, \geq, <, >, =\}$, $Range(x_1) = Range(x_2)$ and $c \in Range(x_1)$.

An **assignment** v of X is a total function which assigns an element of $Range(x)$ to each variable x. The set of all assignments of X is denoted by $Val(X)$. The set of all assignments of X that satisfy a constraint $\varphi \in \Phi(X)$ is denoted by $[\![\varphi]\!]$. φ is related to different sets of variables (because e.g. $x > 5$ is a constraint for both $\{x\}$ and $\{x, y\}$). Therefore, we identify two sets of assignments $V \subseteq Val(X)$ and $W \subseteq Val(X \cup Y)$ iff $W = \{w \in Val(X \cup Y) | \exists v \in Val(X) \ \forall x \in X : w(x) = v(x)\}$ holds.

Now we introduce some notations for a set of assignments $V \subseteq Val(X)$.

- For a variable $x \in X$, the **existential quantification** $\exists x.V$ is defined as set of all assignments of $X \setminus \{x\}$ with the values of all variables but x equal to the values of the same variables in an assignment in V; formally: for $w \in Val(X \setminus \{x\})$, $w \in \exists x.V$ holds iff there exists some $v \in Val(X)$, such that $v(y) = w(y)$ for all $y \in X \setminus \{x\}$.
- For two variables $x \in X$ and $y \notin X$, $V[x \leftarrow y]$ is the set of assignments which is obtained by **renaming** x to y; formally: for a $w \in Val((X \setminus \{x\}) \cup \{y\})$, $w \in V[x \leftarrow y]$ holds iff there exists a $v \in V$, such that $v(x) = w(y)$ and $v(z) = w(z)$ for all $z \in X \setminus \{x\}$.
- For a variable $x \in X$ and a constant $c \in Range(x)$ the **cofactor** $V|_{x=c}$ is defined as $\exists x.(V \cap [\![x = c]\!])$.

A finite relation can be represented by a set of assignments by mapping the arguments of the relation to discrete variables. Let $R \subseteq R_1 \times R_2 \times ... \times R_n$ be a relation and $X = \{x_1, x_2, ..., x_n\}$ a set of discrete variables with $Range(x_i) = R_i$ for all $i \in \{1, 2, ..., n\}$. Then $R(x_1, x_2, ..., x_n)$ denotes the set of assignments of X with $v \in R(x_1, x_2, ..., x_n)$ iff $(v(x_1), v(x_2), ..., v(x_n)) \in R$.

The algorithm for computing all reachable configurations of a parallel composition of n timed automata is shown in Fig. 7. We use the abbreviations introduced in the figure also in the following. We deal only with closed timed automata and the integer semantics as introduced in the previous section. Transfering the results to other discretizations is possible.

Input: parallel composition $\mathcal{A} = \{L, L^0, X, \Sigma, I, E\}$
   with the discrete semantics $[\![\mathcal{A}]\!]_I = (Q, Q^0, \Sigma \cup \mathbb{IN}, \rightarrow)$
   of closed timed automata $\mathcal{A}_i = (L_i, L_i^0, X_i, \Sigma_i, I_i, E_i), i \in \{1, ..., n\}$
   with the discrete semantics $[\![\mathcal{A}_i]\!]_I = (Q_i, Q_i^0, \Sigma_i \cup \mathbb{IN}, \rightarrow_i)$
   and disjoint sets of clocks: $X_j \cap X_k = \emptyset$ for all $j, k \in \{1, ..., n\}$ with $j \neq k$
Output: $Reach_{\mathcal{A}, [\![\mathcal{A}]\!]_I}(q_1, ..., q_n)$,
   with variable q_i corresponding to the configuration $\mathcal{A}_i$ $(Range(q_i) = Q_i)$

$R := Q^0(q_1, \ldots, q_n)$
do
  $R_{prev} := R$
  forall $a \in (\Sigma \cup \{1\})$
    $R := R \cup \left(\exists q_1 ... \exists q_n (R \cap \xrightarrow{a}(q_1, q_1', ..., q_n, q_n')) \right) [q_1' \leftarrow q_1]...[q_n' \leftarrow q_n]$
until $R = R_{prev}$
return R

Fig. 7. Computation of the set of reachable configurations.

For the proof of the upper bound we need a formal definition for BDDs. The following definition is similar to the one from McMillan [McM92]. A BDD is identified with its root node. Let $\vec{x}$ be a vector $(x_1, x_2, ..., x_n)$ of Boolean variables. If $n = 0$, then $\mathcal{B}$ is a **binary decision diagram** over $\vec{x}$ iff $\mathcal{B}$ is the 0-terminal-node (short $\mathcal{B} = 0$) or $\mathcal{B}$ is the 1-terminal-node (short $\mathcal{B} = 1$). If $n > 0$ then $\mathcal{B}$ is a BDD over $\vec{x}$ iff

- $\mathcal{B}$ is a BDD over $(x_2, ..., x_n)$, or
- $\mathcal{B} = (x_1, \mathcal{B}_0, \mathcal{B}_1)$, where $\mathcal{B}_0$ and $\mathcal{B}_1$ are BDDs over $(x_2, ..., x_n)$. $\mathcal{B}$ is called an x_n-node, $\mathcal{B}_0$ is called low child, and $\mathcal{B}_1$ is called high child of $\mathcal{B}$.

A BDD $\mathcal{B}$ over $(x_1, x_2, ..., x_n)$ represents a set of assignments of $\{x_1, x_2, ..., x_n\}$ which are denoted by $[\![\mathcal{B}]\!]$ and defined as follows:

$$[\![\mathcal{B}]\!] = \begin{cases} \emptyset, & \text{if } \mathcal{B} = 0 \\ Val(\{x_1, x_2, ..., x_n\}), & \text{if } \mathcal{B} = 1 \\ ([\![\mathcal{B}_0]\!] \cap [\![x_i = 0]\!]) \cup ([\![\mathcal{B}_1]\!] \cap [\![x_i = 1]\!]), & \text{if } \mathcal{B} = (x_i, \mathcal{B}_0, \mathcal{B}_1) \end{cases}$$

In the sequel we consider only BDDs which are generated by applying only the following rule: Fold together all equal subtrees. The second rule, which is to eliminate nodes with two edges to the same sub-node, we do not apply because we need these nodes for referencing within the formal considerations in the following.

The number of nodes of such a BDD is an upper bound for the number of nodes after applying the second rule. The first rule has more impact on the reduction of the BDD and is more sensitive for the variable ordering than the second rule.

Proposition 1. *Let $\mathcal{B}$ be a BDD over the vector $(x_1, x_2, ..., x_k)$ of Boolean variables and $i \in \{1, ..., k-1\}$. Then the number of x_{i+1} nodes in $\mathcal{B}$ is less than or equal to twice the number of x_i nodes.*

Let $\mathcal{B}$ be a BDD over $(q_1, q_1', ..., q_n, q_n')$, $i \in \{1, ..., n\}$ and x the Boolean variable which is the first in the variable ordering of the variables encoding q_i. Then $|\mathcal{B}|_i$ is used to denote the number of x-nodes in $\mathcal{B}$ and $|\mathcal{B}|_{n+1}$ is used to denote the number of terminal nodes in $\mathcal{B}$. $|\mathcal{B}|$ is the number of all non-terminal nodes in $\mathcal{B}$. For a set of assignments $V \subseteq Val(\{q_1, q_1', ..., q_n, q_n'\})$ and a set of variables $M = \{q_{i_1}, q_{i_1}', ..., q_{i_k}, q_{i_k}'\}$ $(i_1, ..., i_k \in \{1, ..., n\})$, $V|_M$ denotes the set of all cofactors of V regarding the variables in M, i.e. $V|_M = \{V|_{q_{i_1}=c_1, q_{i_1}'=c_1', ..., q_{i_k}=c_k, q_{i_k}'=c_k'} \mid c_l, c_l' \in Q_{i_l} \text{ for all } l \in \{1, ..., k\}\}$. As abbreviating notation $V|_i$ denotes $V|_{\{q_1, q_1', ..., q_{i-1}, q_{i-1}'\}}$ for $i \in \{1, ..., n+1\}$. For a set M, $|M|$ is used to denote the number of elements of M.

Proposition 2. *Let $\mathcal{B}$ be a BDD over $(q_1, q_1', ..., q_n, q_n')$ and $V \subseteq Val(\{q_1, q_1', ..., q_n, q_n'\})$ be a set of assignments with $[\![\mathcal{B}]\!] = V$. Then $|\mathcal{B}|_i \leq |\,V|_i \cup \{\emptyset\}\,|$ holds for all $i \in \{1, ..., n+1\}$.*

Note: Let $x_1, ..., x_s$ be the Boolean variables encoding $q_1, q_1', ..., q_{i-1}, q_{i-1}'$. If there exists an assignment of $\{x_1, ..., x_s\}$ in $V|_i$ which is not an encoding of an assignment of $\{q_1, q_1', ..., q_{i-1}, q_{i-1}'\}$, then we have to consider the empty set as additional cofactor. This is the case if the cardinality of a set Q_k ($k \in \{1, ..., i-1\}$) is not a power of two. Otherwise $|\mathcal{B}|_i = |\,V|_i\,|$.

From the number of cofactors of an assignment we can infer the size of its BDD representation. An upper bound for the number of cofactors of the transition relation is given by the following lemma. The time transitions are taken synchronously for the clocks in all components. We would get additional edges in the communication graph connecting all automata having a clock. This does not give any hint for the variable ordering, and thus, we do not consider them here. In the sequel we consider only the relation of discrete transitions $\rightarrow' = \bigcup_{a \in \Sigma} \xrightarrow{a}$. To regard the communication structure we define a function reflecting the communication between parts of the system. This function depends on the ordering of the components. The set $\mathbf{Comm}_\mathcal{A}(i)$ contains the indices of all components of $\mathcal{A}$ which have an index less than i and communicate with a component having an index greater than or equal to i: $Comm_\mathcal{A}(i) = \{k \mid k < i$ and there exists an $l \geq i$ with $\mathcal{A}_k \rightleftharpoons \mathcal{A}_l\}$.

Lemma 2. *For the transition relation $\rightarrow'$ $(q_1, q_1', ..., q_n, q_n')$ and every $i \in \{1, ..., n+1\}$, the following holds:*

$$|\rightarrow'(q_1, q_1', ..., q_n, q_n')|_i \cup \{\emptyset\}| \leq 4 \cdot \prod_{k \in Comm_\mathcal{A}(i)} |Q_k|^2 + 4$$

Proof. At first we give a lemma used in our computation of the number of cofactors. For all $V, W \subseteq Val(\{q_1, q_1', ..., q_n, q_n'\})$, $i_1, ..., i_k \in \{1, ..., n\}$ and $c_l, c_l' \in Q_{i_l}$ ($l \in \{1, ..., k\}$) the following holds:

$$(V \cap W)|_{q_{i_1}=c_1, q_{i_1}'=c_1', ..., q_{i_k}=c_k, q_{i_k}'=c_k'} \tag{1}$$
$$= V|_{q_{i_1}=c_1, q_{i_1}'=c_1', ..., q_{i_k}=c_k, q_{i_k}'=c_k'} \cap W|_{q_{i_1}=c_1, q_{i_1}'=c_1', ..., q_{i_k}=c_k, q_{i_k}'=c_k'}$$

Equation 1 analogously holds for the union of sets of assignments.

We partition the transition relation $\rightarrow'$ into three subsets. From its cofactors we can conclude the cofactors of $\rightarrow'$ applying equation 1.

Case 1. Discrete transitions concerning only the components $\mathcal{A}_1$ to $\mathcal{A}_{i-1}$:

$$\bigcup_{a \in \Sigma \backslash (\Sigma_i \cup ... \cup \Sigma_n)} \xrightarrow{a}$$

$$= \bigcup_{a \in \Sigma \backslash (\Sigma_i \cup ... \cup \Sigma_n)} \bigcap_{k \in \{1,2,...,n\}} \begin{cases} \xrightarrow{a}_k (q_k, q_k'), & \text{if } a \in \Sigma_k \\ [\![q_k' = q_k]\!], & \text{otherwise} \end{cases}$$

$$= \bigcup_{a \in \Sigma \backslash (\Sigma_i \cup ... \cup \Sigma_n)} \left(\begin{array}{c} \bigcap_{k \in \{1,...,i-1\}} \begin{cases} \xrightarrow{a}_k (q_k, q_k'), & \text{if } a \in \Sigma_k \\ [\![q_k' = q_k]\!], & \text{otherwise} \end{cases} \\ \cap \bigcap_{k \in \{i,...,n\}} [\![q_k' = q_k]\!] \end{array} \right)$$

$$= \bigcup_{a \in \Sigma \backslash (\Sigma_i \cup ... \cup \Sigma_n)} \bigcap_{k \in \{1,...,i-1\}} \begin{cases} \xrightarrow{a}_k (q_k, q_k'), & \text{if } a \in \Sigma_k \\ [\![q_k' = q_k]\!], & \text{otherwise} \end{cases}$$
$$\cap \bigcap_{k \in \{i,...,n\}} [\![q_k' = q_k]\!]$$

Regarding equation 1 for the cofactors we get:

$$\left(\bigcup_{a \in \Sigma \backslash (\Sigma_i \cup ... \cup \Sigma_n)} \xrightarrow{a} \right)\Big|_i \subseteq \left\{ \emptyset, \bigcap_{k \in \{i,...,n\}} [\![q_k = q_k']\!] \right\}.$$

A sketch of the BDD for these cofactors is shown by Fig. 8. In the figure, 'A' denotes a BDD for the part where transitions change the assignments for the variables. 'E' denotes the BDD for the empty set and 'B' denotes the BDD for the assignments with $q_k = q_k'$.

Case 2. Discrete transitions concerning only the components $\mathcal{A}_i$ to $\mathcal{A}_n$:

$$\bigcup_{a \in \Sigma \backslash (\Sigma_1 \cup ... \cup \Sigma_{i-1})} \xrightarrow{a}$$

$$= \bigcap_{k \in \{1,...,i-1\}} [\![q_k' = q_k]\!]$$
$$\cap \bigcup_{a \in \Sigma \backslash (\Sigma_1 \cup ... \cup \Sigma_{i-1})} \bigcap_{k \in \{i,...,n\}} \begin{cases} \xrightarrow{a}_k (q_k, q_k'), & \text{if } a \in \Sigma_k \\ [\![q_k' = q_k]\!], & \text{otherwise} \end{cases}$$

Denoting the second term of the intersection by T, using equation 1 follows:
$$\left(\bigcup_{a \in \Sigma \backslash (\Sigma_1 \cup ... \cup \Sigma_{i-1})} \xrightarrow{a} \right)\Big|_i \subseteq \{\emptyset, T\}. \text{ The BDD representation is shown in Fig. 9.}$$

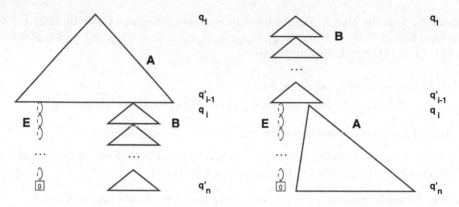

Fig. 8. BDD for Case 1.   **Fig. 9.** BDD for Case 2.

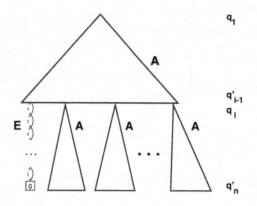

Fig. 10. BDD for Case 3.

Case 3. Discrete transitions concerning components before $\mathcal{A}_i$ as well as components from $\mathcal{A}_i$:

$$\bigcup_{a \in (\Sigma_1 \cup \ldots \cup \Sigma_{i-1}) \cap (\Sigma_i \cup \ldots \cup \Sigma_n)} \xrightarrow{a}$$

$$= \bigcap_{k \in \{1, \ldots, i-1\} \setminus Comm_{\mathcal{A}}(i)} [\![q'_k = q_k]\!]$$

$$\cap \bigcup_{a \in (\Sigma_1 \cup \ldots \cup \Sigma_{i-1}) \cap (\Sigma_i \cup \ldots \cup \Sigma_n)} \bigcap_{k \in Comm_{\mathcal{A}}(i) \cup \{i, \ldots, n\}} \begin{cases} \xrightarrow{a}_k (q_k, q'_k), & \text{if } a \in \Sigma_k \\ [\![q'_k = q_k]\!], & \text{otherwise} \end{cases}$$

Denoting the first term of the intersection as T_1 and the second term as T_2 we get $T_1|_i \subseteq \{\emptyset, \; Val(\{q_i, q'_i, \ldots, q_n, q'_n\})\}$, and, because $T_2 \subseteq Val(\{q_k, q'_k \mid k \in Comm_{\mathcal{A}}(i)\} \cup \{q_i, q'_i \ldots, q_n, q'_n\})$, the following holds: $|T_2|_i| \leq \prod_{k \in Comm_{\mathcal{A}}(i)} |Q_k|^2$.

Applying equation 1,

$$\left| \left(\bigcup_{a \in (\Sigma_1 \cup \ldots \cup \Sigma_{i-1}) \cap (\Sigma_i \cup \ldots \cup \Sigma_n)} \xrightarrow{a} \right) \Big|_i \cup \{\emptyset\} \right| \leq \prod_{k \in Comm_{\mathcal{A}}(i)} |Q_k|^2 + 1$$

holds.

Fig. 10 shows this most interesting part as BDD representation.

Using equation 1 for the union of the three parts of the transition relation the claim follows.   □

From the upper bound of the number of cofactors we derive an upper bound for the BDD's size now. We use $|q_i|$ to denote the number of Boolean variables encoding q_i.

Theorem 3. *Let $\mathcal{B}$ be the BDD over $(q_1, q_1', ..., q_n, q_n')$ with $[\![\mathcal{B}]\!] = \rightarrow' (q_1, q_1', ..., q_n, q_n')$. Then the following holds:*

$$|\mathcal{B}| \leq \sum_{i=1}^{n} \left(2^{2|q_i|} - 1\right) \cdot \left(4 \cdot \prod_{k \in Comm_A(i)} |Q_k|^2 + 4\right)$$

Proof. Lemma 2 states for every $i \in \{1, ..., n\}$:

$$\left|\rightarrow' (q_1, q_1', ..., q_n, q_n')|_i \cup \{\emptyset\}\right| \leq 4 \cdot \prod_{k \in Comm_A(i)} |Q_k|^2 + 4.$$

Using Proposition 2, for every $i \in \{1, ..., n\}$

$$|\mathcal{B}|_i \leq 4 \cdot \prod_{k \in Comm_A(i)} |Q_k|^2 + 4$$

follows. Finally, using Proposition 1, we get the upper bound for the number of all BDD nodes which code q_i and q_i':

$$\sum_{l=0}^{2|q_i|-1} 2^l \cdot \left(4 \cdot \prod_{k \in Comm_A(i)} |Q_k|^2 + 4\right)$$
$$= \left(2^{2|q_i|} - 1\right) \cdot \left(4 \cdot \prod_{k \in Comm_A(i)} |Q_k|^2 + 4\right).$$

Applying the sum over all $i \in \{1, ..., n\}$ we get the claim.   □

The statement of this upper bound for the BDD's size obviously reflects the rules of the previous section: If we order communicating components on neighboring positions in the variable ordering and if we place components communicating with many other components at the beginning of the ordering, then the sets $Comm_A(i)$ have only few elements and the upper bound is relative small.

In the upper bound we used the assumption that q and q' of one component have successive positions within the variable ordering. This makes sense because usually every bit of the successor configuration depends on all bits of the current configuration and thus, there exist a lot of communication within a component. Because a bit of the successor configuration usually is most inter-related to the corresponding bit of the current configuration, we use an interleaved ordering, i.e. each bit of the current configuration is directly followed by the corresponding bit of the successor configuration.

To use the upper bound for the transition relation as size estimation for the BDD representing all reachable configurations we need a modification of Theorem 3. Furthermore, the aim is not to compute an upper bound but to compute an estimation of the BDD's size for comparison of different variable orderings by an algorithm. Therefore, the size estimation should reflect the actual BDD size induced by the variable ordering as good as possible, because the quality of the estimation corresponds directly to the quality of the variable ordering we will "declare as the best".

Differently from the BDDs for transition relations, BDDs for sets of reachable configurations do not contain primed variables for successor configurations. This leads to the following estimation:

$$\sum_{i=1}^{n} \left(2^{|q_i|} - 1\right) \cdot \left(4 \cdot \prod_{k \in Comm_{\mathcal{A}}(i)} |Q_k| + 4\right).$$

Let $\mathcal{B}$ be the BDD over $(q_1, ..., q_n)$ with $[\![\mathcal{B}]\!] = Reach_{\mathcal{A}, [\![\mathcal{A}]\!]_I}(q_1, ..., q_n)$. For $i \in \{1, ..., n\}$, let the variable q_i be encoded by the Boolean variables $x_{i,1}, ..., x_{i,|q_i|}$, such that $\mathcal{B}$ is a BDD over $(x_{1,1}, ..., x_{1,|q_1|}, ..., x_{n,1}, ..., x_{n,|q_n|})$. The estimation contains the pessimistic bound that the number of $x_{i,k+1}$ nodes in $\mathcal{B}$ is twice the number of $x_{i,k}$ nodes $(1 \leq k < |q_i|)$. This assumption is not realistic for variables q_i with large number of bits and the estimation is not very similar to the actual size. To get a better estimation for the number of $x_{i,k+1}$ nodes we can also use a linear or exponential interpolation. In our tool implementation we use a linear interpolation and for our purpose the estimation is sufficient because it reflects the relation between different variable orderings approximately.

5.3   Finding Good Variable Orderings for CTA Models

An algorithm for finding the variable ordering of the best estimation, which considers the bits encoding one component as a unit, must compute the size estimation for all permutations of the sequence $q_1, \ldots, q_n$. Such an algorithm is of exponential time complexity and therefore, it is not relevant for practical use. With a computation of the estimation in $O(n^2)$, the time complexity would be $O(n^2 n!)$

Dynamic programming reduces this complexity to $O(n^3 2^n)$ by storing the results already computed in former iterations for parts of an ordering. But this is not efficient and therefore we need an algorithm of polynomial time complexity. Because of this, exact algorithms are not acceptable, especially for large numbers of components. Thus, we have to accept heuristic solutions, e.g. we can use the arbitrary insertion heuristic [LLKS85]. Using this heuristic we get a time complexity in $O(n^3)$ which is sufficient for our purpose, i.e. to find a good variable ordering regarding our estimation.

Using the structure of CTA models. Cottbus Timed Automata can be considered as composition of timed automata and thus, the algorithms mentioned above can be used. Nevertheless, it is very promising to use special techniques for CTA which use the information about the hierarchical structure as hints for good variable orderings.

The main idea is that the bit-encodings of all objects (variables, automata) contained in the same module instance have successive positions in the variable ordering because objects which are considered as strongly coupled are put together by the model's developer. In the module hierarchy, it is considered that synchronization labels and variables are accessible only where they are really needed. The modules' interfaces should be as small as possible. These considerations lead to a model in which the communication (in the sense of Section 5.1) within a module normally is stronger than the communication of the module with its environment.

We can not guarantee that an algorithm using the hierarchical structure always computes better variable orderings than the algorithm for plain composition of timed automata, but using the structure has the following main advantages:

- The modeller's knowledge about the system is used.
- The problem of variable ordering is partitioned into smaller sub-problems, which results in smaller computation times or that exact algorithms are applicable for these smaller problems, and thus, one might be able to get better variable orderings.

6 Experimental Results

To demonstrate the high performance of our approach we give two examples. We use an algorithm for mutual exclusion to examine the computation of the estimation of the BDD's size and we validate the quality of the variable orderings found using our heuristics by measuring the time and the number of nodes needed for verification of the mutex property. The second example is an AND circuit. We consider the module structure to find good variable orderings for the analysis of this model.

Fischer's protocol. Fischer's protocol is a timing-based mutual exclusion protocol. We verified the mutual exclusion property for Fischer's protocol for n processes. The automaton modeling one process has a location for the critical section. The verification task is to compute all reachable configurations and to check whether there exists a reachable situation in which at least two processes are in the critical section. The communication graph of Fischer's protocol for n processes is shown in Fig. 11. Changing the positions of the process automata in the variable ordering has no effect on the estimation of the BDD's size; only the position of the variable k is important and that the encodings of clock and location of an automaton have neighboring positions. Table 1 reports the results of our experiments with different variable orderings. We give the computation times in seconds on a SUN Ultra-Sparc 1 with 200 MHz processor. We examined five combinations of tools and strategies. The first row of an experiment in the table contains the computation time in seconds and for experiments with our tool the second row displays the growth of the maximal size of the BDD representing reachable configurations.

In the third experiment we used a variable ordering violating the rule that the variables of a component have successive positions. We used the variable

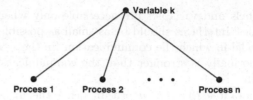

Fig. 11. Communication graph of Fischer's protocol.

ordering (variable k, automaton 1, ..., automaton n, clock 1, ..., clock n). It leads to a very strong growth of the BDD's size.

If we place the variable k on the last position we get $Comm_1 = Comm_{n+2} = \emptyset$ and $Comm_i = \{1, ..., i-1\}$ for $i \in \{2, ..., n+1\}$. We can compute the estimation for the BDD $\mathcal{B}$ of all reachable configurations as follows: We start to compute $|\mathcal{B}|_i = \prod_{k \in Comm_{\mathcal{A}}(i)} |Q_k|$ (we can leave out the 4 because of using the O-notation). Since $Comm_1 = Comm_{n+2} = \emptyset$, we get the estimation 1 for $|\mathcal{B}|_1$ and $|\mathcal{B}|_{n+2}$. For $|\mathcal{B}|_i$ ($i \in \{2, ..., n+1\}$) we get 12^{i-1} since $|Q_k| = 12$ for $k \in \{1, ..., n\}$ (number of configurations for each process = four locations × three clock values) and $Comm_i = \{1, ..., i-1\}$ for $i \in \{2, ..., n+1\}$. Because variable k is on position $n+1$, the biggest term of the sum for the estimation is that for *component* k, which is $\left(2^{|q_{n+1}|} - 1\right) \cdot 12^n$. The estimation for $|\mathcal{B}|$ therefore is in $O(n \cdot 12^n)$ (or $O(log_2 n \cdot 12^n)$ using linear interpolation). The fourth experiment shows that the BDD's size actually grows exponentially.

Placing variable k on first position we have $Comm_1 = Comm_{n+2} = \emptyset$, $Comm_2 = ... = Comm_{n+1} = \{1\}$. The estimation for $|\mathcal{B}|_1$ and $|\mathcal{B}|_{n+2}$ is 1 again, but the estimation for $|\mathcal{B}|_2, ..., |\mathcal{B}|_{n+1}$ is $n+1$ (because $|Q_1| = n+1$). Thus, the estimation for the size of $\mathcal{B}$ is in $O(n^2)$. In the last experiment the estimation matches the actual size (number of nodes) very good.

Table 1 also contains a comparison with the most popular tools for the verification of timed automata, Kronos and Uppaal. These tools use difference bound matrices to represent sets of clock assignments. The first and second experiment in the table show the computation times of our experiments with these tools. The results show that the computation times of Kronos and Uppaal seem to be at least exponential in n, while the computation time of our tool *Rabbit* seems to be polynomial using a good variable ordering (fifth row). A BDD-based version of Kronos is able to verify 14 processes as reported in [BMPY97], which also means exponential growth of computation time.

Table 1. Computation times for the verification of the mutex property of Fischer's protocol. MO means that more than 64 MB memory were needed. The last three experiments belong to our tool Rabbit.

No. proc.	4	5	6	7	8	10	12	14	16	32	64
Kronos	3.0	191	MO								
Uppaal	0.5	13.0	657	MO							
Separated	0.3	1.0	5.0	21.6	110	MO					
No. nodes	828	3053	10983	38515	132245						
k at end	0.3	0.6	1.6	3.9	9.4	46.3	249	MO			
No. nodes	456	1003	2119	4625	9158	36405	145438				
k in front	0.3	0.4	0.8	1.3	2.3	4.0	8.9	13.6	22.7	208	1920
No. nodes	326	544	812	1129	1497	2375	3450	4720	6190	24983	100200

Table 2. Times and BDD's size for computation of all reachable configurations of the 'And4' model. 'N/A' indicates that measured values are not available for that model.

Number of input signals	2	4	8	16
Kronos (BDD): Computation time	N/A	324.7	N/A	N/A
Rabbit: Computation time	0.5	6.0	79.6	1208.7
Rabbit: Number of BDD's nodes	2007	15722	119870	789835

MOS circuit. This section applies our algorithms to the model 'And4' introduced in Section 3. This model has a more complicated communication graph than Fischer's protocol. Table 2 contains the results of our measurements. The computation times are given also in seconds of CPU time on a SUN Ultra-Sparc 1 with 200 MHz processor.

The first row contains a result of the BDD-based version of Kronos. This result, also obtained using a SUN Ultra-Sparc 1, is published in [BMPY97]. The second row of the table shows the computation time needed by our tool *Rabbit* to compute the whole set of reachable configurations. The number of nodes needed to represent this set is given in the third row. (Using a 'stupid' random variable ordering the number of nodes is about 4,000,000 for four input signals.)

7   Summary

To provide efficient verification, symbolic representation of the locations of a timed automaton using a BDD-based representation is the first step. The second step is a finite semantics to be able to use BDDs also for the representation of the continuous part of the model. In extension of [ABK+97,AMP98] we gave a formal definition of a discrete semantics for closed timed automata. We proved the correctness of using this discrete semantics for the computation of all reachable locations.

As the next step towards efficient reachability analysis we use the communication structure of the system to find good variable orderings. Based on the concepts described in this paper we implemented *Rabbit*. This is a tool for the BDD-based reachability analysis of closed timed automata as an extension of our existing model checker using matrices [BR00]. We developed a BDD library following the ideas of [BRB90]. In order to use the modeller's knowledge for finding a good variable ordering we use the modular modeling notation Cottbus Timed Automata [BR98]. This notation enables us to build hierarchical structures of timed automata-based models.

The main result of our paper is that we can compute good variable orderings based on an estimation for the BDD size and that the verification of timed automata using our technique is very efficient. Our experimental results show that for some classes of real-time models the reachability analysis seems to be of polynomial time and space complexity. Based on the communication structure, we can decide whether a model is good-natured or not for BDD-based reachability analysis. An open question is for which classes of models our technique performs well. Currently, we are modeling a production cell consisting of various transport belts and machines. We will also investigate the topic of combining reachability analysis with refinement checking to be able to verify larger models.

Acknowledgements. We thank Andreas Noack for his conceptual ideas and the implementation of the BDD engine, Michael Vogel for developing CTA versions of the case studies, and Heinrich Rust for his valuable hints for improvement of the paper.

References

[ABK+97]   Eugene Asarin, Marius Bozga, Alain Kerbat, Oded Maler, Amir Pnueli, and Anne Rasse. Data-structures for the verification of timed automata. In O. Maler, editor, *Proceedings of the 1st International Workshop on Hybrid and Real-Time Systems (HART'97)*, LNCS 1201, pages 346–360. Springer-Verlag, 1997.

[AD94]   Rajeev Alur and David L. Dill. A theory of timed automata. *Theoretical Computer Science*, 126:183–235, 1994.

[AMP98]   Eugene Asarin, Oded Maler, and Amir Pnueli. On discretization of delays in timed automata and digital circuits. In R. de Simone and D. Sangiorgi, editors, *Proceedings of the 9th International Conference on Concurrency Theory (CONCUR'98)*, LNCS 1466, pages 470–484. Springer-Verlag, 1998.

[ATB94]   Adnan Aziz, Serdar Tasiran, and Robert K. Brayton. BDD variable ordering for interacting finite state machines. In *Proceedings of the 31st ACM/IEEE Design Automation Conference (DAC'94)*, pages 283–288, 1994.

[BDM+98]   Marius Bozga, Conrado Daws, Oded Maler, Alfredo Olivero, Stavros Tripakis, and Sergio Yovine. Kronos: a model-checking tool for real-time systems. In A.J. Hu and M.Y. Vardi, editors, *Proceedings of the 10th International Conference on Computer-Aided Verification (CAV'98)*, LNCS 1427, pages 546–550. Springer-Verlag, 1998.

[BMPY97] Marius Bozga, Oded Maler, Amir Pnueli, and Sergio Yovine. Some progress on the symbolic verification of timed automata. In O. Grumberg, editor, *Proceedings of the 9th International Conference on Computer Aided Verification (CAV'97)*, LNCS 1254, pages 179–190. Springer-Verlag, 1997.

[BR98]   Dirk Beyer and Heinrich Rust. Modeling a production cell as a distributed real-time system with cottbus timed automata. In Hartmut König and Peter Langendörfer, editors, *Tagungsband Formale Beschreibungstechniken für verteilte Systeme (FBT'98)*, pages 148–159. Shaker Verlag, Aachen, June 1998.

[BR99]   Dirk Beyer and Heinrich Rust. A formalism for modular modelling of hybrid systems. Technical Report 10/1999, BTU Cottbus, 1999.

[BR00]   Dirk Beyer and Heinrich Rust. A tool for modular modelling and verification of hybrid systems. In Alfons Crespo and Joan Vila, editors, *Proceedings of the 25th IFAC/IFIP Workshop on Real-Time Programming 2000 (WRTP 2000)*. Elsevier Science, Oxford, 2000.

[BRB90]   Karl S. Brace, Richard L. Rudell, and Randal E. Bryant. Efficient implementation of a BDD package. In *Proceedings of the 27th ACM/IEEE Design Automation Conference (DAC'90)*, pages 40–45, 1990.

[GPV94]   Aleks Göllü, Anuj Puri, and Pravin Varaiya. Discretization of timed automata. In *Proceedings of the 33rd IEEE Conference on Decision and Control*, pages 957–958, 1994.

[HMP92]   Thomas A. Henzinger, Zohar Manna, and Amir Pnueli. What good are digital clocks? In *Proceedings of the 19th International Colloquium on Automata, Languages, and Programming (ICALP'92)*, LNCS 623, pages 545–558. Springer-Verlag, 1992.

[Lam87]   Leslie Lamport. A fast mutual exclusion algorithm. *ACM Transactions on Computer Systems*, 5(1):1–11, 1987.

[LLKS85] E. L. Lawler, J. K. Lenstra, A. H. G. Rinnooy Kan, and D. B. Shmoys, editors. *The Traveling Salesman Problem*. John Wiley & Sons, 1985.

[LPY97]   Kim G. Larsen, Paul Pettersson, and Wang Yi. UPPAAL in a Nutshell. *International Journal on Software Tools for Technology Transfer*, 1(1-2):134–152, October 1997.

[McM92]   Kenneth L. McMillan. *Symbolic Model Checking: an approach to the state explosion problem*. PhD thesis, School of Computer Science, Carnegie Mellon University, 1992. Technical report CMU-CS-92-131.

[RAB+95] Rajeev K. Ranjan, Adnan Aziz, Robert K. Brayton, Carl Pixley, and Bernhard Plessier. Efficient BDD algorithms for synthesizing and verifying finite state machines. In *Workshop Notes of the IEEE/ACM International Workshop on Logic Synthesis (IWLS'95)*, 1995.

[YBO+98] Bwolen Yang, Randal E. Bryant, David R. O'Hallaron, Armin Biere, Olivier Coudert, Geert Janssen, Rajeev K. Ranjan, and Fabio Somenzi. A performance study of BDD-based model checking. In Ganesh Gopalakrishnan and Phillip J. Windley, editors, *Proceedings of the 2nd International Conference on Formal Methods in Computer-Aided Design (FMCAD'98)*, LNCS 1522, pages 255–289. Springer-Verlag, 1998.

Serialising Parallel Processes in a Hardware/Software Partitioning Context

Leila Silva[1], Augusto Sampaio[2], and Geraint Jones[3]

[1] Departamento de Ciência da Computação e Estatística
Universidade Federal de Sergipe
CEP 49100-000, Aracaju - SE - Brazil
{lmas@di.ufpe.br, leila@ufs.br}
[2] Centro de Informática - Universidade Federal de Pernambuco
Caixa Postal 7851 - Cidade Universitária
CEP 50740-540 Recife - PE - Brazil
acas@di.ufpe.br
[3] Oxford University Computing Laboratory
Wolfson Building, Parks Road, Oxford, UK, OX1 3Q
Geraint.Jones@comlab.ox.ac.uk

Abstract. In this paper we present a strategy to serialise parallel processes in occam, in the context of a hardware/software partitioning approach. The strategy takes as input two parallel processes to serialise and applies algebraic rules to perform the serialisation. These rules are derived from the semantics of occam, which guarantees that the serialisation strategy preserves the semantics of the original parallel processes. In particular, the strategy ensures that deadlock is not introduced during the serialisation procedure.

1 Introduction

Embedded systems are dedicated to a specific target application and the majority of them are implemented using general programmable components (software components) and specific application components (hardware components). They can be found in a large variety of applications such as telecommunication systems and in systems for the defence of territory and the environment. Hardware/Software co-design is a new design paradigm for the joint specification, design and synthesis of mixed hardware/software systems.

In the last years several methodologies and tools supporting hardware/software co-design for embedded systems have been published (among them, [5,6,8, 16]). A crucial point in the co-design flow is how to perform the partitioning of a system into hardware and software components. In addition to the approaches mentioned above, many other algorithms have been proposed (as for example, [1,18]) to achieve this goal. Those approaches validate the partitioned system by simulation (for instance, [6,8,16]) or by using formal methods to prove that some desired properties of the original system are preserved after partitioning [5,11].

J.N. Oliveira and P. Zave (Eds.): FME 2001, LNCS 2021, pp. 344–363, 2001.

As embedded systems become increasingly complex and are often used in life critical situations, the validation of the partitioned systems is no longer sufficient to guarantee safety. Thus, the formal verification of the partitioning process is essential to ensure that the behaviour is preserved throughout the co-design flow.

In [2] Barros and Sampaio presented some initial ideas towards a partitioning approach with emphasis on correctness. This work was the seed of the PISH co-design system [3], which comprises all the steps from the partitioning of (an initial description of) the system into hardware and software components to the layout generation of the hardware. The PISH system attempts to address some key points not covered by the approaches mentioned before: the characterisation of the partitioning process as a program transformation task; the use of a same specification and reasoning mechanism (the occam language [15]); the use of formal verification techniques to assure the correctness of the partitioned system, and the automatic generation of the interface among hardware and software components, which is designed to be correct by construction.

The partitioning approach in PISH accepts as input an occam description (according to the grammar given in Section 2) and applies transformation rules to derive the description of the partitioned system. The main reason for choosing occam is that the algebraic laws of occam [17] can be used to carry out program transformation with the preservation of semantics. Furthermore, occam includes features to express parallelism and communication. Note that these are essential to express the result of the partitioning in the programming language itself: the hardware and software components generated by the partitioning are represented as communicating processes.

The PISH approach for partitioning verification comprises two main phases: *splitting* and *joining*. The aim of the splitting phase [20] is to transform the original description of the system into a description which is a set of *simple* parallel processes. These processes have a suitable form for the partitioning analysis regarding its implementation either in hardware or in software. Then, an algorithm is applied [1] to decide which processes will compose each component and the way they should be combined (in series or in parallel). By considering this decision, in the joining phase [21] these processes are effectively combined and the description of the partitioned system is generated. Both in the splitting and in the joining phases, algebraic rules are applied to perform the relevant transformations. These rules are all proved using the laws of occam, as shown in [22].

During the partitioning analysis, it may be required that processes originally in parallel be combined in series, due to economy of resources. Thus, a very important step of that approach is the elaboration of a strategy to serialise parallel processes; this is the central aim of this paper. Although [21] presents the main ideas of the joining strategy, it does not include any result about the serialisation of processes. Thus, the work presented here is the closing step of the methodology for partitioning verification published in [20] and [21].

The serialisation problem is extremely difficult in general, especially when the major concern is conceiving an automatic strategy which preserves correctness by construction. This has forced the approaches to serialisation reported in the literature to impose strong restrictions on the form of processes which are dealt with. As far as we are aware, the work closest to ours is that presented in [23], where Welch and Justo regard serialisation as an optimisation technique, applied automatically at the final stage of the development of parallel occam programs.

The occam processes considered in [23] are on the form of pre-defined templates. A template defines a particular kind of behaviour, that is, a reusable pattern of communication and synchronisation between the process and its environment. Assuming that these templates are deadlock-free, the strategy proceeds by combining them using the occam operators and ensuring that no deadlock is introduced. Our serialisation strategy accepts as input an arbitrary occam description (according to the grammar defined in Section 2) and the only restrictions we impose to the system are: it must be deadlock-free and each channel appears only twice in the description of the system (once for input and once for output).

This paper is organised as follows. Section 2 briefly describes the subset of occam adopted in this work, as well as presents some laws of occam and useful definitions. The approach to partitioning is briefly described in Section 3. Then, the serialisation strategy is presented in Section 4 and in Section 5 we discuss some implementation features of the strategy. A small example is presented in Section 6, for illustration purposes. Finally, in Section 7 we give the conclusions and some directions for future work.

2   A Language of Communicating Processes

The goal of this section is to present the subset of occam adopted in this work, defined by the BNF-style syntax given below. For convenience, we sometimes linearise occam syntax in this paper. For example, we may write $SEQ(P_1, P_2, \ldots, P_n)$ instead of the standard vertical style.

```
P ::= SKIP | STOP | x := e | ch ? x | ch ! e
    | IF (c₁ P₁, c₂ P₂, ..., cₙ Pₙ) | ALT (c₁&g₁ P₁, c₂&g₂ P₂,..., cₙ&gₙ Pₙ)
    | SEQ (P₁, P₂, ..., Pₙ) | PAR (P₁, P₂, ..., Pₙ)
    | VAR x: P | CHAN ch: P
```

In what follows we give a short description of these commands. The SKIP construct has no effect and always terminates successfully. STOP is the canonical deadlock process which can make no further progress. The commands x := e, ch?x and ch!e are assignment, input and output commands, respectively; the communication in occam is synchronous. The commands IF and ALT select a process to execute, based on a condition (IF) or on a guard (ALT). The commands SEQ and PAR denote the sequential and parallel composition of processes, respectively. Processes within a PAR constructor run concurrently, with the possibility of communication among them, and cannot share variables. The constructs VAR and CHAN declare local variables and channels, respectively. Here we avoid mentioning a particular type for the declared variables or channels. A more detailed description of these commands can be found, for example, in [15].

To conduct the partitioning strategy we have extended occam syntax with some new constructs, among them, PARhw, PARsw, PARpar, PARser, PARparFail and PARserFail. These constructs have no semantic effect and can be regarded as annotations added to the occam description. The aim of these constructs is to indicate a hardware (PARhw) or a software (PARsw) component and the way the processes should be combined in each component, that is, in parallel (PARpar) or in series (PARser). The two last constructs indicates that a parallelisation (PARparFail) or a serialisation (PARserFail) of processes, required by the partitioning algorithm, cannot be implemented, as it violates the semantics of the original description.

2.1   Some Algebraic Laws and Useful Definitions

As mentioned in Section 1 occam obeys a set of algebraic laws [17] which can be used to carry out program transformation with the preservation of semantics. Here we present a very small subset of them. Each law is given a number and a name suggestive of its use, and the operational justification for each law is taken from [17].

The SKIP process is the identity of sequential composition.

Law 1 (*SEQ-SKIP unit*) SEQ(SKIP, P) = SEQ(P, SKIP) = P

The SEQ operator runs a number of processes in sequence. If it has no arguments it simply terminates. Otherwise it runs the first argument until it terminates and then runs the rest in sequence. Therefore it obeys the following associative law:

Law 2 (*SEQ assoc*) SEQ(P_1, P_2,..., P_n) = SEQ(P_1, SEQ(P_2, P_3,..., P_n)).

A PAR command terminates as soon as all its components have; the empty PAR terminates immediately. Furthermore, PAR is an associative operator.

Law 3 (*PAR-SKIP unit*) PAR(P, SKIP) = PAR(P) = P

Law 4 (*PAR assoc*) PAR(P_1, P_2,..., P_n) = PAR(P_1, PAR(P_2, P_3,..., P_n))

It is possible to use the previous laws to transform all occurrences of SEQ and PAR operators within a program to binary form. This is why the next laws are cast in binary form. The PAR operator is also commutative.

Law 5 (*PAR sym*) PAR(P_1, P_2) = PAR(P_2, P_1)

The declaration of variables obeys a set of laws. Here we illustrate only one of them, the one which distribute VAR over the first argument of a SEQ.

Law 6 (*VAR-SEQ 1*)
`SEQ(VAR x: P, Q) = VAR x: SEQ(P, Q)`, provided x does not occur in Q.

As we have mentioned, the new constructs have no semantic effect and this fact is captured by algebraic laws, not given in [17]. Thus, for example,

Law 7 (*PARser unit*) `PARser P = PAR P`

Law 8 (*PARserFail unit*) `PARserFail P = PAR P`

Throughout this text we use the following definitions.

Definition 1 (*Free and Bound Variables*) *If* P *is an occam process and* x *is a variable, we say that an occurrence of* x *in* P *is free if it is not in the scope of any declaration of* x *in* P, *and bound otherwise.*

Definition 2 (*Variable (Channel) Disjoint*) *Two processes* P_1 *and* P_2 *are variable (channel)-disjoint if they have no free variable (channel) in common.*

Definition 3 (*Variable-independent Processes*) *Two processes* P_1 *and* P_2 *are variable-independent if no free variable assigned by* P_1 *is free in* P_2, *and, on the other hand, no free variable assigned by* P_2 *is free in* P_1.

Definition 4 (*Independent and Disjoint Processes*) *Two processes are independent if they are variable-independent and channel-disjoint. Two processes are disjoint if they are variable- and channel-disjoint.*

Definition 5 (*Subprocess and Elementary Subprocess*) *Let* P_i *be a process included into a sequential, parallel, conditional or* ALT *process* P. *We say that* P_i *is a subprocess of* P. *The subprocess* P_i *is elementary if either it includes at most one communication command or it includes at most one* ALT *construct, having communication commands only as its input guards and no other communication commands in the subprocess.*

3   The Partitioning Approach

The general structure of the approach to partitioning in which this work is inserted is depicted in Figure 1. The shaded boxes represent the relevant phases of partitioning verification. The phase of definition of components is related to the non-functional issues of the partitioning (the efficient mapping of the system into hardware/software components). The implementation phase comprises the tasks of the co-design flow performed after partitioning, among them, hardware synthesis, software compilation, prototyping and co-simulation.

The splitting phase accepts as input an arbitrary occam description, according to the grammar given in Section 2, and transforms this description into a description in the form of Definition 6. As mentioned in Section 1, this description must satisfy two restrictions: to be deadlock-free and to allow only one point of synchronisation, for each channel.

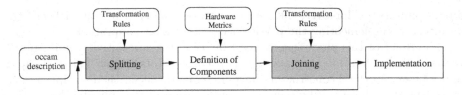

Fig. 1. The partitioning phases.

Definition 6 (*Splitting Normal Form*) *A process is in splitting normal form if it has the structure below:*

CHAN ch_1, ch_2,..., ch_m: PAR(P_1, P_2,..., P_r)

where each P_i, *for* $1 \leq i \leq r$, *is simple.*

Here we will not detail the form of simple processes, nor discuss their suitability to hardware/software partitioning (see [20,22]). For this work it is relevant to mention that ALT constructs are in a *simple* form if they include communication commands only as input guards. If a conditional includes communication commands and is in a *simple* form, it has two branches, of the form IF(c Q, TRUE SKIP). If Q involves communication it can be: an input command, an output command or an ALT construct in the simple form.

To achieve the normal form, a reduction strategy is necessary [20]. This strategy applies algebraic rules (derived from the basic laws of occam) in two main steps. In the first step, ALT and IF constructs are transformed into the simple form mentioned above. In the second step, basically the sequential processes are put in parallel. As original sequential processes may be data-dependent and as parallel processes in occam cannot share variables, we have to introduce communication to perform this transformation. The splitting strategy can be summarised by the following theorem, proved in [20,22]:

Theorem 1 (*Splitting Strategy*) *An arbitrary program* P *(according to the syntax defined in Section 2), deadlock-free and allowing only one point of synchronisation for each channel, can be reduced to the splitting normal form*

CHAN ch_1, ch_2,..., ch_m: PAR(P_1, P_2, ..., P_r)

where each P_i *is simple.*

The description generated by the splitting phase is the input of the phase of definition of components, where heuristics are applied to decide which simple processes will compose the hardware and the software components, as well as in which way these processes should be combined (in series or in parallel). This decision is guided exclusively by implementation metrics, which consider various features of the description, such as non-determinism, mutual exclusion, communication costs, concurrent behaviour, data-dependency and functional similarity among processes. Moreover, the tradeoff between the area and the delay of the architecture implementing the partitioned system is also appraised.

The result of this phase is expressed by using the associativity and commutativity of the PAR operator and the new constructors PARhw, PARsw, PARpar and PARser. As these constructors have no semantic effect, the description generated by this phase can be seen as a permutation of the splitting description rearranged and extended with some useful annotations for the joining phase.

It is important to notice that this phase is responsible only for determining which processes should be combined (in series or in parallel) to form the components, but it does not actually carry out the necessary transformations to combine the processes. These transformations are performed by the joining phase. Like the splitting phase, it applies algebraic rules to effectively combine the processes of the components, according to the way established by the phase of definition of components. During the combination procedure, the communication introduced by the splitting phase is eliminated, whenever possible. It is important to remark that if the phase of definition of components requires a transformation which violates the semantics of the original description, this transformation is not performed by the joining phase and an error is annotated for future designer analysis. The joining strategy can also be summarised by a theorem, proved in [22].

Theorem 2 (*Joining Strategy*) *A program* P *in the splitting normal form*

> CHAN ch_1, ch_2,..., ch_m: PAR(P_1, P_2, ..., P_r),

*with some annotations (*PARhw, PARsw, PARpar *and* PARser*), can be reduced to the joining normal form*

> CHAN ch_1, ch_2,..., ch_s: PAR(Q_1, Q_2, ..., Q_t),

where $s \leq m$, $t \leq r$ *and each* P_i, $1 \leq i \leq r$, *belongs to exactly one* Q_j, $1 \leq j \leq t$. *Moreover, the reduced description has two characteristics: (1) either follows what was established by the phase of definition of components or includes an indication of an error of the requirements, and (2) the communication and variables introduced by the splitting phase are eliminated, whenever this transformation preserves the semantics of the splitting description.*

4   The Serialisation Strategy

As mentioned before, during the phase of definition of components it may be required that processes originally in parallel be serialised, due to economy of resources of the final chip.

To motivate the serialisation problem, consider the fragment of program PAR(ch_1?x, ch_2?y). To serialise these processes, it is necessary to know how the channels ch_1 and ch_2 interact with the environment (the rest of the program). If the environment has the form SEQ(ch_1!e, ch_2!f), ch_1 synchronises before ch_2, and, in this case, the parallel command can be transformed

into SEQ($\mathtt{ch_1?x}$, $\mathtt{ch_2?y}$). On the other hand, if the environment has the form
SEQ($\mathtt{ch_2!f}$, $\mathtt{ch_1!e}$), the transformation must be SEQ($\mathtt{ch_2?y}$, $\mathtt{ch_1?x}$). Furthermore, if $\mathtt{ch_1}$ and $\mathtt{ch_2}$ are in parallel in the environment, the order of serialisation
is irrelevant. In general, the serialisation problem can be stated as follows:

> Let P be an occam program. Given two parallel processes of P, say P_x and
> P_y, we want to find a sequential order of execution of the processes P_x
> and P_y that preserves the semantics avoiding the introduction of deadlock
> in P.

Before introducing the serialisation rules (Section 4.1), as well as the algorithm which guides the rules application (Section 4.2), we will give a more precise
definition of environment. The environment is the context into which the parallel processes to serialise are immersed. In [22, Chapter 8] it is shown that it is
always possible to express the environment as a process E which runs in parallel
with the fragment of program P we want to serialise. Thus, the serialisation rules
which depend on the context have the form:

PAR(P, E) = PAR(Q, E),   provided E can satisfy S.

where S specifies, as defined in what follows, a list of restrictions on the order of
execution of communication commands inside P, in order to guarantee that the
transformation, from P to Q, does not introduce deadlock. The condition of the
above equation expresses the fact that the environment E (running in parallel
with P and Q) must offer the opportunity of a synchronisation which satisfies the
synchronisation restrictions S, given in the sequel. For conciseness reasons, we
abbreviate rules in that form to $P =_{(E,S)} Q$.

Definition 7 (*Synchronisation Restriction*) *Let P be an occam program. Let P_j
and P_k be two independent processes of P. We call by restriction $P_j P_k$ the following
constraint in the order of synchronisation of the channels used by P_j and P_k
with the environment E: the channels used by P_j must synchronise before any
channel of P_k. In particular, if either P_j or P_k does not include a communication
command, we say that the restriction $P_j P_k$ is void.*

Considering the previous example, let P_1 be $\mathtt{ch_1?x}$ and let P_2 be $\mathtt{ch_2?y}$. If
the environment has either the form SEQ($\mathtt{ch_1!e}$, $\mathtt{ch_2!f}$) or PAR($\mathtt{ch_1!e}$, $\mathtt{ch_2!f}$)
it satisfies restriction $P_1 P_2$, and thus P_1 and P_2 can be serialised in this order.
Observe that when the environment is a parallel process, it offers as one of the
possibilities the synchronisation which satisfies $P_1 P_2$. In the sequential case, this
is the only way the environment can synchronise.

4.1   The Serialisation Rules

The serialisation rules can be derived from the basic laws of occam given in
[17] and from Lemma 1 (*PAR-SEQ result*) (proved in [22, Appendix A]), which
is a generalisation of a similar result for disjoint processes presented in [10,
Chapter 7].

352   L. Silva, A. Sampaio, and G. Jones

Lemma 1 (*PAR-SEQ result*)

$$\text{PAR}(\text{SEQ}(Q_1,\ Q_2),\ \text{SEQ}(T_1,\ T_2)) =_{(E,(Q_1T_2,T_1Q_2))} \text{SEQ}(\text{PAR}(Q_1,\ T_1),\ \text{PAR}(Q_2,\ T_2))$$

This result changes the way of execution of the processes Q_1 and T_2 and also Q_2 and T_1. Observe, for example, that Q_1 and T_2 execute in parallel on the left-hand side of the equation and in sequence on the right-hand side. To do this transformation, Q_1 and T_2, as well as Q_2 and T_1 must be independent processes. Moreover, the environment must offer the opportunity of a synchronisation with all channels of Q_1 before synchronising with any channel of T_2 and with all channels of Q_2 before synchronising with any channel of T_1. Three immediate corollaries of this result are given in what follows.

Corollary 1 (*PAR-SEQ derived - 1*)

$$\text{PAR}(Q_1,\ \text{SEQ}(T_1,\ T_2)) =_{(E,Q_1T_2)} \text{SEQ}(\text{PAR}(Q_1,\ T_1),\ T_2)$$

Corollary 2 (*PAR-SEQ derived - 2*)

$$\text{PAR}(\text{SEQ}(Q_1,\ Q_2),\ T_1) =_{(E,Q_1T_1)} \text{SEQ}(Q_1,\ \text{PAR}(Q_2,\ T_1))$$

Corollary 3 (*PAR-SEQ derived - 3*)

$$\text{PAR}(Q_1,\ T_1) =_{(E,Q_1T_1)} \text{SEQ}(Q_1,\ T_1).$$

In this text we implicitly use Law 7 (*PARser unit*) and, therefore, all results applied to the PAR operator can immediately be applied to the PARser construct. Thus, for example, we can refer to Lemma 1 (*PAR-SEQ result*), when the PAR construct is, in fact, a PARser construct.

Now, let P_x and P_y be two parallel processes for which the serialisation is required. The easy case of the serialisation procedure happens when the processes P_x and P_y are independent and satisfy either the restriction P_xP_y or P_yP_x. In this case, Corollary 3 (*PAR-SEQ derived - 3*) (applied to a PARser construct) is enough to serialise P_x and P_y. (This is the case of the fragment of program shown previously.)

When applying Corollary 3 (*PAR-SEQ derived - 3*) to serialise processes P_x and P_y in PARser(P_x, P_y), the symmetry of the PARser operator should be applied to the parallel construct, with the aim of exploring both possibilities of serialisation, that is P_x either before or after P_y. Similar comments will be omited in the remainder of this text.

If this result cannot be applied, the proposed strategy performs a *gradual serialisation* of P_x and P_y. Figure 2 shows a simple example of a gradual serialisation of processes P_u and P_v, where the environment is represented by process P_z. Observe that as the channels of P_u and P_v synchronise in an interleaved way with P_z, Corollary 3 (*PAR-SEQ derived - 3*) cannot be applied (the restriction P_uP_v (or P_vP_u) is violated). Nevertheless, we can perform the serialisation of P_u

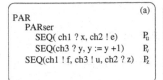
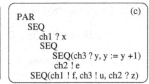

Fig. 2. An example of a gradual serialisation of P_u and P_v.

and P_v by exhaustively serialising their subprocesses, according to the order of execution of the channels in P_z, as shown in Figure 2(b) and (c).

To perform the gradual serialisation of processes, firstly laws 2 (*SEQ assoc*), 1 (*SEQ-SKIP unit*), 4 (PAR assoc) and 3 (*PAR-SKIP unit*) are used to transform into a binary form all occurrences of SEQ and PAR inside P_x and P_y. (This is why each of the remainder of the rules of this section is cast in binary form.) In addition, to simplify the proposed serialisation rules, the laws of declaration (given in [17]) are used to increase the scope of the possible local variables of P_x and P_y to widest scope.

To avoid the introduction of deadlock when P_x and P_y are gradually serialised, all internal synchronisations of these processes must be solved first; this is why we need to introduce the following rule:

Rule 1 (*internal serialisations*)
PARser(F(PAR(Q₁, Q₂)), P₂) = PARser(F(PARser(Q₁, Q₂)), P₂),
provided Q_1 and Q_2 are not channel-disjoint.

The role of the previous rule is to indicate, for future serialisation, the processes that share channels (Q_1 and Q_2) into P_1 (represented by F(PAR(Q₁, Q₂))).

To solve internal serialisations of P_x and P_y, the strategy is applied recursively. To guarantee that the internal serialisations are solved first, the remainder of the rules of this section requires that the processes to serialise do not include any PARser construct. This is also required when we apply Lemma 1 (*PAR-SEQ result*) and its corollaries.

After performing these preliminary transformations, the rules for effectively serialising P_x and P_y are applied. The proposed strategy follows an inductive approach and thus we have *base* and *intermediate* cases. Corollary 3 (*PAR-SEQ derived - 3*) can be considered the base case (0). In addition, we have the following base cases:

- (1) the first subprocess of P_x to serialise is channel-disjoint from P_y and, as a consequence, independent of P_y;
- (2) the first subprocess of P_x to serialise synchronises with P_y.

To solve the base case (1), Corollary 2 (*PAR-SEQ derived - 2*) and Rule 2 (*serialisation - 1*) can be applied.

Rule 2 (*serialisation-1*)

$$\texttt{PARser(PAR(Q_1, Q_2), T_1)} =_{(E, (Q_1Q_2, Q_1T_1))} \texttt{SEQ(Q_1, PARser(Q_2, T_1))}$$

provided the processes involved do not include any PARser process.

Rule 2 (*serialisation-1*) is applied when one process of the PARser construct is a parallel process. The first subprocess to execute is Q_1 and the environment must offer the opportunity of a synchronisation with Q_1 before synchronising with any channel of T_1 and Q_2. In fact, the transformation captured by this rule can be achieved by applying Corollary 3 (*PAR-SEQ derived - 3*) to put Q_1 and Q_2 in sequence and after Corollary 2 (*PAR-SEQ derived - 2*) to serialise Q_1. Nevertheless, due to the expressiveness of this transformation we prefer to capture it as a new rule.

To solve the base case (2), we need to introduce synchronisation rules, given in Section 4.1.

If the first subprocess, say Q, (of either P_x or P_y) to serialise includes more than one communication command it may happen that Corollary 2 (*PAR-SEQ derived - 2*) and Rule 2 (*serialisation - 1*) cannot be applied, due to a violation of the synchronisation restriction expressed in such results. In this case, we need to unnest the first elementary subprocess of Q, in order to apply one result for the base cases. As this elementary subprocess of Q may be inside several levels of SEQ and PAR constructs, we need to exhaustively apply the following results:

- Law 2 (*SEQ assoc*) to transform a pattern of the form SEQ(SEQ(Q_1, Q_2), Q_3) into SEQ(Q_1, SEQ(Q_2, Q_3));
- Rule 3 (*serialisation-2*), given in what follows, to transform a pattern of the form SEQ(PAR(Q_1, Q_2), Q_3) into SEQ(Q_1, SEQ(Q_2, Q_3));
- Corollary 2 (*PAR-SEQ derived - 2*) to transform a pattern of the form PAR(SEQ(Q_1, Q_2), Q_3) into SEQ(Q_1, PAR(Q_2, Q_3));
- Rule 2 (*serialisation-1*) (applied to the PAR construct instead to a PARser construct) to transform a pattern of the form PAR(PAR(Q_1, Q_2), Q_3) into SEQ(Q_1, PAR(Q_2, Q_3)).

Rule 3 (*serialisation - 2*)

$$\texttt{SEQ(PAR(Q_1, Q_2), Q_3)} =_{(E, Q_1Q_2)} \texttt{SEQ(Q_1, SEQ(Q_2, Q_3))}$$

provided none of the processes involves a PARser construct.

Rule 3 (*serialisation-2*) can be derived from Corollary 3 (*PAR-SEQ derived - 3*) and Law 2 (*SEQ assoc*) and follows similar explanation of these results.

Notice that, for the four patterns mentioned above, the depth in which Q_1 is nested decreases by one, after the transformations; this is why the exhaustive application of these rules is able to bring Q_1 to the most external level, whenever possible.

The serialisation strategy cannot be concluded successfully due to a violation of a synchronisation restriction (see [22] for a more detailed discussion).

This can happen basically in two situations: (1) at least one process to serialise includes an ALT construct interacting in a particular way with the environment and (2) the processes to serialise have an apparent mutual dependency. In the first situation, in the environment, the communication commands which include the channels (guards) of the ALT construct execute in an interleaved way with the communication commands which include the channels of the other process to serialise. In the second situation, the order of execution of some communication commands included in the processes to serialise is reverse to the order of execution of communication commands which include these channels, in the environment. In this case, as we assume that the system is deadlock free, necessarily such channels belong to mutual exclusive processes. When these situations happen, we say that the serialisation strategy *fails* and Law 8 (*PARserFail unit*) is applied to indicate such a failure and to finish the serialisation procedure. In the context of our partitioning approach, the required serialisation will be revised by the designer in a later stage of the partitioning flow.

The Synchronisation Rules. Here we can assume that the first subprocess (T_1) to execute of P_y synchronises with the first subprocess (Q_1) to execute of P_x. The subprocesses of P_x and P_y that execute before the synchronisation of P_x and P_y are already serialised, by applying the intermediate and base rules before presented, otherwise a failure has been detected.

As the description is binary, PARser(P_x, P_y) can have one of the following forms (with possibly changing the roles of P_x and P_y), where SEQ/PAR means either a sequential or a parallel process in this context:

> F1: PARser(Q_1, T_1);
> F2: PARser(Q_1, SEQ/PAR(T_1, T_2));
> F3: PARser(SEQ/PAR(Q_1, Q_2), SEQ/PAR(T_1, T_2)).

Forms F1 and F2 are particular cases of Form F3 (due to laws 3 (*PAR-SKIP unit*) and 1 (*SEQ-SKIP unit*)). Thus, here we present only the synchronisation rules for Form F3.

The subprocesses Q_1 and T_1 can be: an output command; an input command; an ALT command; a conditional including an output command; a conditional including an input command; or a conditional including an ALT command. In fact, we need to introduce rules to deal with all possible pairs of these commands. Nevertheless, here we present only the rules involving communication commands inside conditionals and ALT constructs, as the rules for the other possible pair of commands are particular cases of such rules. The full set of synchronisation rules can be found in [22, Chapter 6]. Moreover, we present the rules for the case in which P_x and P_y are sequential processes. The rules for the cases in which one of these processes is a parallel process are similar. In the presentation of such rules we abuse the notation here adopted by expressing the channel, instead of the process, in the synchronisation restriction.

Rule 4 (*sync. IF-in-IF-out-F3*)

$$\text{PARser}(\text{SEQ}(\text{IF}(c_1 \text{ ch ! e, TRUE SKIP}), Q_2),$$
$$\text{SEQ}(\text{IF}(c_2 \text{ ch ? x, TRUE SKIP}), T_2))$$

$=_{DF(E,chQ_2,chT_2)}$

$$\text{SEQ}(\text{IF }(c_1 \text{ x := e, TRUE SKIP}), \text{PARser}(Q_2, T_2))$$
$$\text{provided } c_1 \oplus c_2 = \text{TRUE}.$$

The meaning of this rule is very simple; it expresses the fact that the effect of the synchronisation on the left-hand side of the rule is the assignment of e to x on the right-hand side. Observe that if the program is deadlock free and admits only one point of synchronisation the condition $c_1 \oplus c_2 = \text{TRUE}$ (the symbol $\oplus$ stands for exclusive or) is always valid. This also implies that we can choose between c_1 and c_2 to express the condition on the right-hand side of this rule.

Rule 5 (*sync. IF-out-IF-ALT-F3*)

$$\text{PARser}$$
$$\text{SEQ/PAR}(\text{IF}(c_1 \text{ ch}_1 \text{ ! e, TRUE SKIP}), Q_2)$$
$$\text{SEQ/PAR}(\text{IF}(c_2 \text{ ALT}(b_1 \text{ \& ch}_1?x_1 T_1', \text{ ALT}_{k=2}^n b_k\&g_k T_k'),$$
$$\text{TRUE SKIP}), T_2)$$

$=_{DF(E,ch_1Q_2,ch_1T_2,T'_1Q_2)}$

$$\text{VAR d :}$$
$$\text{SEQ}(\text{SEQ}(d := c_1, \text{ IF } (d \text{ SEQ}(x := e, T_1'), \text{ TRUE SKIP})),$$
$$\text{PARser}(Q_2, \text{ SEQ/PAR}(\text{IF}(\neg d \text{ IF } (c_2 \text{ ALT}_{k=2}^n b_k\&g_k T_k',$$
$$\text{TRUE SKIP}), \text{ TRUE SKIP}), T_2)))$$
$$\text{provided } c_1 \oplus b_1 = \text{TRUE}, \ c_1 \oplus b_k = \text{FALSE}, \text{ for each k},$$
$$c_1 \Rightarrow c_2, \text{ d is a fresh variable and } Q_2 \text{ and } T_2 \text{ do not}$$
$$\text{include any PARser process}.$$

The effect of this rule is also to replace communication with assignment. Observe that as we have assumed that the system is deadlock free originally and has only one point of synchronisation, then necessarily $c_1 \oplus b_1$ always evaluates to TRUE. Moreover, $c_1 \oplus b_k$ is necessarily FALSE. This implies that when c_1 is FALSE, another guard of the ALT construct can be satisfied. Notice also that the case in which c_1 is TRUE and b_1 is FALSE is not possible, as it means that the system would be in deadlock originally. In addition, the process T_1' can modify the value of a variable included in c_1. This is why we need to introduce the new variable d.

To illustrate the proof style of the serialisation rules we develop the proof of Rule 2 (*serialisation-1*). We start with the left-hand side of the equation, and by applying some basic laws and lemmas we obtain the right-hand side.

$$\text{PARser}(\text{PAR}(Q_1,\ Q_2),\ T_1)$$
$$=_{(E,Q_1Q_2)} \{Corollary\ 3(PAR-SEQ\ derived-3)\}$$
$$\text{PARser}(\text{SEQ}(Q_1,\ Q_2),\ T_1)$$
$$= \quad \{Laws\ 1\ (SEQ-SKIP\ unit)\ and\ 7\ (PARser\ unit)\}$$
$$\text{PAR}(\text{SEQ}(Q_1,\ Q_2),\ \text{SEQ}(\text{SKIP},\ T_1))$$
$$=_{(E,Q_1T_1)} \{Lemma\ 1\ (PAR-SEQ\ result)\}$$
$$\text{SEQ}(\text{PAR}(Q_1,\ \text{SKIP}),\ \text{PAR}(Q_2,\ T_1))$$
$$= \quad \{Laws\ 3\ (PAR-SKIP\ unit)\ and\ 7\ (PARser\ unit)\}$$
$$\text{SEQ}(Q_1,\ \text{PARser}(Q_2,\ T_1))\ \square$$

4.2 The Serialisation Algorithm

In what follows we give the algorithm that guides the application of the rules of Section 4.1, using a pseudo functional language, similar to SML [9]. This algorithm basically applies the rules in the order presented in Section 4.1. Thus, initially Corollary 3 (*PAR-SEQ derived - 3*) is applied. After that, the results for preparing the processes involved in the serialisation procedure are applied. Next, the results for the base and the intermediate cases are exhaustively applied. As the synchronisation rules may introduce variables, the laws of declaration are again applied after the application of the results for the base cases. Finally, if a PARser construct remains, Law 8 (*PARserFail unit*) is applied to indicate that the serialisation fails.

All functions accept the global structure p that represents the processes to serialise. Each rule and law applied in the serialisation strategy executes only once. If p is transformed, the application of the rules and laws returns the transformed process; otherwise, it returns p unaltered.

To apply exhaustively one function (which may be the implementation of one rule or law) the function fix is used. This function is implemented as follows:

```
fun fix name_of_function arg =
  let val arg' = name_of_function arg
  in if arg = arg' then arg else fix name_of_function arg'
  end;
```

where name_of_function is the name of the function to apply and arg is the argument of that function. For legibility, we use abbreviations to exhaustively apply each function. For example, to apply exhaustively Rule 2 (*serialisation-1*), function apply_serialisation_1 is introduced.

```
fun apply_serialisation_1 p = fix seq_1 p;
```

Function apply_exhaustively receives a list of functions and an argument. These functions are executed in the order given. If the argument is transformed by the application of one of these functions, apply_exhaustively is called recursively; otherwise the argument is returned unaltered. For example,

```
apply_exhaustively [apply_SEQ_assoc, apply_PAR_assoc] p
```

has the effect of applying Law 2 (*SEQ assoc*) exhaustively and, after that, Law 4 (*PAR assoc*) is also applied exhaustively. If p is transformed during the application of these laws, apply_exhaustively is called recursively and, as consequence, these laws are again exhaustively applied, in this order; otherwise apply_exhaustively returns p unaltered.

The symbol ∘ stands for function composition. For example, the function serialisation, at the beginning of the description of the algorithm, implements the serialisation strategy and is defined as a composition of functions easy_case, binary_description, gradual_serialisation and failure, in this order. This means that firstly the argument p is applied to function easy_case. The result of the application of this function, say p', serves as argument to the application of function binary_description, and so on.

Algorithm 1 (Serialisation Strategy)

```
fun serialisation_strategy p =
  (failure ∘ gradual_serialisation ∘ binary_description ∘ easy_case) p;

fun ease_case p = (PAR_SEQ_derived_3 ∘ PARser_sym ∘ PAR_SEQ_derived_3) p;

fun binary_description p =
  if p is still a PARser process then
    apply_exaustively[apply_SEQ_assoc, apply_SEQ_SKIP_unit,
                      apply_PAR_assoc, apply_PAR_SKIP_unit,
                      apply_laws_of_declaration,
                      apply_internal_serialisation] p
  else p;

fun gradual_serialisation p=
  apply_exhaustively[apply_base_cases012, apply_laws_of_declaration
                     apply_intermediate_rules] p;

(* the function PAR_SEQ_der_2 applies Corollary PAR-SEQ derived - 2, in
   conjunction with Law PAR sym, as in function ease_case. The same
   comment is valid for the other rules. *)

fun base_cases012 p =
  apply_exhaustively[apply_ease_case, apply_PAR_SEQ_der_2,
                     apply_Serialisation_1,
                     apply_synchronisation_rules] p;


fun intermediate p =
  apply_exhaustively[apply_SEQ_assoc, apply_Serialisation_2,
                     apply_PAR_SEQ_der_2, apply_Serialisation_1] p;

fun failure p = apply_PARserFail_unit p;
```

Complexity. This algorithm costs $O((m/2)^2.c\_r)$ (see [22]), where m is the number of elementary subprocesses of P_x and P_y, and c_r is the cost of the implementation of one rule or law.

5   Implementation Features of the Serialisation Strategy

The aim of this section is to briefly discuss some implementation issues related to the applicability of the serialisation strategy (see [22] for a detailed discussion).

The proposed serialisation rules are applied only if the environment can satisfy the restriction imposed on the order of synchronisation of events. Thus, when implementing the rules, we need to introduce an automatic mechanism to identify such an order. A simple possibility is to derive a graph from the environment description, called here *sequence graph*, defined in the sequel.

Definition 8 (*Sequence Graph*) *Let* P *be an occam process deadlock free and allowing only one point of synchronisation for each channel. The sequence graph of* P*, denoted by* $GS(P)$ *is a directed graph whose set of vertices is the set of channel variables of* P*. Two vertices* ch_1 *and* ch_2 *in* $GS(P)$ *are connected by a directed path from* ch_1 *to* ch_2 *if and only if* ch_1 *must synchronise before* ch_2 *in* P*.*

Thus, to identify if restriction P_xP_y is satisfied by the environment E, it is enough to generate $GS(E)$ and to check the following condition:

$$\forall\ ch_i{\in}P_x,\ ch_j{\in}P_y\ .\ \texttt{not(path(}ch_j,\ ch_i,\ \textit{GS(E)}\texttt{))}.$$

where **path** is a function which returns TRUE if there exists a path from ch_j to ch_i in *GS(E)*; otherwise, it returns FALSE. This function may be implemented by using the classic depth-first search algorithm, by taking ch_j as the root of the search.

The algorithm to derive GS of an environment E is given in [22], as well as a proof of its correctness. Here it is enough to mention that there are only two constructs in E that generate edges (mandatory sequences of synchronisation) in GS:

1. the sequential operator (SEQ), which by definition imposes order on the execution of processes included by it;
2. the ALT operator, where the channel belonging to a given guard executes in sequence with the channels included in the process activated when that guard is satisfied.

Figure 3(a) and (b) show an example of an environment and the associated sequence graph, respectively. Notice that, for example, as the channels ch_1 and ch_7 are structured in parallel (and thus have no mandatory sequence of execution), there is no path connecting ch_1 and ch_7 in GS. The same reasoning is applied to channels ch_5 and ch_6, inside the conditional command, and channels ch_2 and ch_4, inside distinct branches of the ALT construct. Nevertheless, notice that channels ch_2 and ch_3 are linked by an edge, as the execution of channel

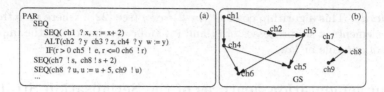

Fig. 3. An example of a program and its associated sequence graph.

ch_3 depends on the execution of channel ch_2. A similar situation happens, for example, to channels ch_1 and ch_2; the channel ch_1 must execute before the channel ch_2, due to the sequential operator. In fact, the conditional and the ALT constructs of this example are not in a simple form. In the context of our approach, processes for which the serialisation is not required (processes belonging to the environment) can include conditionals and ALT constructs in a more flexible form. These commands are encapsulated by a new constructor, with no semmantic effect, not given in Section 2. For conciseness reasons, we have omited the discussion about the form of all simple processes considered here.

Although edges in GS could only be generated by the SEQ and the ALT operators, a path in GS can also be generated by the parallel operator, if two parallel processes synchronise by a given channel. This is the case of the path from ch_7 to ch_9 in Figure 3(b): the synchronisation through channel ch_8 generates the referred path.

6   A Simple Example

Consider Figure 4, which shows the application of the serialisation strategy to processes P and Q. Process E represents the environment. In (a) the description of the processes is given and the sequence graph of the environment, $GS(E)$, is depicted in (b). Frames (c) to (f) shows the transformations of the original PARser construct during the several steps of the strategy. Observe that the conditional of P and the ALT construct of Q are in a reduced form. Thus, the rules of the first step of the strategy are not applied. Then, the description of P and Q is made binary by applying Law 2 (*SEQ assoc*). Next, as ch_1 is the source of all paths in $GS(E)$, Corollary 2 (*PAR-SEQ derived - 2*) is applied to serialise the sequential process of P which includes ch_1, as shown in (c). Now, observe that channel ch_2 is common to the conditional and the ALT constructs. Thus, a particular case of Rule 5 (*sync. IF-out-IF-ALT-F3*) is applied, as shown in (d). After that, Corollary 2 (*PAR-SEQ derived - 2*) is applied to serialise the process which includes ch_3 (see (e)) and Corollary 3 (*PAR-SEQ derived - 3*) is finally applied to serialise the processes which include ch_4 and ch_5 (see (f)).

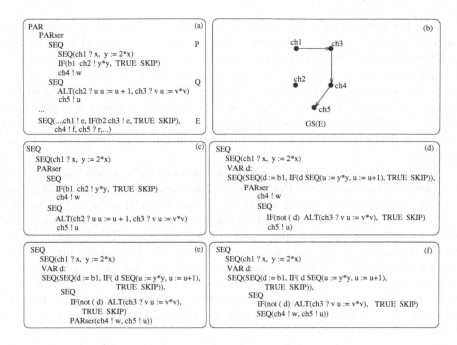

Fig. 4. A simple example of the application of the serialisation strategy.

7   Conclusions

The main contribution of this paper is to present a formal strategy for serialising parallel processes in the context of hardware/software co-design. This strategy is the closing step of the works [20] and [21], which presents an innovative approach to partitioning verification. The formalism used is occam and the algebraic laws which define its semantics. The serialisation of parallel processes is performed by applying algebraic rules, all of them proved from the basic laws of occam, as illustrated here and shown in more detail in [22].

Although this work is inserted into the PISH co-design project, the proposed approach to partitioning verification (which includes the serialisation strategy presented here) is completely orthogonal to the decision about which parts of the system will be implemented in hardware or in software, as well as the way the processes should be combined. This means that the splitting [20], the joining [21] and the serialisation strategy can be used in conjunction with any algorithm for partitioning, provided the internal reasoning mechanism is occam. Moreover, the approach is independent of a possible evolution of the target architecture in which the system will be implemented and also independent of the improvements of the algorithms for partitioning, which are imminent, as research in co-design is in an initial stage.

Another point is that the occam results here presented do not incorporate any co-design particularity. Thus, we believe that they can be used in other areas in which the serialisation of processes is required.

Although this work does not include iteration, the serialisation strategy here presented was extended (see [22]) to consider replicated constructs (useful to deal with arrays of processes) in all constructs of the grammar adopted, enlarging, in this way, the expressiveness of the subset of occam considered here. To deal with procedures, functions and arbitrary loops is our immediate task of future research.

To carry out the partitioning verification automatically, Iyoda [12,13] has developed an environment, the Partitioning Transformation System (ParTS). This tool has been developed as an extension of the occam Transformation System (OTS) [7], which performs general transformations of occam programs. While the basic laws of occam [17] implemented in OTS are useful for program transformation in general, they are not suitable to capture the partitioning problem. ParTS extends OTS with the implementation of the splitting, joining and serialisation rules, as well as the strategies which guide the application of these rules. Each transformation rule is captured in ParTS by a function in the SML [9] language. The strategies are also coded as functions, taking advantage of the pattern matching facilities of SML.

In the context of the PISH system, some small case studies have been developed, among them, the convolution program [22], an intravenous infusion control system [4] and an ATM commuter [13]. To develop medium and large case studies is the immediate task of the PISH team.

Finally, we are not aware of any other work which presents a formalisation of the partitioning problem as done here and in [20] and [21]. Nevertheless, it is worth mentioning that the kind of algebraic framework used here has been used previously to characterise and reason about a number of other applications [14, 17,19]. All these works can be regarded as applications of refinement algebra.

References

1. E. Barros. *Hardware/Software Partitioning Using UNITY*. PhD thesis, Tübingen University, 1993.
2. E. Barros and A. Sampaio. Towards Probably Correct Hardware/Software Partitioning Using Occam. In *Proceedings of the Third International Workshop on Hardware/Software Co-design CODES/CASHE94*, 1994, 210-217, IEEE Press.
3. E. Barros, A. Sampaio, M. E. Lima, L. Silva, R. Jacobi and N. Calazans. The PISH Methodology for Hardware/Software Co-design. In *Workshop of ProTem-CC, CNPq*, Belo Horizonte, Brazil, 1998, 65–98.
4. E. Barros and M. V. D. Santos. A Safe, Accurate Intravenous Infusion Control System. In *IEEE Micro Magazine*, Sept/Oct 1998.
5. M. Chiodo, P. Giusto, H. Hsieh, A. Jurecska, L. Lavagno and A. Sangiovanni-Vicentelli. Hardware/Software Co-design of Embedded Systems. In *IEEE Micro*, August 1994, 26–36.

6. R. Ernst and J. Henkel. Hardware-Software Co-design of Embedded Controllers Based on Hardware Extraction. In *Handouts of the International Workshop on Hardware-Software Co-Design*, October 1992.
7. M. Goldsmith. *The oxford* **occam** *transformation system.* Manual available from the author, Oxford University Computing Laboratory, January 1988.
8. R. Gupta and G. De Micheli. System-level Synthesis Using Re-programmable Components. In *Proceedings of EDAC*, 1992, 2–7, IEEE Press.
9. R. Harper, D. MacQueen and R. Milner. *Standard ML.* Edinburgh University LFCS report series ECS-LFCS-86-2, 1986.
10. C. A. R. Hoare and He Jifeng. *Unifying Theories of Programming.* Prentice-Hall Europe, 1998.
11. R. B. Hughes and G. Musgrave. The Lambda Approach to System Verification. In *Hardware/Software Co-design*, Editors G. De Micheli and M. Sami, Kluwer Academic Publisher, 1996, 427–451.
12. J. Iyoda, A. Sampaio and L. Silva. ParTS: A Partitioning Transformation System. In *Proceedings of FM99 (World Congress on Formal Methods), Lecture Notes in Computer Science*, Springer Verlag, 1999, 1709:1400-1419.
13. J. Iyoda. *ParTS: A Support Tool to Hardware/Software Partitioning.* Master thesis, Federal University of Pernambuco, Brazil, May 2000 (in Portuguese).
14. H. Jifeng, I. Page, and J. Bowen. Towards a Provably Hardware Implementation of occam. In *Correct Hardware Design and Verification Methods (Advanced Research Working Conference, CHARME' 93), Lecture Notes in Computer Science*, Springer Verlag, 1993, 683:214–225.
15. G. Jones and M. Goldsmith. *Programming in occam 2.* Prentice-Hall, 1988.
16. J. Madsen, J. Grode, P. V. Knudsen, M. E. Petersen and A. Haxthausen. Lycos: The Lyngby Co-synthesis System. In *Design Automation of Embedded Systems*, Editor R. Camposano, 1997, 2(2):195-235.
17. A. W. Roscoe and C. A. R. Hoare. The laws of **occam** programming. In *Theoretical Computer Science*, 1988, 60(2):177-229.
18. D. Saha, R. S. Mitra and A. Basu. Hardware/Software Partitioning Using Genetic Algorithm. In *Proc. of 10th International Conference on VLSI Design*, India, 1997, 155-160.
19. A. Sampaio. *An Algebraic Approach to Compiler Design.* Volume 4 of Algebraic Methodology and Software Technology (AMAST) Series in Computing, World Scientific, 1997.
20. L. Silva, A. Sampaio and E. Barros A Normal Form Reduction Strategy for Hardware/Software Partitioning. In *Formal Methods Europe (FME) 97. Lecture Notes in Computer Science*, September 1997, 1313:624-643.
21. L. Silva, A. Sampaio, E. Barros and J. Iyoda. An Algebraic Approach to Combining Processes in a Hardware/Software Partitioning Environment. *7th International Conference on Algebraic Methodology and Software Technology (AMAST) 98, Lecture Notes in Computer Science*, January 1999, 1548:308-324.
22. L. Silva. *An Algebraic Approach Hardware/Software Partitioning.* PhD. Thesis, Federal University of Pernambuco, Recife, Brazil, July 2000.
23. P. Welch and G. R. R. Justo. On the serialisation of parallel programs. *Occam and the Transputer - Current Developments*, 159-180, IOS Press, Amsterdam, 1991.

Verifying Implementation Relations

Jonathan Burton[1], Maciej Koutny[1], and Giuseppe Pappalardo[2]

[1] Dept. of Comp. Sci., University of Newcastle, Newcastle upon Tyne NE1 7RU, U.K.
{j.i.burton, Maciej.Koutny}@ncl.ac.uk
[2] Dipartimento di Matematica e Informatica, Viale A.Doria 6, Università degli Studi di Catania, I-95125 Catania, Italy, pappalardo@dmi.unict.it

Abstract. Implementation relations are a means to relate the behaviour of implementation and specification systems built of communicating processes in the event that respective implementation and specification processes have differing interfaces. In this paper we first present a graph-theoretic statement of such relations, and then derive algorithms for their automatic verification.

Keywords: Behaviour abstraction, communicating sequential processes, compositionality, verification.

1   Introduction

The software development process often involves refining a high-level *specification* into a lower-level or more concrete *implementation*. In the process algebraic context, exemplified by [3,8,9], both specification and implementation may be represented as processes and the notion that a process Q *implements* a process P is based on the idea that Q is more deterministic than (or equivalent to) P in terms of the chosen semantics. However, the *interfaces* ([3,8,9] are only interested in *observable* behaviour) of the specification and implementation processes must be the same to facilitate comparison.

Yet in deriving an implementation from a specification we will often wish to implement abstract, high-level actions at a lower level of detail and in a more concrete manner. As a result, an implementation process may be expressed at a lower (and so different) level of abstraction to a specification process. In the process algebraic context, due to our interest only in *observable* behaviour, this means that verification of correctness must be able to deal with the case that the implementation and specification processes have different interfaces.

The papers [1,5,6] introduced an implementation relation scheme aimed at formalising the notion that a communicating system is an acceptable *implementation* of another *base* or *target* system, in the case that the two systems (respective implementation and specification processes)[1] have different interfaces. Here we present a graph-theoretic restatement of those implementation relations, from which we directly derive algorithms for their automatic verification.

---

[1]   Communicating processes are represented formally in the failure-divergence (FD) model of CSP[9]. Moreover, we assume that the specification processes with which we are dealing are *IO processes* as defined in section 2.

J.N. Oliveira and P. Zave (Eds.): FME 2001, LNCS 2021, pp. 364–383, 2001.

The implementation relation scheme developed in [1] (based on [5,6], and reproduced in section 4) satisfies two light but very natural and useful requirements. The first, *accessibility* or *realisability*, ensures that the abstraction built into the implementation relation may be put to good use; in practice, this means that plugging an implementation into an appropriate environment should yield a conventional implementation of the target. *Distributivity* or *compositionality*, the other constraint on the implementation relation, requires it to distribute over system composition; thus, a target composed of two connected systems may be implemented by connecting two of their respective implementations.

That the implementation relations have the property of *compositionality* has an important consequence when we approach automatic verification. It allows us to verify each component of the implementation system explicitly in terms of its specification component and we avoid one of the great sources of the state explosion problem in concurrency, namely the generation of a state space which is a (substantial) subset of the product of all the state spaces of a set of component processes composed in parallel.

The paper is organised as follows. The next section gives preliminary information. Section 3 describes the motivation behind our approach and defines the notion of extraction pattern, used to encode the relevant interface difference. Section 4 presents the implementation relations themselves. Section 5 deals with computer representations of CSP processes and extraction patterns. In section 6 we show how to relate the representations of processes and extraction patterns, and in sections 7 and 8 we show how the defining conditions for the implementation relations can be verified algorithmically. A preliminary version of this paper appeared as [7]. All proofs can be found in [1].

2   Preliminaries

We use the standard failure-divergence model of CSP (Communicating Sequential Processes) [4,9] in which a process P is a triple $(\alpha P, \phi P, \delta P)$ where αP — *alphabet* — is a non-empty finite set of actions, ϕP — *failures* — is a subset of $\alpha P^* \times 2^{\alpha P}$, and δP — *divergences* — is a subset of αP^*. Moreover, $\tau P = \{t \mid (t, R) \in \phi P\}$ denotes the *traces* of P. We also define *maximal failures* as $max\phi P = \{(t, R) \in \phi P \mid \forall S \subseteq \alpha P : ((t, S) \in \phi P \land R \subseteq S) \Rightarrow R = S\}$.

We use structured actions of the form $b{:}v$, where v is a *message* and b is a communication *channel*. For every channel b, μb is the *message set* of b — the set of all v such that $b{:}v$ is a valid action. $\alpha b = \{b{:}v \mid v \in \mu b\}$ is the *alphabet* of channel b, which is always finite and non-empty. For a set of channels B, $\alpha B = \bigcup_{b \in B} \alpha b$. χa gives the channel on which the action a occurred; for example, $\chi b{:}1 = b$. Moreover, $\chi A = \{\chi a \mid a \in A\}$ for a set of actions A.

We will associate with P a set of channels, χP, and stipulate that the alphabet of P is that of χP. Moreover, χP is partitioned into *input* and *output* channels, respectively denoted by $in\,P$ and $out\,P$. The *composition* of two processes, P and Q, is defined as $P \otimes Q = (P\|Q)\backslash(\alpha P \cap \alpha Q)$ i.e., it is a parallel composition of P and Q with all the interprocess communication hidden.

Throughout the paper we use notations similar to those of [4]. In addition
to that, an infinite sequence of traces $t_1, t_2, \ldots$ is an ω-*sequence* if $t_1 \leq t_2 \leq \ldots$
and $\lim_{i \to \infty} |t_i| = \infty$. A trace $t[c/b]$ is obtained from trace t by replacing each
action $b{:}v$ by $c{:}v$, and $t{\upharpoonright}B$ is obtained by deleting from t all the actions that do
not occur on the channels in B. A mapping from a set of traces to a set of traces
$f : T \to T'$ is *monotonic* if $t, u \in T$ and $t \leq u$ implies $f(t) \leq f(u)$; and *strict* if
$\langle \rangle \in T$ and $f(\langle \rangle) = \langle \rangle$. Moreover, f is a *homomorphism* if $t, u, t \circ u \in T$ implies
$f(t \circ u) = f(t) \circ f(u)$.

The class of base or specification processes comprises all those processes
whose input channels cannot refuse a message purely on the basis of its content.
Formally, a channel c of a process P is *value independent*, denoted $c \in \mathit{vind}\, P$,
if for all $(t, R) \in \phi P$, $c \in \chi R$ implies $(t, R \cup \alpha c) \in \phi P$. An *input-output process*
is a non-diverging process P such that $\mathit{in}\, P \subseteq \mathit{vind}\, P$, and denoted $P \in IO$.

3   Extraction Patterns

In this section, we explain the basic mechanism behind our modelling of behaviour abstraction: the extraction pattern. We then give a formal definition
of extraction patterns, which act as a formal parameter in our implementation
relation scheme.

Consider a pair of IO processes, Snd and Buf, shown in figure 1(a). Snd generates an infinite sequence of 0s or an infinite sequence of 1s, depending on the
signal (0 or 1) received on its input channel, c, at the very beginning of its execution. Buf is a buffer process of capacity one, forwarding signals received on its in-
put channel, d. In CSP, $Snd = \square_{i \in \{0,1\}} c{:}i \to Snd_i$ and $Buf = \square_{i \in \{0,1\}} d{:}i \to B_i$
where $Snd_i = d{:}i \to Snd_i$ and $B_i = e{:}i \to Buf$, for $i = 0, 1$.

Suppose that the signal transmission between the two processes has been
implemented using two channels, r and s, as shown in figure 1(b). The transmissions on d are now duplicated and the two copies sent along r and s. That is,
Snd' sends the duplicated signal, while Buf' accepts a single copy and passes it
on (possibly after a delay), ignoring the other one. The scheme clearly works as
we have $Snd \otimes Buf = Snd' \otimes Buf'$. Suppose now that the transmission of signals
is imperfect and two types of faulty behaviour can occur: $\widetilde{Snd} = Snd' \sqcap stop$ and
$\widehat{Snd} = Snd' \sqcap \overline{Snd}$, where $\overline{Snd}$ is Snd' with all the communication on channel
s being blocked. In other words, $\widetilde{Snd}$ can break down completely, refusing to
output any signals, while $\widehat{Snd}$ can fail in such a way that although channel s
is blocked r can still transmit the signals. $\widehat{Snd}$ could be used to model the following situation: in order to improve performance, a 'slow' channel d is replaced

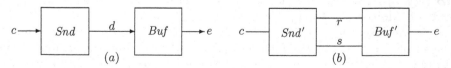

Fig. 1. Two base IO processes and their implementations.

by two channels, a high-speed yet unreliable channel s and a slow but reliable backup channel r. Since $Snd \otimes Buf = \widehat{Snd} \otimes Buf'$ while $\widetilde{Snd} \otimes Buf'$ is not even deadlock-free, $\widehat{Snd}$ is a much 'better' implementation of Snd than $\widetilde{Snd}$.

We will now point at the differences between the two processes and at the same time introduce informally some basic concepts which are subsequently used. We start by observing that the output of $\widehat{Snd}$ can be thought of as adhering to two rules:

R1   The transmissions over r and s are consistent w.r.t. message contents (the set of all traces over r and s satisfying such a property will be denoted by Dom).

R2   Transmission over r is reliable, but there is no such guarantee for s.

The output produced by $\widetilde{Snd}$ satisfies R1 but fails to satisfy R2. To express this formally we need to render the two conditions in some form of precise notation.

To capture the behavioural relationship that exists between Snd and $\widehat{Snd}$ we will employ an (extraction) mapping $extr$ which for traces over r and s returns corresponding traces over d. For example, $\langle \rangle \mapsto \langle \rangle$, $\langle r{:}0 \rangle \mapsto \langle d{:}0 \rangle$, $\langle s{:}0 \rangle \mapsto \langle d{:}0 \rangle$, $\langle s{:}1, r{:}1 \rangle \mapsto \langle d{:}1 \rangle$ and $\langle r{:}1, r{:}0 \rangle \mapsto \langle d{:}1, d{:}0 \rangle$. Notice that the extraction mapping need only be defined for traces satisfying R1, i.e., those in Dom. We further observe that, in view of R2, some of the traces in Dom may be regarded as *incomplete*. For example, $\langle s{:}1, r{:}1, s{:}0 \rangle$ is such a trace since channel r is reliable and so the duplicate of $s{:}0$ (i.e., $r{:}0$) is bound to eventually be offered for transmission. The set of all other traces in Dom — i.e., those which in principle may be *complete* — will be denoted by dom. For our example, dom will contain all traces in Dom where the transmission on s has not overtaken that on r.

Although it will play a central role, the extraction mapping alone is not sufficient to identify the 'correct' implementation of Snd in the presence of faults, since $\tau Snd = extr(\tau \widehat{Snd}) = extr(\tau \widetilde{Snd})$. What one also needs is an ability to relate the refusals of $\widehat{Snd}$ and $\widetilde{Snd}$ with the possible refusals of the base process Snd. This, however, is much harder than relating traces. For suppose that we attempted to 'extract' the refusals of $\widehat{Snd}$. Then, we would have had $(\langle \rangle, \{s{:}0\}) \in \phi \widehat{Snd}$ and $extr(\langle \rangle, \{s{:}0\}) = (\langle \rangle, \{d{:}0\}) \notin \phi Snd$. This indicates that the crude extraction of refusals is not going to work. What we need is a more sophisticated device, which in our case comes in the form of another mapping, ref, constraining the possible refusals a process can exhibit after a given trace $t \in Dom$.[2] More precisely, a sender process can admit a refusal disallowed by $ref(t)$ if the extracted trace $extr(t)$ admits in the target process the refusal of all communication on the corresponding channel and, moreover, the trace t itself is complete, i.e., $t \in dom$. For the example at hand, this roughly amounts to stipulating that an unfinished communication cannot at the same time refuse both $r{:}0$ and $r{:}1$.

Finally, it should be stressed that $ref(t)$ gives a refusal bound on the sender side (more precisely, the process which implements the sender target process).

---

[2] In general, we will only be interested in traces belonging to Dom.

But this is enough since if we want to rule out a deadlock in communication between the sender and receiver, it is now possible to stipulate on the receiver side that no refusal be such that, when combined with any refusal allowed by $ref(t)$, it can yield the whole alphabet of the channels used for transmission. In particular, this means that $ref(t)$ may never allow the whole alphabet of these channels to be refused.

The last notion we will need to establish the correspondence between processes is a partial inverse of the extraction mapping, inv. It will be used to ensure that all the traces of a base process (see section 2) can be extracted from the traces of its implementation.

The previous example can be thought of as modelling a fail-stop communication between two processes (s being a fail-stop channel). The next example is different in that it employs a fault tolerant mechanism based on message retransmission. It is used to illustrate the point that implementations are not forced to preserve the *intuitive* direction of the transfer of messages.

Suppose now that the communication on d has been implemented using two channels, r and s, but now r is a data channel, and s is a feedback channel used to pass acknowledgements. It is, moreover, assumed that a given message is sent at most *twice* since a re-transmission always succeeds. This leads to a simple protocol which can be incorporated into suitably modified original processes. The resulting implementation processes Snd'' and Buf'', are given by:

$$Snd'' = \square_{i \in \{0,1\}} c{:}i \to Snd''_i$$

$$Buf'' = \square_{i \in \{0,1\}} r{:}i \to (s{:}ack \to B'_i \sqcap s{:}nak \to B)$$

where B, Snd''_i and B'_i $(i = 0, 1)$ are auxiliary processes defined thus:

$$Snd''_i = r{:}i \to (s{:}ack \to Snd''_i \square s{:}nak \to r{:}i \to Snd''_i)$$

$$B \quad = \square_{i \in \{0,1\}} r{:}i \to B'_i$$

$$B'_i \quad = e{:}i \to Buf'' \ .$$

It may be observed that $Snd'' \otimes Buf'' = Snd \otimes Buf = Snd[e/d]$. One way of showing this would be to compose the two pairs of processes and prove their equality with $Snd[e/d]$ using, e.g., CSP laws [4]. This would be straightforward for $Snd \otimes Buf$, but less so for $Snd'' \otimes Buf''$, at least by hand. Alternatively, the compositional way in which our approach proceeds is to show that Snd'' and Buf'' are implementations of the respective base processes according to suitable *extraction patterns*, deriving the desired relationship using general results developed in [1], some of which are recalled later in this paper.

Formal definition. The notion of extraction pattern relates behaviour on a set of channels in an implementation process to that on a channel in a target process. It has two main functions: that of interpretation of behaviour necessitated by interface difference and the encoding of some correctness requirements. Formally, an *extraction pattern* is a tuple $ep = (B, b, dom, extr, ref, inv)$ satisfying the following conditions:

EP0 B is a non-empty set of channels (*sources*), and b is a channel (*target*).

EP1   *dom* is a non-empty set of traces over the sources; its prefix-closure is denoted by *Dom*.

EP2   *extr* is a strict monotonic mapping defined for traces in *Dom*; for every t, $extr(t)$ is a trace over the target.

EP3   *ref* is a mapping defined for traces in *Dom*; for every t, $ref(t)$ is a non-empty subset-closed family of subsets of αB such that $\alpha B \notin ref(t)$. It is assumed that if $a \in \alpha B$ and $t \circ \langle a \rangle \notin Dom$ then $R \cup \{a\} \in ref(t)$, for all $R \in ref(t)$.

EP4   *inv* is a homomorphism from traces over the target to traces in *Dom*; for every trace w over the target, $extr(inv(w)) = w$.

As already mentioned, the mapping *extr* interprets a trace over the source channels B (in the implementation process) in terms of a trace over a channel b (in the target process) and defines functionally correct (i.e., in terms of traces) behaviour over those source channels by way of its domain. The mapping *ref* is used to define correct behaviour in terms of failures as it gives bounds on refusals after execution of a particular trace sequence over the source channels. *dom* contains those traces in *Dom* for which the communication over B may be regarded as complete (and so later, it is only for such traces that the sending process is allowed to violate the constraint on refusals given by *ref*).

The extraction mapping is monotonic as receiving more information cannot decrease the current knowledge about the transmission. $\alpha B \notin ref(t)$ will be useful in that for an unfinished communication t we do not allow the sender to refuse all possible transmission. The second condition in EP3 is a rendering in terms of extraction patterns of a condition imposed on CSP processes that impossible events can always be refused. Note that since *inv* is a homomorphism, it suffices to define it for single actions over the target only.

We lift some of the notions to finite *sets* of extraction patterns. Let $ep = \{ep_1, \ldots, ep_n\}$ be a non-empty set of extraction patterns $ep_i = (B_i, b_i, dom_i, extr_i, ref_i, inv_i)$ with distinct targets and disjoint sources; moreover, let $B = B_1 \cup \ldots \cup B_n$ and $C = \{b_1, \ldots, b_n\}$. Then:

EP5 $dom_{ep} = \{t \in \alpha B^* \mid \forall i \leq n : t \restriction B_i \in dom_i\}$.

EP6 $Dom_{ep} = \{t \in \alpha B^* \mid \forall i \leq n : t \restriction B_i \in Dom_i\}$.

EP7 $extr_{ep}(\langle \rangle) = \langle \rangle$ and, for every $t \circ \langle a \rangle \in Dom_{ep}$ with $a \in \alpha B_i$,

$$extr_{ep}(t \circ \langle a \rangle) = extr_{ep}(t) \circ u$$

where u is a (possibly empty) trace and $extr_i(t \restriction B_i \circ \langle a \rangle) = extr_i(t \restriction B_i) \circ u$.

EP8 inv_{ep} is a homomorphism from traces over C to traces over B such that $inv_{ep}(a) = inv_i(a)$, for all $i \leq n$ and $a \in \alpha b_i$.

The u in EP7 is well defined since $extr_i$ is monotonic, and inv_{ep} since $b_i \neq b_j$ for $i \neq j$.

Examples. We have already informally discussed a 'fail-stop' extraction pattern for the example in figure 1(b). It can be formalised as ep_{fs}, where $B = \{r, s\}$, $b = d$ and

$$
\begin{aligned}
dom &= \{t \in \alpha B^* \mid (t{\upharpoonright}s)[r/s] \leq t{\upharpoonright}r\} \\
Dom &= \{t \in \alpha B^* \mid (t{\upharpoonright}s)[r/s] \leq t{\upharpoonright}r \ \vee \ t{\upharpoonright}r \leq (t{\upharpoonright}s)[r/s]\} \\
extr(t) &= \max\{(t{\upharpoonright}s)[d/s], (t{\upharpoonright}r)[d/r]\} \\
ref(t) &= \{R \in 2^{\alpha B} \mid \alpha r \not\subseteq R\} \\
inv(d{:}v) &= \langle r{:}v \rangle .
\end{aligned}
$$

Note that in this case the extraction mapping always returns a trace derived from the longer of the communications over s and r (this is acceptable since these communications are consistent, see Dom). Potentially complete traces are those where r has not fallen behind s in transmitting the signals. The $ref(t)$ component states that if behaviour is not complete on r and s, then at least one event must be possible on r.

For the second example, in order to demonstrate that Snd'' and Buf'' are implementations of respectively Snd and Buf, we will need two kinds of extraction patterns, id_c and ep_{twice}.

An *identity* extraction pattern for a channel c, id_c, is one for which $B = \{c\}$, $b = c$, $dom = Dom = \alpha c^*$, $extr(t) = inv(t) = t$ and $ref(t) = 2^{\alpha c} - \{\alpha c\}$. The idea here is that the extraction mapping interprets the traces over the channel c *verbatim*. Each such communication can therefore be a terminated one. The $ref(t)$ component simply states that a sender process may terminate the sending of messages on a channel c only if it offers no communication on c (i.e. the whole alphabet of c is refused).

For the ep_{twice} extraction pattern, $B = \{s, r\}$ are the source channels and $b = d$ is the target channel; moreover $\mu d = \mu r = \{0, 1\}$ and $\mu s = \{ack, nak\}$. The remaining components of ep_{twice} are defined in the following way, where $t \in dom$ and $t \circ u \in Dom$:

$$
dom = \{\langle r{:}0, s{:}ack\rangle, \langle r{:}0, s{:}nak, r{:}0\rangle, \langle r{:}1, s{:}ack\rangle, \langle r{:}1, s{:}nak, r{:}1\rangle\}^*
$$

$$
extr(t \circ u) = \begin{cases} \langle\,\rangle & \text{if } t \circ u = \langle\,\rangle \\ extr(t) \circ \langle d{:}v\rangle & \text{if } u = \langle r{:}v, s{:}ack\rangle \text{ or } u = \langle r{:}v, s{:}nak, r{:}v\rangle \\ extr(t) & \text{if } u = \langle r{:}v\rangle \text{ or } u = \langle r{:}v, s{:}nak\rangle \end{cases}
$$

$$
ref(t \circ u) = \begin{cases} 2^{\alpha r} & \text{if } u = \langle r{:}v\rangle \\ \{R \in 2^{\alpha r \cup \alpha s} \mid \alpha r \not\subseteq R\} & \text{if } u = \langle\,\rangle \\ \{R \in 2^{\alpha r \cup \alpha s} \mid r{:}v \notin R\} & \text{if } u = \langle r{:}v, s{:}nak\rangle \end{cases}
$$

$$
inv(d{:}v) = \{\langle r{:}v, s{:}ack\rangle\} .
$$

Here, intuitively, we can extract $\langle d{:}v\rangle$ from two sequences of communications: $\langle r{:}v, s{:}ack\rangle$ and $\langle r{:}v, s{:}nak, r{:}v\rangle$. Thus a valid trace in Dom is one which is a concatenation of a series of 'complete' segments of this kind, possibly followed by an initial fragment of one of them. Any trace for which the latter is true, is *incomplete* and belongs to $Dom - dom$; otherwise it belongs to dom.

4   Implementation Relations

Suppose that we intend to implement a base IO process P using another process Q with possibly different communication interface. The correctness of the implementation will be expressed in terms of two sets of extraction patterns, ep and ep'. The former (with sources $in\,Q$ and targets $in\,P$) will be used to relate the communication on the input channels of P and Q, the latter will serve a similar purpose for the output channels.

Fig. 2. Base IO process P and its implementation Q.

Let P be a base IO process as in figure 2, and $ep_i = (B_i, b_i, dom_i, extr_i, ref_i, inv_i)$ be an extraction pattern, for every $i \le m + n$. We assume that the B_i's are mutually disjoint channel sets, and denote $ep = \{ep_1, \ldots, ep_m\}$ and $ep' = \{ep_{m+1}, \ldots, ep_{m+n}\}$. We then take a (not necessarily IO) process Q such that $in\,Q = B_1 \cup \ldots \cup B_m$ and $out\,Q = B_{m+1} \cup \ldots \cup B_{m+n}$, as shown in figure 2, and denote by $\tau_{Dom}Q$ the set of all traces of Q which belong to $Dom_{ep \cup ep'}$. Similarly, $\phi_{Dom}Q$ and $\phi_{dom}Q$ will be the sets of those failures of Q in which the trace component belongs to $Dom_{ep \cup ep'}$ and $dom_{ep \cup ep'}$, respectively. Intuitively, $\tau_{Dom}Q$ — which is subsequently referred to as the *domain* of Q — is the set of those traces of Q which are of actual interest and, consequently, $\phi_{Dom}Q$ is the set of failures of actual interest too. We will say that a channel b_i of P is *blocked* at a failure $(t, R) \in \phi_{Dom}Q$ if either b_i is an input channel and $\alpha B_i - R \in ref_i(t{\restriction}B_i)$, or b_i is an output channel and $\alpha B_i \cap R \notin ref_i(t{\restriction}B_i)$. Note that in both cases this signifies that the refusal bound imposed by the ref_i has been breached.

We then define a number of conditions involving Q and P.

DP If t is a trace of Q such that $t{\restriction}in\,Q \in Dom_{ep}$, then $t \in \tau_{Dom}Q$.

DF $\tau_{Dom}Q \cap \delta Q = \emptyset$.

TE $extr_{ep \cup ep'}(\tau_{Dom}Q) \subseteq \tau P$.

GE If $\ldots, t_i, \ldots$ is an ω-sequence in $\tau_{Dom}Q$, then $\ldots, extr_{ep \cup ep'}(t_i), \ldots$ is also an ω-sequence.

LC If b_i is a channel of P blocked at $(t, R) \in \phi_{Dom}Q$, then $t{\restriction}B_i \in dom_i$.

RE If $(t, R) \in \phi_{dom}Q$ then $(extr_{ep \cup ep'}(t), \alpha B) \in \phi P$, where B is the set of all channels of P blocked at (t, R).

TI $inv_{ep \cup ep'}(\tau P) \subseteq \tau Q$.

RI If $B \subseteq \chi P$ and $(t, \alpha B) \in \phi P$, then

$$(inv_{ep \cup ep'}(t), \{a \in \bigcup_{b_i \in B} \alpha B_i \mid inv_{ep \cup ep'}(t) \circ \langle a \rangle \in Dom_{ep \cup ep'}\}) \in \phi Q .$$

We interpret the above conditions in the following way. DP expresses the *domain preservation* property, which says that if a trace of Q projected on the input channels can be interpreted by ep, then it must be possible to interpret the projection on the output channels by ep'. Note that such a condition is a simple *rely/guarantee* property in the sense of [2]. DF can be interpreted as *divergence freedom* within the domain of Q (in CSP divergences signify totally unacceptable behaviour). TE simply states that within the domain of Q we insist on generating P's *traces after extraction*. GE states that an unboundedly growing sequence of traces in the domain of Q is a sequence of traces unboundedly *growing after extraction*. LC means that going outside the bounds of allowed refusals indicates that the communication on a given channel may be interpreted as *locally completed*. RE states a condition for *refusal extraction*, which means that if a trace is locally completed on all channels, then any local blocking of a channel of P in Q is transformed into the refusal of its whole alphabet in P. TI is a converse of TE and simply states that we insist on generating Q's *traces after inversion*. Finally, RI can be thought of as a converse of RE as it states a condition for *refusal inversion*.

Based on the above conditions, [1] defines three *implementation relations* of increasingly growing discriminative power (all three use the first six conditions above, while the second and third also incorporate TI and RI, respectively).

Crucially, all three implementation relations are preserved by the process composition operation (details can be found in, e.g., [1,5]).

5   Representing CSP Processes and Extraction Patterns

Communicating transition systems. We shall represent a CSP process in terms of a *communicating transition system* (CTS), which is a tuple $CTS = (V, C, D, A, v_0)$ such that: V is a set of states (nodes); $v_0 \in V$ is the initial state; C and D are finite disjoint sets of channels (C will represent input and D output channels); and $A \subseteq V \times (\alpha C \cup \alpha D \cup \{\tau\}) \times V$ is the set of labelled directed arcs, called *transitions*, where τ is a distinguished symbol denoting an *internal* action. We will use the following notation:

- If $(v, a, w) \in A$, we denote $v \xrightarrow{a} w$.
- If $v_1 \xrightarrow{a_1} v_2 \xrightarrow{a_2} \cdots \xrightarrow{a_n} v_{n+1}$, we denote $v_1 \xRightarrow{\langle a_1 \rangle \circ \cdots \circ \langle a_n \rangle} v_{n+1}$ where it is assumed that $\langle \tau \rangle = \langle \rangle$; moreover, $v \xRightarrow{\langle \rangle} v$, for every $v \in V$.
- If $v \xrightarrow{a} w$, we denote $a \in en(v)$ and call a *enabled* at v.
- A state $v \in V$ is *stable* if $\tau \notin en(v)$; V_{stb} denotes the set of stable states.
- If $v \xRightarrow{t} w$, we denote $v \Longrightarrow w$ or $v \xRightarrow{t}$.

We shall assume that a CTS is finite, i.e., both V and A are finite.

The implementation relations which we want to verify algorithmically are all expressed in the denotational semantics of CSP [9], and so we must know how to derive information on divergences, traces and failures from a given CTS.

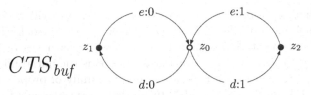

Fig. 3. CTS representing a buffer of capacity one.

For $CTS = (V, C, D, A, v_0)$, we define $P_{CTS} = (C, D, \Phi, \Delta)$ as a tuple such that the following hold (below $\alpha CTS = \alpha C \cup \alpha D$):

$$\Delta = \{t \circ u \in \alpha CTS^* \mid \exists k \geq 1 \, \exists v_1, \ldots, v_k \in V : v_0 \overset{t}{\Longrightarrow} v_1 \overset{\tau}{\longrightarrow} v_2 \cdots v_k \overset{\tau}{\longrightarrow} v_1\}$$

$$\Phi = \{(t, R) \in \alpha CTS^* \times 2^{\alpha CTS} \mid \exists v \in V_{stb} : v_0 \overset{t}{\Longrightarrow} v \, \wedge \, R \cap en(v) = \emptyset\}$$
$$\cup \, \Delta \times 2^{\alpha CTS} \, .$$

P_{CTS} is a CSP process, and if $\Delta = \emptyset$, then $\tau P_{CTS} = \{t \in \alpha CTS^* \mid v_0 \overset{t}{\Longrightarrow}\}$. Figure 3 shows a CTS modelling a buffer of capacity one defined in section 3. Note that $P_{CTS_{buf}} = Buf$.

In order that all sets of nodes representing the same trace may be grouped together, a *normalisation* process is used, as detailed in [9] specifically with respect to the operational semantics of CSP.[3] This normalisation produces a CTS such that there are no τ transitions and each node has at most one successor for each action, and it serves two main purposes. First, it creates a *deterministic* CTS in order that trace inclusion properties may be easily tested for. Second, every node p in the new CTS such that $p_0 \overset{t}{\Longrightarrow} p$ is mapped to a set of stable nodes in the original CTS. The algorithm used for this normalisation process is adapted from [9]. Given a finite $CTS = (V, C, D, A, v_0)$ such that $\Delta = \emptyset$, we form a labelled transition system CTS_{det} with the nodes $V_{CTS_{det}} \subseteq 2^V$ and the initial node p_0, as follows:

1. $p_0 = \mathcal{T}(v_0)$ where, for any node $v \in V$, $\mathcal{T}(v) = \{w \in V \mid v \overset{\langle\rangle}{\Longrightarrow} w\}$ are the nodes reachable under some τ-sequence from v.
2. For each node p generated, we determine the set of non-τ actions enabled at at least one node in p. For each such action a, we form a new node, $p' = \bigcup\{\mathcal{T}(w) \mid \exists v \in p : v \overset{a}{\longrightarrow} w\}$, and then add a transition $p \overset{a}{\longrightarrow} p'$.

We also denote, for every node p of CTS_{det},

$$\kappa_{CTS}(p) = \{en(v) \mid v \in p \wedge \forall w \in p : en(w) \subseteq en(v) \Rightarrow en(w) = en(v)\} \, . \quad (1)$$

In other words, $\kappa_{CTS}(p)$ is the set of minimal sets of actions enabled at stable nodes corresponding to p. Such a set can be used to calculate maximal failures.

---

[3] We use only the first part of that normalisation process and do not deal with nodes which are bisimilar.

Extraction graphs. To represent an extraction pattern we will use an *extraction graph*, which is a tuple $EG = (B, b, V, A, v_0, \varrho, \delta, \imath)$ such that: B is a non-empty finite set of channels; b is a channel; V is a set of nodes; $A \subseteq V \times (\alpha B \times \alpha b^*) \times V$ is a set of labelled arcs; $v_0 \in V$ is the initial node; ϱ is a mapping returning for every node in V a non-empty family of proper subsets of αB; $\delta : V \to \{d, D\}$; and $\imath : \alpha b \to \alpha B^*$. Intuitively, ϱ corresponds to *ref*, d indicates traces in *dom*, D indicates traces in $Dom - dom$, and $\imath$ corresponds to *inv*. We will use the following notation:

- If $(v, a, t, w) \in A$, we denote $v \xrightarrow{a.t} w$.
- If $v_1 \xrightarrow{a_1.t_1} v_2 \xrightarrow{a_2.t_2} \cdots \xrightarrow{a_n.t_n} v_{n+1}$, we denote $v_1 \xrightarrow{\langle a_1, a_2, \ldots, a_n \rangle.t_1 \circ t_2 \circ \cdots \circ t_n} v_{n+1}$;
  moreover, $v \xrightarrow{\langle\rangle.\langle\rangle} v$, for every node v.
- If $v \xRightarrow{u.t} w$, we denote $v \Longrightarrow w$.

We impose the following conditions on an extraction graph EG, where $v \in V$:

- If $R, R' \in \varrho(v)$ and $R \subseteq R'$, then $R = R'$; moreover, if $a \in \alpha B$ and there are no w and t such that $v \xrightarrow{a.t} w$, then $a \in R$.
- $v_0 \Longrightarrow v$.
- If $v \xrightarrow{a.t} w$ and $v \xrightarrow{a.t'} w'$ then $t = t'$ and $w = w'$.   (*)
- If $\delta(v) = D$, then there is $w \in V$ such that $v \Longrightarrow w$ and $\delta(w) = d$.
- If $t = \langle a_1, \ldots, a_k \rangle \in \alpha b^*$, then there is w such that $v_0 \xRightarrow{\imath(a_1) \circ \cdots \circ \imath(a_k).t} w$.

When representing an extraction pattern $ep = (B, b, dom, extr, ref, inv)$, inv can be represented by the mapping $\imath$, giving for every $a \in \alpha b$ the trace $inv(a)$.

Let EG be an extraction graph as above. Then Dom_{EG} is a set of traces, and $ep_{EG} = (B, b, dom_{EG}, extr_{EG}, ref_{EG}, inv_{EG})$ is a tuple, defined as follows.

- $Dom_{EG} = \{u \in \alpha B^* \mid \exists v, t : v_0 \xRightarrow{u.t} v\}$.
- $dom_{EG} = \{u \in \alpha B^* \mid \exists v, t : v_0 \xRightarrow{u.t} v \wedge \delta(v) = d\}$.
- For every $t = \langle a_1, \ldots, a_k \rangle \in \alpha b^*$, $inv_{EG}(t) = \imath(a_1) \circ \cdots \circ \imath(a_k)$.
- By (*) above, for every $u \in Dom_{EG}$, there are *unique* t and v such that $v_0 \xRightarrow{u.t} v$. Then $extr_{EG}(u) = t$ and $ref_{EG}(u) = \{R \mid \exists R' \in \varrho(v) : R \subseteq R'\}$.

ep_{EG} is an extraction pattern, and for every extraction pattern ep there is an extraction graph EG such that $ep = ep_{EG}$. However, we will be interested only in those extraction graphs which are finite, i.e., have a finite number of nodes V. To simplify the presentation, we assume that if $v \xRightarrow{a.t} w$ then $|t| \leq 1$.

6 Unambiguous CTS

Extraction patterns and so extraction graphs are defined for a channel in a base process P and a channel or channels in an implementation process Q. As a result, more than one EG will usually be required to interpret the behaviour of

	δ	ϱ
v_0	d	$\{d{:}0\}, \{d{:}1\}$

	$\imath$
$d{:}0$	$\langle d{:}0 \rangle$
$d{:}1$	$\langle d{:}1 \rangle$

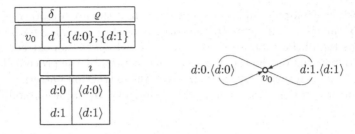

Fig. 4. Extraction graph EG_1.

the implementation process Q as a whole. Moreover, it is possible that the CTS representing Q will be ambiguous (in the sense explained below) with respect to interpretation in terms of the EGs.

Let us consider a base process *Buf* modelling a buffer of capacity one, with input channel d and output channel e, defined in section 3. Recall that it can be modelled by the communicating transition system CTS_{buf} shown in figure 3. We also consider two extraction patterns, ep_1 and ep_2, given by the extraction graphs EG_1 and EG_2, i.e., $ep_i = ep_{EG_i}$ (for $i = 1, 2$). The first extraction graph, for which $ep_{EG_1} = id_d$, is defined in figure 4. The second one, over the sources $\{r, s\}$ and target e, is given in figure 5.

	δ	ϱ
w_0	d	$\{s{:}ack, r{:}0\}, \{s{:}ack, r{:}1\}$
w_1	D	$\{r{:}0, r{:}1\}$
w_2	D	$\{r{:}0, r{:}1\}$

	$\imath$
$e{:}0$	$\langle r{:}0, s{:}ack \rangle$
$e{:}1$	$\langle r{:}1, s{:}ack \rangle$

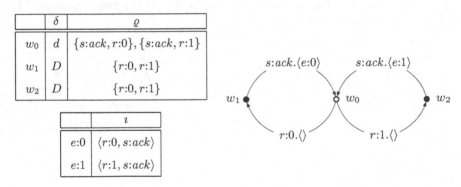

Fig. 5. Extraction graph EG_2.

We would like to verify the implementation conditions, with respect to ep_1 and ep_2, for a process Q_0 such that $in\, Q_0 = \{d\}$ and $out\, Q_0 = \{r, s\}$, and whose behaviour is described by the communicating transition system CTS_Q shown in figure 6, i.e., $Q_0 = P_{CTS_Q}$. Although it is not difficult to see that Q_0 satisfies all eight conditions DP–RI in section 4, it may not be clear what needs to be done to verify this using only the representations of Q_0, *Buf*, ep_1 and ep_2, given in the form of the appropriate communicating transition systems and extraction graphs. In particular, suppose that we want to verify TE, by showing that

$$extr_{\{ep_1, ep_2\}}(\tau Q_0) \subseteq \tau Buf . \tag{2}$$

A possible attempt would be to replace each of the arc annotations in CTS_Q by the 'extracted' string given by the corresponding extraction pattern. This could be done for all the actions except $s{:}ack$ from which we can extract either $\langle e{:}0 \rangle$ or $\langle e{:}1 \rangle$, depending on the previous actions executed by the process. Thus CTS_Q is an *ambiguous* representation of Q_0 given the extraction patterns ep_1 and ep_2. A solution we propose is to remove this ambiguity, by suitably modifying CTS_Q.

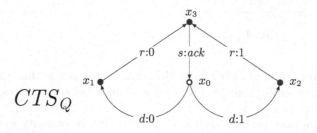

Fig. 6. An implementation of a buffer of capacity one.

Let us split the node x_3 of CTS_Q and separate the two arcs incoming to it, obtaining CTS'_Q shown in figure 7(a). We can now unambiguously interpret each of the arc annotations, which leads to the graph G shown in figure 7(b). To verify that TE holds, it now suffices to check that the traces generated by G are also generated by CTS_{buf}.

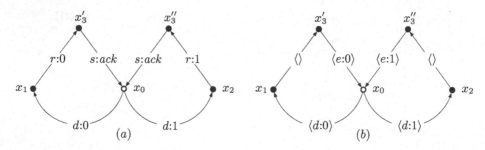

Fig. 7. Disambiguating CTS_Q.

The following algorithm generates an equivalent unambiguous CTS, from a given CTS and a set of extraction graphs.

Algorithm 1. For $i = 1, \ldots, m + n$, let

$$EG_i = (B_i, b_i, V_i, A_i, v_{0i}, \varrho_i, \delta_i, \iota_i)$$

be extraction graphs such that the B_i's are mutually disjoint and the b_i's distinct. Moreover, let $CTS = (V, C, D, A, v_0)$ be a communicating transition system such that $C = B_1 \cup \ldots \cup B_m$ and $D = B_{m+1} \cup \ldots \cup B_{m+n}$. The algorithm generates a communicating transition system CTS^u, in two steps.

Step 1: We generate a labelled directed graph denoted by G, with the nodes $V \times V_1 \times \cdots \times V_n$, as follows. Let $q = (v, v_1, \ldots, v_n)$ be a node in G. The arcs outgoing from q are derived from those outgoing from v; for each arc $v \xrightarrow{a} w$ in CTS we proceed according to exactly one of the following four cases.

1. $a = \tau$. Then we add a transition $q \xrightarrow{\tau} (w, v_1, \ldots, v_n)$.

2. $a \neq \tau$ and there is an arc $v_i \xrightarrow{a.t} w_i$ in EG_i, for some $i \geq 1$.[4]
   Then we add a transition $q \xrightarrow{a} (w, w_1, \ldots, w_n)$ where $w_j = v_i$, for all $j \neq i$. Moreover, we denote $extr(q, a) = \tau$ if $t = \langle\rangle$, and $extr(q, a) = b$ if $t = \langle b \rangle$.

3. $a \in \alpha C$ and there is no arc $v_i \xrightarrow{a.t} w_i$, for any $i \geq 1$. Then we do nothing.

4. $a \in \alpha D$ and there is no arc $v_i \xrightarrow{a.t} w_i$, for any $i \geq 1$. Then we mark permanently q as an *unfinished* node (all the nodes are assumed to be *finished* at the beginning).

Step 2: From the graph G we obtain a communicating transition system CTS^u with the same channels as CTS, by taking $q_0 = (v_0, v_{01}, \ldots, v_{0n})$ as the initial node, and then adding all the nodes reachable from q_0, together with all the interconnecting arcs. If any of the reachable nodes is marked as unfinished, we *reject* CTS^u (since this means that the traces generated by $Q = P_{CTS^u}$ do not satisfy the condition DP, where each ep_i is generated by EG_i).   □

The above algorithm will be executed on the CTS representation of the *implementation* process Q. The result is denoted CTS^u_Q; its main characteristic is that the definition of the nodes allows the unambiguous interpretation of the arc labels through the extraction mappings (see proposition 1). In addition, $\tau P_{CTS^u_Q} = \tau_{Dom} Q$. In practice, one can avoid generating the whole graph G, by performing a depth first search starting from the initial node q_0. Then only the nodes of CTS^u will be visited. In what follows, for a node $q = (w_0, w_1, \ldots, w_n)$ of CTS^u and $0 \leq i \leq m + n$, we will denote $q^{(i)} = w_i$.

CTS^u for the example in figure 6 is shown in figure 8, and is isomorphic to CTS'_Q obtained informally before. Note that $extr((x_3, v_0, w_1), s:ack) = e:0$ and $extr((x_1, v_0, w_0), r:0) = \langle\rangle$.

Proposition 1. *Let* $q_0 \xrightarrow{a_1} q_1 \xrightarrow{a_2} \cdots \xrightarrow{a_k} q_k$ *in* CTS^u *and* $t = \langle a_1 \rangle \circ \cdots \circ \langle a_k \rangle$. *Then* $t \in Dom_{ep \cup ep'}$ *and* $extr_{ep \cup ep'}(t) = u_1 \circ \cdots \circ u_k$ *where* $u_i = \langle\rangle$ *if* $a_i = \tau$ *and* $u_i = \langle extr(q_{i-1}, a_i) \rangle$ *if* $a_i \neq \tau$, *for every* $i \leq k$.

Proposition 2. *Let* $q_0 \xrightarrow{a_1} q_1 \xrightarrow{a_2} \cdots \xrightarrow{a_k} q_k$ *in* CTS^u. *Then* $q_0^{(0)} \xrightarrow{a_1} q_1^{(0)} \xrightarrow{a_2} \cdots \xrightarrow{a_k} q_k^{(0)}$ *in* CTS.

---

[4] There can only be one such EG_i since the B_i's are mutually disjoint.

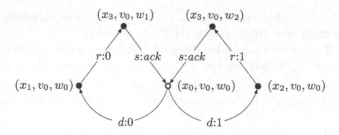

Fig. 8. Applying disambiguating algorithm.

7   Graph Representation of Implementation Relations

We now transfer the implementation conditions formulated in section 4 in terms
of the denotational semantics of CSP, into equivalent conditions expressed in
terms of communicating transition systems and extraction graphs. The latter
will provide, in section 8, a suitable basis for verification algorithms. Below we
list general assumptions which will be used throughout this and the next section.

- P, Q, ep_i (for $i = 1, \ldots, m + n$), ep and ep' are as in section 4.
- CTS_P and CTS_Q are communicating transition systems representing P and
  Q respectively; i.e., $P = P_{CTS_P}$ and $Q = P_{CTS_Q}$.
- For $i = 1, \ldots, m + n$, EG_i is an extraction graph with initial node v_{0i} and
  representing ep_i; i.e., $ep_{EG_i} = ep_i$.
- P_{det} is the *normalised* version of CTS_P. We will use κ_P to denote the mapping defined as in (1) for the nodes of P_{det}, and denote the initial state of
  P_{det} by p_0.
- CTS_Q^u is a disambiguated version of CTS_Q w.r.t. extraction graphs EG_i (see
  algorithm 1). We will denote the initial state of CTS_Q^u by q_0^u.

  The process generated by CTS_Q^u will be denoted by $\widehat{Q}$; i.e., $\widehat{Q} = P_{CTS_Q^u}$.
- Q_{det} is the normalised version of CTS_Q^u. We will use κ_Q to denote the mapping defined as in (1) for the nodes of Q_{det}, and denote the initial state of
  Q_{det} by q_0.

  It may be observed that if v is a node of Q_{det} and $q, r \in v$ then, for all
  $1 \leq i \leq m + n$, $q^{(i)} = r^{(i)}$. We can therefore use $v^{(i)}$ to denote $q^{(i)}$, and
  $extr(v, a) = extr(q, a)$ whenever the latter is defined.

We now proceed with a systematic re-evaluation of the implementation conditions DP–RI. We first obtain the result that testing for DF amounts to checking
for the presence of τ-loops in the graph of CTS_Q^u, and, if there is no such loop,
then testing for DP is done while generating CTS_Q^u.

Proposition 3. *Q satisfies DP and DF if and only if CTS_Q^u has been successfully generated and there are no nodes $v_1, \ldots, v_k$ ($k \geq 2$) in CTS_Q^u such that*
$$v_1 \xrightarrow{\tau} v_2 \cdots \xrightarrow{\tau} v_k = v_1.$$

Below we assume that CTS_Q^u has been successfully generated and does not
contain any τ-loops, and so DP and DF hold. Then it generates a process which
can be used to test for other implementation conditions in place of Q.

Proposition 4. *For each condition TE–RI, Q satisfies the condition if and only if the same is true of $\widehat{Q}$. Moreover, $\tau\widehat{Q} = \tau_{Dom}Q$.*

As we have already seen, DP and DF can be checked directly using CTS_Q^u. In dealing with the remaining conditions, we assume that DP and DF hold, and use Q_{det}, which is the normalised CTS derived from CTS_Q^u. Note that, by propositions 3 and 4, we may assume that $\widehat{Q}$ is an implementation process such that $\delta\widehat{Q} = \emptyset$ and $\tau\widehat{Q} \subseteq Dom_{ep\cup ep'}$.

A relation $sim_{extr} \subseteq V_{Q_{det}} \times V_{P_{det}}$ is an *extr-simulation* if $(q_0, p_0) \in sim_{extr}$ and, for every $(q, p) \in sim_{extr}$,

$$q \xrightarrow{a} q' \implies \exists (q', p') \in sim_{extr} : p \xrightarrow{\langle extr(q,a) \rangle} p' . \tag{3}$$

Proposition 5. *$\widehat{Q}$ satisfies TE if and only if there is an extr-simulation.*

Note that, since P_{det} is deterministic and contains no τ-transitions, if there is at least one extr-simulation, then there exists the smallest one, sim_{extr}^{min}.

From now on, we will additionally assume that $\widehat{Q}$ satisfies TE. Then, testing for GE amounts to checking for extracted τ-loops in the graph of Q_{det}.

Proposition 6. *$\widehat{Q}$ satisfies GE if and only if there are no nodes $v_1, \ldots, v_k$ in Q_{det} such that $v_1 \xrightarrow{a_1} v_2 \xrightarrow{a_2} \cdots \xrightarrow{a_{k-1}} v_k = v_1$ and $extr(v_i, a_i) = \tau$, for all $i \leq k$.*

To prepare the ground for testing of LC and RE, we re-phrase them in terms of maximal failures of $\widehat{Q}$. For every $(t, R) \in \phi\widehat{Q}$, we denote

$$\mathcal{C}_{t,R} = \{b_i \in in\, P \mid \alpha B_i - R \in ref_i(t{\restriction}B_i)\} \cup \{b_i \in out\, P \mid \alpha B_i \cap R \not\in ref_i(t{\restriction}B_i)\} .$$

We also denote $\mathcal{C}_t = \{\mathcal{C}_{t,R} \mid (t, R) \in max\phi\widehat{Q}\}$ and $\overline{\mathcal{C}}_t = \bigcup\{B \mid B \in \mathcal{C}_t\}$. One can see that $\widehat{Q}$ satisfies LC and RE if and only if, for every $t \in \tau\widehat{Q}$, the following hold: (i) if $b_i \in \overline{\mathcal{C}}_t$ then $t{\restriction}B_i \in dom_i$; and (ii) if $t \in dom_{ep\cup ep'}$ then for every $B \in \mathcal{C}_t$ there exists R such that $(extr_{ep\cup ep'}(t), R) \in max\phi P$ and $\alpha B \subseteq R$.

We now introduce notions corresponding to $\mathcal{C}_{t,R}$, $\mathcal{C}_t$ and $\overline{\mathcal{C}}_t$ in the domain of communicating transition systems and extraction graphs. For all $q \in V_{Q_{det}}$ and $A \in \kappa_Q(q)$, we denote

$$\mathcal{C}_{q,A} = \{b_i \in in\, P \mid \exists R' \in \varrho_i(q^{(i)}) : \alpha B_i \cap A \subseteq R'\} \cup$$
$$\{b_i \in out\, P \mid \not\exists R' \in \varrho_i(q^{(i)}) : \alpha B_i - A \subseteq R'\}.$$

We also denote $\mathcal{C}_q = \{\mathcal{C}_{q,A} \mid A \in \kappa_Q(q)\}$ and $\overline{\mathcal{C}}_q = \bigcup\{B \mid B \in \mathcal{C}_q\}$. One can see that if $q_0 \xRightarrow{t} q$ then $\mathcal{C}_q = \mathcal{C}_t$. Moreover, $\mathcal{C}_{q,A} = \mathcal{C}_{t,\alpha Q - A}$ for every $A \in \kappa_Q(q)$ and $\mathcal{C}_{t,R} = \mathcal{C}_{q,\alpha Q - R}$ for every $(t, R) \in max\phi\widehat{Q}$.

Proposition 7. $\widehat{Q}$ *satisfies LC and RE if and only if, for every* $q \in V_{Q_{det}}$:

1. *If* $b_i \in \overline{C}_q$ *then* $\delta_i(q^{(i)}) = d$.
2. *If* $\delta_i(q^{(1)}) = \cdots = \delta_i(q^{(m+n)}) = d$ *then, for every* $B \in C_q$, *and for every* p *such that* $(q, p) \in sim_{extr}^{min}$, *there is* $A \in \kappa_P(p)$ *satisfying* $\alpha B \cap A = \emptyset$.

We now turn to the two remaining implementation conditions. Since the inv_i's are homomorphisms, they can interpret the arc labels directly, without taking into account how a particular node has been reached. However, the situation is complicated by the fact that $inv_i(a)$ will usually be a non-singleton trace.

A relation $sim_{inv} \subseteq V_{P_{det}} \times V_{Q_{det}}$ is an *inv-simulation* if $(p_0, q_0) \in sim_{inv}$ and, for every $(p, q) \in sim_{inv}$,

$$p \xrightarrow{a} p' \implies \exists (p', q') \in sim_{inv} : q \xRightarrow{inv_{ep \cup ep'}(a)} q' . \tag{4}$$

Proposition 8. $\widehat{Q}$ *satisfies TI if and only if there exists an inv-simulation.*

When dealing with RI, we will assume that $\widehat{Q}$ satisfies TI. This does not result in a loss of generality as TI is implied by RI. Note that, since Q_{det} is deterministic and contains no τ-transitions, if there is at least one inv-simulation, then there also exists the smallest one, sim_{inv}^{min}.

To test for RI, we first observe that it can be equivalently expressed in terms of maximal failures. For every $(t, R) \in \phi P$, we denote

$$\mathcal{D}_{t,R} = \{b_i \in \chi P \mid \alpha b_i \subseteq R\} .$$

We also denote $\mathcal{D}_t = \{\mathcal{D}_{t,R} \mid (t, R) \in max\phi P\}$. One can see that $\widehat{Q}$ satisfies RI if and only if, for all $t \in \tau P$ and $B \in \mathcal{D}_t$, there is $(inv_{ep \cup ep'}(t), R) \in max\phi\widehat{Q}$ such that $\bigcup_{b_i \in B} \alpha B_i \subseteq R$.

We now introduce notions corresponding to $\mathcal{D}_{t,R}$ and $\mathcal{D}_t$ in the domain of communicating transition systems. For all $p \in V_{P_{det}}$ and $A \in \kappa_P(p)$, we denote

$$\mathcal{D}_{p,A} = \{b_i \in \chi P \mid \alpha b_i \cap A = \emptyset\}.$$

We also denote $\mathcal{D}_p = \{\mathcal{D}_{p,A} \mid A \in \kappa_P(p)\}$. One can then see that if $p_0 \xRightarrow{t} p$ then $\mathcal{D}_p = \mathcal{D}_t$. Moreover, $\mathcal{D}_{p,A} = \mathcal{D}_{t,\alpha Q - A}$ for every $A \in \kappa_P(p)$ and $\mathcal{D}_{t,R} = \mathcal{D}_{p,\alpha Q - R}$ for every $(t, R) \in max\phi P$.

Proposition 9. $\widehat{Q}$ *satisfies RI if and only if for every* $(p, q) \in sim_{inv}^{min}$, *if* $B \in \mathcal{D}_p$ *then there is* $A' \in \kappa_Q(q)$ *such that* $\bigcup_{b_i \in B} \alpha B_i \cap A' = \emptyset$.

8   Algorithms

We now briefly outline algorithms for checking the implementation relations DP–RI except for DP which is implicitly tested during the generation of CTS_Q^u, provided that DF holds.

To test for DF and GE respectively we use modified versions of the depth-first search algorithm given in [10] to test for strong connectivity.

The algorithm to test for TE is based on proposition 5. We aim to construct the minimal extr-simulation sim_{extr}^{min}, by traversing the product $V_{Q_{det}} \times V_{P_{det}}$. We first map the initial nodes to each other, $(q_0, p_0) \in sim_{extr}$. We then perform a depth-first search, beginning at (q_0, p_0). If the construction is successful, the set of all pairs of nodes reachable from (q_0, p_0) gives the minimal extr-simulation.

The algorithm to test for LC and RE is based on proposition 7 and uses the relation sim_{extr}^{min} calculated during the testing for TE. The pseudo-code is shown in figure 11. It uses three auxiliary functions:

- $LC()$ to test for proposition 7(1) (which captures LC) for q and C_q.
- $RE()$ to test for proposition 7(2) (which captures RE) for q and C_q.
- $getC()$ to calculate the set C_q for a given q.

To test for TI we use proposition 8, aiming to construct the minimal inv-simulation sim_{inv}^{min} by traversing the product $V_{P_{det}} \times V_{Q_{det}}$. We first map the initial nodes to each other, $(p_0, q_0) \in sim_{inv}$. We then perform a depth-first search, beginning at (p_0, q_0). If the construction is successful, the set of all pairs of nodes reachable from (p_0, q_0) gives the minimal inv-simulation. The pseudo-code is shown in figure 10.

The algorithm to test for RI uses the relation sim_{inv}^{min} generated when testing for TI and is based on proposition 9. The pseudo-code is shown in figure 10.

```
function TI()
    outcome ← success
    visit(p₀, q₀, ⟨⟩)
    return outcome


void visit(p, q, invEvents)
    if ⟨⟩ ≠ invEvents = ⟨a⟩ ∘ invEvents'
        then
            if a ∉ en(q)
                then outcome = failure
                else visit(p, q', invEvents') where q ──a──→ q'
        else
            if (p,q) not in jointNodes
                then
                    enter (p,q) in jointNodes
                    for every p ──a'──→ p'
                        visit(p', q, inv_{ep∪ep'}(a'))
    return
```

Fig. 9. Testing for TI.

```
function RI()
    for every p ∈ V_{P_{det}}
        for every A ∈ κ_P(p)
        B ← χP − χA
            for every q such that (p, q) ∈ sim_{inv}^{min}
                matchFound ← false
                for every A' ∈ κ_Q(q)
                    if ⋃_{b_i ∈ B} αB_i ⊆ χQ − χA' then matchFound = true ; break
                if matchFound = false then return failure
    return success
```

Fig. 10. Testing for RI.

9   Concluding Remarks

The algorithms presented here have been derived almost directly from the implementation relations themselves and future work will explore possibilities for optimisation, as well as including a case study to evaluate the performance of the algorithms in practice.

Acknowledgements. The first author was supported in this work by an EPSRC studentship. We would like to thank the anonymous referees for their helpful comments.

References

1. J. Burton, M. Koutny and G. Pappalardo: Modelling and Verification of Communicating Processes in the Event of Interface Difference. Technical Report CS-TR-696, Department of Computing Science, University of Newcastle upon Tyne (2000).
2. P. Collette and C. B. Jones: Enhancing the Tractability of Rely/Guarantee Specifications in the Development of Interfering Operations. Technical Report CUMCS-95-10-3, Department of Computing Science, Manchester University (1995).
3. M. Hennessy: *Algebraic Theory of Processes*. MIT Press (1988).
4. C. A. R. Hoare: *Communicating Sequential Processes*. Prentice Hall (1985).
5. M. Koutny and G. Pappalardo: A Model of Behaviour Abstraction for Communicating Processes. Proc. of *16th Symposium on Theoretical Aspects of Computer Science, STACS'99*, C. Meinel and S. Tison (Eds.). Springer-Verlag, Lecture Notes in Computer Science 1563 (1999) 313-322.
6. M. Koutny, L. Mancini and G. Pappalardo: Two Implementation Relations and the Correctness of Communicated Replicated Processing. *Formal Aspects of Computing* 9 (1997) 119-148.
7. J. Burton and M. Koutny: Verification of Communicating Processes in the Event of Interface Difference. Proc. of *International Workshop on Verification and Computational Logic, VCL2000*, M. Leuschel, A. Podelski, C. Ramakrishnan and U. Ulrich-Nitsche(Eds.). Technical Report DSSE-TR-2000-6, University of Southampton (2000) .
8. R. Milner: *Communication and Concurrency*. Prentice Hall (1989).
9. A. W. Roscoe: *The Theory and Practice of Concurrency*. Prentice-Hall (1998).
10. R. Sedgewick: *Algorithms in C++*. Addison-Wesley (1992).

```
function LC&RE()
   for every q ∈ V_{Q_{det}}
      C_q ← getC(q)
      if LC(q, C_q) = failure or RE(q, C_q) = failure then return failure
   return success


function LC(q, C_q)
   B ← ⋃_{B∈C_q} B
   for every b_i ∈ B
      if δ_i(q^{(i)}) = D then return failure
   return success


function RE(q, C_q)
   if δ_1(q^{(1)}) = ⋯ = δ_{m+n}(q^{(m+n)}) = d
   then
      for every B ∈ C_q
         for every p such that (q, p) ∈ sim_{extr}^{min}
            successful ← false
            for every A ∈ κ_P(p)
               if αB ∩ A = ∅ then successful ← true ; break
            if successful = false then return failure
   return success


function getC(q)
   C_q ← ∅
   for every A ∈ κ_Q(q)
      B ← ∅
      for every b_i ∈ in P
         if ∃R ∈ ϱ_i(q^{(i)}) : αB_i ∩ A ⊆ R then B ← B ∪ {b_i}
      for every b_i ∈ out P
         if ∄R ∈ ϱ_i(q^{(i)}) : αB_i − A ⊆ R then B ← B ∪ {b_i}
      C_q ← C_q ∪ {B}
   return C_q
```

Fig. 11. Testing for LC and RE.

An Adequate Logic for Full LOTOS

Muffy Calder[1], Savi Maharaj[2], and Carron Shankland[2]

[1] Department of Computing Science,
University of Glasgow, Glasgow G12 8QQ, UK
muffy@dcs.gla.ac.uk
[2] Department of Computing Science and Mathematics,
University of Stirling, Stirling FK9 4LA, UK
{savi,carron}@cs.stir.ac.uk

Abstract. We present a novel result for a logic for symbolic transition systems based on LOTOS processes. The logic is adequate with respect to bisimulation defined on symbolic transition systems.

1 Introduction

LOTOS [12] is a popular process description language that has been in use for well over a decade. With the aid of a number of mature verification tools, it has been successfully applied in a number of domains, including protocols and services [17], distributed systems [23,16], and as a semantics for higher level languages such as feature descriptions [22] and use-case maps [1].

A particularly distinctive feature of LOTOS is that it includes a rich set of operators for describing both process control *and* data, which may in turn affect control. However, much of the foundational work, and subsequently the verification tools, has ignored all, or parts, of the data aspect of the language. Specifically, there is no logic for reasoning about LOTOS processes with unconstrained data. This is a serious drawback since it has long been recognised that a more abstract, temporal logic is essential for describing and checking desired (or undesired) properties of processes [11]. Indeed, experience with case studies [21,19,20,17] has shown the benefits of having data in the process description language and the need to express properties of a system in terms of data, as well as actions. Often the properties refer to data, but symbolically, rather than mentioning particular instances. For example, in the classical comparator one such property is *if process* Comp *inputs* x *and* y *on channel* in, *and* x *and* y *are equivalent, then eventually it will output true on channel* out.

There has been a good reason to avoid dealing with data properly: in LOTOS, data introduces infinite branching into the underlying state transition systems. For example, the simple process g?x:Nat; exit results in an infinite choice, one for each member of Nat. This presents a serious obstacle to reasoning, particularly to approaches based on (finite) model-checking. Therefore existing approaches have been restricted to Basic LOTOS [13], or LOTOS with only finite data types [6].

J.N. Oliveira and P. Zave (Eds.): FME 2001, LNCS 2021, pp. 384–395, 2001.
© Springer-Verlag Berlin Heidelberg 2001

Our aim is to provide a complete approach to data. In order to do so, we base our logic on a new semantics for LOTOS which is finitely branching. This is achieved by having a *symbolic* treatment of data; the underlying state transition systems are therefore called symbolic state transition systems (STSs). Our work is heavily influenced by the symbolic transition systems and logic developed by Hennessy, Lin and Liu for CCS [9,10]. However, it is significantly different because of the special characteristics of the STSs that result from LOTOS. These derive from the three (related) features that distinguish LOTOS from most other process algebras: *multi-way (broadcast) synchronisation, value negotiation,* and *selection predicates.* Together, these features make the definition of the similar concepts of symbolic transition, bisimulation and logic, non-trivial.

1.1 Related Work

A symbolic approach to message passing CCS is presented in [9] and a related logic in [10]. We adopt the theory of symbolic transition systems here, but the logic is not so useful for our applications. The logic of Hennessy and Liu is based on a *late* semantics, whereas we adopt an *early* semantics because the standard definition of LOTOS [12] is also early. (The late and early classification relates to binding time of variables to values.) In addition, the modal operators defined rely on the classical CCS distinction between ! and ? data offers (i.e. as corresponding to output and input events). In LOTOS the distinction between these two kinds of data offers is not so clear cut. The logic does have the advantage that it is based on symbolic transition systems, and therefore places no artificial restrictions on data values.

μCRL [8] is, like LOTOS, a process algebra with data. In [7] an extension of the modal mu-calculus [14] is presented which includes quantification over data in the modal operators. The semantics of the logic is over labelled transition systems and therefore is subject to the usual problems of state explosion. The focus of their research is on proof rules for the logic rather than adequacy with respect to some equivalence over μCRL processes.

The CADP toolkit [6] provides a number of tools to analyse Full LOTOS specifications, two of which use logic to provide an abstract description of system properties. The tool *evaluator* takes an alternation free modal mu-calculus [14] formula and assesses its truth with respect to a LOTOS expression. The modal operators are extended to allow more flexibility in dealing with actions with data, for example, precise actions or Unix regular expressions can be matched. However, it is not possible to state general predicates on data, such as *input a value which is less than 42 but more than 3.* The action formulae of this logic treat the values as syntactic entities only, whereas we provide the ability to reason about their semantics too.

Also part of the CADP toolkit is *XTL* [15]. This is an executable temporal language which describes computations over transitions. XTL allows a more general treatment of data actions than the evaluator. For example, variables over data can be declared and matched with actions, and operations over data in the LOTOS source can also be used in the logic. Various logics can be encoded in XTL; in fact, we have encoded a *restricted* form of the logic presented in this paper in XTL and carried out some limited examples.

Two important disadvantages of XTL are that the underlying semantics of labelled transition systems is concrete (i.e. fully instantiated) and that CADP must impose finiteness restrictions on the data types of the language to obtain tractability. So, any logic encoded by XTL cannot handle Full LOTOS effectively or accurately.

1.2   Structure of the Paper

The structure of the rest of this paper is as follows. In Section 2 we introduce the idea of a symbolic transition system, describe how this has had to be adapted for LOTOS, and explain the problem of defining substitution and how this is solved. In Section 3 we present the syntax and semantics of a modal logic called FULL. In Section 4 we give an alternative characterisation of the equivalence induced by the logic by showing that it coincides with bisimulation on symbolic transition systems. Finally, we discuss further work and conclude in Section 5.

2   Symbolic Transition Systems

The standard semantics of LOTOS [12] (labelled transition systems) hard codes concrete data values into the transitions. For example, `g!0; P` offers the single transition labelled `g[0]`, while `g?x:Nat; P` offers the transitions labelled by `g[0]`, `g[succ(0)]`, `g[succ(succ(0))]`, ... (Fig. 1). Thus, event offers of more than one value (i.e. ? offers) correspond to a (possibly infinite) choice over all values of the data type. While this makes the semantics of certain language

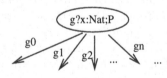

Fig. 1. Standard semantics of `g?x:Nat` event offer

features easier to describe (particularly multiway synchronisation), it makes reasoning about specifications more difficult since transition systems are typically infinite. Existing tools such as CADP [6] deal with this problem by imposing finiteness restrictions on data types, limiting the natural numbers, for example, to a maximum of 256.

An alternative solution is to restate the semantics of the language in a form which exposes the commonalities of actions and the finitary nature of the process specification. This can be done by basing the semantics on *symbolic transition systems* (STSs). These are essentially transition systems whose transitions can have free variables in the data label and are additionally labelled with a *transition condition* representing the conditions under which that transition is available. This approach was first introduced in [9] which gave a symbolic semantics for value passing CCS. In our research [4,3], we have been adapting this theory for use with LOTOS. There are significant differences between LOTOS and value passing CCS which mean that this adaptation is not straightforward.

One difference is that input events in CCS are always unconstrained and there is no analogue of the *selection predicates* which can be used in LOTOS to restrict the values passed in a ? event. For example, LOTOS allows events such as g?x [x > 3] meaning, *input an x which is bigger than 3.* This means that the transition conditions in the LOTOS semantics need to be able to talk about the data associated with the current transition, whereas in CCS these are concerned only with previous transitions.

Another difference is that in order to implement multi-way synchronisation LOTOS permits synchronisation between any combination of ? and ! events, whereas in CCS an input event (?) can synchronise only with an output action (!). This means that the distinction between ? and ! is much less significant in LOTOS than it is in CCS. Essentially, a ! event is associated with an expression using constants and "known" variables while a ? event introduces a new variable. We have found it convenient to remove the !/? distinction from the syntax of data expressions in STSs. We shall still need to be able to tell when a transition introduces a new variable, but this will be determined by comparing the transition's data expression with the free variables of the source of the transition.

We shall assume that we have a countable set of *variables*, Var, ranged over by x, y, etc., and a (possibly infinite) set of *values*, Val, ranged over by v. We also assume a set of *data expressions*, Exp, which includes Var and Val and is ranged over by E, and a set of *boolean expressions*, BoolExp, ranged over by b. We also assume that we have a set of gates, G, ranged over by g. The set of simple events, SimpleEv, ranged over by a, is defined as $G \cup \{i, \delta\}$. (Recall that in LOTOS i is the internal event and δ is the special event which takes place when a process is exited.) The set of structured events, StructEv contains all gate-expression combinations gE, as well as all combinations δE. Since the two kinds of structured events are handled exactly the same, we shall generally ignore δ in this paper, treating it as if it were a member of G. For simplicity, we do not allow structured events consisting of multiple data expressions; only *singleton* data offers are allowed. It is possible, but tedious, to extend our analysis to the case of multiple data offers.

Basically, an STS is a directed graph whose nodes are tagged with sets of free variables, and whose branches are labelled with a boolean condition and an event. Formally, the definition of STS is as follows:

Definition 1. *(Symbolic Transition Systems) A symbolic transition system consists of:*

- *a set of states, containing a distinguished initial state, T_0, with each state T tagged with a set of free variables, denoted $fv(T)$.*

- *a set of transitions written as* $T \xrightarrow{\ b \quad \alpha\ } T'$,
  where $\alpha \in SimpleEv \cup StructEv$ *and* b *is a Boolean expression*
  and $fv(T') \subseteq fv(T) \cup fv(\alpha)$ *and* $fv(b) \subseteq fv(T) \cup fv(\alpha)$ *and*
  $\#(fv(\alpha) - fv(T)) \leq 1$

Following convention, we shall often identify an STS with its initial state. For example, the set of free variables of an STS S, $fv(S)$, is defined as the set of free variables of the initial state of S.

A set of rules presented in [4] define how a symbolic transition system may be constructed from a LOTOS process expression. The resulting transition system is typically a cyclic graph (if recursive processes are involved) and is always of finite width (since only a finite number of branches may be described in a LOTOS process). This paper is concerned with STSs rather than LOTOS processes, though we shall use LOTOS syntax to describe examples.

2.1   Substitution

In the following section we present a logic on symbolic transition systems. Before we can do this, however, we must consider the question of how to define *substitution* on STSs. It is not possible to define a straightforward syntactic substitution on STSs because of the presence of cycles (such as might arise from recursive processes).

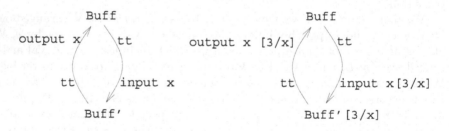

Fig. 2. Failed substitution on `Buff` STS

Consider, for example, the simple buffer `Buff = input?x:Nat; output!x; Buff`. The STS which corresponds to `Buff` is shown in Figure 2. If the first action taken by this process is to input the value 3, then the x at the output gate must also be tied to that value. Since `Buff` is recursive, we expect that the next time round the loop a different value may be input, and therefore a different substitution must be applied. However, if we simply substitute 3 for x in the STS, as shown in Figure 2, we fail to capture this possibility.

In [9], this problem is solved by introducing the concept of a "term": a node in a symbolic transition system paired with a substitution. The same solution can be adapted for LOTOS. Formally, a *substitution* is a partial function from Var to Var $\cup$ Val and a *term* consists of an STS, T, paired with a substitution, σ such that $domain(\sigma) \subseteq fv(T)$. We use t and u to range over terms. For example, since Buff is closed, it can be paired only with the empty substitution to form the term $\text{Buff}_{[\,]}$. The substitution is applied step by step, when necessary, as explained in the rules for transitions between terms (Figure 2). For example, below are some possible transitions starting from the term $\text{Buff}_{[\,]}$. The substitutions capture the fact that the variable x is discarded and then bound afresh upon each pass through the loop, making it possible to process a different value during each pass.

$$\text{Buff}_{[\,]} \xrightarrow{\;tt\quad \text{input } z1\;} \text{Buff'}_{[z1/x]}$$
$$\text{Buff'}_{[z1/x]} \xrightarrow{\;tt\quad \text{output } z1\;} \text{Buff}_{[\,]}$$
$$\text{Buff}_{[\,]} \xrightarrow{\;tt\quad \text{input } z2\;} \text{Buff'}_{[z2/x]} \text{ and so on.}$$

The definition of free variables is extended to terms in the obvious way. Terms, rather than STSs, are used as the basis for defining the logic and bisimulation.

Definition 2. *Transitions on Terms*

$$T \xrightarrow{\;b\quad a\;} T' \text{ implies } T_\sigma \xrightarrow{\;b\sigma\quad a\;} T'_{\sigma'}$$
$$T \xrightarrow{\;b\quad gE\;} T' \text{ implies } T_\sigma \xrightarrow{\;b\sigma\qquad gE\sigma\;} T'_{\sigma'}$$
$$\text{where } fv(E) \subseteq fv(T)$$
$$T \xrightarrow{\;b\quad gx\;} T' \text{ implies } T_\sigma \xrightarrow{\;b\sigma[z/x]\qquad gz\;} T'_{\sigma'[z/x]}$$
$$\text{where } x \notin fv(T) \text{ and } z \notin fv(T_\sigma)$$

In all cases, $\sigma' = fv(T') \lhd \sigma$, that is, the restriction of σ to include only domain elements in the set $fv(T')$.

3   The Modal Logic FULL

In this section we present the syntax and semantics of a modal logic defined over symbolic transition systems. The logic is called Full LOTOS Logic (FULL) and is inspired by the HML presented in [18] and the data extended logic presented in [10]. The logic and the design considerations driving the choice of operators are described fully in [3]; here we simply give the syntax and semantics without discussion.

FULL is made up of two parts. The first set of formulae, ranged over by Φ, applies to closed terms. The second set, ranged over by Λ, is to be used for terms with a single free variable, as would arise from a LOTOS process with a single parameter. (The extension to multiple free variables is straightforward but tedious and is therefore omitted).

Definition 3. *(Syntax of FULL)*

$$\Phi \;::=\; b \;\mid\; \Phi_1 \wedge \Phi_2 \;\mid\; \Phi_1 \vee \Phi_2 \;\mid\; [a]\Phi \;\mid\; \langle a \rangle \Phi$$
$$\mid\; \langle \exists x\ g \rangle \Phi \;\mid\; \langle \forall x\ g \rangle \Phi \;\mid\; [\exists x\ g]\Phi \;\mid\; [\forall x\ g]\Phi$$
$$\Lambda \;::=\; \exists x.\Phi \;\mid\; \forall x.\Phi$$

Definition 4. *(Semantics of FULL) Given any closed term t, the semantics of* $t \models \Phi$ *is given by:*

$$t \models b \quad\quad = \quad b \equiv \text{tt}$$

$$t \models \Phi_1 \wedge \Phi_2 \quad = \quad t \models \Phi_1 \text{ and } t \models \Phi_2$$

$$t \models \Phi_1 \vee \Phi_2 \quad = \quad t \models \Phi_1 \text{ or } t \models \Phi_2$$

$$t \models \langle a \rangle \Phi \quad = \quad \text{there is a } t' \text{ s.t. } t \xrightarrow{\text{tt} \quad a} t' \text{ and } t' \models \Phi$$

$$t \models [a]\Phi \quad = \quad \text{whenever } t \xrightarrow{\text{tt} \quad a} t' \text{ then } t' \models \Phi$$

$$t \models \langle \exists x\ g \rangle \Phi \quad = \quad \text{for some value } v, \text{ either}$$
$$\quad\quad\quad \text{for some } t',\ t \xrightarrow{\text{tt} \quad gv} t' \text{ and } t' \models \Phi[v/x]$$
$$\quad or$$
$$\quad\quad\quad \text{for some } t',\ t \xrightarrow{b \quad gz} t' \text{ and } b[v/z] \equiv \text{tt}$$
$$\quad\quad\quad \text{and } t'_{[v/z]} \models \Phi[v/x]$$

$$t \models \langle \forall x\ g \rangle \Phi \quad = \quad \text{for all values } v, \text{ either}$$
$$\quad\quad\quad \text{for some } t',\ t \xrightarrow{\text{tt} \quad gv} t' \text{ and } t' \models \Phi[v/x]$$
$$\quad or$$
$$\quad\quad\quad \text{for some } t',\ t \xrightarrow{b \quad gz} t' \text{ and } b[v/z] \equiv \text{tt}$$
$$\quad\quad\quad \text{and } t'_{[v/z]} \models \Phi[v/x]$$

$$t \models [\exists x\ g]\Phi \quad = \quad \text{for some value } v,$$
$$\quad\quad\quad \text{whenever } t \xrightarrow{\text{tt} \quad gv} t' \text{ then } t' \models \Phi[v/x] \text{ and}$$
$$\quad\quad\quad \text{whenever } t \xrightarrow{b \quad gz} t' \text{ and } b[v/z] \equiv \text{tt then } t'_{[v/z]} \models \Phi[v/x]$$

$$t \models [\forall x\ g]\Phi \quad = \quad \text{for all values } v,$$
$$\quad\quad\quad \text{whenever } t \xrightarrow{\text{tt} \quad gv} t' \text{ then } t' \models \Phi[v/x] \text{ and}$$
$$\quad\quad\quad \text{whenever } t \xrightarrow{b \quad gz} t' \text{ and } b[v/z] \equiv \text{tt then } t'_{[v/z]} \models \Phi[v/x]$$

Given any term t with one free variable z the semantics of $t \models \Lambda$ *is given by:*

$$t \models \exists x.\Phi \quad = \quad \text{there is some value } v \text{ such that } t_{[v/z]} \models \Phi[v/x]$$
$$t \models \forall x.\Phi \quad = \quad \text{for all values } v,\ t_{[v/z]} \models \Phi[v/x]$$

A property of FULL is that for every formula it is possible to construct the negation, *neg*, of that formula. (We assume that negation is available in the underlying language of boolean expressions.) For example, $neg([\forall x\ g]\Phi)$ is $\langle \exists x\ g \rangle neg(\Phi)$.

To each formula in FULL is associated a *depth*, n, which is defined in the obvious inductive way.

4   Bisimulation and Adequacy of FULL

In developing the logic FULL we were motivated by two goals. The first was to develop a logic which allowed properties concerning data to be expressed in a natural way. The second was to ensure that the logic was *adequate* with respect to other notions of equivalence between processes, in the sense that equivalent processes should satisfy the same set of logical formulae. One important relationship between processes is that of *bisimulation*. In this section we show how bisimulation is defined upon terms and prove that FULL is adequate with respect to bisimulation.

We shall assume we have a function $new(t, u)$ which, given two terms t and u, returns a variable which is not among the free variables of either t or u.

Definition 5. *Bisimulation on terms*
Given two closed terms t and u,

1. $t \sim_0 u$
2. *for all $n > 0$, $t \sim_n u$ provided that:*
   a) **(simple event)**
      whenever $t \xrightarrow{\text{tt } a} t'$, then for some u', $u \xrightarrow{\text{tt } a} u'$ and $t' \sim_{n-1} u'$
   b) **(structured event, no new variable)**
      whenever $t \xrightarrow{\text{tt } gv} t'$, then either
      for some u', $u \xrightarrow{\text{tt } gv} u'$ and $t' \sim_{n-1} u'$
      or
      for some u', $u \xrightarrow{b_u \ gz} u'$ and $b_u[v/z] \equiv$ tt and $t' \sim_{n-1} u'_{[v/z]}$, where $z = new(t, u)$.
   c) **(structured event, new variable)**
      whenever $t \xrightarrow{b_t \ gz} t'$, where $z = new(t, u)$, then, for all v s.t. $b_t[v/z] \equiv$ tt, either
      for some u', $u \xrightarrow{\text{tt } gv} u'$ and $t'_{[v/z]} \sim_{n-1} u'$
      or
      for some u', $u \xrightarrow{b_u \ gz} u'$ and $b_u[v/z] \equiv$ tt and $t'_{[v/z]} \sim_{n-1} u'_{[v/z]}$.
   d), (e), (f) *Symmetrically, the transitions of u must be matched by t.*

Given two terms t and u with free variables $\{x\}$ and $\{y\}$, respectively, $t \sim_n u$ provided that for all values v, $t_{[v/x]} \sim_n u_{[v/y]}$.

The four theorems which follow show that FULL is adequate with respect to bisimulation. Theorems 1 and 2 give the result for closed terms, and are then used to prove the result for terms of one free variable (Theorems 3 and 4).

Theorem 1. *(FULL distinguishes non-bisimilar closed terms) For all n, for all closed terms t and u, if $t \not\sim_n u$ then there is a formula Φ such that $t \models \Phi$ and $u \not\models \Phi$*

Proof *The proof is by induction on n. If $n = 0$ then the result is vacuously true. In the case where $n > 0$, we examine all the ways in which bisimulation can fail and, in each case, construct a formula which is satisfied by t but not by u. We shall illustrate the construction by showing the case where rule (c) of Definition 5 fails. The other cases are simpler and are omitted.*

If rule (c) fails, then there is a transition $t \xrightarrow{b_t \ gz} t'$, where $z = new(t, u)$, but there is some value v such that $b_t[v/z] \equiv$ tt and for all transitions of the form $u \xrightarrow{\text{tt } gv} u'$, $t'_{[v/z]} \not\sim_{n-1} u'$, and for all transitions of the form $u \xrightarrow{b_u \ gz} u'$ where

$b_u[v/z] \equiv$ tt, $t'_{[v/z]} \not\sim_{n-1} u'_{[v/z]}$. *Suppose that that there are k of the first kind of transition and m of the second kind, where k and m are natural numbers. Then, by the induction hypothesis, each of the u'_is of the first kind can be distinguished from $t'_{[v/z]}$ by some formula Φ_i, and for each of the u'_is of the second kind, there is a formula Ψ_i which distinguishes $t'_{[v/z]}$ from $u'_{i[v/z]}$. Then, t and u can be distinguished by the formula $[\exists g\ x](x = v) \wedge \bigwedge\{\Phi_1, ...\Phi_k\} \wedge \bigwedge\{\Psi_1, ...\Psi_m\}$.*

Theorem 2. *(Bisimilar closed terms satisfy the same formulae) For all n, for all closed terms t and u, if $t \sim_n u$ then, for all formulae Φ such that depth$(\Phi) \le n$, $t \models \Phi$ if and only if $u \models \Phi$.*

Proof *The proof is by induction on n. If $n = 0$, then the formula Φ must be of depth 0, and must therefore be a simple boolean b. By the semantics of FULL, it is clear that for any t and u, $t \models b$ iff $u \models b$.*

In the case where $n > 0$, we take any t and u and assume that $t \sim_n u$. We must show that for all formulae Φ such that depth$(\Phi) \le n$, $t \models \Phi$ if and only if $u \models \Phi$. This is done by induction on the structure of Φ. There are 9 cases to consider. We illustrate the arguments used by showing one of the most complex cases:

Consider the case where Φ is of the form $[\forall x\ g]\Phi'$. Suppose that $t \models \Phi$. Then, by the semantics of FULL, for all values v, whenever there is a t' such that $t \xrightarrow{\text{tt}\ gv} t'$ then $t' \models \Phi'[v/x]$, and whenever there is a t' such that $t \xrightarrow{b_t\ gz} t'$ (for some new variable z) and $b_t[v/z] \equiv$ tt then $t'_{[v/z]} \models \Phi'[v/x]$. We must show that $u \models \Phi$. Take any value v. We must consider all u transitions on v. These can be of two kinds:

Case (1) *Suppose there is a transition of the form $u \xrightarrow{\text{tt}\ gv} u'$. By bisimilarity, this is matched by a t transition. There are two possibilities.*

The matching transition may be of the form $t \xrightarrow{\text{tt}\ gv} t'$, where $t' \sim_{n-1} u'$. Then, we know that $t' \models \Phi'[v/x]$ and, by the main induction hypothesis, we get that $u' \models \Phi'[v/x]$.

The matching transition may be of the form $t \xrightarrow{b_t\ gz} t'$, where $z = new(t, u)$ and $b_t[v/z] \equiv$ tt and $t'_{[v/z]} \sim_{n-1} u'$. Then, we know that $t'_{[v/z]} \models \Phi'[v/x]$ and, by the main induction hypothesis, we get that $u' \models \Phi'[v/x]$.

Case (2) *Suppose there is a transition of the form $u \xrightarrow{b_u\ gz} u'$, (for some fresh z) and $b_u[v/z] \equiv$ tt. We wish to show that $u'_{[v/z]} \models \Phi'[v/x]$. Now, since z is fresh, we can replace z by z' where $z' = new(t, u)$. In other words, we are looking instead at the transition $u \xrightarrow{b_u[z'/z]\ gz'} u'_{[z'/z]}$. For this transition, we get that $b_u[v/z'] \equiv$ tt. And, we need to show that $u'_{[v/z']} \models \Phi'[v/x]$.*

By bisimilarity, this transition is matched by a t transition. There are two possibilities.

The matching transition may be of the form $t \xrightarrow{\text{tt}\ gv} t'$, where $t' \sim_{n-1} u'_{[v/z']}$. Then, we know that $t' \models \Phi'[v/x]$ and, by the main induction hypothesis, we get that $u'_{[v/z']} \models \Phi'[v/x]$.

The matching transition may be of the form $t \xrightarrow{b_t \quad gz'} t'$, *where* $b_t[v/z'] \equiv$ tt *and* $t'_{[v/z']} \sim_{n-1} u'_{[v/z']}$. *Then, we know that* $t'_{[v/z']} \models \Phi'[v/x]$ *and, by the main induction hypothesis, we get that* $u'_{[v/z']} \models \Phi'[v/x]$.

Theorem 3. *(FULL distinguishes non-bisimilar open terms) For all* n, *for all terms* t *and* u *with one free variable, if* $t \not\sim_n u$ *then there is a formula* Λ *such that* $t \models \Lambda$ *and* $u \not\models \Lambda$.

Proof *Suppose that the free variables of* t *and* u *are* z_1 *and* z_2, *respectively. Since* $t \not\sim_n u$, *then there is some value* v *such that* $t_{[v/z_1]} \not\sim_n u_{[v/z_2]}$. *By Theorem 1 there is then a formula* Φ *such that* $t_{[v/z_1]} \models \Phi$ *but* $u_{[v/z_2]} \not\models \Phi$. *We construct the formula* $\Lambda = \forall x.(x \neq v) \vee \Phi$. *Then,* $t \models \Lambda$ *but* $u \not\models \Lambda$.

Theorem 4. *(Bisimilar open terms satisfy the same formulae) For all* n, *for all terms* t *and* u *with one free variable, if* $t \sim_n u$ *then, for all* Λ *such that* $depth(\Lambda) \leq n$, $t \models \Lambda$ *if and only if* $u \models \Lambda$.

Proof *This is a straightforward consequence of Theorem 2.*

5 Further Work

The results presented in this paper provide a foundation upon which to build a system for verifying properties of specifications in Full LOTOS. In this section we discuss the further work, both theoretical and practical, which needs to be done to realise this goal.

Extensions of the Logic. The logic we have developed is relatively sparse, and there are several useful ways in which it could be extended and made more expressive. However, care must be taken to ensure that this is not done at the expense of adequacy. Two important features which we intend to focus upon are ways of handling multi-sorted data, and fixpoint operators to handle recursion.

User-defined algebraic datatypes are an important and heavily used feature of LOTOS so it is essential to extend FULL to deal in some way with multiple data types. One obvious way of doing this is to encode types as predicates over values. The details of this need to be worked out and alternative solutions explored.

Recursion is another heavily-used feature of LOTOS, and the usefulness of FULL would be significantly enhanced by the addition of fixpoint operators for reasoning about recursive or infinitary behaviour. This is a topic which has been much studied in the theory of concurrency and we hope to be able to adapt existing solutions to the needs of LOTOS.

Further Theoretical Analysis. Some areas of the theory underlying symbolic transition systems for LOTOS are as yet incomplete. For example, the relationship between our symbolic semantics and the standard semantics of LOTOS has not yet been fully analyzed. We conjecture that the two semantics coincide for closed terms, in the sense that bisimilar terms in the symbolic semantics correspond to bisimilar processes in the standard semantics. The details of this remain to be checked.

Another interesting area of study is *symbolic bisimulation*. The bisimulation presented in this paper is of limited practical use because it requires a possibly infinite number of values to be examined (cf rules *2(c)* and *2(f)* of Definition 5). This problem can be solved by turning to symbolic bisimulation, as introduced in [9]. Symbolic bisimulation solves the problem of infinite values by dividing the value space that must be examined into a finite number of partitions described by boolean expressions. We have defined symbolic bisimulation for LO-TOS [4] and are working on its theoretical underpinnings and the development of a bisimulation-checking tool to support it.

Algorithms and Tools. The eventual goal of this research is the development of tools to support reasoning about specifications in Full LOTOS. Work is in progress on the development of algorithms for reasoning within FULL. In tandem with this, there is also work on the implementation of tools to support reasoning in FULL. At the present time, a restricted version of the logic has been implemented in CADP. The logic is also being implemented in the Ergo theorem prover [2] and in the Maude system [5].

Acknowledgement. The authors would like to thank the Engineering and Physical Sciences Research Council and the Nuffield Foundation Newly Appointed Lecturer scheme for supporting this research.

References

1. D. Amyot, L. Charfi *et al.* Feature Description and Feature Interaction Analysis with Use Case Maps and LOTOS. In M. Calder and E. Magill, editors, *Feature Interactions in Telecommunications and Software Systems VI.* IOS Press, May 2000.
2. H. Becht, A. Bloesch *et al.* Ergo 4.1 Reference Manual. Technical Report 96-31, Software Verification Research Centre, University of Queensland, Australia, November 1996
3. M. Calder, S. Maharaj, and C. Shankland. A Modal Logic for Early Symbolic Transition Systems. *The Computer Journal,* 2001. To appear.
4. M. Calder and C. Shankland. A Symbolic Semantics and Bisimulation for Full LOTOS. To appear as a University of Stirling Technical Report, 2000.
5. M. Clavel, F. Duran *et al.* Maude: Specification and Programming in Rewriting Logic. Maude System documentation. Computer Science Laboratory, SRI, Menlo Park, California, March 1999.
6. J-C. Fernandez, H. Garavel *et al.* CADP (CAESAR/ALDEBARAN Development Package): A Protocol Validation and Verification Toolbox. In R. Alur and T.A. Henzinger, editors, *Proceedings of CAV'96,* number 1102 in Lecture Notes in Computer Science, pages 437–440. Springer-Verlag, 1996.

7. J.F. Groote and R. Mateescu. Verification of Temporal Properties of Processes in a Setting with Data. In *Proceedings of the 7th International Conference on Algebraic Methodology and Software Technology AMAST'98, Amazonia, Brazil*, volume 1548 of *Lecture Notes in Computer Science*, pages 74–90, 1999.

8. J.F. Groote and A. Ponse. The Syntax and Semantics of μ-CRL. In *Proceedings of Algebra of Communicating Processes, Utrecht 1994*, Workshops in Computing. Springer-Verlag, 1995.

9. M. Hennessy and H. Lin. Symbolic Bisimulations. *Theoretical Computer Science*, 138:353–389, 1995.

10. M. Hennessy and X. Liu. A Modal Logic for Message Passing Processes. *Acta Informatica*, 32:375–393, 1995.

11. M. Hennessy and R. Milner. Algebraic Laws for Nondeterminism and Concurrency. *Journal of the Association for Computing Machinery*, 32(1):137–161, 1985.

12. International Organisation for Standardisation. *Information Processing Systems — Open Systems Interconnection — LOTOS — A Formal Description Technique Based on the Temporal Ordering of Observational Behaviour*, 1988.

13. C. Kirkwood. Specifying Properties of Basic LOTOS Processes Using Temporal Logic. In G. v Bochmann, R. Dssouli, and O. Rafiq, editors, *Formal Description Techniques, VIII*, IFIP. Chapman Hall, April 1996.

14. D. Kozen. Results on the Propositional μ-Calculus. *Theoretical Computer Science*, 27:333–354, 1983.

15. R. Mateescu and H. Garavel. XTL: A Meta-Language and Tool for Temporal Logic Model-Checking. In *Proceedings of the International Workshop on Software Tools for Technology Transfer STTT'98 (Aalborg, Denmark)*, 1998.

16. C. Pecheur. Using LOTOS for specifying the CHORUS distributed operating system kernel. *Computer Communications*, 15(2):93–102, March 1992.

17. M. Sighireanu and R. Mateescu. Verification of the Link Layer Protocol of the IEEE-1394 Serial Bus (FireWire): an Experiment with E-LOTOS. *Springer International Journal on Software Tools for Technology Transfer (STTT)*, 2(1):68–88, Dec. 1998.

18. C. Stirling. Temporal Logics for CCS. In J.W. de Bakker, W.-P. de Roever, and G. Rozenberg, editors, *Linear Time, Branching Time and Partial Order in Logics and Models for Concurrency*, LNCS 354, pages 660–672. Springer-Verlag, 1989. REX School/Workshop, Noordwijkerhout, The Netherlands, May/June 1988.

19. M. Thomas. The Story of the Therac-25 in LOTOS. *High Integrity Systems Journal*, 1(1):3–15, 1994.

20. M. Thomas. Modelling and Analysing User Views of Telecommunications Services. In *Feature Interactions in Telecommunications Systems*, pages 168–183. IOS Press, 1997.

21. M. Thomas and B. Ormsby. On the Design of Side-Stick Controllers in Fly-by-Wire Aircraft. *A.C.M. Applied Computing Review*, 2(1):15–20, Spring 1994.

22. Kenneth J. Turner. An architectural description of intelligent network features and their interactions. *Computer Networks*, 30(15):1389–1419, September 1998.

23. A. Vogel. On ODP's architectural semantics using LOTOS. In J. de Meer, B. Mahr, and O. Spaniol, editors, *Proc. Int. Conf. on Open Distributed Processing*, pages 340–345, September 1993.

Towards a Topos Theoretic Foundation
for the Irish School of
Constructive Mathematics (M$_C^{\clubsuit}$)

Mícheál Mac an Airchinnigh

University of Dublin, Trinity College, mmaa@cs.tcd.ie

Abstract. The Irish School of Constructive Mathematics (M$_C^{\clubsuit}$), which extends the VDM, exploits an algebraic notation based upon monoids and their morphisms for the purposes of abstract modelling. Its method depends upon an operator calculus. The School hereto eschewed every form of formal language and formal logic, relying solely upon constructive mathematics.

In 1995 the School committed itself to the development of the modelling of (computing) systems in full generality. This was achieved by embracing Category Theory and by exploring a geometry of formal methods using techniques of fiber bundles. From fiber bundles to sheaves was a natural step. Concurrently, the School moved from the algebra of monoids to categories, and from categories to topoi. Finally, the constructive nature of the School is now coming to terms with formalism and logic through the (natural) intuitionistic logic inherently manifest through topoi.

In this paper we exhibit an accessible bridge from classical formal methods to topos theoretic formal methods in seeking a unifying theory.

Keywords: Cartesian closed category, constructive mathematics, Heyting algebra, intuitionistic logic, modelling, Topos Theory, Unifying Theory, VDM.

1 Prologue

"[...] computer science is in deep crisis, expanding, fragmenting, and specializing faster, faster than any other discipline, faster than anyone can understand, let alone predict. Moreover computer science is increasingly seen as marginal to its applications, and this is particularly true of theoretical computer science" [6, 94].

This quotation of Goguen, taken from his paper *Tossing Algebraic Flowers down the Great Divide*, might it not also be extended to another area of computer science, software engineering and within the embrace of which, formal methods? Has not a great gulf opened up between the overtly very successful practice of software development as manifested especially in recent times on personal computers and by the World-wide Web, and the need to capture, model, codify, and transmit the knowledge gained by this great ongoing scientific computing experiment in which we all participate and that we all experience? How can we build the bridges of various shapes and sizes and function to cross this divide?

J.N. Oliveira and P. Zave (Eds.): FME 2001, LNCS 2021, pp. 396–418, 2001.

As we all well know, every science tries to confirm (and extend) its knowledge by performing experiments based on codified theories expressed in the language of mathematics. There is, of course, a natural relationship between mathematics and logic, and some take the view that 'logic is primary' and conclude that "predicates describing the world are sometimes called Laws of Nature" [8, 26]. However, this view of the world is *not* shared by all [12], as Hoare and He acknowledge [8, 28]. It is moreover very unlikely that Newton, Einstein, and Feynman (*inter alii*) would have formed such an opinion as to the (alleged) priority of logic! The supposed centrality is a very recent invention! Nevertheless, the beautiful work of unification in the text cited is undoubtedly one bridge of a particular shape and function.

In his paper describing some of the 'pre-history' of the VDM, Jones [11, 43] has indicated that Abrial's "Abstract Machine Notation in B does fit more closely with aspects of VDM than Z". He is also reputed to have said recently (2000) that perhaps there might be the possibility of a merging between VDM and B, at least. In his opinion, what really matters is the communication of "the idea of *abstract modelling*" as a way of understanding computer systems [11, 43]. Jones' efforts are clearly another very welcome attempt to provide a specification bridge for the model-theoretic languages.

The Irish School of Constructive Mathematics ($M_C^\clubsuit$), originally founded upon the Irish School of the VDM (est. 1990) and described at length in [17], has hitherto deliberately avoided the issue of the need for a formal logic, even the *Logic of Partial Functions* (LPF) asserted to be part of VDM by Cliff Jones [11, 42], to underpin both the specification of operations and constraints in the mathematical models, and in the application of the well-formulated development steps of its method.

The rationale for the deliberate omission of formal logic was simply based on two factors: (i) that there was a strong *constructive* nature of the specifications and the developments, and that the performing of proofs were effectively either constructions, or algebraic transformations into constructions, in other structures, and (ii) that it was very unlikely that the psychology of (software) engineers was compatible with such formal logic! The nearest one might get to an underlying formal logic was in the specification of well-formedness constraints, invariants, and the *pre-conditions* of the operations of a model which were entirely elementarily set-theoretic. It was certainly not customary to use explicit notations for universal and existential quantifiers! Should one wish to use a formal logic in conjunction with the models constructed in the style of the Irish school then it was considered to be *an extremely eccentric complementary* action. The emphasis was entirely on the algebra.

The specification "language" of the school is deliberately not formal in principle in order to achieve greater mathematical flexibility and expressiveness. Thus no distinction is made between syntax and semantics. All is mathematics. This is a central philosophical tenet of the school. There is nothing whatever, on the other hand, which prohibits the elaboration of a formal language with associated syntax and semantics which respects that philosophical tenet. Colman Reilly explored such a relationship through *Mathematica*[26] and Andrew Butterfield is currently (2000) working on a fully-fledged Clean interpretation. In other words being constructive, specifications in the Irish VDM are necessarily executable.

Another *great divide* is that between state-based formal methods (structure-focussed or state-focussed) and process calculi (action-focussed). Our work was always hitherto focussed on structural aspects of computing and avoided process aspects. In [16] is described an aborted attempt to wed structure with process. We have not ignored process calculi. It is simply the case that we have not been able to reconcile our mathematical understanding of two apparently diverse realities: structure and process, and therefore to find a common language to describe both, in harmony. Recently, and from a very different direction, Malcolm Tyrrell, of our Foundations and Methods Group, has achieved some considerable success in adding *state* to process calculi such as the π-calculus [30]. This brings the two sides closer.

Based upon the success of other unification initiatives in specifications and programming languages we are persuaded within the School to move to a *topos* theoretic foundation for several reasons.

1. the universal properties of category theory and its ubiquity in computing provides a sound semantic basis for both structure and process. See [7, 25–6];
2. topos theory and sheaf theory provide a natural unification of algebra, logic, and geometry. See [22, 1];
3. the intuitionistic logic associated with the topos is compatible with the constructive philosophy of the School;
4. perhaps most important of all, accessible textbooks on the subject of category theory and topos theory are now available for first year undergraduates at University. See especially *Conceptual Mathematics, a first introduction to categories* [15].

To achieve a successful transition to a topos theoretic foundation we do not wish to lose the current 'user-friendliness' of the existing notation. On the other hand we do want to move to expressive forms that are clearly and unambiguously within constructive mathematics and which are sound from a topos theoretic perspective. In addition it is absolutely essential that we meet

"the challenge to make toposes as intuitive from the beginning as they are to experts, especially as concerns topos logic" [23, vii–viii].

What all of this means in practice is that our models and specifications look like classical **constructive** VDM (for VDM read B or Z) models and specifications. On the other hand everything that we model and specify is topos-theoretic and hence universally valid in all possible local computational frameworks including that of the old set-theoretic framework. In practice this means that our (Irish VDM) specifications and models will have the same sort of universal validity as relativistic results have in Natural Science. We are at the dawn of a New Age in Computational Theory.

Mathematics is used to codify scientific knowledge. But there are many different styles of mathematics and notations in which it is expressed. Domain knowledge of computing is codified by abstract modelling using both mathematics and logic. The more views one has of a particular domain concept the better the understanding. That is why algebraic and geometric views of the same concept, say circle, are so valuable. Each provides its own way of understanding and manipulating the object in question. We also need complementary views of computing domain objects. This paper proposes a specific way forward which is being adopted by the School for model-theoretic specification languages.

The rest of the paper is organised as follows.

Section §2 presents three basic operations of the classical model of the spelling checker dictionary: **write**, **read**, and **remove** in order to provide a common basis of understanding for the reason for the need for a bridge to topos theory. In section §3 we introduce the structures of Heyting algebra, Cartesian closed category, and topos and demonstrate how the spelling checker dictionary model may be suitably transformed in order that it conform to the newly introduced structures. This establishes the intuitionistic propositional calculus for the Irish School of Constructive Mathematics. Then, in section §4, we explore the fibering of a classic VDM map and show how intuitionistic quantifiers (and hence intuitionistic predicate calculus) can be introduced naturally. The paper then concludes with some remarks on related work.

2 Classical Spelling Checker Dictionary

"The view that [set and set] membership is primary [in contradistinction to map or function or process] also leads one to believe that [set] membership is global and absolute, whereas in fact it is local and relative" [14, 5].

Essentially, the dictionary we have in mind is like that used in conjunction with the board game SCRABBLE$^{\circledR}$ such as the Official Scrabble Players Dictionary [27]. In the case of a dispute between two players over the spelling of a word there is an agreed procedure whereby the spelling is checked with respect to the occurrence of the word in the "standard dictionary", but only after the player has made the play. If the word is in the dictionary then it is an acceptable word for the play, otherwise . . .

In this real world scenario the essential operation from an end-user's point of view is the checking whether or not a given word is in the dictionary. We call such an operation (in the context of this and other models) a **lookup**. It is the same as the **read** operation in other computing contexts such as data base lookups.

We will model such a dictionary by using sets. We start with a set of words *WORD* and then construct the powerset $\mathcal{P}WORD$. Elements of the powerset, i.e., sets of words, are considered to be dictionaries. We already know that if n is the size of the set *WORD* then there are 2^n possible dictionaries. Naturally, what we have just described is a classic *Gedanken* experiment. In practice, we do **not** start with some set *WORD* and apply the powerset operator to give us our space of dictionaries. Instead we work from a starting point of the empty dictionary and build whatever we need.

More formally, consider the usual domain equation for the most abstract model of the spelling checker dictionary:

$$\delta \in DICT = \mathcal{P}WORD \tag{1}$$

where $\mathcal{P}$ denotes the usual powerset functor. The expression $\mathcal{P}WORD$ provides us with a Boolean algebra $\mathcal{B}$ in a natural way. We will be more general and assume an underlying Heyting algebra $\mathcal{H}$ instead. A formal definition is given in the next section. A Boolean algebra is a Heyting algebra. In other words, the property of being Heyting is more general than the property of being Boolean. The main reasons for the change are fourfold.

1. the Heyting algebra provides an algebraic semantics for propositional intuitionistic logic, whereas the Boolean algebra provides an algebraic semantics for propositional classical logic [22, 48–9], [4, 23].
2. the Heyting algebra itself has a semantics in the set of all the open subsets of a topological space [22, 48–9]; as a corollary one may introduce topological notions directly into computing via the Heyting algebra; more precisely, a (complete) Heyting algebra is a *frame* (geometric view) or *locale* (algebraic view) [22, 472–5];
3. the Heyting algebra is a Cartesian closed category and a Cartesian closed category is of particular universal interest because it has, in an elegant manner, essentially the same expressive power as a typed λ-calculus [1, 175] [13, 41].
4. finally, the step from Cartesian closed category to topos is a small one, but one which introduces the notion of 'truth object', and hence which provides the natural logic to go with the algebra.

The domain equation is read "let δ be an arbitrary element chosen from the model named $DICT$, the structure of which is given by $PWORD$." seeing its Since we are moving away from membership based expressions (in the short term) we will need to find another way of expressing the fact that δ is a typical object in the structure under consideration.

Of immediate importance here, $\mathbb{B}$ denotes the usual two-valued logic and specifically denotes the set of two 'truth values', $\{0, 1\}$ where 1 denotes **true** and 0 denotes **false**. The corresponding set of many truth values will be denoted by $\mathbb{H}$. It is immediately to be noticed that always $\mathbb{B} \subseteq \mathbb{H}$.

Aside: In topos-theoretic terms, the truth-value object $\mathbb{B}$ is often written **2** and denotes the two point set. In a general topos the truth value object is denoted Ω and has the structure of a Heyting algebra. On the road to a topos-theoretic view we have chosen to use the more suggestive $\mathbb{H}$. Finally, the expression $\mathbb{B} \subseteq \mathbb{H}$ is to be read in the general category of sets and total functions S and gives an external view of the relationship between the truth value objects in question.

We shall focus only on the usual **write**, **read**, and **remove** operations, here called **enter**, **lookup**, and **remove**. In the remainder of this section we give the classical form of the specification we have hitherto used.

The write operation: enter the entering of a *new* word into an existing dictionary is captured by

$$Ent: WORD \longrightarrow DICT \longrightarrow DICT \tag{2}$$

$$Ent[w]\delta := \{w\} \cup \delta \tag{3}$$

The expression $\{w\} \cup \delta$ is well-defined within the Heyting algebra and, therefore, does not have to be replaced. This operation is subject to the pre-condition or guard which captures the idea that the word w is *new*:

$$\text{pre-}Ent: WORD \longrightarrow DICT \longrightarrow \mathbb{B} \tag{4}$$

$$\text{pre-}Ent[w]\delta := w \notin \delta \tag{5}$$

The expression $w \notin \delta$ is taken to be equivalent to the predicate $\neg(w \in \delta)$. There are two ideas that need to be examined. The first is that of *set membership*. In a topos-theoretic foundation set membership is not a primary concept. Therefore, we must find a suitable alternative here. The second idea is, of course, that of *negation*. We need to deal with that also.

The read operation: lookup to look up a word in the dictionary is to ask whether or not it is present in that dictionary. There is no pre-condition.

$$Lkp: WORD \longrightarrow DICT \longrightarrow \mathbb{B} \tag{6}$$

$$Lkp[w]\delta := w \in \delta \tag{7}$$

We expect the result of the lookup to be either true or false. The expression $w \in \delta$ is not an appropriate expression within the Heyting algebra. We will have to find an acceptable alternative.

The remove operation: remove the removal of an *existing* word from the dictionary is usually specified by

$$Rem: WORD \longrightarrow DICT \longrightarrow DICT \tag{8}$$

$$Rem[w]\delta := \delta \backslash \{w\} \tag{9}$$

Set removal $\delta \backslash \{w\}$ is not an appropriate expression. We will provide an alternative. This operation is subject to the pre-condition

$$\text{pre-}Rem: WORD \longrightarrow DICT \longrightarrow \mathbb{B} \tag{10}$$

$$\text{pre-}Rem[w]\delta := w \in \delta \tag{11}$$

Let us now examine each operation in turn and consider whether the specification is fully constructive. In order to be complete and, therefore, comprehensive, we also need to say something about the form of the signatures. Finally, we recall the fundamental philosophical distinction between the concept of proof in classical and constructive mathematics.

"In classical mathematics, a proposition is thought of as being true or false independently of whether we can prove or disprove it. On the other hand, a proposition is constructively true only if we have a method of proving it." [24, 11]

3 Intuitionistic Spelling Checker Dictionary

" The Boolean term $S \vee \bar{L}$ is often written as an implication (e.g., $L \supset S$); indeed, the above law,

$$\frac{P \Rightarrow S \vee \bar{L}}{P \wedge L \Rightarrow S} \quad ,$$

together with the inference in the opposite direction, is used in intuitionistic logic to deﬁne implication [... which] is always a predicate [and
being] antimonotonic in its ﬁrst argument, it will rarely be a program " [7,
8].

Who could possibly resist exploring the consequences of such a statement? What is
the nature of implication and its role in intuitionistic logic which would render it almost
useless as a program?

As a first step towards the construction of an intuitionistic spelling checker dictionary
we shall introduce the mathematical structures of Heyting algebra $\mathcal{H}$ and Cartesian closed
category. Then we shall recast each of the operations on the spelling checker dictionary
in terms of these structures. It will be assumed that the reader is already familiar with the
elements of Category Theory. A highly recommended introductory text is *Conceptual
Mathematics, A First Introduction to Category Theory* [15].

For a *working* definition of Heyting algebra we follow [4, 23]. Note that Fitting
uses an "older name" for the Heyting algebra: the pseudo-boolean algebra. We consider
the name Heyting algebra more appropriate. The definition is cast within traditional
Set Theory. Note in particular that we have deliberately 'mapped' the algebra to the
logic. This is in conformance with an old mathematical tradition. Strict formalists (and
logicians) prefer separation. See [4] for details.

DEFINITION I (HEYTING ALGEBRA) *A Heyting algebra is a pair* $\langle \mathcal{H}, \leq \rangle$ *where* $\mathcal{H}$ *is a
non-empty set and* $\leq$ *is a partial ordering relation on* $\mathcal{H}$ *such that for any two elements
A and B of* $\mathcal{H}$:

1. *the least upper bound* $A \vee B$ *exists [to correspond with* logical or *or disjunction];*
2. *the greatest lower bound* $A \wedge B$ *exists [to correspond with* logical and *or conjunc-
   tion];*
3. *the pseudo complement of A relative to B denoted* $A \Rightarrow B$, *defined to be the largest
   $X \in \mathcal{H}$ such that* $A \wedge X \leq B$, *exists [to correspond with* logical implication];
4. *a least element called bottom, denoted* $\perp$, *exists [to correspond with* **false**].

Let the complement of A, denoted $\neg A$, be $A \Rightarrow \perp$ [to correspond with *logical negation*].
Note that the complement of A is the pseudo complement of A relative to $\perp$. Let the top
element, denoted $\top$ be $\neg \perp$ [to correspond with **true**]. Clearly, then $\top = (\perp \Rightarrow \perp)$. In
fact, in general $(A \Rightarrow A) = \top$. Singleton sets of the algebra are called atoms. It is to be
noted that there exist Boolean algebras and hence Heyting algebras which do not have
atoms. See [28, 211]. However, this will not affect our presentation.
    algebra
    In the case of the spelling checker dictionary we take $\mathcal{H} = \mathcal{P}WORD$, $\subseteq$ for the partial
ordering relation, $\perp = \emptyset$, $\top = WORD$, the least upper bound of A and B in $\mathcal{H}$ is given
by $A \cup B$, and the greatest lower bound of A and B in $\mathcal{H}$ is given by $A \cap B$. Note that
the pseudo complement operator $\Rightarrow$ is distinctively new! Its role may be exemplified by
the following diagram where an arrow $P \longrightarrow Q$ denotes $P \subseteq Q$.

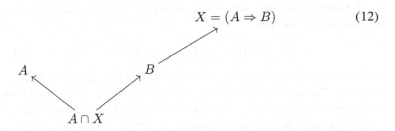

$$X = (A \Rightarrow B) \qquad (12)$$

DEFINITION 2 (BOOLEAN ALGEBRA) *A Boolean algebra is a Heyting algebra with the special property that for every A in $\mathcal{H}$, $\neg A \vee A = \top$.*

It will be demonstrated that, with appropriate modifications, the spelling checker dictionary model, *is* a Heyting algebra.

Before we proceed to that demonstration let us look at the categorical foundations. First, it is well-known that a Heyting algebra is a Cartesian closed category. Following [22, 20] we define a Cartesian closed category.

DEFINITION 3 (CARTESIAN CLOSED CATEGORY) *A category $\mathcal{C}$ is called* Cartesian closed *if it has finite products (i.e., a terminal object and binary products) and if all objects of $\mathcal{C}$ are exponentiable.*

It is a simple exercise to demonstrate that the Heyting algebra is a Cartesian closed category. Let A and B be two objects in the category. Then, if $A \leq B$ we have the map $A \longrightarrow B$. In this view of the Heyting algebra, the terminal object is $1 = \top$. Binary products are given by $\langle A, B \rangle \mapsto A \wedge B$. The exponentiable objects are $B^A = (A \Rightarrow B)$.

Since we will demonstrate that the spelling checker dictionary is a Heyting algebra then it is also a Cartesian closed category.

DEFINITION 4 (ELEMENTARY TOPOS) *An elementary topos $\mathcal{T}$ is a* Cartesian closed category *which has a truth value object Ω.*

Essentially, this means that such a topos provides us with an intrinsic logic. That logic is generally intuitionistic [22, 268]. According to Szabo [29, 190] the internal logic of an elementary topos is "strictly weaker than intuitionistic logic ... certain intuitionistically valid formulas such as $(\forall \xi)\phi(\xi) \Rightarrow (\exists \xi)\phi(\xi)$ no longer hold." Consequently, one needs to be very careful in scoping out a topos of the right shape to accommodate the constructions we are interested in.

3.1 Enter

Recall that the classical specification is

$$Ent: WORD \longrightarrow DICT \longrightarrow DICT \qquad (13)$$
$$Ent[w]\delta := \{w\} \cup \delta \qquad (14)$$

In the context of the Heyting algebra we recognize the dictionary δ as a Heyting subalgebra. The entering of a new word w is the extension of the existing set of atoms of δ by

$\{w\}$. Clearly, therefore, the specification may be interpreted properly as the extension of *structure* denoted by

$$\delta = \{\{a\}, \{b\}, \{c\}, \ldots\} \mapsto \{\{a\}, \{b\}, \{c\}, \ldots, \{w\}\} \tag{15}$$

The Heyting algebra can be recovered by applying the operations $\cup$, $\cap$, and $\Rightarrow$. For example, $\emptyset$ is recovered from $\{a\} \cap \{b\}$, with $\{a\} \neq \{b\}$, and complement is then determined by $\neg\{w\} = (\{w\} \Rightarrow \emptyset)$. In practice, we can use a sequence of words, canonically ordered lexicographically, to represent the set of atoms. This gives us a simple but direct structural implementation of the Heyting algebra and hence of the corresponding spelling-checker dictionary. There is a direct relationship between structure and function which is now becoming evident.

We can extend the original specification to allow for this extra structure:

$$Ent\colon WORD \longrightarrow DICT \times WORD_{\leq}^{*} \longrightarrow DICT \times WORD_{\leq}^{*} \tag{16}$$

$$Ent[w]\langle \delta, \alpha \rangle := \langle \{w\} \cup \delta, \sigma(\langle w \rangle \cdot \alpha) \rangle \tag{17}$$

where α is the ordered sequence of atoms of δ and σ is a sorting morphism on sequences.

There is still the usual need for an invariant here to guarantee that the words in the dictionary $\{w\} \cup \delta$ correspond exactly to the set of atoms in $\sigma(\langle w \rangle \cdot \alpha)$. If we introduce a primitive function **atoms** on a Heyting algebra $\mathcal{H}$ which returns its set of atoms then we may write the appropriate invariant as

$$\text{inv-}Ent\colon WORD \longrightarrow DICT \times WORD_{\leq}^{*} \longrightarrow \mathbb{H} \tag{18}$$

$$\text{inv-}Ent[w]\langle \delta, \alpha \rangle := \text{atoms}(\{w\} \cup \delta) = \text{elems}(\sigma(\langle w \rangle \cdot \alpha)) \tag{19}$$

Now let us take a closer look at the pre-condition for the enter operation. We propose to reject the particular expression $w \notin \delta$ in favour of $\{w\} \cap \delta = \emptyset$. The reasoning for the change is as follows.

The expression $w \notin \delta$ is read as "the word w is not an element of the set δ", which expression we abbreviate as $\neg(w \in \delta)$. Let us first look at the simpler form $w \in \delta$. This expression is interpreted in the context of a membership based set theory such as Zermelo-Fraenkel (ZF) set theory. However, there is a central difference between sets in a *well-pointed topos* and sets approached via membership [23, 215]. To paraphrase McLarty, in the topos of Sets $\mathcal{S}$ we can take a set *WORD* and ask whether a given element w of *WORD* is a member of a given subset δ of *WORD*, but it is pointless to ask whether an element of *WORD* is also an element of some other set, *DUCK*, say.

To comprehend this radically different view of reality one needs to understand how points and elements are defined and used. In general, a point x in a topos $\mathcal{T}$ is a map $1 \xrightarrow{x} A$ from the terminal object 1 to the object A. Objects need not have any points whatsoever. In the category of Sets $\mathcal{S}$ the points of an object A correspond exactly to the elements of the set A. In a general topos $\mathcal{T}$ such points are called global elements. If in a general topos a pair of maps $A \underset{g}{\overset{f}{\rightrightarrows}} B$ are equal, $fx = gx$, for every general element x then the topos $\mathcal{T}$ is said to be well-pointed [22, 236].

A Heyting algebra is not in itself a topos. It seems to fail by a very slight margin. As a Cartesian closed category, the only point is $1 \longrightarrow 1$. This prevents us from having a non-trivial truth object. It appears at first glance to be a strange and worrisome result. However, once one becomes accustomed to the view that a space might reasonably be considered to be composed of parts rather than points [14, 32], then one is freed from a certain blinkered view. Therefore, we need to embed the Heyting algebra in a suitable topos in order to achieve the desired goal. On the other hand, Heyting algebras are plentiful in any topos. Specifically, for any object A in a topos, the power object $\mathcal{P}A$ is a(n internal) Heyting algebra and, as a special case, so is the truth value object $\Omega = \mathcal{P}1$ [22, 201].

For the present section we content ourselves to the transformation of the dictionary in a Heyting algebra compatible form. The choice of suitable topoi, compatible with the VDM, is still under active investigation.

First we observe that $\neg(w \in \delta)$ can be written in terms of the Heyting algebra operations as $\neg(\{w\} \subseteq \delta)$, read as "the atom $\{w\}$ does not belong to the subalgebra δ." If the atom $\{w\}$ does **not** belong to δ then it must belong somewhere and that somewhere is the complement of the subalgebra, denoted $\neg\delta$. In other words we have the **fundamental equivalence**

$$\neg(\{w\} \subseteq \delta) \text{ iff } \{w\} \subseteq \neg\delta \tag{20}$$

way?]

But by the definition of complement in a Heyting algebra $\neg\delta$ is the exponential $\delta \Rightarrow \emptyset$. Hence we have

$$\neg(\{w\} \subseteq \delta) \text{ iff } \{w\} \subseteq (\delta \Rightarrow \emptyset) \tag{21}$$

Now we focus on the expression $\{w\} \subseteq (\delta \Rightarrow \emptyset)$. Since a Heyting algebra is a Cartesian closed category then from the basic adjunction relating products and exponentials

$$\frac{Z \longrightarrow Y^X}{Z \times X \longrightarrow Y} \tag{22}$$

we make the obvious substitutions to obtain [22, 50]:

$$\frac{z \leq (x \Rightarrow y)}{(z \wedge x) \leq y} \tag{23}$$

Now substituting $z \mapsto \{w\}$, $x \mapsto \delta$, $y \mapsto \emptyset$, $\leq \,\mapsto\, \subseteq$, and $\wedge \mapsto \cap$ we obtain

$$\frac{\{w\} \subseteq (\delta \Rightarrow \emptyset)}{(\{w\} \cap \delta) \subseteq \emptyset} \tag{24}$$

This gives us

$$\neg(\{w\} \subseteq \delta) \text{ iff } (\{w\} \cap \delta) \subseteq \emptyset \tag{25}$$

Since $\emptyset$ is bottom then we also have the *fact* that

$$\emptyset \subseteq (\{w\} \cap \delta) \tag{26}$$

Hence

$$\neg(\{w\} \subseteq \delta) \text{ iff } (\{w\} \cap \delta) \subseteq \emptyset \wedge \emptyset \subseteq (\{w\} \cap \delta) \tag{27}$$

$$(\{w\} \cap \delta) = \emptyset \tag{28}$$

and this is our desired pre-condition in the Heyting algebra. We summarise this derivation as follows:

$$\neg(w \in \delta) \tag{29}$$

$$\neg(\{w\} \subseteq \delta) \tag{30}$$

$$\neg(\{w\} \subseteq \delta) \text{ iff } \{w\} \subseteq \neg\delta \tag{31}$$

$$\{w\} \subseteq \neg\delta \text{ iff } \{w\} \subseteq (\delta \Rightarrow \emptyset), \quad \text{by definition} \tag{32}$$

$$\{w\} \subseteq (\delta \Rightarrow \emptyset) \text{ iff } \{w\} \cap \delta \subseteq \emptyset, \quad \text{by adjunction} \tag{33}$$

$$\{w\} \cap \delta = \emptyset \tag{34}$$

Hence the pre-condition or guard for the "enter a new word" operation may be written in the form

$$\textbf{pre-}\textit{Ent}: \textit{WORD} \longrightarrow \textit{DICT} \longrightarrow \mathbb{H} \tag{35}$$

$$\textbf{pre-}\textit{Ent}[w]\delta := \{w\} \cap \delta = \emptyset \tag{36}$$

This is a sensible specification from the point of view of the end-user. This pre-condition may also be expressed in the more 'exotic' forms of

$$\textbf{pre-}\textit{Ent}: \textit{WORD} \longrightarrow \textit{DICT} \longrightarrow \mathbb{H} \tag{37}$$

$$\textbf{pre-}\textit{Ent}[w]\delta := \{w\} \cap \delta \subseteq \emptyset \tag{38}$$

or

$$\textbf{pre-}\textit{Ent}: \textit{WORD} \longrightarrow \textit{DICT} \longrightarrow \mathbb{H} \tag{39}$$

$$\textbf{pre-}\textit{Ent}[w]\delta := \{w\} \subseteq \neg\delta \tag{40}$$

3.2   Remove

Consider the meaning of set difference $A - B$ where A and B are subsets of some ambient or universal set U. We may write $A - B$ in the form $A \cap (-B)$ where $-B$ is the complement of B with respect to U. Now in the Heyting algebra $-B$ is defined to be $B \Rightarrow \emptyset$. Hence we have the definition

$$A - B := A \cap (B \Rightarrow \emptyset) \tag{41}$$

This leads directly to an intuitionistic definition of the removal operation.

$$\textit{Rem}: \textit{WORD} \longrightarrow \textit{DICT} \longrightarrow \textit{DICT} \tag{42}$$

$$\textit{Rem}[w]\delta := \delta \cap (\{w\} \Rightarrow \emptyset) \tag{43}$$

Subject to the pre-condition that w is in the dictionary:

$$\textsf{pre-}Rem: WORD \rightarrow DICT \rightarrow \mathbb{H} \qquad (44)$$

$$\textsf{pre-}Rem[w]\delta := (\delta \cap \{w\}) = \{w\} \qquad (45)$$

Let us consider the definition of the remove operation first. The expression $\delta \cap (\{w\} \Rightarrow \emptyset)$ can hardly be considered intuitive to the end-user *at the present time*. Nor does it seem very constructive. A more end-user friendly form might be $\delta \cap \neg \{w\}$ for which we might agree to use the abbreviation $\delta - \{w\}$ or $\delta \backslash \{w\}$, to get back to where we started.

Turning now to the pre-condition which classically was $w \in \delta$ and which is given here as $(\delta \cap \{w\}) = \{w\}$. Again it is intuitively clear that the new definition is correct. However, it is of interest to attempt to derive this from the classical expression. Already we have agreed above that $\{w\} \subseteq \delta$ is the equivalent to the membership expression. Hence we have a first reasonable and directly accessible specification of a pre-condition:

$$\textsf{pre-}Rem: WORD \rightarrow DICT \rightarrow \mathbb{H} \qquad (46)$$

$$\textsf{pre-}Rem[w]\delta := \{w\} \subseteq \delta \qquad (47)$$

3.3   The Pre-conditions

Let us now take a closer look at the intuitionistic pre-conditions which we have already specified. In the case of **pre-**$Ent[w]$ we replaced $w \notin \delta$ by $\{w\} \cap \delta = \emptyset$ and in the case of **pre-**$Rem[w]$ we replaced $w \in \delta$ by $(\delta \cap \{w\}) = \{w\}$. But we noticed that there were other possibilities. For example, in the case of **pre-**$Rem[w]$ above we suggested the use of $\{w\} \subseteq \delta$. Let us demonstrate formally, that from this expression we can derive algebraically, $\{w\} \subseteq 1$, in much the same way that from $w \in \delta$ one deduces $w \in WORD$ from the containment $\delta \subseteq WORD$.

$$w \in \delta \qquad (48)$$

$$\{w\} \subseteq \delta \qquad (49)$$

$$\delta \cap \{w\} \subseteq \delta \cap \delta \text{ implies } \delta \cap \{w\} \subseteq \delta \qquad (50)$$

$$\delta \cap \{w\} \subseteq \delta \text{ implies } \{w\} \cap \delta \subseteq \delta, \quad \text{by commutativity of } \cap \qquad (51)$$

$$\{w\} \cap \delta \subseteq \delta \text{ iff } \{w\} \subseteq (\delta \Rightarrow \delta), \quad \text{by adjunction} \qquad (52)$$

$$\{w\} \subseteq 1 \qquad (53)$$

$$\text{i.e., } w \in WORD \qquad (54)$$

Perhaps we need to comment upon $(\delta \Rightarrow \delta) = 1$. By definition, $(\delta \Rightarrow \delta)$ is the largest X in $\mathcal{P}WORD$ such that $\delta \cap X \subseteq \delta$. Such an X is clearly $WORD$ and $WORD = 1$ in this Heyting algebra.

3.4   Test

In reflecting upon the structural forms of the intuitionistic pre-conditions for both the enter operation

$$\textsf{pre-}Ent[w]\delta := (\{w\} \cap \delta) = \emptyset \qquad (55)$$

and the remove operation

$$\textsf{pre-}Rem[w]\delta := (\{w\} \cap \delta) = \{w\} \tag{56}$$

it is clear that they both have the general form $A \cap B = C$. Therefore, it seems appropriate to consider a *new* operation on the dictionary that generalises these expressions. For historical reasons we call this the *test* operation. The formal definition is

$$Tst: \mathcal{P}WORD \to DICT \to DICT \tag{57}$$
$$Tst[S]\delta := S \cap \delta \tag{58}$$

Using the *Tst* operation then the pre-conditions for *Ent* and *Rem* become,

$$\textsf{pre-}Ent[w]\delta := Tst[\{w\}]\delta = \emptyset \tag{59}$$

and

$$\textsf{pre-}Rem[w]\delta := Tst[\{w\}]\delta = \{w\} \tag{60}$$

respectively. Knowing that, in practice, one pre-condition is the *opposite* of the other, i.e., that $(\textbf{not } \textsf{pre-}Rem[w]\delta) = \textsf{pre-}Ent[w]\delta$ and assigning "true" to $\textsf{pre-}Rem[w]\delta$ entails assigning "false" to $\textsf{pre-}Ent[w]\delta$. Clearly, we can generalise this to give the truth assignments

$$(Tst[S]\delta = \emptyset) \mapsto \textsf{false}, \text{ if } S \cap \delta = \emptyset \tag{61}$$
$$(Tst[S]\delta = S') \mapsto \text{ the degree of truth measured by } S' \subseteq S \tag{62}$$
$$(Tst[S]\delta = S) \mapsto \textsf{true}, \text{ if } S \cap \delta = S \tag{63}$$

Hence, we do have a natural underlying multi-valued logic. Note in particular that since $(Tst[S]\delta = S \cap \delta) = S$ then the last equation is equivalent to

$$(Tst[S]\delta = 1) \mapsto \textsf{true} \tag{64}$$

in the Heyting subalgebra δ of $\mathcal{P}WORD$.

Aside: Equation (62) calls for some further comment. In the usual category of Sets the natural logic is classical and there are only the possibilities of true or false values [3, 7]. Essentially this means that the kinds of questions which one asks can only have true or false answers. In practice, in formal methods modelling in the Irish School we are intensely interested in what we can construct and in formulating such constructions in words. The construction of equation (62) is clearly natural and can be construed as "Is the set of words S in the dictionary δ ?" The answer is neither yes nor no, corresponding to true and false, respectively. The construction validates the obvious need for us to move to a topos-theoretic foundation where "the idea of inclusion [is] the basis of truth and logic" [15, 344].

3.5   A Simple Proof

To conclude this section we present a simple proof in the new style.

Consider the proof of the assertion that *if one enters a new word w into a dictionary δ and then removes that word the result is the original dictionary δ that one started with.* Constructively, we have

$$(Rem[w] \circ Ent[w])\delta \tag{65}$$

$$= Rem[w](Ent[w]\delta) \tag{66}$$

$$= Rem[w](\{w\} \cup \delta) \tag{67}$$

$$= (\{w\} \cup \delta)\backslash\{w\} \tag{68}$$

$$= (\{w\} \cup \delta) \cap (\{w\} \Rightarrow \emptyset) \tag{69}$$

$$= (\{w\} \cap (\{w\} \Rightarrow \emptyset)) \cup (\delta \cap (\{w\} \Rightarrow \emptyset)) \tag{70}$$

$$= \emptyset \cup \delta \tag{71}$$

$$= \delta \tag{72}$$

The noteworthy aspects of the proof are at (70) where the reduction of $\{w\} \cap (\{w\} \Rightarrow \emptyset)$ to $\emptyset$ may be regarded either as *modus ponens* or as a simple map evaluation in the Cartesian closed category (recall that $\{w\} \Rightarrow \emptyset$ is an exponential), and the reduction $\delta \cap (\{w\} \Rightarrow \emptyset)$ to δ is justified by the pre-condition $\mathsf{pre}\text{-}Ent[w]\delta := \{w\} \cap \delta = \emptyset$.

This concludes the first part of the paper. What we have just accomplished is a demonstration of the intuitionistic propositional calculus in action with respect to a very simple and elementary model. Moreover, it must be noted that in model-theoretic formal methods much of current proof theory reduces to a consideration of set theoretic results. Hence, our Heyting algebraic approach is universally applicable.

The *cognoscente* will recognise how we have kept hidden much of the underlying topos-theoretic justification of the calculation. Moreover (s)he will notice how we have used algebra to do logic in carrying out our proof. (S)he will also notice that it is not a very big step from our algebra to the formal intuitionistic propositional calculus. (See [3]).

Now we turn our attention to the intuitionistic predicate calculus. Again we seek an algebraic version of the usual existential and universal quantifiers. The end result at which we arrive is, of course, already well-established (in Topos Theory). What is for us now astonishing is that the algebraic form of the universal quantifiers emerges as a simple interpretation of basic VDM operations. Our route to that result is via the concept of the fibering of a space, now a natural route. Fibering (a process at the core of fiber bundles and sheaves) occurs very naturally in computer geometry in an obvious constructive sense. It proved to be for us the key link between an algebra and a geometry of formal methods. In our next section we try to exhibit something of that breakthrough. The 'relationists' will note how we Mathematicians normally treat relations as maps.

4 Klinik of Doctors and Their Patients

The usual model of doctors (DOC) and their patients (PAT) that we have become accustomed to use is that which associates with each doctor d in the klinik κ her/his set of current patients S. This is the classical doctor-patient relationship. This model is captured by

$$\kappa \in KLINIK = DOC \longrightarrow \mathcal{P}PAT \tag{73}$$

and a typical klinik κ might have the form

$$\kappa = \begin{bmatrix} c \mapsto \{p,q,r\} \\ d \mapsto \{p,s\} \\ e \mapsto \emptyset \end{bmatrix} \tag{74}$$

It will be noticed that in this model the same patient p might be shared between two doctors c and d, and there is a doctor e with no patients.

This model of a klinik is the most general abstract model of the doctor-patient relation. It is a *directed* model in the sense that the relation is "the doctor d has the set of patients S".

From the perspective of the intuitionistic logic that we are developing it is clear that the codomain may be given the usual structure of a Heyting algebra.

Were one to exclude the possibility of null sets of patients, i.e., maplets of the form $d \mapsto \emptyset$ then one has the classical relational model of doctors and patients which we denote by

$$\kappa' \in \mathit{KLINIK'} = \mathit{DOC} \longrightarrow \mathcal{P}'\mathit{PAT} \tag{75}$$

where $\mathcal{P}'\mathit{PAT} = \mathcal{P}\mathit{PAT}\backslash\{\emptyset\}$.

Being a classical relation, models κ' are invertible. Thus we are led to introduce

$$\nu \in \mathit{CLINIQUE} = \mathit{PAT} \longrightarrow \mathcal{P}'\mathit{DOC} \tag{76}$$

where to each κ' in *KLINIK'* there corresponds its inverse $(\kappa')^{-1} = \nu$.

Being accustomed to working with set-valued maps such as κ in the belief that these were the most interesting and practical models in practice we eschewed the more restricted model domains such as those of the form

$$\mu \in \mathit{CLINIC} = \mathit{PAT} \longrightarrow \mathit{DOC} \tag{77}$$

Our attention was drawn to their significance in a completely round-about manner. Specifically, in the abstract modelling of a hash table, we discovered that it might be cast completely in terms of a fiber bundle [21]. For example, a hash function h may be regarded as a total map $h: \mathit{WORD} \longrightarrow \mathbb{Z}_p$ where $\mathbb{Z}_p$ denotes the finite field of integers modulo p a prime.

The fibering is constructed as shown opposite. To each word u is associated a particular hash value (or hash index) $j = h(u)$. If we construct the Cartesian product $\mathbb{Z}_p \times WORD$ then we obtain all possible hashings. Any section through the fibers then gives a specific hash function. Notably, those words which hash to the same value are then considered to be on the overflow chain. We note in passing that this corresponds to the idea of a level curve in geometry. A hash table with overflow chaining $\lhd_S h$ is then just a restriction to the set of words hashed S.

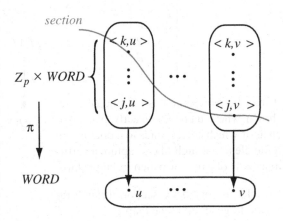

This particular work was a very successful adventure into a geometry of formal methods. From fiber bundles we were led to the more general theory of sheaves and topoi. A good account of the relevance of such theories for our purposes may be gleaned from [22].

It is clear to us that all these models of a klinik belong together. It is also clear that the natural framework is a topos. The basic recasting of all VDM map constructors and operators is the subject matter of a doctoral thesis just being completed (Hughes 2000) and we will report on this outcome at a later stage.

4.1   Klinik as Fibered Space

" Logicians have long thought that the essence of existential quantioca-tion is projection; however, this is merely a special case of the *actual* essence, which is the taking of images. This is why we have adopted the notation $\exists_f(S) = f(S)$"[14, 23].

To complete this section we now explain how quantifiers are introduced. In general, for a total map $f: X \longrightarrow T$, we may consider f as inducing structure on the domain X. In particular, for any t in the codomain T, the inverse image $f^{-1}(t)$ is called the fiber over t. (See Lawvere and Schanuel [15, 81–5] for a brief account of the perspective that a map produces structure in its domain or in its codomain, depending upon the desired model.) Let us consider the model of doctors and patients given by the space of *total* maps

$$f \in CLINIC = PAT \longrightarrow DOC \tag{78}$$

subject to the constraint that f is surjective, i.e., that $\text{rng } f = \text{codom } f$. This condition will guarantee that no fiber is empty. In this highly desirable case one can then taken a (cross-)*section* through the fibers. Such sections provide further modelling concepts.

Consider the typical map

$$f = \begin{bmatrix} p \mapsto c \\ q \mapsto c \\ r \mapsto d \\ v \mapsto d \\ t \mapsto d \end{bmatrix}$$

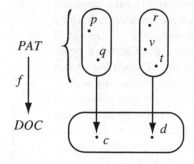

It may be represented as the fibered space shown where there are exactly two fibers each of which corresponds to a doctor. It is quite clear that such fibers capture a particular view of a doctor-patient relationship.

Now let us consider a section through the fibers. In general, a total map $f \colon X \longrightarrow T$ which is surjective has a section $s \colon T \longrightarrow X$ such that $f \circ s = 1_T$, the identity map on T. A section may be considered to be a right-inverse for the map f. Shown here is a typical section σ through the given clinic map f. It is denoted $\sigma = [c \mapsto p, d \mapsto r]$. One interpretation of a section is the scheduling of doctors to patients concurrently within the same time period. There are clearly six possible schedules.

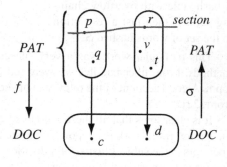

Consider the entire collection of sections $\langle s_1, s_2, \ldots, s_n \rangle$ of the doctor-patient relationship, expressed here in the form of a product (or sequence).

$$DOC \xrightarrow[s_n]{\overset{s_1}{\cdots}} PAT \xrightarrow{f} DOC \tag{79}$$

We can combine these together using a reduction of the form

$$^{*}/\langle s_1, s_2, \ldots, s_n \rangle = s_1 \star s_2 \star \cdots \star s_n \tag{80}$$

where the $\star$ operator is defined by

$$s_i \star s_j := \{ d \mapsto \{ s_i(d) \} \cup \{ s_j(d) \} \mid d \in DOC \} \tag{81}$$

The resulting map $^{*}/\langle s_1, s_2, \ldots, s_n \rangle$ is $\kappa \in KLINIK = DOC \longrightarrow \mathcal{P}PAT$. Hence, instead of using set-valued maps we may fiber and then take a reduction of the sections. Using this approach in general it seems that one may then construct the indexed monoids (i.e., maps with valuations in monoids) which have been a feature of the School since 1993 [18] [19] [20].

The fibering constructed above is not the only one. By considering the map f as a relation, i.e., a set of pairs of the form $\langle p, c \rangle$ each of which corresponds to $p \mapsto c$, one may produce an isomorphic fibering. Here the map ϕ is considered to extend f, where $\phi \langle p, c \rangle = f(p) = c$. It is this fibering which permits us to introduce universal and existential quantifiers as *constructions* into the VDM, following [22, 57].

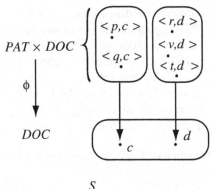

Consider the predicate $S(p, d)$ read "p is a patient of doctor d". Let $S \subseteq PAT \times DOC$ be the set of pairs $\langle p, d \rangle$ for which $S(p, q)$ is true.

Given S we **define** the universal quantifier $(\forall p)S(p, d)$ to be the subset $T \subseteq DOC$ which consists of all those d with $\langle p, d \rangle \in S$. The relationship between S and T is shown by the shaded areas of the diagram. Similarly, **given** S we **define** the existential quantifier $(\exists p)S(p, d)$ to be the subset $U \subseteq DOC$ for which there exists a d with $\langle p, d \rangle \in S$. By construction, it is always the case that

$$(\forall p)S(p, d) \subseteq (\exists p)S(p, d).$$

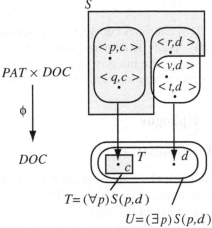

By the isomorphism observed above between the two different fiberings we can generalise the definitions of the universal and existential quantifiers to an arbitrary map f. Again, from [22, 58], we have

$$\forall_f S := \{d \mid \text{for all } p,$$
$$\text{if } f(p) = d, \text{ then } p \in S\}$$

and

$$\exists_f S := \{d \mid \text{there exists a } p,$$
$$\text{with } f(p) = d, \text{ and } p \in S\}$$

We observe that $\forall_f S \subseteq \exists_f S$.

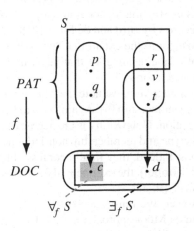

We have referred above to the definition of the quantifiers given by construction. We illustrate this for $\forall_f S$ and $\exists_f S$. Given f and S.

1. Compute the direct image $\exists_f S = f_*(S) = U$.
   [This is guaranteed to be constructive *in practice* since all our structures are finite. For model-theoretic methods such as VDM, Z, B, we may interchange rng f, $f(S) = f_*(S)$, and $\exists_f$ where $S \subseteq \text{dom } f$.]
2. Take the inverse image $X = f^*U = f^*f(S)$.
3. Since $S \subseteq f^*f(S)$ then let $Y = X \backslash S$.
4. Compute the direct image $f_*(Y)$.
5. Then $\forall_f S = \exists_f S \backslash f_*(Y)$.

Elimination of Y gives one (pleasing) form of the result:

$$\forall_f S = \exists_f S \backslash f_*(f^* \exists_f S \backslash S) \tag{82}$$

This completes our algebraic presentation of the existential and universal quantifiers. It may readily be demonstrated that both are adjoints to the inverse image f^* [22, 58]. It is the inverse image which gives us the fibering of the map and validates the overall approach which we adopted in our quest to find a geometry of formal methods.

5 Epilogue

5.1 Related Work

In our School we have always taken the view that maps are primary and that relations are secondary. This was and still is the primary focus. Consequently, the move to categories and topoi is straightforward. There is however a completely opposite well-known and well-established view that relations are primary. The categorical companion to the relation is an allegory. It is not surprising, therefore, to discover that what is here treated in terms of Heyting algebras and topoi is also covered within the chapter on relations and allegories by Bird and de Moor [2, 81–110]. In the same work a passing reference is made to topoi to the extent that "the axioms [introduced by Bird and de Moor] namely those of a tabular allegory that has a unit and power objects, precisely constitute the definition of a topos."

In a similar vein, we note the work on polytypic datatypes and the issue of polytypic datatype membership [9]. Again, as is to be expected, the approach is from the direction of the relation. Noteworthy is the degree of complexity that the authors faced in defining both datatype and membership non-inductively. Their solution to the logic was grounded in a *logos*. Indeed, they finally confessed to "an embarrassment, namely that in certain categories (topoi), the exponential functor is a relator only if the internal axiom of choice is satisfied" [9, 28].

However, we must state categorically that we are of the opinion that neither the Bird and de Moor approach nor the Hoogendijk and de Moor approach (loosely based on Freyd's allegories [5]) are the best way forward for the foundations of the model-theoretic formal methods. Already in 1977 Johnstone, in his comprehensive work on Topos Theory, remarked that he was "personally unconvinced" of Freyd's assertion that the theory of allegories "provides a simpler and more natural basis than topos theory" [10, xix]. At first glance, one might suppose that it is simply a matter of taste or philosophical viewpoint. My (limited) experience (of five years) is that Topos Theory is not only an elementary theory and independent of Set Theory but also that it is more natural for computing (and hence functional programming) and therefore for the modelling of computing systems and for associated intuitionistic logics. Why then are so few people aware of the power and relevance of this extraordinary universal theory? Again, it seems to me to be clear that the problem has been accessibility. Specifically, the "royal road to Topos Theory" is traditionally via the bridge of Category Theory, the learning curve of which is already very steep. The first text to provide a quick access route to Topos Theory in a natural way, was published in 1997 [15]. It was entirely fitting that one of the authors, F. William Lawvere, was also a Patriarch of Topos Theory.

Similarly, in their work on the unified theories of programming, Hoare and He [8, 86–112] have provided a chapter on linking theories wherein comparable material is handled in terms of lattices and Galois connections.

Finally, our attention was drawn to the use of the hash table (presented traditionally in the context of a reification of a 'spelling checker dictionary' as we ourselves are accustomed to do in the VDM, for example) to elaborate upon "Fractal Types" [25]. The author also clearly sees category theory as an essential tool in exploring datatypes and uses generalised hashing to examine concurrency aspects. It is the spirit in which the hashing process is explored that compares with our own use of it for fibered spaces. Indeed the author arrives at exactly the same result in a different way [25, 6] and expresses it in clear though different terminology.

5.2   Conclusions

We now know that Lawvere has done for Computer Science what Cantor did for Natural Science. Elementary Topos Theory is the natural foundation for constructive mathematics (= computing), carrying within it a natural intuitionistic logic. In our opinion the Theory of Allegories, though elegant, is a *cul de sac*. The reason is simple. Allegories (category of sets and relations) contrary to expectation are not natural or prior. One is still confined to the usual category of Sets and one reasons essentially within the confines of classical logic. Topos theory lives in a truly different world.

In order to be able to move towards a topos-theoretic way of thinking and working one needs a bridge. The key concept of Set Theory which must be thrown out immediately is that of set membership. In its place the map is given priority. It is precisely this switch in priority of concepts that allows one to move from Set Theory to Topos Theory.

By picking the spelling-checker dictionary as example we were able to demonstrate precisely the difference in reasoning. Admittedly, to the initiate it might seem that we merely substituted $\subseteq$ for $\in$. However, the entire work was conducted within a Cartesian closed category—the Heyting algebra; we were but one small step away from a topos. By working within the Heyting algebra we effectively calculated the proof in propositional intuitionistic logic.

Our greatest challenge was to find a way in which to move to intuitionistic predicate logic, to introduce the existential and universal quantifiers. The bridging mechanism which proved natural to us was the fibering induced by taking inverse images.

One will have noticed how we did **not** declare in advance which topos we might be working in at any given time. This was deliberate. For example, to restrict one-self *a* *priori* to work within the category of sets and partial maps would be too confining. After all one can work with partial maps in the category of sets and total maps by introducing the partial map f from A to B as the pair of total maps $A \xleftarrow{\ i\ } \text{dom } f \xrightarrow{\ f\ } B$.

By the very nature of Topos Theory, locality is primary. It is to be expected, therefore, that in practical modelling and specification work many topoi will be involved in the elaboration of a single model. We have just begun to move towards that realisation and hence the use of 'towards' in the title of the paper.

Acknowledgements. The members of the Foundations and Methods Group (FMG) at the Department of Computer Science in the University of Dublin, Trinity College, reviewed an earlier draft of this paper and made many valuable suggestions. Particular thanks are due to Andrew Butterfield for pointing out the usual need for a VDM invariant in the refined **enter** operation of the intuitionistic spelling checker dictionary to guarantee that the words in the dictionary $\{w\} \cup \delta$ correspond exactly to the set of atoms in $\sigma(\langle w \rangle \cdot \alpha)$.

A particular debt of gratitude is owed especially to Arthur Hughes who helped me to struggle with what seemed to me to be very strange, difficult and irrelevant concepts (irrelevant that is from the perceived need of real computer scientists and software engineers) in both Category Theory and Topos Theory.

Finally, we are extremely grateful to the careful reviewing of the three anonymous referees whose solicitous remarks encouraged me to try to improve the paper. In particular, we are greatly obliged to the referee who pointed us to the relevant work in polytypic data types [9] and fractal types [25]. We have struggled to accommodate all of their remarks and helpful suggestions in this the final version. Such, however, was the large amount of very useful suggestions for improvement that it was practically impossible to follow them all and stay within, or at least reasonably close to, a twenty page limit. Any errors or incompleteness which remain in the paper are the sole responsibility of the author.

The paper was typeset on a Power Macintosh using BlueSky Textures 2.1.2 and the LaTeX2ϵ format. The style sheet used is Springer-Verlag's *llncs.cls* for the Lecture Notes in Computer Science. Vince Darley's BibTex 1.1.7 was used for the references. Inline category theoretic arrow diagrams were produced using Xy-pic 3.6 of Kristoffer H. Rose and Ross R. Moore. Postscript diagrams were produced using Adobe Illustrator 6.

References

1. Michael Barr and Charles Wells. *Category Theory for Computing Science*. Prentice Hall, London, second edition, 1995.
2. Richard Bird and Oege de Moor. *Algebra of Programming*. Prentice Hall, London, 1997.
3. Michael Dummett. *Elements of Intuitionism*. Number 39 in Oxford Logic Guides. Clarendon Press, Oxford, second edition, [1977] 2000. [ISBN 0 19 850524 8].
4. Melvin Chris Fitting. *Intuitionistic Logic, Model Theory and Forcing*. Studies in Logic and The Foundations of Mathematics. North-Holland Publishing Company, Amsterdam, 1969.
5. Peter J. Freyd and Andre Scedrov. *Categories, Allegories*. Number 39 in North-Holland Mathematical Library. North-Holland, Amsterdam, 1990.

6. Joseph Goguen. Tossing algebraic flowers down the great divide. In C. S. Calude, editor, *People & Ideas in Theoretical Computer Science*, pages 93–129. Springer-Verlag Singapore Pte. Ltd., Singapore, 1999. [ISBN 981-4021-13-X].

7. C. A. R. Hoare. Theories of Programming: Top-Down and Bottom-Up and Meeting in the Middle. In Jeannette Wing, Jim Woodcock, and Jim Davies, editors, *FM'99 World Congress on Formal Methods*, volume 1708 of *Lecture Notes in Computer Science*, pages 1–27. Springer-Verlag, Berlin, 1999.

8. C. A. R. Hoare and Jifeng He. *Unifying Theories of Programming*. Prentice Hall, London, 1998. [ISBN 0-13-458761-8].

9. P. Hoogendijk and O. de Moor. What is a data type? Technical Report 96/16, Eindhoven University of Technology and Programming Research Group, Oxford University, August 1996.

10. P. T. Johnstone. *Topos Theory*. Academic Press, London, 1977.

11. Cliff B. Jones. Scientific Decisions which Characterize VDM. In Jeannette Wing, Jim Woodcock, and Jim Davies, editors, *FM'99 World Congress on Formal Methods*, volume 1708 of *Lecture Notes in Computer Science*, pages 28–47. Springer-Verlag, Berlin, 1999.

12. Stephan Körner. *The Philosophy of Mathematics, an Introductory Essay*. Hutchinson and Company, Limited, London, 1960. [ISBN 0-486-25048-2], The Dover edition is cited; Dover Publications, Inc., New York, 1986.

13. J. Lambek and P. J. Scott. *Introduction to Higher Order Categorical Logic*. Cambridge University Press, Cambridge, 1986.

14. F. William Lawvere. Variable sets etendu and variable structure in topoi. Technical report, University of Chicago, 1975. Notes by Steven Landsburg of Lectures and Conversations.

15. F. William Lawvere and Stephen H. Schanuel. *Conceptual Mathematics, A first introduction to categories*. Cambridge University Press, Cambridge, 1997. [ISBN 0-521-47817-0]. NOTE: An earlier version was published by the Buffalo Workshop Press, 1991, with an Italian translation, Franco Muzzio &c editore spa in 1994.

16. Mícheál Mac an Airchinnigh. *Ph.D. Thesis: Conceptual Models and Computing*. Department of Computer Science, University of Dublin, Trinity College, Dublin, Ireland, 1990.

17. Mícheál Mac an Airchinnigh. Tutorial Lecture Notes on the Irish School of the *VDM*. In S. Prehn and W. J. Toetenel, editors, *VDM'91, Formal Software Development Methods Volume 2: Tutorials, Lecture Notes in Computer Science 552*, pages 141–237. Springer-Verlag, Berlin, 1991.

18. Mícheál Mac an Airchinnigh. Formal Methods & Testing. In *Tutorials of the Sixth International Software Quality Week*, 625 Third Street, San Francisco, CA 94107–1997, May 1993. Software Research Institute.

19. Mícheál Mac an Airchinnigh. Formal Methods & Testing. In *Tutorials of the First International Z User's Meeting (ZUM'95)*, September 1995.

20. Mícheál Mac an Airchinnigh. Mathematics for Formal Methods, a Proposal for Education Reform. In Andrew Butterfield and Sharon Flynn, editors, *2nd Irish Workshop on Formal Methods*, Electronic Workshops in Computing. British Computer Society, London, 1998. http://ewic.org.uk/ewic/workshop/view.cfm/IWFM-98.

21. Mícheál Mac an Airchinnigh and Arthur P. Hughes. The Geometry of Distributions in Formal Methods. In David Duke and Andy Evans, editors, *2nd BCS-FACS Northern Formal Methods Workshop, Ilkley 1997*, Electronic Workshops in Computing. Springer-Verlag, London, 1997. http://www.springer.co.uk/ewic/workshops/.

22. Saunders Mac Lane and Ieke Moerdijk. *Sheaves in Geometry and Logic, A First Introduction to Topos Theory*. Springer-Verlag, New York, 1992. [ISBN 0-387-97710-4].

23. Colin McLarty. *Elementary Categories, Elementary Toposes*. Clarendon Press, Oxford, 1992. [ISBN 0 19 851473 5].

24. Bengt Nordström, Kent Petersson, and Jan M. Smith. *Programming in Martin-Löf's Type Theory, an Introduction*. Number 7 in The International Series of Monographs on Computer Science. Clarendon Press, Oxford, 1990. [ISBN 0-19-853814-6].
25. J. N. Oliveira. Fractal Types: an Attempt to Generalize Hash Table Calculation. Workshop on Generic Programming (WGP'98), Marstrand, Sweden, May 1998. http://www.cs.ruu.nl/people/johanj/wgp98.html.
26. Colman Reilly. Exploring Specifications with Mathematica. In Jonathan P. Bowen and Michael G. Hinchey, editors, *ZUM'95: The Z Formal Specification Notation, Lecture Notes in Computer Science 967*, pages 408–20. Springer-Verlag, Berlin, 1995.
27. Selchow & Righter Company. *The Official SCRABBLE® Players Dictionary*. Merriam-Webster Inc., Springfield, Massachusetts, 1978. [ISBN 0-87779-020-5].
28. Robert R. Stoll. *Sets, Logic, and Axiomatic Theories*. W. H. Freeman and Company, San Francisco, second edition, [1961] 1974. [ISBN 0-7167-0457-9].
29. M. E. Szabo. *Algebra of Proofs*. Number 88 in Studies in Logic and the Foundations of Mathematics. North-Holland Publishing Company, Amsterdam, 1978. [ISBN 0-7204-2286-8].
30. Malcolm Tyrrell, Andrew Butterfield, and Alexis Donnelly. OO-Motivated Process Algebra: A Calculus for CORBA-like Systems. *To appear in the Third Workshop in Rigorous Object-Oriented Methods, York, England*, January 2000.

Faithful Translations among Models and Specifications*

Shmuel Katz

Computer Science Department
The Technion
Haifa, Israel
katz@cs.technion.ac.il

Abstract. Numerous translations exist between the design notations of formal methods tools, usually between two specific notations. In addition, more general translation frameworks are under development. For any translation it is vital that properties true of the semantic interpretations of the source and the translated notations are closely related.

Some possible applications of translations among model descriptions are described and key issues in translating among models with inconsistent features are identified, leading to a source and a target model that do not always preserve the correctness of properties in a simple way. The concept is presented of a *faithful* relation among models and families of properties true of those models. In this framework families of properties are provided with uniform syntactic transformations, in addition to the translations of the models. Three variants are presented, depending on the intended use of the translation, so that the correctness of a property in a model corresponds to the correctness of the transformed property in the translated model. This framework is shown appropriate for common instances of relations among translations previously treated in an ad hoc way. Furthermore, it allows expressing connections among models where one is neither a refinement nor an abstraction of the other. The classes of properties that can be faithful for a given translation provide a measure of the usefulness of the translation.

1 Introduction

Translations among notations for representing models and hardware designs have become common, although often there is no available documentation. Such translations exist from SMV [10,7,26], to PVS[29,30], from Murphi[20] to PVS, from SMV to Spin[18,19], from several notations into Cospan[23], from automata-based notation into Petri nets, and among many other tools. Moreover, individual verification tools often have multiple input formats for models, and internal source-to-source translations. For example, the STeP system [3] and the exposition in [25] allow presenting designs either in a simple C-like programming

---

* This research was partially supported by the David and Miriam Mondry research fund at the Technion

J.N. Oliveira and P. Zave (Eds.): FME 2001, LNCS 2021, pp. 419–434, 2001.

language, or using a modular collection of textual transitions, and internally translates from the former representation to the latter. In addition to translations among formal methods tools, there is increasing interest in translating standard hardware design notations such as Verilog or VHDL (or internal industrial notations) to and from the notations of existing model-checking tools. Such translations introduce formal verification into an existing development process at minimal cost.

More recently, general translation frameworks are being developed, such as the VeriTech project to translate through a simple intermediate notation [13]. That project defines a transition-based core language, and then provides translations between existing notations and the core language, in both directions. At present, VeriTech includes translations between SMV, Murphi, Spin and the core design language, and work is underway to incorporate, among others, PVS, LOTOS[5], STeP and Petri nets[32]. Other such frameworks include the SAL system [2], and the Model Checking Kit[28].

In this paper we present the possible uses of (direct or indirect) translations among model descriptions, show some of the difficulties that must inevitably arise during translation, and provide a theoretical basis to quantify the quality of such translations in a formal framework using *faithful* translations and syntactic transformations of properties. By using this framework, it becomes clear how properties of the original model description and the translated version are related. This in turn provides an evaluation criterion for translations among models: a 'good' translation is faithful for large classes of properties.

Translations among model notations can be used in a variety of ways, and these influence what needs to be true about a translation. Most obviously, a particular property to be verified can be attacked with different tools. For example, if an initial attempt to model check a temporal logic property of a system should fail because of the size of the state space, it is possible to translate the model (either directly or in stages, first to a core representation and then from the core out) to a BDD-based model checker that can handle the problem. Alternatively, the source could be a model description in the SMV language, but for which attempts to verify a property have failed, and the target could be a description appropriate for a tool with a theorem-proving approach like PVS or STeP. Of course, proving the desired property in such a target requires using inductive methods and is not automatic, but at least is not sensitive to the size of the data domain and will not suffer from the state-explosion problem. We shall also see that in many relevant translations the property to be proven in target models will not be identical to the property asserted about the original source model. Nevertheless, a *back-implication* is desired: a property should necessarily hold in the source whenever the related property holds in the target.

In addition, unrelated properties can each be established for a system using a different verification tool, choosing the most convenient tool for each property. This should encourage using different verification tools for various aspects of the same system. For example, a propositional linear-time temporal property might be proven for a finite-state model of the system using a linear-time model checker like Spin. The system model can then be translated to a branching-time model checker like SMV for properties of that type. It can also be translated to a language with real-time notation, such as STeP, or to a theorem proving environment like PVS to treat infinite domains and first-order temporal properties. In this case, we would like to *import* some variant of the properties proven about the source into the target, so that they can be assumed there and used to help prove the new desired property.

As already noted, there are also many translations to and from design notations that do not have associated verification tools. For hardware these include Verilog and VHDL, and for software, Statecharts [15,16] (which provides a hierarchical graphical state-transformation software design notation). Translating from such a notation to one with associated model-checking or other verification tools allows checking properties of existing designs, while a translation in the other direction can introduce a verified high-level design into a development process.

The quality of a translation depends on guaranteeing a close relation between the properties true of the source and those true of the target. This can be used to define the 'correctness' of a model translation. As seen above, the relation among properties can be used in either direction: we may want to 'import' versions of properties already guaranteed true of the original model into the resulting one (so they can be used in showing additional properties without being themselves reproven) or we may want to know that properties shown about the resulting model imply related properties in the original model.

Ideally, the semantic models (e.g., the execution trees) underlying the notations would be identical, making the question trivial in either direction. However, we demonstrate that this is often impossible. In the broader framework proposed here, a translation and transformation of properties will be faithful with respect to families of properties represented as classes of formulas in some temporal logic so that if property X is true of one model, then property Y will be true of the other.

Investigation of these relations can be seen as a step in the research direction proposed in [17], to unify theories of programming. Here those theories used to describe models for formal verification tools are emphasized, rather than full-fledged programming languages. The faithful relation framework shows how to quantify the essential differences among the models, instead of only emphasizing the commonality.

In Section 2 the semantic assumptions we use to compare source and target models are defined, based on fair execution trees as a common underlying semantics. The notion of a faithful relation among models and specifications is defined formally in Section 3, with three variants. In Section 4, we identify the translation issues that prevent a system and its translation from having identical semantics and thus satisfying the exact same properties. We then demonstrate in Section 5 how the inherent model incompatibilities seen in the translation issues lead to natural examples of nontrivial faithful relations among models and their translations. Some of these correspond to specific examples from the literature, others to undocumented 'folk knowledge', and others to new connections among classes of properties. Such identification of faithfulness can serve as a measure of quality for translations, beyond unrealistic assumptions that the semantics of the source and the target are fully identical.

2   The Semantics of Systems and Modules

In order to compare a model in one notation and its translation to a different notation, a uniform semantic basis is required. We will assume that for each notation for describing models a *fair execution tree semantics* can be derived.

Consider the case of a system model given as a collection of textual transitions, each with an applicability condition and a state transformation. Such a collection can define a module, and such modules can be composed into new modules synchronously, asynchronously, or with partial synchronization (handshaking). The global state and the local state of each module are expressed by declaring variables, possibly with initial values. In such a notation, the semantics of a system and of a module can be defined in two stages. First, for semantic purposes only, each definition of a module can be textually expanded ("flattened") to give the module as a list of transitions, replacing instantiations of modules by the collections of transitions they define (including substitution of actual parameters in place of formal ones, and renaming local variables when necessary to avoid conflicts).

Now we can define the semantics of a module with transitions given explicitly, by considering the execution sequences (also called *traces*) that it defines. Of course, this is only for purposes of ensuring the faithfulness of translations: such descriptions of models are not intended to ever 'execute', but rather to describe the collection of all legal computations, which then will be analyzed using a verification tool. Before considering the execution-tree semantics, the state and its components must first be defined: a state of such a system clearly contains the constants and variables declared globally, and also those that follow from the instantiations of modules and their local variables.

Turning to the textual transitions, each can be represented by an *identifier* I, a *precondition* P over states, and a *relation* R between pairs of states. The intended semantics is that a transition $\tau = \langle I, P, R \rangle$ can be activated in a state s if s satisfies P, and such an activation can be seen as constructing a new system state s' from the existing state s of the system, where the pair (s, s') satisfies R. For a system or module defined by a collection of transitions, the possible execution sequences are defined by the sequences of states reached by successive activations of transitions, starting from an initial state.

The initial state has all variable values undefined (e.g., equal to a special value $\perp$), except those with initial values given in their declaration.

The execution sequences are organized into an execution tree, where each state is the parent of the states reachable from it by activation of an enabled transition. If all sequences have the same initial state, that is the root of the tree. Otherwise, a root node with all variables undefined is added, and the possible initializations are the only transitions enabled in that state. (An alternative view would see the semantics as a forest of trees, each with its own initialization, but the single-tree view has the advantage of treating the initializations like other transitions, which can be helpful in some translations. The single-tree view has the disadvantage that usual temporal logic assertions –including invariants– are not intended to hold in the root if all its values are undefined.) Some of the paths in this tree can be declared irrelevant due to an additional *fairness* restriction that can remove infinite paths (criteria for which restrictions are reasonable can be found in [1]). This tree, with fairness restrictions, is the semantic interpretation of a system or module.

This example notation has elements from several existing tools, including the internal representation in the STeP system [3]), Z schemas [33,31], Unity [8] and LOTOS [4,5] composition operators. Other notations can also be given an execution tree semantics, allowing comparisons among translations. The correctness of a translation is defined relative to such trees, and this semantics is sufficient for the specification languages considered here.

Note that a richer semantics is possible, e.g., one that includes what is known as *partial-order* information. For example, if it is possible to ask which execution sequences are equivalent to which other ones under independence of operations in distributed processes, then semantic information on independence of operations is needed [22,21]. This possibility is not considered further here.

In any case, it is important to note that the properties that are to be shown about a system can influence how much of the information in an execution tree is relevant. According to various possible conventions, the tree of a system is 'equivalent' to reduced versions that, for example, eliminate nonessential variables, or remove hidden transitions, without otherwise affecting the system. Moreover, if only linear-time temporal properties will be proven, then the set of traces can be considered, and their organization into a tree structure is irrelevant. Furthermore, if only invariants are of interest, then it is sufficient to consider the set of reachable states. Such considerations will be crucial in understanding the relations needed among models, as will be seen in the continuation.

As part of the specification, additional restrictions can be added to define which traces are relevant. We have already seen that fairness assumptions can be added on the semantic level. There are also contexts in which an assumption of finiteness of the traces is appropriate, excluding the infinite ones.

For specific notations, particularly those defining finite-state systems, it will be convenient to consider also a finite representation of the execution tree by means of a finite state machine. In fact, an (equivalent) alternative semantic basis could be the fair transition system notation used by [25].

3   Faithful Translations

Translations would ideally fully preserve the semantics of the translated system, thus guaranteeing that the source and the target satisfy exactly the same properties. However, as will be demonstrated in Section 4, the semantics of the translated model cannot always be identical to that of the original.

Therefore we loosen the connection between the properties true of the source and those true of the target. Assume we are given two models, M_1 and M_2, possibly defined within two different verification tools. Further assume that the models are related via some model-translation relation. We identify a set of assertions about M_1 and a property-translation relation that connects the assertions in the set of assertions about M_1 to assertions about M_2.

One relation among the translations is that for every assertion in the set, if M_1 satisfies the assertion then M_2 satisfies the translated version of that assertion. The translation is then called *import faithful* with respect to those models and families of properties. We may alternatively establish that if the translated assertion is true of M_2, then the original assertion must have been true about M_1. This translation is then called *back-implication faithful*.

Of course, we may instead require a *strongly faithful* translation that satisfies both of the conditions above.

We require faithfulness to be transitive so that a series of translations can be considered. In particular, for general translation through a core notation, as in VeriTech, it is sufficient that the translations of models and of families of properties are faithful between different tool notations and the core (in both directions, perhaps for different families of properties). The faithfulness of the translation from one tool to another will then result from transitivity arguments.

In classic definitions of the correctness of an implementation, it is common to show a mapping from the states of the implementation to the states of the original system, but under the mapping the same output or key states are required to hold. Here we will be able to treat greater differences among the systems, while still showing the utility of the translation for purposes of verification.

Formally, let $\mathcal{M}_1$, $\mathcal{M}_2$ be two classes of models and $\mathcal{L}_1$, $\mathcal{L}_2$ be sets of properties expressed as formulas in an assertion language for $\mathcal{M}_1$ and $\mathcal{M}_2$, respectively. Let $TR \subseteq \mathcal{M}_1 \times \mathcal{M}_2$ be a *model-translation* relation indicating that a model $M_1 \in \mathcal{M}_1$ is translated to a model $M_2 \in \mathcal{M}_2$. Similarly, $tr \subseteq \mathcal{L}_1 \times \mathcal{L}_2$ is a *property-translation* relation that is total over $\mathcal{L}_1$ (i.e., so that each formula of $\mathcal{L}_1$ is in the relation tr).

TR and tr are *import faithful* for $\mathcal{M}_1$, $\mathcal{M}_2$, $\mathcal{L}_1$, and $\mathcal{L}_2$ if $\forall M_i \in \mathcal{M}_i$ and $f_i \in \mathcal{L}_i, i = 1, 2$, whenever $TR(M_1, M_2)$ and $tr(f_1, f_2)$, then $M_1 \models f_1 \implies M_2 \models f_2$.

TR and tr are *back-implication faithful* for $\mathcal{M}_1$, $\mathcal{M}_2$, $\mathcal{L}_1$, and $\mathcal{L}_2$ if $\forall M_i \in \mathcal{M}_i$ and $f_i \in \mathcal{L}_i, i = 1, 2$, whenever $TR(M_1, M_2)$ and $tr(f_1, f_2)$, then $M_2 \models f_2 \implies M_1 \models f_1$.

TR and tr are *strongly faithful* for $\mathcal{M}_1$, $\mathcal{M}_2$, $\mathcal{L}_1$, and $\mathcal{L}_2$ if $\forall M_i \in \mathcal{M}_i$ and $f_i \in \mathcal{L}_i, i = 1, 2$, whenever $TR(M_1, M_2)$ and $tr(f_1, f_2)$, then $M_1 \models f_1 \iff M_2 \models f_2$.

A relation (rather than a function) is defined among the models in the definitions of faithfulness because internal optimizations or 'don't care' situations can lead to nondeterministic aspects in the translation. Thus, a single source model may be translated to any one of several target programs. The same may be true of the assertion transformations. Note that it follows from the definitions that if tr is a function, it is total over $\mathcal{L}_1$.

In the continuation we express the families of properties as sublanguages of various temporal logics, although other modes of expression are possible. In particular, various forms of automata with infinite acceptance conditions are reasonable alternatives. The sets of languages for which we define faithfulness are not necessarily subsets of the specification languages used by the tools. For example, a compiler translation from Spin into SMV (so we have $TR(Spin, SMV)$) could be back-implication faithful for a transformation tr of properties expressible in linear-time temporal logic. In words, if a linear-time temporal logic property that is the second component in a pair satisfying tr is shown of an SMV model that is the result of activating the compiler on a Spin source model, then the first component will necessarily hold for the Spin source. This holds even though the specification language of SMV is the (restricted) branching-time logic CTL, which cannot express everything expressible in linear-time temporal logic. In such a situation, model checking (in SMV) of a transformed property in the intersection of CTL and linear-time temporal logic will be meaningful for the original Spin model and the appropriate source of the checked property. Clearly, properties not in the range of tr are irrelevant for back-implication. Although they may hold of the target model, they give no information about the source model.

On the other hand, if we show that the translation from Spin to SMV is import faithful for a transformation of all linear temporal logic safety properties of Spin, then we can assume that the SMV model satisfies the transformed versions of all safety properties already shown about the original model in Spin.

To establish that a (TR, tr) pair is faithful for two model notations and subsets of temporal logic properties, semantic abstractions must be established: the semantic models of the source notation and the target notation must be described, as must the abstraction of the model translation, in terms of the changes introduced to the semantic model of the source in going to the target. Two examples of such changes could be that a single transition in the source tree is replaced by a sequence of transitions in the target, or that some of the infinite paths of the source are replaced by finite paths that end in a specially designated *fail* state.

The transformation of temporal logic properties is given syntactically, where the family of properties is also defined by the syntactic structure of a normal form. For this purpose the hierarchy of properties defined for normal forms of linear temporal logic in [25] can be used. For example, safety properties are characterized as having a linear assertion $\mathbf{G}p$, where p only has past operators or is a property of a state with no modalities. Similarly, classes of properties seen in branching-time logics can be useful (e.g., 'forall' CTL* that uses only A and not E [14]). Then it must be shown that the transformed assertion is necessarily true of the target execution tree whenever the original is true of the source tree (for importation) or that the original assertion is necessarily true of the source tree whenever the transformed assertion is true of the target tree (for back-implication).

4   Issues in Translation

Translating between different modeling paradigms requires finding suitable solutions for those modeling aspects that are available in one model but not in the other. Translations generally attempt to keep the translated representation of the model as similar as possible in structure and size to the original system, and in addition to define the relation among the underlying semantic models so that wide categories of properties will be related in the two models.

Even when there is a blow-up in the model representation (the 'program text'), this does not necessarily imply a blow-up in the size of the model (given as an execution tree or a state machine). Below we consider some of the key issues in translation that make it impossible to always maintain the same semantic tree or state machine for a model and the result of its translation.

4.1   Synchrony and Asynchrony

Notations for describing models commonly use three types of composition operators between system modules: synchronous, asynchronous and partially synchronous (for example, in generally asynchronous composition of processes with handshaking communications). Translating among models with the same type of synchrony avoids the specific class of problems of this subsection.

However, we have to resolve cases in which the source model originates from a system with one type of composition while the resulting target model is in a notation that uses a different one.

Assume that we want to translate a synchronous system into an asynchronous tool. In a tool like Murphi, where no synchronization mechanism is available, the translation is done by constructing a Murphi rule for each pair of transitions to be synchronized. In SPIN, on the other hand, the original partition into modules can be preserved and synchronous execution of two transitions is simulated using handshaking communication (via a zero-length buffer, thus adding to the statespace).

Translating from an asynchronous model into a synchronous model (like SMV, in its most common mode of operation) should guarantee that, at each step, at most one module executes a transition while all the others are idle. This can be done by adding a self-loop on each state and a mechanism (a shared variable like **running** in SMV or an additional process) that enables the transitions of one module at a time. In this case the modules correspond to processes. Various fairness constraints can be added to eliminate traces in which all processes are idling forever, one process idles forever (starvation), or all processes idle at the same step (so the global state repeats).

4.2   Unenabled Transitions

In a typical transition system representation, each transition consists of an enabling condition, an optional assignment, and a relation that should hold among values of variables before and after the execution of the transition.

The semantics of the typical transition system notation seen earlier guarantees that a transition is executed only if its enabling condition holds and if its final values satisfy the relation. A precise translation should identify the values for which the enabling condition and the relation hold and construct a transition for these values only. This, however, may not be possible as an atomic operation in the target notation.

One possible solution to this problem is to introduce a special *fail* state in the target program. Transitions in the target program are extended with a conditional statement that results in the original final values if these values satisfy the needed relation, and otherwise results in the *fail* state. Assuming this is the only change caused by the translation, the resulting semantic model has transitions to the *fail* state added to the execution tree, and that state is a leaf (or sink, if we view the addition as adding just one such state).

4.3   Atomicity of Transitions

In many notations, transitions are considered atomic. This means that each transition is performed in isolation, with no interference.

In Murphi each transition (called a *rule*) is also considered atomic. However, there a transition can be defined by any C program. When such a complex transition is translated into a notation with a finer grain of atomicity (e.g., where each transition can be a single assignment to the state), it must be partitioned into a sequence of steps. A *visible* flag (or its equivalent) is typically used to indicate that the intermediate states do not occur in the original model, and are an unavoidable result of the difference in the possible grain of atomicity.

In other tools, like SPIN and LOTOS atomic actions are generally more restricted. SPIN, however, includes a mechanism to define a sequence of statements as atomic. Thus, it is straightforward to maintain the atomicity of Murphi transitions within SPIN. On the other hand, LOTOS does not have such a mechanism. As a result, a translation from any notation with large-grained transitions to LOTOS requires providing a mutual exclusion mechanism that enables the translation of a transition to run from start to end with no intermediate execution of actions from other transitions.

4.4   Variables with Unspecified Next Values

Models of computation differ also by their convention concerning variables whose next-state value has not been specified by the executed transition. One convention, usually taken by asynchronous models, assumes that such variables keep their previous values. This is natural in software, where an assignment to one variable leaves the others unchanged. Another convention, common to synchronous models, assumes that the unassigned variables can nondeterministically assume any value from their domain. This is common in hardware descriptions, because then all options are left open for a variable not updated in one component to be changed in a parallel (synchronously executed) component, and still obtain a consistent result.

If the first convention has been taken and we translate the program into a model where the second holds, then for every transition the resulting program will have to contain an explicit assignment of the previous value for every variable not already explicitly redefined. For the other direction (from a model with any value as a default to one that keeps the previous value), we could use nondeterministic assignments, if they are available in the target model. Otherwise, the resulting program could contain a choice among all possible explicit assignments, for each of the possible values in the domain. Here the blow-up in the size of the resulting program is unavoidable, and auxiliary variables are often needed, but at least the semantics does not otherwise change.

4.5   Partitioning into Components

Partitioning into components (modules, processes, etc.) differs conceptually among languages because they are driven by diverse concerns. In many notations oriented towards programming languages, a component is task-oriented, and a task can change the values of several variables. In hardware description languages like SMV, however, it is more common to collect all possible changes to a single variable into one component. A component then describes, for example, all possible changes to a given register. Such differences sometimes make it difficult to maintain the modular structure of the original system, and may force introducing variables or operations that are global under the partitioning advocated by the target notation.

4.6   State Extensions

The addition of a *visible* flag, or the need to globally declare variables that originally were local in a notation with local modules, or the addition of an explicit mutual exclusion mechanism to simulate differences in the grain of atomicity all mean that the state of the translated program must often be extended. Another common problem is that the target notation may not have the sequencing options of the source. Then the control flow of the original computation is sometimes maintained by adding a program counter as an explicit part of the state, and using it in the enabling condition of the transitions.

Such extensions to the state add variables that are needed to express the model, but usually are not part of the original assertions in the specification of the source. Such variables are called *nonessential* for the purposes of assertions about the model, even though they are needed to express the model itself. Of course, translations can also eliminate such variables, as when explicit control variables are replaced by the sequencing of translated steps, in a notation that does have expressive control commands.

5   Examples of Faithful Translations

Below we present some examples of model-translation relations TR and property-translation relations tr that are faithful for given models and families of specifications. In justifying the faithfulness, semantic proofs on the relations among the execution trees are used. Only outlines of the proofs are given here.

5.1   Operation Refinements

Assume $TR(M_1, M_2)$ if the semantics of M_1 and M_2 are execution trees such that only M_2 uses the *visible* flag, and the *visible* states of M_2 are identical (except for the *visible* flag) to (all of) the states of M_1. Furthermore, the only change in the semantic trees is that each transition of M_1 (edge in the tree) is replaced by a finite sequence of transitions between the corresponding *visible* states of M_2, so that all intermediate states along the sequence have $\neg visible$ and there are no infinite sequences of states with $\neg visible$. (In this case, common terminology will refer to M_2 as a *refinement* of M_1.) Such a translation can arise due to the differences in atomicity seen earlier.

Let $\mathcal{L}_1$ be all properties expressible in some temporal logic. Then tr should relate formulas of $\mathcal{L}_1$ to formulas of $\mathcal{L}_2$ in which the temporal operator next-time ($\mathbf{X}$) is replaced by the temporal operator until ($\mathbf{U}$), in a systematic way. Furthermore, those formulas refer only to *visible* states. If we consider linear-time temporal logic as the language defining the class of properties of both the source and the target of the translation, an atomic state assertion p in $\mathcal{L}_1$ is transformed to $visible \wedge p$. An assertion $\mathbf{X}p$ is transformed to $\mathbf{X}(\neg visible\mathbf{U}(p \wedge visible))$ and $p\mathbf{U}q$ becomes $(visible \rightarrow p)\mathbf{U}(visible \wedge q)$. (From the transformations above, it follows that $\mathbf{F}p$ becomes $\mathbf{F}(visible \wedge p)$ and $\mathbf{G}p$ becomes $\mathbf{G}(visible \rightarrow p)$.)

The translation-transformation pair is strongly faithful for both $\mathcal{L}_1$ and $\mathcal{L}_2$ being linear-time temporal logic. The formula transformation tr is defined for every formula of $\mathcal{L}_1$, as required. Moreover, all formulas obtained as the result of applying the above transformations on a linear-time temporal logic formula are true of M_2 iff the original formula is true of M_1. This claim is true because the only difference between the models is that each next state s has been replaced by a finite sequence of states in which $\neg visible$ holds, ending with a state corresponding to s in which $visible$ holds, so the implication in each direction is immediate from the semantics of the formulas. A formal proof uses induction on the structure of the formulas in $\mathcal{L}_1$. Finally, note that no assertion is made in the definition of faithfulness about formulas of $\mathcal{L}_2$ that are not in the range of the transformation tr.

For this translation, it is also possible to use CTL as the language of interest, and obtain a strongly faithful translation. An assertion of the form $\mathbf{AX}p$ about the source is transformed by tr to an assertion $\mathbf{AXA}(\neg visible\mathbf{U}(visible \wedge p))$ about the target. The result has the necessary alternating of path and state quantifiers and is valid because each edge of the original structure is replaced by a linear subsequence, with no internal branching. A similar transformation can be done for formulas of the form $\mathbf{EX}p$.

If the translation among the models *does* allow infinite sequences of states with $\neg visible$ or paths with a $\neg visible$ state as a leaf, and otherwise satisfies the relation described above, this would correspond to possible loops or 'dead-ends' in the Kripke structure representing $\mathcal{M}_2$. Such a translation could arise from internal attempts to satisfy a condition by 'guessing' values and then testing to see if the condition is satisfied–where the $\neg visible$ paths arise from unsuccessful guesses. In this case, linear temporal logic assertions of M_1 that result in safety assertions about M_2 can be transformed as above and yield a strongly faithful translation. That is, a linear assertion $\mathbf{G}p$ is transformed to $\mathbf{G}(visible \rightarrow p)$.

And indeed p is true in every state of the source if and only if $visible \rightarrow p$ is true of every state in the target. However, liveness properties are not import faithful: $\mathbf{F}p$ is transformed to $\mathbf{F}(visible \wedge p)$, which does not hold for our less strict translation, since there now may be paths where $visible$ never becomes true. However, note that even liveness properties are back-implication faithful: if we *do* succeed in showing $\mathbf{F}(visible \wedge p)$ for a particular p in a target system, then necessarily $\mathbf{F}p$ is true of the source.

For branching-time logics, in this looser translation among models, E-properties (properties that only contain E and not A) are strongly faithful with transformations as above, but A-properties are not import faithful, for reasons similar to those seen above.

5.2 Adding Idle Transitions

A similar situation arises if the only difference between M_1 and M_2 is that some self-loops (idle transitions) have been added to the Kripke structure of M_2. This occurs, for instance, in translations from asynchronous models to synchronous ones. In the execution tree of M_2, there are new paths with finite repetitions of states (due to the idle transitions) appearing between original M_1 states, but the original transitions (and paths) also appear. In addition, the execution tree contains infinite sequences of repeated states due to idle transitions. Since every original path in the tree of M_1 is also a path of M_2, the execution tree of M_2 is greater by the *simulation* preorder [27] than that of M_1.

Consequently, tr taken as the identity relation will be import faithful if both languages are ECTL* [12], i.e., the subset of CTL* that contains only existential path quantifiers. In the other direction, tr as the identity relation will be back-implication faithful for both languages being (ACTL*) [14] i.e., CTL* specifications that contain only universal path quantifiers. This again follows immediately from the fact that the paths of the source M_1 are a subset of those of the target M_2.

If the infinite idle executions are eliminated due to fairness constraints in the models, then the models are *stuttering bisimilar* and tr as the identity will be strongly faithful with respect to full CTL* without the 'next' operator, denoted CTL*$_{-X}$ [6]. The well-known observation of Lamport [24] that linear-time temporal assertions without the next-time operator are insensitive to such 'stuttering' is a special case. Moreover, for this translation of models, we can also define an import faithful transformation tr from all of CTL*, by transforming formulas that include $\mathbf{X}$ to weaker versions without $\mathbf{X}$, e.g., replacing $p \wedge \mathbf{X}q$ of the source by $p \wedge \ p\mathbf{U}q$ in the target. If M_1 satisfies $p \wedge \mathbf{X}q$, it also satisfies $p \wedge \ p\mathbf{U}q$. Since the latter formula does not include $\mathbf{X}$, it will be true of M_2 by the previous arguments.

5.3 Adding Explicit Failures

Assume $TR(M_1, M_2)$ if the execution tree of M_2 is identical to the execution tree of M_1, provided that all *fail* states are truncated along with the transitions into them (see for example Section 4.2).

Assume again that $\mathcal{L}_1$ is a temporal logic. Then tr will relate formulas in $\mathcal{L}_1$ to similar formulas that refer only to paths along which no *fail* occurs ("globally not *fail*"). In linear-time temporal logic, the transformation for any formula f is to $(G\neg fail) \rightarrow f$. A similar transformation is not applicable to CTL. However, it can be expressed using *fair* CTL (CTL^F [10]). In CTL^F, fairness constraints are given by means of a set of CTL formulas. An execution is fair if it satisfies infinitely often each of the constraints, and only fair executions are considered in the semantics of CTL^F formulas. Thus, tr can replace a CTL property f of M_1 by the CTL^F property f together with the fairness constraint $\neg fail$ for M_2. (This transformation is valid because once *fail* becomes *true*, it remains *true* forever. Thus, "infinitely often not *fail*" implies "globally not *fail*".)

5.4 Data Abstraction

Assume $TR(M_1, M_2)$, and M_2 is an abstraction of M_1, where the variables in M_2 are defined over (smaller) abstract domains and the variables in M_1 are defined over concrete domains. Some of the variables of M_1 may not appear at all in the translation M_1. Such a translation may occur in going from a model that needs extra control variables to a target model where nonessential variables might not be needed. In going from theorem prover tools like PVS or STeP to model checkers, such abstractions of variables are also likely, since variables with infinite or very large domains are translated to versions with much smaller domains.

The treatment of abstraction of nonessential variables is easy: the very fact of their being declared as nonessential is equivalent to an assumption that any specification formula of interest does not make assertions about them. Thus in showing (any type of) faithfulness, we can assume that the assertions that define $\mathcal{L}_1$ and $\mathcal{L}_2$ do not include those variables.

For general data abstraction, the abstract model is often obtained by defining an abstraction mapping and grouping concrete states that map into the same abstract state. A transition is in the abstract version if there was a transition between a state that maps to the source and one that maps to the target. A back-implication faithful transformation tr can be defined in this case for the language ACTL*, defined over atomic propositions that relate variables to values from the abstract domain (e.g., $v = a$). The transformation tr replaces each atomic proposition of the form "$v = a$" by the atomic proposition "$v \in \gamma(a)$", where $\gamma(a)$ is the set of all concrete values mapped to the abstract value a [9, 11].

5.5 Changes in the Branching Structure

Assume $TR(M_1, M_2)$ if M_1 and M_2 have the same set of execution paths, but not necessarily the same execution trees. Thus the translation does not preserve the branching structure of the models. If $\mathcal{L}_1$ is all properties expressible in a linear-time temporal logic then tr is the identity relation. If $\mathcal{L}_1$ is a branching-time logic then for the formulas of $\mathcal{L}_1$ which are also linear-time formulas tr is also the identity. Other formulas will have nontrivial tr relations, depending on the changes in the branching structure and the formulas. For example, an assertion $AFAGp$ (eventually on every path there is a subtree with p in every node) can be transformed to the weaker but guaranteed true $AFGp$ (on every path there is a suffix with p true). If additional information is available on the nature of the changes in the branching structure, the translations can be faithful for richer families of properties (languages).

6   Conclusions

Translations among models are already common, and their use is growing rapidly. The ability to easily move among models, properties of interest, and tools extends the practical applicability of formal methods, and reduces the dependence on a single tool. Basic issues in translation, such as the differing grains of atomicity, synchronization primitives, treatment of failures, finiteness or infinity of the state space of the model, often force the models and structure of translations to differ from the original. Thus the framework of a faithful translation between both models and properties is essential to express necessary relations among models and properties of those models.

Faithfulness captures and extends several widespread instances of relations among models previously treated in an ad hoc way. In practice, many translations involve more than one of the types of differences among models that were presented. Thus combinations of the transformations of properties are needed to guarantee faithful relations for interesting classes of properties. For example, one version of a model could concentrate on a particular group of variables, abstracting other parts of the system, while another model could concentrate on different variables. These models are *siblings* where neither is an abstraction of the other, but both are different refinements of some (perhaps implicit) abstraction. Such models can be related by faithful classes of transformed properties, even though in other frameworks they are not comparable.

The quality of translations can be assessed by whether the faithful relations established are sufficient to allow using the models both to import already proven properties into versions automatically true of a translation, and to establish that properties proven of a translation correspond to properties that will then be automatically true of the original model.

References

1. K. R. Apt, N. Francez, and S. Katz. Appraising fairness in languages for distributed programming. *Distributed Computing*, 2:226–241, 1988.
2. Saddek Bensalem, Vijay Ganesh, Yassine Lakhnech, César Muñoz, Sam Owre, Harald Rueß, John Rushby, Vlad Rusu, Hassen Saïdi, N. Shankar, Eli Singerman, and Ashish Tiwari. An overview of SAL. In C. Michael Holloway, editor, *LFM 2000: Fifth NASA Langley Formal Methods Workshop*, pages 187–196, Hampton, VA, June 2000. Available at http://shemesh.larc.nasa.gov/fm/Lfm2000/Proc/.

3. N. Bjorner, A. Browne, E. Chang, M. Colon, A. Kapur, Z. Manna, H.B. Simpa, and T.E. Uribe. Step: The stanford temporal prover - user's manual. Technical Report STAN-CS-TR-95-1562, Department of Computer Science, Stanford University, November 1995.
4. T. Bolognesi and E. Brinksma. Introduction to the ISO specification language LOTOS. *Computer Networks and ISDN Systems*, 14:25–59, 1987.
5. T. Bolognesi, J.v.d. Legemaat, and C.A. Vissars (eds.). *LOTOSphere: software development with LOTOS*. Kluwer Academic Publishers, 1994.
6. M. C. Browne, E. M. Clarke, and O. Grumberg. Characterizing finite kripke structures in propositional temporal logic. *Theoretical Computer Science*, 59(1–2), July 1988.
7. J.R. Burch, E.M. Clarke, K.L. McMillan, D. Dill, and L.J. Hwang. Symbolic model checking: 10^{20} states and beyond. *Information and Computation*, 98:142–170, 1992.
8. K.M. Chandy and J. Misra. *Parallel Program Design*. Addison-Wesley, 1988.
9. E. M. Clarke, O. Grumberg, and D. E. Long. Model checking and abstraction. *ACM Transactions on Programming Languages and Systems (TOPLAS)*, 16, 5:1512–1542, September 1994.
10. E.M. Clarke, E.A. Emerson, and A.P. Sistla. Automatic verification of finite state concurrent systems using temporal logic specifications. *ACM Transactions on Programming Languages and Systems*, 8(2):244–263, April 1986.
11. D. R. Dams, R. Gerth, and O. Grumberg. Abstract interpretation of reactive systems. *ACM Transactions on Programming Languages and Systems (TOPLAS)*, 19(2), March 1997.
12. D.R. Dams, O. Grumberg, and R. Gerth. Abstract interpretation of reactive systems: Abstractions preserving ACTL*, ECTL* and CTL*. In *IFIP working conference on Programming Concepts, Methods and Calculi (PROCOMET'94)*, San Miniato, Italy, June 1994.
13. O. Grumberg and S. Katz. VeriTech: translating among specifications and verification tools–design principles. In *Proceedings of third Austria-Israel Symposium Software for Communication Technologies*, pages 104–109, April 1999. http://www.cs.technion.ac.il/Labs/veritech/.
14. O. Grumberg and D.E. Long. Model checking and modular verification. *ACM Trans. on Programming Languages and Systems*, 16(3):843–871, 1994.
15. D. Harel. Statecharts: a visual formalism for complex systems. *Science of Computer Programming*, 8:231–274, 1987.
16. D. Harel, H. Lachover, A. Naamad, A. Pnueli, M. Politi, R. Sherman, A. Shtull-Trauring, and M. Trakhtenbrot. Statemate: a working environment for the development of complex reactive systems. *IEEE Trans. on Software Eng.*, 16(4):403–414, April 1990.
17. C.A.R. Hoare and He Jifeng. *Unifying Theories of Programming*. Prentice-Hall, 1998.
18. G. Holzmann. *Design and Validation of Computer Protocols*. Prentice-Hall International, 1991.
19. G.J. Holzmann and D. Peled. The state of SPIN. In *Proceedings of CAV96*, volume 1102 of *LNCS*, pages 385–389. Springer-Verlag, 1996.
20. C.N. Ip and D.L. Dill. Better verification through symmetry. *Formal Methods in System Design*, 9:41–75, 1996.
21. S. Katz. Refinement with global equivalence proofs in temporal logic. In D. Peled, V. Pratt, and G. Holzmann, editors, *Partial Order Methods in Verification*, pages 59–78. American Mathematical Society, 1997. DIMACS Series in Discrete Mathematics and Theoretical Computer Science, vol. 29.

22. S. Katz and D. Peled. Interleaving set temporal logic. *Theoretical Computer Science*, 75:263–287, 1990. Preliminary version appeared in the 6th ACM-PODC, 1987.
23. R.P. Kurshan. *Computer-aided Verification of Coordinating Processes*. Princeton University Press, 1994.
24. L. Lamport. What good is temporal logic. In *9th World Congress*, pages 657–668. IFIP, 1983.
25. Z. Manna and A. Pnueli. *The Temporal Logic of Reactive and Concurrent Systems: Specification*. Springer-Verlag, 1992.
26. K. L. McMillan. *Symbolic Model Checking: An Approach to the State Explosion Problem*. Kluwer Academic Publishers, 1993.
27. R. Milner. A formal notion of simulation between programs. Technical Report 14, Swansean University, 1970.
28. http://wwwbrauer.informatik.tu-muenchen.de/gruppen/theorie/KIT/.
29. S. Owre, S. Rajan, J.M. Rushby, N. Shankar, and M.K. Srivas. PVS: Combining specification, proof checking, and model checking. In Rajeev Alur and Thomas A. Henzinger, editors, *Computer-Aided Verification, CAV '96*, volume 1102 of *Lecture Notes in Computer Science*, pages 411–414, New Brunswick, NJ, July/August 1996. Springer-Verlag.
30. Sam Owre, John Rushby, Natarajan Shankar, and Friedrich von Henke. Formal verification for fault-tolerant architectures: Prolegomena to the design of PVS. *IEEE Transactions on Software Engineering*, 21(2):107–125, February 1995.
31. B. Potter, J. Sinclair, and D. Till. *An introduction to Formal Specification and Z*. Prentice Hall, 1991.
32. W. Reisig. *Elements of Distributed Algorithms– Modeling and Analysis with Petri Nets*. Springer-Verlag, 1998.
33. J.M. Spivey. *The Z Notation: a Reference Manual, 2nd. ed.* Prentice Hall, 1992.

Composing Contracts: An Adventure in Financial Engineering

Simon Peyton Jones

Microsoft Research
Cambridge, England
simonpj@microsoft.com

Abstract. Financial and insurance contracts—options, derivatives, futures, and so on—do not sound like promising territory for functional programming and formal semantics. To our delight, however, we have discovered that insights from programming languages bear directly on the complex subject of describing and valuing a large class of contracts. In my talk I will introduce a combinator library that allows us to describe such contracts precisely, and a compositional denotational semantics that says what such contracts are worth. In fact, a wide range programming-language tools and concepts—denotatinoal semantics, equational reasoning, operational semantics, optimisation by transformation, and so on—turn out to be useful in this new setting.
Sleep easy, though; you do not need any prior knowledge of financial engineering to understand this talk!

J.N. Oliveira and P. Zave (Eds.): FME 2001, LNCS 2021, p. 435, 2001.

From Complex Specifications to a Working Prototype. A Protocol Engineering Case Study

Manuel J. Fernández Iglesias*, Francisco J. González-Castaño**,
José M. Pousada Carballo, Martín Llamas Nistal, and Alberto Romero Feijoo

Grupo de Ingeniería de Sistemas Telemáticos.
Departamento de Tecnologías de las Comunicaciones
Universidade de Vigo, Spain
manolo@ait.uvigo.es,
WWW: http://www-gist.ait.uvigo.es/

Abstract. We describe our experience using Formal Description Techniques (FDTs) to support the design of interception systems for GSM networks. Both the GSM protocol and the interceptor have been specified using LOTOS, an FDT standardized by the International Standardization Organization (ISO) to describe communication systems and protocols. This has permitted us to asses the feasibility of the proposed system and speed up further design phases. From the LOTOS model, a simulator has been generated automatically. The TOPO tool set was used across the process. An FTP link to a package containing the specification and the simulator is provided.

1 Introduction

This paper describes our experience using formal methods to support the design process in a realistic situation. Obviously, we can find in the literature other significant reports describing lessons learnt from real experiences [12,18, 23], proposing general guidelines to assist the system engineer when considering a formal approach to design [4,15,16,38], or discussing case studies [1,3,12,13,18, 20], to cite just a few.

However, we think that the adoption of formal methods for *real world* sceneries is less common than it should be, and more reports on successful experiences are needed to contribute to the dissemination of this desgin approach. As we show in this paper, the expected benefits of formal methods will be apparent if the whole design process is carefully organized accordingly, trying at the same time to avoid well known drawbacks.

Having in mind these considerations, we will discuss the design and implementation of a new product that should be integrated into a standard-based

---

* Visiting the International Computer Science Institute, Berkeley, USA, supported by a Spanish CICYT grant.
** Visiting Computer Science Department, University of Wisconsin-Madison, USA, supported by a NATO Scientific Committee Grant.

J.N. Oliveira and P. Zave (Eds.): FME 2001, LNCS 2021, pp. 436–448, 2001.
© Springer-Verlag Berlin Heidelberg 2001

communication system, namely GSM [28,37] networks. In other words, the target product should be flawlessly integrated into an operating GSM network, it should interact with the network according to the corresponding standards, and it should offer the intended service.

Basically, this service consists on the detection and identification of active mobile terminals in a designated closed area, to intercept incoming or outgoing calls when desired. Selective blocking is related to applications where call establishment may be dangerous or simply a nuisance. Examples of designated areas where this system is intended to operate are social areas as concert halls or temples, health care areas [10], or restricted security areas where speech and data transfers are not permitted.

To be able to offer this service, GSM protocols should be analyzed to extract the information related to our problem. Moreover, the results should be verified to guarantee that the new service is consistent with the normal operation of existing GSM networks. Therefore, success has depended dramatically on an initial, comprehensive analysis and understanding of GSM standards, which are scattered through more than 5,000 pages written in natural language.

This scenery is well suited for a formal design approach based on the concept of successive refinements [25]. On one side, this well-established design strategy will prevent designers from going to the next phase until they have a complete mastering of the system at that level of abstraction. As a consequence, design flaws are detected at early stages, speeding up the overall design process. On the other side, the formal approach forces a methodical, comprehensive analysis of the target problem, which, as a first benefit, permits a better understanding of the GSM recommendation set. Furthermore, our group has background both in Formal Methods [8,24,25] and mobile communications security [34]. This approach fosters further collaboration between these research lines.

The rest of this paper is organized as follows: first, we offer a brief description of the intended service to complement the discussion in this introduction. Then, we present an overview of the formal design process, and discuss the lessons learnt. Finally, we offer some conclusions.

2   Service Description

In a few words, the proposed system can be described as a selective and range-limited device to prevent the operation of mobile GSM terminals inside a designated area. A GSM call evolves through a number of protocol messages exchanged between the mobile station (MS) and the corresponding base station (BS). Basically, our system should monitor and capture messages generated by a base station containing mobile station identifiers. These identifiers will then be used to decide if a given MS should be permitted to proceed with call initiation, or should be eventually blocked. This process takes place inside a closed, designated area.

The GSM protocol describes four types of transactions that trigger MS activity: MS location at power-up, BS-initiated MS location update, MS-terminated call, and MS-originated call. For the intended service, a relevant transaction is initiated when a message carrying MS identifier information is detected and captured. Then, it should be decided, either locally or remotely, if the target MS should be blocked.

The GSM standard specifies several control procedures both on network and subscriber side. Nevertheless, none of them is intended to operate in designated closed areas. Therefore, external equipment must be provided to handle the situations described above, that is, to detect specific mobile terminals, and to gather sufficient information from the network to disable them, or to disable specific features when needed.

Note that, as described here, MS blocking is subject to a hard real-time constraint: it must take place before user traffic flow starts or, for some scenarios, even before the call is signaled to the user. Available time to proceed is further restricted because part of the MS-BS dialog is ciphered. A comprehensive quantitative analysis was performed to estimate system feasibility [9].

3   Towards a Formal Model

LOTOS [21] has been selected as the supporting formal language. This formal description technique has been standardized by the International Standardization Organization (ISO) for the specification of open communication protocols and systems. Note that the GSM specification is also compliant with ISO Open Systems Interconnection standard.

LOTOS is based on CCS [30], CSP [14] and CIRCAL [29] (behavior specification) and ACT_ONE [5] (data type specification), and supports the representation of temporal ordering of events, concurrent processes, non-determinism and process synchronization. The TOPO [26,27] tool set offers convenient support for syntactic and semantic analysis, symbolic execution, validation and automatic prototyping through the translation of annotated LOTOS code into C.

The final objective of the formal design process was to assess the feasibility of our target system. For this, we had to evaluate the possibility of interacting with the overall GSM protocol to intercept signaling information. Once determined how the protocol permits such interaction or tampering, we had to identify how and when it should be done. Then, we developed a prototype to field test the proposed solution.

The first task was the identification and formal modelling of the relevant aspects of the GSM transactions that lead to MS activity, as discussed in Sect. 2. An analysis of the GSM protocol [6,7] reveals that they converge after a specific message is sent by the mobile station[1]. This particular message should trigger the interceptor, since a MS identifier is already available. Transactions diverge again at some point after the dialog is ciphered, out of the scope of the interceptor.

---

[1] A *PagingResponse* or similar network message coded into a *Set Asynchronous Balanced Mode* (SABM) link frame.

Thus, we generated a model for the GSM system that only considered those aspects related to our goals, namely MS detection and identification, and call initiation and termination. The model is compliant with GSM standards insofar the modeled functionality is concerned, and permits the feasibility analysis described above. Furthermore, it serves as the basis for the corresponding implementation.

In the next section we discuss the relevant aspects of this process. A package containing the full LOTOS specification, test processes and results, a simulator, and a tool to generate GSM traces can be downloaded from any of the two locations below:

```
ftp://helia.ait.uvigo.es/pub/interceptor/interceptor.tar.gz
http://alen.ait.uvigo.es/interceptor/interceptor.tar.gz
```

4   The Formal Design Process

The next paragraphs present the overall architectural organization, outline the final LOTOS specification for the intended system, and comment some aspects related to testing and validation.

4.1   System Architecture

The formal architecture for our system consists of two communicating processes (see Fig. 1). This layout has been chosen having in mind that a working prototype must be constructed from the formal specification, to assess the feasibility of our interceptor.

The two top-level communicating processes are:

- A process that monitors the radio communication channel to detect MS activation or call initiation. This process (*Monitor* in Fig. 1) is the formal specification of the required functionality, as outlined in Sect. 2.
- A process that models physical level burst generation (i.e. the information that travels through the radio communication channel) for a BS and an undefined number of MS, and generates dialog sequences according to the GSM standard. This process (*Generator* in Fig. 1) is in fact a LOTOS formal specification of the GSM protocol, insofar the relevant functionality is concerned.

These processes interact through gate **burst**, which models the radio channel. *Generator* produces physical-level protocol frames, and *Monitor* captures these frames for further analysis. The system interacts with the environment through gates **trans**, **f12**, **12** and **13**. Through these gates, an external observer can analyze the GSM protocol evolution at the desired level of abstraction, as discussed in Table 1, for individual transactions. For example, gate **trans** signals state changes for transactions between a BS and a MS providing the environment with transaction identifiers and the corresponding present state for that

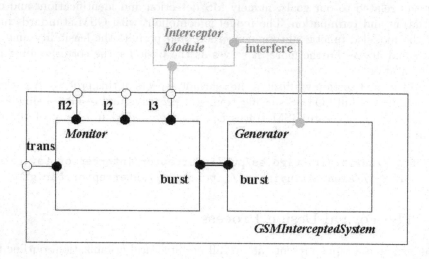

Fig. 1. System Architecture

transaction. The external observer may be another LOTOS process synchronizing with this specification. For example, a testing process that models specific features of the GSM standard. In the case of a symbolic execution tool, the role of the external observer is played by the system engineer interacting with the LOTOS specification through the user interface provided by the tool.

Table 1. Levels of Abstraction for the Observation Gates

Gate	Level of abstraction
trans	Plain TDMA
f12	Physical
l2	Data link
l3	Network

An interceptor can be easily constructed from *Monitor*. For this, an *InterceptorModule* (see Fig. 1) synchronizes at the network level to detect a *PagingResponse* frame (see footnote in Sect. 3) and then disables normal evolution of *Generator* through gate `interfere`. Process *Monitor* is presented in Fig. 2. *SynchroTDMAFrame* models slot synchronization for a Time Division Multiplex

Access (TDMA) burst and acquires information about the distribution of GSM control channels. After synchronization, control is passed to the *Filter* block. *L1Filter* and *L2Filter* capture frames at the corresponding level to construct network-level frames for *Transactions*. This latter process extracts network-level information and assigns transaction identifiers to monitored transactions.

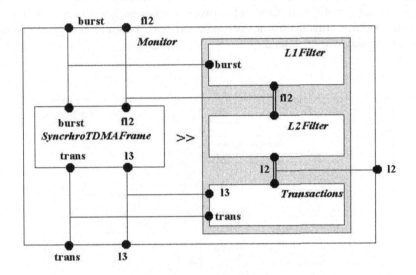

Fig. 2. LOTOS Specification. *Monitor* process

4.2 LOTOS Specification. A Brief Outline

The LOTOS specification includes the behavior description for the target system, abstract data type (ADT) definitions for all relevant data structures, and test processes to validate the system. The text of the specification comprises around 1,300 lines of annotated LOTOS code representing more than 50,000 different states and transitions. Apart from the LOTOS standard library providing basic data types as booleans or natural numbers, ADTs describe the syntax and (equational) semantics of data link and network messages, transaction states, logical channel references, and information fields in bursts, frames and messages. The ADT specification is organized as 16 LOTOS type definitions. These abstract definitions are translated into real C data structures by the TOPO tool set.

Behavior is specified by 16 communicating concurrent processes. Figure 3 outlines the interactions among these processes. *GSMInterceptedSystem, Monitor, Generator, InterceptorModule, SynchroTDMAFrame, L1Filter, L2Filter* and

Transactions have been discussed above. Process *AnalyzeTDMAFrame* monitors the Broadcast Control Channel (BCCH) to acquire information about the distribution of control channels. *Transaction* monitors a specific Standalone Dedicated Control Channel (SDCCH), and checks transaction evolution to compare it with the relevant cases for the intended system. Process *Sabm* monitors the data link protocol in balanced asynchronous mode. This will be the active mode until the end of the active transaction. Other frames in the channel are ignored. Processes *NextInfo0* to *NextInfo4* implement a frame recognition machine, that is, a state machine to sort out different link and network level messages. In Fig. 4 we outline this state machine. Invalid frames are signaled with `tabort`, and valid protocol frames are signaled with `tsend`.

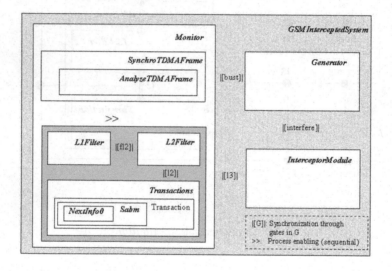

Fig. 3. LOTOS Specification. Process Interaction

The rest of the processes in the LOTOS specification correspond to test sequences. Some of these test sequences are presented in Table 2. For further details on testing this system refer to the discussion below and the package referenced in Sect. 3.

4.3   Protocol Testing and Validation

The final LOTOS specification was obtained through several top-down refinement steps, from an initial specification reflecting only overall architecture design decisions. The final specification included all relevant protocol details needed to assess the feasibility of the target system. The TOPO tool set provided support for:

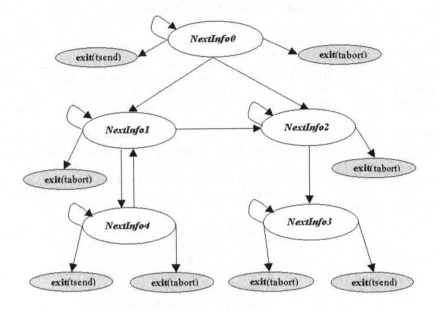

Fig. 4. LOTOS Specification. Frame Analysis

- Checking the syntax and static semantics for each refinement step, that is, checking that each step provided a meaningful LOTOS specification.
- Checking the dynamic semantics for each refinement step, that is, if each step provided a correct LOTOS specification.
- Validating each refinement step, i.e., checking if each new refinement was consistent with the previous one.

For validation, two approaches were initially available. On one hand, test suites where generated to cover all relevant aspects of the intended functionality, as pointed out by the GSM recommendations. A LOTOS test process describes a potential system behavior. An adequate tool (e.g. LOLA [36] from the TOPO tool set) will compose the test process with the target specification to analyze if the test passes or not. Technically, a test process reduces possible system behaviors to those specified by the test. If the resulting behavior does not include all states in the test process, the corresponding test will not pass. Table 2 presents some sample test sequences.

On the other hand, available tools permitted to check if a refinement step was equivalent to the initial specification under bisimulation [31] and testing equivalence [33]. This was feasible only at early refinement stages. State explosion made this approach unfeasible as the results for the successive refinement steps became more and more complex.

This approach forced the design engineer to perform a methodical analysis of the target protocol. The successive refinement strategy, together with the

Table 2. Sample Test Sequences

Process	S	T	D	R	Description
Test0000	2	2	0	MUST	Inactivity timeout if no activity at radio channel
Test0001	6	8	1	MAY	Inactivity timeout if unable to synchronize
Test0002	19	29	1	MAY	Timeout after several unsuccessful synchronization attempts
Test0100	13	17	1	MAY	Configuration captured and successful message reception
Test0101	15	21	1	MAY	Configuration captured and rejection of an incorrect frame
Test0102	15	14	5	REJ	Configuration captured and rejection of a message from an invalid channel
Test0200	124	360	2	MAY	

- Simple transaction, no errors, simple authentication protocol and switching to ciphered mode.
- Aborted transaction due to inactivity.
- Two concurrent simple transactions, one free of errors, another receives a DISConnect.
- Transaction with protocol errors.

Legend: S = states analyzed; T = transitions generated; D = deadlocks found; R = Result of the test: MUST = Must pass, i.e. there is one single trace leading to the successful event in the test; MAY = May pass, i.e. some traces lead to the successful event, other traces are deadlocks or lead to different events; REJ = Reject, i.e. no single trace leads to the defined successful event. In all cases, the results were as expected. Successful event for test Test0102 implied acceptation of the message coming from an invalid channel.

formal support provided by LOTOS, prevented the designer from going on to the next phase until he had a complete understanding of the system at that level of abstraction. As a consequence, design flaws were detected at early stages, speeding up the overall design process.

4.4   Simulation and Rapid Prototyping

Once the successive refinement process terminates with a model of the target system that includes all the desired functionality, we must test how the system under development behaves in a real implementation. Along the formal design process we obtained an abstract model that is functionally equivalent to the final product. Anyway, some aspects only become apparent during the implementation phase. These implementation-dependent aspects are related, for instance, to resource usage or performance.

A Unix executable version of *GSMInterceptedSystem* was generated from the LOTOS final specification using TOPO. The LOTOS code was previously annotated [27], basically to fill the gap between the abstract data types of LOTOS and the data types in C. Annotations define how to translate abstract data types into C data structures, and how to implement other minor architecture-dependent aspects (e.g. file access, output formatting, etc.). Additional code was introduced to play the role of the external environment (i.e. mobile phone subscribers). This code implements a user interface to provide the generator with call establishment events. Sequences of events can be defined and stored in trace files to be easily reproducible during prototype validation. The annotated LOTOS code was translated into around 7,600 lines of C code (roughly 6 automatically generated C code lines for each LOTOS line).

We found that this was a convenient approach to rapid prototyping. In it, a system prototype is generated (almost) automatically from the final specification. This prototype permits a preliminary field test of the desired product that helps to introduce many of the implementation-dependent issues not considered during the formal design process. In our particular case, this approach had further advantages:

First, it permits simple protocol reconfiguration. The protocol has been formally specified in LOTOS and a prototype has been automatically generated using TOPO. Any modification to the protocol can be introduced and formally tested in the LOTOS specification. Then, it can be recompiled to get a new working version of the prototype reflecting the changes.

Besides, the prototype can be tuned up for customized testing. Selected test processes can be included in the system prior to prototype generation. The resulting prototype will have only that functionality specified by the test processes. We can then concentrate in specific features of the system along the prototype evaluation phase.

Additionally, this approach provided full simulation coverage. As the formal model includes both the interceptor and the GSM protocol (process *Generator*), there is no need of an external system to generate events for the interceptor. The prototype will read event trace files from the *Generator*.

5   Concluding Remarks

We have presented in this paper our experience using formal methods for the design of interception equipment for GSM mobile terminals. Although the appropriateness of Formal Methods for the development of industrial computer applications has been and is a controversial issue [2,11,16,35,39], the typical expected benefits of the formal approach to system design were apparent along the design process. Many defects and flaws were detected during the early design stages and, due to the structured top-down style of this approach, it permitted a better understanding both of GSM recommendations and the nature of the pursued system.

LOTOS was selected as the supporting formal language: i) LOTOS is an FDT standardized by ISO (the GSM recommendations were developed into the ISO framework); ii) a broad selection of tools is available to support the design process; and iii) our group had previous experience using LOTOS. Anyway, any formal description technique with comparable expressive power could be equally suitable for this task. Among others, ESTELLE [19], SDL [22], or PROMELA [17], to name some languages the authors have experience with, would also be good choices.

With respect to behavior description, the results obtained using LOTOS were beyond our expectations. The generated code is compact, expressive and permits straightforward verification. Note that, for prototyping, not a single line of code concerning the core of the system (i.e. the corresponding state machine) had to be written by hand. This is particularly interesting because the core of the system is the most complex part and, eventually, the less portable. The only code additions were related to interfacing (e.g. file access and user dialog management) and to data structure translation.

To sum up, the FDT approach was of paramount importance to focus the problem, that is, to separate major from minor aspects and to offer the designer a solid base to support his work.

Acknowledgments. This research has been supported by European Commission/CICYT project grants TIC 1FD97-1485-C02-02 and TIC 97-0669-C03-03. Implementation aspects are subject to Spanish patents P9801903 and P9901114.

Manuel J. Fernández Iglesias was affiliated to the International Computer Science Institute, Berkeley, USA, and Javier González-Castaño was affiliated to the Computer Sciences Department, University of Wisconsin-Madison, USA, when this version was written.

References

1. Bieber, P.: Formal Techniques for an ITSEC-E4 Secure Gateway, Procs. of the 12th, Annual Computer Security Applications Conference, IEEE Computer Society Press, 1996.
2. Bowen, J., Hinchey, M.: Seven more myths of formal methods, IEEE Software, **12**(4) (1995) 34-41.
3. Butler, R., Miller, S., Potts, J., Carreño, V. A.: A Formal Methods Approach to the Analysis of Mode Confusion, in: Procs. of the 17th AIAA/IEEE Digital Avionics Systems Conferenfce, 1998.
4. Easterbrook, S., Callahan, J.: Formal Methods for V&V of Partial Specifications: An Experience Report, in: Procs. of the 3rd IEEE International Symposium on Requirements Engineering (RE'97), IEEE Computer Society Press, 1997.
5. Ehrig, H., Mahr, B.: Fundamentals of algebraic specification 1, EATCS Monographs on Computer Science, Springer Verlag, 1985.
6. ETSI: GSM 03.22: Functions related to mobile station (MS) in idle mode and group receive mode, Digital cellular telecommunications system (Phase 2+) standards suite, ETSI Technical Report ETR 300 930, 1997.
7. ETSI: GSM 04.07: Mobile radio interface signalling layer 3. General aspects, Digital cellular telecommunications system (Phase 2+) standards suite, ETSI Technical Report ETR 300 939, 1997.

8. Fernández-Iglesias, M. J., Llamas-Nistal, M.: Algebraic Specification through Expression Transformation, in: Mizuno, T., Shiratori, N., Higashino, T., Togashi, A., (Eds.), Procs. of the Joint Conference FORTE/PSTV'97, Chapman & Hall, 1997, 355-366.
9. González-Castaño, F. J., Romero-Feijoo, A. et al: Real-Time Interceptor for the GSM Protocol, Technical Report UV/DTC/GRPILF00, Departamento de Tecnologías de las Comunicaciones. Universidad de Vigo, 2000.
10. Grant, H.: Managing electromagnetic compatibility between wireless and medical devices, Compliance Engineering, may-june (1999) 26-31.
11. Hall, J. A.: Seven myths of formal methods, IEEE Software, **7**(5) (1990) 11-19.
12. Hao, R., Lee, D., Sinha, R. K., Vlah, D.: Testing IP Routing Protocols. From Probabilistic Algorithms to a Software Tool, in: Bolognesi, T., Latella, D. Formal Methods for Distributed System Developmen t, Kluwer Academic Publishers, 2000, 249-266.
13. Haxthausen, A. E., Peleska, J.: Formal Development and Verification of a Distributed Railway Control System, IEEE Transactions on Software Engineering, **26**(8) (2000) 687-701.
14. Hoare, C. A. R.: Communicating Sequential Processes, Prentice-Hall, 1985.
15. Holloway, C. M.: Why Engineers Should Consider Formal Methods, in: Procs. of the 16th AIAA/IEEE Digital Avionics Systems Conference, vol. 1, 1.3-16 - 1.3-22, 1997.
16. Holloway, C. M., Butler, R.: Impediments to Industrial Use of Formal Methods, IEEE Computer, **29**(4), (1996) 25-26.
17. Holzmann, G.: Design and Validation of Computer Protocols, Prentice Hall, 1991.
18. Holzmann, G.: Proving the Value of Formal Methods, Procs. of the 7th. Intl. IFIP Conf. on Formal Description Techniques, FORTE'94, North Holland, 1994.
19. ISO: ESTELLE: A formal description technique based on the extended state transition model, International Standard 9074, International Standardization Organization, 1989.
20. Leduc, G., Bonaventure, O., Koerner E., Léonard, L., Pecheur, C., Zanetti, D.: Specification and Verification of a TTP Protocol for the Conditional Access to Services, in: Procs. of the 12th. J. Cartier Workshop on Formal Methods and their Applications, 1996.
21. ISO: LOTOS: A formal description technique based on the temporal ordering of observational behavior, International Standard 8807, International Standardization Organization, 1988.
22. ITU: SDL: Specification and Description Language, CCITT Recommendation Z.100, International Telecommunication Union, 1993.
23. Jonkers, V., Verschaeve, K., Wydaeghe, B., Coypers, L., Heirbaut, J.: OMT*, Bridging the Gap between Analysis and Design, in: Procs. of the 8th. Intl. IFIP Conf. on Formal Description Techniques, FORTE'95, North Holland, 1995.
24. Llamas-Nistal, M., Fernández-Iglesias, M. J., Burguillo-Rial, J. C., Pousada-Carballo, J. M., González-Castaño, F. J., Anido-Rifón, L.: LOTOOL: A Tool for Developing, Verifying and Testing Protocols using Formal Description Techniques, in: Innovations and Quality in Education for Electrical and Information Engineering, European Association for Education in Electronic and Information Engineering, 1997, pp. F1.18-F1.23.
25. Llamas-Nistal, M., Quemada, J., Fernández-Iglesias, M. J.: Direct Verification of Bisimulations, in: Procs. of the Joint Conference FORTE/PSTV'96, Chapman & Hall, 1996.

26. Mañas, J. A., de Miguel, T.: From LOTOS to C, in: K. J. Turner, (Ed), Procs. of FORTE'88, North Holland, 1988, 79-84.
27. Mañas, J. A., de Miguel, T., Salvachúa, J., Azcorra, A.: Tool support to implement LOTOS specifications, Computer Networks and ISDN Systems, **25** (1993) 79-84.
28. Mehrotra, A.: GSM System Engineering, Artech House, 1997.
29. Milne, G.: CIRCAL and the representation of communication, concurrency and time, ACM Trans. on Programming Languages and Systems, **7**(2) (1985) 270-298.
30. Milner, R.: Calculus of communicating systems, Lecture Notes on Computer Science **92**, Springer Verlag, 1980.
31. Milner, R.: Communication and Concurrency, Prentice Hall, 1989.
32. Mouly, M., Pautet, M.-B.: The GSM System for Mobile Communications, Cell & Sys, 1992.
33. de Nicola, R.: Extensional Equivalences for Transition System, Acta Informatica, **24** (1987) 211-237.
34. Pousada-Carballo, J. M., González-Castaño, F. J., Isasi de Vicente, F., Fernández-Iglesias, M. J.: Jamming System for Mobile Communications, IEE Electronic Letters, **34**(22) (1998) 2166-2167.
35. Pfleeger, S. L., Hatton, L.: Investigating the influence of formal methods, IEEE Computer, **30**(2) (1997) 33-43.
36. Quemada, J., Pavón, S., Fernández, A.: Transforming LOTOS specification with LOLA, in: Turner, K. J., (Ed), Procs. of FORTE'88, North Holland, 1988.
37. Redl, S. M., Weber, M. K., Oliphant, M. W.: An introduction to GSM, Artech House, 1995.
38. Steinert, T., Roessler, G.: Generation of Realistic Signalling Traffic in an ISDN Load Test System using SDL User Models, in: Bolognesi, T., Latella, D. Formal Methods for Distributed System Development, Kluwer Academic Publishers, 2000, 219-236.
39. Voas, J.: Software quality's eight greatest myths, IEEE Software, **16**(5) (1999) 118-120.

Coverage Directed Generation of System-Level Test Cases for the Validation of a DSP System

Laurent Arditi[1], Hédi Boufaïed[1], Arnaud Cavanié[2] and Vincent Stehlé[2]

[1] Texas Instruments France. MS 21. BP 5. 06270 Villeneuve Loubet. France.
larditi@ti.com, h-boufaied@ti.com

[2] Esterel Technologies.Twins 2 - 885 av. Julien Lefebvre. 06270 Villeneuve
Loubet. France. cavanie@simulog.fr, stehle@simulog.fr

Abstract. We propose a complete methodology for the automatic generation of test cases in the context of digital circuit validation. Our approach is based on a software model of the system to verify in which some modules are written in the Esterel language. An initial test suite is simulated and the state coverage is computed. New test sequences are automatically generated to reach the missing states. We then convert those sequences into system-level test cases (i.e. instruction sequences) by a technique called "pipeline inversion". The method has been applied for the functional validation of an industrial DSP system giving promising results.

1 Introduction

Although formal verification is now well accepted in the microelectronics industry, it is only a complementary technique and the primary validation and verification methods are still based on simulation. However, it has been shown that formal methods can also raise the quality of simulation-based verification while decreasing its cost[9]: a formal analysis of a circuit can generate tests which are then simulated. The tests are efficient because they are targeted at some meaningful coverage criteria[12][15][2]. That technique is usually called "white-box" verification since it uses the internal structure of the circuit to verify in order to generate the tests.

Our contribution extends this methodology to the system level. It is based on a software model of the system to verify which is partly written in the Esterel language[3]. The functional validation relies on an initial test suite constituted of system-level test cases (i.e. assembly language programs) which is run on the software model. The modules written in Esterel are formally analyzed so that it is possible to get an accurate measure of the state coverage provided by the initial test suite. Test sequences (also called "test vectors") are then automatically generated at the module level[1]. The next step is to translate those sequences into system-level test cases. We propose a technique called "pipeline inversion" to reach that goal.

Section 2 presents the context of our work. We describe in Section 3 our technique to automatically generate tests and in Section 4 their extension to the system-level by pipeline inversion. Practical results are given in the following Section. Finally, we discuss the advantages and weaknesses of our approach, while comparing with related works.

J.N. Oliveira and P. Zave (Eds.): FME 2001, LNCS 2021, pp. 449–464, 2001.

2   Modeling and Validation Flows

This Section describes the existing modeling and validation flows which have been applied before introducing formal methods in the project. We will show in the following Sections how formal methods could have been integrated into those flows to increase the validation efficiency.

2.1   The TMS320C55x™ DSP System

Texas Instruments' TMS320C55x™[22] is a new ultra-low power DSP targeted at the third generation of wireless hand-sets. It is the successor of the popular TMS320C54x™[21]. This is not only a DSP-core but a whole system-on-chip because it includes a CPU (DSP-core) and various system modules such as internal memory controllers, external memory interface, Direct Memory Access (DMA) controller, instruction cache, peripheral bus controller and host-processor interface.

2.2   The Software Model

The final chip which has been designed was synthesized from a hardware model developed in VHDL language[13] at the Register Transfer (RT) level. We call it the "VHDL model". In parallel, a software model of the system was designed. We call it the "C model", because it is written mainly in C/C++ language.

Both models share the same architecture and the same interfaces, down to a single level of sub-modules. From a temporal point of view, the C model is cycle-accurate, meaning that signal commutations done within a cycle happen in the mean time. For each cycle, all output signals are supposed to be equivalent on both C and VHDL models, given that the input signals are equivalent (Section 2.3 details the method for ensuring that equivalency).

There are advantages in having a software model of a hardware system:
- Because software is easier to correct and to modify than hardware, software's development cycle time is shorter than hardware's. A software model is thus functionally ready earlier than the hardware system it represents.
- A software simulator is an environment which provides elegant ways of solving synchronization and probing problems inherent to hardware instrumentation. This facilitates development and performance analysis at the target level.

Those advantages allow to give the customers a usable model of the chip very early, letting them begin development on their side. It also makes possible to write test cases early, ensuring those tests are functionally correct, without waiting for the VHDL code to be ready.

Current development environments based on hardware description languages (HDL) give the designer the possibility to simulate his code. Nevertheless, a separate software model (a simulator) has advantages that a HDL one lacks:
- Simulation based on a software model is faster than HDL simulation by an order of magnitude at least.
- It is possible to decline the software model with various interfaces: command line, GUI, co-design frameworks,...
- It is even possible to wrap it with an HDL interface, providing the best of both worlds.

- The resulting HDL module behaves like the real HDL code would, but it is hardly possible to reverse-engineer this component into HDL code. This elegantly solves the problems of intellectual property and confidentiality which arise when distributing a model of the component to customers.

2.3   Hardware vs. Software Validation

Our C model of TMS320C55x™ provides all the advantages listed above. But its main purpose is to allow validating the real component. This is a multi-step process where:

1. The software model is validated by running the test cases and checking some functional signatures.
2. The hardware model (at the different levels: RT, gate, transistor) is validated by simulating the same test cases. During the run on the software model, the inputs are extracted at each cycle and injected for the simulation of the hardware model. The outputs of both models are then compared and any mismatch is signalled.
3. The physical chip is validated using the same methodology.

That process clearly shows the importance of the set of test cases: if it is too weak, many bugs can reside in the software model and in the final chip.

2.4   Test Cases

Instead of developing test benches and a huge set of test patterns[1], we have developed system-level test cases: they are assembly language programs. System-level test cases are easier to write, debug and maintain than test patterns dedicated to unitary testing. They exercise the whole system, producing inter-module communications, and thus taking into account the behavior of all the system modules. The resulting patterns can not be unrealistic (whereas isolated test patterns could).

Another advantage of having test cases instead of test patterns is that it eases the functional testing. Indeed, our flow offers two ways to ensure a test case is correctly executed. One is to cross-check the results obtained on the software model with the ones obtained on the hardware model as explained in Section 2.3. The other is to insert functional signatures in the test case. This may be done by the test case developers or automatically by dedicated tools. The signatures check values of registers, memory locations, etc. and compare them with some expected values.

We mainly deal with three sorts of test-cases: completely hand-written test-cases, completely generated ones, and a hybridation of both.

- Hand-written test cases are a good starting point when starting the validation afresh. Moreover, one often needs to hand-write dedicated test-cases to reproduce "bugs".
- A different approach is to completely generate assembly test-cases with only a small description of the low-level functionnalities one wishes to test (control-flow instructions, data manipulations...). Dedicated generators have been developed for this purpose.
- Finally, hybrid test cases are obtained by declining a hand-written test-case in many "flavours". For example, a given hand-written test case doing memory ac-

---

[1] Test patterns are sequences of inputs/outputs at the boundary of a given module.

cesses can easily be declined to access different memory areas with different configurations.

The rest of this paper shows how test cases can be generated to increase the state coverage of the system modules.

3   Automatic Generation of Tests

3.1   Choosing a Coverage Metrics

When we started our work on automatic test generation we already had an initial database of test cases. Each one targets a given functionality of our system. Our goal was then to answer the following two questions:

- Do we cover enough functionalities and their possible combinations?
- If not, how can we efficiently, and if possible automatically, increase the coverage?

To answer these questions, one must first precisely define a coverage criterion[10][2]. Coverages based on statements, expressions, conditions, etc. are too weak when dealing with concurrent systems. We have chosen to focus on *state coverage* which appears to be a good compromise. Indeed, each system module is a Finite State Machine (FSM) which state coverage can be accurately measured and it is likely that an uncovered state reflects an untested scenario. However, directly coding FSM is not suitable for modeling and maintaining complex systems. The Esterel language will help us solving this problem as described below.

3.2   The Esterel Language

Esterel[3] is an imperative language dedicated to the modeling of control-dominated reactive systems. It provides powerful primitives for expressing concurrency, communication and preemption. It has a formally defined semantics in terms of FSMs which makes Esterel programs behave deterministically. The Esterel compiler can generate C code, and, as it focuses on control aspects, data-handling is imported from the C language.

From a programming point of view, Esterel is more convenient than C for modeling many of our system's modules: its dedicated primitives make the code simpler, shorter, more readable and maintainable than C code. For short, it is closer to a specification while still remaining executable.

From a validation point of view, the benefit is that Esterel programs are compiled into well defined formalisms such as netlists or explicit automata[2]. This opens the door to the use of formal verification and analysis tools such as SIS[19], VIS[23], SMV[16] and Xeve[4].

Applying our methodology to the whole system at once is unrealistic: first, because of its size, second it would have needed to remodel all the modules in Esterel, including

---

[2] A netlist is a circuit at the gate level. It is represented as a set of Boolean equations assigning values to output signals and registers in function of input signals and previous values of the registers. The netlist implements an FSM but its size is usually much smaller than the equivalent explicit automata (polynomial vs. exponential).

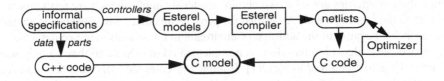

Fig. 1. Development of C model.

the CPU. Thus, we have chosen to apply it at the module level first and to extend it at the system level.

Seven of our system's modules which are control-dominated have been remodeled in Esterel. These modules are compiled into a netlist which is optimized using SIS[19][20]. The netlist is then converted into a C++ code so that it can be integrated in the rest of the C-model (see Figure 1).

We discuss in Section 6.1 the advantages of using a high-level language such as Esterel compared to other formalisms.

3.3   Formally Evaluating State-Coverage

Having embedded the Esterel modules, we are now able to run a simulation and, for each module (noted M), get the *reached state set* (noted *Red*). It simply consists in adding the current state of M to *Red* after each simulation cycle.

To get a coverage measure, we must now determine the number of theoretically reachable states. The formal verification tool Xeve[4] is used for this purpose: taking as input the same netlist we used to generate the C++ code, it builds the Binary Decision Diagram (BDD) [5] of the *reachable state set* (noted *Rable*). The BDD is then traversed and explicitly enumerated. Notice that we do not need to abstract the model in order to extract its control as in [17]. This is because we prohibit the modeling of data in the Esterel models. Therefore, the states we consider are only control states.

The *state coverage* is then defined as the ratio between the number of reached states and the number of reachable states. The difference between these two sets is called the *missing state set* (noted *Miss*).

3.4   Generation of Test Sequences

We have shown how to measure the state coverage. We now detail our method to automatically generate test sequences in order to increase that coverage. It is based on well-known techniques of reachability analysis.

We call a *test sequence* for M a sequence of input vectors applicable to M. To increase M's state coverage, we need to find test sequences leading to the missing states of M:

1. We first exploit *Miss*. For each of its elements S, we add one new output O_S to M's netlist so that O_S is active iff the FSM of M is in the state S.
2. We then use a formal model checker (we have used Xeve[4] and SMV[16]), asking for each O_S to prove the property "O_S is never active".

When these properties are false, we obtain counter-examples which are test sequences leading to the missing states. A verified property means that a missing state is actually not reachable because of the addition of environment constraints (see Section 3.5).

A dedicated algorithm has also been implemented into Xeve so that we only need to input the netlist and *Red* to Xeve[1]. It implicitly computes *Miss* and automatically generates the corresponding test sequences. The whole validation flow starting from the Esterel description of a module to the generation of test sequences reaching missing states has been fully automated.

3.5   Taking Environment Constraints into Account

The computation of *Rable*, and consequently of *Miss*) as presented above does not take into account potential constraints imposed on the module by its environment (i.e. CPU and other modules). The existence of such constraints often makes many theoretically reachable states actually unreachable. Taking these constraints into account is mandatory to contain the state explosion and to get a realistic evaluation of the state coverage. The other reason for considering these constraints relates to test sequence generation: a generated test sequence that does not respect the module's constraints is unusable since it is impossible to produce in practice. The set of constraints applied to a given module is determined by the informal documents describing the module and the ones connected to it. In some cases that set is not maximal. Fortunately that does not corrupt the validity of our method but may only reduce its efficiency. A more important point one must take care of is the correctness of the constraints:

- They must not be contradictory, otherwise "false-positive" results will be returned because $false \rightarrow anything$. Thus, we first prove the constraints are not always false.
- They must not be too restrictive: they must at least allow to reach all the states we know they are reachable in the context of the real system. To do so, we benefit from the fact that our methodology is based on simulation. Indeed, we first verify that *Red* is included in *Rable* even after *Rable* has been reduced by the constraints. The efficiency of that cross-checking depends on the quality of the initial test suite: in the worst case, *Red* is empty and thus always included in *Rable* whatever the constraints are.

It is therefore an important task to also regularly manually review the constraints. In practice, we apply the following iterative process:

1. Get *Red* by simulation, compute *Rable* and *Miss*.
2. Write a constraint set *Constr*.
3. If *Constr* is always *false,* it includes contradictory conjunctions, goto 2.
4. If *Constr* does not hold for all elements of *Red*, it is too strong, goto 2.
5. Generate test sequences to reach all elements of *Miss* under the constraint *Constr*.
6. If some test sequences are unrealistic, *Constr* is too weak, goto 2.

Both Xeve and SMV allow taking constraints into account. One way is to express them is to write an observer in Esterel (i.e. a module which monitors inputs/outputs and signals constraint violations). But it has some limitations because liveness constraints are not expressible. In SMV, constraints, including liveness ones, are expressed in temporal logics LTL or CTL: Linear Temporal Logic (LTL) and Computation Tree Logic (CTL) are logics with additional timing operators: G (always), F (eventually), U (until), X (next step), A (all execution paths), E (some execution paths) [7].

3.6 From Test Sequences to Test Cases

A *test case* is a program. It may be written in C, assembly or any other language, but in the end it is a binary code executed by the system. Unlike a test sequence, a test case is not relative to any module in particular but to the whole system. We say that a *test case realizes a test sequence* if the execution of the test case eventually generates the test sequence.

As we have already mentioned, it is mandatory that our methodology is able to produce test cases and not only module-level test sequences. The task of generating test cases from test sequences may be automated in some cases but it strongly depends on the targeted module M.

The problem has already been addressed in [15] and [2] but those works are in the most convenient case where the module to verify is the decoder of a processor. Therefore, generating input sequences for the module is nearly equivalent to generating instructions: the gap between test sequences and test cases is narrow and easy to cross. We are in a more general situation because the modules being verified are not part of the CPU but are connected to it, directly or not. They are also connected to other modules which are sometimes not formally defined.

The communication protocol between the CPU and the module is a key factor for the automation of the test case generation. Indeed, suppose test sequences have been generated for a module M which is directly connected to the CPU and only to it. Suppose there is a defined set of instructions which can send control signals to M in a deterministic way. Then it is possible to automate the generation of the test cases. But if M is not directly connected to the CPU, if several different modules can drive signals to M, it is difficult to deterministically and automatically convert test sequences into test cases. These two situations are the best and worst cases. We consider the later below and the former in Section 4.

3.7 Manual Generation of Test Cases

We address here the critical case where there is no automatic way to translate test sequences into test cases. Test cases must be manually written but the sequences are of great interest in order to target the effort. Indeed, the sequences accurately show the functionalities and their combinations which have not been exercised. It is the task of the verification engineers to first ensure the asked sequences are realistic, and, if they are, to write programs which realize them.

Let us assume the module under test is M, an automatically generated sequence T is targeted at a missing state S. If T is realistic, an engineer writes a program P which should realize T and so reach S. We provide different tools in order to ensure that assumption. The first and obvious one is to run P and check that S is now included in the new reached state set. Another way is to dump the sequence T' of inputs at M's boundary while running P. It then remains to verify that T' includes T. Indeed, that would mean the trace of inputs T' makes M pass through the state S.

The manual generation of test cases is only usable and valuable when the number of missing states is manageable. But we have experienced an hybrid approach which consists in manually writing a few test cases and then automatically deriving them so that they exercise similar functionalities on different modules and with different configurations. We can also introduce some random parameters. The number of resulting test cases may be large but the effort to produce them is reduced. We show in Section 5.3 how we used that approach, and how it helped increasing the state coverage.

4 Generation of Test Cases by Pipeline Inversion

We have presented our methodology to automatically generate test sequences targeted at state coverage. These sequences may be manually converted into test cases but it is of course preferable to provide a fully automatic flow from missing states to test cases as we propose below.

4.1 Pipeline Inversion

Let M be a module connected to the CPU. Starting with a test sequence for M, the problem is to go backward across the CPU back to a program. Doing so needs a model of the CPU. Then an automated tool can show the input sequences at the CPU level which generate the targeted input sequences at M's level. Input sequences at the CPU level are assembly instruction sequences which are converted into real test cases in a straightforward way. We call that mechanism "pipeline inversion" and we formalize it here below.

We note I_M (respectively O_M) a sequence of inputs (resp. outputs) at the boundary of M. $M(I_M) = O_M$ means that M eventually outputs O_M when its inputs are I_M but the timing between I_M and O_M is not specified. Similarly, $CPU(I_{CPU}) = O_{CPU}$ means that the CPU eventually outputs O_{CPU} when its inputs are I_{CPU} (i.e. the execution of the program I_{CPU} generates the outputs O_{CPU}). As we are in a synchronous framework driven by a single clock, there is a one-to-one mapping between each sequence couple.

The pipeline inversion of O_{CPU} consists in finding a sequence I_{CPU} so that $CPU(I_{CPU}) = O_{CPU}$. The methodology presented in Section 3 allows to generate I_M given O_M. Considering that $I_M = O_{CPU}$, a pipeline inversion of I_M would then convert the test sequence at M's level into a test case. A first alternative to do so is:

1. Generate I_M,
2. Make a pipeline inversion of I_M so that I_{CPU} is generated.

But this approach is too weak, it may produce false-negative results: it may fail to generate I_{CPU} because the pipeline inversion of I_M is impossible. Suppose we want to generate a test case to produce O_M and that all the following conditions are met:

$$\exists I_M, M(I_M) = O_M \qquad (1)$$
$$\exists J_M, (M(J_M) = O_M) \wedge (J_M \neq I_M) \qquad (2)$$
$$\forall I_{CPU}, CPU(I_{CPU}) \neq I_M \qquad (3)$$
$$\exists J_{CPU}, CPU(J_{CPU}) = J_M \qquad (4)$$

The test sequence generation algorithm can show only one input sequence satisfying a given output, if any. Therefore, the algorithm may show only I_M at step 1 (by Equation 1) and thus fails to generate any test case at step 2 (because of Equation 3). But if step 1 would have shown J_M (by Equation 2), the pipeline inversion would have succeeded and generated J_{CPU} (by Equation 4).

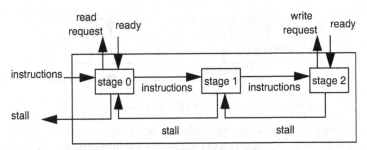

Fig. 2. Overview of the pipeline architecture.

To overcome this drawback, we have extended the technique by connecting the model of the CPU to the model of M, and performing the generation of M input sequences under the constraint of the pipeline inversion. Thus, instead of running the two-step process presented above, we run a single-step process: Find I_{CPU} so that $M(CPU(I_{CPU})) = O_M$. Doing so, the formal analysis will succeed in generating all the O_M which can be produced by M and the CPU together.

That methodology rises performance issues since it requires a computation of the state space for the M-CPU product FSM instead of computing the state spaces for M and for CPU alone. The difference is not negligible in practice since it represents one to two orders of magnitude in computation time. To reduce that weakness, we propose to first use the two-steps approach which is quite fast. We use the single-step approach only for the states which could not have been reached by the two-steps approach.

4.2 Our Pipeline Model

We have applied pipeline inversion to internal memory controllers DARAM, SARAM and APIRAM. Therefore the model of the pipeline we have described in Esterel is an abstraction of the real one which accurately models the communication with the memory controllers but not more. That abstraction is mandatory in order to avoid a state explosion. Here is the list of the abstractions we did:

- The pipeline model describes the execution of 50 instructions whereas the real set includes more than 400 instructions.
- The effects of the instructions are only described for the data control signals. That means the model describes for each instruction at which pipeline stages the requests are sent to the memory controllers and at which stages the ready are awaited.
- The model is pipelined but has only 3 stages whereas the real one has 7. We modeled only the stages at which the pipeline communicates with the memory controllers. For example the instruction fetch and decode stages are not relevant. Instead we express some simple constraints which are true if the running program is mapped into a fast access memory, and if interrupts which could perturb the regular instruction fetch mechanism do not happen.
- The model is not super-scalar whereas the real CPU can execute two instructions in parallel. When needed, the parallel instruction pairs are modeled as pseudo-instructions with equivalent behaviors.

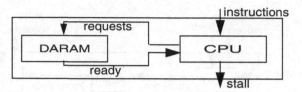

Fig. 3. Connection of DARAM to the pipeline model.

Our Esterel model of the pipeline resembles the one proposed in [18]. It is built as follows (see also Figure 2). At the top-level, inputs are the instructions (one signal for each of the 50 possible instructions), and the acknowledgement signals (ready from memory controllers). The outputs are the request signals (to the memory controllers) and a general stall signal. The top-level consists of three sub-modules: stage 0, 1 and 2. Instruction signals are connected to stage 0 and are propagated to stage 1 and stage 2 when the pipeline is not stalled.

When an instruction arrives to stage 0, if it needs to perform read operations, requests are sent. On the next cycle, if all the awaited ready signals are active, the instruction may either "die" or it is propagated to stage 1 if it also needs to perform write operations. If the ready signals are not present, the pipeline is stalled. That means the instructions are not propagated and that no new instruction is accepted. Stage 2 is similar to stage 0 except that requests concern write operations and that instructions are not propagated any more.

4.3 Pipeline Inversion in Practice

We illustrate here the pipeline inversion on the validation of the DARAM module. DARAM is an internal memory controller which is connected to the CPU. Figure 3 shows how they are connected.

The DARAM and CPU models are compiled as netlists from the Esterel codes and optimized. DARAM's netlist is instrumented to add outputs corresponding to the missing states (see Section 3.4). The two netlists are then connected and converted into a code suitable for the SMV model checker[16].

Additional constraints are written to express pipeline features not specified in the Esterel model. For each instruction, there is an input signal $instr_i$ which is active when the instruction has been fetched and decoded. Examples of constraints expressed in LTL are given below:

- No more than one instruction is decoded at each cycle:

  $G(\forall i, instr_i \rightarrow \forall j \neq i, \neg instr_j)$.

- No instruction is decoded when the CPU is stalled:

  $G(stall \rightarrow \forall i, \neg instr_i)$.

- Some instructions need a relocation of the stack pointer before being executed. In the same program, if one instruction relocates the stack pointer, then all following instructions must use the same location:

  $G(\forall i, instr_i \rightarrow XG(\forall j, instr_j \rightarrow (stack_i = stack_j)))$

All the constraints form an assertion called *rel* which is proved to be true an all elements of *Red* as explained in Section 3.5. Finally we express temporal properties allowing to

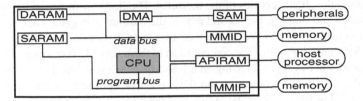

Fig. 4. The DSP system.

generate traces reaching the missing states. Those properties have the form $P_k : rel \rightarrow G \neg O_k$ where O_k is an output activated iff DARAM is in the missing state S_k.

We then ask SMV[3] to prove all P_k properties. If P_k is *true*, that means S_k is actually not reachable because of the pipeline behavior or of *rel*. The set of reachable states is thus reduced. When P_k is *false*, SMV produces a counter-example. It is a trace of the signals (including the $instr_i$ inputs) which leads to the emission of the output O_k, thus which reaches S_k.

We have developed an automatic tool in order to process SMV counter-examples and generate assembly language test cases. That tool selects only the signals named $instr_i$ in the counter-example. It translates them into assembly-language instructions which are included into a template program. Functional signatures are automatically inserted, the program is directly run on the software model and the new number of reachable states can be computed.

5 Practical Results

5.1 Module Description

We have applied the methodology presented above on different kinds of modules building a derivative of TMS320C55x™ system[22]. The modules we focused on are shown on Figure 4: DARAM, SARAM and APIRAM (internal memory controllers), SAM (bus controller which handles communications with external peripherals), MMIP and MMID (external memory interfaces), DMA (direct memory access controller). They were modeled in Esterel. The development time was significantly shorter than the one required to model the same modules in C or in VHDL languages.

Module	DARAM	SARAM	APIRAM	SAM	MMIP	MMID	DMA
# inputs/outputs	18 / 101	32 / 164	35 / 159	33 / 122	22 / 59	49 / 157	24 / 46
#regs init/optim	63 / 30	91 / 27	91 / 26	86 / 80	78 / 30	95 / 67	98 / 73
time optim	41 sec	302 sec	83 sec	82 sec	286 sec	43 sec	428 sec
#reachable init	556	827	422	400	46,513	>1.3M	309
#reachable final	481	368	237	400	46,513	>1.3M	278
time reachable	2.1 sec	3.8 sec	2.5 sec	7.09 sec	40.7 sec	24 hours	23.2 sec
time enum	0.1 sec	0.1 sec	0.1 sec	0.7 sec	3.6 sec	-	0.7 sec

Table 1. System modules on which we applied the generation of test cases.

---

[3] We used SMV for that purpose. But any other model checker is usable.

Table 1 shows the characteristics of the modules. The first row indicates the number of primary inputs and outputs, the second row is the number of registers before and after optimization using SIS[19]. We were faced to a state explosion for MMID: we could not use SIS because it requires the computation of the reachable state space. Instead, we reduced the number of registers using an ad-hoc approach which is less efficient. "time optim" is the CPU time[4] required to run the sequential optimization. "#reachable init" (resp. "#reachable final") gives the number of reachable states obtained without (resp. with) environment constraints. That last number will be our basis for state coverage. The two last rows report the CPU time needed to implicitly build the reachable state sets with Xeve[4] and to explicitly enumerate them. One can see that, except for MMID, the computation and the enumeration of the reachable state spaces is fast. This is mainly due to the sequential optimization.

5.2 Generation of the Initial Reached States

We have compiled all the modules as C code and integrated them into the software model of the complete DSP system. We have then run the initial test suite which serves the designers for non-regression checking[5]. That test suite has been developed along the project during more than two years by several verification engineers. It consists of 48,268 test cases, running for more than 385 Millions of cycles. The simulation time is 120 hours. The initial state coverages obtained after the simulation of that test suite are given in Table 2. The rows show the number of states reached by the test suite, the state

Module	DARAM	SARAM	APIRAM	SAM	MMIP	MMID	DMA
#reached init	166	106	35	217	650	2289	218
coverage init	35%	29%	15%	54%	1%	?	78%
#missing	315	262	202	183	45863	?	60

Table 2. Resulting state coverage after simulation of initial test suite.

coverage it provides and the number of missing states. Notice that the traditional code coverage metrics[10] (statement, condition,...) obtained after the simulation of the same test suite on the VHDL model are in the 90-100% range, even for the modules where state coverage is actually very low. This clearly shows the danger of assimilating code coverage with state coverage.

5.3 Generation of New Test Cases

We have applied our test sequence and test case generation methodology. Table 3 shows the results. The two first rows reports the number of test sequences which have been automatically generated and the CPU time required for that task. "#test cases final" is the number of system-level test cases which have been generated from the test

---

[4] All CPU times are measured on a 360Mhz UltraSparc-II with 1Gb of physical memory and 2Gb of virtual memory.

[5] We have also run real-world applications, representing several Billions of cycles. Those applications are Digital Signal Processing algorithms which exercise the CPU but do not increase the coverage of the system modules.

Module	DARAM	SARAM	APIRAM	SAM	MMIP	MMID	DMA
#test sequences	315	261	201	80	-	-	60
time sequences	5,246 sec	18,836 sec	611 sec	140 sec	-	-	1,139 sec
#test cases final	315	248	201	32	13,752	10,560	10
#reached final	481	254	162	321	2,328	6,382	234
coverage final	100%	69%	68%	80%	5%	?	84%
cov final/cov init	2.9	2.4	4.5	1.48	5	2.8	1.1

Table 3. Generated test sequences, test cases and final state coverage.

sequences, automatically or manually. The three last rows show the coverage obtained after having run the new test cases and how it has increased compared to the coverage provided by the initial test suite.

5.4 Remarks

For DARAM, SARAM and APIRAM, the generation of the test sequences is slow because it uses the pipeline inversion technique as described in Section 4.3. But the advantage is that the test cases are directly and automatically derived. This is the case for DARAM for which we could directly get a 100% coverage. The new tests are very efficient if we consider the number of new states reached over the simulation time: they allow to reach 315 states in 37 seconds whereas the initial test suite covers only 166 states in 120 hours. If we run only the 127 test cases of the suite which where hand-written to validate DARAM specifically, only 132 states are reached in 325 seconds.

Our pipeline models only the CPU data requests but SARAM and APIRAM are also connected to the instruction fetch unit, the DMA and the host processor. Therefore, the pipeline inversion generated incomplete test cases. We then automatically derived them so that they are executed with different combinations of requests from the instruction fetch unit, the DMA and the host processor. It allowed to reach a coverage a little bit less than 70%. It is not clear whether the remaining missing states are really reachable. We think the environment constraints we modeled are too tolerant (but not to restrictive).

For the SAM module, we did not use pipeline inversion because most of the requests are not originated by the CPU. The generation of test sequences is thus fast. From the 80 proposed sequences, we manually wrote 32 test cases we considered as being realistic and the most important ones. That allowed to significantly increase the coverage.

MMIP and MMID have too many states to try to generate test sequences reaching all the missing states. For MMIP, we generated just a few sequences, manually converted them into test cases and automatically derived them into several versions: different memory latencies, protocol configurations,... That approach is not rigorous enough to provide an acceptable coverage. However, we could multiple the coverage by a factor of 5. We did not investigate that methodology more deeply but we believe it is promising, especially if random parameters are introduced for massive test generation. We did not generate any test sequence for MMID but we reused the ones of DARAM that we derived into several test cases so that MMID is addressed instead of DARAM. The coverage of MMID could thus almost be tripled.

For DMA, we generated the missing test sequences and manually converted some into test cases. The other ones seemed to be unrealistic.

5.5 Bugs Found

Our methodology and tools arrived late in the project life so that they have been applied after many bugs had already been found and fixed. However, the generated test cases have shown unknown bugs in various modules, in the software model as well as in the hardware model.

The most interesting conclusion of our experiments is that very often, bugs were not located in the modules we were testing. For example, one of the test cases generated for MMID highlit a possible dead-lock in the DMA. We also found bugs in the CPU while running test cases of DARAM and APIRAM. This remark is important: it shows that a system-level validation approach has several advantages, one of them being that it can show bugs in parts of the system which were not directly being validated.

6 Conclusions

We have shown in this paper a methodology to automatically generate new test sequences targeted at state coverage. They may be automatically converted into system-level test cases using a technique called "pipeline inversion". This validation flow has been integrated into a real world design project and allowed to significantly increase the coverage of system modules.

6.1 Comparison with Related Works

Early works (e.g. [6] and [14]) have investigated the use of formal methods to automatically generate tests. But they took place in an Automatic Test Pattern Generation context, thus at a low level where the tests are not intended to verify the functionalities of the systems but to detect possible fabrication problems.

Our work is more related to [12][15] and [2]: methodologies to automatically generate tests targeted at state and transition coverages are proposed. They show applications for the verification of parts of real processors like an instruction decoder, allowing to easily turn test sequences into test cases. We are in a more general situation where the test sequences generated do not apply to a CPU, thus the need of the pipeline inversion technique to convert the test sequences into system-level test cases. This has been discussed in Section 3.6.

We also think a major advantage of our approach is that the models are written in the Esterel language. The models of [2] and [17] are explicit FSMs hand-written in the Murφ[8] and SMV[16] verification languages and are not reusable for any other purposes like simulation. With Esterel, the FSMs are not explicitly specified but automatically synthesized from a high-level form. The Esterel models are also executable allowing to build software simulators we release to our customers. The extraction of the control parts of the module is automatic: we do not need to work on data abstractions as in [12] or [17].

6.2 Perspectives

Our methodology suffers from some weakness we need to address. The main one is the fact that the state explosion stops the test case generation flow. Indirect approaches are still efficient (see results for MMIP and MMID) but not satisfactory. We have already used reduction techniques but they only help keeping the BDD representation of the states compact. The sequential optimization does not help for modules having a too large state space (e.g. MMID). We are currently working on modular optimization which may allow to progress. Automatic abstraction is also being investigated.

Our current approach needs at least one step where a state set is explicit (*Miss* or *Red*). This is a limitation which could be overridden: the idea is to build *Red* as a BDD during the simulation. Therefore the operation $Miss = Rable - Red$ could be done on BDDs. The generation of test sequences or test cases using the pipeline inversion would then need to use heuristics to produce tests so that each one pass through the maximum number of missing states. This would allow to generate a manageable number of test cases even if the number of missing states is large.

Other coverages may be considered[10][2][11]. The next step is to apply the methodology on transition coverage. We have conducted a first experiment showing that fully automatically generated test cases could raise the transition coverage from 10% up to 90% for DARAM.

We are currently applying our methodology on a new project, at a larger scale, earlier in the project life, with a very limited initial test suite. Our future work also involves the generation of test cases for data-dominated modules and of test generation with tight constraints for final production test.

References

1. L. Arditi, A. Bouali, *et al.* "Using Esterel and Formal Methods to Increase the Confidence in the Functional Validation of a Commercial DSP". In *Workshop on Formal Methods for Industrial Critical Systems*, Trento, Italy, 1999.
2. M. Benjamin, D. Geist, *et al.* "A Study in Coverage-Driven Test Generation". In *36th Design Automation Conference*, 1999.
3. G. Berry, G. Gonthier. "The Esterel synchronous programming language: Design, semantics, implementation". In *Science of Computer Programming*, 19(2), 1992.
4. A. Bouali. "XEVE, an Esterel Verification Environment". In *Computer Aided Verification*, LNCS 1427, 1998.
5. R. Bryant. "Graph-based algorithms for boolean manipulation". In *IEEE Transactions on Computers*, C-35(8), 1986.
6. H, Cho, G. Hachtel, F. Somenzi. "Fast Sequential ATPG Based on Implicit State Enumeration". In International Test Conference, 1991.
7. E.M. Clarke, E.A. Emerson, A.P. Sistla. "Automatic Verification of Finite-State Concurrent Systems Using Temporal Logic Specifications". In *ACM Transactions on Programming Languages and Systems*, 8(2), 1986.
8. D.L. Dill. "The Murφ verification system". In *Computer Aided Verification*, LNCS 1102, 1996

9. D.L Dill. "What's Between Simulation and Formal Verification?". In *35th Design Automation Conference*, 1998.

10. D. Drake, P. Cohen. "HDL Verification Coverage". In *Integrated Systems Design Magazine*, June 1998.

11. F. Fallah, P. Ashar, S. Devadas. "Simulation Vector Generation from HDL Descriptions for Observability-Enhanced Statement Coverage". In *36th Design Automation Conference*, 1999.

12. R.C. Ho, C. Han Yang, M.A. Horowitz, D.L. Dill. "Architecture Validation for Processors". In *International Symposium of Computer Architecture*, 1995.

13. *VHDL language reference manual*. IEEE standard 1076-1993. IEEE Press, 1994.

14. T. Kropf, H.-J. Wunderlich. "A Common Approach to Test Generation and Hardware Verification Based on Temporal Logic". In International Test Conference, 1991.

15. D. Lewin, D. Lorenz, S. Ur. "A Methodology for Processor Implementation Verification". In *Formal Methods in Computer Aided Design*, LNCS 1166,1996.

16. K. McMillan. *Symbolic Model Checking: An Approach to the State Explosion Problem*. Kluwer Academic, 1993.

17. D. Moundanos, J. Abraham, Y. Hoskote."Abstraction Techniques for Validation Coverage Analysis and Test Generation". In *IEEE Transactions on Computers*, 47(1), 1998.

18. S. Ramesh, P. Bhaduri. "Validation of Pipelined Processor Designs using Esterel Tools: A Case Study". In *Computer Aided Verification*, LNCS 1633, 1999.

19. E.M. Sentovitch, K.J. Singh, *et al.* "Sequential Circuit Design Using Synthesis and Optimization". In *International Conference on Computer Design*, 1992.

20. E.M. Sentovitch, H. Toma, G. Berry. "Latch Optimization in Circuits Generated from High-Level Descriptions". In *International Conference on Computer-Aided Design*, 1996.

21. *TMS320C54x DSP CPU Reference Set*. Texas Instruments, Literature Number SPRU131F, Apr. 1999.

22. *TMS320C55x DSP CPU Reference Guide*. Texas Instruments, Literature Number SPRU371A, Feb. 2000. See also http://www.ti.com/sc/c5510

23. The VIS Group. "VIS: A system for Verification and Synthesis", In *Computer Aided Verification*, LNCS 1102, 1996.

Using Formal Verification Techniques to Reduce Simulation and Test Effort

O. Laurent[1], P. Michel[2], and V. Wiels[2]

[1] EADS-Airbus SA, A/BTE/SY/MS
316 route de Bayonne,
31000 Toulouse cedex 03, France
odile.laurent@airbus.aeromatra.com
[2] ONERA-CERT/DTIM
BP 4025, 2 avenue E. Belin,
31055 Toulouse Cedex 4, France
{michel,wiels}@cert.fr

Abstract. This paper describes an experiment in using formal methods in an industrial context. The goal is to use formal verification techniques in order to alleviate the simulation and test activities. The application is a flight control computer of the Airbus A340.

Introduction

Aerospatiale has used formal methods for several years in the development of embedded systems for Airbus and it has already significantly increased productivity. Embedded systems are specified using SCADE [8] a commercial tool based on the Lustre language [1,3]. The SCADE environment provides a qualified automatic code generator, so there is no gap between the specification and the embedded code. This eliminates the need for unit test: only the specification needs to be validated. The development cycle is no more a "V", but a "Y". This use of formal methods thus already implies cost savings.

But it is possible to go further. For the moment, specifications are validated using simulation and test. The goal of the project presented in this paper is to study whether formal verification techniques could be used to verify some properties on these specifications in order to reduce the simulation and test phases which are still very costly. Several tools exist that allow verification of Lustre specifications and we would like to study the feasability of using these tools in an industrial context.

Section 1 presents the case study chosen for the project and the methodology. Section 2 describes the first part of the project which has consisted in identifying and formalising properties of the system. In section 3, we present the ongoing experiments of verification of such properties. Section 4 gives conclusions and suggests avenues for future work.

J.N. Oliveira and P. Zave (Eds.): FME 2001, LNCS 2021, pp. 465–477, 2001.

1   Methodology and Case Study

The case study we are working on for this project is the Flight Control Secondary Computer (FCSC) which is part of the A340 flight control system. The flight control surfaces of an Airbus A340 are all electrically controlled and hydraulically activated. The sidesticks are used to fly the aircraft in pitch and roll. The flight control system computes the order to be applied to the surfaces from the pilot inputs and the current state of the aircraft. Moreover, regardless of the pilot's input, computers will prevent excessive maneuvers and going beyond the safe flight envelope.

For safety reasons, the flight control system presents several redundancy levels:

- Reconfiguration redundancy by duplication of the computers: when an active computer detects a failure, it is replaced by the following one in a reconfiguration list. Each aircraft control surface has its own reconfiguration list, the number and the order of the involved computers depends on the surface.
- Conceptual redundancy. Two kinds of computers have been developed: Flight Control Primary Computer (FCPC) and Flight Control Secondary Computer (FCSC). The A340 flight control system is composed of 3 FCPCs and 2 FCSCs.

FCPCs have been defined to control all kinds of surfaces except flaps and slats. An FCSC can control all kinds of surfaces except flaps, slats and Trimable Horizontal Stabilizer (THS). It uses laws generated by an FCPC in a normal configuration, but when this fails, it generates direct pitch, roll and yaw laws itself. The computer operates as long as the aircraft is electrically energized.

Figure 1 shows the surfaces managed by the flight control system.

The FCSC specification consists of approximately 600 SCADE sheets, dealing with validation of inputs, logic, flight laws and servocommands. The validation of inputs part is concerned with acquiring inputs from pilot, copilot and from different sensors, and with assuring that only valid inputs are used. Logic consists in selecting the right laws with respect to the current state of the aircraft and the pilot inputs. The flight laws computes the values of the orders to be applied to the surfaces. Finally, servocommands are responsible for commanding the surfaces.

In the current development process, the code is automatically generated from the SCADE specifications and validation is done by simulation and test. Two major steps are carried out in the validation process:

- tests in a simulation environment to verify the design of the system,
- tests on the iron bird with the target computers to validate the system within the real environment.

The goal of our study is to replace or alleviate tests performed during the simulation phase of the validation.

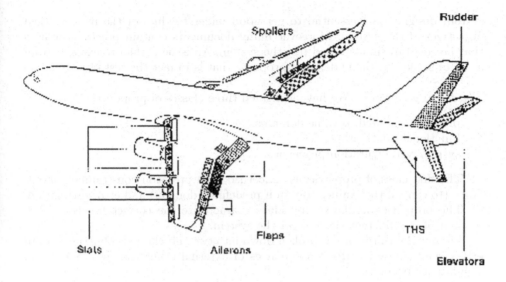

Fig. 1. Plane surfaces.

Our approach is broken down into three steps:

– identification of properties that are to be satisfied,
– expression of these properties in logic,
– verification.

The methodology must allow:

– identification of properties on the inputs and outputs of the system or of a main part of the system which will be called subsystem. Indeed, we want to be able to express properties without entering into the detailed description of *how* the system works.
– automatization of the process.

The first two steps of the approach are described in the next section, and the third one in section 3.

2   Identifying and Expressing Properties

2.1   Identification

Properties have been identified by two means: discussions with designers of the system and study of different design and validation documents such as Safety Requirement Document, Verification and Validation plan or System Descritpion Notes.

This step is a difficult one. It is hard to identify the relevant properties for the system which address inputs and outputs. Detailed discussions with the system designers are essential to get good understanding of the more critical objectives of the system. Moreover many documents contain precise scenarios that are used to simulate and test the system. An issue is then to extract, from a list of scenarios, the underlying property that is in fact the test objective.

Classes of properties. We have identified three classes of properties:

- properties related to value domains,
- functional safety properties,
- system reconfiguration properties.

The first class of properties is concerned with precision constraints, surveillance (to control that values stay in a predefined domain) and error estimation.

The properties in the second class characterize the correct functional behaviour of the different elements of the system.

Finally, the third class is broken down into two sub-classes: robustness properties, which describe the consequences of external events on the system and redundancy properties.

Examples. In this paper, we consider two examples of properties. The first one is a functional safety property concerning the sidesticks. The informal expression of the property (which was given to us by a designer) is the following:

P1: *if we suppose that the two sidesticks cannot be faulty at the same time, there is always an active stick.*

The second one is a redundancy property on inner ailerons. The reconfiguration list for these surfaces mentions two primary computers PC1 and PC2 followed by two secondary computers SC1 and SC2. If we focus on the first FCSC, the redundancy property can be expressed, in a first attempt, as :

P2: *if the two primary computers PC1 and PC2 are faulty, then the secondary computer SC1 becomes operational.*

2.2   Formal Expression of the Properties

The next step is to find a formal expression of the informal properties that were identified. This step is also difficult and requires good knowledge of the application.

P1. In the case of P1, the difficulty is to define what an "active" sidestick means. There are two sidesticks (pilot and copilot), the position of the sidesticks define an order which will correspond to an angle to apply to the surfaces. The sidesticks position and several sensors to detect problems are inputs to the system, the output is the order that must be transmitted to the plane surfaces. The system consists in a fault management part to determine if the sticks are faulty, a priority management part: one sidestick can take priority over the other and finally an order computation part. Property P1 expresses that, if we suppose that the two sidesticks cannot be faulty at the same time, then there is always one of the two sidesticks that can have an effect on the plane surfaces (i.e. that is "active").

The first idea we had was to define "active" in terms of transmission of order: the order from the pilot or the order from the copilot will indeed be transmitted to the surfaces. So we stated:

$$P1 : (PILOT\_ORDER \neq 0) \vee (COPILOT\_ORDER \neq 0)$$
$$\rightarrow (TRANSMITTED\_ORDER \neq 0)$$

that is to say if the pilot order is different from 0 or the copilot order is different from 0 then the transmitted order is different from 0.

But this expression is not correct and we detected it by looking at the counter-example found when we first tried to verify the property: the tool gave us a case where one sidestick was faulty, the other was operational but with value 0. The property was false while it is a valid case. The problem is that a correct order from an active sidestick can be 0.

If we want to express the property in terms of transmission of order, we would have to go into the specification more thoroughly (because of course the value of the transmitted order is not exactly the value of the input order) and this would be in contradiction with our methodology. So we tried to express the property in a different way and we obtained:

$$P1 : \neg((PILOT\_PRIORITY \wedge PILOT\_STICK\_FAULT) \vee$$
$$(COPILOT\_PRIORITY \wedge COPILOT\_STICK\_FAULT))$$

which means it is never true that the pilot has priority and his sidestick is faulty or that the copilot has priority and his sidestick is faulty.

This example illustrates the difficulty of going from an informal text to a formal expression.

P2. If we look more carefully at the property P2, we can see that the expression given in section 2.1 is incomplete. Two implicit but important features are hidden in this formulation:

- Firstly, we can be more precise, saying that when the primary computers PC1 and PC2 are faulty, secondary computer SC1 becomes operational only "if it is possible". If SC1 cannot become operational, then secondary computer SC2 is requested and becomes operational if it is possible.
- Secondly, the property P2, as formulated in §2.1, is a conditional expression without a counterpart (i.e. without else part). But it is obvious for the designers that secondary computer SC1 cannot be operational if the two primary computers PC1 and PC2 are not simultaneously faulty. This counterpart has to be expressed in a rigorous approach.

So, taking into account these two observations and using a semi-formal notation, we can give a more accurate formulation of P2:

```
P2: if (the two primary computers PC1 and PC2 are faulty)
    then if (possible)
             then (the secondary computer SC1 becomes operational)
             else (the secondary computer SC2 is requested)
      else (the secondary computer SC1 is not operational)
```

It is important to note here that this property concerns only one kind of surface, i.e. the inner ailerons, and when we read "SC1 is not operational", we must understand that SC1 is not operational for the inner ailerons, but can be operational for another kind of surface.

This property is now quite complex and should be broken down into several sub-properties. We will focus here on the "else" part which involves fewer propositions and is easier to express than the direct part. If it is expressed alone, the "else" part gives the P2b sub-property:

```
P2b: if not (the two primary computers PC1 and PC2 are faulty)
     then not (the secondary computer SC1 is operational)
```

which can be formulated in the following simpler reverse way:

```
P2b: if (the  secondary computer SC1 is operational)
     then (the two primary computers PC1 and PC2 are faulty)
```

For this property, we have to express the behavior of several computers from the point of view of one of them. Inside the secondary computer SC1, we have to express the following two propositions: " secondary computer SC1 is operational" and "the two primary computers PC1 and PC2 are faulty".

SC1 can check to be operational by the fact that two of the gates it manages are closed. In the SC1 specification, these gates are represented by two output parameters G1 and G2.

Two boolean input parameters of computer SC1, respectively $PRIMARY\_COMPUTER1\_OK$ and $PRIMARY\_COMPUTER2\_OK$ express that computers PC1 and PC2 operate correctly. The second proposition is then represented by a conjunction on the negations of these two booleans.

So we obtained the following formulation for P2b:

$P2b:\ ((G1 = 1) \wedge (G2 = 1)) \rightarrow$
$((\neg PRIMARY\_COMPUTER1\_OK) \wedge (\neg PRIMARY\_COMPUTER2\_OK))$

3   Verifying Properties

We first briefly describe SCADE (based on the Lustre language) and the observer technique which is the usual way of proving properties of Lustre specifications. Then we explain the practical problems we have to solve in order to implement verification. Finally, we give the current results of the project.

3.1 Formal Verification in Lustre

SCADE. The SCADE environment [8] was defined to assist the development of critical embedded systems. This environment is composed of three tools:

- a graphical editor,
- a simulator,
- a code generator that automatically translates graphical specifications into C code.

The SCADE language is a graphic data flow specification language that can be translated into Lustre [1,3].

Lustre. Lustre is a synchronous data flow specification language. A system is described by several interconnected nodes. A node computes values for its outputs from values of its inputs. A node is defined by a set of equations and assertions. An equation `VAR=EXPR` specifies that the variable `VAR` is always equal to `EXPR`. An assertion **assert** `BOOLEXPR` means that the boolean expression `BOOLEXPR` is assumed to be always true during the execution of the program.

Any variable or expression is considered to represent the sequence of values it takes during the whole execution of the system and Lustre operators operate globally over these sequences. For example, `VAR=EXPR` means that the sequences of values associated with `VAR` and `EXPR` are identical.

Expressions are made of variable identifiers, constants, usual arithmetic, boolean and conditional operators and two specific temporal operators: previous **pre** and followed-by **->**.

- If E is an expression denoting the sequence $(e_0, e_1, e_2, ...)$, then **pre(E)** denotes the sequence $(nil, e_0, e_1, ...)$ where nil is an undefined value.
- If E and F are two expressions of the same type respectively denoting the sequences $(e_0, e_1, e_2, ...)$ and $(f_0, f_1, f_2, ...)$, then E **->** F is an expression denoting the sequence $(e_0, f_1, f_2, ...)$.

Synchronous observers. Properties are also expressed in Lustre. Verification is done using synchronous observers [2]. Synchronous observers are used to express invariant properties, i.e. properties that should always hold. The idea behind synchronous observers is to add an extra output to the system which states if the property holds at each time instant.

More precisely, the observed system S is considered as a black box and only its interface (i.e. the input and output variables) can be involved in the formulation of a property P. In order to prove that a property P is satisfied by a system S under a set of hypotheses H, we build a system S' by composition of S, P, H as shown on figure 2.

The only output of S' is the boolean value of P. The verification then consists in checking that output of system S' is always true.

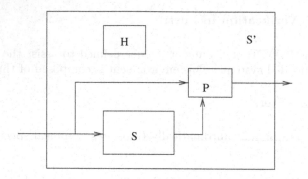

Fig. 2. Observer for a property P on a system S.

Verification tools for Lustre.   Lesar [6,9] is the model checker associated with Lustre. Lesar can apply three verification techniques: an exhaustive enumeration of the states of the system, similar to standard model checking; a symbolic construction of the set of states which satisfy the property, analogous to symbolic model checking; and a symbolic construction of the set of states violating the property.

Another verification tool for Lustre is available: NP-TOOLS with the Lucifer translator [5,4]. NP-TOOLS is a general purpose formal verification toolbox for combinatorial circuits based on Stalmarck's method [7]. Lucifer is a translator from Lustre to NP-TOOLS. The technical difficulty in the translation is that Lustre models dynamic systems, i.e. systems whose outputs depend on the current inputs and all previous inputs while NP-TOOLS deals with static systems whose outputs depend only on the current inputs. The dynamics of Lustre models has to be modelled in NP-TOOLS. This is done by representing each Lustre node as an NP-TOOLS macro with additional inputs corresponding to the memory of the node. For example, an edge detector is specified in Lustre as follows:

```
node edge(x: bool) returns (e: bool);
let
    e = false -> x and not pre x;
tel
```

It uses two temporal operators: `pre` and `->`. It is modelled in NP-TOOLS by adding two inputs: `pre(x)` representing the memory of x, and `init` a boolean that is only true at the initial time. In fact, the NP-TOOLS circuit represents the transition function of the corresponding Lustre node. To model a dynamic Lustre system, several instances of the NP-TOOLS circuit can be connected. The `init` boolean is only true in the first instance. The output x of the first instance is connected to the input `pre(x)` of the second one, and so on. This unrolled specification can then be used to verify the properties of the system.

We plan to experiment both tools in the project. We have mostly used Lucifer and NP-TOOLS up to now and have just begun experimenting with Lesar.

3.2   Practical Problems

Several practical problems had to be solved before starting the experiments.

Building the sub-system.   In order to verify a property on a part of the system, we have to be able to identify the nodes involved in the property and then to build the main node corresponding to the sub-system. The set of nodes which are necessary to build this main node are manually identified using the variables involved in the property. The main node is then automatically generated in Lustre from the list of selected nodes (connections are made between inputs of a node and outputs of another node if they have the same name).

Symbols.   The specification includes several symbols. Symbols are numerical functions that were implemented directly in C for efficiency or simplicity reasons. Some of these functions have now been written in SCADE, but there are still a few symbols that are only implemented in C.

The solution is to define assertions characterising the behaviour of these symbols and to add them to the specification.

Reals.   The SCADE specification of the case study contains a lot of real variables. But Lucifer does not allow reasoning on reals, it can only handle booleans and integers. We thus had to translate reals to integers. As we wish to be as automatic as possible, we have adopted the following method: we first find the precision needed, then we multiply every real to translate it into an integer. In the case study, we multiplied reals by 100. But of course, this translation makes value intervals notably bigger and this may cause problems for the verification.

Lesar accepts real values, it is able to handle numerical properties if the computations are linear.

3.3   Current Results

We present here the current status of the ongoing experiments. These experiments are done on the real system description from which the embedded code is automatically generated.

Property P1.   Let us recall the informal expression of property P1: *if we suppose that the two sidesticks cannot be faulty at the same time, there is always an active stick.*

Ten nodes were selected concerning this property, nodes that express the relationship between the inputs (pilot and copilot order, faulty sticks) and the outputs (transmitted order, priorities). These nodes are essentially composed of nodes for the management of priorities, nodes for monitoring and nodes for the functional part. Then a main node was automatically built from these selected nodes.

Symbols used in this subsystem are written in SCADE so we had no problem for that part. Reals were translated by hand using the technique described previously for Lucifer. No translation was needed for Lesar.

We first made several attempts with our first formal expression of the property using the transmitted order:

$$P1 : (PILOT\_ORDER \neq 0) \lor (COPILOT\_ORDER \neq 0)$$
$$\rightarrow (TRANSMITTED\_ORDER \neq 0)$$

It leads us to several refinements of the property to finally get a more detailed expression that was found valid. This was a first interesting result, but

- Several assertions were necessary on inputs of the subsystem for the property to be valid. These assertions have to be assessed by designers or proved on another subsystem.
- We had to enter in the details of *how* the subsystem was implemented. This is in contradiction with the methodology defined at the beginning.

Consequently, we decided to make other experiments using the second formal expression of the property:

$$P1 : \neg((PILOT\_PRIORITY \land PILOT\_STICK\_FAULT)\lor$$
$$(COPILOT\_PRIORITY \land COPILOT\_STICK\_FAULT))$$

This property was proved valid with no assertion except the initial one stating that the two sticks were not faulty at the same time. This assertion was very easy to express because there was a boolean in the specification corresponding exactly to the fact that both sticks were faulty: TWO_STICKS_FAULTY. So the assertion simply was:

$$assert(\neg TWO\_STICKS\_FAULTY)$$

Both properties were proved by Lucifer and Lesar. Verification was efficient in both cases (a few seconds).

Property P2. A difficulty which often arises when we want to express properties on a system like SC1 is to select the relevant variables among hundreds of inputs and outputs that the system holds. That was the case for P2 and the first step was to select the right input and output variables to get the formulation shown in §2.2.

Then, we had to select a sub-part of the SC1 specification. Our process was twofold :

- in a first attempt, we selected the nodes whose topic is "inner aileron" (the topic is given at the head of the SCADE sheets) plus the nodes used by these sheets;
- then, we selected the nodes using the variables involved in the property, as suggested in §3.2.

Fortunately, these two ways gave the same result, and led to the selection of thirteen nodes.

The selected sub-part of the specification uses some symbols. Most of them are quite simple and were already described by Lustre specifications. We could use these specifications for our purpose, except for one symbol whose specification was rewritten. So it was not necessary to describe the behaviour of symbols by assertions.

The rewritten symbol was a little less simple than the other symbols. It mainly consists in interpolation calculus between real values. In order to use Lucifer and NP-TOOLS, we had to transform it into a function on integers. This was done using the conversion presented in §3.2 (multiplication of reals by their precision to get integer values).

The conversion from reals to integers mainly consists in changing declarations of real variables into declarations of integers and to adapt some calculus involving multiplication or division operations in order to respect the conversion. This happened only three times in the considered sub-system. We made these changes manually, but they can easily be automated and integrated in the Lucifer translator.

The selected sub-system uses temporal operators which induce an initial phase where the system behaviour is not stabilised and where some properties which are normally valid in the current phases may not be satisfied. This is the case for property P2. We have defined the following *begin_ok* operator, which masks the value of a boolean expression E during the n first instants, in order to skip the initial phase and to focus on the current behaviour of the system.

```
node begin_ok (E:bool; n:int)  returns(S:bool);
var  ct : int;
let
  ct = 0 -> (pre (ct) + 1) ;
  S = (ct < n) or E ;
tel;
```

Property P2b has been modified, as shown below, and was checked and proved by Lucifer.

$$P2b : ((G1 = 1) \wedge (G2 = 1)) \rightarrow$$
$$((\neg PRIMARY\_COMPUTER1\_OK) \wedge (\neg PRIMARY\_COMPUTER2\_OK))$$

$$P2b' : begin\_ok(P2b, 5)$$

4   Conclusion and Future Work

In this paper, we have presented ongoing experiments on the use of formal verification for critical systems in an industrial context. We only have qualitative results for the moment and more experiments are needed to get quantitative results as well.

However, current results are encouraging. This first use of such techniques in an industrial environment shows it is a valid way to replace some simulation activities. Once the property is formalised, it is straightforward to verify it with the tool. We sometimes had problems understanding counter-examples, but the reason was we lacked knowledge about the application. Designers would not have such difficulties. This technique thus allows an exhaustive check of the system with respect to a given property.

The next essential step is the integration of these techniques in the current verification and validation process. Three major issues need to be addressed in order to complete this integration:

- automation of the different steps of the proof process described above (construction of the main node, translation of real variables);
- integration in the SCADE environment with a suitable user friendly interface in order for it to be directly usable by the system designers;
- definition of a methodology to help designers express expected behaviors as properties instead of describing them as lists of scenarios.

The goal of the Common Airbus Requirements Engineering (CARE) project is to address the last issue. This project will provide a common set of processes, methods and means to identify, analyse, validate, trace, exchange and manage requirements.

As an attempt to address the other issues, a prototype called L4 is under development at Prover Technology. L4 is an extension module that adds formal verification capabilities to SCADE. It provides the same functionalities as Lucifer but with a user-friendly interface and a full integration with SCADE. The first version of this tool is available since november 2000.

Finally, it is necessary to study more deeply how verification techniques complement the test and simulation phases. We have to be able to find a way to determine which parts of test and simulation can be eliminated and to measure the benefit in practice. The correspondance between properties and scenarios could help in understanding the complementarity.

References

1. P. Caspi, N. Halbwachs, P. Pilaud, and P. Raymond. The synchronous dataflow programming language Lustre. *Proceedings of IEEE, Another Look at Real-time programming*, 79(9):1305–1319, September 1991.
2. N. Halbwachs, Lagnier F., and Raymond P. Synchronous observer and the verification of reactive systems. In *Third International Conference on Algebraic Methodology and Software Technology, AMAST'93*, Twente, June 93.
3. N. Halbwachs, F. Lagnier, and C. Ratel. Programming and verifying real time systems by means of the synchronous data-flow language Lustre. *IEEE Transactions on Software Engineering, special issue on the specification and analysis of real time systems*, september 1992.
4. Magnus Ljung. Formal modelling and automatic verification of Lustre programs using np-tools. Master's thesis, Royal Institute of Technology, Department of Tele-informatics, 1999.

5. Prover Technology AB. *NP-Tools 2.4 Reference manual*, 1999.
6. C. Ratel. *Définition et réalisation d'un outil de vérification formelle de programmes Lustre : le système LESAR*. PhD thesis, Institut National Polytechnique de Grenoble, Juillet 1992.
7. Mary Sheeran and Gunnar Stalmarck. A tutorial on Stalmarck's proof procedure for propositional logic. In *Proceedings of the International Conference on Formal Methods in Computer Aided Design (FMCAD)*, LNCS. Springer Verlag, 1998.
8. Verilog. *SCADE Language - Reference Manual 2.1.*
9. Verimag. Lustre/lesar home page. http://www-verimag.imag.fr/SYNCHRONE/ lustre-english.html.

Transacted Memory for Smart Cards

Pieter H. Hartel[1,2], Michael J. Butler[2], Eduard de Jong[3], and Mark Longley[2]

[1] Dept. of Computer Science, Univ. of Twente, The Netherlands.
pieter@cs.utwente.nl
[2] Dept. of Electronics and Computer Science, Univ. of Southampton, UK.
{phh, mjb}@ecs.soton.ac.uk
[3] Sun Microsystems, Inc. Palo Alto, CA 94043 USA.
Eduard.deJong@Sun.COM

Abstract. A transacted memory that is implemented using EEPROM technology offers persistence, undoability and auditing. The transacted memory system is formally specified in Z, and refined in two steps to a prototype C implementation / SPIN model. Conclusions are offered both on the transacted memory system itself and on the development process involving multiple notations and tools. [1]

1 Introduction

The purpose of transaction processing [1] is to provide atomic updates of arbitrarily sized information. Smart cards need such a facility as any transaction can easily be aborted by pulling the smart card out of the Card Acceptance Device (CAD). Smart cards provide limited resources. High-end smart cards today offer 64KB of ROM, 64KB of EEPROM and 2KB of RAM. These limitations make techniques developed for mainstream transaction processing systems inappropriate for smart cards.

Current smart card solutions, including Java [2] Card implementations [13,14] typically maintain a log/backup of old values, while an updated value is being constructed [4]. The log is cleared once the transaction is committed. If required, the logs can be used to provide the audit trail for security.

Current smart card implementations, by their very nature, view the memory as a resource, used to support a transaction processing API. We present a novel (patented) view [3], which embeds the transaction capabilities into the memory system itself. Transacted memory allows an arbitrary sequence of items to be written as a single transaction to the memory. The space required for such a sequence may even exceed the size of the RAM. An audit trail is automatically provided. The disadvantage of our system is an increased EEPROM requirement

---

[1] This work was supported by Sun Microsystems Inc, USA and by Senter, The Netherlands under contract nr ITG94130
[2] Java and all Java-based trademarks and logos are trademarks or registered trademarks of Sun Microsystems, Inc. in the U.S. or other countries, and are used under license.

J.N. Oliveira and P. Zave (Eds.): FME 2001, LNCS 2021, pp. 478–499, 2001.

to at least twice the size of the data. The permanent RAM requirements are NIL, transient RAM requirements are of the order of a few bytes.

Transacted memory does not impose structural constraints on the information stored, nor does it provide marshaling and unmarshalling capabilities. These are intended to be implemented, for instance by an API on top of the transacted memory.

The current work is part of a series of formally specified components [7, 6] of smart card systems. We hope that we will eventually be able to design, specify and implement a complete smart card operating system kernel that can be subjected to Common Criteria at evaluation level EAL7 [12].

The work of Sabatier and Lartigue [13] is different from ours in the sense that it describes a classical transaction facility for smart cards, using a backup area of old values. Theirs is a much simpler design than ours. Their approach is in similar in that they refine an abstract specification into a C implementation. Unlike ours, Sabatier and Lartigue's development is fully formal, discharging all of some 1500 proof obligations.

Transacted memory is not to be confused with transactional memory [8], which is a technique for supporting lock free data structures on multi processor architectures. The implementation of transactional memory is an extension of the cache coherence protocol of such machines [8]. We consider a different problem domain with severe resource constraints.

We present a high level specification of the system (using Z) and discuss two refinements (in Z) of the system, ultimately leading to executable code (using C). A number of properties of the high level specifications have been proved (by hand), and the prototype implementation has been subjected to assertion checking (using SPIN).

The contributions of the paper are:

- A presentation of the novel smart card transacted memory manager.
- A discussion of the lessons learned by systematically translating a Z specification with proofs into C code with assertion checking. This complements the results reported in our earlier paper [5].

1.1   The Process

Figure 1 describes the specifications and the prototype implementation of the memory management system. Z was chosen as the specification language because at the time the project was started, (Summer of 1996) this appeared to be the specification language most acceptable by industry.

The abstract specification was produced after initial discussions between the inventor of transacted memory (Eduard de Jong) and the specification team (the other authors). After further rounds of consultation the abstract specification was revised, and a first refinement was produced to reflect the reality of the EEPROM technology as documented in Section 3.

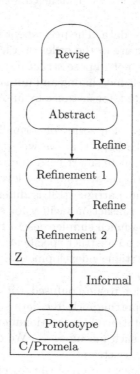

Fig. 1. The process.

In 1997 a second data refinement was produced to reflect the possibilities of errors arising by interrupting EEPROM write operations. In 2000, the final specification labelled "prototype" was produced manually by interpreting the second refinement as literally as possible. The prototype is at the same time an executable specification (because it is a SPIN model) and a C program. Some macros are used to transfer from a common notation to either SPIN or C.

The prototype is a proper implementation, it is as memory efficient as possible. It is not as time efficient as possible, because often-used information is recomputed instead of cached. However the prototype is a useful yardstick to measure progress of further implementations by, which would explore space / time tradeoffs. The prototype also allows for a considerable degree of parallelism to be exploited in a hardware implementation of the memory system.

1.2   The Idea

Transacted memory is designed around two notions: a tag and an information sequence. A tag is merely a unique address, e.g. identifier of a particular information sequence. An information sequence is the unit of data stored and retrieved.

An information sequence would be used to store a collection of objects that are logically part of a transaction.

There may be several generations of the information associated with a tag. Operations are provided to write a new generation, and to read the current or older generations. All generations associated with a tag have the same size, although this could be generalised.

The transaction processing capability of the memory is supported by a commit operation, which makes the most recently written information the current generation. The oldest generation is automatically purged should the number of generations for a tag exceed a preset maximum.

Transacted memory thus provides undoability (by being able to revert to a previous generation) and persistence (by using EEPROM technology). These are precisely the ingredients necessary to support transactions [11].

To provide this functionality, transacted memory maintains a certain amount of book-keeping information. In its most abstract form, the book-keeping information records three items:

- The size of the information sequence that may be associated with the tag.
- The different generations of information associated with each tag. It is possible that there is no information associated with a tag.
- Which tags are currently committed.

Having sketched the ideas, we will now make this precise by presenting an abstract Z specification.

2   Abstract Specification

The abstract specification assumes the existence of tags used to address the memory, and the existence of information to be stored in the memory. No further assumptions are made about either.

$[Tag, Info]$

The existence of a finite set of available tags is assumed ($tags$), as well as limits on the size of the memory ($msize$) and the maximum number of generations that may be associated with any tag ($maxgen$):

$$
\begin{aligned}
&tags : \mathbb{F}\ Tag \\
&msize : \mathbb{N}_1 \\
&maxgen : \mathbb{N}_1
\end{aligned}
$$

Two partial functions $assoc$ and $size$ and a set $committed$ specify the memory system. The derived value $usage$ is included to aid the presentation:

```
┌─ AMemSys ─────────────────────────────────────────────
│ assoc : tags ⇸ seq(seq Info)
│ size : tags ⇸ N₁
│ committed : P tags
│ usage : N
├───────────────────────────────────────────────────────
│ dom assoc = dom size
│ committed ⊆ dom assoc
│ ∀ t : tags | t ∈ committed • assoc t ≠ ⟨⟩
│ ∀ t : tags | t ∈ dom assoc • #(assoc t) ≤ maxgen ∧
│     (∀ i : N₁ | 1 ≤ i ≤ #(assoc t) • #(assoc t i) = size t)
│ usage = Σ(t : tags | t ∈ dom assoc • #(assoc t) * size t)
│ usage ≤ msize
└───────────────────────────────────────────────────────
```

The *assoc* function associates a tag with a sequence of sequences of information, the most recent generation is at the head of the sequence. The *size* function gives the length of the information sequences associated with a tag. The *committed* set records those tags whose most recent generation of information has been committed. The two functions must have the same domain, the committed set must be a subset of this domain and all the information sequences associated with a tag must be of the length given by the size function. The total amount of information associated with all the tags should not exceed the size of the memory system. The non-standard Z construct Σ sums all values of the expression $\#(assoc\ t) * size\ t$.

The initial state of the memory system is described as follows:

```
┌─ AInitialMemSys ──────────────────────────────────────
│ AMemSys
├───────────────────────────────────────────────────────
│ dom assoc =
└───────────────────────────────────────────────────────
```

The *ANewTag* operation returns an unused tag. The size of the information sequences to be written to the tag is specified as an argument $n?$ to this operation.

```
┌─ ANewTag ─────────────────────────────────────────────
│ ΔAMemSys
│ n? : N₁
│ t! : tags
├───────────────────────────────────────────────────────
│ t! ∉ dom assoc
│ assoc' = assoc ∪ {t! ↦ ⟨⟩}
│ size' = size ∪ {t! ↦ n?}
└───────────────────────────────────────────────────────
```

The operation returns an unused tag (one that has no associated sequence of information sequences), marks the most recent generation as empty, and records the expected length of the information sequences.

The *AReadGeneration* operation reads the information sequence of a given generation g? associated with a tag. The tag t? must have an associated information sequence of the given generation, numbered relative to the current generation.

```
┌─ AReadGeneration ─────────────────────────────────
│ ΞAMemSys
│ t? : tags
│ g? : ℕ
│ info! : seq Info
├───────────────────────────────────────────────────
│ t? ∈ dom assoc
│ assoc t? ≠ ⟨⟩
│ g? ≤ (#(assoc t?) − 1)
│ info! = assoc t? (g? + 1)
└───────────────────────────────────────────────────
```

The schema *CurrentGeneration* constrains a generation argument to the current generation:

```
┌─ CurrentGeneration ───────────────────────────────
│ g? : ℕ
├───────────────────────────────────────────────────
│ g? = 0
└───────────────────────────────────────────────────
```

The *ARead* operation reads the current generation of information associated with a tag. It is specified using schema conjunction and hiding.

$$ARead == (AReadGeneration \wedge CurrentGeneration) \setminus (g?)$$

The *ARelease* operation releases all the information associated with a tag. The operation does this by removing the tag from the domains of the functions *assoc* and *size*, and from the *committed* set.

```
┌─ ARelease ────────────────────────────────────────
│ ΔAMemSys
│ t? : tags
├───────────────────────────────────────────────────
│ t? ∈ dom assoc
│ assoc' = {t?} ◁ assoc
│ size' = {t?} ◁ size
│ committed' = committed \ {t?}
└───────────────────────────────────────────────────
```

The operation *ACommit* commits the current generation of information associated with a tag. The tag must have an associated information sequence, which is flagged as committed.

```
┌─ ACommit ─────────────────────────────────────────
│ ΔAMemSys
│ t? : tags
├───────────────────────────────────────────────────
│ t? ∈ dom assoc
│ assoc t? ≠ ⟨⟩
│ committed' = committed ∪ {t?}
└───────────────────────────────────────────────────
```

The operation $AWrite$ writes a sequence of information to a tag. This operation has a number of different cases depending on the state of the sequence of generations associated with the tag and whether the current generation has been committed.

The first write to a tag by $AWriteFirst$, after $ANewTag$, must make sure there is enough room to write the new information. The association for the tag with a singleton sequence containing the new information sequence is replaced.

```
┌─ AWriteFirst ─────────────────────────────────────
│ ΔAMemSys
│ t? : tags
│ info? : seq Info
├───────────────────────────────────────────────────
│ t? ∈ dom assoc
│ #info? = size t?
│ assoc t? = ⟨⟩
│ (usage + #info?) ≤ msize
│ assoc' = assoc ⊕ {t? ↦ {1 ↦ info?}}
└───────────────────────────────────────────────────
```

Writing to a tag whose current generation is not committed, by the operation $AWriteUncommitted$, does not need any extra room.

```
┌─ AWriteUncommitted ───────────────────────────────
│ ΔAMemSys
│ t? : tags
│ info? : seq Info
├───────────────────────────────────────────────────
│ t? ∈ dom assoc
│ #info? = size t?
│ assoc t? ≠ ⟨⟩
│ t? ∉ committed
│ assoc' = assoc ⊕ {t? ↦ (assoc t? ⊕ {1 ↦ info?})}
└───────────────────────────────────────────────────
```

Writing to a tag whose current generation has been committed by the operation $AWriteCommitted$ requires extra room for the new information. In this case the new association is obtained by concatenating the new sequence in front of the existing one and then cropping the sequences of sequences by the maximum allowed generation.

__ *AWriteCommitted* _____

$\Delta AMemSys$
$t? : tags$
$info? : \text{seq } Info$

$t? \in \text{dom } assoc$
$\#info? = size\ t?$
$assoc\ t? \neq \langle\rangle$
$t? \in committed$
$(usage + \#info?) \leq msize$
$assoc' = assoc \oplus \{t? \mapsto ((1 \mathinner{..} maxgen) \lhd (\{1 \mapsto info?\} ^\frown (assoc\ t?)))\}$
$committed' = committed \setminus \{t?\}$

Using schema disjunction the $AWrite$ operation is specified as follows:

$$AWrite == AWriteFirst \lor AWriteUncommitted \lor AWriteCommitted$$

This completes the presentation of the abstract specification of the transacted memory. In the following sections we will present the principles and the data structures of two refinements. The full specifications may be found in our technical report [2].

3   First Refinement

EEPROM technology normally supports byte reads but only block writes. The block size is typically of the order of 8 ... 32 bytes. EEPROM technology allows a full block to be written efficiently, and we assume that a block is written atomically. It may be necessary to use a low level block write operation to achieve this. EEPROM lifetime is limited, so repeated writes to the same block must be avoided.

3.1   Data Structures

To acknowledge these technological constraints, the first refinement introduces atomic operations over "pages" in terms of which all operations must be described. The two mappings $assoc$ and $size$, and the set $committed$ of the abstract specification are refined by four more concrete data structures. Before describing these, we introduce the definitions needed by the refinement. The first definition introduces a boolean flag.

$\mathbb{B} ::= False \mid True$

The EEPROM is treated as a sequence of pages, where each page contains a small amount of book-keeping information and a payload consisting of a single item of information from one of the original information sequences. The page size would typically be the block size of the EEPROM technology. The type

Loc below represents the locations of the pages in the memory. The type *Page* represents the actual data stored in each page, together with the book-keeping:

$$Loc == 0 \mathinner{\ldotp\ldotp} (msize - 1)$$
$$Page == Info \times \mathbb{B} \times tags \times \mathbb{N} \times \mathbb{N}$$

The type *Page* contains five components:

1. *Info* represents one item from an information sequence, the actual payload.
2. The boolean flag states whether the page is actually in use.
3. *tags* represents the tag with which the current information sequence is associated.
4. The fourth component gives the generation index of the current information sequence.
5. The fifth component gives the page number of the item within the information sequence.

The refinement needs a small table, which records the essential data for each tag as type *TagData*.

$$TagData == \mathbb{B} \times \mathbb{N}_1 \times \mathbb{B} \times \mathbb{N} \times \mathbb{N}$$

The type *TagData* contains five components:

1. The first boolean flag states whether the tag is actually in use.
2. The second component states the size of the information sequence associated with this tag.
3. The third component states whether the current generation associated with the tag has been committed.
4. The fourth component gives the number of generations associated with the tag.
5. The fifth component gives the generation index of the current information sequence.

Having introduced the relevant types we are now in a position to show the four data structures that represent the state of the transacted memory.

```
┌─ CMemSys ───────────────────────────────────
│  data : tags → TagData
│  mem : Loc → Page
│  freetags : ℙ tags
│  freelocs : ℙ Loc
│ ───────────────────────
│  . . .
└─────────────────────────────────────────────
```

For brevity, we have omitted the invariant representing the consistency of the variables of *CMemSys*. Full details may be found in the technical report [2]. The abstraction invariant between *AMemSys* and *CMemSys* is represented by the following schema:

Abstraction

CMemSys
AMemSys

$dom(assoc) = \{ t : tags \mid data(t) = (True, \_, \_, \_, \_) \}$
$\forall t : tags; \; I, J, G, i, j, g : \mathbb{N}; \; d : Info \bullet$
    $t \in dom(assoc) \; \wedge$
    $data(t) = (True, J, True, I, G) \; \wedge$
    $i \leq I \; \wedge \; j \leq J \; \wedge$
    $(d, True, t, g, j) \in ran(mem) \; \wedge$
    $g = (G + i) \bmod max\_index$
    $\Rightarrow$
        $size(t) = J \; \wedge$
        $\#assoc(t) = I \; \wedge$
        $assoc(t)(i)(j) = d$

The last line of this abstraction invariant shows how the jth information component d for a tag t and generation i is extracted from the concrete memory system. The specifications of the operations on the concrete memory system may be found in [2]. The present refinement has not been verified, but we have verified an earlier refinement for a system without generations.

4   Second Refinement

The second data refinement describes the error states that may arise when a sequence of atomic page writes is interrupted. This may happen at any point, leaving the memory in error states not found during normal operation. These error states are therefore not present in the abstract specification or in the first refinement.

There are two different ways to handle erroneous states. The first approach is to modify the higher level specifications to allow for such erroneous states. The second refinement could then simply allow such states but avoid discussing how they might be handled. The problem with this approach is that while error states can be detected, by the absence or duplication of pages, there is no way to recognise the cause of the error and therefore no way to perform error recovery. To solve this problem the memory manager would have to record some indication of its current state in the memory in such a way as to allow for subsequent error recovery. The recording of such a state in a form that relates to the memory operations as seen by an application require repeated writes of the state information to some page in memory. This has to be avoided, so as not to wear out the EEPROM.

The second way to cope with erroneous states would allow all the error detection and recovery to be contained within the second refinement and hidden at some level within the final implementation of the system. This has been adopted and is described below. Read and write operations of the second refinement recover from error states by tidying up the memory before reading data or writing new data if necessary.

4.1   Realistic Constraints

There are a number of new constraints that were used as goals when preparing the second refinement. The first constraint was actually the motivation for the development of the tagged memory management system. However, the abstract specification and the first refinement did not take this into account and in that sense it is new in this specification:

- a given page should be written as few times as possible. This means that a page should only be written to when there is no choice:
  - When writing new pages of information.
  - When superseding pages of information.
  - When removing an association between a page and a tag.
  All the information required to track the state of the memory manager should be stored using only these write operations. The second refinement satisfies all these constraints while imposing only a slight memory cost on the memory manager.
- Memory is limited so the memory management system should use as little as possible itself.
- The only write operation that may be performed on the memory is the atomic writing of a page.
- Any sequence of atomic write operations can be interrupted at any point. It should be possible to detect the resulting erroneous state and then to tidy up the memory.
- Lost memory should be recoverable when an atomic operation sequence is interrupted.
- All the constraints employed in the previous specifications should be retained, such as the main correctness requirement that the information read from a tag is equal to that previously written to that tag.

4.2   Causes of Error States

There are four contexts in which a sequence of atomic operations can be interrupted to give rise to a distinct error state:

- When writing a new generation of information not all the required pages may be successfully written.
- Writing a new version of the current generation may fail to write all the pages of the new version or to supersede all the pages of the old version.
- When releasing the pages of an old generation in order to provide space for a new generation some of the pages of the old generation may not be released.
- When deallocating all the pages for a tag for the Release operation, some of the pages may not be released.

It is not possible to record a separate flag to track the current state of the memory manager as we would have to pick a page to keep it in which would then suffer from repeated writes as the state changed. Instead the presence of page zero has been chosen to indicate the presence of all the other pages of a generation. In addition, the information otherwise stored in a page is elaborated by a further piece of data:

– A cyclic, three state flag that makes it possible to determine the relative age of two versions of the same generation.

Here is the Z specification of the flag:

$$Version ::= VA \mid VB \mid VC$$

Each page in a given version will have the same value in this flag, the pages of a new version will all take the successor state to that of the current version.

4.3   Data Structures

The type $DPage$ represents the refinement of the type $Page$:

$$DPage == \mathbb{B} \times tags \times Info \times \mathbb{N} \times \mathbb{N} \times Version$$

The type $DPage$ contains six components, which is a little more than the information kept by the first refinement:

1. The boolean flag states whether the page is actually in use.
2. $tags$ represents the tag with which the current information sequence is associated.
3. $Info$ represents one item from an information sequence, the actual payload.
4. The first number gives the generation index of the current information sequence.
5. The second number gives the page number of the item within the information sequence.
6. $Version$ is the cyclic flag that we mentioned in Section 4.2.

The type $DTagData$ represents the refinement of the type $TagData$.

$$DTagData == \mathbb{B} \times \mathbb{N}_1 \times \mathbb{B}$$

The type $DTagData$ contains three components, i.e. considerably less than the information kept for the same purpose in the first refinement.

1. The first boolean flag states whether the tag is actually in use.
2. The second, numeric component states the size of the information sequence associated with this tag.
3. The last boolean flag states whether the current generation associated with the tag has been committed. This flag is only false upto the occurrence of the first write.

The data structures of the second refinement show the mappings that represent the state of the memory. No further data structures are used to maintain the transacted memory. Both mappings are supposed to be stored in EEPROM.

```
 ___ DMemSys _____
|  ddata : tags → DTagData
|  dmem : Loc → DPage
|_____
|  . . .
|_____
```

The abstract Z specification of Section 2 is (almost) standard Z notation. In the two refinements we felt the need to deviate more from standard Z to express important constraints such as the writing of pages to memory in a particular order. While it would be possible to specify this in Z, the specifications we came up with contained some elements that were less intuitive than say a simple for loop. Therefore we will not present further details of the Z version of the two refinements here [2]. Instead we discuss the essential elements of the SPIN and C version of the second refinement.

5   SPIN and C Prototype

The Prototype implements the two mappings *ddata* and *dmem* that form the core of the memory system as arrays. This is efficient, both in Promela (the modelling language of the SPIN tool) and in C:

```
#define   msize     10
#define   tsize     2
#define   DTagData byte
#define   DPage     short

DTagData ddata[tsize] ;
DPage     dmem[msize] ;
```

The domains of the mappings, *tags* and *Loc*, are represented by integers. The types *DTagData* and *DPage* are represented as a **byte** and a **short** respectively. Depending on the actual size of an information item, and the number of tags in the system larger sizes would be required. In any case the information must be tightly packed, as in a production implementation. An alternative would have been to use a **struct**. This would have been made it difficult to achieve the same information density, and it would not model reality accurately.

As a consequence, the various fields of the range types, as specified in Section 4.3, are accessed by a collection of macros. These macros work equally well in Promela as they do in C. For example reading the 'in use' flag of an element of the **ddata** array, and writing an entry in the same array are modelled as follows:

```
#define read_ddata1(t, u) \
   u =(ddata[t] >> inuse_shift) & inuse_mask
```

```
#define write_ddata3(t, u, s, c) \
    ddata[t] = \
        ((u) << inuse_shift) | \
        ((s) << size_shift) | \
        ((c) << committed_shift)
```

The shifts and masks are appropriately defined to pack and unpack the information. The remaining access operations are defined in a similar way.

5.1   DNewTag in C

Below is the C version of the *DNewTag* operation. Noteworthy is the `for` loop, which (inefficiently) locates a tag that is not is use, as stipulated by the predicate $t! \notin$ dom *assoc* in the Z specification.

```
Tag DNewTag( Size size ) {
    Tag   tag ;
    bool taginuse ;

    for( tag = 0; tag < tsize; tag++ ) {
        read_ddata1(tag, taginuse) ;
        if( ! taginuse ) {
            write_ddata3(tag, true, size, false) ;
            break ;
        }
    }
    return tag ;
}
```

The Z specification also states that the *DNewTag* operation is undefined if the preconditions are not met, i.e. if there is no available tag. The C and SPIN prototype refine this specification by returning a value for `tag` that is outside the permitted range of 0 .. `tsize-1`.

Given the encapsulation of the memory read and write operations by the macros `read_ddata1` and `write_ddata3`, the C version of the *DNewTag* operation is clear and concise.

5.2   DNewTag in Promela

The next point of interest is to compare the C version of *DNewTag* to the Promela version shown below. The first issue to be addressed is that Promela does not offer a function call mechanism. Instead function call/return must be simulated trough process creation and message passing [9]. This requires four steps.

The first step introduces a number of tags to distinguish the various messages required:

```
mtype {MSize, MTag, Mabort, Mdone, ... } ;
```

The second step introduces two channels – one to pass arguments to the simulated procedure, and another to return the results:

```
chan go_DNewTag   = [0] of { mtype, Size } ;
chan done_DNewTag = [0] of { mtype, Tag } ;
```

The third step models a procedure as a process, which continually waits for a message on its `go_...` channel, and responds on its `done_...` channel. A typical call to a procedure would send on the `go_...` channel and receive from the `done_...` channel:

```
{
    ...
    go_DNewTag ! MSeq, 2 ;
    done_DNewTag ? MTag, tag ;
    ...
}
```

To allow SPIN to help discover errors in the specification a fourth step is needed. Each procedure call may either complete successfully or it may abort. An abort would be triggered by a failed write operation to the EEPROM. Actual calls to a procedure call must therefore be prepared for two different kinds of response:

```
{
    ...
    go_DNewTag ! MSeq, 2 ;
    if
    :: done_DNewTag ? MTag, tag -> ...
    :: done_DNewTag ? Mabort -> ...
    fi
}
```

The Promela version of the *DNewTag* operation is shown below. A nondeterministic choice is made at the second `if` statement either to perform the write to the EEPROM, or to abort the operation. Otherwise the code is the same as in the C version.

```
active proctype DNewTag( ) {
    Size size ;
    Tag  tag ;
    bool taginuse ;

endloop:
    do
    :: go_DNewTag ? MSeq, size ->
        tag = 0 ;
        do
```

```
    :: tag < tsize ->
       read_ddata1( tag, taginuse ) ;
       if
       :: ! taginuse ->
          if
          :: done_DNewTag ! Mabort ;
             goto endloop
          :: write_ddata3( tag, true, size, false ) ;
             break
          fi ;
       :: else -> skip
       fi ;
       tag = tag + 1
    :: else -> break
    od ;
    done_DNewTag ! MTag, tag
 od
}
```

It is apparent that loops and other control statements are a bit more verbose in Promela than they are in C.

The SPIN model uses processes only to simulate procedures, not to introduce concurrency. Otherwise there could be no simple correspondence between the SPIN model and the C implementation. The SPIN model does use the non-determinism offered by SPIN to choose between successful and failed EEPROM writes.

5.3   DTidy

A second operation of interest is the *DTidy* operation, which cleans up the memory in four phases. The *DTidy* operation should be used once only, upon restart of the system i.e. after an aborted write operation.

The first phase of the operation is shown below. It detects and frees the locations in the dmem array that are marked as being in use by a tag that is itself marked as not in use, or that is not committed.

```
void DTidy( ) {
    Loc     loc ;
    bool    pageinuse ;
    Tag     tag ;
    Info    dpi ;
    Gen     dpx ;
    PageNo  dpn ;
    Ver     dpv ;
    bool    taginuse ;
    Size    size ;
    bool    committed ;
```

```
for( loc = 0; loc < msize; loc++ ) {
    read_dmem6( loc, pageinuse, tag, dpi, dpx, dpn, dpv ) ;
    if( pageinuse ) {
        read_ddata3( tag, taginuse, size, committed ) ;
        if( ! taginuse || ! committed ) {
            write_dmem6( loc, false, tag, dpi, dpx, dpn, dpv ) ;
        }
    }
}
...
}
```

Here the scan of the entire tag array and the memory is unavoidable as the Tidy operation is intended to be used when the memory system is restarted after an aborted write. Short of scanning the entire collection of pages there is no way of knowing which pages belong to an aborted transaction.

The salient aspects of the C prototype and the SPIN model have now been covered. The complete list of data structures and functions of the transacted memory is shown in Table 1. The write operations will write the complete information sequence only if sufficient space is available.

5.4   Testing and Assertion Checking

The interest of the development of the prototype is in testing (C) and assertion checking (SPIN). Assertion checking in SPIN involves executing all possible execution paths of a finite program and testing assertions at various points in the execution paths.

To gain confidence in the prototype we wrote a simple test program. After some initialisation, the test program writes 16 generations of information for one particular tag. After each write operation, the test program reads back all existing generations and asserts that the information read back is correct. For the most recent generation the assertion is:

```
DWrite( tag, info ) ;
DCommit( tag ) ;
assert( DRead( tag ) == info ) ;
```

Each write operation will be interrupted at least once, leading to an error state. The DTidy operation is then called upon to recover from the error. Since DTidy performs write operations as part of the recovery process, these writes may be interrupted as well, leading to further calls to the DTidy operation.

The test performs over 2000 successful write operations and assertions, and 65 aborted writes. The test does not violate a single assertion.

The above protocol initially revealed a number of assertion failures, due to clerical errors made while interpreting the Z specification in the transition to the prototype. Once these errors were corrected a number of more serious issues were found. These will be discussed in the next section.

Table 1. Transacted Memory data structures and functions for C.

```
typedef struct { Gen old, new ; byte cnt ; } GenGenbyte ;
```
structure used to hold the number of the oldest and newest generation, and the number of generations.

```
typedef struct { Size size ; Info data[ssize] ; } InfoSeq ;
```
structure used to hold an information sequence and its size.

```
GenGenbyte DGeneration( Tag ) ;
```
Return all available information for the given tag. The result is undefined if the tag is not in use.

```
Tag DNewTag( Size ) ;
```
Return an unused tag of the specified size. The result is undefined if no tag is available.

```
void DTidy( ) ;
```
Recover from all possible interrupted writes.

```
InfoSeq DReadGeneration( Tag, Gen ) ;
```
Read the information sequence of a given tag and generation. The information sequence is undefined if the tag is not in use.

```
InfoSeq DRead( Tag ) ;
```
Read the information sequence of the current generation associated with the given tag.

```
void DCommit( Tag ) ;
```
Commit the current generation for the given tag. The operation has no effect if the tag is already committed.

```
void DRelease( Tag ) ;
```
Release all information associated with the given tag. The operation has no effect if the tag is not in use.

```
void DWriteFirst( Tag, InfoSeq ) ;
```
Write the to a tag immediately after the $DNewTag$ operation. The result is undefined if insufficient space is available.

```
void DWriteUncommitted( Tag, InfoSeq ) ;
```
Write to a tag whose current generation is uncommitted.

```
void DWriteCommittedAddGen( Tag, InfoSeq ) ;
```
Write to a tag whose current generation has been committed, and whose maximum number of generations has *not* been reached.

```
void DWriteCommittedMaxGen( Tag, InfoSeq ) ;
```
Write to a tag whose current generation has been committed, and whose maximum number of generations *has* been written. The oldest generation will be dropped.

6   Lessons Learned

A variety of lessons were learned, about the specification process, and about the transacted memory system itself. We will discuss each, starting with the process.

The specifications indicated in Figure 1 were made by different authors. Butler started with an abstract specification and a refinement of an initial version of the system. This refinement was formally verified by hand. The further refinements of the revised version were not formally verified but the development of abstraction invariants did help to increase the confidence in the refinements.

The next step in the development process was an evaluation of the specifications, leading to a revised version and further refinement of the specification (by Longley). Then the prototype was created (by Hartel) on the basis of the earlier specifications. At each stage there was a fresh opportunity for making mistakes, from which, of course, we learn.

The original Z specifications contain three non-standard Z constructs.

- The abstract specification contains a summation construct Σ (See Section 2). The summation was introduced because it is a valuable, standard symbol in mathematics, that can be used without ambiguity in most contexts. In Z by contrast different symbols are required depending on the data type over which summation is to take place.
- Procedures and for loops were introduced in the two refinements to suggest a close, and we believe valuable correspondence with the implementation. For example the 'Z schema' expressing the release of a set of tags would be:

> $PROCEDURE$
> $release : DMemory \times \mathbb{P}\,Loc \rightarrow DMemory$
> $release(mem, lset) = FOR\ l\ IN\ lset\ DO\ write(mem, l, \ldots)$

The presence of the three non standard Z constructs made it impossible for tools such as ZTC [10] to be used. To asses whether this would be a serious problem we commented the Σ construct out of the abstract specification and ran it through ZTC. This revealed a number of clerical errors:

- Three occurrences were found by the ZTC syntax check of missing parentheses, writing $\#f(x)$ instead of $\#(f(x))$.
- Five occurrences were found of a misspelled variable name by the ZTC syntax check.
- One occurrence of a missing operator was found by the ZTC type checking, where we wrote $\#x = y$ instead of $\#x = \#y$.
- One occurrence was found by the ZTC type checker of an incorrectly used operator ($a \times b$ instead of $a * b$).

The abstract specification is relatively small (2 pages, or 10 schemas and two auxiliary definitions). Yet we found 10 clerical errors.

During the manual translation from the second refinement into Promela a number of errors were found, some of which of a serious nature.

- Two occurrences were found of misspelled identifiers.
- One occurrence was found of an auxiliary function whose definition was missing.
- Three occurrences were found of an auxiliary function definition part of an earlier refinement that was implicit reused in a later refinement.
- Consider the following Z example, consisting of state and an operation on the state:

$$
\begin{array}{|l}
\hline
\underline{\;A\;} \\
\quad a : \mathbb{N} \\
\quad b : \mathbb{N} \\
\hline
\end{array}
$$

Assume that the operation $Inca$ increments a but leaves b untouched.

$$
\begin{array}{|l}
\hline
\underline{\;Inca\;} \\
\quad \Delta A \\
\hline
\quad a' = a + 1 \\
\hline
\end{array}
$$

Some operations in the two refinements explicitly constrain $b' = b$, and some omit this. This is clearly inconsistent.

Three serious problems were found:

- In the second refinement the two committed write operations made the tag uncommitted instead of committed. This error was found by inspection.
- Instead of the correct version given in Section 5.3, the second refinement stated the equivalent of this if statement:

```
if( ! taginuse ) {
    write_dmem6( loc, false, tag, dpi, dpx, dpn, dpv ) ;
}
```

The incorrect version thus failed to release pages with uncommitted data. This error was found by C testing.
- $ACommit$ as specified in Section 2 lacks a predicate $t? \notin committed$ and thus permits the $ACommit$ operation to be repeated. The interpretation leading to the prototype was created in a 'defensive' style, by systematically excluding all states in which an operation was not considered to be applicable. This lead to a discrepancy between the more permissive specification and the more restrictive prototype. The discrepancy was found by Spin's assertion checking.

Consistent with our earlier findings [5], we believe that using more than one tool/notation has benefits that contribute to the accuracy of the resulting specifications/implementations. In the present case, the prototype was created in 10 days, using the second refinement as a starting point. Creating the second refinement took several months to complete. The cost of providing a 'second opinion' on a specification by translating it into a different language/notation can thus be qualified as low.

7 Conclusion and Future Work

Our ideas of the transacted memory manager have become more and more accurate as progress was made on the various, more and more detailed specifications. The specifications served as a clear and unambiguous basis for discussions.

The combination of creating high level specifications in Z and detailed specification in Promela worked well for the memory manager. The high level Z specifications are clearer than the SPIN models would have been and conversely, the detailed SPIN models are clearer than the detailed Z specifications. The manual translation from the Detailed Z specification to a SPIN model is the weakest link in the chain of specifications. In principle we could have proved that our implementation satisfied the Detailed Z specification, but this was not attempted. Instead we used assertion checking on the SPIN model with assertions derived from the high level Z specification. This helped increase our confidence in the implementation.

An ad-hoc common notation has been used, from which both a SPIN model and C prototype are generated by expedient use of simple macros. This gives a reasonable degree of confidence that the C prototype is consistent with the SPIN model. SPIN's concurrency has not been used, but its facility for making a non-deterministic choice has.

Using different languages and associated tools to specify and prototype a specification automatically provides a second, and even a third opinion on various important issues. We discovered a considerable number of problems in earlier specifications when working on later specifications. The cost of providing a second opinion on the transacted memory manager was low.

Each operation of the prototype requires only a small, constant amount of RAM space, proportional to the number of generations associated with a tag. No RAM space is retained in between operations. However, to speed up some of the operations, a further refinement could be made to cache often used data.

The transacted memory that we have presented offers the basic facilities for building a type safe transaction facility. In addition, such a facility would also require a marshalling and unmarshalling capability. We are currently pursuing this for the use with Java.

The many for loops in the prototype may seem to introduce considerable inefficiency. However, we intend to produce further refinements down to the hardware level, where for loops taking a fixed number of steps could be 'unrolled' to form parallel hardware structures. The intention is to develop an FPGA based prototype.

One of our goals is to achieve certification of the transacted memory manager at EAL7 of the Common Criteria. This would require verification of the two the refinement steps as well as further formal refinements down to the hardware level.

References

1. Ph. A. Bernstein and E. Newcomer. *Principles of Transaction Processing*. Morgan Kaufman, San Francisco, 1997.
2. M. J. Butler, P. H. Hartel, E. K. de Jong, and M. Longley. Applying formal methods to the design of smart card software. Declarative Systems & Software Engineering Technical Reports DSSE-TR-97-8, University of Southampton, 1997.
3. E. K. de Jong and J. Bos. *Arrangements for storing different versions of a set of data in separate memory areas and method for updating a set of data in a memory*. Dutch Patent Application, 2000.
4. D. Donsez, G. Grimaud, and S. Lecomte. Recoverable persistant memory of smart-card. In J.-J. Quisquater and B. Schneier, editors, *3rd Int. Conf. Smart card research and advanced application (CARDIS), LNCS 1820*, page to appear, Louvain la Neuve, Belgium, Sep 1998. Springer-Verlag, Berlin.
5. P. Hartel, M. Butler, A. Currie, P. Henderson, M. Leuschel, A. Martin, A. Smith, U. Ultes-Nitsche, and B. Walters. Questions and answers about ten formal methods. In S. Gnesi and D. Latella, editors, *4th Int. Workshop on Formal Methods for Industrial Critical Systems, Vol II*, pages 179–203, Trento, Italy, Jul 1999. ERCIM/CNR, Pisa, Italy.
6. P. H. Hartel, M. J. Butler, and M. Levy. The operational semantics of a Java secure processor. In J. Alves-Foss, editor, *Formal Syntax and Semantics of Java, LNCS 1523*, pages 313–352. Springer-Verlag, Berlin, 1999.
7. P. H. Hartel and E. K. de Jong Frz. Towards testability in smart card operating system design. In V. Cordonnier and J.-J. Quisquater, editors, *1st Int. Conf. Smart card research and advanced application (CARDIS)*, pages 73–88, Lille France, Oct 1994. Univ. de Lille, France.
8. M. Herlihy and J. E. B. Moss. Transactional memory: Architectural support for Lock-Free data structures. In *Int. Symp. in Computer Architecture (ICSA)*, pages 289–300, San Diego, California, May 1993. Computer Architecture News, 21(2).
9. G. J. Holzmann. *Design and Validation of Computer Protocols*. Prentice Hall, Englewood Cliffs, New Jersey, 1991.
10. Xiaoping Jia. *ZTC: A Type Checker for Z – User's Guide*. Dept. of Comp. and Inf. Sci, DePaul Univ.,Chicago, Illinois, May 1995.
11. S. M. Nettles and J. M. Wing. Persistence+undoability=transactions. In *25th Hawaii International Conference on System Sciences (HICS)*, pages 832–43. IEEE Comput. Soc. Press., Los Alamitos, California, 1991.
12. National Institute of Standards and Technology. *Common Criteria for Information Technology Security Evaluation*. U. S. Dept. of Commerce, National Bureau of Standards and Technology, Aug 1999.
13. D. Sabatier and P. Lartigue. The use of the B formal method for the design and the validaion of the transaction mechanism for smart card applications. In J. M. Wing, J. Woodcock, and J. Davies, editors, *World Congress on Formal Methods in the Development of Computing Systems (FM), LNCS 1708*, pages 348–368, Toulouse, France, Sep 1999. Springer-Verlag, Berlin.
14. Sun. *Java Card 2.1 Runtime Environment (JCRE) Specification*. Sun Micro systems Inc, Palo Alto, California, Jun 1999.

Houdini, an Annotation Assistant for ESC/Java

Cormac Flanagan and K. Rustan M. Leino

Compaq Systems Research Center
130 Lytton Ave., Palo Alto, CA 94301, USA
{cormac.flanagan,rustan.leino}@compaq.com

Abstract. A static program checker that performs *modular checking* can check one program module for errors without needing to analyze the entire program. Modular checking requires that each module be accompanied by annotations that specify the module. To help reduce the cost of writing specifications, this paper presents Houdini, an annotation assistant for the modular checker ESC/Java. To infer suitable ESC/Java annotations for a given program, Houdini generates a large number of candidate annotations and uses ESC/Java to verify or refute each of these annotations. The paper describes the design, implementation, and preliminary evaluation of Houdini.

1 Introduction

The Compaq Extended Static Checker for Java (ESC/Java) is a tool for finding defects in Java programs [4,13,8,14]. It relies on the programmer to supply annotations describing program properties such as method preconditions, postconditions, and object invariants. These annotations allow ESC/Java to catch software defects using a method-local analysis. During this analysis, ESC/Java verifies that the annotations are consistent with the program, and it also uses the annotations to verify that each primitive operation (such as a dereference operation) will not raise a run-time exception (as might happen, for example, if a dereferenced pointer is null).

Other static checkers that follow this modular approach include conventional type checkers, which rely on type annotations to guide the type checking process, and rccjava [6], a static race condition checker, which relies on annotations describing the locking discipline.

A limitation of the modular checking approach is the burden on the programmer to supply annotations. Although programmers have grown accustomed to writing type annotations, they have been reluctant to provide additional annotations. In our experience, this reluctance has been the major obstacle to the adoption of ESC/Java. This annotation burden appears particularly pronounced when faced with the daunting task of applying ESC/Java to an existing (unannotated) code base.

To make ESC/Java more useful in catching defects in legacy code, we have developed Houdini, an *annotation assistant* that infers suitable ESC/Java annotations for an unannotated program. Houdini reuses ESC/Java as a subroutine

J.N. Oliveira and P. Zave (Eds.): FME 2001, LNCS 2021, pp. 500–517, 2001.

when inferring these annotation. Essentially, Houdini conjectures a large number of possible *candidate* annotations, and then uses ESC/Java to verify or refute each of these annotations.

This paper describes the design, implementation, and preliminary evaluation of Houdini. Our experience indicates that this approach is capable of inferring many useful annotations. These annotations significantly reduce the number of false alarms produced by ESC/Java (as compared with checking the original, unannotated program), and we have found that using Houdini reduces the programmer time required to statically catch defects in unannotated programs.

The presentation of our results proceeds as follows. The following section starts by reviewing ESC/Java. Section 3 introduces the basic architecture of Houdini. Section 4 describes the heuristics for generating candidate annotations. Section 5 describes how Houdini handles libraries. Section 6 describes Houdini's user interface. Section 7 describes our experience using Houdini to catch defects in four test programs totaling 50,000 lines of code. Houdini is actually a third-generation annotation assistant; Section 8 outlines some prior approaches we have tried. Section 9 describes related work, and we conclude in Section 10.

2   Review of ESC/Java

ESC/Java is a tool for finding common programming errors in Java programs. It takes as input a Java program, possibly annotated with ESC/Java light-weight specifications, and produces as output a list of warnings of possible errors in the program. Because of its static and automatic nature, its use is reminiscent of that of a type checker. Under the hood, however, ESC/Java is powered by a more precise semantics engine and an automatic theorem prover.

ESC/Java performs modular checking: Every routine (method or constructor) is given a specification. ESC/Java checks that the implementation of each routine meets its specification, assuming that all routines called meet their specifications. The specification comes from user-supplied annotations. Note that ESC/Java does not trace into the code of a callee, even if the callee code is also given to the tool to be checked. By performing modular checking, ESC/Java can be applied to a class, or even a routine, at a time, without needing the entire program.

Figure 1 shows a simple Java class that demonstrates the use of typical ESC/Java annotations. The class implements an n-tuple of non-null values (of type Object), where n can be changed over the lifetime of the object. The constructor creates an empty tuple and the put method sets element j of the tuple to the given value p, extending the tuple size by 1 if j==n, and returning the previous value, if any, of this tuple element.

ESC/Java annotations are given as specially formatted Java comments. If the first character within the Java comment is an @-sign, ESC/Java parses the comment and expects to find legal annotations. The expressions occurring in ESC/Java annotations are mostly just side-effect free Java expression, but with

```
class Tuple {
  int n;
  //@ invariant 0 <= n;

  Tuple() { ... }                        // constructor

  //@ requires 0 <= j;
  //@ requires j <= n;
  //@ requires p != null;
  //@ ensures j == n || \result != null;
  Object put(int j, Object p) { ... }

  ...

  Object a[];
  //@ invariant a != null;
  //@ invariant (\forall int i; 0 <= i && i < n ==> a[i] != null);
  //@ invariant n <= a.length;
}
```

Fig. 1. Examples of typical ESC/Java annotations.

some additions, including quantified expressions and some special keywords and functions.

The example in Figure 1 shows the put method to have some pre- and post-conditions. The **requires** keyword declares a precondition and the **ensures** keyword declares a postcondition. The occurrences of j and p in these annotations refer to the method's parameters and n refers to the field declared in the class. The postcondition uses the special keyword \result to refer to the value returned by the method. Since this is a light-weight specification, it does not specify all aspects of the method's behavior.

The example also shows several declarations of object invariants. ESC/Java checks that these are established by the constructor and maintained by other routines. (The details are described in the ESC/Java user's manual [13].) One of the invariant declarations uses a universal quantification and the ESC/Java implication operator ==>.

To make ESC/Java simpler, it contains some degree of unsoundness by design. That is, it sometimes fails to detect genuine errors. In practice, this limitation does not negatively affect the usefulness of ESC/Java. Also, since the properties that it attempts to check are undecidable in the worst case, ESC/Java is also incomplete and may produce spurious warnings.

3   Houdini Architecture

Although ESC/Java works well on annotated programs, catching defects in legacy, unannotated programs using ESC/Java is an arduous process. It is possible to run ESC/Java on an unannotated program, but this produces an excessively large number of false alarms. Alternatively, one can manually insert appropriate annotations into the program, but this is a very time-consuming task for large programs. Preliminary experience with ESC/Java indicates that a programmer can annotate an existing, unannotated program at the rate of a few hundred lines per hour, or perhaps at a lower rate if the programmer is unfamiliar with the code.

Therefore, we would like to automate much of the annotation process by developing an *annotation assistant* that infers suitable ESC/Java annotations for a legacy, unannotated program. The following *Houdini* algorithm implements an annotation assistant. This algorithm leverages off ESC/Java's ability to perform precise method-local analysis.

> *Input*: An unannotated program P
> *Output*: ESC/Java warnings for an annotated version of P
> *Algorithm*:
> generate set of candidate annotations and insert into P;
> **repeat**
>   invoke ESC/Java to check P;
>   remove any refuted candidate annotations from P;
> **until** quiescence;
> invoke ESC/Java to identify possible defects in P;

The first step in the algorithm is to generate a finite set of *candidate annotations*. This set is generated from the program text based on heuristics about what annotations might be useful in reasoning about the program's behavior. For example, since a common precondition in manually-annotated programs is that an argument of reference type is non-null, the candidate annotation set includes all preconditions of this form. Other useful heuristics for guessing candidate annotations are described in Section 4.

Many of the candidate annotations will of course be incorrect. To identify these incorrect annotations, the Houdini algorithm invokes ESC/Java on the annotated program. Like any invocation of ESC/Java, this invocation may produce two kinds of warnings. The first kind concerns potential run-time errors, such as dereferencing the null pointer. These warnings are ignored by the Houdini algorithm.

The second kind of warning concerns invalid annotations. During the checking process, ESC/Java may discover that the property expressed by an annotation may not hold at a particular program point (for example, a method precondition may not hold at a call site of the method). The annotation assistant interprets such warnings as refuting incorrect guesses in the candidate annotation set, and removes these refuted annotations from the program text.

Since removing one annotation may cause subsequent annotations to become invalid, this check-and-refute cycle iterates until a fixpoint is reached. This process terminates, because until a fixpoint is reached, the number of remaining candidate annotations is strictly decreased with each iteration. The resulting annotation set is clearly a subset of the candidate set, and is *valid* with respect to ESC/Java, that is, ESC/Java does not refute any of its annotations. The inferred annotation set is in fact a maximal valid subset of the candidate set. Furthermore, this maximal subset is unique. For a proof of these properties, and also a more efficient version of the basic algorithm presented here, we refer the interested reader to our companion paper [7].

Note that the Houdini algorithm works also for recursive methods. The candidate preconditions of a recursive method will be refined (by removing refuted preconditions) until the resulting set of preconditions holds at all call sites of the method, both recursive and non-recursive call sites.

After the check-and-refute loop terminates, the final step in the Houdini algorithm is to run ESC/Java one more time to identify potential run-time errors in the (now annotated) program. These warnings are then presented to the user, and are used as a starting point in identifying defects in the program.

4   Generating the Candidate Annotation Set

The usefulness of the inferred annotations depends crucially on the initial candidate annotation set. Ideally, the candidate set should include all annotations that are likely to be useful in reasoning about the program's behavior. However, the candidate set should not be too large, because this would increase the running time of the algorithm. Based on an inspection of a variety of hand-annotated programs and on our experience with ESC/Java and Houdini, we have developed the following heuristics for generating candidate annotations.

For any field `f` declared in the program, we guess the following candidate invariants for `f`:

Type of `f`	Candidate invariants for `f`
integral type	`//@ invariant f` *cmp* *expr* `;`
reference type	`//@ invariant f != null;`

array type	`//@ invariant f != null;`
	`//@ invariant \nonnullelements(f);`
	`//@ invariant (\forall int i; 0 <= i && i <` *expr*
	`                              ==> f[i] != null);`
	`//@ invariant f.length` *cmp* *expr* `;`

boolean	`//@ invariant f == false;` `//@ invariant f == true;`

Many of these candidate invariants are intended to help verify the absence of index-out-of-bounds errors. For each integral field `f` we guess several inequalities relating `f` to other integral fields and constants. The comparison operator *cmp* ranges over the six operators <, <=, ==, !=, >=, and >, and *expr* is either an integral field declared earlier in the same class or an *interesting constant*. Interesting constants include the numbers -1, 0, 1, and also constant dimensions used in array allocation expressions (*e.g.*, `new int[4]`). For each field `f` of an array type, we also guess a number of inequalities regarding `f.length`. Although some of these inequalities are more useful than others, we include all of them for completeness.

Some of these guessed invariants are mutually inconsistent. For example, if a class declares an integral field `f` we will guess several invariants, including:

```
//@ invariant f < 0;
//@ invariant f >= 0;
```

Such inconsistent guesses do not cause a problem. When checking a constructor for the class, ESC/Java will refute at least one of these invariants, since the constructed instance cannot simultaneously satisfy both invariants.

We also guess candidates invariants that help verify the absence of null dereference errors. For each field `f` of a reference type, we guess `f != null`. For each field `f` of an array type, in addition to guessing the invariant `f != null`, we also guess the invariant `\nonnullelements(f)`, which states that each entry in the array is not null, and we guess an invariant that all entries in `f` up to *expr* (a field or an interesting constant) are not null. We have found this last property to be useful in reasoning about the behavior of stack-like data structures implemented using arrays.

We generate candidate preconditions and postconditions in a similar manner for each routine declared in the program. Candidate preconditions may include inequalities relating two argument variables, or relating an argument variable to a field declared in the same class. Candidate postconditions may relate the result variable `\result` to either argument variables or fields. In addition, we generate the candidate postcondition

```
//@ ensures \fresh(\result);
```

which states that the result of a method is a newly-allocated object, and hence not an alias of any previously existing object.

As an aid in identifying dead code, we generate the candidate annotation

```
//@ requires false;
```

for every routine in the program. An unrefuted `requires false` annotation indicates that the corresponding routine is never called.

For correctness reasons, we require that all applicable candidate annotations hold in the program's initial state. Hence, for the program entry point

```
public static void main(String args[]) { ... }
```

we only generate the following precondition, which is ensured by the Java runtime system:

```
//@ requires \nonnullelements(args);
```

5   Dealing with Libraries

So far, we have described Houdini as a system that infers annotations based on an analysis of the entire program. However, the program may be linked with a library (or with several libraries) that we cannot analyze, either because we do not have source code for the library or because the size of the library makes the analysis impractical.

If the library in question already includes ESC/Java annotations that specify its interface, or if we are willing to write such an interface specification, then it is straightforward to adapt the Houdini algorithm to analyze and annotate the remainder of the program with respect to this specification. In many cases, however, the size and complexity of the library makes writing an interface specification quite tedious. Hence, we would like to be able to infer annotations for a program even in the absence of ESC/Java specifications for all of the libraries used by the program.

Therefore, we extend Houdini so that it can analyze a program with respect to *guessed* specifications for these libraries. There are two main strategies for guessing library specifications. The first strategy is to make *pessimistic* assumptions, for example, that all pointers returned by library methods may be null. Since many of these pointers will never be null, such pessimistic specifications cause Houdini to produce a large number of false alarms in the rest of the program, and we have not found this approach cost-effective for static debugging. (ESC/Java provides pessimistic assumptions by default in the absence of library annotations.)

An alternative strategy is to make *optimistic* assumptions about the behavior of libraries, for example, that all pointers returned by library methods will be non-null. Since some of these pointers may sometimes be null, this assumption is unsound, and may cause Houdini to miss certain run-time errors. However, in library clients, Houdini will still detect many other run-time errors, and since the optimistic specifications lead to many fewer false alarms, this appears to be a more cost-effective strategy for guessing library specifications.

For libraries, we need to be careful not to guess contradictory annotations. To illustrate this idea, suppose that we generated the two contradictory post-conditions

```
//@ ensures \result < 0;
//@ ensures \result >= 0;
```

for a library method that the program does not override. Since the implementation of the library method is not checked, neither of these guessed annotations will be refuted. ESC/Java would then infer that the method never returns and would not check code following a call to this method. Therefore, we only guess the following consistent postconditions for each library method:

Result type	Optimistic postconditions
integral type	`//@ ensures \result >= 0;`
reference type	`//@ ensures \result != null;`
array type	`//@ ensures \result != null;` `//@ ensures \nonnullelements(\result);`

We guess optimistic preconditions and invariants in a similar manner.

The modified Houdini algorithm for dealing with libraries is as follows:

> *Input*: An unannotated program P
> A set of libraries S with specifications
> A set of libraries L without specifications
> *Output*: ESC/Java warnings for an annotated version of P
> *Algorithm*:
> generate and insert candidate annotations into P;
> generate and insert optimistic annotations into L;
> **repeat**
>   invoke ESC/Java to check P with respect to L and S;
>   remove any refuted candidate annotations from P;
>   remove any refuted optimistic annotations from L;
> **until** quiescence;
> invoke ESC/Java to identify possible defects in P with respect to L and S;

6   User Interface

To catch defects using Houdini, a user starts by inspecting Houdini's output, which includes the set of warnings that ESC/Java produces for the annotated version of the program. Unlike using ESC/Java, where a warning in one routine often points to a problem with that routine's implementation or specification, the warnings produced by Houdini are more often caused by some other part of the program. For example, suppose one of the warnings points out a possible null dereference of t in the following method:

```
char getFirstChar(String t) { return t.charAt(0); }
```

A user's first reaction might be: But I only intend **getFirstChar** to be called with non-null arguments! The ESC/Java user would then add the precondition t != null, which suppresses the spurious warning. (This precondition is then checked at call sites.) But the Houdini user will instead ask: Why didn't Houdini infer this precondition?

In our experience with looking at Houdini output, we constantly asked questions such as these. We developed a simple user interface to help answer these questions. The user interface generates a collection of HTML pages. The root

page of this collection presents a summary of the kinds of warnings that the
final call to ESC/Java produces, followed by the actual list of warning messages.
Each warning message contains a hyperlink to the source view of the code at the
location of the offending program line.

In the source code view (shown in Figure 2), the user interface displays all of
the candidate annotations guessed by Houdini. A refuted annotation is grayed
out and hyperlinks to the source line where ESC/Java issued the warning that
refuted the annotation. We also insert the warning messages into the code in the
source view.

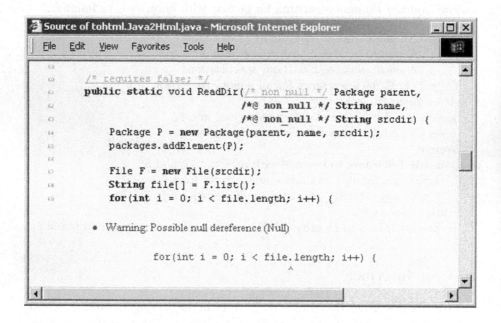

Fig. 2. Screen shot showing the source view of Houdini's user interface. (Declaring a
parameter, like `parent`, with the ESC/Java modifier `non_null` serves as an alternate
way of writing the precondition `requires parent != null;`).

Thus, in the example above, the Houdini user would look at the preconditions
that Houdini guessed initially for `getFirstChar`. These would include a grayed-
out precondition `t != null`, and clicking on this refuted annotation would bring
the user to a call site where, as far as ESC/Java could tell, the actual parameter of
t may be null. This may lead the user to understand whether the null dereference
warning in `getFirstChar` is a real problem with the program or a spurious
warning, or this may just be one of a number of similar steps required to get to
the source of the problem. Surprisingly, our experience indicates that presenting
the *refuted* annotations and the causes thereof is the most important aspect of
the user interface.

7   Experience

We have applied Houdini to tens of thousands of lines of unannotated program code. Here we report on four programs that have been subjected to many test runs of various versions of the tool. They are:

- Java2Html [12], a 500-line program that turns Java programs into color-coded HTML pages,
- WebSampler, a 2,000-line program that performs statistical samplings of trace files generated by the web crawler Mercator [11],
- PachyClient, the 11,000-line graphical user interface of the web-based email program Pachyderm [15], and
- "Cobalt", a proprietary 36,000-line program.

These programs had been tested and used, in some cases extensively, before Houdini was applied to them.

Table 1 shows some statistics for the first three programs. For each program, the table shows three columns. The first of these columns indicates the number of checks performed by ESC/Java to verify various correctness properties. These correctness properties include proving that various run-time exceptions will not occur and that libraries are used in a manner consistent with their manually written specifications.

Table 1. A breakdown of the checks performed by ESC/Java and the warnings produced by ESC/Java before and after applying Houdini.

warning or exception type	Java2Html checks	warnings before	after	WebSampler checks	warnings before	after	PachyClient checks	warnings before	after
NullPointerException	145	41	2	328	87	12	2619	1016	392
IndexOutOfBoundsExn.	8	3	2	228	112	19	294	57	24
ClassCastException	8	7	7	5	4	3	152	117	103
ArithmeticException	0	0	0	23	2	2	25	7	7
NegativeArraySizeExn.	1	0	0	16	2	0	20	4	2
ArrayStoreException	0	0	0	5	2	0	6	0	0
library annotations	22	5	0	147	43	5	376	49	17
all	184	56	11	752	252	41	3492	1250	545

Checking that NullPointerException is not raised is by far the most common check. The row for IndexOutOfBoundsException counts every array dereference as two separate checks, one for the lower bound and one for the upper bound. ClassCastException checks arise from type cast expressions, which are commonly used with container classes. ArithmeticException is raised in the case of integer division by zero. NegativeArraySizeException is raised if an attempt is made to allocate an array with a negative size. The need for ArrayStoreException checks comes from Java's co-variant array subtyping rule. The libraries we used in checking these programs contained some manually inserted light-weight ESC/Java specifications. The library annotations row shows the number of checks in the program arising from these specifications.

The second and third columns for each program in Table 1 show the number of these checks that ESC/Java is not able to statically verify. Each such unverified check corresponds to a warning produced by ESC/Java. The second column is the number of warnings produced for an unannotated program and the third column is the number of warnings produced after running Houdini to infer annotations for the program.

Java2Html was something of a lucky draw: of the 4 non-cast warnings reported, all 4 indicate real errors in the source code. For example, the program will crash if a line in the input exceeds 1024 characters or if the system call `File.list()` returns null (see Figure 2). Houdini currently does not have support for guessing the annotations needed to verify cast checks. For this reason, Houdini actually uses a command-line option to ESC/Java to suppress all cast warnings, since we have found it more cost effective for users to investigate warnings of other kinds.

The warnings produced on WebSampler led us to find 3 real errors. One of these was part of a class that was borrowed from the web crawler Mercator: the method

```
int read(byte[] b);
```

of `java.io.InputStream` is supposed to read characters into the given array `b`, returning -1 if the input stream is at end-of-file or returning the number of characters read otherwise. However, a Mercator subclass of `InputStream` erroneously returned 0 whenever the length of `b` was 0, even if the stream was at end-of-file.

Houdini also issued several warnings pointing out places where WebSampler assumed its input to have a particular format. For example, in some situations, WebSampler assumed the next line of input to be at least 4 characters long and to consist only of characters that can be interpreted as a decimal number. The warnings pointing out these infelicities were considered spurious, since WebSampler is only intended to work on well-formed input.

We have inspected only about a dozen of the PachyClient warnings. Nevertheless, two of these pointed out infelicities that compelled the author of the code to make code changes. Technically, one can argue that these infelicities were not errors, but they did make the code overly brittle. The author changed the code to guard against possible future failures.

Table 2 shows some statistics for the Cobalt program. Rather than using hand-annotated libraries, we analyzed this program using the two strategies of pessimistic and optimistic library assumptions. For each of these two strategies, Table 2 shows the number of checks that ESC/Java performs to verify various correctness properties, and the number of these checks that ESC/Java is not able to statically verify before and after running Houdini.

The table shows that the use of optimistic library annotations can significantly reduce the number of null-dereference and bounds warnings that Houdini produces.

Table 2. A breakdown of the checks performed by ESC/Java on the Cobalt program, and the warnings produced by ESC/Java before and after applying Houdini, using both pessimistic and optimistic library annotations.

warning or exception type	no lib. anns.			optimistic lib. anns.		
	checks	warnings		checks	warnings	
		before	after		before	after
NullPointerException	10702	3237	1717	10702	2438	488
IndexOutOfBoundsExn.	982	151	75	982	118	52
ClassCastException	347	278	234	347	271	234
ArithmeticException	17	0	0	17	0	0
NegativeArraySizeExn.	60	13	11	60	1	0
ArrayStoreException	18	0	0	18	0	0
library annotations	0	0	0	9385	787	0
all	12126	3679	2037	21511	3615	774

One hundred of the non-cast warnings of Cobalt were inspected and revealed 3 real errors in the code.

For the first three programs, we did not measure the user time required to inspect the warnings, but in the case of Cobalt, this time was measured to be 9 hours to inspect one hundred warnings. Toward the end of this time, the inspection proceeded at a higher pace than in the beginning, partly because of getting more familiar with the tool's output and partly because of repeated spurious warnings. This experience suggests that using Houdini, a user can inspect a program for errors at a rate upwards of 1000 lines per hour.

Despite the precision of ESC/Java, Houdini still produces many false alarms. A major cause of false alarms is that Houdini may fail to guess the right annotations for a given program. In particular, Houdini does not guess disjunctions, such as in the following postcondition of the method **put** from Figure 1:

```
//@ ensures j == n || \result != null
```

Another cause of false alarms in Houdini is the incompleteness of ESC/Java, comprising the incompleteness of the underlying theorem prover, the incompleteness of ESC/Java's axiomatization of Java's operators (for example, the semantics of bitwise-and is not completely axiomatized), and the incompleteness of ESC/Java's light-weight annotation language. An ESC/Java user would know to insert **nowarn**, **assume**, and **axiom** annotations to make up for any such incompleteness (see the ESC/Java user's manual [13]), but Houdini does not infer such annotations.

After inspecting a serious warning, a user would normally fix the error in the program. If instead the user determines the warning to be spurious, a prudent course of action is to convey to Houdini the missing pieces of information. For example, if the cause of a spurious warning is that Houdini didn't guess some annotation, possibly with a disjunction like the one shown above, then the user can manually insert the missing annotation into the program.

Thus, experienced Houdini users are likely to manually insert ESC/Java annotations into the program, just like ESC/Java users would. However, Houdini users insert many fewer annotations. We predict that leaving such a small number of annotations in the code will be acceptable to most programmers.

These manually-inserted annotations give future runs of Houdini more information about the program, which may cause Houdini to generate fewer spurious warnings. Thus, experienced users are likely to rerun Houdini after adding some manual annotations. This iterative process can be quite cost effective, because even small manual interventions can prevent what otherwise might have resulted in a cascade of spurious refutations.

A consequence of this iterative process is that the Houdini running time must not be too long. Since Houdini, like all other static debuggers, competes in practice with software testing, it seems reasonable that a dozen iterations may be done over the course of a couple of weeks. This means that each run of Houdini must be fast enough to complete overnight, say, finishing within 16 hours.

The version of Houdini reported on in this paper does not meet the overnight challenge: the running time on the 36,000-line Cobalt program was 62 hours. We remain optimistic, however, for several reasons. First, some preliminary experiments with algorithmic improvements seem promising. Second, measurements of the work performed during each of Houdini's iterations suggest the operations of Houdini to be parallelizable. And third, we have built a prototype of a dynamic refuter, which creates an instrumented version of the program that, when run, records which candidate annotations are violated (*i.e.*, refuted) during the execution. This significantly reduces the number of candidate annotations that are left to be refuted by ESC/Java.

Since a run of Houdini may take many hours, an important aspect of Houdini's usability is that it is restartable. The system periodically writes a snapshot of its current state to disk, so that if that particular run is abruptly terminated (for example, by a power failure), it can later be restarted at the most recent snapshot.

Finally, we give some measurements that provide a preliminary idea of the effectiveness of the various heuristics described in Section 4 for generating candidate annotations. Table 3 shows the number of candidate annotations generated for the Cobalt program by these heuristics, and the percentage of these annotations that are actually valid. In this table, the count of valid annotations includes many annotations that hold in all Java programs (for example, `a.length >= -1`) and annotations that are subsumed by other annotations (for example, `x != -1` is subsumed by `x > 0`); it remains for future work to avoid such valid but redundant annotations.

8   Other Annotation Assistants

The design of Houdini was inspired by the experience with two other ESC/Java annotation assistants that we developed. The annotations inferred by Houdini

Table 3. Numbers of candidate annotations generated on the Cobalt program by the heuristics of Section 4, and the percentages of these annotations that are valid.

Type of annotation	Preconditions		Postconditions		Invariants		Total	
	guessed	%valid	guessed	%valid	guessed	%valid	guessed	%valid
f == *expr*	2130	18	985	18	435	14	3550	17
f != *expr*	2130	35	985	35	435	38	3550	35
f < *expr*	2130	26	985	27	435	24	3550	26
f <= *expr*	2130	31	985	32	435	36	3550	33
f >= *expr*	2130	25	985	21	435	19	3550	32
f > *expr*	2130	31	985	36	435	35	3550	23
f != null	509	92	229	79	983	72	1721	79
\nonnullelems(f)	54	81	21	62	36	64	111	72
(\forall ...)	841	27	260	37	125	59	1226	32
f == false	47	36	51	25	39	10	137	20
f == true	47	28	51	24	39	8	137	25
\fresh(\result)	0	0	229	30	0	0	229	30
false	780	17	0	0	0	0	780	17
exact type	37	19	11	36	14	57	62	31
Total	15095	30	6762	30	3846	40	25703	31

have been significantly more useful than the annotations inferred by these earlier annotation assistants.

The first annotation assistant starts with an unannotated program and iteratively added annotations. To support this annotation assistant, ESC/Java was modified to output a suggestion with each warning, whenever possible. For example, if a warning points to the dereference of a formal parameter p that is not changed by the routine body being checked, the suggestion is to add a precondition p != null. Each suggestion has the property that by following the suggestion and rerunning ESC/Java, the warning will be suppressed (but other, new warnings may be generated). The annotation assistant iteratively runs ESC/Java and follows the suggestions until ESC/Java produces no more suggestions.

Although many of the suggestions are good, this annotation assistant has two severe limitations. First, it is hard to produce enough suggestions. Not only do new heuristics become increasingly more complicated, but because of the requirement of only suggesting measures that are sure to suppress the warning, the heuristics for when to make a suggestion frequently have side conditions that are not met (such as "... and the formal parameter is not assigned to by the body"). Second, the suggested annotations are not always correct. The cascading effects of incorrect annotations limit the effectiveness of the annotation assistant.

The second annotation assistant uses a whole-program set-based analysis [5, 10] to identify which variables and fields are never null and inserts corresponding annotations into the program. These annotations are useful in verifying many dereference operations. However, the inferred annotations do not include numeric inequalities (which are necessary for verifying the absence of array bounds errors) and do not include properties such as

```
//@ invariant (\forall int i; 0 <= i && i < expr ==> f[i] !=
null);
```

(which are necessary for checking stack-like data structures implemented using arrays).

Like the first annotation assistant, Houdini uses ESC/Java as a powerful subroutine. Like the second annotation assistant, Houdini infers only valid annotations. Furthermore, since Houdini's iterative check-and-refute machinery does not depend on the particular annotations contained in the candidate set, Houdini provides a flexible architecture for inferring many kinds of annotations.

Another advantage of the Houdini algorithm is its generality: it is not closely dependent on the underlying checker and can be used to infer annotations for a variety of modular static checkers. We have successfully ported Houdini to a second checker, the race condition checker for Java [6]. This checker extends Java's type system with additional checks that verify the absence of race conditions. The checker relies on additional type annotations to describe aspects of the locking discipline, for example, the protecting lock of each field. Adapting the Houdini algorithm to guess many such type annotations was straightforward, and, as with ESC/Java, we have found the annotations inferred by the system to be useful.

9   Related Work

Predicate abstraction is a technique for analyzing an infinite state system, given a set of predicates over the state space of the system [9]. This technique finds a boolean combination of the predicates that holds in all reachable states, and that holds in a minimum of unreachable states.

The Houdini algorithm can be viewed as a variant of predicate abstraction in which each candidate annotation corresponds to a predicate. Interestingly, the Houdini algorithm does not consider arbitrary boolean formulae over these predicates; it only considers conjunctions of predicates. This restriction means that Houdini cannot infer disjunctions or implications of candidate predicates. For example, given the two predicates `j == n` and `\result != null`, Houdini could not infer the property

```
j == n || \result != null
```

This restriction reduces the maximum number of iterations of the algorithm from exponential to linear in the number of predicates; however, it also increases the number of false alarms produced by the system.

Abstract interpretation [2] is a standard framework for developing and describing program analyses. We can view the Houdini algorithm as an abstract interpretation, where the abstract state space is the power set lattice over the candidate annotations and the checker is used to compute the abstract transition relation. As usual, the choice of the abstract state space controls the conservative approximations performed by the analysis. In our approach, it is easy to tune these approximations by choosing the set of candidate annotations appropriately, provided that this set remains finite and that the annotations are understood by the checker.

An interesting aspect of our approach is that the checker can use arbitrary techniques (for example, weakest preconditions in the case of ESC/Java) for performing method-local analysis. If these local analysis techniques allow the checker to reason about sets of intermediate states that cannot be precisely characterized using the abstract state space, then the Houdini algorithm may yield more precise results than a conventional abstract interpretation that exclusively uses abstract states to represent sets of concrete states.

PREfix is a static programming tool that warns about possible errors in C and C++ code [1]. There are no annotations involved in using PREfix, which is mostly an advantage. We find the presence of annotations in Houdini's output, including the refuted annotations, helpful when inspecting the tool's output. Annotations also provide a general and convenient way for users to supply the tool with missing, uninferred facts. The technology underlying PREfix is different from the precise semantics engine and automatic theorem prover that underly ESC/Java, but perhaps the differences are bigger than they need to be.

Daikon is a system that uses an empirical approach to find probable invariants [3]. These invariants are found by creating an instrumented version of the program that records a trace of intermediate program states, running the instrumented program on a test suite, and then analyzing the generated traces off-line to determine properties that hold throughout all runs. Given a suitably complete test suite, the inferred properties are likely to be true program invariants.

10   Conclusions

This paper describes a technique for building an annotation assistant for a modular static checker. The annotation assistant reuses the checker as a subroutine; it works by guessing a large number of candidate annotations and using the checker to verify or refute each candidate annotation.

We have used to this technique to develop an annotation assistant, called Houdini, for the modular program checker ESC/Java. Houdini is capable of inferring a large number of useful annotations, which significantly reduce the number of false alarms produced by ESC/Java (as compared with checking an unannotated program). These inferred annotations also reduce the programmer time required to check an existing, unannotated program for defects.

In our experience, a natural strategy for using Houdini is to maintain a code base with a few manually-inserted annotations that Houdini cannot infer, and to rely on Houdini to infer additional annotations whenever the code needs to be checked. Thus, we expect that Houdini will be considered by users as a static checker in itself, and not just as an annotation assistant for the underlying checker ESC/Java.

A number of issues remain for future work, including refining the heuristics for the generation of the candidate annotations, improving the performance of Houdini (significant progress has already been made in this direction), and enhancing the user interface. However, the system developed to date has already proven capable of catching defects in several real-world programs.

Acknowledgements. We are grateful to our colleagues who contributed in various ways to the Houdini project: Yuan Yu suggested and helped us develop the dynamic refuter. He also helped inspect the Houdini output on WebSampler. Steve Freund ported Houdini to `rccjava`. Raymie Stata helped create the earlier annotation assistant that used set-based analysis. Jim Saxe helped think about how to get the underlying theorem prover to work well with Houdini's demands. Lawrence Markosian and Dr. Maggie Johnson of Reasoning, Inc., Mountain View, CA inspected the Houdini output on Cobalt. Roy Levin suggested "Houdini" as the name of "the great ESC wizard".

References

1. William R. Bush, Jonathan D. Pincus, and David J. Sielaff. A static analyzer for finding dynamic programming errors. *Software—Practice & Experience*, 30:775–802, 2000.
2. Patrick Cousot and Radhia Cousot. Abstract interpretation: a unified lattice model for static analysis of programs by construction or approximation of fixpoints. In *Conference Record of the Fourth Annual ACM Symposium on Principles of Programming Languages*, pages 238–252, January 1977.
3. Michael D. Ernst, Adam Czeisler, William G. Griswold, and David Notkin. Quickly detecting relevant program invariants. In *Proceedings of the 22nd International Conference on Software Engineering (ICSE 2000), Limerick, Ireland*, June 2000.
4. Extended Static Checking home page, Compaq Systems Research Center. On the Web at `research.compaq.com/SRC/esc/`.
5. Cormac Flanagan. *Effective Static Debugging via Componential Set-Based Analysis*. PhD thesis, Rice University, Houston, Texas, May 1997.
6. Cormac Flanagan and Steven N. Freund. Type-based race detection for Java. In *Proceedings of the 2000 ACM SIGPLAN conference on Programming Design and Implementation (PLDI)*, pages 219–232, 2000.
7. Cormac Flanagan, Rajeev Joshi, and K. Rustan M. Leino. Annotation inference for modular checkers. *Information Processing Letters*, 2001. To appear.
8. Cormac Flanagan and James B. Saxe. Avoiding exponential explosion: Generating compact verification conditions. In *Conference Record of the 28th Annual ACM Symposium on Principles of Programming Languages*. ACM, January 2001. To appear.
9. S. Graf and H. Saidi. Construction of abstract state graphs with PVS. In O. Grumberg, editor, *CAV 97: Computer Aided Verification*, Lecture Notes in Computer Science 1254, pages 72–83. Springer-Verlag, 1997.
10. Nevin Heintze. Set-based analysis of ML programs. In *Proceedings of the ACM Conference on Lisp and Functional Programming*, pages 306–317, 1994.
11. Allan Heydon and Marc A. Najork. Mercator: A scalable, extensible web crawler. *World Wide Web*, 2(4):219–229, December 1999.

12. Java2html, Compaq Systems Research Center. On the Web at
    `research.compaq.com/SRC/software/`.
13. K. Rustan M. Leino, Greg Nelson, and James B. Saxe. ESC/Java user's manual.
    Technical Note 2000-002, Compaq Systems Research Center, October 2000.
14. K. Rustan M. Leino, James B. Saxe, and Raymie Stata. Checking Java
    programs via guarded commands. In Bart Jacobs, Gary T. Leavens, Peter
    Müller, and Arnd Poetzsch-Heffter, editors, *Formal Techniques for Java Programs*, Technical Report 251. Fernuniversität Hagen, May 1999. Also available as Technical Note 1999-002, Compaq Systems Research Center, from
    `research.compaq.com/SRC/publications/`.
15. The Pachyderm email system, Compaq Systems Research Center. On the Web at
    `research.compaq.com/SRC/pachyderm/`, 1997.

A Heuristic for Symmetry Reductions with Scalarsets[*]

Dragan Bošnački[1], Dennis Dams[2], and Leszek Holenderski[1]

[1] Dept. of Computing Sci., Eindhoven University of Technology
PO Box 513, 5600 MB Eindhoven, The Netherlands
[2] Dept. of Electrical Eng., Eindhoven University of Technology
PO Box 513, 5600 MB Eindhoven, The Netherlands

{D.Bosnacki,D.Dams,L.Holenderski}@tue.nl

Abstract. We present four versions of a new heuristic for coping with the problem of finding (canonical) representatives of symmetry equivalence classes (the so-called *orbit problem*), in symmetry techniques for model checking. The practical implementation of such techniques hinges on appropriate workarounds of this hard problem, which is equivalent to graph isomorphism. We implemented the four strategies on top of the Spin model checker, and compared their performance on several examples, with encouraging results.

1 Introduction

One way to combat the state explosion problem in model checking [5,8] is to exploit symmetries in a system description. In order to grasp the idea of symmetry reduction, consider a mutual exclusion protocol based on semaphores. The (im)possibility for processes to enter their critical sections will be similar regardless of their identities, since process identities (pids) play no role in the semaphore mechanism. More formally, the system state remains behaviorally equivalent under permutations of pids. During state-space exploration, when a state is visited that is the same, up to a permutation of pids, as some state that has already been visited, the search can be pruned. The notion of behavioral equivalence used (bisimilarity, trace equivalence, sensitivity to deadlock, fairness, etc.) and the class of permutations allowed (full, rotational, mirror, etc.) may vary, leading to a spectrum of symmetry techniques.

The two main questions in practical applications of symmetry techniques are how to find symmetries in a system description, and how to detect, during state-space exploration, that two states are equivalent. To start with the first issue: as in any other state-space reduction method based on behavioral equivalences, the problem of deciding equivalence of states requires, in general, the construction of the full state space. Doing this would obviously invalidate the approach, as

---

[*] This research has been supported by the VIRES project (Verifying Industrial Reactive Systems, Esprit Long Term Research Project #23498).

it is precisely what we are trying to avoid. Therefore, most approaches proceed by listing sufficient conditions that can be statically checked on the system description. The second problem, of detecting equivalence of states, involves the search for a *canonical* state by permuting the values of certain, symmetric, data structures. In [4] it was shown that this *orbit problem* is at least as hard as testing for graph isomorphism, for which currently no polynomial algorithms are known. Furthermore, this operation must be performed for every state encountered during the exploration. For these reasons, it is of great practical importance to work around the orbit problem. In practice, heuristics for the graph isomorphism problem can be reused to obtain significant speedups. In case these do not work, one can revert to a suboptimal approach in which (not necessarily unique) *normalized* states are stored and compared.

The use of symmetry has been studied in the context of various automated verification techniques. We mention here only a few papers that are most closely related to our work, which is in the context of asynchronous systems. For a more complete overview we refer to the bibliography of [19]. Emerson and Sistla have applied the idea to CTL model checking in [10], with extensions to fairness in [13] and [15]. In [10] they outlined a method for efficient calculation of a canonical representative for a special case when the global state vector consists only of individual process locations (program counters), i.e., no variables are allowed. In [11], Emerson and Trefler extended the concepts to real-time logics, while in [12] they considered systems that are *almost* symmetric and they also adapted the method for finding a canonical representative from [10] in the context of symbolic model checking. Clarke, Enders, Filkorn, and Jha used symmetries in the context of symbolic model checking in [4] where they proposed a heuristic involving multiple representatives of equivalence classes. Emerson, Jha, and Peled, and more recently Godefroid, have studied the combination of partial order and symmetry reductions, see [9,14]. Our work draws upon the ideas of Dill and Ip [17,18,19]. They introduce, in the protocol description language Murφ, a new data type called *scalarset* by which the user can point out (full) symmetries to the verification tool. The values of scalarsets are finite in number, unordered, and allow only a restricted number of operations, that do not break symmetry; any violations can be detected at compile time.

We take the approach of Ip and Dill as the starting point. In order to work around the orbit problem, we follow their idea of *splitting* the state vector — the following is adapted from [17]:

> We separate the state into two parts. The leftmost (most significant) part is canonicalized (by picking the lexicographically smallest equivalent as a representative). Because the same lexicographical value may be obtained from different permutations, we may have a few canonicalizing permutations for this part of the state. The second, rightmost part is *normalized* by one of the permutations used to canonicalize the first part. The result is a normalized state of a small lexicographical value.

In this paper, we improve on this idea by exploiting another degree of freedom, namely the freedom to choose the ordering of variables in the state vector, on which the lexicographical ordering is based. Viewed differently, we reshuffle the positions of variables in the state vector — but only *conceptually* so! — before splitting it. In doing so, the goal is to move certain variables to the left so as to reduce the number of permutations that is determined by canonicalizing the leftmost part. Reshuffling of the state vector is done by searching for an array that is indexed by a scalarset type. This *main array* is then conceptually positioned at the leftmost end of the state vector. This results in a new heuristic for normalization, called the *sorted strategy*. A second improvement ensues by not using one of the permutations obtained from canonicalizing the leftmost part of the state vector, but using all of them in order to *canonicalize* the second part. This *segmented strategy* induces the same reduction as canonicalization of the state vector without splitting—which we have also implemented for reference purposes (*full strategy*)—but involves a much smaller overhead in time, as is demonstrated by our experiments.

We have also implemented a variation on this, which is particularly useful when no main array occurs in the system description. Namely, in the case that the process identities are of type scalarset, a main array can be coined by putting the program counters of the individual processes together in an array. The resulting strategies are called *pc-sorted* and *pc-segmented*.

In order to compare these 5 strategies, we have implemented them on top of the Spin model checker [16]. Building upon results reported in [9], our extension is compatible with Spin's partial order reduction algorithm, which is another, orthogonal approach to reduce the state space, and indeed one of the major strengths of the Spin tool. A more detailed description of the implementation can be found in [3]. In this paper we concentrate more on the theoretical aspects and the methodology.

We are aware of only one other attempt to extend Spin with symmetry reductions [21]. With their implementation the user himself (herself) has to write a function that computes the normalized state. As a consequence, it is hard to see how this approach can be generalized. Moreover, it might require quite a deep knowledge of Spin's internal workings.

Our current implementation preserves all safety properties. A large number of experiments have been conducted that show good results (Section 5).

2   Preliminaries

A *transition system* is a tuple $T = (\mathcal{S}, s_0, \rightarrow)$ where $\mathcal{S}$ is a set of states, $s_0 \in \mathcal{S}$ is an initial state, and $\rightarrow \subseteq \mathcal{S} \times \mathcal{S}$ is a transition relation. We assume that $\mathcal{S}$ contains an error state $e \neq s_0$ which is a sink state (whenever $e \rightarrow s$ then $s = e$).

An equivalence relation on $\mathcal{S}$, say $\sim$, is called a *congruence* on T iff for all $s_1, s_2, s_1' \in \mathcal{S}$ such that $s_1 \sim s_2$ and $s_1 \rightarrow s_1'$, there exists $s_2' \in \mathcal{S}$ such that $s_1' \sim s_2'$ and $s_2 \rightarrow s_2'$. Any congruence on T induces a quotient transition system $T/\!\!\sim = (\mathcal{S}/\!\!\sim, [s_0], \Rightarrow)$ such that $[s] \Rightarrow [s']$ iff there exists a transition $q \rightarrow q'$, such that $q \in [s]$, $q' \in [s']$.

A bijection $h : \mathcal{S} \to \mathcal{S}$ is said to be a *symmetry* of T iff $h(s_0) = s_0$, $h(e) = e$, and for any $s, s' \in \mathcal{S}$, $s \to s'$ iff $h(s) \to h(s')$. The set of all symmetries of T forms a group (with function composition).

Any set A of symmetries generates a subgroup $G(A)$ called a *symmetry group* (induced by A). $G(A)$ induces an equivalence relation $\sim_A$ on states, defined as

$$s \sim_A s' \text{ iff } h(s) = s', \text{ for some } h \in G(A)$$

Such an equivalence relation is called a *symmetry relation* of T (induced by A). The equivalence class of s is called the *orbit* of s, and is denoted by $[s]_A$.

Any symmetry relation of T is a congruence on T (Theorem 1 in [18]), and thus induces the quotient transition system $T/\sim_A$. Moreover, s is reachable from s_0 if and only if $[s]_A$ is reachable from $[s_0]_A$ (Theorem 2 in [18]). This allows to reduce the verification of safety properties of T to the reachability of the error state $[e]$ in $T/\sim_A$ (via observers, for example).

In principle, it is not difficult to extend an enumerative model checker to handle symmetries, i.e., to explore $T/\sim_A$ instead of T. Provided with a set A of symmetries and a function $rep : \mathcal{S} \to \mathcal{S}$ which for a given state s picks up a representative state from $[s]_A$, one can explore $T/\sim_A$ by simply exploring a part of T, using $rep(s)$ instead of s. A generic algorithm of this type is given in Section 4. In the sequel, by a *reduction strategy* we mean any concrete rep.

When choosing a reduction strategy one has to deal with two contradictory requirements: rep should both lead to a substantial reduction of the explored state space and be computationally inexpensive. Obviously, the best reduction of the state space is obtained if rep is *canonical* (i.e., $rep(s) = rep(s')$ whenever $s \sim_A s'$) since then the explored part of T is isomorphic with $T/\sim_A$. On the other hand, a canonical rep may be computationally costly and the time overhead caused by using it can substantially exceed the time savings gained by exploring a smaller state space.

In Section 3 we formally define several reduction strategies and then, in Section 5, compare their performance on several examples.

3   Reduction Strategies

Assume a model is specified by a program in a programming language based on shared variables. The variables are typed, and the types are of two kinds only: *simple* types (say, finite ranges of integers) and *array* types. An array type can be represented by a pair $I \mapsto E$ of types where I is the type of indices and E is the type of elements. I must be simple while E can be any type that does not depend on $I \mapsto E$. Let $\mathcal{D}_T$ denote the set of all values of type T then a value of an array type $I \mapsto E$ is a function $a : \mathcal{D}_I \to \mathcal{D}_E$. We write $a[i]$ instead of $a(i)$.

We assume that a program specifies a set of processes run in parallel, and that the processes use only global variables. (The latter assumption is not essential. We use it only to simplify the presentation.) Let $\mathcal{V}$ denote the set of variables used in the program and $\mathcal{D}$ denote the union of $\mathcal{D}_T$, for all types T used in the program. A program P induces a transition system T_P, via a formal semantics of the programming language. We assume that in the semantics states are pairs $(s_\mathcal{V}, s_{PC})$ where $s_\mathcal{V} : \mathcal{V} \to \mathcal{D}$ is the valuation of program variables and s_{PC} represents the values of program counters, for each process in P. For $s = (s_\mathcal{V}, s_{PC})$ and $v \in \mathcal{V}$, $s(v)$ means $s_\mathcal{V}(v)$.

In order to simplify the detection of symmetries in T_P, we assume a special simple type called Pid which is a scalarset (i.e., an unordered subrange of integers from 0 to $n - 1$, for some fixed n). Its elements are called $pids$ (for $process$ $identifiers$). We assume that all programs are of the form $B\|C_0\| \cdots \|C_{n-1}$ where B is a $base$ process and $C_0, \ldots, C_{n-1}$ are instances of a parameterized family $C = \lambda i : Pid \ . \ C_i$ of processes. Notice that Pid can be used as any other simple type, for example, to index arrays.

For such a class of programs, it is convenient to treat the program counters of the family C as an array indexed by pids, and to consider it as a global variable. Thus, in $s = (s_\mathcal{V}, s_{PC})$, the program counters of the family C are in fact "stored" in the component $s_\mathcal{V}$, and s_{PC} represents only the program counter of B.

Let $\mathcal{P}$ denote the set (in fact, the group) of all pid permutations. A pid permutation $p : Pid \to Pid$ can be lifted to states, via $p^* : \mathcal{S} \to \mathcal{S}$. Intuitively, p^* applies p to all values of type Pid that occur in a state, including the pids used as array indices. Formally, for $s = (s_\mathcal{V}, s_{PC})$, we have $p^*(s) = (\lambda v.\bar{p}_{type(v)}(s_\mathcal{V}(v)), s_{PC})$ where $\bar{p}_T : \mathcal{D}_T \to \mathcal{D}_T$ is defined as

$$\begin{aligned} \bar{p}_T(d) &= d \qquad \text{if } T \text{ is a simple type other than } Pid \\ \bar{p}_{Pid}(d) &= p(d) \\ \bar{p}_{I \mapsto E}(a) &= \lambda i \in \mathcal{D}_I . \bar{p}_E(a[\bar{p}_I(i)]) \end{aligned}$$

In fact, p^* is a symmetry of T_P (Theorem 3 in [18]). Moreover, $\mathcal{P}^* = \{p^* : p \in \mathcal{P}\}$ is a symmetry group of T_P (since $(\cdot)^*$ preserves the group operations of $\mathcal{P}$). In fact, $\mathcal{P}$ and $\mathcal{P}^*$ are isomorphic (with $(\cdot)^*$ as an isomorphism).

All the reduction strategies considered in this paper have the same pattern. For a given state, a set of pid permutations is generated, and each permutation is applied to the given state. All the states obtained in this way are equivalent w.r.t. the symmetry relation, and we choose one of them as a representative. Formally, this process is specified by a function $rep : \mathcal{S} \to \mathcal{S}$ defined as

$$rep(s) = \mu(\{p^*(s) : p \in \pi(s)\})$$

where $\mu : 2^\mathcal{S} \to \mathcal{S}$ is a choice function (i.e., $\mu(X) \in X$, for any nonempty $X \subseteq \mathcal{S}$) and $\pi : \mathcal{S} \to 2^\mathcal{P}$ generates a set of pid permutations for a given state.

We call such rep a $general$ reduction strategy since it is parameterized by π and μ. A $concrete$ reduction strategy is obtained from rep by fixing some π, and is denoted by rep_π. In the sequel, we consider several concrete strategies which we call full, sorted, segmented, pc-sorted and pc-segmented. The names denote the respective π functions in rep_π, and whenever we say "strategy π" we really mean "strategy rep_π".

In the full strategy, all pid permutations are taken into account, thus $\mathsf{full}(s) = \mathcal{P}$. Since this strategy is canonical, for any choice function μ, it leads to the best reduction of the state space. However, it is computationally intensive.

In order to improve the full strategy we make two assumptions. In fact, the assumptions are needed only for presentation purposes (we want to *derive* the improvements to full, and not just state them). As it will turn out later, they can be dropped.

First, we assume a choice function of a particular kind, namely the one which picks up the lexicographically smallest state, under some lexicographical ordering of states. Formally, let us assume that each simple type used in a program is totally ordered, and that the order of pids is just the natural order of the set $\{0, \ldots, n-1\}$.[1] As usual, such a total order can be lifted to the lexicographical order on arrays (by considering them as vectors), and then to states (by considering them as vectors).

Second, we assume that program P uses a variable $M : Pid \mapsto E$ which is an array indexed by pids and whose elements do not involve pids. M is called a *main array*. Most real protocols specified in a language based on shared variables, and of the form $B||C_0|| \cdots ||C_{n-1}$, use such an array, either directly or indirectly. (Notice that each local variable declared in the parametric program $C = \lambda i : Pid \, . \, C_i$, and whose type does not involve Pid, can be considered an element of an array indexed by Pid, when lifted to the global level.) We further assume that M dominates in the total order used by our particular choice function μ, in the sense that the main array is located at the beginning of the state vector. (If it is not the case, the state vector can be reshuffled.)

Let us consider a state s. Notice that if $rep_{\text{full}}(s) = s'$ then $s'(M)$ must be sorted, w.r.t. the ordering of E, due to our particular choice of μ. So instead of considering all pid permutations in full it is enough to consider only those which sort $s(M)$. (Notice that there may be more than one sorting permutation, if $s(M)$ contains repeated values.) Let $\vec{s}(M)$ denote the set of all sorting permutations.

In the sorted strategy we consider just one pid permutation $\vec{p} \in \vec{s}(M)$ obtained by applying a particular sorting algorithm to $s(M)$. (Formally, sorted$(s) = \{\vec{p}\}$.) Obviously, the rep_{sorted} strategy is faster then rep_{full}. Unfortunately, it is not canonical since $\vec{p}$ minimizes only $s(M)$ and not necessarily the whole s. (If $s(M)$ contains repeated values then there may be another sorting permutation p such that $p^*(s)$ is smaller than $\vec{p}^*(s)$.)

In the segmented strategy we consider all the permutations in $\vec{s}(M)$.[2] (Formally, segmented$(s) = \vec{s}(M)$.) Obviously, $rep_{\text{segmented}}$ is canonical, for the particular choice function we have assumed. Moreover, $rep_{\text{segmented}}(s) = rep_{\text{full}}(s)$, for any s.

As an example, consider the following picture showing a state vector before and after sorting its main array M.

---

[1] This is not inconsistent with the assumption that Pid is a scalarset, and thus unordered. In fact, a scalarset can be ordered but a program that uses such a scalarset must not depend on the order (all the models of the program obtained under different orderings must be isomorphic).

[2] The name "segmented" comes from the way we have implemented the computation of segmented(s). We first sort $s(M)$, locate all the segments of equal values in the sorted array, and permute these segments independently.

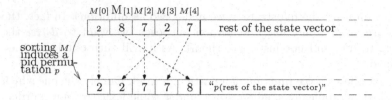

M is indexed by pids, which in this case range from 0 to 4. M's elements are the numbers 2, 7, and 8, taken from some type that differs from Pid. Suppose that the particular sorting algorithm being used sorts M as indicated by the dashed arrows. This particular sorting induces the pid permutation $p = \{0 \mapsto 0, 1 \mapsto 4, 2 \mapsto 2, 3 \mapsto 1, 4 \mapsto 3\}$, which is then applied to the rest of the state vector in order to obtain the representative under the **sorted** strategy. If we applied *all* pid permutations to the upper state vector in the picture, then the lexicographical minimum among the results, call it $s_{\min}$, would start with the same values as the lower state vector, namely 2, 2, 7, 7, 8. However, the rest of $s_{\min}$ need not coincide with the rest of the lower state vector. The reason is that there are other pid permutations that yield the same initial values, for example $p' = \{0 \mapsto 1, 1 \mapsto 4, 2 \mapsto 3, 3 \mapsto 0, 4 \mapsto 2\}$, but may give smaller results than p. The **segmented** strategy applies all the permutations that sort M (in this example there are four of them) on the whole state vector, and selects the smallest among the results, which is then guaranteed to be $s_{\min}$.

The requirement that program P uses an explicit main array can be dropped, by observing that in every program of the form $B||C_0||\cdots||C_{n-1}$ there is, in fact, an implicit array indexed by pids, namely the array of program counters for processes $C_0,\ldots,C_{n-1}$. Thus, we can consider the variants of **sorted** and **segmented** in which we use the array of program counters instead of M. The variants are called **pc-sorted** and **pc-segmented**, respectively. If P contains a main array as well then both **sorted/segmented** and **pc-sorted/pc-segmented** are applicable to P, so the question arises which of the combinations is better. We cannot say much about **sorted** versus **pc-sorted**, in general. However, **segmented** and **pc-segmented** are both canonical, so they are equally good, as far as the reduction of a state space is considered.

The following result allows us to drop the assumption about our particular μ function.

Theorem 1. *For any choice function μ, rep*_{segmented} *is canonical.*

Proof. Let $P(s) = \{p^*(s) : p \in \mathsf{segmented}(s)\}$. We have to show that if $s \sim s'$, i.e., there exists a pid permutation p such that $p^*(s) = s'$, then $\mu(P(s)) = \mu(P(s'))$. In order to show it for any choice function μ, it is enough to show that $P(s) = P(s')$. Assume $s_1 \in P(s)$ then $s_1 = p_1^*(s)$ for some pid permutation p_1, where p_1^* sorts the array M in s. Observe that $s = (p^{-1})^*(s')$ where p^{-1} is the inverse of p. Hence, $s_1 = p_1^*((p^{-1})^*(s'))$. Since $p_1^* \circ (p^{-1})^*$ sorts the array M in s', $s_1 \in P(s')$. Similarly, if $s_1 \in P(s')$ then $s_1 \in P(s)$.

Remark 1. In the proof, the only step specific to the segmented strategy is the observation that if p establishes the equivalence of states s and s', and p_1^* sorts the array M, then also $p_1^* \circ (p^{-1})^*$ sorts the array M. Thus, the theorem can be generalized to any strategy π that preserves pid permutations in the following sense: if p establishes the equivalence of states s and s' then for any $p_1 \in \pi(s)$, $p_1^* \circ (p^{-1})^* \in \pi(s')$. For example, this condition holds for the full and pc-segmented strategy as well.

The theorem has an important practical consequence. Suppose we want to extend an existing enumerative model checker with symmetry reductions. Usually, a model checker stores a state in a continuous chunk of memory. A very efficient way of implementing μ is to choose the lexicographically smallest chunk by simply comparing such memory chunks byte by byte (for example, in C, the built-in function memcmp could be used for this purpose). By Theorem 1, such μ is a choice function, no matter where the main array resides in the memory chunk. Thus, the requirement that the main array dominates in the total order used by μ is not needed. Also, the array of program counters, used in pc-sorted and pc-segmented, need not even be be contiguous. As a consequence, we do not need to reshuffle a state vector in order to use the presented strategies.

Finally, the assumption that programs are of the form $B||C_0|| \cdots ||C_{n-1}$ with process indices in the scalarset *Pid* is only needed to formalize the pc-sorted and pc-segmented strategies. For segmented and sorted, the only essential assumption about *Pid* is that it is a distinguished scalarset.

In Section 5 we compare, on several examples, the performance of all the concrete strategies introduced above.

4   Extending Spin with Symmetry Reductions

In order to compare the performance of the various reduction strategies in practice, we have embedded them into the enumerative model checker Spin [16]. In principle, extending an existing enumerative model checker to handle symmetries is not difficult, once the *rep* function is implemented. Instead of using a standard algorithm for exploring $T = (\mathcal{S}, s_0, \rightarrow)$, as depicted in Fig. 1, one explores the quotient $T/\sim$ using a simple modification of the algorithm, as depicted in Fig. 2. (This modification is borrowed from [18].)

In practice, we had to overcome several problems, due to idiosyncrasies of Spin. For example, it turned out that the operation "add $rep(s')$ to *unexpanded*" is difficult to implement reliably, due to a peculiar way Spin represents the set *unexpanded* as a set of "differences" between states rather than states themselves. For this reason, we had to change the exploration algorithm given in Fig. 2. In our[3] algorithm, the original states, and not their representatives, are used to generate the state space to be explored, as depicted in Fig. 3.

Obviously, our algorithm is still sound. Moreover, it allows to easily regenerate an erroneous trace from the set *unexpanded*, in case an error is encountered.

---

[3] We acknowledge a remark from Gerard Holzmann which led us to this algorithm.

$$reached := unexpanded := \{s_0\};$$
$$\text{while } unexpanded \neq \varnothing \text{ do}$$
$$\qquad \text{remove a state } s \text{ from } unexpanded;$$
$$\qquad \text{for each transition } s \rightarrow s' \text{ do}$$
$$\qquad\qquad \text{if } s' = \textbf{error} \text{ then}$$
$$\qquad\qquad\qquad \text{stop and report error;}$$
$$\qquad\qquad \text{if } s' \notin reached \text{ then}$$
$$\qquad\qquad\qquad \text{add } s' \text{ to } reached \text{ and } unexpanded;$$

Fig. 1. A standard exploration algorithm

$$reached := unexpanded := \{rep(s_0)\};$$
$$\text{while } unexpanded \neq \varnothing \text{ do}$$
$$\qquad \text{remove a state } s \text{ from } unexpanded;$$
$$\qquad \text{for each transition } s \rightarrow s' \text{ do}$$
$$\qquad\qquad \text{if } s' = \textbf{error} \text{ then}$$
$$\qquad\qquad\qquad \text{stop and report error;}$$
$$\qquad\qquad \text{if } rep(s') \notin reached \text{ then}$$
$$\qquad\qquad\qquad \text{add } rep(s') \text{ to } reached \text{ and } unexpanded;$$

Fig. 2. A standard exploration algorithm with symmetry reductions

$$reached := \{rep(s_0)\}; \; unexpanded := \{s_0\};$$
$$\text{while } unexpanded \neq \varnothing \text{ do}$$
$$\qquad \text{remove a state } s \text{ from } unexpanded;$$
$$\qquad \text{for each transition } s \rightarrow s' \text{ do}$$
$$\qquad\qquad \text{if } s' = \textbf{error} \text{ then}$$
$$\qquad\qquad\qquad \text{stop and report error;}$$
$$\qquad\qquad \text{if } rep(s') \notin reached \text{ then}$$
$$\qquad\qquad\qquad \text{add } rep(s') \text{ to } reached \text{ and } s' \text{ to } unexpanded;$$

Fig. 3. Our exploration algorithm with symmetry reductions

Since Spin explores the state space in a depth first manner, the set *unexpanded* is in fact structured as a stack. When an error is encountered the stack contains the sequence of states that lead to the error, and its contents can directly be dumped as the erroneous trace. In the algorithm from Fig. 2, the stack would contain the representatives of the original states, and since the representatives are not necessarily related by the transition relation in the original model, the stack would not necessarily represent an existing trace in the original model.

If *rep* is canonical, both algorithms explore the same state space (since they agree on the *reached* set). However, notice that there could still be a difference in their execution times, if the numbers of the successor states s' considered in the loop "for each transition $s \rightarrow s'$ do" were different. It can easily be proved that this is not a case. Whenever our algorithm computes the successors of s, the algorithm in Fig. 2 computes the successors of $rep(s)$. Since s and $rep(s)$ are related by a symmetry, they must have the same number of successors (recall that any symmetry is a bijection).

If *rep* is not canonical, then the number of explored states and transitions differs between the two algorithms and depends on the choice of *rep*. The algorithms are incomparable in this case: It can happen that our algorithm explores fewer states and/or transitions than the algorithm in Fig. 2, or vice versa.

We also put an effort into efficiently implementing the 5 variants of the `rep` function. For example, it turns out that all the sets of pid permutations used in our reduction strategies can always be enumerated starting with an initial permutation and then composing it with transpositions (permutations that swap two elements). As a consequence, the most costly operation p^* (that applies a given pid permutation to a given state) can be optimized by using two versions of p^*. In addition to the general version that is applicable to any pid permutation, we also use a restricted (and more efficient) version that is only applicable to transpositions. Our implementation is described in [3].

In the verification experiments described in the next section, we used Spin in two ways: with and without its partial order reduction (POR) algorithm. Allowing Spin to use its POR algorithm together with our symmetry reductions is sound due to Theorem 19 in [9] which guarantees that the class of POR algorithms to which the Spin's POR algorithm belongs, is compatible with the generic symmetry reduction algorithm. With a straightforward modification, the theorem's proof is valid for our algorithm as well.

It can be shown [1] that the nested depth-first search algorithm of [6], which is used in Spin for cycle detection, remains correct with the symmetry reduction. This implies that we can go beyond safety properties, or more precisely, the full class of ω-regular correctness properties can be handled by Spin.[4]

5   Experimental Results

We tried our prototype implementation on several examples. The experiments showed that there is no favorite among the reduction strategies regarding the space/time ratio. This suggests that it makes sense to have all strategies (maybe except full) as separate options of the extended model-checker. In most of the cases there was a synergy between the symmetry and the partial order reductions. The two reduction techniques are orthogonal because they exploit different features of the concurrent systems, therefore, their cumulative effect can be used to obtain more efficient verification.

In the sequel, we present the results for three of the examples. All experiments were performed on a Sun Ultra-Enterprise machine, with three 248 MHz UltraSPARC-II processors and 2304MB of main memory, running the SunOS 5.5.1 operating system. Verification times (in the rows labeled with "t") are given in seconds $(s.x)$, minutes $(m{:}s)$, or hours $(h{:}m{:}s)$; the number of states (in the rows labeled with "s") is given directly or in millions (say, 9.1M); *o.m.* stands for out of memory, and *o.t.* denotes out of time (more than 10 hours); +POR and -POR mean with and without POR, respectively.

---

[4] In fact, as pointed out in [4,10], the property to be checked should also be symmetric. More precisely, the property should be invariant under any permutation of Pids.

528   D. Bošnački, D. Dams, and L. Holenderski

Peterson's Mutual Exclusion algorithm [20]. For this well known example[5] we verified the mutual exclusion property. The results for different numbers N of processes are shown below.

Table 1. Results for Peterson's mutual exclusion algorithm

N		2		3		4		5		6		7	
		+POR	-POR	+POR	-POR	+POR	-POR	+POR	-POR	+POR	-POR	+POR	-POR
no sym.	s	154	263	4992	11318	202673	542921	9.1M	o.m.	o.m.	o.m.	o.m.	o.m.
	t	6.5	5.6	6.8	6.3	25.0	1:09	19:04	—	—	—	—	—
full	s	89	134	980	1976	9634	24383	86112	262749	700543	2.5M[a]	5.3M[a]	o.m.
	t	6.5	5.6	6.7	5.9	10.4	19.3	2:35	12:02	2:04:03	o.t.	o.t.	—
seg.	t	6.7	5.6	6.6	5.8	8.5	12.4	38.0	2:31	7:36	44:40	1:56:00	—
pc-seg.	t	6.5	5.6	6.6	5.8	8.4	11.3	37.4	1:59	10:01	40:46	4:26:32	—
sorted	s	113	160	1877	3967	35644	88489	595843	1.8M	8.8M	o.m.	o.m.	o.m.
	t	6.5	5.6	6.6	6.1	11.0	21.6	1:42	8:13	28:37	—	—	—
pc-sort.	s	92	137	1149	2396	20339	46804	401423	942786	9.6M	o.m.	o.m.	o.m.
	t	6.5	5.6	6.6	5.8	10.2	15.0	1:36	4:53	54:53	—	—	—

[a] The number of states is obtained with segmented and pc-segmented.

The gain due to the symmetry reduction is obvious. The obtained reductions, ranging from 49% (for $N = 2$) to 99% and more (for $N \geq 5$) are close to the theoretical maxima, which can be explained with the high degree of symmetry in the protocol. The verification times are also better, even with the straightforward full strategy, due to the smaller number of states that are generated during the search. We used both symmetry and partial order reduction (which is default in standard Spin), separately and in combination. Standard Spin with partial order reduction could not handle more than 5 processes. However, the segmented versions of the symmetry heuristics alone were sufficient for $N = 6$. For $N = 7$ we had to use a combination of both reduction techniques in order to stay inside the available memory.

The sorted strategies are comparable with their segmented counterparts only for small values of N. For greater values they deteriorate and even the possible gain in time over the segmented versions disappears because of the greater number of states that have to be explored.

One can also expect that as N increases pc-segmented and pc-sorted will loose the advantage they have over segmented and sorted, for smaller values of N. The reason is that the number of different elements in the main array of segmented and sorted increases as N increases, while the number of values of the pc counter stays the same. (We use as a main array the array of flags. Whenever process i enters the competition for the critical section, it sets flag i to a value between 1

---

[5] In our implementation the global predicate that guards the entry in the critical section is checked atomically. As this guard ranges over all process indices, the atomicity was necessary due to the restrictions on statements that can be used such that the state space symmetry is preserved.

and $N - 1$. The default value is 0. Notice that the values of the flag array are not of type *Pid*, although their range is the same as the *Pid* type range.) Intuitively, the greater versatility of the values in the main array, the fewer permutations have to be generated on average, in order to canonicalize the state. This tendency is already visible for $N = 6$ (for which sorted is winning over pc-sorted) as well as for $N = 7$ (for which segmented is better than pc-segmented).

Data Base Manager [22]. The system that we consider consists of $N \geq 2$ data base managers, which modify a data base and exchange messages to ensure the consistency of the data base contents. Our model deals with the procedural part of the protocol, i.e., with the message exchange, by abstracting form the actual modification of the data base. Initially all managers are in inactive state until one of them modifies the data base. This manager in one atomic step reserves the data base for itself and sends a message to every other manager. After that it waits for acknowledgments from the other managers. All other managers concurrently perform a two step sequence: reception of the message, and sending of an acknowledgment. When all acknowledgments are available, the manager who initially modified the data base and started the whole procedure, reads them. At the same moment it also releases the data base so that it can be modified by the other managers, after which it returns to inactive state. We checked the model for absence of deadlock.

Table 2. Results for the Data Base Manager example

N		7		8		9		10		11		12	
		+POR	-POR	+POR	-POR	+POR	-POR	+POR	-POR	+POR	-POR	+POR	-POR
no sym.	s	100	5112	130	17506	164	59060	202	196842	244	649552	290	2.1M
	t	0.0	0.5	0.0	1.9	0.0	8.2	0.0	32.1	0.0	2:11	0.0	8:27
full	s	16	31	18	39	20	48	22	58	24	69	—	—
full	t	0.5	2.0	4.6	24.5	48.0	6:16	9:08	1:27:40	1:55:09	22:07:36	o.t.	o.t.
seg.	t	0.3	0.4	2.8	3.8	28.3	39.1	5:22	7:20	1:06:32	1:30:53	o.t.	o.t.
pc-seg.	t	0.1	0.1	0.8	1.0	7.3	9.1	1:16	1:33	15:16	17:14	o.t.	o.t.
sorted	s	27	250	31	505	35	1016	39	2039	43	4086	47	8181
sorted	t	0.0	0.0	0.0	0.1	0.0	0.2	0.0	0.6	0.0	1.3	0.0	3.1
pc-sort.	s	16	58	18	91	20	155	22	245	24	415	26	659
pc-sort.	t	0.0	0.0	0.0	0.0	0.0	0.0	0.0	0.1	0.0	0.1	0.0	0.3

Our experiments agree with the theoretically predicted results from [22]: Both symmetry and POR applied separately reduce the exponential growth of the state space to quadratic, and in combination they give linear growth. Unlike in the previous example, this time pc-segmented strategy is a clear winner over segmented. The explanation is again in the diversity of the elements occuring in the sorted array – the only possible values of the main array for **segmented** are 0 and 1, while the pc counter has 7 different values. (The main array consists of boolean flags which are set to 1 when a manager reserves the data base and sends a message to all the other processes.) It is interesting that **pc-sorted** in combination with POR is by far the most successful strategy. It achieves the same reduction as the canonical strategies, but within much shorter time. It remains to be seen whether this is just a peculiarity of this model, or it occurs for a wider class of examples.

Base Station. The third example is a simplified version of MASCARA – a telecommunication protocol developed by the WAND (Wireless ATM Network Demonstrator) consortium [7]. The protocol is an extension of the ATM (Asynchronous Transfer Mode) networking protocol to wireless networks. Our model represents a wireless network connecting $N \geq 2$ mobile stations (MS) that may communicate with each other, using a limited number ($M \geq 1$) of radio channels provided by one base station BS. More specifically, when MS A wants to send a message to MS B it must request a channel from BS. Provided there are channels available, A is granted one, call it c. If B wants to receive messages, it queries BS. As there is a pending communication for B through c, BS assigns c to B. After the communication has taken place, both A and B return the channel to BS. The results given below are for checking for unreachable code, with $M = 2$.

Table 3. Results for the Base Station example

N		2		3	
		+POR	-POR	+POR	-POR
no sym.	s	15613	15621	*o.m.*	*o.m.*
	t	7.6	6.4	—	—
full	s	7808	7812	3.4M	3.4M
	t	7.5	6.3	17:39	13:00
seg.	t	5.8	6.3	12:10	9:46
pc-seg.	t	5.9	6.4	13:24	10:18
sorted	s	7856	7860	3.9M	3.9M
	t	7.2	6.3	12:58	9:48
pc-sort.	s	8282	8286	5.1M	5.1M
	t	7.5	6.3	16:48	12:57

For $N = 2$ the symmetry reduction approaches the theoretical limit of 50%. For $N = 3$ standard Spin ran out of memory, while with symmetry reduction it was possible to verify the model. In this example POR did not play a significant role. Also, there was no clear preference between segmented, pc-segmented and sorted.

6   Conclusions and Future Work

We have presented four variants of a new heuristic for coping with the orbit problem in symmetry reduction. Their strength is based on the observation that the lexicographical ordering on state vectors may be tuned to optimize the splitting heuristic of [17]. Of the resulting strategies, the segmented/pc-segmented versions indeed produce canonical representatives of orbits, while sorted/pc-sorted are only normalizing. The sorted and segmented strategies presuppose the presence of a main array in the program. Their pc variants exploit the array of program counters in programs containing a family of similar processes.

We have implemented these strategies in Spin, as well as the full reference strategy, and compared their effects on three programs. The experimental results show that there is no uniform winner: It depends on the program which of the strategies performs best. In some cases, this was in fact predicted by the form of the program. Thus, it make sense to have all strategies (maybe except full) as separate options of the extended model-checker.

The results obtained with this experimental implementation are sufficiently encouraging in order to integrate the symmetry strategies more completely into the Spin tool. One concern here is to ensure the compatibility of the symmetry reduction with Spin's other features. So far, we have focussed on the partial order reduction. Our recent results [1] show that the correctness of Spin's cycle detection algorithm, which lies at the heart of its capability to handle the full class of ω-regular correctness properties, is preserved. Furthermore, the symmetry is compatible with the recent extension to timed systems, DTSpin ([2]). It should be added that the present implementation is able to deal with multiple scalar sets and multiple process families. Also, almost all Promela features are handled, including queues. For the latter there is still the restriction though that the the queue elements have to be simple, non-structured types.

Also, the restrictions on the scalarset variables are as yet not automatically checked. Next, we plan to extend the symmetry algorithm itself with other system topologies, like rings[6]. An interesting question is whether the choice of an appropriate strategy can be automated, based on syntactic clues.

Acknowledgments. The authors would like to thank the anonymous referees for their helpful comments.

---

[6] The group of *shift* permutations can be handled by a simplification of our approach, where instead of sorting the main array, it is cyclically shifted until it starts with a minimal element.

532   D. Bošnački, D. Dams, and L. Holenderski

References

1. D. Bošnački, *Enhancing State Space Reduction Techniques for Model Checking*, Ph.D. Thesis, Department of Computer Science, Eindhoven University of Technology, expected in 2001.
2. D. Bošnački, D. Dams, Integrating real time into Spin: a prototype implementation, in S. Budkowski, A. Cavalli, E. Najm (eds), *Proc. of FORTE/PSTV'98 (Formal Description Techniques and Protocol Specification, Testing and Verification)*, pp. 423–438, Paris, France, 1998.
3. D. Bošnački, D. Dams, L. Holenderski, Symmetric Spin, *SPIN'2000 (The 7th International SPIN Workshop on Model Checking of Software)*, pp. 1–19, LNCS 1885, 2000.
4. E.M. Clarke, R. Enders, T. Filkorn, S. Jha, Exploiting symmetry in temporal logic model checking, *Formal Methods in System Design*, Vol. 19, pp. 77–104, 1996.
5. E.M. Clarke, O. Grumberg, D.A. Peled, *Model Checking*, The MIT Press, 2000.
6. C. Courcoubetis, M. Vardi, P. Wolper, M. Yannakakis, Memory efficient algorithm for the verification of temporal properties, *Formal Methods in System Design I*, pp. 275-288, 1992.
7. I. Dravapoulos, N. Pronios, S. Denazis *et al*, The Magic WAND, Deliverable 3D2, *Wireless ATM MAC*, Sep 1997.
8. E.A. Emerson, Temporal and modal logic, in Jan van Leeuwen (ed.), *Formal Models and Semantic*, Vol. B of *Handbook of Theoretical Computer Science*, Chap. 16, pp. 995–1072, Elsevier/The MIT Press, 1990.
9. E.A. Emerson, S. Jha, D. Peled, Combining partial order and symmetry reductions, in Ed Brinksma (ed.), *Proc. of TACAS'97 (Tools and Algorithms for the Construction and Analysis of Systems)*, LNCS 1217, pp. 19–34, Springer, 1997.
10. E.A. Emerson, A.P. Sistla, Symmetry and model checking, in C. Courcoubetis (ed.), *Proc. of CAV'93 (Computer Aided Verification)*, LNCS 697, pp. 463–478, Springer, 1993.
11. E.A. Emerson, R.J. Trefler, Model checking real-time properties of symmetric systems, *Proc. of the 23rd International Symposium on Mathematical Foundations of Computer Science (MFCS)*, pp. 427–436, Aug. 1998.
12. E.A. Emerson, R.J. Trefler, From asymmetry to full symmetry: new techniques for symmetry reduction in model checking, *Proc. of CHARME'99 (The 10th IFIP WG10.5 Advanced Research Working Conference on Correct Hardware Design and Verification Methods)*, Bad Herrenalb, Germany, Sep. 1999.
13. E.A. Emerson, A.P. Sistla, Utilizing symmetry when model-checking under fairness assumptions: an automata-theoretic approach, *ACM Transactions on Programming Languages and Systems*, 19(4):617–638, July 1997.
14. P. Godefroid, Exploiting symmetry when model-checking software, *Proc. of FORTE/PSTV'99 (Formal Methods for Protocol Engineering and Distributed Systems)*, pp. 257–275, Beijing, Oct. 1999.
15. V. Gyuris, A.P. Sistla, On-the-fly model checking under fairness that exploits symmetry, in O. Grumberg (ed.), *Proc. of CAV'97 (Computer Aided Verification)*, LNCS 1254, pp. 232–243, Springer, 1997.
16. G.J. Holzmann, *Design and Validation of Communication Protocols*, Prentice Hall, 1991. Also: http://netlib.bell-labs.com/netlib/spin/whatispin.html
17. C.N. Ip, D.L. Dill, Better verification through symmetry, in D. Agnew, L. Claesen, R. Camposano (eds), *Proc. of the 1993 Conference on Computer Hardware Description Languages and their Applications*, Apr. 1993.

18. C.N. Ip, D.L. Dill, Better verification through symmetry. *Formal Methods in System Design*, Vol. 9, pp. 41–75, 1996.
19. C.N. Ip, *State Reduction Methods for Automatic Formal Verification*, Ph.D. thesis, Department of Computer Science of Stanford University, Dec 1996.
20. N.A. Lynch, *Distributed Algorithms*, Morgan Kaufmann Publishers, 1996.
21. R. Nalumasu, G. Gopalakrishnan, Explicit-enumeration based Verification made Memory-efficient, *Proc. of CHDL'95 (Computer Hardware Description Languages)*, 617-622, Chiba, Japan, Aug. 1995.
22. A. Valmari, Stubborn sets for reduced state space generation, *Advances in Petri Nets 1990*, LNCS 483, pp. 491–515, Springer, 1991.

View Updatability Based on the Models of a Formal Specification*

Michael Johnson[1] and Robert Rosebrugh[2]

[1] Macquarie University, Sydney, Australia,
mike@ics.mq.edu.au
[2] Mount Allison University, NB, Canada
rrosebru@mta.ca

Abstract. Information system software productivity can be increased by improving the maintainability and modifiability of the software produced. This latter in turn can be achieved by the provision of comprehensive support for *views*, since view support allows application programs to continue to operate unchanged when the underlying information system is modified. But, supporting views depends upon a solution to the *view update problem*, and proposed solutions to date have only had limited, rather than comprehensive, applicability. This paper presents a new treatment of view updates for formally specified information systems. The formal specification technique we use is based on *category theory* and has been the basis of a number of successful major information system consultancies. We define view updates by a universal property in a subcategory of models of the formal specification, and explain why this indeed gives a comprehensive treatment of view updatability, including a solution to the view update problem. However, a definition of updatability which is based on models causes some inconvenience in applications, so we prove that in a variety of circumstances updatability is guaranteed independently of the current model. The paper is predominantly theoretical, as it develops the theoretical basis of a formal methods technique, but the methods described here are currently being used in a large consultancy for a government Department of Health. Because the application area, information systems, is rarely treated by formal methods, we include some detail about the formal methods used. In fact they are extensions of the usual category theoretic specification techniques, and the solution to the view update problem can be seen as requiring the existence of an initial model for a specification.

Keywords: View update, database, formal specification, information system, category theory, conceptual modelling, data model.

---

* Research partially supported by the Australian Research Council, NSERC Canada, and the Oxford Computing Laboratory. The authors are grateful for that support, and also for the advice of the anonymous referees.

J.N. Oliveira and P. Zave (Eds.): FME 2001, LNCS 2021, pp. 534–549, 2001.

1   Introduction

Much of the progress of software engineering has been based on limiting the ramifications of software modifications. After correctness, and avoiding gross inefficiencies, producing modifiable code is of prime concern.

In the information systems field, the need for maintainable and easily modifiable software is becoming consistently more important with the dependency on legacy code and the growth of the need for systems interoperability, whether for business-to-business transactions, internet based interfaces, or interdivisional cooperation within an organisation.

Many information systems attempt to address this issue by providing a *view* mechanism. Views allow data derived from the underlying information system to be structured in an appropriate way. Provided that views are used as the interface between an information system and other software, the information system can be modified and, as long as the view mechanism is correspondingly modified, the external software will continue to work.

Typically, the "appropriate" structure for a view is a database interface, allowing data to be queried, inserted, or deleted, as if the system were a stand-alone database. But importantly, not all view inserts and deletes can be permitted since the view data are derived from the underlying information system, and apparently reasonable changes to the view may be prohibited or ambiguous when applied to the information system. We will see examples below, but for a text book treatment the reader is referred to Chapter 8 of [13]. The *view update problem* is to determine when and how updates of views can be propagated to the underlying information system.

Views have been the subject of considerable research, including for example [22], [23], [29], and [1]. The difficulty of obtaining a comprehensive solution to the view update problem has led to systems which offer only limited view mechanisms. Furthermore, the relatively limited use of formal methods (as opposed to semi-formal methodologies) in information system specification has resulted in views being defined either informally, or solely in terms of the underlying information system's schema. Both of these hamper the use of the view mechanism in facilitating program reuse when the underlying information system changes significantly.

The authors and their coworkers have, over a number of years, been developing a formal method for information system specification based on category theory. The impetus for its development came from a very large consultancy [7] which compelled us to use formal methods to manage the complexity. The techniques we use, recently called the *sketch data model* because they are based upon the category theoretic notion of mixed sketch [3], have since been developed considerably and tested in other consultancies including [10] and [8].

This paper develops a detailed approach to views and view updatability based on the sketch data model. After defining the sketch data model in Section 2 we define views (Section 3) in a manner that is designed to permit a wide range of data accessible from the underlying information system to be structured in the view in any manner describable in the sketch data model.

A solution to the view update problem needs to determine when and how view updates can be propagated to the underlying information system. Typically the *when* is determined by definition — certain view updates are defined to be updatable, and then for those updates the *how* is given by specifying the translation of each view update into an update of the underlying information system. Unfortunately this approach can lead to ad hoc treatments as each discovery of new *hows* leads to an adjustment of the defined *whens*, and naturally we should not expect such solutions to be complete — they really represent a list of those view updates that a system is currently able to propagate. Instead, in Section 4 we define the *when* and *how* together using a universal property [26], and we indicate how the nature of the universal property ensures a certain completeness.

Interestingly the universal property we use is based upon the *models* of the specification when previous solutions have usually defined updatability in terms of schemata (the signatures of the specifications). This is very important for the theoretical development. Nevertheless, in Section 5 we prove a number or propositions that show that, for a range of schemata, view updatability can be determined independently of the models. Such results considerably simplify the application of the theory in industry.

After reviewing related work in Section 6, we conclude by enumerating the limitations and advantages of our approach. We note that it is presumably the appeal of schemata based view updatability that has drawn previous workers into defining updatability in terms of schemata. We would argue that it is this that has led to view updatability being seen as a difficult problem.

2   Category Theoretic Information System Specification

This section provides the mathematical foundation for the sketch data model. It is based on categorical universal algebra, which is the basis of widely used formal method specification techniques [16]. We assume some familiarity with elementary category theory, as might be obtained in [3], [26] or [30]. The graphs we use will always be what have sometimes been called "directed multi-graphs, possibly with loops", see for example [3] page 7. The limits and colimits we will deal with will all be finite in our applications.

Definition 1 A *cone* $C = (C_b, C_v)$ in a graph G consists of a graph I and a graph morphism $C_b : I \longrightarrow G$ (the *base* of C), a node C_v of G (the *vertex* of C) and, for each node i in I, an edge $e_i : C_v \longrightarrow C_b i$. *Cocones* are dual (that is we reverse all the edges of G which occur in the definition, so the new definition is the same except that the last phrase requires edges $e_i : C_b i \longrightarrow C_v$). The edges e_i in a cone (respectively cocone) are called *projections* (respectively *injections*).

Definition 2 A *sketch* $\mathbb{E} = (G, \mathbf{D}, \mathcal{L}, \mathcal{C})$ consists of a graph G, a set $\mathbf{D}$ of pairs of directed paths in G with common source and target (called the commutative diagrams) and sets of cones ($\mathcal{L}$) and cocones ($\mathcal{C}$) in G.

Every category has an underlying sketch: Let G be the underlying graph of the category, $\mathbf{D}$ the set of all commutative diagrams, and $\mathcal{L}$ (respectively $\mathcal{C}$) the set of all limit cones (respectively colimit cocones). Of course underlying sketches are usually not small. The advantage of the theory of sketches is that we can frequently use a sketch to give a finite presentation of an infinite category.

Definition 3 Let $\mathbb{E} = (G, \mathbf{D}, \mathcal{L}, \mathcal{C})$ and $\mathbb{E}' = (G', \mathbf{D}', \mathcal{L}', \mathcal{C}')$ be sketches. A *sketch morphism* $h : \mathbb{E} \longrightarrow \mathbb{E}'$ is a graph morphism $G \longrightarrow G'$ which carries, by composition, diagrams in $\mathbf{D}$, cones in $\mathcal{L}$ and cocones in $\mathcal{C}$ to respectively diagrams in $\mathbf{D}'$, cones in $\mathcal{L}'$ and cocones in $\mathcal{C}'$.

Definition 4 A *model* M of a sketch $\mathbb{E}$ in a category $\mathbf{S}$ is a graph morphism from G to the underlying graph of the category $\mathbf{S}$ such that the images of pairs of paths in $\mathbf{D}$ have equal composites in $\mathbf{S}$ and cones (respectively cocones) in $\mathcal{L}$ (respectively in $\mathcal{C}$) have images which are limit cones (respectively colimit cocones) in $\mathbf{S}$.

Equivalently, a model is a sketch morphism from $\mathbb{E}$ to the underlying sketch of the category $\mathbf{S}$. We can also express models in terms of functors as follows.

To each sketch $\mathbb{E}$ there is a corresponding *theory* [3] which we denote by $Q\mathbb{E}$. The theory corresponding to $\mathbb{E}$ should be thought of as the category presented by the sketch $\mathbb{E}$. For our applications this will be the free category with finite limits and finite colimits generated by the graph G subject to the relations given by $\mathbf{D}$, $\mathcal{L}$ and $\mathcal{C}$, or some subcategory thereof.

Using the evident inclusion $G \longrightarrow Q\mathbb{E}$ we will sometimes refer to nodes of G as objects, edges of G as arrows and (co)cones of $\mathbb{E}$ as (co)cones in $Q\mathbb{E}$. If $\mathbf{S}$ has finite limits and finite colimits then a model M of $\mathbb{E}$ in $\mathbf{S}$ extends uniquely to a functor $QM : Q\mathbb{E} \longrightarrow \mathbf{S}$ which preserves finite limits and finite colimits.

Definition 5 If M and M' are models a *homomorphism* $\phi : M \longrightarrow M'$ is a natural transformation from QM to QM'. Models and homomorphisms determine a category of models of $\mathbb{E}$ in $\mathbf{S}$ denoted by $\mathrm{Mod}(\mathbb{E}, \mathbf{S})$, a full subcategory of the functor category $[Q\mathbb{E}, \mathbf{S}]$.

We speak of (limit-class, colimit-class) sketches when $\mathcal{L}$ and $\mathcal{C}$ are required to contain (co)cones only from the specified (co)limit-classes. When the specified classes do not include all finite (co)limits we can restrict the theory corresponding to such a sketch to be closed only under the specified limits and colimits and the functor QM will only need to preserve the specified limits and colimits. For example, (finite-product, $\emptyset$) sketches correspond to (multi-sorted) algebraic theories, their theories are categories with finite products and their model functors QM preserve finite products.

Definition 6 An *SkDM sketch* $\mathbb{E} = (G, \mathbf{D}, \mathcal{L}, \mathcal{C})$ is a (finite limit, finite coproduct) sketch such that

- There is a specified cone with empty base in $\mathcal{L}$. Its vertex will be called 1. Arrows with domain 1 are called *elements*.
- Nodes which are vertices of cocones whose injections are elements are called *attributes*. Nodes which are neither attributes, nor 1, are called *entities*.
- The graph of G is finite.

An SkDM sketch is used for specifying information systems. An SkDM sketch is sometimes called *a* sketch data model, while *the* sketch data model usually refers to the sketch data modelling formal methodology.

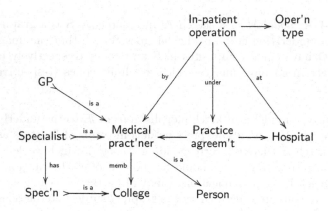

Fig. 1. A fragment of a graph for an SkDM sketch

Example 7 Figure 1 is part of the graph of an artificial SkDM sketch, derived from a fragment of a real sketch data model [8]. The other components of this SkDM sketch are as follows: **D** contains both triangles; $\mathcal{L}$ contains the empty cone with vertex 1 (not shown), the square (whose diagonal, one of the projections, is also not shown) and three further cones intended to ensure that the three arrows indicated $\rightarrowtail$ are realised as monics; and $\mathcal{C}$ contains the cocone with vertex Medical practitioner and base Specialist and GP (short for General practitioner), along with a number of cocones with attributes (not shown) as vertices.

Briefly, we expand on each of these components in turn, indicating what they, as a specification, correspond to in models.

- The graph is a type diagram. The three monic arrows indicate subtypes. The other arrows are functions (methods) which given an instance of their domain type will return an instance of their codomain type.
- The commutativity of the two triangles represents a typical real-world constraint: Every in-patient operation conducted at a particular hospital by a particular medical practitioner must take place under a practice agreement

(a type of contract) between that hospital and that practitioner. If, instead the left hand triangle were not required to commute (that is, was not in **D**) then it would still be the case that every operation took place under an agreement, but Dr X could operate under Dr Y's practice agreement. In many information models, situations like this do not even include the arrow marked under, and thus they store the contractual information, but do not specify the constraint — it is expected to be added at implementation time (this is one example of why information modelling is *not* usually a formal specification technique).

- The inclusion of the square in $\mathcal{L}$ ensures that in models it will be a pullback. This ensures that the specialists are precisely those medical practitioners who are members of a college which occurs in the subtype Specialisation. This is important because the registration procedures (not shown) for specialists are different from those for other medical practitioners. Similar pullbacks can be used to specify other subtypes, for example, the medical practitioners with a specific specialisation, say otorhinolaryngologists.

- Subtype inclusion arrows, and other arrows that are required to be monic in models, are so specified using pullbacks. Specifically, requiring that

be a pullback is another way of saying that m must be monic. Incidentally, we could include just two such cones since elementary properties of pullbacks ensure that if the square is realised as a pullback and its bottom arrow as a monic then its top arrow will necessarily be monic. Notice also that the arrow into Person is not required to be monic. A single person might appear more than once as a medical practitioner, as for example, when the person practises both as a GP and as a specialist, or practises in more than one specialisation. This is a minor point, but the distinction between people and the roles they play is an important distinction in many real world applications.

- The cocone with vertex Medical practitioner ensures that the collection of medical practitioners is the disjoint union of the collection of specialists and the collection of GPs. Specifications which don't include this constraint could be used to allow other vocations, say physiotherapists, to be treated as medical practitioners.

- As is common practice, attributes are not shown in Figure 1, but they are important. They are usually large fixed value sets, often of type `integer` (with specified bounding values), `string` (of specified maximum length), `date` etc. Some examples for this model include the validity period of a practice agreement, the name and the address of a person, the classification of a hospital, the date of an operation, the provider number of a medical practitioner and many more. Strictly, they are all part of the graph, but in practice they are usually listed separately in a data dictionary.

Definition 8 A *database state* D for an SkDM sketch $\mathbb{E}$ is a model of $\mathbb{E}$ in $\mathbf{Set}_0$, the category of finite sets. The *category of database states of* $\mathbb{E}$ is the category of models $\mathrm{Mod}(\mathbb{E}, \mathbf{Set}_0)$ of $\mathbb{E}$ in $\mathbf{Set}_0$.

A database state or model of the SkDM sketch of Example 7 is a collection of finite sets and functions satisfying the constraints. The set corresponding to, for example, In-patient operation should be thought of as the collection of all operations currently stored in the information system.

Sketch data modelling can be viewed as an extension of entity-relationship (ER) modelling [6],[28]. An ER diagram can be used to generate in a systematic way a graph for a sketch data model (the details are dealt with in [19]). The theory corresponding to a sketch data model includes objects representing the queries (first noted in [11]). The extra "semantic" power of the sketch data model comes from the non-graph components: $\mathbf{D}$ can be used to specify constraints, and $\mathcal{L}$ and $\mathcal{C}$ can be used to specify the calculation of query results based on other objects, and then these query results can be used to specify further constraints, and so on. It is not surprising that this extra power, by providing a much richer set of possibilities for specifying constraints, is of benefit in information modelling, and it has been the basis of our successful consultancies which have used the sketch data model as a formal information system specification technique.

3   Views

Views are important tools in software engineering. In information systems a view allows a user to manipulate data which are part of, or are derived from, an underlying database. For example our medical informatics graph (Figure 1) represents a view of a large health administration database. It in turn might provide views to an epidemiologist who only needs to deal with the two triangles, with Operation type, and with their associated attributes; or to an administrator of a College of Surgeons who needs to deal with data in the inverse image of that college, and not with any of the data associated only with other colleges.

Views have generally been implemented in very limited ways so as to avoid difficulties related to the view update problem. For example, allowable views might be restricted to be just certain row and column subsets of a relational database. However, we seek to support views which can be derived in any way from the underlying database, so views might include the result of any query provided by the database, and we argue that views ought to be able to be structured in any way acceptable under the data model in use.

For the sketch data model we now provide a definition of view which supports the generality just described.

Recall from Section 2 that for each sketch $\mathbb{E}$ there is a corresponding theory, often called the classifying category, denoted $Q\mathbb{E}$. We observed in [11] that the objects of the classifying category correspond to the queries of the corresponding information system. This motivates the following definition.

Definition 9 A *view* of a sketch data model $\mathbb{E}$ is a sketch data model $\mathbf{V}$ together with a sketch morphism $V : \mathbf{V} \longrightarrow Q\mathbb{E}$.

Thus a view is itself a sketch data model **V**, but its entities are interpreted via V as query results in the original data model E. In more formal terms, a database state D for E is a finite set valued functor $D : QE \longrightarrow \mathbf{Set}_0$, and composing this with V gives a database state D' for **V**, the V-view of D.

Remark 10 The operation *composing with* V is usually written as V^*. Thus $D' = V^*D$. In fact, V^* is a functor, so for any morphism of database states $\alpha : D \longrightarrow C$ we obtain a morphism $V^*\alpha : D' \longrightarrow V^*C$.

Following usual practice we will often refer to a database state of the form V^*D as a view. Context will determine whether "view" refers to such a state, or to the sketch morphism V. If there is any ambiguity, V should be referred to as the *view schema*.

4   Updatability

We have defined *view* above so as to ensure that views have the widest possible applicability. A view is a sketch data model, and so it can appear in any structural form acceptable to the sketch data model formal specification technique. The use of a sketch morphism V guarantees that the constraints on the view imposed by the diagrams, limits and colimits in the view's sketch data model are compatible with the constraints on the underlying database. And the fact that V takes values in QE permits any data derivable from the model of the underlying database to appear in the view.

Views support software maintenance — as long as the view mechanism is maintained, the logical structure (the design) of a database can be changed without needing to modify applications programs which access it through views. The only risk is that needed data might actually be removed from the database. If, on the other hand, the data is there in any form it can be extracted as an object of $Q(E)$ and accessed via a view. The breadth of the definition of view is important to ensure that this support for maintenance can be carried out in the widest possible range of circumstances.

The view update problem is to determine under what circumstances updates specified in a view can be propagated to the underlying information system, and how that propagation should take place. The essence of the problem is that not all views are updatable, that is, an insert or a delete which seems perfectly reasonable in the view, may be ill-defined or proscribed when applied to the underlying information system. For example, a college administrator can alter the medical practitioner attribute values for a member of the college, but even though such administrators can see the practice agreements for members of their college, they cannot insert a new practice agreement for a member because they cannot see (in the inverse image view) details about hospitals, and every practice agreement must specify a hospital.

In the sketch data model, view updates can fail in either of two ways [12]:

1. There may be no states of the database which would yield the updated view. This usually occurs because the update, when carried to the underlying database, would result in proscribed states. For example, a view schema might include the product of two entities, but only one of the factors. In the view, inserting or deleting from the product seems straightforward, after all, it looks like an ordinary entity with a function to another entity. But in the underlying database the resulting state of the product might be impossible, as for instance if the numbers of elements in the product and the factor become coprime.

2. There may be many states of the database which would yield the updated view. The simplest example of this occurring is when a view schema includes an entity, but not one of its attributes. Inserting into the entity seems straightforward, but in the underlying database there is no way to know what value the new instance should have on the invisible attribute, and there are usually many choices.

Thus we define

Definition 11 Let $V : \mathbf{V} \longrightarrow Q\!E$ be a view of E. Suppose $t : T \rightarrowtail T'$ consists of two database states for $\mathbf{V}$ and a database state monomorphism, with T' being an insert update of T and with $T = V^*D$ for some database state D of E. We say that the insert t is *propagatable* when there exists an initial $m : D \rightarrowtail D'$ among all those database states D'' with $m' : D \rightarrowtail D''$ for which $V^*D'' = T'$ and $V^*m' = t$. Initial here means an initial object in the full subcategory of the slice category under D. The state D' is then called the *propagated update* (sometimes just the update). The definition of propagatable delete is dual (so we seek a terminal D' among all those $D'' \rightarrowtail D$).

Since a view is just a database state, we know how to insert or delete instances. Intuitively a specified view insert/delete is then propagatable if there is a unique "minimal" insert/delete on the underlying information system whose restriction to the view (via V^*) is the given view insert/delete.

Notice that propagatability (view updatability) is in principle dependent on the database state (the model of the specification) which is being updated — we have defined when an insert or delete of a view (database state) is propagatable, rather than trying to determine for which view schemata inserts and deletes can always be propagated. In fact we can often prove that for given view schemata, all database states are updatable. Such results are important for designers so that they can design views that will always be updatable. The next section provides some propositions analysing this.

It is important to note that by defining updatability in terms of models we obtain the broadest reasonable class of updatable view inserts and deletes. Whenever there is a canonical (initial or terminal) model of the underlying information system among those models that could achieve the update of the view we say that the view is updatable. The only invalid view updates are those which are in fact impossible to achieve in the underlying information system, or those which could be derived from multiple non-isomorphic minimal or maximal models of the underlying information system.

5   Schema Updatability

Definition 12 A view $V : \mathbf{V} \longrightarrow Q\!E$ is called *insert* (respectively *delete*) *updatable* at an entity $W \in \mathbf{V}$ when all inserts (respectively deletes) into (respectively from) W are propagatable, independently of the database state. (Note that an insert or delete *at* W changes the database state's value only at W — the values in the model of other entities and attributes remain unchanged.)

In this section we establish insert or delete updatability at $W \in \mathbf{V}$ (sometimes loosely just called *updatability*) for a variety of circumstances. As well as being technically useful in applications, these results help to show that the definitions above correspond well to our intuitions about what should and should not be updatable. In most cases we will deal in detail with the insert case as it is the more interesting and slightly harder case.

To establish notation, assume that $V : \mathbf{V} \longrightarrow Q\!E$ is a sketch morphism, that T and T' are models of $\mathbf{V}$, that T' is an insert or delete update of T at W, and that D, D' and D'' are models of E. Suppose further that $T = V^*D$ and that $T' = V^*D' = V^*D''$. When dealing with inserts we will suppose $t : T \rightarrowtail T'$, $m : D \rightarrowtail D'$ and $m' : D \rightarrowtail D''$ are insert updates. Deletes will be treated dually $(t : T' \rightarrowtail T$ etc). In either case we suppose that $V^*m = V^*m' = t$.

In most of the following propositions we will suppose for simplicity that E has no cones except the empty cone with vertex 1, and no cocones except attribute cocones. With care the propositions can be generalised to sketches E which do not meet this restriction, provided that W is not in any of the cones or cocones except perhaps as specified explicitly in the hypotheses. Similarly we will assume for simplicity that V is an injective sketch morphism. We begin by considering cases where V is just a view of a part of E.

Proposition 13 *Suppose* $VW \in E$. *If* VW *is not the initial node in any commutative diagram in* E *and all of the arrows out of* VW *in* E *are in the image of* V, *then* V *is insert updatable at* W. *Conversely, if all of the arrows into* VW *in* E *are in the image of* V, *then* V *is delete updatable at* W.

Proof. We prove only the insert case. The delete case is a straightforward dual argument, except that there is no need to be concerned about commutative diagrams (deleting an element cannot spoil commutativity but inserting an element can).

Let D' be defined by $D'X = DX$ for X not equal to W and $D'W = T'W$, and $D'f = Df$ for arrows f not incident at VW, $D'f = T'f$ for arrows f out of VW, and $D'f = t_W Df$ for arrows f into VW. The natural transformation m has the evident identities and inclusion as components.

Now D' is a model since the limits and colimits are the same as in D and commutativity cannot be spoiled because arrows into $D'W$ factor through DW and naturality of t ensures that for arrows f and g composed through W, $D'gD'f = D'gt_WDf = DgDf$. Furthermore $m : D \rightarrowtail D'$ is initial among the appropriate $m' : D \rightarrowtail D''$ since it is initial at each component.

Proposition 13 says that a view which can "see enough" is updatable. For example, if the view were to include Medical practitioner, Practice agreement, and Hospital, along with the two arrows between them (see Figure 1), then the view is insert updatable, but not delete updatable, at Practice agreement.

In many of the following propositions W is assumed to be the only entity in the view, and E will be very simple. This might seem rather restrictive. In fact, the single entity view is in accord with common practice where views are frequently required to be the result of a single query, so the view should be a single object $\{W\} = \mathbf{V}$ with its image in QE. In our applications we encourage larger structured $\mathbf{V}$, but the following propositions are nevertheless useful then because we can search for parts of $\mathbf{V}$ which match the premises of the propositions and either find a counterexample to updatability at W, or partition $\mathbf{V} - \{W\}$ and argue that updatability for each partition as a view, whether concurrently or serially, implies the updatability of $\mathbf{V}$ at W. Similarly the propositions can be applied to large complex E because updatability is a "local" phenomenon: Inserts or deletes at W will be updatable according as to whether they are updatable in the restriction of E to objects "near" W.

Proposition 14 *Suppose that* $\mathbf{V} = \{W\}$, *and* E *has a graph including* $f : VW \longrightarrow A$ *where* A *is a non-trivial attribute, that is, the vertex of a cocone of at least two elements. Then* V *is not insert updatable at* W.

Proof. Choose two distinct elements $a, b : 1 \longrightarrow A$. If the insert is non-trivial and atomic then there is an element $w : 1 \longrightarrow T'W$ which is not in TW and $T'W = TW + \{w\}$. Consider D' and D'' defined by $D'W = D''W = T'W$, and of course $D'A = D''A = T'A = TA$ (attributes are constant for all models), with $D'fw = a$ and $D''fw = b$ and $D'f = D''f = Tf$ when restricted to TW. But now $D \longrightarrow D'$ and $D \longrightarrow D''$ are incomparable but minimal so there is no initial object and the view update is not propagatable.

Thus we should require that W has all of its attributes in its view. For simplicity we will in fact assume that W has no attributes for the remainder of this section, but the propositions can be generalised to arbitrary W provided all of the attributes of W do appear in $\mathbf{V}$.

The next proposition is the first in which W is a non-trivial query based on E. These are essentially selection queries.

Proposition 15 *Suppose that* $\mathbf{V} = \{W\}$, *and* $\mathbb{E}$ *has as graph* $f : B \longrightarrow A$ *where* A *has an element* $a : 1 \longrightarrow A$. *Let* VW *be the pullback*

$$
\begin{array}{ccc}
VW & \longrightarrow & B \\
\downarrow & & \downarrow f \\
1 & \xrightarrow{\ a\ } & A
\end{array}
$$

Then V *is insert updatable at* W.

Proof. Write $T'W = TW + W_0$ with t the inclusion of the first summand, which we can do since T' is an insert update of T (writing $+$ for disjoint union in $\mathbf{Set}_0$). Let $D'B = DB + W_0$, and $D'A = DA$, and define $D'f$ to be the function whose components on $D'B$ are Df and the constant at a (that is the unique function $W_0 \longrightarrow 1$ composed with the element $a : 1 \longrightarrow A$). Then D' is a model, $m : D \rightarrowtail D'$ is given by the evident inclusion and identity, and, calculating the pullback in $\mathbf{Set}$, $V^*D' = T'$ and $V^*m = t$. Suppose $m' : D \rightarrowtail D''$ is another such model. Then there is a unique natural transformation $i : D' \longrightarrow D''$ commuting with m and m' since with $D''1 = 1$ and with DA and DB fixed inside $D''A$ and $D''B$, $D''f$ must have as fibre over a, $(Df)^{-1}(a) + W_0$ in order for the pullback to be $T'W$, and these fully determine the components on i. Thus, V is insert updatable.

This is an important proposition. At first it might seem surprising that V is insert updatable since the arrow $VW \longrightarrow B$ is rather like that in Proposition 14. But the fact that VW arises as a pullback determines the values that the function must take, and that all those values must be fibred over a.

Proposition 15 is also important because it is an example of an update that many view systems would prohibit [13] despite its practical importance. As an example which arises naturally consider a view of Figure 1 which arises from choosing a particular specialisation. This is the view used by an administrator of a particular college, and it should be updatable.

If the hypotheses of Proposition 15 were generalised to replace 1 by an entity C the proposition would no longer hold. However, if C is included in the view along with the pullback VW and the arrow between them then we recover insert updatability.

Alternatively, the hypotheses can be generalised to allow C in place of 1, but strengthened to require that the arrows $C \rightarrowtail A$ and $B \rightarrowtail A$ be monic. In that case V is again insert updatable.

Proposition 16 *Suppose that* $\mathbf{V} = \{W\}$, *and* $\mathbb{E}$ *has two entities* A *and* B. *Let* VW *be the coproduct of* A *and* B. *Then* V *is not insert updatable.*

Proof. (Sketch:) The two models D' and D'' obtained by adding the set difference $T'W - TW$ to A and B respectively are incomparable and minimal.

Proposition 17 *Suppose that* $\mathbf{V} = \{A_0 \longrightarrow W\}$, *and* $\mathbb{E}$ *has two entities* A *and* B. *Let* $VA_0 = A$ *and let* VW *be the coproduct of* A *and* B. *Then* V *is insert updatable.*

Proof. (Sketch:) In contrast to the proof of the previous proposition, this time an element of $T'W - TW$ corresponds to an element of $T'A_0$ or not. In the first case we define D' by adding the element to DA, and in the second case by adding it to DB. (As noted at the beginning of this section, a strict reading of "insert at W" would mean that only the second case could arise.) In either case D' so constructed is initial, and the view is insert updatable at W.

Proposition 18 *Suppose that* $\mathbf{V} = \{W\}$, *and* $\mathbb{E}$ *has two entities* A *and* B. *Let* VW *be the product of* A *and* B. *Then* V *is not insert updatable.*

Proof. As noted in Section 4 if, as is usually the case, adding 1 to TW leads to its number of elements being coprime to the number of elements in DA and in DB then there are no models D' such that $V^*D' = T'$ and a fortiori no initial such, in which case the view insert is not propagatable.

There are many more results of similar interest and considerable utility. This section has provided a sample of results indicating a range of circumstances that can easily be dealt with.

For the record, the hypotheses of all but the last proposition result in delete updatability.

6   Related Work

In the last decade there has been considerable growth in the use of sketches to support data modelling. Among this work Piessens has obtained results on the algorithmic determination of equivalences of model categories [27] which were intended to support plans for view integration. Meanwhile Diskin and Cadish have used sketches for a variety of modelling purposes including for example [14] and [15]. They have been concentrating on developing the diagrammatic language of "diagram operations". Others, including Lippe and ter Hofstede [25], Islam and Phoa [17], and Baklawski et al [4], have been using category theory for data modelling.

Recent work on updating problems has included work by Atzeni and Torlone [2] who developed a solution to the problem of updating relational databases through weak instance interfaces. While they explicitly discuss views, and state that their approach does not deal with them, the technique for obtaining a solution is analogous to the technique used here. They consider a range of possible solutions (as we here consider the range of possible updates $D \rightarrowtail D''$) and they construct a partial order on them, and seek a greatest lower bound (analogous with our initial/terminal solution). A similar approach, also to a non-view problem, appears in [24].

Meanwhile, the authors have recently been futher testing the techniques presented here. Johnson and Dampney [9] have used the techniques in a case study; Dampney, Johnson and Rosebrugh [12] explore the implications for semantic data modelling and present a simplified form of the techniques to the database community; and Johnson and Rosebrugh [20] show how the techniques can be used for database interoperability for computer supported cooperative work. Johnson, Rosebrugh and Wood [21] have developed a new mathematical foundation that unifies the treatment of specifications, updates, and model categories. And in current work the present authors are exploring the relationship between our approach to the view update problem and the frame problem in software engineering [18], [5].

7   Conclusion

After defining the sketch data model in Section 2 we defined views (Section 3) in a way that ensures that the view structure is itself a sketch data model, and that offers maximum generality in the sense that the view can be constructed from any data that can be obtained from queries of the underlying database. In this framework we have proposed a new solution to the view update problem (Section 4), and shown in Section 5 how we can still obtain results about the updatability of schemata.

The work presented here has a number of limitations:

1. Views take values in $Q\!I\!E$ which contains all structural queries, but no arithmetic queries that could summarise, rather than extract and manipulate, data.
2. The updates dealt with are only insert and delete updates. We don't yet treat modifications of data in situ.
3. We provide no special treatment of nulls (in agreement with, for example, Date's recommendation [13] that systems should not support nulls).
4. We have not given detailed consideration to implementational issues. In particular the treatment of both the *when* and the *how* of view updating by universal properties does not directly address implementational issues (but see the remarks below on computational category theory).

Each of these is the subject of ongoing current research.

Despite the limitations, the new approach to views has significant advantages:

1. The sketch data model has been extended to incorporate views, and the extension is very general allowing data based on any structural query to be viewed in any sketch data model schema, subject only to the compatibility with the underlying information system implied by V being a sketch morphism (and this last is as we would expect — we can't constrain the data in the view more than it is constrained in the underlying information system since the former is derived from the latter).

2. View updatability is defined once and for all in a single consistent framework based on a universal property among models. Arguably the universal property gives the most general reasonable definition to view updatability possible.
3. The framework presented here links well with computational category theory work being carried out in Italy, the UK, Canada and Australia. That work has developed repositories, graphical tools, and elementary algorithms, that amount to a rapid prototyping tool for systems specified using the sketch data model.
4. The "closedness" obtained by having a view be itself a sketch data model allows views of views etc. It also supports well proposals for using views as the interface for database interoperability and for federated information systems.
5. The propositions presented in section 5 and similar propositions allow us to work with schema updatability (rather than model based updatability) in the usual way, and the proofs of the propositions embody the code required to carry out the update without resorting to general universal property algorithms.

These developments have depended fundamentally on using a formal methods framework, rather than the more usual semi-formal methodologies, and this led to the universal property being based on models rather than the more usual schema based definitions.

References

1. Serge Abiteboul and Oliver M. Duschka. Complexity of Answering Queries Using Materialized Views. *ACM PODS-98*, 254–263, 1998.
2. P. Atzeni and R. Torlone. Updating relational databases through weak instance interfaces. *TODS*, 17:718–743, 1992.
3. M. Barr and C. Wells. *Category theory for computing science*. Prentice-Hall, second edition, 1995.
4. K. Baklawski, D. Dimovici and W. White. A categorical approach to database semantics. *Mathematical Structures in Computer Science*, 4:147–183, 1994.
5. A. Borgida, J. Mylopoulos and R. Reiter. And Nothing Else Changes: The Frame Problem in Procedure Specifications. *Proceedings of the Fifteenth International Conference on Software Engineering*, IEEE Computer Society Press, 1993.
6. P. P. -S. Chen. The Entity-Relationship Model—Toward a Unified View of Data. *TODS*, 2:9–36, 1976.
7. C. N. G. Dampney and Michael Johnson. TIME Compliant Corporate Data Model Validation. Consultants' report to Telecom Australia, 1991.
8. C. N. G. Dampney and Michael Johnson. Fibrations and the DoH Data Model. Consultants' report to NSW Department of Health, 1999.
9. C. N. G. Dampney and Michael Johnson. A formal method for enterprise interoperability: A case study in a major health informatics information system. *Proceedings of the Thirteenth International Conference on Software and Systems Engineering*, CNAM Paris, vol 3, 12-5, 1–6, 2000.

10. C. N. G. Dampney, Michael Johnson and G. M. McGrath. Audit and Enhancement of the Caltex Information Strategy Planning (CISP) Project. Consultants' report to Caltex Oil Australia, 1994.

11. C. N. G. Dampney, Michael Johnson, and G. P. Monro. An illustrated mathematical foundation for ERA. In *The Unified Computation Laboratory*, pages 77–84, Oxford University Press, 1992.

12. C. N. G. Dampney, Michael Johnson, and Robert Rosebrugh. View Updates in a Semantic Data Model Paradigm. Proceedings of ADC, IEEE Computer Society, in press, 2001.

13. C. J. Date. *Introduction to Database Systems, Volume 2*. Addison-Wesley, 1983.

14. Zinovy Diskin and Boris Cadish. Algebraic graph-based approach to management of multidatabase systems. In *Proceedings of The Second International Workshop on Next Generation Information Technologies and Systems (NGITS '95)*, 1995.

15. Zinovy Diskin and Boris Cadish. Variable set semantics for generalised sketches: Why ER is more object oriented than OO. In *Data and Knowledge Engineering*, 2000.

16. H. Ehrig and B. Mahr. *Fundamentals of algebraic specifications*. Springer-Verlag, 1985.

17. A. Islam and W. Phoa. Categorical models of relational databases I: Fibrational formulation, schema integration. Proceedings of the TACS94. Eds M. Hagiya and J. C. Mitchell. *Lecture Notes in Computer Science*, 789:618–641, 1994.

18. D. Jackson. Structuring Z Specifications with Views. *ACM Transactions on Software Engineering and Methodology*, 4:365–389, 1995.

19. Michael Johnson and C. N. G. Dampney. On the value of commutative diagrams in information modelling. In Algebraic Methodology and Software Technology, *Springer Workshops in Computing*, 1994.

20. Michael Johnson and Robert Rosebrugh. Database interoperability through state based logical data independence. *Proceedings of the Fifth International Conference on Computer Supported Cooperative Work in Design*, IEEE Hong Kong, 161–166, 2000.

21. Michael Johnson, Robert Rosebrugh, and R. J. Wood. Entity-relationship models and sketches. Submitted to *Theory and Applications of Categories*, 2001.

22. Rom Langerak. View updates in relational databases with an independent scheme. *TODS*, 15:40–66, 1990.

23. A. Y. Levy, A. O. Mendelzon, D. Srivastava, Y. Sagiv. Answering queries using views. *ACM PODS-95*, 1995.

24. C. Lecluse and N. Spyratos. Implementing queries and updates on universal scheme interfaces. *VLDB*, 62–75, 1988.

25. E. Lippe and A ter Hofstede. A category theoretical approach to conceptual data modelling. *RAIRO Theoretical Informatics and Applications*, 30:31–79, 1996.

26. Saunders Mac Lane. *Categories for the Working Mathematician*. Graduate Texts in Mathematics 5, Springer Verlag, 1971.

27. F. Piessens and Eric Steegmans. Selective Attribute Elimination for Categorical Data Specifications. Proceedings of the 6th International AMAST. Ed. Michael Johnson. *Lecture Notes in Computer Science*, 1349:424-436, 1997.

28. J. D. Ullman. *Principles of Database and Knowledge-Base Systems*. Volume 1, Computer Science Press, 1988.

29. J. D. Ullman. Information integration using logical views. *ICDT-97*, 1997.

30. R. F. C. Walters. *Categories and Computer Science*. Cambridge University Press, 1991.

Grammar Adaptation

Ralf Lämmel

CWI, Kruislaan 413, NL-1098 SJ Amsterdam
Vrije Universiteit, De Boelelaan 1081a, NL-1081 HV Amsterdam
Email: ralf@cwi.nl
WWW: http://www.cwi.nl/~ralf/

Abstract. We employ transformations for the adaptation of grammars. Grammars need to be adapted in grammar development, grammar maintenance, grammar reengineering, and grammar recovery. Starting from a few fundamental transformation primitives and combinators, we derive an operator suite for grammar adaptation. Three groups of operators are identified, namely operators for refactoring, construction and destruction. While refactoring is semantics-preserving in the narrow sense, transformations for construction and destruction require the consideration of relaxed notions of semantics preservation based on other grammar relations than equality of generated languages. The consideration of semantics and accompanying preservation properties is slightly complicated by the fact that we cannot insist on reduced grammars.

1 Introduction

Grammar adaptation. We consider formal transformations facilitating the stepwise adaptation of grammars. These transformations model common schemes of restructuring (e.g., based on fold and unfold), and local changes (e.g., restriction, generalisation or removal of phrases). We focus on grammar transformations mimicking simple adaptation steps which are performed by "grammar programmers" in grammar development manually otherwise. The amount of grammar programming should not be underestimated. Our approach is relevant for grammar development, maintenance, reengineering, and recovery.

Grammar recovery. The transformations formalised in the present paper proved to be valuable in actual grammar recovery projects. Grammar recovery is concerned with the derivation of a language's grammar from some available resource such as a semi-formal language reference. Grammar transformations can be used to correct, to complete, and to restructure the raw grammar extracted from the resource in a stepwise manner. Grammar recovery is of prime importance for software reengineering—in particular for automated software renovation [5,3]. The Y2K-problem or the Euro-conversion problem are some well-recognized reengineering problems. Tool support in software renovation, e.g., for grammar-based software modification tools, relies on grammars for the languages at hand. Suitable grammars are often not available, since one might be faced with ancient languages including all kinds of COBOL dialects, or with in-house languages and language extensions. Thus, there is a need for grammar recovery. In one

J.N. Oliveira and P. Zave (Eds.): FME 2001, LNCS 2021, pp. 550–570, 2001.

particular recovery project, we obtained the first publicly available, high-quality
COBOL grammar [8]. The effort for this undertaking was relatively small compared to other known figures (refer to [9] for details). The use of grammar transformations was crucial to make this process accessible for tool support, traceable
regarding the many steps and decisions involved, and measurable to allow for
formal reasoning and claims like correctness and completeness. A global account
on grammar recovery and grammar (re-) engineering from a software engineering
perspective is given in [14,9].

2.7.8 REDEFINES-clause

```
___ Format _____
|                                                                  |
| >>__level-number_____REDEFINES__data-name-2____><   |
|                   |_data-name-1_|                                |
|                   |_FILLER_____|                                |
|_____|
```

Fig. 1. An incorrect syntax diagram from [7]

Sample adaptation. In recovering the VS COBOL II grammar [8] from the IBM
reference [7], we were faced with a surprising number of problems regarding the
syntax definition contained in the reference.[1] There were errors and omissions
in the narrow sense. The syntax definition also suffered from the use of informal
comments to regulate syntax. It is actually the lack of (use of) formal methods
that causes such important documents to be incorrect and incomplete. One incorrectness is shown in the syntax diagram in Fig. 1. The diagram is supposed to
define the syntax of a REDEFINES-clause which is an optional clause of a COBOL
data item. For convenience, we also define the piece of syntax from the diagram
in extended BNF notation:[2]

REDEFINES-clause ::=
    level-number (data-name | "FILLER")? "REDEFINES" data-name

The diagram or its integration in the overall grammar is incorrect because the
diagram does not just define the structure of a REDEFINES-clause, but rather the
structure of a data item *with* a REDEFINES-clause. A proper REDEFINES-clause
is simply of the form of "REDEFINES" data-name. The problem can easily be
recognized by parsing approved code if the (prototype) parser is derived directly
from the diagrams as described in [9]. To correct the diagram or the grammar
resp., we need to delete the phrase which does not belong to a proper REDEFINES-
clause. Using a corresponding transformation operator for grammar adaptation,
this removal can be expressed as follows:

delete level-number (data-name | "FILLER")? in {REDEFINES-clause}

---

[1] About 300 transformation steps were needed to derive [8] from [7].
[2] We enclose terminals in double quotes ("..."). "|" separates alternatives. "?" is a
postfix operator for optionals. Grouping is done with "(...)".

552   R. Lämmel

Benefit of the transformational approach. Transformational grammar adaptation improves on ad-hoc manual adaptation in several respects. Transformations add traceability since changes can be recorded. In actual grammar development, maintenance, recovery etc., it is important to state clearly what changes were needed. The resulting adaptation scripts are also reusable in part for grammars of dialects, or if some adaptation decisions are altered. The properties of transformation operators immediately qualify a certain adaptation accordingly. For those operators, which are not semantics-preserving in the narrow sense, we provide corresponding relaxed notions characterising the impact of the operators. In the above sample, we non-ambiguously identify the phrase to be removed. Also, since the transformation is performed in a focus, we document the intended area for the local change. In grammar programming, it is indeed important to understand the impact that a change might have, since grammars serve as contracts for language tools [6]. In general, we envision that our approach to grammar adaptation contributes to completeness and correctness claims for grammars.

Structure of the paper. In Section 2, we propose a variant of context-free grammars particularly useful to cope with evolving grammars. In Section 3, binary grammar relations and induced transformation properties are studied to enable formal reasoning for transformational grammar adaptation. The contribution of this section is that we go beyond semantics-preservation in the narrow sense. In Section 4, a transformation framework is developed. It offers primitives and combinators for grammar transformation. In Section 5, operators for grammar adaptation, e.g., the operator delete used in the example above, are derived in the transformation framework. The paper is concluded in Section 6.

Acknowledgement. This work was supported, in part, by *NWO*, in the project *"Generation of Program Transformation Systems"*. I am grateful for advice by the FME'01 anonymous referees. I am also grateful to Jeremy Gibbons, Jan Heering, Merijn de Jonge, Paul Klint, Chris Verhoef, Joost Visser, Guido Wachsmuth, and Dave Wile for encouraging discussions, and for helpful suggestions. Some results from the present paper have been presented at the 54th IFIP WG2.1 ("Algorithmic Languages and Calculi") meeting in Blackheath, London, April, 3th–7th, 2000, and at the 2nd Workshop Software-Reengineering, Bad Honnef, May, 11th–12th, 2000.

2   Grammar Fragments

We derive a simple variant of context-free grammars as the object language for grammar transformations. We call this variant *grammar fragments*. The idea of grammar adaptation implies that we cannot assume reduced context-free grammars. We rather have to cope with evolving grammars.

2.1   Standard Context-Free Grammars

A context-free grammar G is a quadruple $\langle N, T, s, P \rangle$, where N and T are the disjoint finite sets of nonterminals resp. terminals, $s \in N$ is called start symbol, and P is a finite set of productions or (context-free) rules with $P \subset N \times (N \cup T)^\star$. A production $\langle n, u \rangle \in P$ with $n \in N$ and $u \in (N \cup T)^*$ is also written as $n \to u$. It is common to assume reduced grammars, that is, each production can be used in some derivation of a terminal string from the start symbol.

2.2 Deviation

We slightly deviate from the standard. We do not insist on the identification of a start symbol s because this is definitely not sensible for incomplete grammars. Furthermore, we do not explicitly declare nonterminals and terminals. A grammar is represented just by its productions. Nonterminals and terminals originate from different universes of grammar symbols, that is, $\mathcal{U}_N$ for nonterminals, and $\mathcal{U}_T$ for terminals. We call the resulting deviation *grammar fragments*. We do not require grammar fragments to be terminated, that is, there can be nonterminals which are used, but not defined. We call these nonterminals *bottom nonterminals*. The domains of all context-free productions $\mathcal{R}$ (or rules for short) and grammar fragments $\mathcal{G}$ are defined as follows:[3]

$$\mathcal{R} = \mathcal{U}_N \times (\mathcal{U}_N \cup \mathcal{U}_T)^*$$
$$\mathcal{G} = \mathcal{P}_{fin}(\mathcal{R})$$

We use γ possibly indexed or primed to range over $\mathcal{G}$. The terms $\mathcal{T}(\gamma) \subset \mathcal{U}_T$ and $\mathcal{N}(\gamma) \subset \mathcal{U}_N$ are used to denote terminals and nonterminals of γ. These and other relevant sets of grammar symbols are defined in Fig. 2.

$$\mathcal{D}(\gamma) = \{n \in \mathcal{U}_N \mid n \to u \in \gamma, u \in (\mathcal{U}_N \cup \mathcal{U}_T)^*\}$$
$$\mathcal{U}(\gamma) = \{n' \in \mathcal{U}_N \mid n \to u\, n'\, v \in \gamma, n \in \mathcal{U}_N, u, v \in (\mathcal{U}_N \cup \mathcal{U}_T)^*\}$$
$$\mathcal{N}(\gamma) = \mathcal{D}(\gamma) \cup \mathcal{U}(\gamma)$$
$$\mathcal{T}(\gamma) = \{t \in \mathcal{U}_T \mid n \to u\, t\, v \in \gamma, n \in \mathcal{U}_N, u, v \in (\mathcal{U}_N \cup \mathcal{U}_T)^*\}$$
$$\bot(\gamma) = \mathcal{U}(\gamma) \setminus \mathcal{D}(\gamma)$$
$$\top(\gamma) = \mathcal{D}(\gamma) \setminus \mathcal{U}(\gamma)$$
$$\emptyset(\gamma) = \{n \in \mathcal{N}(\gamma) \mid \not\exists w \in (\bot(\gamma) \cup \mathcal{T}(\gamma))^*.\ n \Rightarrow^*_\gamma w\}$$

Fig. 2. Defined nonterminals $\mathcal{D}(\gamma)$, used nonterminals $\mathcal{U}(\gamma)$, nonterminals $\mathcal{N}(\gamma)$, terminals $\mathcal{T}(\gamma)$, bottom nonterminals $\bot(\gamma)$, top nonterminals $\top(\gamma)$, looping nonterminals $\emptyset(\gamma)$

Bottom nonterminals capture some important properties of a grammar fragment γ. In grammar development, a bottom nonterminal might correspond to a nonterminal lacking a definition. Alternatively, a bottom nonterminal might indicate a connectivity problem, that is, the intended definition is given with a

---

[3] $\mathcal{P}_{fin}(x)$ denotes the finite subsets of x.

different nonterminal symbol on the left-hand side. There is also the notion of *top nonterminals* which is somewhat dual to the notion of bottom nonterminals. As Fig. 2 details, the set $\top(\gamma)$ of top nonterminals consists of all nonterminals defined but not used in γ. A start symbol usually meets this condition.[4] An incomplete and/or incorrect grammar usually exhibits several such top nonterminals. Thus, in a sense, top nonterminals provide an indication to what extent a grammar fragment is connected. The set $\emptyset(\gamma)$ of looping nonterminals which is also introduced in Fig. 2 will be explained later.

2.3   Semantics

Terminal strings. The common semantics for context-free grammars is based on derivation ($\Rightarrow$ etc.). The language $\mathcal{L}(G)$ generated by a common context-free grammar $G = \langle N, T, s, P \rangle$ is usually defined as follows:

$$\mathcal{L}(G) = \{ w \in T^\star \mid s \Rightarrow^+_G w \},$$

i.e., as the set of terminal strings derivable from the dedicated start symbol. Of course, one can also consider the terminal strings derivable from an arbitrary nonterminal n. We are going to denote the semantics of n w.r.t. a grammar fragment γ as $[\![n]\!]_\gamma$. Adopting the idea of generated terminal strings, we get a first approximation of the ultimate denotation of n, namely:

$$[\![n]\!]_\gamma \supseteq \{ w \in \mathcal{T}(\gamma)^\star \mid n \Rightarrow^+_\gamma w \}$$

It easy to acknowledge that terminal strings are not sufficient since grammar fragments are not necessarily terminated. Productions which contain bottom nonterminals can never contribute to the set of derivable terminal strings. The sets of terminal strings generated by some defined nonterminals will even be empty. Consider, for example, the incomplete grammar γ_1 in Fig. 3 (the other content of the figure will be explained later). Indeed, the defined nonterminal s (the definition of which refers to the bottom nonterminal b) generates the empty set of terminal strings. This is not convenient for a semantics because a grammar fragment is not fully reflected by derivable terminal strings. Thus, terminal strings can only provide a lower bound for the ultimate denotation $[\![n]\!]$ of a nonterminal n.

Sentential forms. Instead of pure terminal strings, sentential forms can be taken into account. As we will see, sentential forms correspond to an upper bound for the ultimate denotation. Thus, we have the following:

$$[\![n]\!]_\gamma \subseteq \{ w \in (\mathcal{N}(\gamma) \cup \mathcal{T}(\gamma))^\star \mid n \Rightarrow^*_\gamma w \}$$

Sentential forms are too sensitive. They do not even provide a basis to state the semantics preservation of fold/unfold modulations. Such modulations are obviously very useful in refactoring a grammar.

---

[4] A relaxed definition of top nonterminals is favourable: A top nonterminal might be used in the rules for the nonterminal itself. This definition is useful to cope with recursive start symbols and to provide a strong criterion for safe elimination of nonterminals.

$$\gamma_1 \qquad\qquad\qquad\qquad\qquad\qquad\qquad\qquad\qquad \gamma_2$$

$$[b]^{\emptyset}_{\gamma_1} = \emptyset \;=\; [b]^{\emptyset}_{\gamma_2} = \emptyset$$

$s \to a\,b$

$a \to \epsilon$

$a \to \text{``A''}\, a$

$$[b]^{\perp(\gamma_1)}_{\gamma_1} = \{b\} \;\supset\; [b]^{\perp(\gamma_2)}_{\gamma_2} = \emptyset$$

$$[b]^{\perp(\gamma_1)\cup\emptyset(\gamma_1)}_{\gamma_1} = \{b\} \;\subset\; [b]^{\perp(\gamma_2)\cup\emptyset(\gamma_2)}_{\gamma_2} = \{b, \text{''B''}\, b, \ldots\}$$

$s \to a\,b$

$a \to \epsilon$

$a \to \text{``A''}\, a$

$b \to \text{''B''}\, b$

Fig. 3. Illustration of incomplete grammars

Observable nonterminals and sentential forms. We need to restrict the sentential forms so that only particular nonterminals are *observable*. It is sensible to require at least the bottom nonterminals to be observable. Then we can still derive all "interesting" sentential forms for γ_1 in Fig. 3. To be slightly more flexible regarding observable nonterminals, we consider an augmented variant of the semantic function with a superscript ψ for the observable nonterminals:

$$[n]^{\psi}_{\gamma} \stackrel{\text{def}}{=} \{w \in (\psi \cup \mathcal{T}(\gamma))^\star \mid n \Rightarrow^*_{\gamma} w\} \text{ where } \psi \subseteq \mathcal{N}(\gamma)$$

We can read $[n]^{\psi}_{\gamma}$ as the semantics of n according to γ assuming the nonterminals in ψ are observable. We call the corresponding sentential forms observable, too. The semantics restricted to sentential forms consisting solely of bottom nonterminals and terminals is then denoted by $[n]^{\perp(\gamma)}_{\gamma}$. These sentential forms provide a better lower bound for the ultimate semantics than the one we had before (i.e., terminal strings). Thus, we have the following:

$$[n]_{\gamma} \supseteq [n]^{\perp(\gamma)}_{\gamma}$$

We have to explain why observing bottom nonterminals only leads to a lower bound. Consider grammar γ_2 in Fig. 3 for that purpose. Although, b is defined, b does not generate strings over $\perp(\gamma_2) \cup \mathcal{T}(\gamma_2)$. This is caused by the particular definition of b in γ_2, that is, the definition is *looping* because there is no base case for b.

Looping nonterminals. We resolve the above problem by observing also the set $\emptyset(\gamma)$ of all looping nonterminals as defined in Fig. 2. Finally, we are in the position to define the denotation of n w.r.t. γ in the ultimate way as follows:

$$[n]_{\gamma} \stackrel{\text{def}}{=} [n]^{\perp(\gamma)\cup\emptyset(\gamma)}_{\gamma}$$

This semantics assumes the minimum of observable nonterminals without causing the denotation of some nonterminal to be empty.

3   Formal Reasoning

We are interested in comparing grammars, and in characterising the properties of grammar transformations. For this purpose, we define certain relations on $\mathcal{G}$ starting from the equivalence of grammar fragments. Finally, the grammar relations are employed for defining several forms of semantics-preservation.

3.1   Equivalent Grammars

Definition 1 (Equivalence ($\equiv$)). γ and γ' are equivalent *($\gamma \equiv \gamma'$) if:*

1. $\mathcal{N}(\gamma) = \mathcal{N}(\gamma')$,
2. $\forall n \in \mathcal{N}(\gamma).\ \llbracket n \rrbracket_\gamma = \llbracket n \rrbracket_{\gamma'}$,
3. $\perp(\gamma) = \perp(\gamma')$, $\mathcal{D}(\gamma) = \mathcal{D}(\gamma')$.[5]

This relation is useful to characterize fold/unfold modulations. All grammar relations will be exemplified in Fig. 4. As for equivalence, it holds $\gamma_1 \equiv \gamma_2$. Note that γ_1 and γ_2 are indeed related via unfold: The definition of y is unfolded in the first rule of γ_2. The way in which the grammars γ_3–γ_6 differ from γ_1 goes beyond equivalence.

γ_1	γ_2	γ_3	γ_4	γ_5	γ_6
$x \rightarrow y$	$x \rightarrow z$	$x \rightarrow y$	$x \rightarrow z$	$x \rightarrow y$	$x \rightarrow y$
$y \rightarrow z$	$y \rightarrow z$	$y \rightarrow z'$		$y \rightarrow z$	$y \rightarrow z$
				$y \rightarrow z'$	$z \rightarrow \epsilon$

Fig. 4. Illustration of grammar relations

3.2   Beyond Equivalence

Equivalence is often too restrictive to characterise related grammars. Completing a grammar, or revising a grammar, we still would like to characterise the relation between input and output grammar. We can think of various relations on two grammars γ and γ':

- γ and γ' are only equivalent modulo renaming.
- γ' contains definitions for nonterminals neither defined nor used in γ.
- It does not hold $\llbracket n \rrbracket_\gamma = \llbracket n \rrbracket_{\gamma'}$, but $\llbracket n \rrbracket_\gamma \subseteq \llbracket n \rrbracket_{\gamma'}$ for some n.
- Some bottom nonterminals from γ are defined in γ'.

These relaxations are formalised in the following definitions.

Definition 2 (Equivalence modulo renaming ρ ($\stackrel{\rho}{=}$)). γ and γ' are equivalent modulo renaming ρ *($\gamma \stackrel{\rho}{=} \gamma'$) if:*

1. ρ is a bijective function of type $\rho : \mathcal{N}(\gamma) \rightarrow \mathcal{N}(\gamma')$,
2. $\forall n \in \mathcal{N}(\gamma).\ \rho(\llbracket n \rrbracket_\gamma) = \llbracket \rho(n) \rrbracket_{\gamma'}$,[6]
3. $n \in \perp(\gamma)$ implies $\rho(n) \in \perp(\gamma')$, and $n \in \mathcal{D}(\gamma)$ implies $\rho(n) \in \mathcal{D}(\gamma')$.

In Fig. 4, it holds that $\gamma_1 \stackrel{id[z'/z]}{=} \gamma_3$.[7]

---

[5] The third condition is not implied by the first due to pathological cases for looping nonterminals. Add, for example, $z \rightarrow z$ to γ_1 from Fig. 4. The resulting grammar satisfies the first and the second condition, but not the third.

[6] Here, we assume that ρ cannot just be applied to nonterminals, but also to sets of strings over terminals and observable nonterminals through natural lifting.

[7] *id* denotes the identity function. $id[z'/z]$ denotes the update of *id* at z to return z'.

Definition 3 (Subgrammar relation ($\overset{\leq}{\equiv}$)). γ is a subgrammar of γ' $(\gamma \overset{\leq}{\equiv} \gamma')$ *if:*

1. $\mathcal{N}(\gamma) \subseteq \mathcal{N}(\gamma')$,
2. $\forall n \in \mathcal{N}(\gamma). \; [\![n]\!]_\gamma = [\![n]\!]_{\gamma'}$,
3. $\bot(\gamma) \subseteq \bot(\gamma'), \; \mathcal{D}(\gamma) \subseteq \mathcal{D}(\gamma')$.

In Fig. 4, it holds that $\gamma_4 \overset{\leq}{\equiv} \gamma_1$ (but of course not vice versa). As the definition details, the super-grammar γ' might employ more nonterminals than the subgrammar γ (cf. 1.). The denotations of γ are preserved (cf. 2.). Also, nonterminals of the subgrammar do not change their status to be a defined or a bottom nonterminal (cf. 3.). Thus, we can only add definitions for fresh nonterminals.

Definition 4 (Enrichment relation ($\overset{\subseteq}{\equiv}$)). γ' is richer than γ $(\gamma \overset{\subseteq}{\equiv} \gamma')$ *if:*

1. $\mathcal{N}(\gamma) \subseteq \mathcal{N}(\gamma')$,
2. $\forall n \in \mathcal{N}(\gamma). \; [\![n]\!]_\gamma \subseteq [\![n]\!]_{\gamma'}^{\bot(\gamma')\cup\emptyset(\gamma')\cup\emptyset(\gamma)}$,
3. $\bot(\gamma) \subseteq \bot(\gamma'), \; \mathcal{D}(\gamma) = \mathcal{D}(\gamma')$.

In Fig. 4, it holds that $\gamma_1 \overset{\subseteq}{\equiv} \gamma_5$. The above definition essentially says that γ' is richer than γ if γ' generates more than γ, i.e., $[\![n]\!]_\gamma \subseteq [\![n]\!]_{\gamma'}$. However, the actual definition also observes the looping nonterminals from γ for the denotation of γ'. Thereby, the relation is made robust regarding the particular case that γ' is obtained from γ by providing a base case for a looping nonterminal. While the subgrammar relation is concerned with the addition of definitions for fresh nonterminals, the enrichment relation is concerned with the extension of existing definitions. What remains, is a relation which covers the addition of definitions for bottom nonterminals.

Definition 5 (Instance relation ($\overset{\Rightarrow^*}{\equiv}$)). γ' is an instance of γ $(\gamma \overset{\Rightarrow^*}{\equiv} \gamma')$ *if:*

1. $\mathcal{N}(\gamma) \subseteq \mathcal{N}(\gamma')$,
2. $\forall n \in \mathcal{N}(\gamma). \; \forall x \in [\![n]\!]_\gamma. \; \exists y \in [\![n]\!]_{\gamma'}. \; x \Rightarrow^*_{\gamma'} y$,
3. $\forall n \in \mathcal{N}(\gamma). \; \forall y \in [\![n]\!]_{\gamma'}. \; \exists x \in [\![n]\!]_\gamma. \; x \Rightarrow^*_{\gamma'} y$,
4. $\mathcal{D}(\gamma) \subseteq \mathcal{D}(\gamma'), \; \mathcal{D}(\gamma') \setminus \mathcal{D}(\gamma) \subseteq \bot(\gamma)$.

In Fig. 4, it holds that $\gamma_1 \overset{\Rightarrow^*}{\equiv} \gamma_6$ because the bottom nonterminal z of γ_1 is resolved in γ_6. In the definition, the second condition means that strings from $[\![n]\!]_\gamma$ can be completed into strings from $[\![n]\!]_{\gamma'}$ using $\Rightarrow^*_{\gamma'}$. The third condition states that all strings from $[\![n]\!]_{\gamma'}$ have to be reachable in this manner to make sure that the enrichment relation is not subsumed by the instance relation. A notion which can be characterised by the instance relation is context-free substitution.

3.3 Grammar Transformers

The above grammar relations can be employed to define various preservation properties for grammar transformations. We model grammar transformations as partial functions on grammars, say partial *grammar transformers.*

Definition 6 (Preservation properties). *Given a partial function $f : \mathcal{G} \nrightarrow \mathcal{G}$, we use $Rel(f) \subset \mathcal{G} \times \mathcal{G}$ to denote the relation encoded by f, that is, $Rel(f) = \{\langle \gamma, \gamma' \rangle \in \mathcal{G} \times \mathcal{G} \mid \gamma' = f(\gamma)\}$. The function f is*

1. strictly semantics-preserving *if $Rel(f) \subset \equiv$,*
2. semantics-preserving modulo renaming ρ *if $Rel(f) \subset \overset{\rho}{\equiv}$,*
3. introducing *if $Rel(f) \subset \overset{\leq}{\equiv}$,*
4. eliminating *if $Rel(f) \subset \overset{\leq}{\equiv}{}^{-1}$,*
5. increasing *if $Rel(f) \subset \overset{\subseteq}{\equiv}$,*
6. decreasing *if $Rel(f) \subset \overset{\subseteq}{\equiv}{}^{-1}$,*
7. resolving *if $Rel(f) \subset \overset{\Rightarrow^*}{\equiv}$,*
8. rejecting *if $Rel(f) \subset \overset{\Rightarrow^*}{\equiv}{}^{-1}$.*

The ultimate goal is to come up with transformation operators which separate the preservation properties, and to show that the resulting operator suite for grammar adaptation is reasonably orthogonal, complete, and usable.

4   The Transformation Framework

We define a simple framework for grammar transformations offering transformation primitives and combinators. We give a denotational semantics of the operators using partial grammar transformers as denotations. We discuss a number of supplementary concepts such as focus, constraints and symbolic operands.

4.1   Primitives

All the operators we have in mind are derivable from primitives the syntax of which is defined in Fig. 5. There are the constant operators id corresponding to the identity function on grammars, fail modelling the undefined grammar transformation, and reset denoting the grammar transformer returning the empty set of rules. There are primitives to add and to subtract a rule from the given grammar. There are also primitives to substitute nonterminals, and to replace phrases by other phrases in rules. We will see later that the operator delete used in the introductory example is derived from the operator replace.

In Fig. 6, the simple interpretation of the primitives is given by recursive functions in the style of denotational semantics. We use partial grammar transformers as denotations.[8] In the definition of substitute and replace, we employ an auxiliary function *rhs* to traverse right-hand sides of rules using list-processing functions *head* and *tail*.[9]

---

[8] The given semantics does not rely on *cpos* as semantic domains because general recursion is not involved. The undefined value corresponds to failure. We assume a strict failure model, that is, transformations cannot observe or recover from failure. For brevity, we do not spell out the propagation of failure.

[9] The *rhs* traversal for substitute adheres to the map scheme for lists (of grammar symbols), whereas the *rhs* traversal for substitute relies on associative matching.

$$Trafo ::= \text{id} \mid \text{fail} \mid \text{reset} \mid \text{add } Rule \mid \text{sub } Rule$$
$$\mid \text{substitute } Nt \text{ by } Nt \mid \text{replace } Phrase \text{ by } Phrase$$
$$Nt ::= \mathcal{U}_N$$
$$Phrase ::= (\mathcal{U}_N \cup \mathcal{U}_T)^*$$
$$Rule ::= Nt \to Phrase$$

Fig. 5. Syntax of the transformation primitives

$$\mathcal{IT} \qquad\qquad : Trafo \to (\mathcal{G} \nrightarrow \mathcal{G})$$
$$\mathcal{IT} \; [\![\text{id}]\!] \; \gamma \quad = \gamma$$
$$\mathcal{IT} \; [\![\text{fail}]\!] \; \gamma \quad = \text{undefined}$$
$$\mathcal{IT} \; [\![\text{reset}]\!] \; \gamma \; = \emptyset$$
$$\mathcal{IT} \; [\![\text{add } r]\!] \; \gamma = \gamma \cup \{r\}$$
$$\mathcal{IT} \; [\![\text{sub } r]\!] \; \gamma = \gamma \setminus \{r\}$$
$$\mathcal{IT} \; [\![\text{substitute } n \text{ by } n']\!] \; \gamma = \{ren(n) \to rhs(u) \mid n \to u \in \gamma\}$$

where
$$ren(m) = id[n'/n](m)$$
$$rhs(u) = \begin{cases} \epsilon, & \text{if } u = \epsilon \\ ren(head(u)) \; rhs(tail(u)), & \text{otherwise} \end{cases}$$

$$\mathcal{IT} \; [\![\text{replace } p \text{ by } p']\!] \; \gamma = \{n \to rhs(u) \mid n \to u \in \gamma\}$$

where
$$rhs(u) = \begin{cases} \text{undefined}, & \text{if } p = \epsilon \\ \epsilon, & \text{if } u = \epsilon \\ p' \; rhs(v), & \text{if } u = p \, v \\ head(u) \; rhs(tail(u)), & \text{otherwise} \end{cases}$$

Fig. 6. Semantics of the transformation primitives

The primitives do not satisfy any convenient preservation properties except a few trivial ones. The denotations $\mathcal{IT} \; [\![\text{id}]\!]$ and $\mathcal{IT} \; [\![\text{fail}]\!]$, for example, are strictly semantics-preserving. More interesting preservation properties will be enabled if we consider suitably restricted applications of the other operators. Consider, for example, the transformation substitute n by n'. The substitution is semantics-preserving modulo renaming if n' is fresh in the given grammar. Indeed, our operator suite for grammar adaptation will consist of such suitably restricted combinations.

4.2   Combinators

We need several combinators for grammar transformations. Firstly, there is a simple combinator $T_1 ; T_2$ for sequential composition of the transformations T_1 and T_2. Secondly, there is a form of a conditional if C then T_1 else T_2 to perform either the transformation T_1 or the transformation T_2 depending on the condition C. We postpone discussing possible forms of conditions. Thirdly, there is a combinator $T_{/\psi}$ to apply a transformation T in a focus, that is, for certain nonterminals ψ only. Recall the introductory example: Some phrase had to be deleted in the definition of REDEFINES-clause (but not elsewhere). Finally, there is a trivial combinator $T!$ to enforce that a given transformation has an effect. An adaptation step, which has no effect, usually indicates an error. In Fig. 7, the syntax for the combinators is summarised.

$Trafo ::= \cdots \mid Trafo; Trafo \mid \text{if } Cond \text{ then } Trafo \text{ else } Trafo \mid Trafo_{/Focus} \mid Trafo!$
$Focus ::= \{Nt, \ldots, Nt\}$

Fig. 7. Syntax of the transformation combinators

The semantics of the combinators is defined in Fig. 8. The interpretation of sequential composition and of the if-construct is straightforward. In the equation for a focused transformation $T_{/\psi}$, we use an auxiliary operator $\gamma_{/\psi}$ to restrict a grammar γ to a set of nonterminals ψ. The operator is defined as follows:

$$\gamma_{/\psi} = \{n \to u \in \gamma \mid n \in \psi\}$$

The interpretation of $T_{/\psi}$ details that the remainder of the grammar outside of the focus, that is, $\gamma_{/\mathcal{D}(\gamma) \setminus \psi}$, is preserved. Note also that an invalid focus (i.e., $\psi \not\subseteq \mathcal{D}(\gamma)$) leads to an undefined result. The equation for the interpretation of $T!$ formalises what we mean by a transformation that has an effect on the given grammar. The transformation $T!$ only succeeds if T succeeds *and* the resulting grammar is different from the given grammar. Here, we assume structural equality on grammars. Let us consider two examples. The transformation id! unconditionally fails. The transformation substitute n by n'! fails if there are no occurrences of n in the given grammar, or if $n = n'$.

$\mathcal{IT}$ $\qquad\qquad\qquad\qquad$: $Trafo \to (\mathcal{G} \rightharpoonup \mathcal{G})$
$\mathcal{IT}$ $[\![T_1; T_2]\!]\, \gamma$ $\qquad\qquad$ $= \mathcal{IT}$ $[\![T_2]\!]\, (\mathcal{IT}$ $[\![T_1]\!]\, \gamma)$

$\mathcal{IT}$ $[\![\text{if } C \text{ then } T_1 \text{ else } T_2]\!]\, \gamma = \begin{cases} \mathcal{IT} \ [\![T_1]\!]\, \gamma, \text{ if } c = true \\ \mathcal{IT} \ [\![T_2]\!]\, \gamma, \text{ if } c = false \end{cases}$
$\qquad\qquad\qquad\qquad\qquad\quad$ where $c = \mathcal{IC}$ $[\![C]\!]\, \gamma$

$\mathcal{IT}$ $[\![T_{/\psi}]\!]\, \gamma$ $\qquad\qquad$ $= \begin{cases} \gamma', \qquad\quad \text{if } \psi \subseteq \mathcal{D}(\gamma) \\ \text{undefined, otherwise} \end{cases}$
$\qquad\qquad\qquad\qquad\qquad\quad$ where $\gamma' = (\mathcal{IT}$ $[\![T]\!]\, \gamma_{/\psi}) \cup \gamma_{/\mathcal{D}(\gamma) \setminus \psi}$

$\mathcal{IT}$ $[\![T!]\!]\, \gamma$ $\qquad\qquad$ $= \begin{cases} \gamma', \qquad\quad \text{if } \gamma \neq \gamma' \\ \text{undefined, otherwise} \end{cases}$
$\qquad\qquad\qquad\qquad\qquad\quad$ where $\gamma' = \mathcal{IT}$ $[\![T]\!]\, \gamma$

Fig. 8. Semantics of the transformation combinators

4.3 Constraints

In order to derive operators which satisfy some interesting preservation properties, we need means to constrain transformations. One constraint which we already encountered is that a transformation has to be effective. Other constraints can be formulated using conditionals (if C ...). In Fig. 9, some forms of conditions C are defined. In practice, further forms might be relevant. There are conditions which are concerned with the kinds of nonterminals (fresh, bottom, etc.). Such conditions are valuable if we need to enforce assumptions on the nonterminals occurring as operands in transformations. There is a further form of condition, namely u covers v. Roughly, the condition attempts to test if u generates at least what v generates. Such tests are useful, for example, to constrain increasing and decreasing transformations.

Syntax
$Cond ::=$ fresh $Nt \mid$ bottom $Nt \mid$ top $Nt \mid$ used $Nt \mid$ defined $Nt \mid$ looping Nt
$\qquad \mid Nt \in Focus \mid Phrase$ covers $Phrase$

Evaluation
$\mathcal{IC}$ $\qquad\qquad : Cond \rightarrow (\mathcal{G} \multimap \{false, true\})$
$\mathcal{IC} \; [\![\text{fresh } n]\!] \; \gamma \quad = n \notin \mathcal{N}(\gamma)$
$\mathcal{IC} \; [\![\text{bottom } n]\!] \; \gamma = n \in \bot(\gamma)$
$\dots$
$\mathcal{IC} \; [\![n \in \psi]\!] \; \gamma \quad = n \in \psi$
$\mathcal{IC} \; [\![u \text{ covers } v]\!] \; \gamma = u \leadsto_\gamma v$

Coverage
$u \leadsto_\gamma u$
$n \leadsto_\gamma u$ where $n \rightarrow u \in \gamma$
$u \leadsto_\gamma n$ where $\gamma_{/\{n\}} = \{n \rightarrow u\}, n \notin \emptyset(\gamma)$
$\quad \dots$

Abbreviations
$C\,?$ $\qquad$ = if C then id else fail
$\neg\,C\,?$ $\qquad$ = if C then fail else id
u equiv $v\,?$ = u covers $v\,?\,; v$ covers $u\,?$

Fig. 9. Syntax and evaluation of conditions

The evaluation of the conditions concerned with the various kinds of nonterminals simply refers to the corresponding sets of nonterminals defined earlier. In the evaluation of u covers v, we use an auxiliary binary relation $\leadsto_\gamma$. Conceptually, $u \leadsto_\gamma v$ should hold if the observable strings derivable from v are also derivable from u (but not necessarily vice versa). In practice, we use a pessimistic heuristic as indicated in Fig. 9 to check for coverage. Such a heuristic checks if the two given phrases can be made (structurally) equal by a finite number of symbolic derivation steps in the sense of $\Rightarrow_\gamma$.[10]

---

[10] Of course, we cannot determine in general if the strings generated by v are also generated by u because otherwise we would claim that the subset relationship for context-free grammars is decidable.

We also define some convenient abbreviations in Fig. 9 for transformations which serve solely as guards. The transformation C? models a guard with a positive condition C, whereas $\neg\, C$? models a guard with a negated condition C. We will use such guards to model pre- and post-conditions of transformation operators. The last abbreviation is a guard u equiv v? for checking two phrases to be equivalent by a "conjunction" checking coverage in both directions.

Finally, we should comment on the interaction of the focus-construct and the evaluation of conditions. Since conditions are evaluated w.r.t. a given grammar, it matters if a guard is performed before or after restriction, and before or after re-unification with the grammar outside a focus. Usually, one wants to place conditionals before restriction or after re-unification. We cannot check, for example, that a nonterminal is fresh by just looking at a restricted grammar. One can think of other more flexible semantic models for the focus-construct, e.g., a model where the restriction is not performed by the focus-construct itself, but rather by the unconditional primitives in the last possible moment. Such a model has the drawback that the propagated focus has to be kept consistent. This is not straightforward.

4.4   Symbolic Operands

So far, transformations only operate on *concrete* nonterminals, phrases, rules, focuses as operands due to the definition of *Nt*, *Phrase*, *Rule*, and *Focus* (cf. Fig. 5 and Fig. 7). This is not always convenient. Sometimes, we also would like to formulate *symbolic* operands for transformations.

Syntax
Phrase ::= $\cdots$ | definition of *Nt*
Focus ::= $\cdots$ | all

Normalisation
definition of $n \to_\gamma u$ where $\gamma_{/\{n\}} = \{n \to u\}$
all $\to_\gamma \mathcal{D}(\gamma)$

Fig. 10. Two forms of symbolic operands

Let us consider examples. A symbolic form of phrase is definition of n which denotes the right-hand side of the rule defining n assuming there is only a single rule with n on the left-hand side. This form is convenient, for example, in the context of unfolding, where a nonterminal is replaced (in terms of the primitive replace) by the right-hand side of the definition of the nonterminal. We are relieved from actually pointing out the definition itself. Another symbolic form is all. It denotes all nonterminals defined in the grammar at hand. This form is useful if an operator expecting a focus parameter should be applied globally. We are relieved from enumerating all defined nonterminals. In practice, other forms are relevant, too. We can think of, for example, a form to turn a phrase into the corresponding permutation phrase [4]. If extended BNF is taken into account, all forms for alternatives, optionals, lists also need to be dealt with symbolically.

The question is how symbolic forms should be evaluated. Recall that conditions are evaluated by the semantic function $\mathcal{IC}$ which in turn is invoked if conditionals are interpreted via $\mathcal{IT}$. We could adopt this approach for symbolic forms, and introduce corresponding evaluation functions for Nt, $Phrase$, $Rule$ and $Focus$ which are then invoked during interpretation of the transformations. For pre- and post-conditions it is sensible, that they are evaluated w.r.t. intermediate grammars in a compound transformation. It is not sensible for symbolic forms. Consider, for example, a transformation for unfolding the definition of n in the focus of $\{n'\}$. The definition of n is not available for evaluation after the restriction to the focus $\{n'\}$. We propose that symbolic forms of a given transformation corresponding to an *indivisible adaptation step* are eliminated before interpretation. This model provides referential transparency. In Fig. 10, elimination rules for the above examples of symbolic forms are shown.[11]

5   The Operator Suite

We are now in the position to derive operators which are immediately useful for actual grammar adaptation. Indeed, the derived operators are meant to mimic the roles one naturally encounters while adapting grammars manually.

5.1   Overview

A *stepwise adaptation* can be conceived as a sequence $T_1; \ldots; T_m$ of transformation steps, where the T_i correspond to applications of the operators from the suite. A transformational grammar programmer does neither use primitives nor combinators. He solely uses operators of the suite. In particular, a programmer does not restrict the focus of transformations himself. Instead, operators expose a focus parameter if necessary. The T_i are exactly those indivisible adaptation steps assumed for the evaluation model of symbolic operands.

The definitions of all the operators covered in this section are shown in Fig. 11. The operators can be subdivided into three groups, namely refactoring, construction, and destruction. These groups are discussed in detail below. Note that several of these operators are more interesting if extended BNF expressiveness was considered. Properties of the operators, mainly semantics preservation properties, will be summarised at the end of the section.

5.2   Refactoring

Refactoring is useful to restructure grammars so that comprehensibility is improved, or subsequent adaptation steps are easier to perform. Refactoring operators are semantics-preserving in the narrow sense. Note how the guards in the

---

[11] We conceive these elimination rules (performed w.r.t. a grammar γ) as rewrite rules to be used for normalisation. If the resulting normal form still contains symbolic forms, we consider that as an error, and we will not interpret the corresponding transformation.

Refactoring

preserve P in F as P'	$= P$ equiv P'?; replace P by $P'!_{/F}$; P equiv P'
fold P in F to N	$=$ introduce N as P; preserve P in F as N?
unfold N in F	$=$ preserve N in F as definition of N
introduce N as P	$=$ fresh N?; add $N \to P$
eliminate N	$=$ reject $\{N\}$; fresh N?
rename N to N'	$=$ fresh N'?; substitute N by N'!

Construction

generalise P in F to P'	$= P'$ covers P?; replace P by $P'!_{/F}$; P' covers P?
include P for N	$=$ defined N?; add $N \to P$!
resolve N as P	$=$ bottom N?; add $N \to P$
unify N to N'	$=$ bottom N?; $\neg$ fresh N'?; replace N by N'

Destruction

restrict P in F to P'	$= P$ covers P'?; replace P by $P'!_{/F}$; P covers P'?
exclude P from N	$=$ sub $N \to P$!; defined N?
reject F	$=$ reset$_{/F}$
separate N in F as N'	$=$ fresh N'?; replace N by $N'!_{/F}$; $\neg$ fresh N?
delete P in F	$= \neg P$ covers ϵ?; replace P by $\epsilon!_{/F}$

Fig. 11. Operator suite for grammar adaptation

operator definitions describe pre- and post-conditions. Also note that the operators check themselves if they actually affect the given grammar (either directly by "!", or more indirectly).

A fundamental refactoring operator is **preserve**. The operator allows to replace a phrase by an equivalent one. There is a focus parameter (cf. ... in ...), i.e., one can restrict the replacement to a certain focus. The constraint that the old and the new phrase have to be equivalent is checked before and after replacement.[12] Operators for folding and unfolding nonterminal definitions can be directly derived from the operator **preserve**. Folding and unfolding are common transformations discussed for various formalisms elsewhere (cf. [12]). Nonterminals which should be unfolded have to be defined by exactly one rule.[13] The operator **preserve** is not restricted to folding and unfolding. In general, it can be used, if a grammar needs to be simplified, e.g., to remove an ambiguity, or if a grammar should be restructured to adhere to a certain style, e.g., for turning recursive nonterminals into extended BNF notation for lists.

Let us consider the remaining refactoring operators. Introduction and elimination of nonterminals is facilitated by the operators **introduce** and **eliminate**. Introduction can be clearly conceived as semantics-preserving in the narrow sense because all previous definitions are preserved. We consider elimination also as

---

[12] The post-condition is needed to cope with pathological cases. Consider, for example, **preserve definition of** n **in** $\{n\}$ **as** n, i.e., a transformation where the definition of a nonterminal n is replaced by n itself. The definition of n would be damaged by this replacement.

[13] This is implied by the use of **definition of** ... in the definition of **unfold**.

semantics-preserving in the narrow sense because we can only eliminate nonterminal definitions which are not needed in the remaining grammar anyway. Here, we assume that a grammar programmer has a clear perception of what the primary nonterminals of a grammar are, e.g., in the sense of a start symbol, and that such primary nonterminals are not eliminated. Finally, there is the operator rename for renaming of nonterminal symbols. The pre-condition fresh N' ? for rename N to N' makes sure that N is not renamed to a nonterminal N' which is already in use in the given grammar. This requirement qualifies substitution to perform renaming.

There is an insightful asymmetry between folding and unfolding. The operator fold performs introduction on the fly, whereas the operator unfold does not perform elimination. This asymmetry is sensible for pragmatic reasons. Unfolding is often performed in a focus and not globally. Thus, elimination is usually impossible. By contrast, folding is usually performed to identify a subphrase and to introduce a nonterminal for it. Otherwise, the operator preserve can be used.

5.3   Construction

The second group of operators in Fig. 11 facilitates construction. The term construction is meant here in a rather broad sense, that is, grammar substitution, extension, completion and others. Let us discuss the various operators in detail.

generalise P in F to P' The phrase P is replaced by the more general phrase P' in all occurrences focused by F. This is one convenient way to extend the generated language. As the pre-condition details, P' has to cover P.

include P for N Another straightforward way to extend the generated language is to add a rule $N \to P$ for a nonterminal N already defined in the given fragment. In fact, the pre-condition makes sure that there is a definition to be extended. Compared to the operator generalise, the operator include works at the rule level and not inside rules.

resolve N as P This operator is used to provide the definition for a bottom nonterminal N. Note that both include and resolve add rules, but due to the guards, the roles of increasing and resolving transformations are separated.

unify N to N' The bottom nonterminal N is unified with another nonterminal N' in the sense that N is replaced by N'. The operator unify is useful, if a bottom nonterminal should be resolved in terms of an existing definition (cf. first scenario in Fig. 12), or if two bottom nonterminals intentionally coincide (cf. second scenario in Fig. 12).

The operators for construction are useful in grammar development to complete and to connect a grammar. Missing rules are added by include. Too restrictive phrases are generalised with generalise. Missing definitions of nonterminals are established via resolve. Nonterminals are unified with unify.

5.4   Destruction

The third group of operators in Fig. 11 is useful for destructing grammars. Again, destruction is meant here in a broad sense. The destruction group pro-

$$
\begin{array}{lll}
x \rightarrow \dots b \dots & & x \rightarrow \dots z \dots \\
y \rightarrow \dots b \dots & \xRightarrow{\text{unify } b \text{ to } z} & y \rightarrow \dots z \dots \\
z \rightarrow \dots & \xleftarrow{\text{separate } z \text{ in all as } b} & z \rightarrow \dots
\end{array}
$$

$$
\begin{array}{lll}
x \rightarrow \dots b \dots & & x \rightarrow \dots b' \dots \\
y \rightarrow \dots b' \dots & \xRightarrow{\text{unify } b \text{ to } b'} & y \rightarrow \dots b' \dots \\
z \rightarrow \dots b' \dots & \xleftarrow{\text{separate } b' \text{ in } \{x\} \text{ as } b} & z \rightarrow \dots b' \dots
\end{array}
$$

Fig. 12. Illustration of the operators unify and separate

vides essentially the inverse operators of the construction group.[14] The operator restrict replaces a phrase by a more restrictive phrase in a given focus. The operator exclude excludes one rule for a given nonterminal. The post-condition makes sure that exclude behaves as a decreasing rather than a rejecting operator. The latter role is solely modelled by the operator reject, and accordingly enforced by its post-condition. The operator separate "breaks up connections" in the grammar, that is, it replaces nonterminal occurrences by a fresh nonterminal as illustrated in Fig. 12. The post-condition ensures that the separation does not degenerate to a renaming. Finally, the operator delete removes a phrase from the focused rules. It has been illustrated in the introduction. The pre-condition of delete is insightful because it makes sure that this removal cannot be done in a more modest way, that is, by restricting the phrase of concern to ϵ via the more disciplined operator restrict.

As the operators for construction are useful in grammar development to complete and to connect a grammar, the destruction operators are useful for correction or revision. Too general phrases can be restricted. Superfluous rules or definitions can be excluded or rejected, respectively. Accidentally unified phrases can be separated by introducing new nonterminals in certain occurrences. Refactoring steps usually precede construction and destruction.

5.5   Discussion

Let us discuss the properties of the various operators. The semantics-preservation properties are summarized in Fig. 13. The figure also shows the (sometimes only approximative) inverse operator for each operator. The operators from the refactoring group are semantics-preserving in the narrow sense, say strictly semantics-preserving, semantics-preserving modulo renaming, introducing, or eliminating. The operators for construction and destruction are not semantics-preserving in the narrow sense. Several operators experience the grammar relations for enrichment and instances, that is, the corresponding transformations are increasing, decreasing, resolving or rejecting.

The properties from Fig. 13 are implied by simple arguments. Let us consider a few examples. The operator preserve is strictly preserving because equiv-

---

[14] Exception: The operator delete has no counterpart in the construction group.

Operator	Semantics Preservation	Inverse
Refactoring		
preserve	strict	preserve
fold	introducing	unfold
unfold	strict	fold
introduce	introducing	eliminate
eliminate	eliminating	introduce
rename	modulo renaming	rename
Construction		
generalise	increasing	restrict
include	increasing	exclude
resolve	resolving	reject
unify	essentially resolving	separate
Destruction		
restrict	decreasing	generalise
exclude	decreasing	include
reject	rejecting	resolve
separate	essentially rejecting	unify
delete	"zig-zag"	

Fig. 13. Properties of the derived operators

alence of the phrases (w.r.t. generation of observable strings) involved in replacement implies equivalence of grammars. Since unfolding is solely defined in terms of preserve, strict semantics-preservation for unfold is implied. The operator introduce is introducing because it adds a rule for a fresh nonterminal. This is a direct implementation of the notion of a super-grammar. The operator fold is introducing because it is defined as a sequence of an introducing transformation and a strictly semantics-preserving transformation. A rigorous proof for the properties is beyond the scope of the paper.

The distribution of the various preservation properties in Fig. 13 documents a kind of orthogonality of the operator suite. Most operators experience exactly one kind of preservation property in a pure way. All operators except unify, separate, and delete are pure in that sense. All grammar relations or preservation properties resp. are covered by the pure operators. The impure operators have been introduced for convenience. In practice, a few further impure operators are convenient, too. In fact, the impure operators can be reconstructed in terms of the pure operators. These reconstructions are also useful to understand the exact preservation properties of the impure operators. We only show the reconstruction of unify:[15]

unify N to N' $=$ ¬ fresh N'?; resolve N by N'; unfold N in all; eliminate N

---

[15] Reconstruction of separate and delete in terms of the pure operators is slightly more tedious since we need fresh nonterminals for some temporary definitions. This is also the reason why we favoured a more compact (impure) definition solely based on replace in Fig. 11.

Superficially, unify is a resolving operator since it "connects" one nonterminal N to another N', that is, N is defined in terms of N'. As we see, the transformation sequence above is indeed essentially a resolving transformation. However, the nonterminal N is only defined temporarily. The definition is eliminated after unfolding. The complete transformation sequence is not strictly resolving because the instance relationship does not hold without the temporary definition.

6   Concluding Remarks

Towards proper grammar engineering. As for common practice, grammar development is usually done in ad-hoc manner. Grammar development is often conceived as coding effort, as grammar (conflict) hacking. As for research, grammars are not too much of a topic anymore. Grammars deserve more attention both in practice and academia. Grammars should be regarded much more as real engineering artifacts. Research should supply the methods useful in grammar development. The present paper contributes in this context. The paper lays down the foundations of an adaptive style for grammar development. Grammars are adapted by well-behaved program transformations. The ultimate grammar programmer probably does not write down verbose transformations, but he rather uses an interactive tool which automatically deduces grammar transformations. One can think of a proper grammar engineering environment providing not just support for interactive adaptation but also for grammar assessment, testing by parsing, coverage measurement, and others. Similar tools are envisioned and described (to some extent) in [14,9].

Semantics-preservation and relaxation. To call one group of adaptation operators refactorings, has been inspired by the idea of refactoring in (object-oriented) programming [10]. Indeed, the intentions coincide, that is, programs or grammars resp. are adapted in a semantics-preserving manner to improve their structure, and to prepare subsequent extensions or even revisions. Recall that the other groups of adaptation operators discussed in the paper are not semantics-preserving in the narrow sense. The major body of research on transformational programming assumes semantics-preservation [11,12]. The present paper contributes a set of weaker preservation notions which are suitable to characterise revisions, extensions and others. The style of adaptive grammar programming developed in the paper scales up to practically relevant grammar projects [9], and it helps to actually make these projects feasible and predictable.

Perspective. The present paper does not explore several dimensions in depth. The operator suite is complete in a trivial sense: One can derive any grammar with it.[16] We are interested in more global notions than preservation properties, e.g., if a grammar is *improved* in some sense along some transformation sequence. This is a challenging research topic. Another issue ignored in the present paper is the interaction of context-free syntax and semantic functions as relevant for attribute grammars. This issue is in fact practically relevant for the application

---

[16] An extreme strategy is the following. The input grammar is discarded by reject all. The output grammar is constructed (from scratch) via introduce, resolve, and include.

of compiler compilers like YACC. At a more general level, this interaction issue can be rephrased as the question how clients of a grammar such as compiler compiler inputs, rewrite rules have to be adapted if the grammar serving as contract changes. This issue is an open research problem. Finally, we would like to integrate our approach with other scenarios of grammar adaptation, and applications for grammar transformations. We just mention a few. In [16], grammar transformations are used for the development of domain-specific languages starting from reusable syntax components. In [15], grammar transformations are used to derive abstract syntaxes from concrete syntaxes. In several contexts, schematic adaptation is often relevant as opposed to stepwise adaptation favoured in the present paper. For schematic adaptation, one needs to formulate transformation *schemes* which are then systematically applied all over the grammar either exhaustively or according to some heuristics. In grammar reengineering [14], one is, for example, concerned with DeYACCification, that is, the systematic introduction of optionals, lists and that alike. In parser implementation [2,1,13], schematic adaptation is needed to systematically eliminate list constructs, to optimise grammars w.r.t. certain grammar classes, or for grammar class migration.

References

1. J. Aycock and N. Horspool. Faster Generalized LR Parsing. In S. Jähnichen, editor, *Proc. of the 8th International Conference on Compiler Construction (CC'99)*, volume 1575 of *LNCS*, pages 32–46. Springer-Verlag, 1999.
2. D. Blasband. *Automatic Analysis of Ancient Languages*. PhD thesis, Free University of Brussels, 2000.
3. M. Brand, M. Sellink, and C. Verhoef. Generation of components for software renovation factories from context-free grammars. *Science of Computer Programming*, 36(2–3):209–266, 2000.
4. R. D. Cameron. Extending context-free grammars with permutation phrases. *ACM Letters on Programming Languages and Systems*, 2(4):85–94, Mar. 1993.
5. E. Chikofsky and J. Cross. Reverse engineering and design recovery: A taxonomy. *IEEE Software*, 7(1):13—17, 1990.
6. M. de Jonge and J. Visser. Grammars as Contracts. In *Proc. of GCSE 2000*, LNCS, Erfurt, Germany, 2001. Springer-Verlag. to appear.
7. IBM Corporation. *VS COBOL II Application Programming Language Reference*, 1993. Release 4, Document number GC26-4047-07.
8. R. Lämmel and C. Verhoef. VS COBOL II Grammar Version 1.0.3. http://www.cwi.nl/~ralf/grammars, 1999–2001.
9. R. Lämmel and C. Verhoef. Semi-automatic Grammar Recovery. Submitted, available at http://www.cwi.nl/~ ralf/, July 2000.
10. W. F. Opdyke. *Refactoring Object-Oriented Frameworks*. PhD thesis, University of Illinois at Urbana-Champaign, 1992.
11. H. A. Partsch. *Specification and Transformation of Programs*. Springer-Verlag, 1990.
12. A. Pettorossi and M. Proietti. Rules and Strategies for Transforming Functional and Logic Programs. *ACM Computing Surveys*, 28(2):360–414, June 1996.
13. J. J. Sarbo. Grammar transformations for optimizing backtrack parsers. *Computer Languages*, 20(2):89–100, May 1994.

570   R. Lämmel

14. M. Sellink and C. Verhoef. Development, assessment, and reengineering of language descriptions. In J. Ebert and C. Verhoef, editors, *Proceedings of the Fourth European Conference on Software Maintenance and Reengineering*, pages 151–160. IEEE Computer Society, March 2000.
15. D. S. Wile. Abstract syntax from concrete syntax. In *Proc. of the 1997 International Conference on Software Engineering*, pages 472–480. ACM Press, 1997.
16. D. S. Wile. Integrating Syntaxes and their Associated Semantics. Draft, 1999.

Test-Case Calculation through Abstraction

Bernhard K. Aichernig

Institute for Software Technology, Graz University of Technology
Inffeldgasse 16b, A-8010 Graz, Austria
`aichernig@ist.tu-graz.ac.at`

Abstract. This paper discusses the calculation of test-cases for interactive systems. A novel approach is presented that treats the problem of
test-case synthesis as an abstraction problem. The refinement calculus
is used to formulate abstraction rules for calculating correct test-case
scenarios from a formal contract. This abstraction calculus results
in a synthesis method that, does not need to compute a finite state
machine. This is in contrast to previous work on testing from state-based
specifications. A well known example from the testing literature serves
to demonstrate this unusual application of the refinement calculus in
order to synthesize tests rather than implementations.

Keywords: testing, test-case synthesis, refinement calculus, abstraction
rules, scenarios, contract.

1 Introduction

In the past of computer science a large gap between the testing and the formal
methods community could be realized. Testers did not believe in the applicability
of formal verification techniques to real world problems, and formal method's
advocates could not accept testing-techniques as an adequate verification method
for producing correct software. However, today the gap is closing.

Today, light-weight approaches to formal methods invite engineers to gain
the advantages of formal specification techniques without focusing solely on correctness proofs. Having precise and unambiguous formal specifications available,
is the pre-requisite in order to automate black-box testing. This functional testing approach, in which the system under test is considered as a black-box, has
become more and more important: There is a growing awareness that a combination of black- and the more traditional white-box testing uncovers more defects
than applying a technique solely. Especially, the object-oriented paradigm and
the increasing use of Components Of The Shelf (COTS), shifted the focus of
interest towards black-box approaches [8].

The process of testing, and so its automation, can be divided into two main
activities: first, the synthesis of test-cases, second, the execution and evaluation
of the tests. In [3] the author has presented techniques for automating the latter by using an abstract requirements specification in the Vienna Development
Method Specification Language (VDM-SL) as a test-oracle for black-box testing.
In this paper we focus on the synthesis of test-cases.

J.N. Oliveira and P. Zave (Eds.): FME 2001, LNCS 2021, pp. 571–589, 2001.

1.1   Motivation

The motivation for this work originates in two previous industrial projects, where explicit VDM specifications and IFAD VDMTools [13] have been used to support the conventional synthesis of system-level test-cases. Both projects in the area of voice communication for air-traffic control demonstrated the need for formality.

In the first project the formalization of the requirements uncovered 64 ambiguous, contradictory, unclear or erroneous issues in the informal system documents. Furthermore, the execution of the formal prototype with the system test-cases in use lead to the realization that only 80% of the system's radio functionality had been covered — an unacceptable low percentage for a safety-critical system [17,18].

The second project's formalization raised 108 questions concerning the requirements, with 33 of them resulting in changes in the requirements document. Furthermore, 16 errors in the 65 original test-cases have been found [4]. This time, the conventional test-cases were designed in a very thorough manner: for each requirement one or more test-cases have been specified resulting in a 100% expression coverage. Thus, we realized that this coverage metric of VDMTools was too weak for finding more advanced test-cases.

The following observations motivate the formal test-synthesis method presented here. (1) The quality of system-level test-cases heavily relies on the quality of the based requirements. Formal specification techniques have proved to raise this quality. (2) Executable specifications tend to become too low-level with respect to abstraction. Therefore, a test-case synthesis approach should rather be based on more general relational than on functional specifications. (3) In our case, the safety-critical system is a highly interactive systems. Hence, the formalism used should be capable of capturing interaction. (4) Typical test-cases of such complex systems are scenarios of usage. Thus, a testing strategy must rather focus on scenarios than on input-output behavior. (5) In practice, many change requests have to be considered and test-cases should be easily adaptable. (5) Existing test-synthesis approaches do not satisfy our needs, as will be explained in more detail below.

1.2   Related Work on Testing

Since our approach is based on the refinement calculus, test-case generation from model-based specifications mostly relate to our own work. Model-based specifications use mathematical objects like sets, sequences and finite mappings for modeling a system's state explicitly.

One of the most cited works on test-case generation from model-based specifications is [11]. Dick and Faivre describe the method for an automated calculation of an finite state machine (FSM) based on a partitioning of the state spaces as well as the involved operations. A prolog tool has been developed for calculating the partitions based on a disjunctive normal form (DNF) transformation of the specification.

Most of the later work on testing from formal specifications is based on their observations. In Stocks' PhD thesis and his subsequent work, this formal partitioning technique is applied to Z [30,29,28,9] for the first time.

Stepney realized the abstraction relation between test-cases and object-oriented Z specifications [27]. Her group developed a tool for interactively calculating partition abstractions and to structure them for reuse. Our work can be seen as an extension of this view on testing.

In [16] a Z-based tool for partitioning is presented. As in our previous work, the specification is used as a test-oracle. The work presented in [15] demonstrates that a theorem prover like Isabelle can be used to generate such test-classes based on DNF rewriting. In order to reduce the number of possible partitions the classification tree method is applied for selecting only interesting partitions in [26]. Furthermore, in [25] testing from combined Z and statechart specifications is discussed.

In [2] the DNF method is applied to B [1]. Furthermore, B prototypes have been used for preparing tests [31], similar to our own industrial projects using VDM. Recently, Derrick and Boiten [10] discussed the refinement of test-cases calculated from a Z specification. Again, the approach is based on calculating a FSM.

Another class of approaches starts directly from behavioral specifications like finite state machines or finite labeled transition systems. For example [23, 24] reports on the test-case generation from CSP specifications for embedded systems.

As we do, MacColl and Carrington are planing to develop a testing framework for interactive systems. They use a combination of Z and behavioral specifications (the process algebras CSP and CCS) for specifying such systems [21]. In [14] such behavioral specifications are combined with algebraic testing techniques.

As can be seen, a lot of work has been done on generating test-cases from formal specifications. However, this paper demonstrates that there is still space for new contributions.

1.3   Contribution

Unlike the work above, our approach is based on program synthesis techniques. Since test-case generation is a synthesis process we find it more natural to use a development method like the refinement calculus in order to calculate test-cases.

The innovation in the work presented here is that the synthesis of test-sequences (scenarios) is considered as an abstraction problem. Especially, the reverse application of a refinement calculus for calculating the test-cases is new. In general, refinement is known as the process of concretization from an abstract specification towards an implementation while preserving its correctness. In contrast to the usual application of refinement techniques (see [12,20,22,6]), where a program is developed, in this approach the possible user interactions are specified on an abstract level and then further abstracted towards a valid sequence of user-actions – a test-scenario. Here Back and von Wright's theory of refinement [6] is applied in order to calculate correct abstractions.

Finally, our sequencing technique does not calculate the complete FSM prior to test-case selection and thus differs from the approaches above. In an environment, where change requests are common, calculating the whole FSM is not very efficient. Our method focus on the impact on the possible scenarios by systematically analyzing interaction compositions.

2   Testing Based on Contracts

2.1   Contracts

The prerequisite for testing is some form of contract between the user and the provider of a system that specifies what it is supposed to do. In case of system-level testing usually user and software requirement documents define the contract. Formal methods propose mathematical languages to define such a contract unambiguously and soundly. In this work the formal contract language of [6] is used. It is a generalization of the conventional pre- and post-condition style of formal specifications of VDM, B and Z. The logic of the contract language is higher-order logic (HOL).

A system is modeled by a global state x of type Σ denoted by $x : \Sigma$. Functionality is either expressed by functional state transformers f or relational updates R. A state transformer is a function $f : \Sigma \to \Gamma$ mapping a state space Σ to the same or another state space Γ.

A relational update $R : \Sigma \to \Gamma \to$ Bool specifies a state change by relating the state before with the state after execution. In HOL, relations are modeled by functions mapping the states to Boolean valued predicates. For convenience, a relational assignment $(x := x'|b)$ is available and generalizes assignment statements. It sets a state variable x to a new state x' such that b holds.

The language further distinguishes between the responsibilities of communicating agents in a contract. Here, the contract models the viewpoint of one agent called the *angel* who interacts with the rest of the system called the *demon*. In our work following [6,5], the user is considered the angel and the system under test the demon. Relational contract statements denoted by $\{R\}$ express relational updates under control of the angel (user). Relational updates of the demon are denoted by $[R]$ and express updates that are non-deterministic from the angel's point of view. Usually, we take the viewpoint of the angel.

The contract statement $\langle f \rangle$ denotes a functional update of the state determined by a state transformer f. There is no choice involved here, neither for the angel nor the demon agent, since there is only one possible next state for a given state.

Two contracts can be combined by sequential composition $C_1; C_2$ or choice operators. The angelic choice $C_1 \sqcup C_2$ and the demonic choice $C_1 \sqcap C_2$ define non-deterministic choice of the angel or demon between two contracts C_1 and C_2. Furthermore, predicate assertions $\{p\}$ and assumptions $[p]$ define conditions the angel, respectively the demon, must satisfy. In this language of contract statements $\{p\}; \langle f \rangle$ denotes partial functions and $\{p\}; [R]$ pre-postcondition specifications. Furthermore, recursive contracts are possible for expressing iteration.

2.2   Semantics

The semantics of the contract statements is defined by weakest precondition predicate transformers. A predicate transformer $C : (\Gamma \to \mathsf{Bool}) \to (\Sigma \to \mathsf{Bool})$ is a function mapping postcondition predicates to precondition predicates. The set of all predicate transformers from Σ to Γ is denoted by $\Sigma \mapsto \Gamma \mathrel{\hat{=}} (\Gamma \to \mathsf{Bool}) \to (\Sigma \to \mathsf{Bool})$. Following the convention, we identify contract statements with predicate transformers that they determine. The notation $f.x$ is used for function application instead of the more common form $f(x)$. For details of the predicate transformer semantics, we refer to [6].

2.3   Refinement

The notion of contracts includes specification statements as well as programming statements. The latter can be defined by the basic contract statements presented above. The refinement calculus provides a synthesis method for refining specification statements into programming statements that can be executed by the target system. The refinement rules of the calculus ensure by construction that a program is correct with respect to its specification.

Formally, refinement of a contract C by C', written $C \sqsubseteq C'$, is defined by the pointwise extension of the subset ordering on predicates: For Γ being the after state space of the contracts, we have

$$C \sqsubseteq C' \mathrel{\hat{=}} \forall q \in (\Gamma \to \mathsf{Bool}) \cdot C.q \subseteq C'.q$$

. This ordering relation defines a lattice of predicate transformers (contracts) with the lattice operators meet $\sqcap$ and join $\sqcup$. The top element $\top$ is $\mathsf{magic}.q \mathrel{\hat{=}} \mathsf{true}$, a statement that is not implementable since it can magically establish every postcondition. The bottom element $\bot$ of the lattice is $\mathsf{abort}.q \mathrel{\hat{=}} \mathsf{false}$ defining the notion of abortion. The choice operators and negation of contracts are defined by pointwise extension of the corresponding operations on predicates. A large collection of refinement rules can be found in [6,22].

3   Test-Cases Are Abstractions

Abstraction is dual to refinement. If $C \sqsubseteq C'$, we can interchangeable say C is an abstraction of C'. In order to emphasize rather the search for abstractions than for refinements, we write $C \sqsupseteq C'$ to express C' is an abstraction of C. Trivially, abstraction can be defined as

$$C \sqsupseteq C' \mathrel{\hat{=}} C' \sqsubseteq C$$

This ordering relation of abstraction $\sqsupseteq$ defines the dual lattice on predicate transformers. Consequently, dual laws about the predicate transformer lattice can be constructed by interchanging $\sqsubseteq$ and $\sqsupseteq$, $\top$ and $\bot$, $\sqcup$ and $\sqcap$ in the original law.

In the following we will demonstrate that test-cases common in software engineering are in fact contracts – highly abstract contracts. To keep our discussion simple, we do not consider parameterized procedures, but only global state manipulations. In [6] it is shown how procedures can be defined in the contract language. Consequently, our approach scales up to procedure calls.

3.1   Input-Output Tests

The simplest form of test-cases are pairs of input i and output o data. We can define such an input-output test-case TC as a contract between the user and the unit under test:

$$\mathsf{TC}\; i\; o \mathrel{\hat=} \{x = i\}; [y := y' | y' = o]$$

Intuitively, the contract states that if the user provides input i, the state will be updated such that it equals o. Here, x is the input variable and y the output variable.

In fact, such a TC is a formal pre-postcondition specification solely defined for a single input i. This demonstrates that a collection of n input-output test-cases TCs are indeed pointwise defined formal specifications:

$$\mathsf{TCs} \mathrel{\hat=} \mathsf{TC}\; i_1\; o_1 \sqcup \ldots \sqcup \mathsf{TC}\; i_n\; o_n$$

Moreover, such test-cases are abstractions of general specifications, if the specification is deterministic for the input-value of the test-case, as the following theorem shows.

Theorem 1. *Let* $p : \Sigma \to \mathit{Bool}$ *be a predicate,* $Q : \Sigma \to \Gamma \to \mathit{Bool}$ *a relation on states, and* $TC\; i\; o$ *a test-case with input* i *in variable* x *and output* o *in variable* y . *Then*

$$\{p\}; [Q] \sqsupseteq \mathsf{TC}\; i\; o \;\equiv\; (x = i) \subseteq p \wedge |x = i|; Q \subseteq |y := o| \,,$$

where $|p|$ *and* $|f|$ *denote the coercion of predicates (here* $x = i$*) and state transformers (here* $y := o$*) to relations. Furthermore the composition operator* ; *is overloaded for relations.*

Theorem 1 shows that only for deterministic specifications, simple input-output test-cases are sufficient, in general. The theorem becomes simpler if the whole input and output is observable.

Proof.

$\{p\}; [Q] \sqsupseteq \mathsf{TC}\ i\ o$

$\equiv$ by definitions

$\forall\ \sigma\ r \cdot p.\sigma \wedge Q.\sigma \subseteq r \Leftarrow (x = i).\sigma \wedge [y := y'|y' = o].r$

$\equiv$ by definition of demonic relational assignment

$\forall\ \sigma\ r \cdot p.\sigma \wedge Q.\sigma \subseteq r \Leftarrow (x = i).\sigma \wedge (\forall\ y' \cdot (y' = o) \Rightarrow r[y := y'])$

$\equiv$ by simplification of update

$\forall\ \sigma\ r \cdot p.\sigma \wedge Q.\sigma \subseteq r \Leftarrow (x = i).\sigma \wedge r[y := o]$

$\equiv$ by definition of substitution $r := (y := y'|y' = o).\sigma$

$\forall\ \sigma\ \cdot p.\sigma \wedge Q.\sigma \subseteq (y := y'|y' = o).\sigma \Leftarrow (x = i).\sigma$

$\equiv$ distributivity, subset definition

$(\forall\ \sigma\ \cdot (x = i).\sigma \Rightarrow p.\sigma) \wedge$

$(\forall\ \sigma\ \sigma' \cdot (x = i).\sigma \wedge Q.\sigma.\sigma' \Rightarrow (y := y'|y' = o).\sigma.\sigma')$

$\equiv$ definitions

$(x = i) \subseteq p \wedge |x = i|; Q \subseteq |y := o|$

$\square$

Corollary 1. *Let* $p : \Sigma \to Bool$ *be a predicate,* $Q : \Sigma \to \Gamma \to Bool$ *a relation on states, and* $TC\ i\ o$ *a test-case, where the whole change of state is observable. Thus, input* $i : \Sigma$ *and output* $o : \Gamma$*. Then*

$$\{p\}; [Q] \sqsupseteq \mathsf{TC}\ i\ o \equiv p.i \wedge Q.i.o$$

Proof. The corollary follows from Theorem 1 and the assumption that $i : \Sigma$ and $o : \Gamma$. $\square$

The fact that test-cases are indeed formal specifications and as Theorem 1 shows abstractions of more general contracts explains why test-cases are so popular. They are abstract, and thus easy to understand. Furthermore, they are formal and thus unambiguous.

Furthermore, the selection of certain test-cases out of a collection of test-cases can be considered as abstraction:

Corollary 2.

$$\mathsf{TC}\ i_1\ o_1 \sqcup \ldots \sqcup \mathsf{TC}\ i_n\ o_n \sqsupseteq TC\ i_k\ o_k$$

where $1 <= k <= n$.

Proof. The theorem is valid by definition of the join operator $a \sqcup b \sqsupseteq a$ or $a \sqcup b \sqsupseteq b$, respectively. $\square$

3.2   Partition Tests

Partition analysis of a system is a powerful testing technique for reducing the possible test-cases: Here, a contract is analyzed and the input domains are split into partitions. A partition is an equivalence class of test-inputs for which the tester assumes that the system will behave the same. These assumptions can be based on a case analysis of a contract, or on the experience that certain input values are fault-prone.

In case of formal specifications, the transformation into a disjunctive normal form (DNF) is a popular partition technique as already mentioned in the discussion of the related work in Section 1. This technique is based on rewriting according the rule $A \vee B \equiv (A \wedge B) \vee (\neg A \wedge B) \vee (A \wedge \neg B)$.

A *partitioning* of a contract statement $\{p\}; [R]$ is a collection of n disjoint partitions $\{p_i\}; [R_i]$, such that

$$\{p\}; [R] = \{p_1\}; [R_1] \sqcup \ldots \sqcup \{p_n\}; [R_n]$$

and

$$\forall i, j \in \{1, \ldots, n\} . i \neq j \Rightarrow p_i \cap p_j = \emptyset$$

These partitions describe classes of test-cases, here called partition test-cases. Often in the literature, if the context is clear, a partition test-case is simply called a test-case.

Partition test-cases are abstractions of specifications, too:

Theorem 2. *Let* $\{p_i\}; [R_i]$ *be a partition of a specification* $\{p\}; [R]$. *Then*

$$\{p\}; [R] \sqsupseteq \{p_i\}; [R_i]$$

Proof. The result follows directly from the definition of partitioning above, and the definition of $\sqcup$. $\square$

Above, only the commonly used pre-postcondition contracts have been considered. They are a normal form for all contracts not involving angelic actions. This means that arbitrary contracts excluding $\sqcup$ and $\{R\}$ can be formulated in a pre-postcondition style. (see Theorem 26.4 in [6]). However, our result that test-cases are abstractions holds for general contract statements involving user inter-action. In order to justify this, user-interaction has to be discussed with respect to testing. The next section will introduce the necessary concepts.

4   Testing Interactive Systems

The synthesis of black-box tests for an interactive system has to consider the possible user actions. Furthermore, simple input-output test-cases are not sufficient for practical systems. Moreover, sequences of interactions, called scenarios, are necessary for setting the system under test into the interesting states. Consequently, scenarios of the system's use have to be developed for testing.

Scenarios are gaining more and more popularity in software engineering. The reasons are the same as for other test-cases: Scenarios are abstractions of an interactive system. For a comprehensive introduction into the different roles of scenarios in software engineering see [19]. In this work, the focus is on validation and verification.

4.1   User Interaction

Testing interactive systems, typically involves the selection of a series of parameters. Some of these parameters can be entered directly, some have to be set up, by initiating a sequence of preceding actions. Adequate test-cases should distinguish between these two possibilities of parameter setup. Therefore, simple pre-postcondition contracts are not sufficient to specify test-cases. Moreover, the tester's interaction with the system has to be modeled.

We define an atomic *interaction* IA of a tester, as a composition of the testers system update T and the following system's response Q.

$$\text{IA} \triangleq \{T\}; [Q]$$

The fact that we define an atomic interaction by means of angelic and demonic updates does not exclude other contract statements for modeling interaction. Theorem 13.10 in [6] states that $\{T\};[Q]$ is a normal form, thus arbitrary contract statements can be defined by means of interactions.

In this context a simple input-output test-case $\mathsf{TCl}\ i\ o$ involves the actual setting of the input variable to i.

$$\mathsf{TCl}\ i\ o \triangleq \{x := x' | x' = i\}; [y := y' | y' = o]$$

Again the abstraction relation holds for this kind of test-cases.

Theorem 3. *Let* $T : \Sigma \to \Gamma \to Bool$ *and* $Q : \Gamma \to \Theta \to Bool$ *relations on states, and* $\mathsf{TCl}\ i\ o$ *a test-case with input i in variable x and output o in variable y. Then*

$$\{T\}; [Q] \sqsupseteq \mathsf{TCl}\ i\ o \ \Leftarrow\ |x := i| \subseteq T \wedge Q \subseteq |y := o|$$

Proof. The theorem holds by homomorphism and monotonicity properties. For abstracting an interaction, demonic updates may be weakened and angelic updates strengthened. $\square$

The proof is similar to that of Theorem 1.

4.2   Iterative Choice

The application of an *iterative choice* statement for specifying and refining interactive systems have been extensively discussed in [5]. This statement, introduced in [6], is defined as a recursive selection of possible interactions S.

$$\text{do } \Diamond_i^n\ g_i\ ::\ S_i \text{ od} \triangleq (\mu X \cdot \{g_1\}; S_1; X \sqcup \ldots \sqcup \{g_n\}; S_n; X \sqcup \text{skip})$$

The skip statement, models the user's choice of stopping the dialog with the system. μ denotes the least fix-point operator. In general, a recursive contract $\mu X \cdot S$ is interpreted as the contract statement S, but with each occurrence of statement variable X in S treated as a recursive invocation of the whole contract.

The iterative choice statement follows a common iteration pattern, called angelic iteration. This iteration construct over S is defined as the following fixpoint:

$$S^{\Phi} \mathrel{\hat=} (\mu X \cdot S; X \sqcup skip)$$

Therefore, we have

$$\textbf{do } \Diamond_i^n \; g_i \; :: \; S_i \textbf{ od} = (\{g_1\}; S_1 \sqcup \ldots \sqcup \{g_n\}; S_n)^{\Phi}$$

Iterative choice should not be mixed with guarded command iterations used by Dijkstra [12]. Guarded command iterations are strong iterations defined by $S^{\omega} \mathrel{\hat=} (\mu X \cdot S; X \sqcap skip)$ with, in contrast to angelic iteration, the termination out of a user's control.

In [5] refinement rules for iterative choice are given. However, for testing we need abstraction rules for the synthesis of test-cases — scenarios are our goal.

4.3   Scenarios

An arbitrary scenario SC of an interactive system with n possible interactions S_i and of length l is a sequence of l sequential user interactions S_i. We write a sequence comprehension expression

$$\langle S_i(k) \mid (1 \leq i \leq n) \wedge (1 \leq k \leq l)\rangle$$

to denote such arbitrary sequences, where k is the position in the sequence. It should be mentioned that this sequence comprehension expression is not a valid predicate transformer, but rather serves as a scheme for sequences of predicate transformers. We use sequence comprehensions as a convenient notation, but they cannot be defined in higher-order logic.

Scenarios are abstractions of interactive systems, modeled by iterative choice, as the following theorem shows.

Theorem 4.

$$\textbf{do } \Diamond_i^n \; g_i \; :: \; S_i \textbf{ od} \sqsupseteq \langle (\{g_i\}; S_i)(k) \mid (1 \leq i \leq n) \wedge (1 \leq k \leq l)\rangle$$

Proof. The theorem is valid by definition of the angelic iteration statement and thus by definition of iterative choice:

$$\textbf{do } \Diamond_i^n \; g_i \; :: \; S_i \textbf{ od}$$
$$\equiv \; skip \sqcup \{g_1\}; S_1 \sqcup \{g_2\}; S_2 \sqcup \{g_1\}; S_1; \{g_1\}; S_1 \sqcup \{g_1\}S_1; \{g_2\}S_2 \sqcup \ldots$$

Hence, by definition of $\sqcup$ any arbitrary choice of sequence is an abstraction. $\square$

However, for test-case generation, we are only interested in valid scenarios. A scenario is considered a test-scenario if it terminates from every possible state. Thus its weakest precondition should be true:

$$\langle S_i(k) \mid (1 \le i \le n) \wedge (1 \le k \le l) \rangle.true = true$$

Consequently, the abstraction should not equal the abort statement. Since abort is the bottom element $\perp$ of the predicate transformer lattice, it is the trivial abstraction of every statement. Therefore, we define a notion of testing abstraction $\sqsupseteq_T$

$$S \sqsupseteq_T T \triangleq S \sqsupseteq T \sqcap \text{abort}$$

and get the abstraction rule for testing scenarios:

Theorem 5. *Let $g(k)$ denote the guard at the kth position in a scenario and assume that the system specification is consistent. Hence we assume that for all interactions $S_i.true \subseteq g_i$. Furthermore, $g(l+1) \ne false$ should be an arbitrary predicate called the **goal**.*

$$\text{do } \Diamond_i^n \; g_i \; :: \; S_i \text{ od } \sqsupseteq_T$$
$$\langle (\{g_i\}; S_i)(k) \mid (1 \le i \le n) \wedge (1 \le k \le l) \wedge g_i(k) \subseteq S_i(k).g(k+1) \wedge g(1) = true \rangle$$

Proof. Abstraction follows from Theorem 4. Termination is valid by induction: The weakest precondition of the first interaction is true, due to the assumption that for all interactions $S_i.true \subseteq g_i$ and $g(1)$ chosen to be true. Consequently $S_i(1)$ terminates. An interaction $S_i(k+1)$ terminates due to the fact that its pre-condition $g(k+1)$ can be reached by definition. $\square$

This abstraction rule defines the calculation of valid test scenarios. The goal predicate is a condition towards a sequence should be developed. Trivially, it is chosen to be true. For developing a scenario for setting a system to a certain state, this goal predicate represents the corresponding state description.

The theorem above shows that the question if a scenario terminates, can be reduced to the question if two following interactions are compositionable. From this observation a new testing strategy will be derived in the next section.

5   Calculating Scenarios for Testing

5.1   Critics on FSM Approaches

In previous related work on test-sequencing for model-oriented specifications, authors have been concentrated solely on the approach proposed by Dick and Faivre in [11]. This strategy first calculates partitions of the available operations and states. Then a finite state machine (FSM) is calculated by searching transitions from one state to the other. In this graph, nodes are state partitions and transitions are operation partitions. To derive test-sequences (scenarios) the tester follows the paths in the resulting graph. See the related work summarized in Section 1 for examples of this approach.

One disadvantage of this approach is that the whole FSM has to be calculated in advance, even if full coverage is out of the tester's scope due to resource limitations. This situation is even worse: Due to the focus on state partitions, the number of states increases exponentially with the number of partitioned state variables. Hence, rather large FSMs have to be calculated in advance. The second disadvantage is that a state based testing strategy is enforced, although the contract does not emphasize states but, like for interactive systems, possible interactions are the central paradigm of description.

In the following, a scenario oriented testing strategy is proposed. We call it a lazy technique, since the test-cases are calculated by need. It does not calculate a FSM, since it is not based on states. It is based on atomic scenarios, called compositions.

5.2   Compositions

We define a composition of an interactive system as a terminating sequential composition of two interactions. The following corollary follows directly from Theorem 5 and defines a rule for calculating such *compositions*.

Corollary 3. *For a consistent specification of interactions we have that*

$$(p \cap g_a) \subseteq S_a.g_b \Rightarrow \mathsf{do}\ \Diamond_i^n\ g_i\ ::\ S_i\ \mathsf{od}\ \sqsupseteq_T \{p \cap g_a\}; S_a; \{g_b\}; S_b$$

where $1 \leq a, b \leq n$ holds and p is an arbitrary predicate such that $p \neq$ false.

In practice, we will not calculate the compositions from the original specification, but will previously perform a partition analysis on the interactions, leading to more (partition) interactions. However, the approach keeps the same. These compositions should be calculated for all interaction partitions of interest. Next, these compositions are combined into scenarios.

5.3   Scenario Synthesis

The following rule defines the general calculation of scenarios by combining two compositions of interest.

Corollary 4. *Let the interactions with indices $1 \leq i, j, k \leq n$ be interactions of an interactive system with n interaction partitions, then*

$$\mathsf{do}\ \Diamond_i^n\ g_i\ ::\ S_i\ \mathsf{od}\ \sqsupseteq_T \{p_1 \cap g_i\}; S_i; \{g_j\}; S_j \sqcap \{p_2 \cap g_j\}; S_j; \{g_k\}; S_k\ \wedge$$
$$p \cap p_1 \cap g_1 \subseteq S_j.(p_2 \cap g_2) \Rightarrow$$
$$\mathsf{do}\ \Diamond_i^n\ g_i\ ::\ S_i\ \mathsf{od}\ \sqsupseteq_T \{g_i\}; S_i; \{g_j\}; S_j; \{g_k\}; S_k$$

In order to generate valid scenarios, a tester can e.g. start by an initial interaction with a guard equal to *true* and then he further searches for compositions leading to his test-goal. Which scenarios and how many scenarios are tested, depends on the testing strategy.

5.4   Scenario Based Testing Strategies

The new test approach can be divided into three phases:

1. calculation of interesting partitions for each interaction.
2. calculation of compositions.
3. combination of compositions to validate or to generate test-scenarios.

Different test-coverage strategies can be derived, determined by the strategy for combining the compositions. Interesting scenario analysis strategies are:
  Derive scenarios that include for each partition

- one composition consisting of the partition: for each partition one scenario.
- all possible compositions consisting of the partition: for each partition, one scenario for each interaction reaching the partition.
- all possible combinations of compositions between two interactions of interest: all scenarios leading from one interaction of interest to another.
- all possible combinations of compositions: all possible scenarios

The strategies are similar to the testing strategies used in data-flow testing [7]. The difference is that here atomic scenarios, called compositions, are considered, and in data-flow testing data-objects. An example will serve to demonstrate the approach at work.

6   Example: Process Scheduler

In this section, the application of our test synthesis method is demonstrated by an example, well known in the formal methods testing literature. It is the process scheduler introduced in [11] and translated to Back and von Wright's contract notation. We have chosen this example, although it is not new, because it allows a comparison to the traditional FSM approach most easily. Test-cases for industrial examples from our projects have been calculated, too. These more complex examples will be published in future publications.

6.1   Interactive Process Scheduler

The system consists of processes either *ready* to be scheduled or *waiting* to become ready and, optionally, a single *active* process. These processes are identified by a unique Pid $\hat{=}$ Nat. A process cannot be both ready and waiting, and the active process is neither ready nor waiting. In addition, there must be an active process whenever there are processes ready to be scheduled. The scheduling algorithm is not further specified.

We can model the interactions with this process scheduler as shown in Figure 1. In this specification a : Pid | nil is a global variable representing an optional active process, the global variable r : set of Pid and w : set of Pid represent the sets of ready and waiting processes. Furthermore, p : Pid is a global input variable solely used for setting a parameter.

$Init \;\hat{=}\;\;\;\; [a, r, w := a', r', w' | a' = \mathsf{nil} \wedge r' \cup w' = \emptyset]$

$New \;\hat{=}\;\;\;\; \{p := p' | p' \neq a \wedge p' \notin (r \cup w)\}; [w := w' | w' = w \cup p_{set}]$

$Ready \;\hat{=}\;\;\; \{p := p' | p' \in w\}; [a, r, w := a', r', w' | w' = w - p_{set} \wedge$
$\qquad\qquad\qquad\qquad\qquad\qquad\qquad a = \mathsf{nil} \Rightarrow (r' = r \wedge a' = p) \wedge$
$\qquad\qquad\qquad\qquad\qquad\qquad\qquad a \neq \mathsf{nil} \Rightarrow (r' = r \cup p_{set} \wedge a' = a)]$

$Swap \;\hat{=}\;\;\;\; \{a \neq \mathsf{nil}\}; [a, r, w := a', r', w' | r = \emptyset \Rightarrow (a' = \mathsf{nil} \wedge r' = \emptyset) \wedge$
$\qquad\qquad\qquad\qquad\qquad\qquad r \neq \emptyset \Rightarrow (a' \in r \wedge r' = r - a'_{set}) \wedge$
$\qquad\qquad\qquad\qquad\qquad\qquad w' = w \cup a_{set}]$

Fig. 1. Contracts of the process scheduler's initialization and interactions.

New introduces another process, *Ready* puts a process into the ready state, and *Swap* changes the active process. In order to prevent a confusion with assertions, p_{set} and a_{set} are used for denoting the sets $\{p\}$, $\{a\}$ containing the single element p and a. *Swap* is a good example, how we separate preconditions on the internal state from conditions for the parameter selection. Here, the fact that *Swap* is only defined if $\{a \neq \mathsf{nil}\}$ is documented as a precondition.

The interactive process scheduler can be defined by iterative choice of these interactions. The initialization statement should be executed once prior to user interaction. In Figure 2 this model is shown. Note that the precondition of *Swap* has become a guard. Furthermore, necessary conditions such that a parameter selection is possible are documented in the guards. Here $w \neq \emptyset$ is such a precondition of *Ready*.

6.2   Interaction Partitioning

For test-case synthesis, we first partition the basic interactions. Here, our partition strategy will be based solely on the case distinctions in the contract. As a consequence, the interaction *New* is not partitioned. Figure 3 presents the new partitions after some simplification.

Further partitioning based on interesting states would be possible. Here, for example, *New* may be further partitioned into cases where $w = nil$ and $w \neq nil$.

$Scheduler \;\hat{=}\; Init;\; \mathsf{do}\;\; \mathsf{true} :: New$
$\qquad\qquad\qquad \Diamond \quad w \neq \emptyset :: Ready$
$\qquad\qquad\qquad \Diamond \quad a \neq \mathsf{nil} :: Swap$
$\qquad\qquad\qquad \mathsf{od}$

Fig. 2. Contract of the interactive process scheduler.

$Ready_1 \,\hat{=}\, \{a = \mathsf{nil}\}; \{p := p'|p' \in w\}; [a, r, w := a', r', w'|w' = w - p_{set}\ \wedge$
$$r' = r \wedge a' = p\,]$$

$Ready_2 \,\hat{=}\, \{a \neq \mathsf{nil}\}; \{p := p'|p' \in w\}; [a, r, w := a', r', w'|w' = w - p_{set}\ \wedge$
$$r' = r \cup p_{set} \wedge a' = a]$$

$Swap_1 \,\hat{=}\, \{a \neq \mathsf{nil} \wedge r = \emptyset\}; [a, r, w := a', r', w'|(a' = \mathsf{nil} \wedge r' = \emptyset) \wedge$
$$w' = w \cup a_{set}]$$

$Swap_2 \,\hat{=}\, \{a \neq \mathsf{nil} \wedge r \neq \emptyset\}; [a, r, w := a', r', w'|(a' \in ready \wedge r' = r - a'_{set}) \wedge$
$$w' = w \cup a_{set}]$$

Fig. 3. Partitioned process scheduler.

Any partition is possible and can be formulated as a rewriting rule, such that the resulting partitions are correct abstractions as stated in Theorem 2.

As a consequence of this partitioning, a new interactive system contract can be given. In this new description shown in Figure 4, the partition preconditions are incorporated into the guards. This is necessary such that our scenario synthesis approach works.

6.3   Compositions

The next step, is the calculation of atomic scenarios — the compositions. The calculation is done by applying the rule of Corollary 3 to the partitioned interactive system contract. In many cases, the precondition p of a composition is stronger than the guard g_a of the first interaction S_a. In the formula of Corollary 3 this means that $p \neq \mathsf{true}$. The reason for the additional constraint p is that the interaction S_a does not guarantee that g_b is satisfied. This fits perfectly into our approach, since precondition strengthening is in fact abstraction. However, such strengthening indicates paths that are more difficult to establish. In the trivial case $p = g_b$, which means that the precondition of the composition is the conjunction of the two guards g_a and g_b.

$Scheduler' \,\hat{=}\, Init;$ **do** true :: New
$\qquad\qquad \Diamond \quad w \neq \emptyset \wedge a = \mathsf{nil} :: Ready_1$
$\qquad\qquad \Diamond \quad w \neq \emptyset \wedge a \neq \mathsf{nil} :: Ready_2$
$\qquad\qquad \Diamond \quad a \neq \mathsf{nil} \wedge r = \emptyset :: Swap_1$
$\qquad\qquad \Diamond \quad a \neq \mathsf{nil} \wedge r \neq \emptyset :: Swap_2$
$\qquad\qquad$ **od**

Fig. 4. Partitioned contract of the interactive process scheduler.

$\{a = \mathsf{nil}\}; New; Ready_1$
$Swap_1; Ready_1$

$\{a \neq \mathsf{nil}\}; New; Ready_2$
$\{\text{card } w > 1\}; Ready_1; Ready_2$
$\{\text{card } w > 1\}; Ready_2; Ready_2$
$Swap_2; Ready_2$

$\{r = \emptyset\}; Ready_1; Swap_1$
$\{r = \emptyset \wedge a \neq \mathsf{nil}\}; New; Swap_1$
$\{\text{card } r = 1\} Swap_2; Swap_1$

$\{\text{card } r > 1\}; Swap_2; Swap_2$
$Ready_2; Swap_2$
$\{a \neq \mathsf{nil}\}; New; Swap_2$

$S; New$

Fig. 5. Compositions of the process scheduler.

The compositions of the scheduler are listed in Figure 5. In this presentation the guard assertions g are skipped. Only if a guard g has been strengthened by a precondition p the additional assertion is shown as the precondition $\{p\}$ of the composition of the two interactions.

This collection of possible compositions has several advantages: (1) Several scenarios can be calculated stepwise, without calculating the weakest precondition for the whole sequence of interactions again and again. (2) It carries the information which interactions are easily established and which are difficult to set up. For setting up a goal as quick as possible, choosing simple compositions will lead to shorter scenarios. On the other hand, strong preconditions indicate that these combinations are complicated to carry out. A tester should include such complex combinations.

The compositions are grouped by the second statement, which is more practical for searching scenarios backwards. Backwards scenario development is more useful if scenarios are used to reach a certain test goal, as will be seen next.

6.4   Scenarios

Applying the rule for composing two compositions, correct scenarios can be synthesized in a systematic way. In Figure 6 one scenario for testing each partition is presented. For each scenario the additional precondition to be established is documented. $Scenario_3$ serves to discuss the synthesis process in more detail.

The actual scenario synthesis starts with the last statement. Here, this is $Ready_2$, the interaction to be tested. From Figure 5 it can be seen that four compositions are available. $Ready_1$ is chosen because a scenario for $Ready_1$ is already available. However, the new precondition forces to choose New twice.

New is chosen, because it is the most promising: Here, New can follow each statement S, since it has the precondition true. It is a general strategy to choose interactions with weak guards.

$Scenario_4$ and $Scenario_5$ shows that scenarios can be reused for setting a system in a state of interest.

$Scenario_1 \,\hat{=}\, Init;$ (Testing New)
                 New

$Scenario_2 \,\hat{=}\, Init;$ (Testing $Ready_1$)
                 $\{a = \mathsf{nil}\}; New;$
                 $Ready1$

$Scenario_3 \,\hat{=}\, Init;$ (Testing $Ready_2$)
                 $\{a = \mathsf{nil}\}; New;$
                 $\{a = \mathsf{nil} \wedge \mathsf{card}\ w > 0\}; New;$
                 $\{\mathsf{card}\ w > 1\}; Ready_1;$
                 $Ready_2$

$Scenario_4 \,\hat{=}\, Scenario_2;$ (Testing $Swap_1$)
                 $Swap_1$

$Scenario_5 \,\hat{=}\, Scenario_3;$ (Testing $Swap_2$)
                 $Swap_2$

Fig. 6. Testing scenarios for the process scheduler.

Based on the table of possible compositions, all scenarios according to one of the selection strategies that have been presented in the previous section can be calculated. Here, we applied the first strategy: One scenario for each partition.

It should be noted that for this simple strategy, not all compositions have to be calculated in advance. However, compositions carry the information which combinations are most easily achieved, those with the weakest additional precondition. Trivially, it equals true.

7 Conclusions

What we have presented, is to our present knowledge, the first application of the refinement calculus for generating test-cases. We formally defined our notion of test-cases for simple input-output tests, partition tests and extended this definition to test scenarios for interactive systems.

For all these classes of test-cases, we demonstrated that they are in fact formal abstractions. This realization lead to formal abstraction rules for calculating correct test-cases. The presented synthesis rules define an alternative method for finding scenarios of interactions. In contrast to finite state machine (FSM) based approaches, the focus is on finding possible compositions of interactions. Which compositions are possible is determined by the abstraction rules. A well-know example has been translated into an interactive contract specification and served for illustrating purposes of the method.

As future work we intend to investigate the application of abstraction techniques further. We will apply the method to our industrial projects. However, for large industrial examples the method needs automation. Theorem provers and model-checkers could be used for interactively verifying the abstraction relations.

We hope that the presented work stimulates further research on test-synthesis based on other program-synthesis approaches. Especially, the application of program synthesis and transformation tools for testing could be a topic of future research.

References

1. Jean-Raymond Abrial. *The B-Book: Assigning Programs to Meanings*. Cambridge University Press, Trumpington Street, Cambridge CB2 1RP, Great Britain, 1996.
2. Lionel Van Aertryck. *Une méthode et un outil pour l'aide à la génération de jeux de tests de logiciels*. PhD thesis, Université de Rennes, January 1998.
3. Bernhard K. Aichernig. Automated black-box testing with abstract VDM oracles. In M. Felici, K. Kanoun, and A. Pasquini, editors, *Computer Safety, Reliability and Security: proceedings of the 18th International Conference, SAFECOMP'99, Toulouse, France, September 1999*, volume 1698 of *Lecture Notes in Computer Science*, pages 250–259. Springer, 1999.
4. Bernhard K. Aichernig, Andreas Gerstinger, and Robert Aster. Formal specification techniques as a catalyst in validation. In *Proceedings of the 5th Conference on High-Assurance Software Engineering, 5th–7th November 2000, Albuquerque, New Mexico, USA*. IEEE, 2000. To be published.
5. Ralph Back, Anna Mikhajlova, and Joakim von Wright. Reasoning about interactive systems. In Jeannette M. Wing, Jim Woodcock, and Jim Davies, editors, *FM'99 — Formal Methods, World Congress on Formal Methods in the Development of Computing Systems, Toulouse, France, September 1999, Proceedings, Volume II*, volume 1709 of *Lecturen Notes in Computer Science*. Springer, 1999.
6. Ralph-Johan Back and Joakim von Wright. *Refinement Calculus, a Systematic Introduction*. Graduate Texts in Computer Science. Springer, 1998.
7. Boris Beizer. *Software Testing Techniques*. Van Nostrand Reinhold, New York, 2nd edition, 1990.
8. Boris Beizer. *Black-Box Testing: Techniques for Functional Testing of Software and Systems*. John Wiley & Sons, Inc., 1995.
9. D. Carrington and P. Stocks. A tale of two paradigms: Formal methods and software testing. In *Proceedings of the 8th Z User Meeting*. Springer-Verlag, 1994.
10. John Derrick and Eerke Boiten. Testing refinements of state-based formal specifications. *Software Testing, Verification and Reliability*, 9:27–50, July 1999.
11. Jeremy Dick and Alain Faivre. Automating the generation and sequencing of test cases from model-based specifications. In J.C.P. Woodcock and P.G. Larsen, editors, *FME'93: Industrial-Strength Formal Methods*. Springer-Verlag, April 1993.
12. E.W. Dijkstra. *A Discipline of Programming*. Prentice-Hall International, 1976.
13. John Fitzgerald and Peter Gorm Larsen. *Modelling Sytems, Practical Tools and Techniques*. Cambridge University Press, 1998.
14. Marie-Claude Gaudel and Perry R. James. Testing algebraic data types and processes: A unifying theory. *Formal Aspects of Computing*, 10(5 & 6):436–451, 1998.
15. Steffen Helke, Thomas Neustupny, and Thomas Santen. Automating test case generation from Z specifications with Isabelle. In *ZUM'97*, 1997.
16. E.M. Hörcher and E. Mikk. Test automation using Z specifications. In *"Tools for System Development and verification", Workshop, Bremen, Germany*, BISS Monographs. Shaker Verlag, 1996.

17. Johann Hörl and Bernhard K. Aichernig. Formal specification of a voice communication system used in air traffic control, an industrial application of lightweight formal methods using VDM++ (abstract). In J.M. Wing, J. Woodcock, and J. Davies, editors, *Proceedings of FM'99 – Formal Methods, World Congress on Formal Methods in the Development of Computing Systems, Toulouse, France, September 1999*, volume 1709 of *Lecture Notes in Computer Science*, page 1868. Springer, 1999. Full report at ftp://ftp.ist.tu-graz.ac.at/pub/publications/IST-TEC-99-03.ps.gz.

18. Johann Hörl and Bernhard K. Aichernig. Validating voice communication requirements using lightweight formal methods. *IEEE Software*, pages 21–27, May/June 2000.

19. Mathias Jarke and Reino Kurki-Suoni (editors). Special issue on scenario management. *IEEE Transactions on Software Engineering*, 24(12), 1998.

20. Cliff B. Jones. *Systematic Software Development Using VDM*. Series in Computer Science. Prentice-Hall, second edition, 1990.

21. Ian MacColl and David Carrington. A model of specification-based testing of interactive systems (abstract). In J.M. Wing, J. Woodcock, and J. Davies, editors, *Proceedings of FM'99 – Formal Methods, World Congress on Formal Methods in the Development of Computing Systems, Toulouse, France, September 1999*, volume 1709 of *Lecture Notes in Computer Science*, page 1862. Springer, 1999. Full report at http://www.csee.uq.edu.au/ ianm/model.ps.gz.

22. Carrol C. Morgan. *Programming from Specifications*. Series in Computer Science. Prentice-Hall International, 1990.

23. Jan Peleska. Test Automation for Safety-Critical Systems: Industrial Application and Future Developments. In Marie-Claude Gaudel and Jim Woodcock, editors, *FME'96: Industrial Benefit and Advances in Formal Methods*, pages 39–59. Springer-Verlag, March 1996.

24. Jan Peleska and Michael Siegel. From Testing Theory to Test Driver Implementation. In Marie-Claude Gaudel and Jim Woodcock, editors, *FME'96: Industrial Benefit and Advances in Formal Methods*, pages 538–556. Springer-Verlag, March 1996.

25. S. Sadeghipour and H. Singh. Test strategies on the basis of extended finite state machines. Technical report, Daimler-Benz AG, Research and Technology, 1998.

26. Harbhajan Singh, Mirko Conrad, and Sadegh Sadeghipour. Test case design based on Z and the classification-tree method. In *Proceedings of the 1st International Conference on Formal Engineering Methods (ICFEM '97)*, 1997.

27. Susan Stepney. Testing as abstraction. In J. P. Bowen and M. G. Hinchey, editors, *ZUM '95: 9th International Conference of Z Users, Limerick 1995*, volume 967 of *Lecture Notes in Computer Science*. Springer, 1995.

28. P.A. Stocks and D.A. Carrington. Test templates: A specification-based testing framework. In *Proceedings of the 15th International Conference on Software Engineering*, pages 405–414, August 1993.

29. Phil Stocks and David Carrington. Test template framework: A specification-based testing case study. In *Proceeddings of the International Symposium on Software Testing and Analysis*, pages 11–18, 1993.

30. Philip Alan Stocks. *Applying formal methods to software testing*. PhD thesis, The Department of computer science, The University of Queensland, 1993.

31. H. Treharne, J. Draper, and S. Schneider. Test case preparation using a prototype. In Didier Bert, editor, *B'98*, volume 1393 of *LNCS*, pages 293–311. Springer, 1998.

A Modular Approach to the Specification and Validation of an Electrical Flight Control System*

M. Doche[1]**, I. Vernier-Mounier[2], and F. Kordon[2]

[1] Department of Electronics and Computer Science
University of Southampton, Highfield
Southampton SO17 1BJ, United-Kingdom
mfd@ecs.soton.ac.uk
[2] Laboratoire d'Informatique de Paris 6, 4 place Jussieu,
F-75252 Paris Cedex 05, France
{Isabelle.Vernier-Mounier, Fabrice.Kordon} @lip6.fr

Abstract. To study a part of an Electrical Flight Control System we have developed a tool-supported method dedicated to the incremental specification and validation of complex heterogeneous systems. Formal description of a system is structured in modules that interact.

We combine two modular approaches that share the same view of modularity but offer complementary validation procedures: model checking and functional test generation. We have adapted these validation procedures to take care of the modular aspects of our specification. They are performed incrementally. We first consider basic modules, then the communication between modules and finally composed modules.

To support our method, we have adapted existing tools, dedicated to non-modular specifications, to deal with modular constraints. These tools are integrated into a common platform to build a coherent execution environment.

Keywords. Heterogeneous Specification, Modularity, Verification, Test Generation, Case Tools.

1 Introduction

Critical embedded systems must ensure fault tolerance requirements. They are more and more complex as their functions increase and become more sophisticated. These systems are structured in several heterogeneous components strongly interconnected. Components may represent software as well as hardware parts of the system. They may be specified in several specification languages. Components are often independently well-known and reused from one

---

* This work was supported by the *VaMoS* project, one of the four projects of the French action FORMA (http://www.imag.fr/FORMA/)
** This work was done when she was working at ONERA-CERT/DTIM, Toulouse.

J.N. Oliveira and P. Zave (Eds.): FME 2001, LNCS 2021, pp. 590–610, 2001.

version of a system to a new one. The main difficulty lies in the number and the diversity of interactions between components. So, we present in this paper a tool-supported method to formally specify and analyze modular specifications of embedded systems. The integration of various tools in a common framework allowed us to apply our method to a significant industrial application : a part of an Electrical Flight Control System (EFCS). This industrial application is proposed by Sextant Avionique and is significant both for its size and complexity, representative of a wide range of embedded architectures. Specification, verification and test case generation results obtained on this system are given in the corresponding sections of the paper.

There exist well-tried methods and tools to specify and validate specifications. Their application to non-trivial software or process control remains difficult, but some recent results are promising [4,28,29,10]. To overcome these difficulties modular specification and verification methods dealing with components are needed [12]. Problems appear with the specification of communications between components, decomposition of global properties into a set of properties that deal with a single component at a time, incremental specification and verification.

Several modular methods are proposed in the literature on verification [2,3] or test generation [5,27]. Our approach is to propose a set of modular methods to deal with each steps of the software development. We verify structural properties of components to ensure that their compositions are possible and lead to the expected result. These constraints are expressed by means of composition links, *morphisms*, between two components. This allows us to separate the specification coherence verification from the behavioral properties verification and test case generation. Furthermore, if the specification coherence is verified, a module can also be reused several times.

We combine two modular approaches. MOKA [26] is a tool-supported method dedicated to the specification and composition of modules. The coherence between interfaces and different parts of modules is checked before composition. Combined with the metric temporal logic TRIO [22], we generate functional test cases at different level of abstraction [17]: basic components, interactions and clusters (i.e. components resulting from the composition of others). The OF-Class [14] language is dedicated to object oriented specification and behavioral verification. It allows the verification of each module independently, by computing an abstraction of the components that communicate with it, i.e. its *environment*. The two approaches offer complementary verification procedures and share a same view of the modularity. Therefore, it was valuable to integrate them in a unified modular method and to support it by integrating the two related sets of tools into the FrameKit platform [25].

Section 2 describes our specification language, the *VaMoS* language and the *structural verification* of the coherence of our specifications. Section 3 shows how to analyze the behavior of the model, by verifying constraints on the specified behavior. In Section 4 we describe the generation of test cases at each level of abstraction we consider.

Moreover, we have integrated the different validation tools (structural verification, behavioral verification and test cases generation) into a platform presented in Section 5. A graphical interface helps to design modular specification and we ensure the coordination of the validation process with *note files*, which contain information on the state of the validation.

We conclude and present future works in Section 6.

2   The *VaMoS* Language

VaMoS is a modular language to the specification and the validation of complex systems. A component is described in two steps. The first one deals with the modular aspects of the specification. We define the components of the system and their interactions with the environment. The second step is the description of the internal behavior for each component.

2.1   Modularity in *VaMoS Language*

For complex systems with heterogeneous components, a modular specification highlights the interface of each component and its interaction with the environment. Then we can define links between components and build clusters of components according to modular operations.

Module, Reusability, and Modular operations. A module is composed of four specifications. The *Param* part contains the parameters of a generic module. The *Import* part contains the items imported by the module and the conditions under which these elements can be used. The *Export* part contains the items supplied by the component and the conditions under which the environment can use them. These three parts constitute the interface of the module. The *Body* part represents the internal behavior of the module. It specifies how the imported elements are used and how the exported ones are computed

The four specifications are interconnected by four internal morphisms, which ensure safe formal connections between the specifications (cf. Figure 1 and 4). A morphism maps the items of a *source* specification to the items of a *target* specification with two constraints: both the linked items have the same type and the behavior of the source specification is preserved in the target specification [1]. In the particular case of a module, *Param*, *Import* and *Export* do not contain behavior description but properties which describe conditions on their items. So the second constraint means in this case that the properties of the interface can be deduced from the behavior specification of *Body*. The internal morphisms allow us to verify the coherence of both the four parts of the module and its interface.

---

[1] Our modular framework is based on the category theory and thus our morphisms correspond to theory morphisms as defined in [23] by Goguen and Burstall. The notion of module is adapted from the work of Ehrig and Mahr [20]. For more details of this aspect of our framework see [26,31].

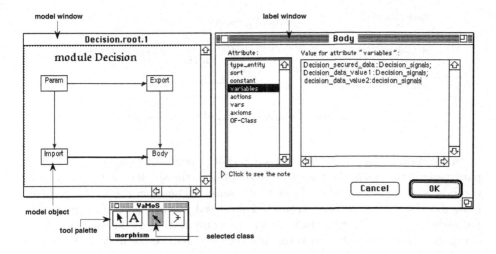

Fig. 1. VaMos formalism in FrameKit

To reuse a module, we just have to verify that the environment in which we want to plug it respects the *Import* and *Export* conditions. Several implementations of a same module share the same *Import* and *Export*, they only differ by the *Body* and *Param* parts. To refine the behavior of a module, we just have to verify the coherence between both the new *Body* specification and the interfaces (cf. 2.3).

A cluster is the component that results from the composition of two others. The links between components and the interface of the resulting cluster depend upon relationships between these components. Composition operations are defined by external morphisms that identify items of the interfaces of the composed modules[2]. The four parts and the four internal morphisms of the cluster module are automatically computed. Thus, we incrementally build a *system module*, which entirely specifies the system. For more details on module concepts and calculus, see [26,31].

Case study. The presented case study is a part of an Electrical Flight Control System (EFCS). It is proposed by Sextant Avionique and is a significant industrial application both for its size and complexity, representative of a wide range of embedded architectures (for instance in A330-40 aircraft [7]). Hardware and software techniques must ensure fault tolerance requirements. Therefore the code correctness is highly critical ([16,1]).

We consider here the part of the EFCS that manages the spoilers of an airplane during takeoff and landing. Opening angles applied to the spoilers are computed with respect to the value given by sensors (altitude, speed, ...) and the angle the pilot wants to apply.

---

[2] Such operations on modules have been defined by Ehrig and Mahr [20]. In terms of the categories theory, the resulting module is computed by several colimits on the different parts of the components.

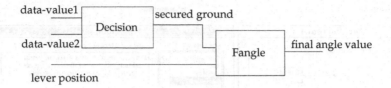

Fig. 2. Modular composition of the case study

A function **Fangle** computes an angle that depends on two parameters. One parameter is the angle the pilot wants to apply to the spoilers, it is identified by the position of a lever and confirmed by a sensor. The other one is a signal that indicates if the airplane is on ground. This signal, *secured ground*, is secured by redundancy of the function dedicated to its computation. A decision procedure compares the two results and transmits their common value if they match or a pre-defined one otherwise. Figure 2 describes this system.

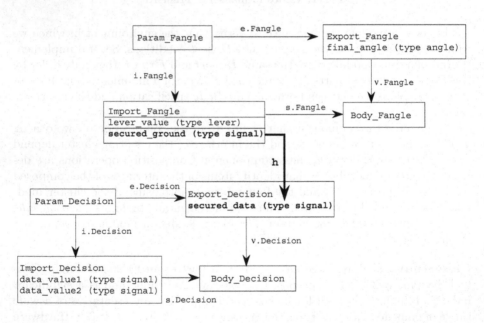

Fig. 3. Definition of the partial composition of modules Fangle and Decision

We specify this mechanism by composition of two modules: **Decision** and **Fangle**. Then we define the interfaces of the modules:

– The **Decision** module imports two signal values (data_value1 and data_va-lue2) computed from values of the sensors by two components that are not represented and provides a secured value of the detection of the presence of the airplane on ground.

- The **Fangle** module imports a lever position value provided by the environment and the secured data provided by the module **Decision** and computes an angle value to apply to spoilers.

We specify now the relationships between the components. Modules **Decision** and **Fangle** are composed by a *partial composition* operation. **Decision** is a supplier and **Fangle** is a user. The *Export* part of **Decision** satisfies partially the *Import* part of **Fangle**. The external morphism *h* identifies the secured data exported by **Decision** with the secured one imported by **Fangle**. Figure 3 shows the four parts of each module.

The cluster module, represented by Figure 4, imports the lever position and the two values that are imported by **Decision**. It exports the angle value computed by **Fangle**. Its internal morphisms are automatically computed.

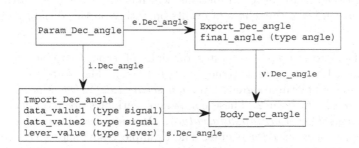

Fig. 4. Result of the partial composition of modules Fangle and Decision

In such a case study, where redundant mechanisms appear often, the genericity and reusability capabilities of our formalism are very useful: for the whole case study, composed of 18 components, we have specified only 6 modules.

2.2   VaMoS Specification Language

We show how behavioral specifications are handled within modules. Each part of a *VaMoS* module contains :

- The declaration of the names of items used to describe the behavior of the system and the signature of actions. It is denoted *Vocabulary*.
- The logical description of constraints on items of the interface for the *Param*, *Import* and *Export* parts. For the *Body* part it contains the logical description of the behavior. It is denoted *Formulae section*.
- The description of the actions performed by the module for the *Body* part only. It identifies the actions, explicitly describes them as well as their control system. This description is denoted *Imperative language section*.

The *Formulae* and *Imperative language* sections of the *Body* part allow us to manage conjointly logical and behavioral views of the same component.

The language used to specify the *Formulae section* is a linear temporal logic. We have chosen the TRIO logic. It provides a description well adapted to test case generation. A set of TRIO logic formulae represents the logical links between the actions and the properties they must satisfy.

The language used to specify the *Imperative language section* is a C-like language (automatically translated into Colored Petri Nets (CPN)). Properties are expressed apart from the behavior description in the TRIO logic. Therefore, they can be verified by model checking.

Vocabulary. The vocabulary consists of four declaration parts:

- *Sorts* is a set of types;
- *Constants* declares constant functions;
- *Variables* declares variable functions, which describe the state of the system;
- *Actions* models occurrences of events operating on the variables of the system.

The **Decision** module operates on data of type *Decision_signals*. The specific signal values are t (true) and f (false). The state of the component is described by three signals *Decision_secured_data*, *Decision_data_value*1, and *Decision_data_value*2. These component variables are modified when one of the actions *Decision_imp_data_value*1, *Decision_imp_data_value*2 or *Decision_compute_secured_data* occurs. The example below shows the vocabulary part of the *Body* specification of **Decision** module.

$Specification\ Decision =$
    $Sorts : Decision\_signals;$
    $Constants :$
        $t : Decision\_signals;$
        $f : Decision\_signals;$
    $Variables :$
        $Decision\_secured\_data : Decision\_signals;$
        $Decision\_data\_value1 : Decision\_signals;$
        $Decision\_data\_value2 : Decision\_signals;$
    $Actions :$
        $Decision\_imp\_data\_value1(Decision\_signals);$
        $Decision\_imp\_data\_value2(Decision\_signals);$
        $Decision\_exp\_secured\_data(Decision\_signals);$
  $ImperativeLanguage : ...$
  $Formulae : ...$
  $endSpecification$

An occurrence of the action *Decision_imp_data_value*1 (respectively *Decision_imp_data_value*2) allows the acquisition of a unique value, which is stored in the local variable *Decision_data_value*1 (respectively *Decision_data_value*2). The local variable *Decision_secured_data* takes the value t if and only if both previous variables take the value t.

Imperative Language. The OF-Class [13] language is dedicated to modular specification. Modules are composed regarding the interface specification of the modules. From the *Imperative language section* ,the OF-Class compiler automatically generates a CPN from one or several components [14].

The compiler represents each variable by a place. Interfaces places represent imported and exported variables. Actions are represented by transitions. The composition of modules is performed by identification of interfaces places.

Figure 5 represents significant elements of the CPN automatically generated from the specification of the **Decision** module. The declaration part of the CPN defines classes (types) associated with places (variables) used by the specification. Double-circled places represent the interface variables. Black transitions are actions identified in the vocabulary declaration; they represent the importation and exportation actions. Transitions *compute_t* and *compute_f* represent the two possible ways to compute the secured data. The OF-Class compiler adds information to express the control of the variables. The complete automatically computed CPN holds 11 transitions, 16 places and 46 arcs.

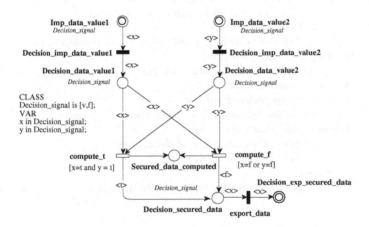

Fig. 5. Part of the Petri net of the Decision module

Formulae. The part *Formulae* of a *VaMoS* specification contains TRIO formulae generated from vocabulary items, and logical connectors. TRIO ([22]) is a first order linear temporal logic. A TRIO formula is composed of atoms and logical connectors: classical ones (& and, | or, ∼ not, → implies, ↔ equivalent), quantifiers (∀ for all and ∃ exists) or temporal operators. Moreover, TRIO language holds the basic temporal operator : $Dist(F, \delta)$ means that formula F is true at δ time units from the current instant (δ can be positive or negative).

The TRIO operators allows us to derive all the classical linear temporal operators, in particular the following ones:

- *Next state(F)* is true iff F is true in the next state.
- *AlwF(F)* is true means F is true in all the following instants.
- *SomF(F)* is true if F means true in at least one of the following instants.
- *Until(F, G)* is true if F means true until G becomes true.

To describe the behavior of the system, we define a set of axioms, each of them being a TRIO formula. The following set of formulae is the TRIO specification of these axioms.

> *Specification Decision = ...*
> *Formulae :*
> > *Vars :*
> > > $x, y : Decision\_signal;$
> > *Axioms :*
> > > $Decision\_signal\_availability\_value1 :$
> > > $Alw(\exists\ x\ (Decision\_imp\_data\_value1(x)\&$
> > > $\qquad \forall y(Decision\_imp\_data\_value1(y) \rightarrow x = y)));$
> > > $Decision\_signal\_availability\_value2 :$
> > > $Alw(\exists\ x\ (Decision\_imp\_data\_value2(x)\&$
> > > $\qquad \forall y(Decision\_imp\_data\_value2(y) \rightarrow x = y)));$
> > > $Decision\_local\_copy\_value1 :$
> > > $Alw(\forall\ x\ (Decision\_imp\_data\_value1(x) \rightarrow Decision\_data\_value1 = x));$
> > > $Decision\_local\_copy\_value2 :$
> > > $Alw(\forall\ x\ (Decision\_imp\_data\_value2(x) \rightarrow Decision\_data\_value2 = x));$
> > > $Decision\_secure\_result :$
> > > $Alw(Decision\_secured\_data = t \leftrightarrow$
> > > $\qquad Decision\_data\_value1 = t\ \&Decision\_data\_value2 = t);$
> > > $Decision\_publish\_secure\_result :$
> > > $Alw(\forall\ x\ (Decision\_exp\_secured\_data(x) \leftrightarrow$
> > > $\qquad x = Decision\_secured\_data));$
> *endSpecification*

In the example we have chosen to associate an axiom to each condition on an action:

- *Decision_signal_availability_value1* (respectively *Decision_signal_availability_value2*) states how the action *Decision_imp_data_value1* (respectively *Decision_imp_data_value2*) occurs at each time instant.
- *Decision_local_copy_value1* (respectively *Decision_local_copy_value2*) asserts that, each time a signal is acquired, its value is stored in the adequate local variable.
- *Decision_secure_result* specifies how the secured local value *Decision_secured_data* is computed using the value of the other local parameters.
- *Decision_publish_secured_result* characterizes the action *Decision_exp_secured_data*.
- At each time instant, the action publishes one and only one secured value: *Decision_secured_data*.

2.3   Structural Verification

A preliminary step of validation (we call it "structural verification") verifies the consistency of a modular specification based on the modules and the composition operations presented in section 2.1.

For each module, we check the four internal morphisms, which means for each morphism :

- The source vocabulary is included in the target vocabulary depending on morphism and two linked items have the same type. The MOKA tool, developed at ONERA-CERT ([26,31]), performs type checking of the morphisms.
- The constraints defined in the specifications of the interface can be deduced from the *Body* specification :
  - In CPN, the properties that represent the constraints are verified on the Petri net specification by model checking.
  - In TRIO, we prove that axioms of the source can be deduced from the set of axioms of the target. The MOKA tool only generates a *"proof obligation"* that has to be proved by some other tool (for example a prover on TRIO logic).

Then, for each specification we check the consistency of both description parts by classical means (parsers and type checkers dedicated to each language).

For modular operation definition, to control the validity of each interconnection, we must check the external morphisms as we check internal morphisms. This verification, performed by the MOKA tool, leads to the automatic computation of the four parts of the cluster module.

This ensures that what is needed by a module is offered by the one with which it is composed. Several verification, as behavioral or test case generation, are needed to ensure that what is offered is exactly what was expected.

3   Behavior Verification of Modular Specifications

To verify properties we use a model checker. The first step is to decompose the properties into a set of local properties and a set of communication ones. Each local property concerns the internal behavior of a module. Its verification can be performed independently of the other modules. The communication properties express relations between modules. Before their verification, the composition of the concerned components must be computed.

3.1   Modular Aspects

The CPNs, generated by the OF-Class compiler, are dedicated to modular verification. Each module is viewed as a function that imports data, computes results and exports them. The computation of results is an internal action. Therefore, once a module has collected all the needed values, its environment has no impact on the way the results are computed. Composition preserves all the properties on the computation step, for example properties that express links between the values of the imported data and the value of the results.

To independently study each module, a representation of its environment is computed when it is translated into a Petri net. It represents the production of all the possible imported data and the use of the exported ones. There is no restriction on the possible values of the imported data and they are provided each time they are needed. Therefore, no deadlock results from this specification of the environment and it does not restrict the possible behaviors of the module. This representation is used to verify local properties that deal with the relation between the values of the imported data and the exported ones or internal deadlocks. If a local property is verified in this representation, it is verified whatever the environment of the module may be. But, if the property is not verified, no conclusion is possible. As the OF-Class components do not have pre-conditions, the *bad* values produced by the represented environment are not *filtered* even if they are not produced by the real environment. To obtain a certitude, we consider the module in its real environment.

To verify properties that concern the communications between several modules, we have to compose them. Such properties may be the detection of deadlocks in the system. In this case the composition of the whole system is necessary. The environment of several modules is represented by the same way as for one module. Therefore, incremental verification is possible. In [4] the authors model the abstraction of the environment to check a part of a case study, but this is manually performed.

3.2   Abstractions

Despite important results in the state space representation [9], the state space explosion problem happens even for one module. Therefore we have worked on abstractions of the specification.

The first identified abstraction is due to data having a large set of possible values (speed, altitude, ...). Very often, for several values of a same variable, the execution sequence is the same. The domain is partitionned into sub-domains that lead to different sets of instructions (such an approach can be related to uniformity hypotheses of testing).

The second abstraction depends upon the property to verify. Instructions without incidence on the result of the verification are suppressed. Rules to perform abstractions and simplifications have been identified and their implementation is in progress. These rules have been applied on the example above leading to a reduction factor of 100 to 1000 depending upon the verified properties. The same principle is applied in [10].

The computation of abstractions is not yet tool supported but rules have been identified and applied on the example presented in the paper. The state space reduction we obtain is significant.

3.3   Practical Application

CPN [24] are well adapted to describe the control of systems and to support behavior verification. We use PROD[3] : a Petri net reachability analysis tool that supports on the fly verification of linear time temporal properties as well as verification of branching time properties. Moreover, linear temporal logic formulae supported by PROD can be expressed in TRIO logic. This allows us to complete or to confirm this verification step with tools dedicated to the TRIO language.

3.4   Example

The redundancy introduced to support failures needs some adaptation of the software to manage the fact that two identical functions do not give the same result. In our example, **Fangle** must provide a neutral angle value (i.e., 0 value) if **Decision** imports two different values. The temporal specification of this property is:"at each instant, (**Decision** imports two different values) implies (there is an instant in the future such that **Fangle** exports 0)". It is a liveness property. The TRIO formulae are:

$$CommunicationProperty \equiv AlwF(DecisionProp \Rightarrow SomF(FangleProp))$$
$$DecisionProp \equiv \exists x1, x2 \ Decision\_imp\_data\_value1(x1) \ \&$$
$$Decision\_imp\_data\_value2(x2) \ \& \ (x1 \neq x2)$$
$$FangleProp \equiv \forall sp \ Fangle\_compute\_angle(sp, 0)$$

We decompose *CommunicationProperty* in three lemmas that highlight the signal exported by **Decision** and imported by **Fangle**. Lemma L1 concerns **Decision**. It shows the consequence of *DecisionProp* on the value of the exported signal. Lemma L2 concerns **Fangle**. It shows the conditions that must be satisfied by the imported signal to ensure *FangleProp*. Lemma L3 concerns the relationship between the modules. It ensures that if **Decision** exports the signal value f, **Fangle** imports the same value.

$$CommunicationProperty \equiv (L1 \ \& \ L2 \ \& \ L3)$$
$$L1 \equiv AlwF(DecisionProp \Rightarrow Decision\_exp\_secured\_data(\mathrm{f}))$$
$$L2 \equiv AlwF(Fangle\_imp\_data\_signal(\mathrm{f}) \Rightarrow SomF(FangleProp))$$
$$L3 \equiv AlwF(Decision\_exp\_secured\_data(\mathrm{f}) \Rightarrow Fangle\_imp\_data\_signal(\mathrm{f}))$$

Initial specification. The state space of the module **Decision**, computed in 16 seconds, holds 80 states and 93 arcs. Property L1 has been verified in 26 seconds on it. The state space of module **Fangle**, computed in 4 minutes and 8 seconds, holds 9,247 states and 19,250 arcs. The state space of the global system, computed in 18 hours 54 minutes 20 seconds, holds 818,390 states and 2,605,318 arcs. The verifications have not been performed on this specification.

---

[3] PROD is developed at the Helsinki University of Technology ([30]).

Abstraction of data domains. Fangle uses angle variables that belong to the interval [0..46]. Variables of this domain are only compared with the maximum value. As all values in [0..45] lead to the execution of the same instructions we have mapped the interval on [0..1]. Values [0..45] are identified with 0 and 46 with 1. This does not modify the possible behaviors of the components. Of course, such an abstraction may not be applied for a property dealing with the exact value of a variable in the domain. The reduced state space of **Fangle**, computed in 16 seconds, holds 113 states and 135 arcs. Property L2 has been verified in 27 seconds on it.

Abstraction regarding property L3. This abstraction is significant for the property that ensures that if *Decision* exports value "f" then **Fangle** imports the same value. The way values are computed is not important, only communication instructions affect the property. We reduce the size of the specification by deleting the instructions that do not affect the communications between the two modules. This abstraction is applied jointly with the one on data domains. The state space of the global system has been computed in 27 seconds. It holds 176 states and 318 arcs. Property L3 has been verified in 1 minute and 11 seconds.

4   Test Case Generation from Modular Specifications

To complete the validation process, and to verify the implementation, we also generate functional test cases.

Many works deal with test cases generation from non-modular formal specifications [21,8], but many techniques are limited by the size of the specifications. We take advantage of our modular structure to assist the test cases generation at different levels of abstraction:

- First, *unit level* tests independently (and in detail) little parts of the system or basic components. The generation is based on basic modules describing the basic components.
- Then, *integration level* tests interactions between components. For this step, we focus on interfaces of modules and morphisms defined in a modular operation to describe links between components.
- Finally, *cluster level* allows to detect global errors of the system. The generation is achieved by composition of test cases from basic modules according to the modular operations.

Moreover, we generate, at each step, a correct test set as defined in [6]. A set of test cases is *unbiased* if it does not reject a correct program and it is *valid* if it accepts only correct programs. To avoid state space explosion problem, we define test hypotheses to reduce the size of the set (for example uniformity hypotheses on the data domain).

4.1 Modular Aspects

In our approach, we want to reuse as often as possible classical generation techniques from non-modular specifications, which are often based on the generation of models of the specification (see [21,8] for a description of different techniques). But during the generation process from modular specifications, new constraints appear due to the modular aspects:

Encapsulation of data: at unit and cluster level, we want to generate test cases that contain only data of the interface.

Renaming according to the morphisms: at integration level, we want to base the generation on the interface of several modules and on morphisms which describe links between the items of the interfaces.

Composition according to modular operations: at cluster level, we want to reuse test cases defined at unit level and to compose them to obtain test cases for the cluster.

In the sequel, we describe how we perform encapsulation, renaming and composition; we illustrate them on our example (more details can be found in [17,15]). How these processes preserve correctness is described in [18,15].

Encapsulation. A module encapsulation allows to hide non-visible items. These items must neither be observed nor commanded during functional test steps. However the test cases generated from the module are possible executions of its internal specified behavior. To deal with test generation at unit level:

– We generate test cases from the *Body* specification of the module. Indeed, by construction and structural verification, this part contains the complete description of the behavior of the module and constraints on its interface. For this purpose, we use existing test case generation method from non-modular formal specification.

– We project the resulting test cases on the vocabulary of the interface (parts *Export, Import* and *Param*) such that the new test cases contain only visible items.

Assuming that the structural verification has succeeded, if we succeed to generate a correct test set from the *Body* specification, its correctness is preserved during the projection step. Indeed, projection step reduces items of the test cases, so they accept at least all programs accepted before projection step and an unbiased test set remained unbiased. Its validity is preserved due to conditions on the internal morphisms and structure of the module (see [15]).

Renaming. Interactions between components are described using a set of morphisms between the interfaces of the modules, according to a modular operation. To verify the modular specification, we generate and prove proof obligations on these morphisms (see section 2.3), which allow to check that the behavior of the target specification of a morphism maps the behavior of its source specification. We need to make the same check on the implementation: each possible behavior of the target specification meets the constraints stated by the source specification. So to deal with integration level, we follow for each morphism of a modular operation the following procedure:

- We generate test cases from the source specification of the morphism by a classical non-modular technique. They describe the constraints stated by this specification.
- We rename each test case according to the morphism, to obtain test cases defined on the vocabulary of the target, for the constraints of the source specification.

Validity and unbias of the test set are preserved during the renaming step because of the condition on the morphism (see section 2.3). For more details of these approaches, see [18].

Composition. Application of a module composition creates a new module (see section 2.1). A naive but inefficient approach in practice would be to incrementally generate the global system and to generate test cases for it. Therefore, we reuse the test cases generated for unit level and we rely on properties of modular operations to complete the test cases.

For example, let us consider the partial composition described in section 2.1. The TRIO tool generates two sets of test cases for the user **Fangle** and for the supplier **Decision**. We merge, by pair, any test case of **Fangle** with any compatible test case of **Decision** to obtain a test case of the resulting module. Compatibility means that all common items of the both modules have the same evaluation at a given instant in the both test cases. That will be illustrated in the following example.

Once again, correctness is ensured by the correct definition of the cluster module and the external morphisms between both basic modules. A priori generated test cases accept at the most programs accepted by the test sets of both basic modules, so validity is preserved. Internal structure of the basic modules and external morphisms between these modules ensure that the generated test set remains unbiased. For more details of these approaches, see [18].

To achieve test case generation at cluster level, this composition step must be followed by a projection step to obtain test cases defined on the interface of the cluster.

4.2   Practical Application

To generate correct test cases from the specifications of a module, we use the TRIO Model generator[4]. It is founded on the TRIO language and a semantics

---

[4] A TRIO formal specification environment for complex real-time system specifications has been developed by CISE, supported by Politechnico Di Milano, under a contract of ENEL/CRA ([11]).

tableaux algorithm. It generates temporal finite partial models (called *histories*) from a specification. We define a *temporal window*, which is an interval of integer, and which represents the time scale [22]. Each history is considered as an abstract test case and is composed with a set of pertinent evaluation of items at any instant of the temporal window (the items can represent different values according to the test hypotheses). The set of all possible histories generated from a specification forms a correct test set for this specification.

To achieve an entirely tool supported method, we develop tools to deal with modular aspects: encapsulation, renaming and composition [15].

4.3 Example

Test cases generation from the body specification. Let us consider the module **Decision**: for a temporal window of two units the TRIO model generator has generated 16 test cases in 3.9 seconds.

Encapsulation of data on a unitary test case. We project each test case generated from the body on the vocabulary of the interface. The projection of the test case c generated from the Body of **Decision** on the vocabulary of the interface of **Decision** leads to the test case k:

$$
c = \qquad\qquad\rightarrow\qquad\qquad k =
$$

$$
\begin{pmatrix}
Decision\_secured\_data = f & : 1\\
\sim Decision\_exp\_secured\_data(t) : 1\\
Decision\_exp\_secured\_data(f) & : 1\\
Decision\_data\_value1 = f & : 1\\
\sim Decision\_imp\_data\_value1(t) : 1\\
Decision\_imp\_data\_value1(f) & : 1\\
Decision\_data\_value2 = t & : 1\\
\sim Decision\_imp\_data\_value2(f) : 1\\
Decision\_imp\_data\_value2(t) & : 1
\end{pmatrix}
\qquad
\begin{pmatrix}
\sim Decision\_exp\_secured\_data(t) : 1\\
Decision\_exp\_secured\_data(f) & : 1\\
\sim Decision\_imp\_data\_value1(t) : 1\\
Decision\_imp\_data\_value1(f) & : 1\\
\sim Decision\_imp\_data\_value2(f) : 1\\
Decision\_imp\_data\_value2(t) & : 1
\end{pmatrix}
$$

"*Decision_secured_data* = f : 1" means that the variable *Decision_secured_data* takes the value f at the instant 1.

Generation of integration test cases. Assume s is a test case of the source specification of the morphism h (a part of the *Import* of **Fangle**). After renaming according to h, we obtain the test case t, defined on the vocabulary of the *Export* of **Decision**:

$$
s = \qquad\qquad\rightarrow\qquad\qquad t =
$$

$$
\begin{pmatrix}
\sim Fangle\_imp\_secured\_ground(t) : 1\\
Fangle\_imp\_secured\_ground(f) & : 1\\
...
\end{pmatrix}
\qquad
\begin{pmatrix}
\sim Fangle\_imp\_secured\_data(t) : 1\\
Fangle\_imp\_secured\_data(f) & : 1\\
...
\end{pmatrix}
$$

Generation of cluster test cases. Assume l is a projected test case of **Fangle**; it merges the test case k to obtain m. Actions that are linked by an external morphism are identified in m. It is possible only if they have the same value. Otherwise, the test cases cannot be merged. Actions of l and k that are not linked by the external morphism appear in m. In our example, the external morphism h identifies the action $Decision\_exp\_secured\_data$ of the $Export$ of **Decision** to the action $Fangle\_imp\_secured\_data$ of the $Import$ of **Fangle**:

$$
\begin{aligned}
& k \\
& + \\
& l = \\
& \begin{pmatrix} \sim Fangle\_imp\_secured\_data(t) : 1 \\ Fangle\_imp\_secured\_data(f) \quad : 1 \\ Fangle\_imp\_lever\_data(f) \qquad : 1 \\ ... \end{pmatrix}
\end{aligned}
\quad \rightarrow \quad
\begin{aligned}
& m = \\
& \begin{pmatrix} \sim Decision\_exp\_secured\_data(t) : 1 \\ Decision\_exp\_secured\_data(f) \quad : 1 \\ \sim Decision\_imp\_data\_value1(t) \; : 1 \\ Decision\_imp\_data\_value1(f) \qquad : 1 \\ \sim Decision\_imp\_data\_value2(f) : 1 \\ Decision\_imp\_data\_value2(t) \qquad : 1 \\ Fangle\_imp\_lever\_data(f) \qquad\quad : 1 \\ ... \end{pmatrix}
\end{aligned}
$$

Conversely, the following projected test case k' of **Decision** cannot be merged with the test case l because l and k' disagree on the evaluation of action $Decision\_exp\_secured\_data$ and $Fangle\_imp\_secured\_data$.

$$
k' = \begin{pmatrix} \sim Decision\_exp\_secured\_data(f) : 1 \\ Decision\_exp\_secured\_data(t) \qquad : 1 \\ \sim Decision\_imp\_data\_value1(t) \quad : 1 \\ Decision\_imp\_data\_value1(f) \qquad : 1 \\ \sim Decision\_imp\_data\_value2(f) \quad : 1 \\ Decision\_imp\_data\_value2(t) \qquad : 1 \end{pmatrix}
$$

5   Implementation of a CASE Environment

To efficiently test our methodology and build a coherent execution environment we have integrated the required tools into FrameKit [25]. FrameKit is a generic platform dedicated to the rapid prototyping of CASE environment. Its implementation follows the guidelines of the ECMA-NIST reference model [19]. In FrameKit, presentation and display of services are strongly constrained. A polymorphic editor engine, Macao [25], provides a unified look and feel for the manipulation of models as well as access to services integrated in FrameKit. FrameKit manages three kinds of entities: *formalisms*, *models* and *services*. A formalism describes representation rules of a knowledge domain. A model is the description of a given knowledge using a formalism; it is a "document" composed with objects defined in the formalism. A service is a tool function that corresponds to operations in a design methodology. For example *VaMoS* modules and CPN are formalisms for which the user may define several models. The MOKA verifier, the TRIO test case generator and the Petri net model checker PROD are services. FrameKit allows the use of several formalisms. Furthermore, it manages shared data, versions of model specifications and provides good facilities for fast integration of new tools that were not initially designed for it.

5.1   Multi-formalism Management

Parameterization of Macao and the services management of FrameKit allows us to specify and handle multiple formalisms.

Editor and User Interface. Macao is parameterized using external files that describe components of the formalism. Thus, the construction of a new formalism does not imply any recompilation. Of course, Macao deals with syntactical aspects only, semantical ones are a convention between the user and the tool.

Figure 1 shows the graphical representation of the *VaMoS* formalism presented in section 2.1. The four nodes represent the four parts of a module, the four internal morphisms that link them and the labels associated with the body part.

Services management. Each service is relevant for an identified set of formalisms. FrameKit holds an instantiation mechanism that identifies the formalism of a model and creates the list of dedicated services. Therefore, the user can only ask for services that are relevant for his specification.

5.2   Open Platform

FrameKit is an open platform that may be enriched by new services. To achieve this enrichment, a procedure called integration has been defined. We distinguish two types of tool integration : *a priori* and *a posteriori*.

The *a priori* integration concerns tools that are especially designed to run in the FrameKit environment. The compiler from OF-Class to CPN was developed to be integrated in FrameKit; it was implemented to an *a priori* implementation.

The *a posteriori* integration concerns already designed tools (sometimes, source files may not be available) to be integrated in the FrameKit environment. It requires an adaptation of the imported software. A translation of the FrameKit file format into the file format expected by the tool is necessary. The opposite translation is necessary to store results. Moreover, for interactive tools, such as MOKA and PROD, functions to drive the user interface are provided. MOKA, PROD and TRIO are *a posteriori* integrated tools.

Figure 6 shows how the integrated tools are linked. If some syntax errors or interface incoherence are detected, the specification must be modified. No verification tool can be applied. Such a mechanism is automatically handled by FrameKit

5.3   Note Files

A note file is attached to each specification module. It is a structured file containing all the information related to the analysis of the model. A note is associated to a property and gives:

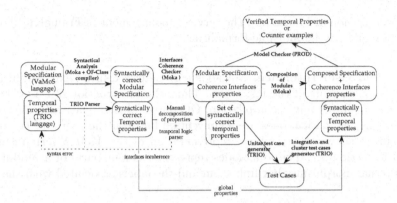

Fig. 6. Modular specification and validation methodology

- its identification,
- the method used to verify it,
- the part of the module concerned by the verification,
- the way the property has been identified (by the model checker, the interfaces coherence checker, ...),
- the status of the verification (done, in progress, to do),
- the context of the verification (abstraction of the model, computation of the state space, ...).

The defined syntax of some note attributes allows the exploitation of the same note file by several tools. These *note files* may be used to produce an analysis report any time. Files associated with a model may be shared between several tools.

6   Conclusion

We have presented a tool-supported approach dedicated to the specification and validation of critical embedded systems. We deal with the complexity of the system using a modular methodology, which provides generic and reusable modules. Our homogeneous specification language allows us to manage conjointly two views of a same specification: a logical one and a behavioral one. Each of them is well adapted to a specific verification procedure (model checking and test cases generation). We are now identifying the common semantic aspects of Petri nets and MOKA components to strengthen the links between both views.

The modular structure of our specifications is exploited to perform the verification of the system. We have improved these approaches to deal with a realistic industrial application ([1]). We are implementing a CASE environment integrating these tools into the FrameKit platform . This allows us to trace the development process in both views, with note files to exchange information and version management. However, some steps of the validation methods are not yet tool supported. To improve these points, the semantics aspects can help us to increase the cooperation between the two approaches. Especially, we will study how validation tools can interact and how to use results of one step in the other. For example, TRIO model generator automatically computes data domain abstractions that are relevant for the model checker PROD. The model checker PROD defines possible execution scenarios that can be used to define sequences of test cases to test on the system.

Acknowledgments. We would like to thank the other members of the VaMoS project for fruitful discussions and useful comments on early version of this paper: Jacques Cazin, Alioune Diagne, Pascal Estraillier, Pierre Michel, Christel Seguin, Virginie Wiels.

References

1. Action FORMA. *Maîtrise de systèmes complexes réactifs et sûrs*, Journée au MENRT: Bilan de la 1ere année, Paris, January 1998. http://www.imag.fr/FORMA/.
2. R; Alur, T.A. henzinger, F.Y.C. Mang, S. Qadeer, S.K. Rajamani, and S. Tasiran. Mocha : Modularity in model checking. In *proceedings on the 10th International Conference on Computer-Aided Verification*, pages 521–525. Springer Verlag, 1998.
3. H.R. Andersen, J. Staunstrup, and N. Maretti. A comparison of modular verification techniques. In *Proceedings of FASE'97*. Springer Verlag, 1997.
4. R.J. Anderson, P. Beame, S. Burns, W. Chan, F. Modugno, D. Notkin, and J.D. Reese. Model checking large software specifications. In *Proceedings of the 4th ACM SIGOFT Symposium on the Foundations of Software engineering*, pages 156–166, 1996.
5. S. Barbey, D. Buchs, M-C. Gaudel, B. Marre, C. Péraire, P. Thévenod-Fosse, and H. Waeselynck. From requirements to tests via object-oriented design. Technical Report 20072, DeVa ESPRIT Long Term Research Project, 1998. http://www.laas.research.ec.org/deva/papers/4c.pdf.
6. G. Bernot, M-C. Gaudel, and B. Marre. Software testing based on formal specifications: a theory and a tool. *Software Engineering Journal*, 6, November 1991.
7. D. Brière and P. Traverse. Airbus a320/a330/a340 electric flight controls: a family of fault-tolerant systems. *FTCS*, 23:616–623, 1993.
8. E. Brinksma. Formal methods for conformance testing: Theory can be practical. In *CAV'99*, number 1633 in LNCS, pages 44–46. Springer Verlag, July 1999.
9. J.R. Burch, E.M. Clarke, D.E. Long, K.L. McMillan, and D.L. DILL. Symbolic model checking for sequential circuit verification. *IEEE Trans. on Computer-Aided Design of Integrated Circuits and Systems 13*, 4:401–424, 1994.
10. W. Chan, R.J. Anderson, P. Beame, and D. Notkin. Improving Afficiency of Symbolic Model Checking for State-Based System Requirements. In *proceedings of the 1998 International Symposium on Software Testing and Analysis* , 1998.
11. E. Ciapessoni, E. Corsetti, M. Migliorati, and E. Ratto. Specifying industrial real-time systems in a logical framework. In *ICLP 94 - Post Conference Workshop on Logic Programming in Software Engineering*, 1994.

12. E.M. Clarke and J.M. Wing. Formal Methods: State of the Art and Future Directions. Technical report, Carnegie Mellon University, 1996.
13. A. Diagne. *Une Approche Multi-Formalismes de Spécification de Systèmes Répartis: Transformations de Composants Modulaires en Réseaux de Petri*. Thèse, LIP6, Université Paris 6, 4, Place Jussieu, 75252 Paris Cedex 05, May 1997.
14. A. Diagne and F. Kordon. A multi-formalisms prototyping approach from conceptual description to implementation of distributed systems. In *Proceedings of the 7th IEEE International Workshop on Rapid System Prototyping (RSP'96)*, Porto Caras, Thessaloniki Greece, June 1996.
15. M. Doche. *Techniques formelles pour l'évaluation de systèmes complexes. Test et modularité*. PhD thesis, ENSAE, ONERA-CERT/DTIM, Décembre 1999.
16. M. Doche, J. Cazin, D. Le Berre, P. Michel, C. Seguin, and V. Wiels. Module templates for the specification of fault-tolerant systems. In *DASIA'98*, May 1998.
17. M. Doche, C. Seguin, and V. Wiels. A modular approach to specify and test an electrical flight control system. In *FMICS-4, Fourth International Workshop on formal Methods for Industrial Critical Systems*, July 1999. Available at http://www.cert.fr/francais/deri/wiels/Publi/fmics99.ps.
18. M. Doche and V. Wiels. Extended institutions for testing. In *AMAST00, Algebraic Methodology And Software Technology*, LNCS, Iowa City, May 2000. Springer Verlag. Available at http://www.cert.fr/francais/deri/wiels/Publi/amast00.ps.
19. ECMA. A Reference Model for Frameworks of Software Engineerings Environments. Technical Report TR/55 (version 3), NIST Report, 1993.
20. H. Ehrig and B. Mahr. *Fundamentals of Algebraic Specification 2 : Modules specifications and constraints*, volume 21 of *EATCS Monographs on Theoretical Computer Science*. Springer-Verlag, 1990.
21. M-C. Gaudel. Testing can be formal, too. In *TAPSOFT'95*, pages 82–96. Springer Verlag, 1995.
22. C. Ghezzi, D. Mandrioli, and A. Morzenti. A model parametric real-time logic. *ACM Transactions on programming languages and systems*, 14(4):521–573, October 1992.
23. J. A. Goguen and R. Burstall. Institutions: Abstract model theory for specification and programming. *Journal of the ACM*, 39(1):95–146, January 1992.
24. K. Jensen. *Coloured Petri Nets, Basic Concepts, Analysis Methods and Practical Use, Volumes 1, 2 and 3*. Springer-Verlag, 1992.
25. MARS-Team. MARS Home page. http://www.lip6.fr/mars.
26. P. Michel and V. Wiels. A Framework for Modular Formal Specification and Verification. In *LNCS 1313, Proceedings of FME'97*, September 1997.
27. A. Morzenti, P. San Pietro, and S. Morasca. A tool for automated system analysis based on modular specifications. In *ASE98*, pages 2–11. IEEE Computer Society, 1998.
28. R. Pugliese and E. Tronci. Automatic verification of a hydroelectric power plant. In *LNCS 1051, FME'96: Industrial Benefit and Advances in Formal Methods, 3rd International Symposium of Formal Methods Europe*, pages 425–444, 1996.
29. T. Sreemani and J.M. Atlee. Feasibility of model checking software requirements: A case study. In *COMPASS'96, Proceedings of the 11th Annual Conference on Computer Assurance*, pages 77–88, 1996.
30. K. Varpaaniemi, J. Halme, K. Hiekkanen, and T. Pyssysalo. PROD Reference Manual. Technical Report ISBN 951-22-2707-X, University of technology, Departement of Computer Science, Digital Systems Laboratory, 1995.
31. V. Wiels. *Modularité pour la conception et la validation formelles de systèmes*. PhD thesis, ENSAE - ONERA/CERT, October 1997.

A Combined Testing and Verification Approach for Software Reliability

Natasha Sharygina and Doron Peled

Bell Laboratories, 600 Mountain Ave.,
Murray Hill, NJ, USA 07974
{natali,doron}@research.bell-labs.com

Abstract. Automatic and manual software verification is based on applying mathematical methods to a *model* of the software. Modeling is usually done manually, thus it is prone to *modeling errors*. This means that errors found in the model may not correspond to real errors in the code, and that if the model is found to satisfy the checked properties, the actual code may still have some errors. For this reason, it is desirable to be able to perform some consistency checks between the actual code and the model. Exhaustive consistency checks are usually not possible, for the same reason that modeling is necessary. We propose a methodology for improving the throughput of software verification by performing some consistency checks between the original code and the model, specifically, by applying software testing. In this paper we present such a combined testing and verification methodology and demonstrate how it is applied using a set of software reliability tools. We introduce the notion of a *neighborhood* of an error trace, consisting of a tree of execution paths, where the original error trace is one of them. Our experience with the methodology shows that traversing the neighborhood of an error is extremely useful in locating its cause. This is crucial not only in understanding where the error stems from, but in getting an initial idea of how to redesign the code. We use as a case study a robot control system, and report on several design and modeling errors found during the verification and testing process.

1 Introduction

Software reliability can be enhanced by applying various different analysis methods based on mathematical theories. This includes software verification and testing. Software testing is the more commonly used technique in the software industry. It involves generating test suites and sampling the execution of the code according to them. It usually can be applied directly to the actual code. Its main disadvantage is that it is not exhaustive. Thus, although it practically helps in detecting many of the program errors, it has a high probability of missing some of them. Automatic software verification is more exhaustive, but it is usually limited to finite state systems with a 'reasonable' amount of program states, due to the problem of 'state space explosion'. Because of these limitations, model checking is usually applied to a *model* of the checked code rather than to the

J.N. Oliveira and P. Zave (Eds.): FME 2001, LNCS 2021, pp. 611–628, 2001.

actual code directly. This model is obtained by manual translation through a process called "modeling". The process of manual translation may induce some errors in the model. This means that errors found in the model during its verification may not correspond to real errors in the code, and vice versa. Thus, even if the model is found to satisfy the checked properties, the actual code may still have some errors.

The correspondence between the actual code and the model can be addressed using different techniques. Simulation of the model execution and testing based on formal descriptions of the functional and behavioral specifications [3], [8] can be useful for checking that the implementation is behaviorally equivalent to the design. Another approach is to develop mapping algorithms to connect the implementation and the model [12], [16]. Verifying the correspondence between the code and the model can also be done formally, e.g., using theorem proving technology. In most approaches, consistency checks are performed informally basis, and not exhaustively.

In this paper we explore a combination of testing and verification methods. We present a hybrid methodology to software reliability that combines program analysis and verification techniques. This methodology addresses the issue of minimizing the number of errors introduced into the model during the translation process. It also helps identifying the causes of the conceptual errors found during the verification along with facilitating the software redesign process.

The fundamental principals of our combined testing and verification methodology include application of the testing process both during system modeling prior to the actual verification and during evaluation of the counterexample produced by the verifier after the verification is complete. The fact that testing methods are applied to the modeled software allows us to validate the translation. The idea is to use a testing tool for the examination of the execution paths of the model, while comparing them with the behavior of the actual code. During this process, modeling errors, as well as possible conceptual errors, may be uncovered.

The common model checking approach is to apply the verification to the model, and if a counterexample is found, to compare it with the original code in order to check whether it is indeed an error (if it is not, it is called a 'false negative'). Doing any conformance testing on the checked model with respect to the actual code increases the dependability of model checking. We introduce the notion of a neighborhood of an error trace, which consists of a tree of execution paths, where the original error trace is one of them. Our experience with this methodology shows that traversing the neighborhood of an error is extremely useful in locating its cause. This is crucial not only in understanding where the conceptual error stems from, but in getting an initial idea of how to correct the code.

We demonstrate the methodology using a case study taken from robotics, namely a robot control software. Our proposed methodology does not depend on the choice of specific tools. We have used it with the following combination of tools: as the verification tool, we used the SPIN model checking system [11] and as a testing tool, we used the PET system [7]. The errors, found in different stages of the verification process, consist of modeling and design errors. These errors led to changes in the design.

Section 2 provides the description of the combined testing and verification methodology. Section 3 describes application of the methodology to the verification of the robot control system and presents its results. Section 4 provides conclusions and describes future research.

2   The Combined Methodology: Testing and Verification

One of the main problems of software verification is that it is applied to a *model* of the software, rather than to the software directly. This stems from mathematical limitations on dealing with infinite state systems, limitations on memory usage, and the use of different kinds of notations and programming languages in different tools. As a consequence, a discrepancy in functionality can exist between the actual code and the checked model. The possible danger is twofold: errors found in the checked model may not correspond to actual executions of the original code. On the other hand, a positive verification result may not have taken into account all the executions of the actual code.

The usual practice in this case is that a model is constructed and verified, and error traces found later during the verification are compared against the original code. If these error traces are not compatible with the code, then the model needs to be modified accordingly. Because of a possible modeling error, when model checking does not come up with an error, there is sometimes very little that we know about the correctness of the checked property.

In order to minimize the effect of the possible discrepancy between the model and the code, we suggest a methodology of testing the checked model against

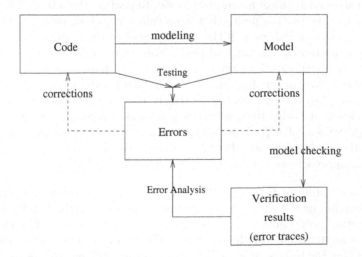

Fig. 1. The combined methodology

the actual code, as part of applying formal methods. This is done by integrating interactive 'white box testing' of the model [15] with the verification process. We examine execution paths of the model and compare them to the original code. Detected discrepancies usually reflect modeling errors and result in modification of the model. Moreover, in some cases, the testing process can result in the discovery of errors in the original code.

Figure 1 is used to illustrate our methodology. It adds into the verification process a testing tool, which can be used to simulate execution paths of the model. A testing tool that supports interactive and visual representation of the program's structure would benefit the process of simulation and examination of the program execution the most. The interactive testing approach we use is based on a flow graph notation. We remind the reader this commonly used formalism. A node in a flow graph is one of the following: *begin, end, predicate, random* (i.e., nondeterministic choice), *wait* (for a certain global predicate to hold, in a concurrent program), *assign, send* or *receive*. The *begin* and *end* nodes appear as ovals, the *predicate, wait* and *random* nodes appear as diamonds, labeled by a condition, or the word *random*, in the latter case. *Assignment* and message *send* or *receive* nodes appear as boxes labeled by the corresponding statement. Each node, together with its output edge constitutes a *transition*, i.e., an atomic operation of the program, which can depend on some condition (e.g., the current program counter, an *if-then-else* or a while *condition* in the node, the nonemptiness of a communication queue) and make some changes to the program variables (including message queues and program counters). White box testing (specifically, unit testing) can be performed by examining paths in flow graphs. Different *coverage techniques* [15] suggest criteria for the appropriate coverage of a program by different paths.

Consider an execution path in the flow graph of a sequential program. A *related path* of the flow graph can be obtained from it by selecting at some point an alternative edge out of a condition node. Repeating this process of obtaining alternative paths (with a prefix that is mutual with a previously selected path), we obtain a tree, which we call the *neighborhood* of the original path. This tree includes in particular the original path. Note that for each path there can be multiple neighborhoods. Intuitively, if an execution path contains an error, then its neighborhood (rather than just the path alone) contains enough information for understanding the error and correcting it. In concurrent code, a trace consists of a sequence of nodes from different processes. Projecting on the processes, the neighborhood of a path generates a single tree for each process. Figure 2 represents a path (emphasized) and its neighborhood.

In our approach we use testing in two different ways:

White box testing of the model We perform interactive software testing before performing model checking, comparing it with the original code. Traversing execution paths allows us to better understand the code. Errors found in this way are usually modeling errors. They lead to changing the model, and repeating the testing process. There is no clear guidance to how much testing is needed to obtain confidence that the model reflects the code properly.

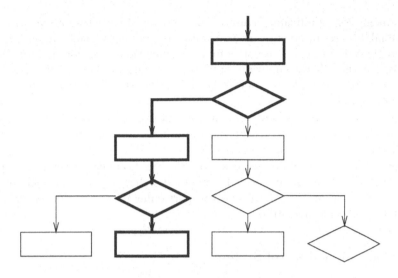

Fig. 2. A neighborhood

Testing the neighborhood of an error trace. After an error trace is found with a model checker, a testing tool is used to traverse the neighborhood of that trace. We explore the neighborhood until the relevant part of the code is understood, and the cause for the error is detected. The main point is that it is not only a single error trace that is used to detect an error, but also some related execution paths, namely the neighborhood. Errors that are found in this way can be both modeling or conceptual errors. Thus, a fix is needed in either the model or the original code, respectively.

Our methodology proceeds as follows. The verification process starts with modeling. Then white box testing is performed as long as modeling errors are found, and until a certain degree of confidence in the verification model is obtained. Then, we start performing model checking. Upon finding an error, neighborhood testing is performed. Analyzing the error results in fixing the original code or the model.

3   The Methodology in Practice

As a working example for our methodology, we examine a Robot Control System (RCS). It is a subset of a multiple criterion decision support software [1], used for controlling redundant robots (i.e., robots that have more than six degrees of freedom). Redundant robots are widely used for sophisticated tasks in uncertain and dynamic environments in life-critical systems. This includes space and underwater operations, nuclear cleanup, and bomb disposal. Failure recovery is one of the examples of redundancy resolution applications: if one actuator fails, the controller locks the faulty joint and the redundant robot continues operating. The robot control algorithms support redundancy resolution. They combine requirements for significant computations, hard real-time responsiveness, stringent reliability requirements, and distributed and networked implementation. This combination of characteristics makes application of formal methods highly desirable. Although we analyze a simplified version of the RCS in this paper, this is not a toy example, and its study and verification is of high interest to the robotics research.

The robot control system controls the motion behavior of the robot arm and includes kinematics algorithms and interfaces to the robotic computational libraries, which are the components of the OSCAR [13] system.

In the following sections we describe the functionality of the RCS, specify properties that we formally verified using model checking, and present the combined verification and testing process in particular using the SPIN verifier, and the PET path exploration tool.

3.1   The Robot Control System

The design of the RCS is done using the ObjectBench [19] notation. It is an object-oriented development and analysis environment, which has been used for the automatic generation of C++ code that can be used for controlling the robot. [1] In the description of the RCS we use the convention that the names of the processes in ObjectBench representation of the RCS that are in italics and start with a capital letter. The names of the variables are in italics and start with a lowercase letter.

A robot arm consists of several joints and one end-effector. The end-effector is the last link of the robot, used to accomplish a task. The end-effector may be holding a tool, or the end-effector itself may be a tool. In this paper we assume that the robot arm consists only two joints. These physical entities are represented by the processes *Arm*, *Joint1*, *Joint2* and *EndEffector* in the software design.

For each joint we specify an angle, representing a rotation of the joint relative to its neighboring link, as a vector of three components. The end-effector *Current_position* is given as a vector of positions (cp_x, cp_y, z) and orientation angles (α, β, γ). The system's task is to move the end-effector along the specified path. We examine a simplified instance, in which the end-effector moves only in the horizontal, i.e., the x direction.

The control algorithm starts with defining an initial end-effector position given the initial joint angles. This is done by solving a forward kinematics problem [6]. The next step is to get a new end-effector position from a predefined path. The system calculates the joint angles for this position, providing the solution of the inverse kinematics problem [6] and configures the arm.

---

[1] Some abstraction was already used in creating the ObjectBench description. In fact, the ObjectBench code itself can actually be seen as a model for the real system. However, the fact that there are two levels of abstraction is orthogonal to our methodology, and might be misleading. We thus treat the ObjectBench description as the 'code' and ignore the lower level of the robot control system.

At each of the steps described above, a number of physical constraints has to be satisfied. The constraints include limits on the angles of joints and on the end-effector position. If a joint angle limit is not satisfied, a fault recovery is performed. The faulty joint is locked within the limit value. Then, the value of the angle of another joint is recalculated for the same end-effector position. If the end-effector position exceeds the limit, the algorithm registers the undesired position, which serves as a flag to stop the execution. A *Checker* process controls the joints that pass or fail the constraints check. If all the joints meet the constraints, the *Checker* issues the command to move the end-effector to a new

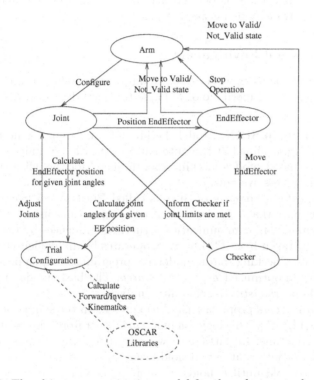

Fig. 3. The object communication model for the robot control system

position. Otherwise it sends a command to the *Arm* process indicating its invalid state.

During the development of this software, one is mainly concerned with the satisfaction of the reliability requirements. In the presented RCS, the ultimate goal is to ensure that the end-effector is moving only when the arm is indeed in a valid state.

The concurrent behavior of the robot components makes it difficult to analyze the overall behavior of the system. In particular, the calculations of the movement of different parts of the robot are done in a distributed way. A major concern is that different parameters that correspond to previous and future moves may be used incorrectly. This may result in an improper combination, leading to a faulty behavior of the arm. In order to prevent such situations, formal verification is applied.

The object communication model of the RCS is presented in Figure 3. It displays the flow of events of the RCS in terms of the control signals exchanged among the objects in the system. Exchange of data in the model is represented by an arrow originating from a source object to a destination object.

The state transition diagram shown in Figure 4 specifies a lifecycle of one of the processes of the RCS, the *EndEffector* process. It consists of nodes, representing states and their associated actions to be performed, and event arcs, which represent transitions between states.

3.2   Experimental Environment

In order to verify the RCS, we have selected tools for model checking and testing, which can support our methodology. These tools are described below.

Model Checking in SPIN. Model checking [2], [5], [18] is a generic name for a family of algorithms aimed at the automatic verification of finite state systems. SPIN is a state-based model-checking tool designed for the efficient verification of distributed process systems.

The specification language of SPIN is called PROMELA. PROMELA is a programming language that includes sequential constructions inspired by Dijkstra's Guarded command [4], communication structures influences by Hoare's CSP [9] and expressions taken from **C** [14]. SPIN operates by an explicit enumeration of reachable states. Checking that a model of a program satisfies a property is done by performing an optimized *depth-first-search*. The basic mode of operation of SPIN is based on *exhaustive* reachability analysis.

Specific correctness properties can be expressed in the syntax of Linear Temporal Logic (LTL) [17]. This logic include *modal* operators, expressing properties that change over time. In particular, we can write $\Box \varphi$ to express that φ holds forever, $\Diamond \varphi$ to denote that φ will hold eventually, and $\varphi \, U \, \psi$ to denote that φ will continue to hold until ψ holds. Combining several modalities allows us to express more complicated formulas. For example, $\Diamond \Box \varphi$ means that φ will eventually start to hold and would then continue to do so forever. The formula $\Box \Diamond \varphi$ means that φ would hold infinitely often. The formula $\Box(request \rightarrow \Diamond granted)$ can be used to assert that at any point in the execution, if a request was made, it is eventually granted.

Testing using PET. The PET system works with a sequential program, or with a concurrent program consisting of several processes with shared variables and a synchronous communication. The processes are written in a language that is an extension to the programming language PASCAL.

PET automatically generates the flow graph of the tested processes. It then allows the user to select concurrent execution paths of these processes. PET leaves

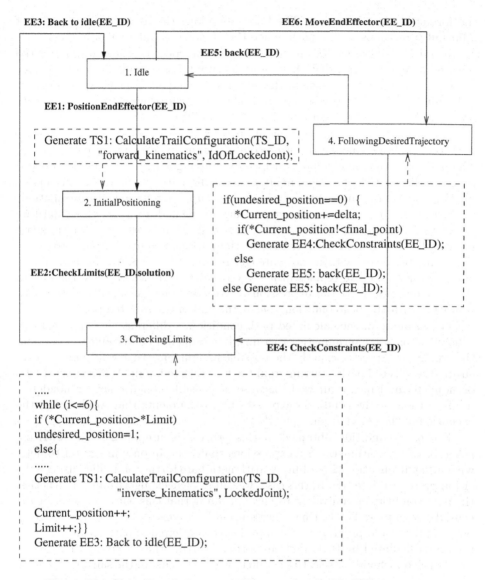

Fig. 4. The ObjectBench Transition Diagram for the *EndEffector* process

the choice of the paths to the user. The user can choose a path by clicking on the appropriate nodes of a flow graph. A path can also consist of an interleaving of nodes from multiple concurrent processes. The user can also create a variant of a path by backtracking to a *predicate* (or *random*) node, and making an alternative selection. Another way to alter a path is to use the same transitions but allow a different interleaving of them. When dealing with concurrent programs, the way the execution of transitions from different nodes are interleaved is perhaps the foremost source of errors. The PET tool allows the user to flip the order of adjacent transitions on the path, when they belong to different processes.

In order to make the connection between the code, the flow graph and the selected path clearer, sensitive highlighting is used. For example, when the cursor points at some predicate node in the flow graph window, the corresponding text is highlighted in the process window. The code corresponding to a predicate node can be, e.g., an *if-then-else* or a *while* condition.

Once a path is chosen, the condition to execute it is calculated, based on repeated symbolic calculation of preconditions, as in program verification [10]. The path condition is calculated backwards, starting with *true*. Thus, we proceed from a *postcondition* of a node, in order to calculate its *precondition*. In calculating the path condition, we progress backwards, applying various transformations to the current running condition, depending on the nodes we encounter, until we arrive to the beginning of the paths. For a transition consisting of a predicate p with the 'yes' outedge, we transform the current condition from c to $c \wedge p$. The same predicate with a 'no' outedge, results in $c \wedge \neg p$. For an assignment of the form $x := e$, we replace in p every (free) occurrence of the variable x in the postcondition c by the expression e. We start the calculation of the path condition with the postcondition *true* at the end of the selected path.

The meaning of the calculated path condition is different for sequential and concurrent or nondeterministic programs. In a sequential deterministic program, the condition expresses exactly the possible assignments that would *ensure* executing the selected path, starting from the first selected node. When concurrency or nondeterminism are allowed, because of possible concurrency or nondeterministic choices, the condition expresses the assignments that would make the execution of the selected path *possible*.

The path condition obtained in this process is simplified using rewriting rules, based on arithmetic. Subexpressions that contain only integer arithmetic without multiplication (Pressburger arithmetic) are further simplified using a decision procedure (see [7]). In this case, we can also check algorithmically whether the path condition is equivalent to *false* (meaning that this path can never be executed), or to *true*. The testing process using PET consts of repeatedly selecting paths in the tested program and comparing the anticipated path conditions with the ones calculated by PET. PET supports modifying the selected path, traversing its neighborhood, or selecting a different interleaving of the same transitions.

3.3   Verification of the RCS

We have performed a manual translation of the ObjectBench code into a SPIN model, written in the programming language PROMELA. At the same time we translated the same code into a PET model. The target programming language of PET is only syntactically different from PROMELA. Moreover, there is a one to one correspondence in their sequential syntactic constructs (e.g., loops, conditionals) and the concurrency features (e.g., shared variables and communication). Thus, although SPIN and PET do not accept exactly the same input, we could use PET to perform the white box testing of the ObjectBench code with the SPIN code (with the obvious possibility of having introduced additional typos).

In order to reduce the complexity of checking the original code we had to abstract and restrict some calculations. In particular, in the ObjectBench code the robot arm movement calculations are done through the interface with the OSCAR libraries [13]. In this example we abstracted away actual calculations and replaced them with nondeterministic assignments of small natural numbers. Scaling of the object attribute values has been enforced in order to avoid dealing with the rational numbers that were widely used in the original code. Figure 5 graphically represents a flow graph of the *Arm* process. The events *to_joint1!1*, *to_joint2!1* are used to initiate movements of the joints and the *arm_status* variable is used to store information about the status of the arm configuration. Below we present the PROMELA code for the *EndEffector* process. The actions associated with the events of the *EndEffector* process, as specified in the Transition Diagram in Figure 4, are presented as the comments in the PROMELA code.

```
proctype endeffector (){
byte m;
byte c_p_y=0, c_p_z=0, c_a_alpha=0, c_a_beta=0, c_a_theta=0, k;
  do
  :: c_i<2  -> {
     to_endeffector?m;
     c_i=c_i+1;
     if
     :: c_i==2 -> {
        to_trialconf!1;                        //PositionEndEffector
        to_arm!0;
        do
        :: end_position==0 ->
           ee_reference=0;
           if
           :: endeffector_status==1-> {
              to_endeffector?k;
              if
              :: abort_var==1 -> break
              ::else -> skip
              fi;
              c_p_x=c_p_x+delta;               //MoveEndEffector
              to_recovery!0,0;
              to_arm!0;
              ee_reference=1}
           ::else -> skip
           fi;
           if
           :: c_p_x<=finale -> {
           if                          //CheckConstraints
           ::( (c_p_x<=max_x) && (c_p_y<=max_y) && (c_p_z<=max_z) &&
               (c_a_alpha<=max_a) && (c_a_beta<=max_b) &&
               (c_a_theta<=max_t) ) -> {
```

```
           if
              ::endeffector_status==0 ->
              to_joint2!1;
              endeffector_status=1    }
              ::else-> to_trialconf!0   //CalculateTrialConfiguration

           fi }
           ::else -> { end_position=1;
                              to_arm!3;
                              break}
           fi     }
           ::else ->{
           end_position=1;
           to_arm!2;
           break}
              fi    }
        od }
     ::else -> skip
     fi      }
  ::else -> break
od  }
```

3.4   Testing and Verification Results

During our testing and verification process, we formed four generations of SPIN
models. *Model 0* is the first model created by translation from ObjectBench
code into PET's internal language, and at the same time into a PROMELA model.
Model 1 is obtained after making some corrections based on the white box testing
results. *Model 2* corresponds to an improved version that includes several changes
from *Model 1*, which where made as a result of finding modeling errors. *Model
3* is our final model of the RCS, whose implementation underwent some design
changes in order to correct the conceptual errors found during the testing and
model checking processes.

We checked a collection of correctness requirements specifying the coordinated behavior of the RCS processes. The requirements were encoded as LTL
formulas. We expressed all the formulae in terms of state predicates. Since SPIN
prefers specifying properties over states, rather than over events, we sometimes
needed to encode the occurrence of some important events by adding new state
variables.

We demonstrate the advantages of using the combined testing and verification methodology using a selection of the specifications that failed the formal
checking. We then discuss how the proposed methodology was used for the redesign of the original code.

Consider the following description of the checked properties. We refer in this
description to the states appearing in the state transition diagrams in Object-
Bench. An example appears in Figure 4.

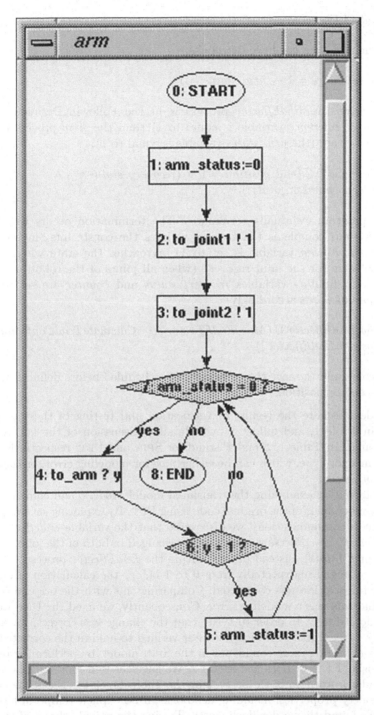

Fig. 5. Flow graph representation of the *Arm* process using PET tool

1. *DeadlockFreedom*

The model does not have deadlocks.

2. $\Box(ee\_reference = 1 \rightarrow arm\_status = 1)$

Whenever the *EndEffector* process is in the FollowingDesiredTrajectory
state (*ee_reference* variable is equal to 1) than the *Arm* process is in the
"Valid" state (the *arm_status* variable is equal to 1).

3. $abort\_var = 0 \, \mathrm{U} \, (end\_position = 1 \lor (recovery\_status = 1 \land$
   $counter = number\_joints))$

The program eventually terminates. The termination occurs when either
the system completes the task or violates the constraints (in both cases
the *end_position* variable is set to 1) or reaches the state where there is
no solution for the fault recovery (when all joints of the robot arm violate
the joint limits - variables *recovery_status* and *counter* are set to 1 and
number_of_joints accordingly).

4. $\neg MoveEndEffector \, \mathrm{U} \, (MoveEndEffector \land (\neg CalculateTrialConfiguration$
   $\mathrm{U} \, PositionEndEffector))$

No command to move the end-effector is scheduled before defining an initial
end-effector position.

We demonstrate the results of verification and testing of these properties
(*Prop*) in Table 1, and follow it by a detailed discussion of the nature of the
errors found. In Table 1, S and P stand for SPIN and PET, respectively, *Err tp*
defines an error type, which can be either *mod* for modeling error, or *concept* for
conceptual error.

We started by examining the translated model *Model 0* and comparing it to
the known behavior of the original code using PET. By exploring several possible
interprocess communications, we discovered that the variable *endeffector_status*
of the *EndEffector* process was mistakenly changed in both of the joint processes
(*Joint1* and *Joint2*), instead of only within the *EndEffector* process. This variable was changed unexpectedly from 0 to 1 before the calculation of an initial
end-effector position was completed. Comparing this with the original code, we
found that this was a modeling error. Consequently, we fixed the PET and SPIN
models accordingly. In order to verify that the change was correct, we specified
Property 4 (see Table 1), which was later verified to hold in the corrected *Model
1*. After obtaining more confidence in the SPIN model, by performing repeated
testing using PET, we obtained *Model 1*. We have checked *Model 1* for deadlocks
(the deadlock-freedom is Property 1 in the Table 1). SPIN checks the code for
several safety properties, including deadlocks, if no explicit temporal formula is
given. We found that a deadlock exists. Tracing the neighborhood of the deadlock using PET, we could realize the cause for it. We observed that in the model,

Table 1. Experimental results

	Model 1			Model 2			Model 3	
Prop	Tools	Result	Err tp	Tools	Result	Err tp	Tools	Result
1	S +P	False	mod	S +P	False	concept	S	True
2	n/a	n/a		S +P	False	concept	S	True
3	n/a	n/a		S +P	False	concept	S	True
4	n/a	n/a		S	True		S	True

the *counter* variable of the *Checker* process is not reset to zero when it was equal to *number_joints*, as opposed to the original code.

Thus, another modeling error was identified. We have fixed this error. At this point, after these corrections to the model, we have obtained *Model 2*. We repeated the SPIN verification for Property 4 (the cause of the previous deadlock) on this model, and this check succeeded. Nevertheless, we found using SPIN that a deadlock still occurs. After examination of the error track that led to the deadlock situation, and studying its neighborhood with PET, we realized that this was due to a conceptual error in the fault recovery algorithm.

To confirm this fact we formulated and checked Property 3, which was aimed at checking whether the system terminates properly. This property did not hold for *Model 2* and the examination of the error track led us to the conclusion that the system does not terminate in the case where there is no solution for the fault recovery. We will remind the reader that the fault recovery procedure is activated in the RCS if one of the robot joints does not satisfy the specified limits. In fact, if during the process of fault recovery some of the newly recalculated joint angles do not satisfy the constraints in their turn, then another fault recovery procedure is called. Analysis of the counterexample provided by SPIN for Property 3 indicated that a mutual attempt was made for several faulty joints to recompute the joint angles of other joints while not resolving the fault situation.

Specifically, Property 3 failed since in our example it can be shown that requests originated from *Joint1* and *Joint2* to recompute the angles of these joints could continue indefinitely: if *Joint1* does not respect the limit then the fault recovery is called and *Joint1* is locked with the angle limit value. The *Joint2* angle is being recalculated for the original *EndEffector* position. If the new angle of *Joint2* does not satisfy its limit then another fault recovery procedure is called, which attempts to find a new angle for *Joint1* while *Joint2* angle is locked. If there is no resolutions that satisfies the limit for *Joint1* than fault recovery is called again. This is also a confirmation of the above deadlock situation.

Another conceptual error found during verification of *Model 2* indicated a problem of coordination between the *Arm* and the *EndEffector* processes. The original design assumed a sequential execution pattern. In fact, it was expected that the *arm_status* variable of the *Arm* process would be repeatedly updated before the *EndEffector* would switch to the FollowingDesiredTrajectory state, where the *ee_reference* variable changes its value from 0 to 1. An interaction

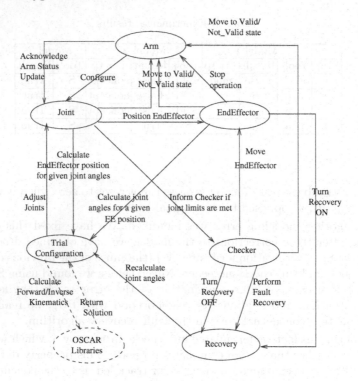

Fig. 6. The modified model of the robot control system

between the processes led to the situation where the update of the *ee_reference* variable precedes the change of the *arm_status* value. This was the reason for Property 2 to fail.

In order to fix these conceptual errors a redesign of the original system was required. Figure 6 reflects the changes made. The corresponding model is then *Model 3*. We had to introduce a new process called *Recovery*, whose functionality provides a correct resolution of the fault recovery situation described above. Additionally we added several exchanges of messages between the processes *Arm* and *Joint* in order to fix the coordination problem reported earlier. Formal verification of the redesigned model confirmed that a new design satisfies all of the properties described above.

4   Conclusions

Model checking and testing techniques provide two complimentary ways of improving the reliability of software, however, traditionally they have been used separately. In fact, they are usually being advocated by different communities. We have proposed a methodology that combines the two techniques. This is done by applying testing to check the model created for the process of model checking. Further, testing is used to examine the results of model checking and locating the possible causes for the detected error.

The conformance testing between the source code and the model is based on the application of an interactive testing tool. Our approach assumes that a testing team knows the expected behavior of the source code.

We have demonstrated our methodology on a real application, consisting of a robot control system. Several algorithms that are in current use are known to have design errors. Several of these errors were identified using our methodology. We used a collection of formal methods tools, namely, the PET interactive testing system, and the model checking system SPIN. One of the major achievements of this experiment is that we could find conceptual errors and correct them quite quickly, namely within a month of work of one person. This included learning of the tools that were used.

We used the notion of *neighborhood*. This is a collection of execution sequences that are simple variants of the error trace found during the automatic verification. The PET tool was helpful in testing neighborhoods. Model checking is often used to verify the control part of a system. It is less effective in debugging the data dependent (sometimes called 'data path') part of the system. The data dependent part often provides a conceptually infinite state space, or at least one that is too big to be automatically verified using current tools. In our methodology, we can extend the testing process to deal with the data dependent part of the system, which are not handled by finite state model checking techniques.

For example, we can extend the RCS model, to deal with 'painting' a surface. The painting is controlled by the RCS. A mathematical equation is used to control the painted area, e.g., to make sure that we are within a radius r from some origin, we check that the relation between the radius and the x and y coordinates position is $x^2 + y^2 \leq r^2$. We can use PET to generate the necessary path conditions for executions that include the painting. This can be used in testing the behavior of the extended model.

As a consequence of our experiment with the tools SPIN and PET, and with the presented methodology, we suggest a new tool that combines the verification and testing process described in this paper. Along with the automatic verification process, the tool will have the ability to display an error trace and the capability of tracing the neighborhood of an error. The tracing will be connected visually with the code and with its graphical representation as a flow graph. We have found such a combination (by joining the capabilities of the above mentioned tools) useful in a rapid process of verification and redesign of the example software.

Acknowledgement. We acknowledge the counsel of Prof. J.C. Browne in constructing the ObjectBench representation of the RCS model. We also would like to thank Nina Amla for reading the manuscript and making suggestions for improvements.

References

1. Cetin, M., Kapoor, C., Tesar, D.: Performance based robot redundancy resolution with multiple criteria, Proc. of ACME Design Engineering Technical Conference, Georgia (1998)
2. Clarke, E.M., Emerson, E.A.: Design and synthesis of synchronization skeletons using branching time temporal logic. Workshop on Logic of Programs, Yorktown Heights, NY. Lecture Notes in Computer Science, Vol. 131. Springer-Verlag, Berlin Heidelberg New York (1981)
3. Clarke, E.M., Grunberg, O., and Peled, D.: Model Checking, MIT Press (1999)
4. Dijkstra, E.W.: Guarded commands, nondeterminacy and formal derivation of programs, Comm. ACM, Vol. 18(8) 1975 453-457
5. Emerson, E.A., Clarke, E.M.: Characterizing correctness properties of parallel programs using fixpoints, Lecture Notes in Computer Science, Vol. 85, Springer-Verlag, Berlin Heidelberg New York (1980) 169-181
6. Graig, J.J: Introduction to Robotics: Mechanics and Control. Addison-Wesley (1989)
7. Gunter, E.L., Peled, D.: Path Exploration Tool, Proceeding of TACAS 1999, Amsterdam, The Netherlands, (1999) 405-419
8. Harel, D.: From Play-In Scenarios to Code: An Achievable Dream, Proceedings of FASE 2000, Berlin, Germany, Lecture Notes in Computer Science, Vol. 1783, Springer-Verlag, Berlin Heidelberg New York (2000) 22-34
9. Hoare, C.A.R.: Communicating Sequential Processes, Comm. ACM, Vol. 21(8) (1978) 666-677
10. Hoare, C.A.R.: An axiomatic basis for computer programming, Comm. ACM, Vol. 12 (1969) 576-580
11. Holzmann, G.J.: Design and Validation of Computer Protocols, Prentice Hall Software Series, (1992)
12. Jackson, D.: Aspect: Detecting Bugs with Abstract Dependencies. ACM Transactions on Software Engineering and Methodology, Vol. 4(2) (1995) 279-295
13. Kapoor, C., and Tesar, D.: A Reusable Operational Software Architecture for Advanced Robotics (OSCAR), The University of Texas at Austin, Report to U.S. Dept. of Energy, Grant No. DE-FG01 94EW37966 and NASA Grant No. NAG 9-809 (1998)
14. Kernighan, B., and Ritchie, D.: The C programming Language, Prentice Hall (1988)
15. Myers, G.J.: The Art of Software Testing, Wiley (1979)
16. Murphy, G., Notkin, D., and Sullivan, K: Software Reflexion Models: Bridging the Gap between Source and High-Level Models, In Proceedings of SIGSOFT'95 Third ACM SIGSOFT Symposium on the Foundations of Software Engineering, ACM (1995) 18-28
17. Pnueli, A.: The temporal logic of programs, Proc. of the 18th IEEE Symp. on Foundation of Computer Science (1977) 46-57
18. Quielle, J.P., and Sifakis, J.: Specification and verification of concurrent systems in CESAR, Proceedings of the 5th International Symposium on Programming (1981) 337-350
19. SES inc., ObjectBench Technical Reference, SES Inc. (1998)

Author Index

Agha, Gul   197
Aichernig, Bernhard K.   571
Alagar, Vasu S.   173
Arditi, Laurent   449
Arvind   43

Bellegarde, F.   2
Beyer, Dirk   318
Bošnački, Dragan   518
Boufaïed, Hédi   449
du Bousquet, Lydie   242
Burton, Jonathan   364
Butler, Michael J.   478

Calder, Muffy   384
Cavalcante, Sérgio   278
Cavanié, Arnaud   449
Chechik, Marsha   72
Currie, Andrew   99

Dams, Dennis   518
Darlot, C.   2
Derepas, Fabrice   119
Doche, M.   590
Dupuy-Chessa, Sophie   242

Easterbrook, Steve   72

Fernández Iglesias, Manuel J.   436
Flanagan, Cormac   500
Flores, Andres   223

Gastin, Paul   119
González-Castaño, Francisco J.   436

Hartel, Pieter H.   478
Helke, Steffen   20
Holenderski, Leszek   518

Jackson, Daniel   1
Johnson, Michael   534
Jones, Geraint   344
de Jong, Eduard   478
Jürjens, Jan   135
Julliand, J.   2

Katz, Shmuel   419
Kordon, F.   590
Kouchnarenko, O.   2

Koutny, Maciej   364

Lämmel, Ralf   550
Laurent, O.   465
Leino, K. Rustan M.   500
Leuschel, Michael   99
Llamas Nistal, Martín   436
Longley, Mark   478

Mac an Airchinnigh, Mícheál   396
Maharaj, Savi   384
Mantel, Heiko   153
Massart, Thierry   99
Michel, P.   465
Misra, Jayadev   222
Moore, Richard   223

Pahl, Claus   259
Pappalardo, Giuseppe   364
Paynter, Stephen E.   300
Peled, Doron   611
Petrovykh, Victor   72
Peyton Jones, Simon   435
Plainfossé, David   119
Pousada Carballo, José M.   436

Reynoso, Luis   223
Romero Feijoo, Alberto   436
Rosebrugh, Robert   534

Sampaio, Augusto   278, 344
Santen, Thomas   20
Shankland, Carron   384
Sharygina, Natasha   611
Shen, Xiaowei   43
Sherif, Adnan   278
Silva, Leila   344
Stehlé, Vincent   449
Stoy, Joseph   43

Talcott, Carolyn   197

Venkatasubramanian, Nalini   197
Vernier-Mounier, I.   590

Wiels, V.   465

Xi, Zheng   173

Lecture Notes in Computer Science

For information about Vols. 1–1924
please contact your bookseller or Springer-Verlag

Vol. 1925: J. Cussens, S. Džeroski (Eds.), Learning Language in Logic. X, 301 pages 2000. (Subseries LNAI).

Vol. 1926: M. Joseph (Ed.), Formal Techniques in Real-Time and Fault-Tolerant Systems. Proceedings, 2000. X, 305 pages. 2000.

Vol. 1927: P. Thomas, H.W. Gellersen, (Eds.), Handheld and Ubiquitous Computing. Proceedings, 2000. X, 249 pages. 2000.

Vol. 1928: U. Brandes, D. Wagner (Eds.), Graph-Theoretic Concepts in Computer Science. Proceedings, 2000. X, 315 pages. 2000.

Vol. 1929: R. Laurini (Ed.), Advances in Visual Information Systems. Proceedings, 2000. XII, 542 pages. 2000.

Vol. 1931: E. Horlait (Ed.), Mobile Agents for Telecommunication Applications. Proceedings, 2000. IX, 271 pages. 2000.

Vol. 1658: J. Baumann, Mobile Agents: Control Algorithms. XIX, 161 pages. 2000.

Vol. 1756: G. Ruhe, F. Bomarius (Eds.), Learning Software Organization. Proceedings, 1999. VIII, 226 pages. 2000.

Vol. 1766: M. Jazayeri, R.G.K. Loos, D.R. Musser (Eds.), Generic Programming. Proceedings, 1998. X, 269 pages. 2000.

Vol. 1791: D. Fensel, Problem-Solving Methods. XII, 153 pages. 2000. (Subseries LNAI).

Vol. 1799: K. Czarnecki, U.W. Eisenecker, Generative and Component-Based Software Engineering. Proceedings, 1999. VIII, 225 pages. 2000.

Vol. 1812: J. Wyatt, J. Demiris (Eds.), Advances in Robot Learning. Proceedings, 1999. VII, 165 pages. 2000. (Subseries LNAI).

Vol. 1932: Z.W. Raś, S. Ohsuga (Eds.), Foundations of Intelligent Systems. Proceedings, 2000. XII, 646 pages. (Subseries LNAI).

Vol. 1933: R.W. Brause, E. Hanisch (Eds.), Medical Data Analysis. Proceedings, 2000. XI, 316 pages. 2000.

Vol. 1934: J.S. White (Ed.), Envisioning Machine Translation in the Information Future. Proceedings, 2000. XV, 254 pages. 2000. (Subseries LNAI).

Vol. 1935: S.L. Delp, A.M. DiGioia, B. Jaramaz (Eds.), Medical Image Computing and Computer-Assisted Intervention – MICCAI 2000. Proceedings, 2000. XXV, 1250 pages. 2000.

Vol. 1936: P. Robertson, H. Shrobe, R. Laddaga (Eds.), Self-Adaptive Software. Proceedings, 2000. VIII, 249 pages. 2001.

Vol. 1937: R. Dieng, O. Corby (Eds.), Knowledge Engineering and Knowledge Management. Proceedings, 2000. XIII, 457 pages. 2000. (Subseries LNAI).

Vol. 1938: S. Rao, K.I. Sletta (Eds.), Next Generation Networks. Proceedings, 2000. XI, 392 pages. 2000.

Vol. 1939: A. Evans, S. Kent, B. Selic (Eds.), «UML» – The Unified Modeling Language. Proceedings, 2000. XIV, 572 pages. 2000.

Vol. 1940: M. Valero, K. Joe, M. Kitsuregawa, H. Tanaka (Eds.), High Performance Computing. Proceedings, 2000. XV, 595 pages. 2000.

Vol. 1941: A.K. Chhabra, D. Dori (Eds.), Graphics Recognition. Proceedings, 1999. XI, 346 pages. 2000.

Vol. 1942: H. Yasuda (Ed.), Active Networks. Proceedings, 2000. XI, 424 pages. 2000.

Vol. 1943: F. Koornneef, M. van der Meulen (Eds.), Computer Safety, Reliability and Security. Proceedings, 2000. X, 432 pages. 2000.

Vol. 1944: K.R. Dittrich, G. Guerrini, I. Merlo, M. Oliva, M.E. Rodriguez (Eds.), Objects and Databases. Proceedings, 2000. X, 199 pages. 2001.

Vol. 1945: W. Grieskamp, T. Santen, B. Stoddart (Eds.), Integrated Formal Methods. Proceedings, 2000. X, 441 pages. 2000.

Vol. 1946: P. Palanque, F. Paternò (Eds.), Interactive Systems. Proceedings, 2000. X, 251 pages. 2001.

Vol. 1947: T. Sørevik, F. Manne, R. Moe, A.H. Gebremedhin (Eds.), Applied Parallel Computing. Proceedings, 2000. XII, 400 pages. 2001.

Vol. 1948: T. Tan, Y. Shi, W. Gao (Eds.), Advances in Multimodal Interfaces – ICMI 2000. Proceedings, 2000. XVI, 678 pages. 2000.

Vol. 1949: R. Connor, A. Mendelzon (Eds.), Research Issues in Structured and Semistructured Database Programming. Proceedings, 1999. XII, 325 pages. 2000.

Vol. 1950: D. van Melkebeek, Randomness and Completeness in Computational Complexity. XV, 196 pages. 2000.

Vol. 1951: F. van der Linden (Ed.), Software Architectures for Product Families. Proceedings, 2000. VIII, 255 pages. 2000.

Vol. 1952: M.C. Monard, J. Simão Sichman (Eds.), Advances in Artificial Intelligence. Proceedings, 2000. XV, 498 pages. 2000. (Subseries LNAI).

Vol. 1953: G. Borgefors, I. Nyström, G. Sanniti di Baja (Eds.), Discrete Geometry for Computer Imagery. Proceedings, 2000. XI, 544 pages. 2000.

Vol. 1954: W.A. Hunt, Jr., S.D. Johnson (Eds.), Formal Methods in Computer-Aided Design. Proceedings, 2000. XI, 539 pages. 2000.

Vol. 1955: M. Parigot, A. Voronkov (Eds.), Logic for Programming and Automated Reasoning. Proceedings, 2000. XIII, 487 pages. 2000. (Subseries LNAI).

Vol. 1956: T. Coquand, P. Dybjer, B. Nordström, J. Smith (Eds.), Types for Proofs and Programs. Proceedings, 1999. VII, 195 pages. 2000.

Vol. 1957: P. Ciancarini, M. Wooldridge (Eds.), Agent-Oriented Software Engineering. Proceedings, 2000. X, 323 pages. 2001.

Vol. 1960: A. Ambler, S.B. Calo, G. Kar (Eds.), Services Management in Intelligent Networks. Proceedings, 2000. X, 259 pages. 2000.

Vol. 1961: J. He, M. Sato (Eds.), Advances in Computing Science – ASIAN 2000. Proceedings, 2000. X, 299 pages. 2000.

Vol. 1963: V. Hlaváč, K.G. Jeffery, J. Wiedermann (Eds.), SOFSEM 2000: Theory and Practice of Informatics. Proceedings, 2000. XI, 460 pages. 2000.

Vol. 1964: J. Malenfant, S. Moisan, A. Moreira (Eds.), Object-Oriented Technology. Proceedings, 2000. XI, 309 pages. 2000.

Vol. 1965: Ç. K. Koç, C. Paar (Eds.), Cryptographic Hardware and Embedded Systems – CHES 2000. Proceedings, 2000. XI, 355 pages. 2000.

Vol. 1966: S. Bhalla (Ed.), Databases in Networked Information Systems. Proceedings, 2000. VIII, 247 pages. 2000.

Vol. 1967: S. Arikawa, S. Morishita (Eds.), Discovery Science. Proceedings, 2000. XII, 332 pages. 2000. (Subseries LNAI).

Vol. 1968: H. Arimura, S. Jain, A. Sharma (Eds.), Algorithmic Learning Theory. Proceedings, 2000. XI, 335 pages. 2000. (Subseries LNAI).

Vol. 1969: D.T. Lee, S.-H. Teng (Eds.), Algorithms and Computation. Proceedings, 2000. XIV, 578 pages. 2000.

Vol. 1970: M. Valero, V.K. Prasanna, S. Vajapeyam (Eds.), High Performance Computing – HiPC 2000. Proceedings, 2000. XVIII, 568 pages. 2000.

Vol. 1971: R. Buyya, M. Baker (Eds.), Grid Computing – GRID 2000. Proceedings, 2000. XIV, 229 pages. 2000.

Vol. 1972: A. Omicini, R. Tolksdorf, F. Zambonelli (Eds.), Engineering Societies in the Agents World. Proceedings, 2000. IX, 143 pages. 2000. (Subseries LNAI).

Vol. 1973: J. Van den Bussche, V. Vianu (Eds.), Database Theory – ICDT 2001. Proceedings, 2001. X, 451 pages. 2001.

Vol. 1974: S. Kapoor, S. Prasad (Eds.), FST TCS 2000: Foundations of Software Technology and Theoretical Computer Science. Proceedings, 2000. XIII, 532 pages. 2000.

Vol. 1975: J. Pieprzyk, E. Okamoto, J. Seberry (Eds.), Information Security. Proceedings, 2000. X, 323 pages. 2000.

Vol. 1976: T. Okamoto (Ed.), Advances in Cryptology – ASIACRYPT 2000. Proceedings, 2000. XII, 630 pages. 2000.

Vol. 1977: B. Roy, E. Okamoto (Eds.), Progress in Cryptology – INDOCRYPT 2000. Proceedings, 2000. X, 295 pages. 2000.

Vol. 1978: B. Schneier (Ed.), Fast Software Encryption. Proceedings, 2000. VIII, 315 pages. 2001.

Vol. 1979: S. Moss, P. Davidsson (Eds.), Multi-Agent-Based Simulation. Proceedings, 2000. VIII, 267 pages. 2001. (Subseries LNAI).

Vol. 1983: K.S. Leung, L.-W. Chan, H. Meng (Eds.), Intelligent Data Engineering and Automated Learning – IDEAL 2000. Proceedings, 2000. XVI, 573 pages. 2000.

Vol. 1984: J. Marks (Ed.), Graph Drawing. Proceedings, 2001. XII, 419 pages. 2001.

Vol. 1987: K.-L. Tan, M.J. Franklin, J. C.-S. Lui (Eds.), Mobile Data Management. Proceedings, 2001. XIII, 289 pages. 2001.

Vol. 1989: M. Ajmone Marsan, A. Bianco (Eds.), Quality of Service in Multiservice IP Networks. Proceedings, 2001. XII, 440 pages. 2001.

Vol. 1990: I.V. Ramakrishnan (Ed.), Practical Aspects of Declarative Languages. Proceedings, 2001. VIII, 353 pages. 2001.

Vol. 1991: F. Dignum, C. Sierra (Eds.), Agent Mediated Electronic Commerce. VIII, 241 pages. 2001. (Subseries LNAI).

Vol. 1992: K. Kim (Ed.), Public Key Cryptography. Proceedings, 2001. XI, 423 pages. 2001.

Vol. 1993: E. Zitzler, K. Deb, L. Thiele, C.A.Coello Coello, D. Corne (Eds.), Evolutionary Multi-Criterion Optimization. Proceedings, 2001. XIII, 712 pages. 2001.

Vol. 1995: M. Sloman, J. Lobo, E.C. Lupu (Eds.), Policies for Distributed Systems and Networks. Proceedings, 2001. X, 263 pages. 2001.

Vol. 1998: R. Klette, S. Peleg, G. Sommer (Eds.), Robot Vision. Proceedings, 2001. IX, 285 pages. 2001.

Vol. 2000: R. Wilhelm (Ed.), Informatics: 10 Years Back, 10 Years Ahead. IX, 369 pages. 2001.

Vol. 2003: F. Dignum, U. Cortés (Eds.), Agent Mediated Electronic Commerce III. XII, 193 pages. 2001. (Subseries LNAI).

Vol. 2004: A. Gelbukh (Ed.), Computational Linguistics and Intelligent Text Processing. Proceedings, 2001. XII, 528 pages. 2001.

Vol. 2006: R. Dunke, A. Abran (Eds.), New Approaches in Software Measurement. Proceedings, 2000. VIII, 245 pages. 2001.

Vol. 2007: J.F. Roddick, K. Hornsby (Eds.), Temporal, Spatial, and Spatio-Temporal Data Mining. Proceedings, 2000. VII, 165 pages. 2001. (Subseries LNAI).

Vol. 2009: H. Federrath (Ed.), Designing Privacy Enhancing Technologies. Proceedings, 2000. X, 231 pages. 2001.

Vol. 2010: A. Ferreira, H. Reichel (Eds.), STACS 2001. Proceedings, 2001. XV, 576 pages. 2001.

Vol. 2013: S. Singh, N. Murshed, W. Kropatsch (Eds.), Advances in Pattern Recognition – ICAPR 2001. Proceedings, 2001. XIV, 476 pages. 2001.

Vol. 2015: D. Won (Ed.), Information Security and Cryptology – ICISC 2000. Proceedings, 2000. X, 261 pages. 2001.

Vol. 2021: J. N. Oliveira, P. Zave (Eds.), FME 2001: Formal Methods for Increasing Software Productivity. Proceedings, 2001. XIII, 629 pages. 2001.

Vol. 2024: H. Kuchen, K. Ueda (Eds.), Functional and Logic Programming. Proceedings, 2001. X, 391 pages. 2001.